Global Mans

UNIVERSITY OF
GLOUCESTERSHIRE
at Cheltenham and Gloucester

Global Management Principles

RONNIE LESSEM
Reader in International Management
City University Business School

PRENTICE HALL

New York   London   Toronto   Sydney   Tokyo   Singapore

First published 1989 by
Prentice Hall International (UK) Ltd
66 Wood Lane End, Hemel Hempstead
Hertfordshire, HP2 4RG
A division of
Simon & Schuster International Group

Printed and bound in Great Britain at the
University Press, Cambridge

British Library Cataloguing in Publication Data

Lessem, Ronnie
  Global management principles.
  1. Management
  I. Title
  658

    ISBN 0-13-357344-3

Library of Congress Cataloging-in-Publication Data

Lessem, Ronnie.
  Global management principles / Ronnie Lessem.
     p.   cm.
  Includes bibliographical references.

    ISBN 0-13-35744-3 : $40.00
    1. Comparative management. 2. Career development.
  3. Organizational change. I. Title.
  HD30.55.L47   1990
  658.4—dc20   89–23194
                                      CIP

2 3 4 5 93 92 91 90

To my mother and father,
who gave me a global perspective,
on life and on business.

Contents

Acknowledgements

Before I say more I must acknowledge my very great debt to Eugene Horan, Director of the Ashridge MBA in the UK, who did such a meticulous editing job on this text. Similarly, I owe a great deal to Maggie McDougall, my product champion at Prentice Hall, and to Cathy Peck.

This book draws upon a majestic tree of knowledge, without which it would never exist. Without Adam Smith and Michael Polanyi, Frederick Taylor and Mary Parker Follett, George Land and Rudolph Steiner, David Bohm and Fritjof Capra, the book would have no roots. It would lack originality.

Without Tom Peters, Peter Drucker, Bernard Lievegoed and Harrison Owen the book would have no core. It would lack substance. Without Gifford Pinchot and Mary Kay, Koontz and O'Donnell and Warren Bennis, Pascale and Athos and Abraham Maslow, Tom Thiss and Kevin Kingsland, it would have no branches. It would lack form.

Without 3M and Mondragon, Rank Xerox and F International, the Sogo Shosha and Yugoslav Self Management, as well as the Bank of Credit and Commerce, it would bear no fruit, and hence no business application.

Without, moreover, John Myser at 3M and Hilary Cropper at F International, Shigeru Kobayashi at Sony and John Hilberry at BCC, Ray Stata at Analog Devices and Nelli Eichner at Interlingua, John Harvey Jones of ICI and Steve Shirley at F, V. H. Abidi at BCC and John Sculley of Apple, Terence Conran of Storehouse and Joyce Choto at the University of Zimbabwe, there would be no practicing managers on which to base my management theory.

Finally, and perhaps most importantly, without the whole of the globe, from which to draw my management theory and practice, there would be no global management text. I want to thank Australia and Austria, Canada and China, Cyprus and Czechoslovakia, France and Germany, Holland and Hong Kong, India and Indonesia, Italy and Japan, Nigeria and Pakistan, the Soviet Union and Spain, Yugoslavia and the United Kingdom, the United States and Zimbabwe for directly, and the rest of the world for indirectly, contributing to my thinking.

Preface

Introduction

Introducing the management domain

This is a book about 'domains' of managment, drawing on global principles and practices, and relating them to you, as an individual manager.

Such a domain is more than a 'school' or 'concept' or 'practice' of management. It is a whole set of beliefs, attitudes, and values associated with an individual manager, organization or society, at a particular stage of their development.

Domain

... a territory governed or right over which is exercized, a region distinctively marked or wholly overspread or dominated by some particular feature; a field of control or range of governance; a distinctly delimited sphere of knowledge, or of intellectual, institutional or cultural activity; a circumscribed realm of human concern; the realm of applicability of an idea or notion or the range of values within which a variable may govern.

Webster's Third New International Dictionary

Managing difference

This book, firstly then, is about your job of managing, as a particular individual, in a particular part of the globe. It is secondly a book about managing, at a specific stage of your, and of your organization's, development.

Place

So, first it describes how management in the West (America) is different from management in the North (Europe) is different from management in the East (Japan) is different from management in the South (developing countries). It also indicates how the job of managing for one type of individual is different from the job of managing for another.

Time

Second, it illustrates how management in youth (twenties) is different from management in adulthood (thirties) is different from management in midlife (forties) is different from management in maturity (fifties onwards). It also indicates how the management desired at one stage of an organization's development is different from that required at another.

Place and time

Management domains, therefore, vary by place – according to culture and personality – and by time – according to the stage of an individual's or organization's development.

In this book we are concerned with management as a whole, rather than with its functions, such as marketing or finance. However, management, for us, is differentiated according to personal space (you) and cultural space (your country), and according to individual time (your phase of life) and organizational time (its stage of development). I shall start with the place domains.

Place domains

Global trends

For thousands of years trade was conducted in isolated pockets around the world. Only in the nineteenth century did we begin to see signs of international trade on any significant scale. Yet it was only towards the middle of the twentieth century that multinational enterprises really began to flourish. Moreover, it is only now, in the 1980s, that a globally based business operation is becoming a criterion for survival – for any enterprise to be commercially significant.

Geography

So, business management today is becoming global in origin and scope. Not only do General Motors, IBM or ICI do business all over the world, but their competition comes from Hyundai in Korea, from Olivetti in Italy or from Mitsubishi in Japan.

Managers in Korea, Italy and Japan, while sharing some common management principles, are fundamentally different. Their indigenous cultures are rooted in soils other than those in Los Angeles or London, Boston or Paris, where many a management text has been written. They therefore inhabit distinct geographical domains.

To perform as a globally oriented manager you will need to be familar with those differences.

The idea that a single set of management principles can be applied across the globe, or to any individual, is no longer tenable.

Individuality

Business and management today is becoming increasingly concerned with the individual. Not only are markets being segmented according to individual tastes and lifestyles, but professional managers are seeking to do things their own way, in their own time, and even – thanks to advances in communications technology – in their own place.

More specifically, a variety of individual management styles, and orientations, is becoming the norm in progressive organizations. In other words entrepreneurs, enablers and innovators are being welcomed rather than suppressed.

The idea that a single flavor of managerial individuality should be adopted across the board is no longer tenable.

Time domains

Management trends

Business management is coming of age. It has grown up from its childhood and youth, at the turn of this century, into its adulthood, in the forties and fifties. Whereas the early managers were trumped up entrepreneurs, paying lip service to management, their counterparts fifty years later – at least in the United States of America – were fully fledged business administrators. They had become responsible managers in their own right.

In the sixties and seventies the discipline of management entered its midlife crisis. Classical and 'bureaucratic' approaches were increasingly called into question. There was some new management thinking, particularly in the area of *organization development*. However, the thinking remained fuzzy, and was only haphazardly applied. Today management is still working through its midlife crisis. On the one hand, the conventionally analytical American–European approach is beset by a spirited challenge from Japan. On the other hand, management itself is being challenged by a new entrepreneurism, which threatens to return it to its infancy. Yet this very crisis represents an opportunity. For if the discipline of management is to mature, coherence will have to be created out of confusion.

In fact, it is our task, through this book, to establish such coherence. In the process we shall be identifying four distinct conceptual domains that have been emerging, in management, over the past fifty years. They will be called, respectively, 'primal', 'rational', 'developmental' and 'metaphysical'. Each of these represents a fundamentally different orientation, accessible, in turn, to managerial instinct, intellect, insight and imagination.

As a complete manager you will need to understand, if not become fluid in, all four of these evolving domains.

Organization development

An organization, like management or society at large, also undergoes its phases of development. The managerial approach to be adopted by a youthful and pioneering enterprise is fundamentally different from the one that should be applied to an adultlike and established organization. Similarly, but less clearly apparent to us, as a company approaches midlife, and is in need of business renewal, yet another form of management becomes appropriate. Finally, and even less apparently, the mature corporation, in need of organizational transformation, requires a fourth distinctive management approach.

The idea, then, that there are a set of management principles governing all the stages of an organization's development is no longer tenable.

Individuation

Finally, like the organization, an individual manager like yourself undergoes phases of adult development. Although their individual character will be affected by the type of person you are, the underlying strands of development – if you wish to develop as a manager – remain constant.

Youth, in your twenties, is a time for exploration, experimentation, enthusiasm and enterprise. While some of you carry such youthful qualities even into old age, these attributes will necessarily be curtailed as you mature.

Adulthood, in your thirties, is a time for consolidation, responsibility, clarity and structure. While the conventional manager may extend these qualities into midlife, and beyond, he or she may be inclined to overextend, rather than develop and renew them.

Midlife, in your forties, is a time for review, reflection, for self-discovery and self-renewal. While these sorts of activities will inevitably be undertaken at earlier stages of your managerial life, they should become more purposeful and intensive at the midlife stage.

Finally, maturity, in your fifties and beyond, is a time for centering and for transformation of yourself and your organization. It is potentially the most creative phase of your managerial life. It is also the time when you are able to accommodate and to balance the attributes of all four phases both in yourself and in others.

The idea, then, that there is one set of management principles and practices to cater for you at every age and stage of your life is no longer tenable.

Managing place and time differences

In summary, there are different 'domains' of management to reflect different cultures and individuals, on the one hand, and different stages of personal and organizational development, on the other. Fortunately, for us, there is a lot of potential overlap. Although these categories, both in themselves and in relation to each other, will seem rather foreign to you at the outset. I would hope that during the course of this text you will be able to turn confusion into clarity.

Let me start, then, with the first and primal domain.

Domains of management

The primal domain

> We believe the word management should be discarded and leadership installed in its place. Such leadership involves giving everyone in the organization space to innovate ... making things work. Listening to customers, and to your people, and asking both of them for their ideas. Then acting on them. Wandering around: with customers, your people, suppliers. Pay attention to pride, trust, enthusiasm, passion and love.
>
> Peters and Austin *A Passion for Excellence*[1] 1985

The primal domain of management, or of 'leadership by wandering about', represents a return to basics, to tangible, uncomplicated people and things. It incorporates entrepreneurship and shared values applied with passion.

The passion for excellence represents a vigorous, youthful reaction against the rational management that preceded it, and is particularly applicable to younger and to enterprising managers, particularly in the context of new, or rejuvenated ventures.

The rational domain

> To be effective is the job of the executive. To effect, and to execute, are, after all, near –
> synonyms. Whether he works in a business or in a hospital, in a government agency or in a

labour union, an executive is expected to get the right things done ... Intelligence, imagination and knowledge are essential resources, but only effectiveness converts them into results.

Peter Drucker *The Effective Executive*[2] 1967

The tone and orientation of rational management is entirely different from its primal counterpart. The means are abstract – effective management of resources, rather than concrete – visible leadership of people by wandering about. The end is rational – converting capabilities into results, rather than primal – generating pride, enthusiasm, passion and love.

Peter Drucker, the leading academic force in rational management, is originally European (Northern) whereas Tom Peters operates in California. Drucker believes that the same codified principles of management can be applied in any organization, whereas Peters is of the opinion that a good leader must be physically in tune with a particular industry and enterprise. Finally, Drucker is responsibly adult in his orientation, whereas Peters is energetically youthful in his approach. Rational management is particularly appropriate to those of you, in your thirties, seeking to consolidate your managerial or professional positions, or to those who have a personal leaning towards role or project-based management.

Finally such rational management, for the past thirty years, has represented the conventional wisdom in established organizations. Primal management, over the last ten, has vigorously rocked the rational boat. For twenty years, though, barely noticed until the art of Japanese management was uncovered, developmental management has been infiltrating the establishment. The Eastern approach to management is more contemplative than active, thus providing more long term insight than short term impact. The Dutch organizational psychologist, Bernard Lievegoed, has drawn upon this Eastern tradition, while linking it with a European approach to individual self-development. The full developmental approach to management, therefore, crosses the East–West divide.

The developmental domain

The management of the future will need to acquire two sorts of knowledge: insight into the development of the human being during the course of his life, so that he can handle his development in all his plans; understanding of the development of social structures, and in particular of commercial organizations and of society in general.

Bernard Lievegoed *The Developing Organization*[3] 1980

Developmental management does not attempt to replace rational, or even primal management, but merely to supplement them. The developmental manager claims that products and markets, as well as individuals and organizations, evolve in stages. As each evolves it becomes progressively more complex. In that sense the Dutchman, Bernard Lievegoed – the leading light amongst developmental theorists – directly contradicts the Californian (back to basics) Tom Peters.

Above all, for Lievegoed, a manager needs to be able to anticipate, and to cope with the respective pioneering, established and renewal stages of a business' development. Moreover, in healthy organizational midlife, collaboration overtakes competition and coordination as the dominant form of business activity. It is in that context that 'Japanese Inc.', in the East, has risen to its global ascendancy.

Developmental management, then, will particularly appeal to those of you who are either innately sensitive to potential in people or things, or else are open to your own development in midlife.

Management personnel around the globe are currently grappling with primal, rational, and – less evidently – with developmental approaches to managing their enterprises. At the same time, if rather uniquely, a fourth management domain has appeared on the business horizons, *via* the developing countries, and through the 'real' management philosophy developed at the Bank of Credit and Commerce (BCC).

The metaphysical domain

> Should we as corporate managers confine ourselves to empirical wisdom and its application? Or should we attempt to reach beyond that through the process of humility and interfusion of the streams of the energy psyche of individual human beings with the main stream of the cosmic energy psyche? We may ask ourselves if wisdom is merely human reason and perception confined within the prison of the human ego, or is wisdom nature, its laws and its principles. We in BCC have attempted to give precedence to nature.
>
> Agha Hasan Abedi, President BCC *Real Management*[4] 1985

The principles and practices of 'real' management have turned BCC into a major, multinational bank, over the course of fifteen years. In its involvement with 'spirit' as well as matter, it is not far removed from the developmental approaches of major Japanese companies. What is unique is the way in which it has conceptualized its approach into a coherent body of metaphysically based management knowledge.

Those of you willingly entering, or anticipating maturity in your fifties, will be open to this metaphysical approach, particularly if vision and imagination are a part of your managerial character. Similarly, large and mature organizations are ripe for the kind of organizational transformation that BCC has brought about. In fact, those of you operating in the South and East may be more receptive to the kind of spirit and energy involved than those of us based, primarily, in the North and West.

'Real' management, in the final analysis, draws on natural laws, governing the functioning of all physical and human phenomena, and applies them to the conduct of business enterprise. Placing particular emphasis on energy – that is its flow, velocity, quality and quantity – it draws from a philosophical and experimental base that is now common to both ancient wisdom and to modern physics.[5]

Now it is time for us to consider the overall plan of this book, using the analogy of a tree to help us along.

The tree of knowledge

Because management is approaching maturity there are four distinct domains of knowledge and skill from which to draw. Not only does each represent different stages of individual, managerial and organizational evolution, but each one draws off different personalities and cultures. The four management domains, therefore, reflect different time phases and different places of origin.

To put it another way – using a living analogy – each domain is planted in particular soils (see Fig. 1), has its own variety of roots to draw on, possesses a distinctive core, cultivates its own size and shape of branches, and yields uniquely colored foliage and uniquely flavored fruit.

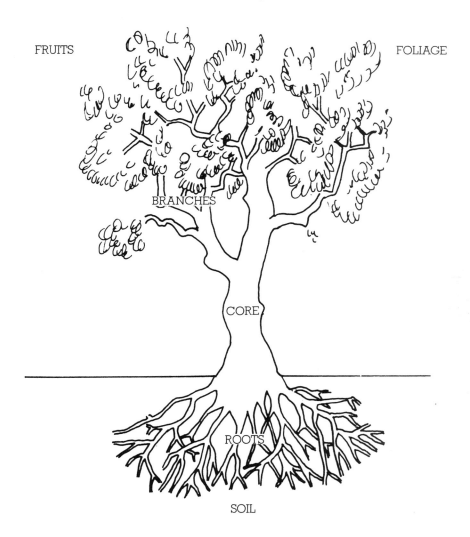

FRUITS

FOLIAGE

BRANCHES

CORE

ROOTS

SOIL

Fig. 1 The tree of management knowledge.

The soils, like the surrounding atmosphere, provide cultural enrichment of a particular kind, to the domain in question. The roots provide the academic underpinning on which the core concept is based. The core concept, in its turn, provides visibility, clarity, firmness and coherence. The branches provide the leading edge theories, which extend the core of management into everyday application, and the fruits represent the case examples, through which the particular domain is successfully and prominently exemplified. Finally, the foliage, attached to the branches and also taking in the surrounding atmosphere, represents the two role models – hard and soft – that typify each domain.

Continuing with the analogy, I shall start with the youthful plant, or primal domain of management, and end with the mature or metaphysical one. The plan of this book is to cover the roots, the core, the branches and the fruits of each management domain, before discussing specifically how you can develop yourself in each managerial respect.

Youthful management

Primal soil

The youthful manager, or young sapling, has been characteristically planted in fertile American soils, although Hong Kong, Singapore, and other parts of the world that have been populated by immigrant Chinese, Indians and Jews, are also rich in enterprise. In fact, the most fertile of such cultural soils combines free enterprise with binding community.

Primal roots

The primal management domain, which flourishes in young and rejuvenated enterprises, is rooted in political and cultural economics. These two disciplines provide its basic underpinning.

Primal core

The core of primal management has only recently become visible to the management establishment, as it was previously relegated to 'fringe' business literature, and to small business enterprise. A new primal core was re-presented to management in response to the Japanese threat to American commercial domination. The main person responsible for this primal renewal was Tom Peters, who depicted it as a search and passion for excellence.

Primal branches

Primal branches of management, as in all other domains, come in both hard and tough, as well as soft and tender, varieties. The hard branch is represented by intrapreneuring, which has become a concept in its own right, depicting entrepreneurship within organizations. The soft one is reflected in people management, which is a more instinctive, and down to earth version of personnel or human resource management.

Primal fruit and foliage

I have chosen, as my primal fruit, 3M (Minnesota Mining and Manufacturing), in America, and the Mondragon cooperatives of Northern Spain. They represent, respectively, personal and cooperative enterprise, both on a major scale and of prime quality.

As the outstanding primal managers (foliage), I have selected the American President of Analog Devices as a dynamic entrepreneur, Ray Stata, and the Czech founder, Nelli Eichner, of what is now the largest interpreting and translations company in the world – Interlingua/TTI – as a loving 'animateur'.

The President of 3M (Canada), finally, is the intrapreneur, who combines both the hard (entrepreneur) and soft (animateur) primal elements together.

Adultlike management

Rational soil

The rational manager, or well established plant, is characteristically grown in European soil, most noticeably in central Europe, but spread more thinly across all the industrialized countries, where large-scale enterprise has proliferated. The most fertile of such soils combines institutional order with personal freedom.

Rational roots

Management's rational roots are very strongly entrenched in two complementary fields, those of administrative and behavioral science. Whereas the hard, administrative sciences, including so called 'scientific management' in its traditional form, reach down to the late nineteenth century, the softer behavioral sciences – including psychology, sociology, and political science – are a phenomenon of the last fifty years. The core of rational management, then, is a direct and combined outcome of these root sources.

Rational core

The rational core spans business, management and organizational functions and behavior, duly focused upon management for results. Its academic leader, over the past forty years, has been the European-American, Peter Drucker, who has maintained that rationally based principles of management can be communicated and learnt, through a combination of theory and practice. He has also proposed that accountable enterprise should replace free enterprise as business' reason for being.

Rational branches

The rational branches are more prolific, by far, than any of the other domains. On the 'administrative' side, management skills, organization structure and corporate strategy have each been conceptualized and applied in very considerable detail. On the 'behavioral' side, management style and organizational behavior have been covered to a similar extent, though business behavior has commanded comparatively less academic attention.

Rational fruits and foliage

As case examples of rational management, duly combining institutional order with individual freedom, I have selected two UK based communications companies. Rank Xerox (International) is the better known one commercially with its strong comparative focus on organizational order, and F International is the better known one socially with its strong comparative focus on individual freedom. As the outstanding rational managers I have chosen, as an executive, a Chairman of the multinational chemicals company, ICI, John Harvey Jones, and, as a change agent, Steve Shirley, the founder of F International. As a combination of the two, that is a manager of change, I have cited the current Managing Director of F International (UK), Hilary Cropper.

Midlife management

Developmental soil

The developmental soil is particularly widespread, and therefore widely diffused. Unlike primal and rational management, therefore, its origins and applications are difficult to trace. Overall, its origins are more easily uncovered in the East than in the West, especially in Japan, where a Western approach to technology and business development has been successfully grafted on to a uniquely Eastern approach to organizational development.

At the same time, the fertile soil for personal development has been in Europe and America rather than in Japan. As a result, and in the context of this text, the developmental soils are spread across East, and possibly South for organizational harmony, and across West and North for manager self-development.

Developmental roots

The academic roots of developmental management lie not so much in the behavioral sciences, as may be expected, as in developmental biology and social ecology. Because of the somewhat tenuous connections between these disciplines and management, the developmental roots are still rather distantly connected to the developmental core.

Developmental core

Such a developmental core emerges from the work of the Dutchman, Bernard Lievegoed, into the developing organization. Lievegoed, in fact, is a disciple of the Austrian philosopher, economist, biologist and psychologist, Rudolph Steiner. Steiner's ideas on 'social ecology', including his cooperative approach to economics, and his evolutionary approach to individual and organizational life, lie at the core of the developing organization.

Lievegoed's focus on the phases of business development, from the pioneering enterprise to the interdependent organization, straddles the individual self-development and social harmony characterizing West and East.

Developmental branches

Because of the still delicate links between roots and core the branches of developmental management are still emerging. On the one hand, there are the softer branches of the developing self, with the American Abraham Maslow's work on 'self-actualization' at the leading edge. On the other hand, there are the harder branches of Japanese management, with Kenichi Ohmae's concept of global business harmony leading the way.

Developmental fruits and foliage

The harder fruits of developmental management are successfully borne out in Japan, and exemplified by their trading companies – the *sogo shosha* – and, for example, by Sony Corporation. The softer fruits are more difficult to find, though I have identified the Yugoslav approach to self-management as an example.

The two exemplars, as developmental managers, are the adopter – an imitator and harmonizer and the enabler – who harnesses the potential of people and things. An instance of the first is the Indian General Manager of the Bank of Credit and Commerce in the UK, V. H. Abidi, and an instance of the second is Apple's chief executive, John Sculley. The two role models combined into one result in what I termed a 'corporate architect', exemplified by a plant manager, Shigeru Kobayashi, at Sony in Japan in the seventies.

Mature management

Metaphysical soil

The metaphysical soil, like the developmental, is difficult to uncover. It lies, seemingly, deeply set under the ground. However, my researches have led me to believe that it is closer to the surface in the South and East than in the North and West. For the cultural conditions that support metaphysical management are a closeness to nature and to natural energy, on the one hand, and a capacity to dream, or to envision, on the other.

Metaphysical roots

Strangely enough, the roots of metaphysical management are lodged in two apparently opposite places. On the one hand sources of ancient wisdom, from all around the globe, point towards a unity between the material and the spiritual. On the other hand, and more relevant for our purposes, modern physics is pointing in the same direction.

Metaphysical core

As might be expected, the roots and core of metaphysical management are still tenuously connected. However, the recent emergence of corporate culture and of so-called organizational transformation have swung the pendulum in both primal and metaphysical directions. On the metaphysical side Harrison Owen,[6] an American lay preacher and management consultant, has focused on 'spirit', as the ultimate management resource. His work *Spirit, Transformation and Development in Organizations*, together with his focus on myth and ritual, has focussed in the same direction as BCC's 'real' management.

Metaphysical branches

'Real' management, then, is one applied branch of metaphysical management. It bases itself upon the harnessing of energy, through an understanding of the laws of nature. The transformation of such energy into spirit, and vice versa, takes place when action is transformed into vision, and also vision is converted into action.

Metaphysical fruits and foliage

Metaphysically based companies are few and far between. The Bank of Credit and Commerce is one; Bodyshop International, which manufactures and distributes naturally based cosmetics, is another. Both are strongly rooted in the Third World, the Bank through its transactions and Bodyshop through its products. The two exemplars, in this metaphysical domain, are the business adventurer, Joyce Choto, and the business innovator, Terence Conran, from Zimbabwe and Britain respectively. A key director at BCC, an Englishman with a strong affinity with the South, is the visionary, John Hillbery, who combines adventure with innovation.

Conclusion

The plan of this book

In conclusion, this book is divided into seven sections. You may choose to tackle the book as a whole, or else more selectively. If you want to be more selective – depending on personal or educational needs and circumstances – turn to 'Fulfilling your personal needs', p. xxiii.

Studying the book as a whole

Section A: Introduction
In Section A you are introduced to the stages of development that characterize growing organizations (Chapter 1); to the cultural soils from which the four management domains are drawn – East/West (Chapter 2) and North/South (Chapter 3); to the hard and soft edges of evolving management (Chapter 4) and to the global management principles (Chapter 5) that emerge.

Section B: Primal management
Section B is liable to be the most popular one in this text, especially amongst those of you still in your twenties, and also those who are bursting with initiative and enthusiasm. After being introduced to the 'intrapreneur', you will cover the whole of primal management, that is its economic roots (Chapter 6); its core of excellence (Chapter 7); its hard intrapreneurial branches (Chapter 8), its soft people-oriented ones (Chapter 9); and finally its fruits, that is 3M and the Mondragon Cooperatives (Chapter 10).

Section C: Rational management
Section C is the most prolific one in this text, covering twice the ground of the other three domains, and is the most respectable and well established. It will particularly suit those of you who want to understand the conventional wisdom. After being introduced to the 'manager of change', you will cover the whole of rational management, that is its administrative and behavioral roots (Chapter 11); its management core (Chapter 12); its functional (Chapters 13, 14 and 15) and behavioral (Chapters 16, 17 and 18) branches – covering management, organization and business respectively; and finally its fruits, that is Rank Xerox and F International (Chapter 19).

Section D: Developmental management
Section D is especially for those of you seeking to renew yourselves in midlife, being a bridge between past and future. It also offers a bridge between East and West.

After you have been introduced to the role of the 'corporate architect', you will cover the whole of developmental management, that is its biological and ecological roots (Chapter 20); its core in the developing organization (Chapter 21); its hard synergetic branches (Chapter 22) and its self-actualizing ones (Chapter 23); and finally the fruits of developmental management in Japan and Yugoslavia (Chapter 24).

Section E: Metaphysical management

Section E is the most speculative of them all, but at the same time the most powerful. It will suit those of you willingly entering the age of wisdom, and may hold particular appeal in the South. After you have been introduced to the 'visionary', you will cover the whole of metaphysical management, that is its ancient and modern roots (Chapter 25); its core, in organizational transformation (Chapter 26); its hard branches, from vision to action (Chapter 27), and its soft ones in 'real' management (Chapter 28); and finally its fruits in BCC (Chapter 29).

Section F: Developing your managerial self

In Section F you will be invited to recognize and develop yourself, prospectively, as a primal (Chapter 30), rational (Chapter 31), developmental (Chapter 32), or metaphysical manager (Chapter 33) of either the tough or tender variety! You will therefore be able to choose from one of eight – not just four – alternative, managerial selves.

Section G: Conclusion

Finally, you should be able to tie all the threads together in the concluding chapters (34 and 35), balancing theory and practice, youth and age, West and East as well as North and South, and one domain with the other.

Fulfilling your personal needs

You may wish to study this text, selectively, in order of relevance to yourself, depending on the following:

1. Your age.
2. Your personality.

Table 1 Your personal plan for this book

	Sections, priority and sequence
Your age	
20s	A, B, C, D, E, F, G
30s	A, C, B, D, E, F, G
40s	A, D, C, B, E, F, G
50s	A, E, D, C, B, F, G
Your personality	
Primal	A, B, C, D, E, F, G
Rational	A, C, B, D, E, F, G
Developmental	A, D, F, C, B, E, G
Metaphysical	A, E, D, C, B, F, G
Stage of your organization	
1	A, B, C, G
2	A, C, B, D, E, G
3	A, D, C, B, E, F, G
4	A, E, D, C, B, F, G
Geographical domain	
West	A, B, C, E, F, D, G
North	A, C, B, D, F, E, G
East	A, D, C, B, E, F, G
South	A, E, D, B, C, F, G

3. Your nationality and country of residence.
4. The stage of development of the organization for which you work.

If so, you may choose to follow the sequence indicated in Table 1. In fact, you may choose whether your age, personality, stage of organizational development, or cultural identity should assume priority.

Pursuing management themes

Finally, particularly if you are following a formal programme of studies, you may wish to pursue particular management topics, through the course of the book. The most popular amongst these are likely to be as shown in Table 2.

Table 2 A thematic plan for this book

Theme	Chapters and sequence
Business foundations	6, 11, 20, 25
Business policy and strategy	1, 17, 18
Career/self-development	22, 30, 31, 32, 33
Corporation culture	2, 3, 4, 9, 26
Corporate social responsibility	18, 19, 28, 29
Entrepreneurial/intrapreneurship	7, 8, 10
In pursuit of excellence	7
Human resource management	7, 12, 19, 21, 24, 26, 30, 31, 32, 33, 34
International management	2, 3, 24, 29
Japanese management	2, 22, 24
Joint ventures	2, 22, 24
Management in the Third World	3, 6, 9, 10, 29
Management principles	11, 12, 13
Management style	5, 14
Marketing management	2, 3, 17, 34
Mergers and acquisitions	10, 22, 26
Operations management	19, 34
Organizational behavior	4, 11, 15, 16, 19, 20, 21, 22, 24, 28
Organization development	20, 21, 22, 24

Having worked out how you wish to tackle this text, you are now in a position to move on.

References

1. T. Peters and N. Austin, *A Passion for Excellence*, Collins (1985), p. 9.
2. P. Drucker, *The Effective Executive*, Heinemann (1967), p. 1.
3. B. Lievegoed, *The Developing Organization*, Celestial Arts (1980), pp. 9–10.
4. A. H. Abedi, *Real Management*, BCC (1985).
5. R. Weber, *The New Unity: a Dialogue with Scientists and Sages*, Routledge & Kegan Paul (1987).
6. H. Owen, *Spirit, Transformation and Development in Organizations*, Abbott Publishing, (1987).

Section A
Introduction

Introduction

In the introductory section to this text I want to establish the building blocks for the subsequent managerial investigation. In fact, before arriving at our global management principles (Chapter 5) we need to uncover the following:

1. The stages of business and economic development (Chapter 1).
2. The global context of business operations, specifically comparing and contrasting the East and West (Chapter 2) and the North and South (Chapter 3).
3. The 'soft' and 'hard' edges of management (Chapter 4).

Managing in stages

International economic development

The global economy has been developing in approximately four stages, vestiges of each being still in evidence. As it has evolved, an alternating series of structure building and structure changing phases have emerged.

For thousands of years some form of international trade has been undertaken, though it is only in the last two hundred that it has taken place on a significant scale.

A hundred years ago the first multinational businesses began to arrive on the world's stage, based in Europe and America, but opening up subsidiary operations in other countries. Some seventy years later these companies were approaching their heyday.

In the sixties and seventies, particularly with the economic emergence of the Middle East, joint business ventures evolved. At the same time, the phenomenon of 'production sharing' whereby bits of manufacturing operations were shared around the globe, became increasingly prevalent. We began to see the emergence of the transnational enterprise, crossing international boundaries at the drop of a hat.

Finally, and most recently, we have seen one or two examples of truly global corporations, like BCC, without any single national identity, but with a truly global orientation.

Business and organization development

Like individuals on the one hand, and whole economies on the other, business enterprises can be seen to develop in phases, interspersed with structure-changing transitions. Each phase contains within it the hard and soft attributes to which we shall be continually referring.

The first structure building phase is that of the pioneering enterprise, appearing out of obscurity, which mirrors the industrial revolution, and combines entrepreneurial flair with communally shared values.

The second phase, usually emerging out of a crisis of authority, is that of the structured organization, mirroring the managerial revolution and combining competitive strategy with cooperative teamwork.

The third phase, often arising out of a crisis of bureaucracy, is that of corporate renewal, mirroring the recent design revolution, and combining planned evolution with a cooperative strategy.

The fourth, and most remote phase of development, probably emerging out of a moral crisis, is that of organizational transformation, mirroring what may be called a consciousness revolution, and combining a spiritually based vision with an interfusion of energy.

East–West

Japan

East and West, most visibly – in business terms – representing Japan and America, reflect, particularly strongly, two out of the four stages of development.

Japan has spearheaded the joint ventures, outside the country, and public–private cooperation, within, that characterize the third stage of transnational and inter-organizational development. Japanese organizations, moreover, have played a leading part in exposing the comparative disharmony of large-scale enterprises in the West. In effect, the Japanese way has managed to combine adaptation (including imitation) with harmony in a uniquely Eastern context. Unfortunately, to date, neither China nor India, on the one hand, nor Eastern Europe, on the other, has developed indigenously and sufficiently for us to be able to make culturally based conclusions. Doubtless, in the next decade or so, especially in China and Russia – what with *Glasnost* – this situation will change.

America

The United States of America is geographically, and in many ways philosophically, at an opposite position to the Japanese. Although both run free enterprise economies, their innate approaches to business are fundamentally different. Whereas Japan focuses on the group, America focuses on the individual; where America separates public from private enterprise, Japan integrates them. The American way, then, is not to focus on adaptation and harmony so much as to concentrate on enterprise and community. Whereas the Americans excel at the pioneering stage, and sometimes at the organizational one, the Japanese are at their best at the developmental stage.

North–South

Europe

Although there is considerable overlap between Western Europe and the United States, significant differences remain. The Europeans value structure and rationality more than their American counterparts, although there are variations within Europe. The central Europeans veer more towards order and hierarchy, and the Scandinavians towards freedom and networks. The British find themselves positioned in between not only the central and northern Europeans, but also between Europe and America. As a whole, though, Europe is attempting to reconcile order and freedom, at the second stage of a business' development.

Africa

Whereas America, Europe and now Japan, have given expression to their natural, and culturally biased approaches to business, none of the Southern countries have yet managed to express their business selves, at least on any significant scale. For until such expression is given, in its 'adult' and conceptualized form, we are left in a state of confusion and doubt. For all too many countries, around the globe, business has remained underdeveloped in its primal form. This is the result of a combination of under-development in the South and East, and overdevelopment (or exploitation) from the North and West. As a result, both the world in general and business in particular remains impoverished. However, from my own, and rather subjective, knowledge of one Southern country – that of my birth – Zimbabwe, I have come to the conclusion that the fourth stage of development, if the other three were allowed to unfold, is its natural one. In fact, it is the combination of vision and energy, facilitated by the closeness to nature and to 'spirit', that stimulates organizational transformation.

In conclusion, each quarter of the globe potentially contributes its part to the developing business' whole. The combination of primal competitiveness, rational effectiveness, developmental cooperativeness and metaphysical consciousness from West–North–East–South, makes for the best of all worlds.

The soft and hard edges of management

Each stage of business development, and each quarter of the globe, brings both hard and soft qualities into business. The hard ones are enterprise, order, adaptability and vision; the soft ones are community, freedom, harmony, and energy. (See Table 3.)

Table 3 Soft and hard edges of management

State of development	Quarter of the globe	Soft attribute	Hard attribute
1	West	Community	Enterprise
2	North	Freedom	Order
3	East	Harmony	Adaptability
4	South	Energy	Vision

Yin and yang

From ancient times this division between 'soft' and 'hard' has been considered fundamental to development in life, if not in business. The ancient Chinese introduced the terms 'yin' and 'yang' to represent these complementary attributes. For some, the division between 'feminine' and 'masculine' parallels yin and yang, but this association often causes controversy. It must be emphasized that feminine attributes can be possessed by men and vice versa.

The two sides of the brain

Recent research into the two sides of the brain has revealed some striking similarities between the left brain (right hand) and right brain (left hand), and so-called masculine and feminine traits. Whereas the left brain controls our more analytical and focussed consciousness, the right brain controls our more intuitive and diffuse awareness. At each of the developmental stages, and for each management domain, we require a combination of soft and hard qualities, of a continually changing nature.

Global principles of management

Stages, cultures and domains

Variations in time – phases of development, and in place – quarters of the globe, provide the heterogeneous building blocks through which global principles of management can be developed. Moreover, the combinations of hard and soft attributes provide the stability and the fluidity, the life building and life changing structures, to enable the management principles to evolve and mature.

The four domains that combine together to form the global principles of management, are drawn out of our diverse cultures and life phases. However, it is essential to note, for example, that primal management and the first stage of business development, though they overlap, are not the same thing. Tom Peters has stretched his 'primal' point to make it apply to all stages of an organization's development, though at some stage it will be made to stretch too far. There does remain a vital connection between pioneering enterprise and primal management.

The same will apply to the other domains. Peter Drucker maintains that there are rational principles that guide the entrepreneur, although it is the established organization that lends itself particularly well to his scientifically based concepts. Similarly, whereas particular cultures do favor particular domains – for example the West Germans and rational management get on very well – the argument is by no means watertight. After all, most of the textbooks on rational management come from that bastion of primal enterprise, the USA.

Table 4 Domains of theory

Domain	Source
Primal	Hunters and gatherers
Rational	Administrative and behavioral sciences
Developmental	Organization development and Japanese management
Metaphysical	Organization transformation and BCC

Domains of theory

As we enter the domains of theory (See Table 4), then, we shall find only a rough correspondence between culture and concept. I have nevertheless done my best to comb the globe for major business concepts and applications.

Primal. Primal theory, not surprisingly, is firmly based in America, but I trace its origins back to the gatherers as well as to the hunters in our traditional societies. Unfortunately the gatherer heritage is all too often lost in our management textbooks.

Rational. Rational concepts of course abound, though again there is a bias. The administrative tradition has been consistently followed through, whereas the behavioral one, whose leading instigator was Mary Parker Follett in the twenties, has almost completely bypassed the latter, as its most highly evolved source of influence.

Developmental. Developmental theory is much more difficult than its rational counterpart to uncover, and more widely spread. Unfortunately, too, its supposedly most important source of theory and application, that is 'organization development', has all too often been twisted into rational shape. At the same time, the developmentally oriented Japanese tend not to write about themselves, but to leave it to culturally biased others.

Metaphysical. Finally, metaphysical concepts are inevitably embryonic in their development, and we must be indebted to Harrison Owen in America and to BCC in the developing countries, for their uniquely imaginative exposition on this domain.
Let us proceed, then, to manage in stages.

1 Managing in stages

Contents

Key concepts

Once you have fully understood this chapter you should be able to define the following concepts in your own terms:

Cartels   Comparative advantage

Consciousness revolution   International business
Design revolution   Joint venturing
The developing business   Managerial revolution
Developmental attributes   Multinational business
Entrepreneurial attributes   Production sharing
Entrepreneurial revolution   Structure building
Executive attributes   Structure changing
Global corporation   Transnational business

Objectives

Upon completing this chapter you should be able to do the following:

1. Outline the four stages of global economic development.
2. Describe the four stages of business development.
3. Compare and contrast structure-changing transitions and structure-building phases.
4. Describe the comparative entrepreneurial, executive, developmental and transformation attributes.
5. Compare and contrast 'soft' and 'hard' attributes at each stage of a business' development.

Introduction

The scope of global management

Most management texts are written with the conventionally managed American or British company in mind. This one is different in two respects. Firstly, it covers the management of a business over time at each stage of its development. Secondly, it encompasses management theory and practice across national boundaries from around the globe.

Management over time

There are distinct stages in a healthily growing business' development. These encompass, respectively, the independent *enterprise*, the multinational *organization*, the transnational *business*, and the global *corporation*. Each of these embodies different domains of management.

Management across space

There are acknowledged centers of management theory, and geographically emergent ones. The acknowledged centers are American (West), European (North), and Japanese (East). Emergent theories from the developing world, I associate – somewhat arbitrarily – with the South.

Global management in context

Both individual business and the international economy develop in stages. As this development takes place there is a change in the nature and extent of differentiation and integration both within the business and without. As a result the business' nature is progressively transformed.

This development takes place through alternating processes of transition, or structure changing, and of stabilization, or structure building. Such development takes place at both the level of the global economy and of the individual firm. I shall start with the macro, global approach and then move on to the micro level of the firm.

Global business development

Stage one: economic

Structure building

In the first developmental stage, spanning some two thousand years, business is conducted in small and isolated pockets within local regions across the globe. Contacts between these regions is made through middlemen, that is through itinerant adventurers and traders. Such contact is restricted to individual and commercial dealings based on economic motives. Economic differentiation and integration is achieved through the free workings of the market-place. But trading is so limited and scattered that it hardly warrants being termed international.

In fact international trade only begins to take place in the nineteenth century, as economic and political motives begin to merge. Economic trade and political ambitions intermingle as merchant adventurers like Robert Clive of India and Cecil Rhodes in Africa make their weighty impact.

Structure changing

International cartel arrangements, in the first half of this century, mark an extension of the in between phase linking economic and organizational integration. This is the transition between a vigorous and youthful international economy and a more cautious and adult one.

Stage two: organizational

Structure building

Once we enter into the second stage of business and economic development 'free' international trade is transformed. It turns into systematically coordinated multinational organization. In other words middlemen are replaced, at least in part, by a company's own manufacturing and distribution units. Contact with indigenous peoples changes from one based on trade to another based on organization and management. Organizational differentiation and integration between parent and subsidiary, between home and host governments now supercedes trading relationships.

Structure changing

Between the second and third stages is another transition period. The centrally directed multinational begins to lose its old controlling identity, by delegating power and authority. But it has not yet found a new role. While perhaps wishing its internationally based managers to be 'citizens of the world', 3M, for example, remains 'Minnesota Mining and Manufacturing'. Such a company, like IBM or most multinationals, is yet to enter wholeheartedly into the third stage of their development.

Stage three: social

Structure building

In the third stage, multinational business is replaced by a transitional business architecture. Wholly owned subsidiaries recede into the background and joint ventures become the norm. The recent spate of joint ventures, particularly in the automobile and electronics industries, reflects that growing trend. The increasing number of partnerships between small and large firms is another feature of this phase.

In fact, in this transnational stage, cooperation replaces competition as the overriding business ethic. Competition does not disappear, but it now plays second fiddle. As a result production sharing arrangements become commonplace and private – public partnerships the rule rather than the exception. Interdependent relationships replace both independent and dependent ones. Therefore social differentiation and integration replaces its economic and organizational equivalents, as the new force that divides and unites. Recognizing and relating human beings as well as commercial entities, of different individualities and nationalities, becomes the greatest priority.

Structure changing

In between the third and fourth phases there is a final transition, from interweaving of different individuals and cultures to their genuine 'interfusion' (see Chapter 28). Attention now shifts from the personal, social and economic development of particular individuals, organizations and nations to the transformation of the relationships between them.

Stage four: cultural

Structure building

The fourth, and most rarely attained stage of development, consists of the truly global corporation. For a company like the Bank of Credit and Commerce (BCC) not only understands and accommodates the spirit of different nations but also aims to transform them (see Chapters 24–26). It is achieving this through a process of business and cultural transformation spearheaded by a shared vision. As one rare example of such a global corporation, BCC is engaged in cultural differentiation and integration through international banking. Its ultimate and transcendent mission is the attainment of world peace.

Structure changing

A global corporation like BCC is inevitably in a state of flux, moving to and fro within itself, in between both economic, organizational, social and cultural differentiation and also integration. For business is never finished.

I now want to analyze, more closely, each stage of global development in turn.

International business

Structure changing

The advent of economics

Accounts of barter of goods or of services among different peoples can be traced back almost as far as the record of human history. International trade, however, involves economic exchange between different nations, and accounts of such only begin with the rise of the modern nation state. That rise was paralleled by a new attitude to material gain amongst the peoples of Western Europe. It may strike one as odd, in fact, that the idea of systematic material gain is a relatively modern one. We are inclined to believe that man is an essentially acquisitive creature. Yet the idea that each man should constantly strive to better his material lot was quite foreign to the great lower and middle strata in Ancient Egypt, Greece or Rome. It was also largely absent from Eastern civilization and had only a scattered application throughout the Renaissance and Reformation.

In fact in Shakespeare's time, according to the American economist Robert Heilbronner, the object of life for the ordinary citizen was not to advance his lot, but to maintain it. Even for America's pilgrim forefathers, Heilbronner says: 'the idea that gain might be a tolerable – even a useful goal – in life, would have appeared nothing short of a doctrine of the devil'.[1] The whole world, until the sixteenth and seventeenth centuries could not even envisage the market system. For land, labour and capital did not yet exist. It had to be invented by Adam Smith and the world's first political economists. Of course people were aware of the existence of soil, of human beings and of hand tools, but these had not yet become depersonalized economics entities.

Following in the wake of these inventions, including the concept of the market-place, was 'the principle of comparative advantage', developed in England by the economist, David Ricardo.

The principle of comparative advantage

If it takes two man days to produce a given quantity of cloth in Portugal and one man a day to produce the same in England while it takes three man days to produce a given quantity of wine in England and two man days in Portugal why then, Portugal should concentrate on producing wine and England on cloth!

David Ricardo *Principles of Economics*[2] 1817

In an age of production sharing, joint venturing, and complex cross-licensing agreements, it is amazing how little our economic theory has advanced since Ricardo's law.

The rise of the merchant adventurers

While Adam Smith and David Ricardo were developing their economic theories, the merchant adventurers had arrived. The notion of economic gain was now entering the national agenda, most particularly in Western Europe. Columbus, Cortez and Francis Drake were becoming not only national heroes, but also agents of economic progress. In the seventeenth and eighteenth centuries a new economic man was being thrust into the forefront with the trading company well to the wings. He became the stuff from which the tales of Kipling and Conrad were drawn.

To start with the overriding emphasis was on gold, the emerging symbol of national power. But, by the eighteenth century, that emphasis was beginning to look a trifle naive. New schools of thought were growing up which focussed on commerce as the great source of national vitality. The question to which Western European nations addressed themselves was no longer how to corner the gold market. They now looked for ways to create ever more wealth by assisting the rising merchant class of adventurers.

It was such adventurers as Robert Clive of India and Cecil Rhodes in Africa who carried out the imperial mission. The mission was to acquire both territory and wealth for the home country. Imperial expansion brought with it the massive exploitation of raw materials to feed the industrial revolutions in Europe and America. Gold and diamonds from South Africa, cotton from India and rubber from Malaysia fuelled Britain's economic growth. In the nineteenth century most overseas business enterprises were run by venturesome entrepreneurs.

Structure building

Innovative forerunners of international business

The real forerunners of the international businesses were the scientifically based entrepreneurs who expanded out of their home base in the 1860s. One such entrepreneur was Frederick Bayer, who took a stake in an aniline plant in New York in 1865, two years after establishing his chemical plant near Cologne. Another was Alfred Nobel, the Swedish inventor of dynamite, whose company subsequently became part of ICI. In 1866 Nobel established an explosive plant in Hamburg.

Both Nobel and Bayer were pioneering innovators and entrepreneurs whose businesses were extensions of themselves. Yet they also created organizations that were to take on a life of their own. These were to become today's multinationals. Organizational management and integration would then supercede entrepreneurism and free international trade.

In 1867 the US Singer sewing machinery company built its first overseas factory in Glasgow. Singer was the original company to manufacture and to mass market a product in basically the same form across the world. It began to specialize, standardize, centralize and establish dependent relationships with its overseas operations. It had a strong claim to be regarded as the first truly international business. No more was the romance of the man abroad to fill the pages of many a Somerset Maugham saga. Technology had changed things; suddenly, there appeared the international company which employed him, the organization that the jargon of our times has named the international enterprise.

Business growth and expansion

By the end of the nineteenth century America had become quite prepared to challenge the older industries of Europe on its own territory. While international businesses had originated in Europe they subsequently proliferated in America. Each company that went in search of higher profits had its own particular reason for doing so. But there were a number of facts that influenced them all. Industrial enterprises were becoming larger, and mass production in response to mass markets was developing. The improvement in transport and communications drew the attention of manufacturers to foreign opportunities and made it possible for them to exercise control over foreign subsidiaries. They discovered that it could be cheaper to manufacture in a foreign market than to do so at home.

However, the most important reason for the growth of international companies in the last thirty years of the nineteenth century was the spread of protectionism. Nationalism was growing apace, and the First World War was on Europe's doorsteps. By 1914 the concept of the international company was well established. This was especially true of those industries, such as cars, oil, chemicals and aluminium, which are so important today. But the scale of international activity in relation to total economic activity was very small. The multinational company was yet to enter its heyday.

Structure changing

The great cartels

The period of instability, in the interwar years, heralded an important change in the shape of international enterprise. The period saw the emergence of the great cartels. The underlying objective was to maintain prices and profits, and to provide some mechanism whereby companies could reconcile their conflicts of interest without loss of blood. The cartels foisted stability and exclusivity on to an unstable world, increasingly dominated by industrial giants from Europe and America.

The cartels, in fact, tended to break down under stress. The companies they represented were often dominated by autocratic leaders, who lay halfway between the traditional and idiosyncratic entrepreneur and the contemporary and rational chief executive. The cartels, then, were a step on the way to today's multinationals. They can be seen as both predecessors of, and successors to, the structured organization. On the one hand their structures were brittle and their management haphazard, and their value system one of exploitation. On the other hand – at least to some extent – they gave their management an understanding of national differences and of the need to modify business practices to take these into account. Instead of thinking primarily of supplying their home markets, and exporting surpluses, cartel managers became accustomed to approaching the problems of their industries on a world basis. They were operating within and across all four quarters of the globe.

Multinational business

Structure building

The emergence of the multinational company

The period since the Second World War has seen the full realization of the powers of competitive strategy making and of structured organization on a global scale. The period has been marked by an explosive expansion in international direct investment which for much of the time has been rising at twice the world's GNP. The 'multinational' company has become the characteristic industrial organization of the third quarter of the twentieth century.

Organizational differentiation and integration
Christopher Tugendhat, an English observer of the multinational scene some seventeen years ago, was one of the first to comment on the nature and extent of multinational enterprise.

Coordinated from the center

The most striking characteristic of the modern multinational company is its central direction. However large it may be, and however many subsidiaries it may have scattered across the globe, all its operations are coordinated from the center.

Christopher Tugendhat *The Modern Multinational*[3] 1971

There have been variations on the centralization theme and in his book *The Multinational Man*,[4] Thomas Aitken presents a more balanced view: 'Multinational arrangements', he says,

> consist of two vertical spheres; a naturally and culturally decentralized base structure designed to deal with pluralistic conditions, through strong semi-autonomous entities at the national and local levels; and, a centralized super-structure to guide and coordinate the organization as a whole on the international level.

Whatever the precise balance, the basic model of coordination at the center, and division-alization at the periphery, prevailed throughout the fifties and sixties. Differences arose in the way that territories, product lines and management functions were allocated, but these again were mere variations on a theme. The theme began to change in the seventies.

Transnational business

Structure changing

The interdependent multinational
During the 1960s multinationals had begun to experiment with joint ventures, especially when their hand was forced by the developing countries. Peter Drucker forecast in 1974 that the 'joint venture' would become increasingly important in the future. He added, at the same time: 'It is the most demanding and difficult of all tools of diversification, and the least understood'.[5] This is hardly surprising. For the very spirit of joint venturing is as alien to the entrepreneur's competitive drive as it is foreign to the manager's analytical mind. The West and the North, therefore, have played a back seat role in the development of transnational enterprise.

In fact it has been initially the Middle East, subsequently Japan, and most recently China which have obliged multinational management to reconsider their approach. Not surprisingly, in all these Eastern countries, heart and feeling supersede head and thinking, albeit in different ways in each case.

The emergence of production sharing

Earlier on I cited Ricardo's principle of comparative advantage, as an economic basis for international trade. Today it is being overtaken by the more complex and synergistic notion of production sharing. Once again it is Peter Drucker who first drew our attention to it, in his book *Management in Turbulent Times*. Drucker refers to production sharing, in the late seventies, as a vehicle for transnational integration. 'In production sharing', he says, 'the resources of the developing countries – their abundant labor for traditional jobs – are brought together with the resources of the developed countries – their management, their technology, their educated people, their markets and purchasing power'.[6] He then cites several examples of this. The electronic calculator is one.

The hand held electronic calculator may carry the name plate of a Japanese company, but that may be the only part of it that is 'Made in Japan'. The electronic chips probably come from Texas or from Silicon Valley. They may have been assembled in Singapore, in Indonesia, or perhaps in Nigeria. The casing may be the product of an Indian steel mill and of course the final product will be sold all over the world. The design, the quality control and the marketing will have been done in a highly developed country, Japan, and the labor-intensive work in developing countries. Whereas the former has expertise readily on tap the latter have surplus labor on hand.

There is more to production sharing than comparative costs alone and yet there is no acknowledged theory to explain this new pattern of international trading: 'We are about to enter the stage of integrated trade, for this is what production sharing means. Yet economists and policy makers are totally unprepared for the challenge'.[7] Drucker claims that the multinational of tomorrow will need to be organized quite differently from its predecessor. It will be organized around two focal points, technology (or design) and marketing.

Instead of being a multinational corporation, he says, it will have to become a transnational confederation. The local subsidiary 'will not be a business as it has traditionally been, one that produces and markets the full range of the company's products, but only in its own country. The products it makes will be sold all over the world'.[8]

Tomorrow, Drucker says, the developing countries will matter to the multinationals as they have not mattered before. They will provide the manufacturing work. The parent company should thus become increasingly dependent on them. Top management will lead an orchestra rather than an army.

Production sharing, Drucker tells us, makes high demands on design, quality control and marketing, and even higher ones on the management skills of planning, organizing, integrating and coordinating. So production sharing lies half way between second and third stage thinking. There is evidence of interdependence and a need for mutual trust, but conventional management skills are still most strongly emphasized.

Peter Drucker's production sharing paves some of the way towards a new, integrated business outlook. But it still falls short of the kind of technological, economic and cultural interdependency that I now see around me. To take a step further we need to go and enter into the full spirit of joint venturing, as a vehicle for economic, organizational and social differentiation and integration.

Structure building

The rise of joint venturing
The first global business revolution turned trading companies into international businesses, with foreign manufacturing and marketing facilities. International entrepreneurs were transformed into national and meta-national managers. Sophisticated structures and procedures took the place of intuitive deals and informal relationships. As the international businesses grew in scale and geographical diversity they began to see themselves as multinational. However, in most instances, they only entered into the true and interdependent spirit of multinationality, when their hands were forced.

This was especially true, in the seventies, when the Arabs and the Japanese both began to assert themselves as equals on the world's trading scene. They added a political to an economic imperative, obliging American and European companies to enter into joint ventures with them, if they wanted to survive. In fact, John Walmsley, an inveterate joint venturer with GKN, who has spearheaded a British multinational's growth in the Middle East, has said: 'Almost without exception, the Middle East that we see today represents the product of joint business ventures'.[9]

The same picture is today emerging in China. The spate of recent joint ventures in fact dates back to the republic's new economic policy, reflected in the edict of July 1979: 'With a view to expanding international economic cooperation and technological exchange, the People's Republic of China permits foreign companies to incorporate themselves, within the territory of China, into joint ventures with Chinese companies, on the principle of equality and mutual benefit'.[10]

The more closely, in fact, we look at today's international business scene, the more convinced I become that there is an 'invisible hand' at work. But it is not Adam Smith's. In a sense the business scene works against it. It is not self-interest but mutual interest which is becoming the invisible guide. In this respect it is the Japanese who have led the way.

Technology and transnational interdependence
The Japanese have not only taken the business world by storm in recent years, but have also posed it with a fundamental dilemma. On the one hand they have forced Europe and America to become more competitive; on the other they have encouraged them to become either more cooperative or more isolationist!

In his recent book *Triad Power*,[11] Ohmae makes two key points, one spurred on by the competition and the other by the need for cooperation. His first point is that major companies in America, Europe and Japan (the Triad) have all now to plan and implement their strategies globally. Nothing else will do. This is the new economic imperative for any large company that wants to remain competitive. In order to compete, and here lies the irony, companies need to cooperate. Ohmae's reasoning is not founded, like Drucker's, on the comparative availability of labor on the one hand, and on comparative management and design expertise, on the other. No, Ohmae's argument is centered upon today's technology. As the development and commercialization of new technological breakthroughs become increasingly costly, he argues, there is a threefold movement towards integration and cross fertilisation. The need for integration arises first downstream, to control interfaces with the customer; second upstream, to acquire new technologies; and third horizontally, to share complementary technologies prior to joint market exploitation.

Ohmae then cites the example of the IBM personal computer. The interface with the customer is controlled not directly by IBM but through a group of third party companies, such as the consumer retail experts of Sears Roebuck. IBM moved upstream, to acquire new technologies, by adopting Intel processors that originate from Hitachi; finally, by linking up with an Epson printer IBM shared the exploitation of the small business market with a competitor. How odd it is, Ohmae goes on to say, that the general public holds on to the perception of Detroit fighting against Japan. For never before have the respective national car makers been so close to one another.

GM, as the biggest of the Detroit three, in 1985 boosted its equity in Isuzu of Japan to 34 per cent. It also has a 5 per cent share in Suzuki motors, from which it is gleaning minicar technology and for which it serves as a marketing arm in the States. That is the way companies now cooperate and mutually benefit as a result.

It is only by combining forces with other people, enterprises and nations that one really gets to know another, for good or for ill. Moreover, the current wave of consortia or joint venture is very different from the conventional merger or acquisition. For a start the thrust is more international in spirit and scope. Secondly, according to Ohmae, the consequences are different: 'The current consortia and joint ventures encourage dynamic competition; mergers tend to choke it'.[12]

To my mind it is no accident that a Japanese business consultant should have become the first to perceive the multinational arena in such interdependent terms. For all their fierce competitiveness, the Japanese, as I shall be describing in greater detail in Chapter 23, are much more attuned to reciprocity than we are in the West and North.

Technological, economic and social integration

But the times are rapidly changing. Europe, if not also America, is shedding its old, divided skin and is very tentatively beginning to grow a new, more cohesive one. An article that appeared in London's *Financial Times* in the summer of 1985, was entitled 'a divided continent in search of its lost vitality'. The correspondent wrote: 'Much of the vigour and self confidence that Europe had for almost three decades after the Second World War have evaporated'. As part of the same series of articles, the correspondent also happened to mention: 'Last year saw a record increase in commercial and technical cooperation agreements between European companies'. In fact the Chairman of Bull, the French state-owned computer group, was quoted as saying: 'Collaboration is a magic word in Europe today'.[13] Bull, in fact, had already been involved in a cooperative venture with the US computer manufacturer, Honeywell.

So the rules of the game have been changing. In 1989, competitive product and market strategies, and the economies of scale to support them, remain critical. But, at one and the same time, technical and commercial collaboration, and the synergy that goes with it, have become enormously important. Everyday in the European financial press another joint venture is announced, with Phillips in Holland, Olivetti in Germany and Siemens in Germany playing particularly prominent roles. Both commerce and technology have become too complex for single companies and homogeneous cultures to handle.

While Silicon Valley is populated by Europeans, Chinese, Indians and Americans,

Europe is populated by Latins, Anglo Saxons, Teutonics ... As one of the leading influences behind the European Eureka collaborative chip manufacturing project, Yves Stourdze, has said: 'Europe's technological renaissance requires the coming together of different intellectual backgrounds, nationalities and cultures'.[14]

So Europe is poised for a new phase of cooperation and integration, reaching towards 1992. The third phase of its business and economic development is on hand if only the constituent enterprises and nations will rise to the challenge. Ironically they will only succeed in doing so if they manage to imbibe the interdependent outlook of the East, in order to turn their analytical managers into business architects.

The global corporation

Structure changing

Transition to maturity
Multinational business then, is approaching maturity, as dependent relationships and political constraints are replaced by economic, cultural, technological and political interdependence. All of this reflects the third stage of international business development.

In the fourth, transformative phase the focus shifts from interdependent development to physical, economic and cultural transformation. This is the phase that the Bank of Commerce and Credit has entered. Its overriding mission is to help Third World Countries to transform themselves economically, through cultural and technological 'interfusion'. All the major multinationals have at least touched this fourth stage by virtue of the size and scope of their activity. The oil companies, for example, are engaged in physical and cultural transformation whether they recognize it or not. The impact of their activities is global, to the extent that the resources and environment they transform affects the whole planet. As we shall see, 3M's involvement with space research hurtles the company into this transcendent domain.

Because it acknowledges its power to transform the economic and cultural fabric of the entire globe, the Bank of Commerce and Credit has laid its own underlying spiritual foundations. These foundations, the Japan watchers Pascale and Athos claim[15], are singularly lacking in the West. I would argue that the main reason for this lack is, not our failure to look East, but a failure to turn towards the South.

Global transitions
To my mind, the 'invisible hand' is leading international companies from a period of rugged independence, to a stage of imposed dependence, then towards a period of mutual interdependence, followed by a glimpse of transcendence. In the process economic, organizational, social and cultural integration succeed one another in overlapping phases. For in the first developmental stage trade is the central and limiting means of global integration. In stage two the need for organizational coordination, at a global level, arises. Stage three marks a required sharing of meaning amongst fellow human beings, and stage four heralds an era of cocreation.

The great historian Arnold Toynbee had great hopes of world corporations becoming the instruments of global unity.[16] Toynbee argued that the nation state as we know it is a relative new comer to the world scene. It has spurted out of dying institutions or ancient empires – like the European nations out of the Roman state. We are beginning to see for the first time, multinationals looking for opportunities of achieving unity through cultural diversity, rather than by imposing their particular brand of national uniformity. To the extent that any world corporation succeeds, it will need to accommodate the full scale development of its people, within and without, and its organization. This remains something still to be accomplished. I now want to investigate how the individual business develops.

Business and enterprise development

Having investigated the development of global business, emerging out of its origins in international trade, I now want to review the development of the global corporation, emerging out of its origins in the industrial revolution. Whereas my initial orientation was a macro one I now want to focus on business development from a micro point of view. I shall start with the 'age of enterprise', encompassing both the entrepreneurial revolution and also the pioneering firm.

Stage one: the age of enterprise

The entrepreneurial revolution
The nineteenth century brought with it an age of industrial enterprise. At a time when management was as yet unheard of, Victorian engineers in Great Britain, railroad barons and maverick financiers in America, as well as scientifically trained entrepreneurs in Germany and Sweden, were making business history. So transport, manufacturing, and commerce were transformed by heroic individuals. They had plenty of guts, and abounded in frontier spirit. Swashbuckling entrepreneurs were willing to put their money and reputation, and sometimes even their life and limb, on the line. They also had boundless enthusiasm and were able to capture the imagination of their supporters.

Although ingenious Britons in the North got the whole process going, courageous Americans in the West reaped the full entrepreneurial dividends. The Americans took even bigger risks than the Europeans, operating over larger spans of territory, and by the late nineteenth century represented the true bastion of free enterprise. The North was thus eclipsed by its Western counterpart.

Starting up a business
Starting up a business, like each phase of business development, requires both hard and soft qualities – in this case, respectively, a spirit of enterprise and an affinity with people.

Enterprise
The entrepreneurial revolution is relived every time a person starts up a new enterprise. As anyone who has done it knows only too well, it takes lots of emotional resilience – a willingness to take personal and financial risks – as well as hard work, native wit, a capacity to improvize and enough imagination to see round corners.

People
Business is also about people. In fact there could be no business without people. The

ability to enthuse others, and to feel out a market need are indispensable, within the early stages of business development. More specifically, in my book *The Roots of Excellence*[17], I have identified seven particular entrepreneurial attributes, which are centered around finely honed business instincts (see Table 5).

Table 5   Entrepreneurial junctions and attributes

Function	Attribute
Physical	Capacity to work hard, very hard
Social	Enthusiasm, and the ability to arouse it
Mental	Mental agility, or native wit
Emotional	Will, risk-taking capacity, and emotional resilience
Analytical	Capacity to improvize, rather than organise
Intuitive	Gut feel, and eye for a chance
Imaginative	Imagination enough to see around corners

These are all innate qualities, that can only be acquired through personal observation, experience and learning, as a result of living and working vigorously. There are both thrusting qualities, like hard work and emotional resilience, and binding ones, like enthusiasm and improvization. A new business requires the thrust of hard work, native wit, emotional resilience and basic imagination. At the same time it requires the coherence created by innate enthusiasm, improvized organization and customer feel. The hard and soft qualities change their precise shape and form, however, as a business evolves.

The transition from enterprise to organization

Ironically, it is these instinctive business qualities which can prove to be the entrepreneur's downfall, as his business expands. In other words, the very success of the business enterprise can eventually lead to its demise. Thus Ford Motors grew too big for Henry Ford to effectively handle. In trying to hold on to the reins of power, he almost destroyed what he had created. More recently Steve Jobs, founder of Apple Computers, has been eclipsed by the professional management that he himself sought.

Stage two: the age of reason

The managerial revolution

During the entrepreneurial revolution, guts were primary, and brains were secondary! The same goes for the start up phase of a business. During the managerial revolution, as well as in the administered phase of an organization's development, the roles are reversed. The science of management replaces the art of entrepreneurship. Brains become primary and guts secondary.

Intellectual aptitudes, structures of organization, and concepts of strategy, therefore surpass purely instinctive, entrepreneurial qualities. In other words, businessmen and businesses become more conscious, explicit, self-aware, scientific. Administrative and behavioural science overtake classical economics and anthropology. Business instinct is not able to cope with the advancing organizational and environmental complexity.

Although it has been American business enterprises, once they expanded and consolidated, that have applied management theory most extensively, the theory was orginally conceived in Europe. It was a German sociologist, Max Weber, who, in the late nineteenth century developed his rational approach to organization. He called it 'bureaucracy'. Weber's motive was healthy enough. He wanted to counteract the nepotism and corruption of his day. Healthy motives only become unhealthy when they are plucked out of their right time and place and put into the wrong ones. French industrialist, Henri Fayol, wrote the first book on 'Industrial Management' at the turn of the century. Also, in the 1920s the first chairman of the Imperial Chemical Industries in Britain, Alfred Mond, saw his great challenge to be that of developing a true science of organization. These early ideas, hatched in the European North, subsequently came to roost in the American West, though, I would argue, never in as pure a form as in Germany or France.

The transition from entrepreneurship to administration

American corporations, during the course of the twentieth century, were growing so large that codified principles of management just had to be applied to their operation. Today the transition from enterprise to management is acknowledged as a necessity, if a company is to grow and prosper (see Table 6).

Entrepreneurship and bureaucracy

The initiating act of business is always and inescapably entrepreneurial – that is, an undertaking of creativity or of innovative change by someone who pursues the belief that the inherent uncertainty of the future will turn out favourably to his undertaking.

Successive acts to sustain the originating achievement require the formalization of repetitive procedures, to economize on the scarce entrepreneurial capacity. That requires bureaucracy.

Ralph Horwitz *Entrepreneurial Management*[18] 1978

Managing for results

Strategy and structure

In the 1950s the American business historian, Alfred Chandler, wrote his pathbreaking book, entitled *Strategy and Structure*.[19] In it he laid the ground rules for the professional manager, illustrating how a rationally designed structure follows from a rationally devised strategy. The company to which he referred most extensively was General Motors. It was Alfred Sloane's very success in structuring a divisionalized and functionally based organization, that led to the extraordinarily successful General Motors. In its day, GM surpassed Ford because Sloane had mastered the basic principles of strategy formulation and structure formation. In a period of sustained growth and in an environment that was largely ordered and predictable, rational management won many a day. Such an approach involves a conversion of instinctive and personalized attributes into formalized and depersonalized ones. Northern formality takes over from Western informality.

Style and behavior

Administrative formality, however, does not rule out participative management. A balance between task and relationships orientation is quite plausible within the progress-ive and rationally managed organization. In fact, a 'human relations' orientation falls well within the second stage of a business' development. Such behavioral and stylistic interventions provide the soft edge, while administrative and strategic thrust provide the hard ones.

Table 6 Executive versus entrepreneurial attributes

Entrepreneurial attribute	Executive attribute
Hard work	High productivity
Raw enthusiasm	Effective teamwork
Native shrewdness	Management control
Sheer willpower	Competitive strategy
Improvization	Formal organization
Market instinct	Analytical marketing
Imagination	Systematized innovation

The person who has done more than anyone else this century to spread this kind of rational awareness is Peter Drucker. The principles and functions of management, business policy and strategy, the theory of organization and the practice of managing by objectives were all developed or refined by this formidable man!

Drucker is an Austrian by birth who has been resident for many years in America. He is very much an amalgam of West and North, in that he is emotionally influenced by the spirit of enterprise and intellectually driven by the science of management. The hard thrust that Drucker introduces is analytical and result-oriented; the soft coherence is integrative and integrity oriented.[20] The analytical thrust of high productivity, management control, corporate strategy, formalized organization, analytical marketing and systematized innovation takes over from hard work, native wit, entrepreneurial flair, improvised organization, and market instinct. The softer attribute of effective teamwork takes over from innate enthusiasm.

To my mind Drucker is the last – following in the footsteps of Max Weber, Henri Fayol, Alfred Mond and Alfred Sloane – of the great apostles of scientific management. Times have again changed. The managerial revolution is being superceded by another one, as yet un-named. The degree of rigidity, impersonality, and insularity created by the rational manager creates dysfunctional inertia. Alienation within the organization and without sets in. A new healing and growing force is required.

Stage three: the age of renewal

The design revolution

As the industrialized nations evolve, so their entrepreneurial base is converted into managed organizations, if not also into a managed economy. While the entrepreneurial base is still clearly apparent in the West, especially in Texas and California, the managed organizations have reached their pinnacle in the North, especially in West Germany. Much less clear, then, is what happens afterwards.

J. K. Galbraith, the controversial American political economist, has maintained that a 'heightened design awareness' accompanies economic maturity. The design revolution taking place in Britain today would certainly seem to endorse Galbraith's view. Whereas the entrepreneur concentrates on the market, thereby generating a source of profitability, the executive attends to the organization, thereby increasing efficiency, and the designer focuses on the product, thereby attaining quality. Profit has material 'body' to it, efficiency is a product of the rational mind, and quality is the outcome not only of thought but also of feeling. That is one of the reasons why the Japanese, with their strong aesthetic awareness, have taken so naturally to that originally American theory, 'quality circles'. Today the industrialized nations in general, are going through a design revolution. Designers are coming into their own because, as societies evolve, people seek more meaning, beauty and fulfilment in their lives. Walter Teague, perhaps the greatest of America's automobile designers, was already making the point in the 1940s.

Form and beauty

As a thing becomes perfectly adapted to the purpose for which it is made, and so approaches its ultimate form, it also advances in that power to please us, which we call beauty.

Use is the primary source of form. The function of a thing is its reason for existence, its justification and its end. It is a sort of life urge thrusting through a thing and determining its development. It is only by realizing its destiny, and revealing that destiny with candour and exactness that a thing acquires significance and validity of form.

This means much more than utility, or even efficiency. It means the kind of perfected order we find in natural organisms, bound together in such precise rhythms that no part can be changed without wounding the whole.

Walter Teague *American Automobile Designer*[21] 1946

The developing organization

Corporate synergy
As the individual business evolves, and becomes more self-conscious, so entrepreneurial instinct and managerial intellect are replaced by intuitive individual and organizational development. At present most intuitive design departments are divorced from organizational, if not business development and thus are not yet fully evolved. Yet in the Japanese culture a whole tradition of aesthetic awareness has been converted into organizational sensitivity, as reflected in their concept of, and feeling for, harmony. For the Japanese, as should be the case at this third stage of business development, feeling (heart) is primary, and thinking (mind) as well as doing (guts) are secondary. That is why consensus forms such an important part of decision making.

Manager self-development
Whereas the Japanese have made a major contribution towards the design of a new corporate architecture, it is the Europeans and Americans who have contributed more towards the design of a new and individualized lifestyle. The notion of 'quality of life', as opposed to sheer quantity of material gain, has, in the last thirty years, begun to impinge itself on the managerial mind. In that context, the development of the person as a whole is allied with the development of the business and organization as a whole, towards what

the American organizational psychologist, Abraham Maslow, has called self-actualization.[22] The self-actualized individual, moreover, is 'in tune' with the rest of society.

As the business advances, then, from its independently managed structure to its interdependently economic and social design so developmental replaces rational management as the guiding business force. (See Table 7.) So fluidity of process displaces rigidity of structure at this third stage. As interdependence supplants dependence or independence, joint ventures are replacing autonomous or wholly owned companies, as the norm.

Table 7 Rational and developmental attributes

Executive	Developmental
High productivity	Intense interactivity
Effective teamwork	Quality circles
Management by objectives	Manager self-development
Competitive strategy	Cooperative strategy
Formal organization	Corporate architecture
Corporate planning	Planned evolution
Managed innovation	Corporate renewal

In summary, then, during the entrepreneurial revolution the industrialized nations advanced from economic stagnation to rapid take off. In the same way a new enterprise emerges from nothing at all into something commercial and tangible. The result is material wealth and economic 'body'.

During the managerial revolution planned and coordinated expansion and consolidation took place at both macro and micro levels. This kind of development is the product of a well oiled organizational and managerial 'mind'. Today the design revolution is bringing with it, for the first time in business and economic history, a conscious and often integrated development of people, technology and business. This gives new 'heart' to the economy and to the firm, both of which may have been acquiring paralysis through analysis! The adaptive thrust of intense interactivity, manager self-development, planned evolution and corporate renewal takes over from high productivity, management control, corporate planning and systematic innovation. The harmonious coherence of quality circles, cooperative strategies and the new corporate architecture takes over from effective teamwork, competitive strategies and formal organization.

Yet we still have one more stage, or revolution, to go. For the problem with the new corporate architecture is that it can become too diffuse, the alliances too loosely held, the developing individuals too remote from one another. What is now required is a new, transforming center.

Stage four: the age of transformation

The consciousness revolution

Any businessman who has spent time recently in the United States will have recognized that 'corporate culture' has become a prevailing management concern. In fact this represents a fundamental shift in business and human consciousness. This re-orientation forms part of our global economic development.

The entrepreneurial revolution in the nineteenth century followed a leap forward in man's acquisitive impulses. As the American economic historian Robert Heilbronner puts it in *The Wordly Philosophers*, it is only in the last 200 years that the desire for systematic material gain has entered mankind's immediate horizons. The managerial revolution, in its turn, heralded an era of not only material expansion and growth, but also of the advancement of 'human capital'. The subsequent design revolution reflects a shift in orientation towards quality as opposed to mere quantity.

Mythology

Now that 'culture', and its associated myth and ritual, has entered into the corporate mainstream, we are witnessing a further evolutionary step. For it is the great myths throughout the ages – whether in the East, West, North or South – that have stirred man's inner spirit. Ultimately it is a business' or a nation's spirit which controls its destiny. Thanks to people like Peters and Waterman[23] this is now becoming recognized within the corridors of corporate power. Corporate culture, myth and ritual therefore mark the end of the journey from physical matter towards human spirit *via* mind and heart. This form of corporate being is still the least manifest of all stages of business development.

The transformed corporation

The transition from youth to maturity

As businessmen or women develop their new enterprises into structured organizations, they have to undergo the sort of mental and emotional transformation that comes with difficulty to a Steve Jobs (Apple Computers) or to a Clive Sinclair (Sinclair Research). As an independent entrepreneur each required guts to break out of a mould, and to lead by example, through both good times and bad. But then followed the crisis of delegation.

In a certain sense entrepreneurs have to grow up from a state of childlike independence, into a state of strong dependence on others. At the same time, they have to accept the adultlike responsibility of having others dependent on them. Formal structure is required in place of improvization. Mind is needed to functionally differentiate and to organizationally integrate. Once this crisis of dependence is resolved the business can move on. However, the stage will inevitably be reached, with further growth and expansion, when the hierarchy of dependence will begin to collapse.

The increasingly turbulent and interdependent world eventually wreaks havoc upon rigidly authoritarian structures. Youthful enterprises have to grow up and become mature reciprocating organizations within a community of interdependent technologies, functions, business ventures, or institutional partners. Sensitive harmonies are required at the front line, in place of rigid forms. Heart is needed to stimulate evolution and to foster interdependence. Yet even the adaptable, evolutionary and interdependent corporation cannot last forever. It has breadth but it lacks depth. It can evolve but it cannot continuously innovate. In order to grow up, from midlife to maturity, it has to advance from interdependence to transcendence.

From vision to action

The global corporation, then, has to transcend its personal, company or inter-organizational identity, and assume a universal one. So a corporation, like the Bank of Credit and Commerce that has reached the fourth stage of its development, aspires towards the establishment of conditions for world peace by transforming the economic conditions around the globe. In order to do this its visionary leaders have to embark on a heroic journey, so as to transform their global vision into local action.

'Natural' management

Such a journey cannot be taken without enlisting the support of the fundamental, laws of nature. There are four of these, according to the President of BCC (see p. 57): nature operates as an integrated system in its dynamic state; we live within the fold of change; infinity is the container of existence; and the moral governs all that is material. In other words, the global corporation needs to 'interfuse' with the rest of the world's economy and environment, to recognize and flow with natural energy forces, to operate within a context of limitless possibilities, and to develop a spiritually based mission which guides its material one.

In summary, the attributes of business transformation – as compared with renewal – contain both thrust and coherence. (See Table 8.) Thrust is provided by the energy flow, by process and change, by the principles of natural management and by the spiritually based vision. These can be contrasted against intense interactivity, manager self-development, the new corporate architecture and corporate renewal. Coherence is provided by the corporate culture, by business interfusion, and by unlimited possibility. This can be compared to quality circles, business cooperation and planned evolution.

Table 8 Attributes of transformation

Renewal	Transformation
Intense interactivity	Energy flow
Quality circles	Corporate culture
Manager self-development	Process and change
Cooperative strategy	Business interfusion
Corporate architecture	Natural management
Planned evolution	Unlimited possibility
Corporate renewal	Spiritually based vision

In the final analysis, whereas commercial enterprise calls on sharply honed instinct, and managed organization on broadly based intellect, business renewal requires finely tuned insight and corporate transformation powerful imagination. These, between them, constitute the four domains of management with which this text will be concerned.

Conclusion

Business reality

Although business transformation apparently represents the ultimate stage of development, a final point is in fact never quite reached. Life and business involve a journey rather than a destination. All four developmental stages, like the four quarters of the globe, will be contained in some part of a continuously developing business. Any major corporation will have embryonic and youthful as well as middle aged and mature sectors within it. Parts of the organization, if not the whole of it, will also be in states of transition, in between stages. Finally, it may well be that a business needs to regress before it can progress.

Moreover, many, if not most, businesses, stop growing in quantitative or in qualitative terms. They may never evolve beyond adulthood, that is beyond the rationally managed organization. In such a case they will be forced to regress to an earlier stage, in order to survive in the short to medium term. Ultimately, they will die, but it is impossible to predict how long they might endure.

Domains of management

The stages of development that a business undergoes lead directly into four management domains which characterize each (see Fig. 2). However, because development is an up and down, intermittent and inconsistent process, the domains only fit approximately into developmental boxes. In other words, and for example, elements of commercial enterprise have their place within a managed organization like 3M (see Chapter 10), while aspects of corporate transformation may already be in place within a youthful enterprise, like Apple (see pp. 641–4). All depends on the individual founder(s), and on the industry dynamics, as well as on the laws of development.

As a result all four management domains, which I shall be calling primal, rational, developmental and metaphysical, may, to some degree, coexist at a particular stage of a business' development. While the 'primal' domain, for example, is likely to predominate at an earlier stage, it may overstay its welcome, because of an entrepreneur who is reluctant to let go of the reins, or make a return visit at a later point, because the company is in trouble. Similarly, the 'rational' stage may make an early start because of the sober character of the business founder, or the complexity of the industry (e.g. biotechnology), or methodical bias of the national culture in which the firm is based (e.g. Germany).

All the same, I have come to the conclusion that there are distinctive domains of management, each of which does bear a strong relationship to the respective stages of business development. Each of these domains has groups of related management theories, and is inevitably culturally biased. Furthermore, within each one there are both 'softer' and 'harder' attributes.

The implication of all this is that the 'whole' manager must become familiar with all the stages of a business' development, with a diverse set of cultures, and with the two sides of his or her brain! To uncover, at this stage, what kind of managerial personality you might have, you are invited to complete the 'spectral' inventory included in the appendix

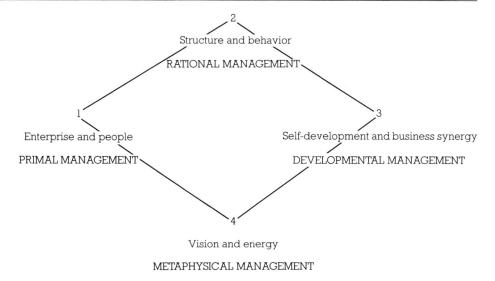

Fig. 2 The developing business.

to this chapter. Once you have completed it we can investigate the diverse cultures of the globe and, thereafter, the two sides of the brain associated with the 'yin' and 'yang' of management.

Appendix

Introduction

The spectral inventory, which is based on a model of communication and management developed by Kevin Kingsland and myself over the past twenty years, is designed to 'profile' both your personality and management style. The inventory, like any such instrument based on purely verbal responses, can inevitably be no more than a rough and ready guide to the managerial sub-domain that you inhabit. Whatever result you come up with should be checked against the perceptions, firstly of yourself, and secondly of your close family, friends and colleagues.

Pay particular attention to your top score, which is an indicator of your preferred domain of operation, but remember that other scores are indicative of the closeness of other types of manager to you. The more access you have to a particular managerial domain, within yourself, the easier will be your communications with that kind of person in the external world. For example if your top score was 'entrepreneur' and your second one 'executive' you may be an entrepreneurial manager with easy access to your executive personality. At the same time, if you scored lowest, for example, on the 'enabler' category you will find it particularly difficult to access that part of yourself. If you tied your top score, or there is only a difference of one between two or three categories, make your own subjective judgement of your managerial preference.

In fact, it is as if we all live in a building with eight floors, each representing one managerial sub-domain. One floor is particularly brightly lit, and one of two others are likely to shine fairly brightly as well. However, there will inevitably be one or more floors which are rather dimly lit. In the final analysis, though, this particular inventory gives no indication of how successful you are within any one domain, or sub-domain. It merely indicates your preferences, that is where you prefer to operate. Also, do bear in mind that there may be some blurring between who you actually are, and who you would like to be. The information that comes out can only be as accurate as that which is put in.

Method of assessment

Rank the statements in the following eight sets in order, from 8 (highest) to 1 (lowest), in each case. Ensure that no two statements are ranked equally, tempted as you may be to score them so.

The easiest way to go about your ranking is to decide on the highest and the lowest ones, and then to rank the rest, in order, in between. For example, in number (1), you may decide that (a) is most definitely you, because you are so physically active, and (c) is most definitely not, because you hate being out of control. So you rate (a) 8 and (b) 1, and then you rank the rest between 7 and 2, on the right hand side of the page. When you have finished, add up all the ('a's), all the ('b's) and so on, until you have totalled all eight from the ('a's) to the ('h's). Then plot your scores on the graph provided. As you can see, it is quite easy to become what you want to be rather than what you are. In fact, you may choose to do the exercise twice, once for the manager you would like to be, and the other time for the person you think you are.

The spectral inventory

Score

1.
(a) I am an active person who likes to keep physically on the go.
(b) I am generally inclined to create something out of nothing, something which is completely original.
(c) I tend to let things flow, until something or someone meaningful emerges.
(d) I tend to be the one in authority, so I keep people and things under control.
(e) I am inclined to take calculated, financial risks.
(f) I respond to every situation differently.
(g) I enjoy being sociable.
(h) I am essentially a humble person.

2.
(a) I have lots of energy to do things.
(b) I think in pictures, using image and metaphor to portray my ideas.
(c) I really enjoy seeing people develop to their full potential.
(d) I welcome the responsibility of organizing people.
(e) I like to be up front.
(f) I enjoy being mentally stimulated.

(g) I value friendship above all else.
(h) I am wholly receptive to what goes on around me.

3.
(a) I love taking physical risks.
(b) I like to dream, that is, to build up a picture in my imagination of how I want things to be.
(c) I rely on intuition rather than logic.
(d) I follow procedures thoroughly.
(e) I love challenges.
(f) I like to keep my options open.
(g) I enjoy celebrations.
(h) My ambition is collectively rather than personally based.

4.
(a) I act quickly and don't look back.
(b) I am an inspired person.
(c) I am often the one to create harmony between people.
(d) I am good at putting people and information into categories.
(e) I have to be totally committed, or else not at all.
(f) I am flexible in my approach to people and situations.
(g) I am usually the one who gives emotional support to individual people around me.
(h) Once I trust people, I trust them completely.

5.
(a) I need to keep physically stimulated in one way or another.
(b) I can totally transform a situation from one minute to the next.
(c) I can see the pattern in events or relationships.
(d) I like to be clear in my role.
(e) I have to see a financial return for my efforts.
(f) I am constantly seeking novelty in my work.
(g) I find it easy to establish a warm atmosphere whereby people around me immediately feel at home.
(h) I have a line of destiny to follow.

6.
(a) I love to travel to unknown territories.
(b) I am obsessed by my vision.
(c) I am a person with insight, who can understand people or things in depth.
(d) I am good at creating order out of chaos.
(e) My life and work are full of emotional ups and downs.
(f) Living and learning is what it is all about for me.
(g) I want to be seen as a nice person.
(h) I have subordinated myself to a higher purpose.

7.

(a) I am a physical person.

(b) I feel compelled to realize my dreams.

(c) I can identify the real meaning behind things.

(d) I welcome a clearly defined chain of command.

(e) I am very persistent in achieving my aims.

(f) I can adapt to most situations.

(g) I spend lots of time with people I like.

(h) When I'm absorbed in my work I'm at peace with myself.

8.

(a) I love my sport.

(b) Creativity is my life.

(c) I like dealing with opposites, in people or ideas.

(d) I am good in turning vague ideas into clearcut concepts.

(e) I like uncertain situations, where there is room for maneuver.

(f) I hate to be tied down.

(g) I am a feeling sort of person.

(h) I have no 'ego' to defend.

Scoring procedure

Now note down your scores in Table 9, for each of the sets (1 to 8) of statements – (a) to (h) – and add up the totals for a, b, c, d, e, f, g, h.

Table 9 Total scores

	a	b	c	d	e	f	g	h
1								
2								
3								
4								
5								
6								
7								
8								
Total								

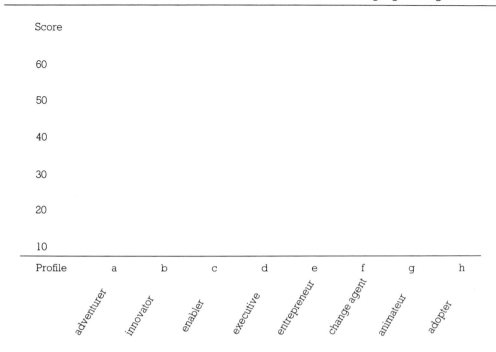

Fig. 3 Your management spectrum.

References

1. R. Heilbronner, *The Worldy Philosophers*, Penguin (1968), p. 23.
2. D. Ricardo, *Principles of Economics* (1817).
3. C. Tugendhat, *The Modern Multinational*, Eyre & Spottiswoode (1971), p. 26.
4. T. Aitken, *The Multinational Man*, Allen & Unwin (1973).
5. P. Drucker, *Management in Turbulent Times*, Heinemann (1979), p. 93.
6. P. Drucker, *op. cit.*, p. 96.
7. P. Drucker, *op. cit.*, p. 98.
8. P. Drucker, *op. cit.*, p. 101.
9. J. Walmsley, *Handbook of International Joint Ventures*, Graham & Trotman (1982), p. 31.
10. J. Walmsley, *op. cit.*, p. 14.
11. K. Ohmae, *Triad Power*, Free Press (1985).
12. K. Ohmae, *op. cit.*, p. 145.
13. Y. Stourdze, 'A divided continent in search of its lost vitality', *Financial Times*, (26 June 1985).
14. Y. Stourdze, *op. cit.*
15. Pascale and Athos, *The Art of Japanese Management*, Penguin (1982).
16. A. Toynbee, *A Study of History*, Thames & Hudson (1972).
17. R. Lessem, *The Roots of Excellence*, Fontana (1986), p. 16.
18. R. Horwitz, *Entrepreneurial Management*, Westhall Books (1978), p. 37.
19. A. Chandler, *Strategy and Structure*, Doubleday (1954).
20. P. Drucker, *Managing for Results*, Pan (1974).
21. W. Teague, quoted in Bailey, S., *The Shape of Design*, Design Council (1982).
22. A. Maslow, *Motivation and Personality*, Harper & Row (1964).
23. T. Peters and B. Waterman, *In Search of Excellence*, Harper & Row (1982).

 2 East–West

Contents

Key concepts

Once you have fully understood this chapter you should be able to define the following concepts in your own terms:

Ai	Melting pot
Amae	*Ma*
Family spirit	*Oyaban*
Frontier spirit	Self-made man
Gumption	*Shusse*
Ko-gaisha	*Uchi*

Objectives

Upon completing this chapter you should be able to do the following:

1. Outline, in essence, the background and context of the Western approach to primal management.
2. Describe, in outline, the background and context of the Eastern approach to developmental management.
3. Compare and contrast the Western and Eastern approaches.
4. Identify the reasons why Japanese and American managers may have communication problems.
5. Relate the Western and Eastern approaches to your own management style, acknowledging where you have the greatest ease, and difficulty, in comprehension.

Introduction

Global business reach

In the previous chapter we examined the course of business' development over time. Now, in the next two chapters, we shall examine its origins and development, in different places. We shall be looking West and East, at America and Japan, and North and South, at Great Britain and Africa. Because of the broad sweep taken in these chapters, they will inevitably be impressionistic and general in nature.

Global management principles

The whole of management, in this text, has been divided into four major sets of principles and practices.[1] Moreover, each one has found itself particularly fertile ground in a quarter of the globe. More specifically, I have associated the West (United States), with a primal or basic approach to management. This approach is focussed on the pursuit of 'excellence', through combining 'personal enterprise' with 'shared values'. The North (Europe) I associate with rational management. This approach is centered upon the pursuit of individual freedom within organizational order. I have associated the East, and particularly Japan, with a developmental approach to business and management. This approach is oriented towards the pursuit of 'quality', through combining 'commercial adaptability' with 'organizational harmony'. Finally, and exercizing a little foresight, I identify the South with a metaphysical approach to management. This approach is centered on the pursuit of business 'vision', through combining 'human energy' with 'collective spirit'. Needless to say, however, some instances of primal, rational and metaphysical management can be found all over the globe.

The West: enterprise and shared values

The passion for excellence

In the late seventies two American business consultants, Tom Peters and Bob Waterman[2] went out 'in search of excellence'. They sought to make out what really made successful American companies what they are. In the process they overturned the erudite management theories that had prevailed for some fifty years in America, and concluded that basically two things prevailed in 'excellent' companies in their country – 'fired up champions' and 'shared values'.

The spirit of America

Peters' and Waterman's conclusions are not altogether surprising, given America's particular history, and identity. The historian Henry Commager[3] has in fact identified four characteristics that together reflect the spirit of the United States. Three of them relate to enterprise (fired up champions) and the fourth relates to community (shared values).

Enterprise. The first attribute involves a search for the neverending frontier of human activity through pilgrimage, through exploration, through experimentation and change. The second, set in the context of that vast and often hostile territory – the land of America – is the battle for survival, the compulsion to move or die.

The third and probably most important constituent of the American enterprising spirit is the theme of opportunity, of individual achievement, of competition, of capitalism and of wealth creation!

Community. The fourth and final one of Commager's characteristics encompasses equality, community, and the assimilation of a diverse group of people into the American melting pot. It forms the basis for the family feeling, the closeness to customers and the shared values of many an American enterprise. It also fuels the parochial competitiveness that is typically American.

Enterprise and community. The crucial American dilemma, then, is how to reconcile enterprise – the frontier spirit, an inherent restlessness and a desire to stand out, with community – their melting pot.

The spirit of enterprise

The frontier spirit

Americans have always been possessed with an urge to cross frontiers, geographically, technologically and commercially. They are quick to believe that everything familiar about their lives is subject to constant change. Restless movement is their guiding image. America belongs to the New World, which, by definition, is never complete. Americans have always been willing to move on and start again.

Ready, fire, aim!

One of the most quotable lines from Peters and Waterman is 'ready, fire, aim!' The Americans are certainly one of the most action-oriented nations round the world and their sport, their business and their entertainment bear this out.

The American dream

While the frontier spirit, and an action orientation are both characteristic of enterprising man, it is the desire to accumulate wealth which lies at the heart of the 'American Dream'.

Self-made man

When Steve Jobs made millions almost overnight by creating Apple computers, he fulfilled the American Dream. When Lee Iaccoca turned Chrysler around, in a similarly short period of time, he too became an American hero. Both struck it rich. It is very difficult by now to distinguish between money making in America, as a route to freedom and dignity, and making money as a passionate obsession in and of itself.

Becoming a champion

When Peters and Waterman went out in search of excellence, one message, as they put it, came through particularly poignantly. People like to think of themselves as winners. They then proceeded to describe how excellent companies had designed systems to reinforce this notion. What Peters and Waterman have brought back to American business life is that particular kind of respect for the individual which is so important to free enterprise. The excellent companies have a deeply ingrained philosophy that says, in effect: 'respect the individual, make people winners and let them stand out'.

The hero of the American corporation, then, is no longer the brainy executive, but that slight modification of the rugged entrepreneur, the appropriately named 'champion'. The dynamic and attention grabbing activity that Peters and Waterman observed 'revolves around fired up champions and around making sure that the potential innovator, a champion, comes forward, grows and flourishes'. The champion, they say, is not a blue sky dreamer or an intellectual giant. Above all, 'he's the pragmatic one who grabs on to someone else's theoretical construct, if necessary, and bullheadedly pushes it to fruition'. The combination of relentless ambition and stubborn competitiveness carries him through. Yet tough ambition and competitiveness, without a tender family feeling accompanying each, would leave America and its constituent enterprises out in the cold.

Community spirit

The melting pot

For all the geographical and ethnic diversity within the United States, there is a remarkable degree of conformity in outlook and spirit, amongst all its people. Hence the analogy of the melting pot that is so often used.

The IBM way

IBM's founder, Watson Senior felt that employment at IBM was not solely a job, but a life commitment. The company was, similarly, engaged not only in operating and expanding a business, but in propagating a faith, setting a standard and an example of industrial morality, and demonstrating in action the premise that prosperity was an open doorway to human happiness.

Rogers Think[4] (1969)

Go out and carry the IBM banner, take pride in your profession and play fair. Make the calls, give the service, for it's the little things that count in business. My motto through the years has been, have faith in God, my country, my fellow man, and my product, and I thank IBM for giving me the opportunity to become a happy and successful salesman.

H. R. Bergmann, IBM salesman[5] (1969)

This focus on shared values and beliefs, is very much part of America's heritage. It is reinforced through active programmes of cultural assimilation, and in the proud and frequent displays of the American flag. It is a much more effective means of bonding people together than is corporate strategy making or management by objectives.

The family spirit

In the 1960s and 1970s business was inundated with management theory on human relations, motivation and communication and on interpersonal processes. Yet, in spite of all that supposedly relevant theory, impersonal and bureaucratic organization expanded relentlessly. What had happened was that corporations – all but the 'excellent' ones – had lost touch with the basic family spirit. That spirit, of family and community, had always pervaded at least the 'silent majority' of the American nation. What Peters and Waterman and their followers have done is to replace modern 'interactive processes' with old fashioned teamwork, closeness to the customer, family and community spirit.

Community center for employees

If you look at the entrepreneurship of American industry it's wonderful. On the other hand, if you look at the paternalism and discipline of the Japanese companies, it's wonderful too ... There are certain companies that have evolved into a blend of these two, and 3M is one of them ... Companies like 3M have become a sort of community center for employees, as opposed to just a place to work.

We have employee clubs, intramural sports, travel clubs, and a choral group. This has happened because the community in which people live has become so mobile it is no longer an outlet for the individual. The schools are no longer a social center for the family. The churches have lost their drawing power as social, family centers.

With the breakdown of these traditional structures certain companies have filled the void. They have become sort of mother institutions, but have maintained their spirit of entrepreneurship at the same time.

Lew Lehr, Chairman, 3M[6] 1985

Community and enterprise

The United States has been purpose built for pioneering enterprise. Its people seem to have guts enough for the whole world. The nation's technologists and managers also have sufficient nouse to sustain and create vast, managed organizations, albeit not as efficiently as the Germans or Japanese.

In some strange and almost incomprehensible way America has also managed to take in many, many different cultures and then melt them into one. That vast community spirit has provided the supportive environment for the American Dream, for the relentless spirit of personal enterprise, for the continuing Westward journey. That Western approach is, as we shall now see, virtually diametrically opposite to the Eastern orientation of the Japanese.

The East: adaptability and harmony

America and Japan: the need to achieve differently

The Japanese are an enigma. Particularly for those of us looking at their business behavior through American or European eyes it is remarkably difficult to get inside their skin. In fact the world renowned anthropologist, Ruth Benedict, pointed this difficulty out soon after the last war, after she had been sent by the American government to discover what made the Japanese tick.

The enigmatic Japanese

The Japanese are, to the highest degree, both aggressive and inaggressive, both militaristic and aesthetic, both insolent and polite, rigid and adaptable, submissive and resentful of being pushed around, loyal and treacherous, brave and timid, conservative and hospitable to new ways.

Ruth Benedict *The Chrysanthemum and The Sword*[7] (1946)

Both America and Japan hunger for success, which makes them such powerful economic rivals. However, whereas in America the passion for excellence is fuelled by personal enterprise and communally shared values, in Japan both the cultural and economic source and outlet are entirely different. More specifically, whereas the Westerner's drive is personal and materially rooted, the Easterner's is collectively motivated and spiritually stimulated.

Cultural adaptability

The Japanese have been collectively conditioned over the centuries to feel a profound sense of dissatisfaction, according to Japan's eminent psychiatrist Takeo Doi.[8] This endures until they have completed whatever task they have embarked upon, or whatever goal they have set themselves. When the goal is a great one, therefore, there is no end to the dissatisfaction that the Japanese feel. They set themselves to work at a furious pace to relieve the dis-ease they experience when confronted with something unresolved. The pursuit of quality, and the relentless capacity for adaptation, both stem from this collective urge for meaning and for resolution.

Group harmony

With the fall of the feudal system in 1868, the new government began an intensive campaign to raise the level of the Japanese economy to that of Europe and America. An important part of this campaign was a concerted effort to imbue every child in the country with a concept of success, known as '*Risshin Shusse*'.

Shusse is distinctive in that it places major emphasis on the group rather than the individual. So already we have a particular Japanese flavor. The success of the individual is seen to depend on the success of the group. The process of rising to eminence begins with the immediate work group and, by extension, goes all the way up to include the whole country.

As a result, and at all levels, reciprocal obligation vertically, and harmony of intention, laterally, is all important. *Shusse*, moreover, is not measured in terms of wealth, but in relation to social position. Therefore it is not the extent of Japan's wealth, but its social and economic standing in the world which is ultimately seen to count.

Societal adaptability

Adaptability, for the Japanese, carries the same weight and influence as enterprise, for the Americans, albeit in a group context. But its source and direction is rather different. In place of frontier spirit there is 'gumption', instead of an action orientation there is reflective contemplation, and in place of the American Dream there is the 'Japanese Godhead'.

Exercising 'gumption'

The American social philosopher, Robert Pirsig, wrote a book in the seventies that became an immediate bestseller. In *Zen and the Art of Motorcycle Maintenance*[9] Pirsig uses his motorcycle as a metaphor for technology as a whole. I have adapted his intentions just a little[10] to take into account business, technology and society.

If you are going to repair a motorcycle (turn around a company), Pirsig says, an adequate supply of 'gumption' is the first and most important tool. A person filled with gumption does not sit around dissipating time and stewing about things. He is at the front line of his own awareness, watching attentively to see what lies ahead, and meeting it when it comes. The gumption, then, is the psychological gasoline that keeps your personal vehicle going. Pirsig goes on to identify 'gumption traps'. Of these the most widespread and pernicious is 'value rigidity'. This involves an inability to revalue what one sees because of a commitment to previous values. The next trap is 'ego'. If one has a high opinion of oneself the ability to recognize new facts is weakened. So as we can see, gumption begins to look less and less like the direct equivalent of American 'enterprise'.

Attaining peace of mind

The central theme of Pirsig's book is not gumption, an interesting sideline, but quality. The mountain of achievement, he says, represents quality discovered in the outer direction only. So externalized achievement is relatively meaningless, as well as often unobtainable, unless taken together with 'the ocean trenches of self-awareness'. This self-awareness arises from peace of mind, which is in its turn the key to quality's inner direction. Notice again how the emphasis shifts from the restless pursuit of gain to the restful attainment of quality. Quality, or its absence, does not reside in either the subject, that is the person, or in the object, that is the product. It lies in the relationship between the two. When there is genuine caring by the producer for the product, quality results. The secret behind the Japanese capacity to adapt is not any spirit of enterprise, as understood in the Western sense, but rather a mixture of religious and aesthetic qualities.

The Japanese godhead

No-thing ('mu')

The religious influence comes from Zen Buddhism. The way that Robert Pirsig has put it is that the 'Godhead' can be found just as easily in the gears of a motorcycle transmission as in the heavens above. In order to come to that sort of realization a person has to acquire the habit of complete openness, through which he or she lives totally in the present. By virtue of living totally in the present the individual, paradoxically, is wholly open to the future. No preconceptions get in the way. The mind is kept hollow and therefore takes in completely what is happening around it. One finds symbols of this kind in a Japanese garden, where a few large rocks stand alone in a sea of pebbles. Translated into business terms, it is reflected in the market niche that nobody has yet spotted. It has been standing alone in a sea of already fulfilled needs.

Adaptability and enterprise

In conclusion, the extraordinary ability that the Japanese have to adapt to, and to adopt, new technologies and markets, results from a combination of qualities that are largely alien to us in the West. The combination of Japanese gumption, contemplation and quality, provides the Eastern business thrust. It is very different in origin, if not in impact, to American wealth creation, active experimentation and quantity. If that combination is the source of the ongoing Japanese challenge, where does the culture's inner cohesiveness come from?

Group harmony

To understand the source of cultural cohesion, whether within society at large, or in business, we need to turn from the individual person or group to the family or household.

Collective household ('uchi')

The Japanese family system differs from the American, European, African or even Chinese. Family ethics are not based on individual relationships between husband and wife or between brothers and sisters, but on the collective family group. The household, as a whole, rather than any particular member of it, has the ultimate integrating power. As a result, in a Japanese organization, there is no clearcut division of responsibility between a manager and his subordinates. So whereas patterns of reciprocal responsibility are woven into the organizational fabric no individual holds ultimate power.

In fact the Japanese language has no word for the term 'leadership'. For the so-called leader is expected to be so thoroughly involved in the group that his personal identity disappears. The extent to which the Japanese employee is dependent upon both his work group and his lifetime employer is absolute. A new employee is in just about the same position as a newly born family member, or a newly adopted son-in-law. Indeed the relationship between employer and employee cannot be explained in contractual terms. They are bound together as one by fate.

Reciprocal obligation ('oyabun')

Give and take

The core of the Japanese family, ancient and modern, is the parent–child relationship, and not that between husband and wife. The basis for mutuality in Japanese organizational life is therefore formed by this relationship, as it exists in the family. The ready acceptance of an order by a junior predisposes the senior in his favor, and the accumulation of such give and take strengthens the bond between the two. The relationship between the larger Japanese employer and his employees is, therefore, not primarily an economic one. The average employer gets from his workers an inordinate degree of loyalty, cooperation and effort. In turn, the employer feels responsible for his employees' social and spiritual as well as his economic wellbeing. This reciprocal parent/child-like relationship is replicated at each level of organization, as we shall see at the Sony Corporation (see Chapter 26).

The parent/child relationship also extends beyond the boundaries of an individual firm. A characteristic of Japanese industry, in fact, is for each of the larger firms to attach themselves to a host of smaller subsidiaries. These are known as 'ko-gaisha' or child companies. The same principles of reciprocal obligation apply in these external relationships as in the internal ones, though the extent of the alignment is determined by the degree of dependence. Dependence, of course, is regarded in a positive light in Japan, unlike in America.

Rank and status

Japanese organization, therefore, involves an extremely subtle balance between obligation and mutuality, dependence and interdependence, that outsiders, including myself, find difficult to describe. Certainly there is an aspect to Japanese business and life that, as Ruth Benedict affirms, appears to be extremely regimented, if not outright authoritarian.

Everything in its place

'*Ai*' means specifically the love of a superior for his dependents. A Westerner might perhaps feel that it meant 'paternalism', but in its Japanese usage it means more than that. It is a word that means affection . . . Love from above to below. The Japanese way of life allocates proper authority and defines its proper sphere. It gives much greater deference – and therefore freedom of action – to 'superiors' than Western cultures do, but they must keep their station. Japan's motto is: everything in its place.

Ruth Benedict *The Chrysanthemum and the Sword*[11] 1946

The Japanese then, especially those born before 1945, have a very shallow and fragile concept of themselves as individual entities. As a result the professional in Japan ranks very low, and can even be disregarded if the company for which he works is not of high status. Status and ranking is all important to the Japanese. Every person, every company, every university, and probably every nation is ranked. In fact, the particular strength of the typical large-scale organization today springs from the traditional social manners and ethics as they were developed in feudal times. For centuries people were told to respect authority and to work cooperatively. These attitudes were also reinforced by the Confucian influence from Ancient China. In return for this respect the same people were guaranteed a livelihood and protection. The system was made to hold together by minutely defined obligations, through a highly refined etiquette system, and through an acknowledgement of dependence.

Dependence and interdependence

Takeo Doi, to whom I have already referred, wrote a book entitled *The Anatomy of Dependence*. In it he describes '*amae*' as the oil of Japanese life. His American interpreter, Boye De Mente[12] goes so far as to say that *amae* is the pillar around which the traditional character of the Japanese is built. *Amae* is literally the quality of absolute love that an infant receives from its mother. In practical terms a Japanese person does not feel right in any relationship if that feeling of complete trust and confidence is absent. As a result the person who can 'safely' encourage such dependence, in its purest form, is best qualified for leadership. The Japanese are therefore reluctant to extend their friendship to anyone with whom they do not share complete trust. To form such a relationship takes a great deal of time and careful nurturing. This applies to not only individuals in a work group, but also to customers, suppliers, and to people engaging in joint ventures with them. The Japanese therefore require a degree of intimacy and a quality of 'mothering' which is quite alien to business people in the North and West. These, then, have been the external influences that have helped to shape the Japanese character. As a result a cohesive organizational form, constructed out of a subtle combination of mutuality and obligation, dependence and interdependence, has supported the assertive force, the national and adaptive drive for achievement.

Conclusion

In conclusion the Japanese economic miracle is the result of a very subtle blend of forces. The combination of adaptivity and harmony, transposed from an Eastern cultural context into a modern business context, has resulted in a developmental approach to management. Such an approach, combining gumption with aesthetic awareness, and contemplation with a sense of reciprocal obligation, is by now well analyzed but poorly synthesized, Whereas the American is individually enterprising, the Japanese is collectively adaptive; whereas the West shares personal values within an independent and corporate melting pot, the East harmonizes group values within an interdependent Japanese Inc.

The 'developmental' approach to management is, in fact, constructed upon foundations of individual and organizational interdependence that cut completely across the American spirit of independence. I now want to turn North–South, to investigate the cultural foundations of first, the rational and second, the metaphysical approaches to management.

References

1. R. Lessem, *The Global Business*, Prentice Hall (1987).
2. T. Peters and B. Waterman, *In Search of Excellence*, Harper & Row (1982).
3. H. Commager, *America in Perspective*, Mentor (1948), p. 35.
4. T. Rogers, *Think*, Weidenfeld & Nicolson (1969).
5. Ex T. Rogers, *op. cit.*
6. L. Lehr, personal interview, (1985).
7. R. Benedict, *The Chrysanthemum and the Sword*, (1946).
8. T. Doi, ex Opie Nakane, *Japanese Society*, Weidenfeld & Nicolson (1970).
9. R. Pirsig, *Zen and the Art of Motorcycle, Maintenance*, Corgi (1976), p. 289.
10. R. Lessem, *op. cit.*
11. R. Benedict, *op. cit.*, p. 74.
12. B. De Mente, *The Japanese Way of Doing Business*, Prentice Hall (1981), p. 132.

3 North–South

Contents

Key concepts

Once you have fully understood this chapter you should be able to define the following concepts in your own terms:

Archetypes	Order
Collective unconscious	Primal management
Developmental management	Quality
Dream	Rational management
Flow principle	Scientific revolution
Freedom	Story
Integrity principle	Totality principle
Latency principle	Vision
Metaphysical management	

Objectives

Upon completing this chapter you should be able to do the following:

1. Outline, in essence, the background and context of the Northern approach to rational management.
2. Describe, in outline, the background and context of the Southern approach to metaphysical management.
3. Compare and contrast the Northern and Southern background and approaches to management.
4. Identify the essential differences between the American, British, Japanese and African approaches to management.
5. Relate all these to your own management style, acknowledging where you have the greatest ease, and difficulty, in comprehension.

Introduction

Whereas in moving from West to East the focus of management shifts from personal enterprise and communally shared values to corporate adaptability and organizational harmony, in moving North–South we confront another set of polarities. In essence, European management, in the North, has the job of reconciling individual freedom with organizational order, while the South has the particular managerial task of reconciling physical energy with creative spirit.[1] While the former is the task of rational management, the latter is the subject of what I have termed metaphysical management. I shall begin in the European North, and then proceed to the African South.

The spirit of Britain

In presenting you with the North I had great difficulty in selecting a manageable focus. Ideally I should have liked to consider Europe in its richly varied entirety. But that prospect proved too much for me, and may well have turned out to be confusing for you. So I opted for Great Britain because of its apt geographical and historical position.

Freedom *versus* order

Fertile grounds for order, in a British setting, are found in two places. The one contains a spirit of tolerance, and the other an orientation towards quality. Thus fertile grounds for organizational order do not lie in regimented and class-based authority but in a sense of fairness and justice (tolerance), coupled with a sense of aesthetic balance and appreciation (quality). Similarly, fertile grounds for individual freedom in Britain are to be found in two other places. The one contains a spirit of creativity and the other a love of recreation. Thus fertile grounds for personal freedom lie not in 'bucking the system' for its own sake, nor even in 'making your pile'. Rather it lies in a combination of subtle humor, scientific inventiveness and artistic illumination (creativity), coupled with a sense of fun and a love of play (recreation). Let me now investigate each of these in turn.

Order within freedom

The most fertile grounds for organizational order, in Great Britain in particular if not in Europe in general, combine the pursuit of quality with a spirit of tolerance. Similarly unfertile business grounds, derived from the same cultural source, would combine overdue product orientation with a spirit of apathy or indifference.

The pursuit of quality

> Productivity is higher in New York, Dusseldorf, Paris and Stockholm. There is a nervous intensity in these towns; crowds hustle along city streets, heads down, business-like. People in London streets tend to amble round, move more slowly. This hurts the growth rate, but it may ease the psyche.[2]

The ideal businessman
The above quotation from a correspondent with the Washington Post, Bernard Nossiter, may be less applicable to Thatcherite Britain than to the sixties and seventies, but a strong grain of truth remains. John Ruskin, the nineteenth century English writer and philosopher, described his ideal businessman, as one dedicated to a code of honor instead of a calculus of advantage, and 'taking as his duty the enhancement of the quality, not the quantity of life'. J. A. Hobson, the economic historian, followed Ruskin in arguing that the true value of a thing is neither the price paid for it, nor the amount of present satisfaction it yields to the customer, but the intrinsic service it is capable of yielding by its right use. Those goods that have a capacity for satisfying wholesale human wants provide 'wealth', whereas those that are detrimental to man he called 'ilth'.[3] A. H. Marshall, the influential economist of the late nineteenth century, suggested that money should be incidental to the task of doing a job well. He hoped to encourage the spread of such 'economic chivalry' amongst the nation's business élite. In fact, just before he died he wished he might have devoted his life to psychology rather than to economics.

Quality consciousness
In recent years, that is over the course of the twentieth century, much of this quality-con- sciousness has gone underground because the nation's pride in itself has slipped. Yet

interestingly enough, in the 1980s it has resurfaced, in the form of a strongly heightened design awareness. The Conservative party has made design a key feature of its economic policies. The furniture designer Terence Conran, featured as one of the visionaries in this text (see pp. 649–52) has fought a personal crusade in this respect. It is as if, in Britain, quality and mass production could never be entirely reconciled. Now that the microchip is enabling us to combine freedom of choice with order in production – through flexible manufacturing systems – the UK may once more come into its own. To pursue this argument we need to move on to the spirit of tolerance.

The spirit of tolerance

> The country has never been torn apart by prolonged bloody revolution; its rulers have accommodated themselves to change and reform.[4]

We're a mixed lot!

As a refugee from an oppressive regime in the country of my birth, I can vouch for the fact that British society is a relatively tolerant one. The nature and extent of this tolerance has only become apparent to me through a study of history. It came as a complete eye opener to me when I picked up Toynbee's monumental *Study of History*[5] and discovered Great Britain's real roots. I have reproduced his diagram (Fig. 4),[6] as an indication of how cosmopolitan this nation really is.

Learning to live and let live

English, if not British history, concerns a people who, five hundred years before the birth of Christ, first settled on an island off the coast of continental Europe. Our island was created by an Atlantic flood which, eight thousand years ago, cut it off from the European mainland. Like the rest of Europe, Great Britain, after the ending of glacial times, was settled by perhaps three ethnic stocks: Nordic, Alpine and Mediterranean. Then, around 500 BC, the relatively recent settlers followed from France, Germany, Holland and Scandinavia:

> Refugees from the mainland, they were from the beginning a mixed lot, and their story is a standing refutation of all theories that claim racial purity to be a recipe for national success.[7]

Unable to find sufficient food to maintain themselves, the immigrants sought richer soil. Many of them were Celts whose forebears, in prehistoric times, had spread from the steppes of Southern Russia into Central Europe. In classical times the Celts had been warlike, for in 390 BC they sacked Rome, but by 100 BC they had settled down, to mingle with the native population. They learnt, as a result of bitter struggle and difficulty, to live with and tolerate other peoples. Successive invasions of Romans, Jutes, Angles and Saxons, Danes, Norwegians and Normans never completely broke this pattern of tolerance for diversity:

> The survival of racial minorities, defying yet ultimately intermingling with the predominant majority, together with the island climate and situation, shaped English history. Long, tall and broad, short build and tall, dark pigmentation and blonde ... such intermixture in so small an island helped to make its people many-sided and versatile.[8]

Fig. 4 Britain's roots in European cultures.

So much diversity among neighbours was a constant stimulus and education. Yet England was fortunate in that the invasions which gave her so mixed an ancestry were separated by long periods. This enabled each new influence to be digested, and saved the island from anarchy, at one extreme, and complacency at the other. Moreover, left to themselves the Anglo Saxons of a thousand years ago might have settled down to a sluggish torpor. But they were harried by the Danes and Norsemen, and subsequently conquered by the Normans. In the face of these powerful minorities the Anglo Saxons had to struggle for centuries to retain their customs, institutions and language. Moreover, behind their well-ploughed shires, lurked the vibrant and artistic Celts.

The immigrants kept on coming

After the Norman conquest of 1066, the steady stream of immigrants continued, no longer invaders, but refugees flying to England's shores from poverty and persecution. Flemings came in the fourteenth and sixteenth centuries, Huguenots in the seventeenth, Jews in the eighteenth, and West Indians and Pakistanis in our own day. Added to these have been, in recent times, more than a sprinkling of immigrants, from the old colonies and America, who have been attracted to Great Britain by the liberal atmosphere and cultural stimulus. With the advent of international business, particularly in the City of London, a mix of faces and cultures from all over the globe has descended on the British Isles. The fact that English is an international language has reinforced this tendency, and provided educational opportunities that foreigners take up here.

Value in diversity

Over 2,500 years, each of the invading or immigrant populations brought something distinctive, which has never been lost. The Celts were a vibrant and artistic nation, who treated their women as equals – a trait which has only recently begun to return to modern civilizations. The Romans built the first roads, aqueducts and solidly constructed buildings. The Anglo Saxons were the early farmers, and the Normans were the great advocates of law and order. It was the Danes, however, who introduced the first juries, and these Viking colonists were the early sailors, adventurers and tradesmen. They, in fact, taught the Anglo Saxons much in the line of trade, a field of activity which has been strongly developed by the Jews and Asians more recently. The West Indians, in their turn, have brought with them music, and a sporting prowess, which is gradually spreading into many fields of physical and prospectively commercial endeavor.

Quality and tolerance

The fertile, orderly grounds within British culture are, therefore, distinctive. They involve a blend of craftsmanship and aesthetic appreciation with accommodation of diversity in people and things. This qualitative order is best represented not within established industrial organizations but in the picturesque rural landscapes, throughout the United Kingdom. What is so striking about the countryside in the UK is its extraordinary patchwork structure. It combines, in the most fascinating way, unconventional order with conventional disorder. The basic principle of an English garden is that it must be carefully planned to look as unplanned and natural as possible. There must be no formal symmetry. The object is to make the garden appear as if it were part of the natural landscape and not an artificial pattern imposed by man. Nature must be given, or seen to be given, its head and not cut down to size. Within this framework, which is instinctive rather than theoretical, an immense amount of variety is possible. Along with this variety comes a balance of shape, timing and form, (whereby the heights of various flowers and shrubs, and the different times at which they will flower, are taken into account). The same might apply to an organization structured along those innate lines.

Freedom within order

Whereas the pursuit of quality and a spirit of tolerance constitute the fertile grounds for order, a love of recreation and a spirit of creativity constitute the grounds for freedom – of the most fertile variety. We start with the love of recreation.

The love of recreation

The preference for leisure over goods applies chiefly to those toiling in mines or on assembly lines, labouring at routine tasks in huge white collar bureaucracies, public and private. This work cannot, does not enlarge personality; quite the contrary. It diminishes it. They work because they must, to earn enough to support themselves and their families. It is these workers who have decided there are limits to how long and hard they will labour for extra goods. Britons, in short, appear to be the first citizens of the post-industrial age who are choosing leisure over goods on a large scale ... It reflects an attitude, a lifestyle, a choice. .[9]

A sense of fun, the pursuit of hobbies, a love of play, and a spirit of adventure, is innate to the British. 'Play', in this context, is not the American variety, involving lots of physical exertion, nor the Mediterranean version, involving a lot of social activity. The British version is more reflective and introverted in character. Moreover, as Nossiter has indicated, it affects working life as well as leisure. Generalizing from this, many would argue that the Briton gets more satisfaction from his unpaid work than from his job. This is because, perhaps, Britons are such rugged individualists.

Rugged individualism

The more frustrated the British become, working for some bureaucratic department, the more energy they put into DIY, community work, gardening, the local computer user's club, or some such recreation. Yonedi Masuda has extrapolated this trend a stage further. As a Japanese futurist who has written a book on *The Information Society*, he claims that:

> If the goal of industrial society is represented by volume consumption of durable consumer goods or realization of heavy mass consumption, the information society may be termed one of highly intellectual creativity where people may draw future designs on an invisible canvas, and pursue and release individual lives worth living.[10]

Anthony Glyn, in his book *The Blood of a Britishman*,[11] maintains that the object of work to the average Briton is to do something, produce something, repair something, complete something. The work is a means to an end, not an end in itself. One of the reasons that so many mindless bureaucrats occupy certain positions of mediocrity in certain large establishments, is because, deep down, they cannot see the purpose in what they do. This is of course different from the attitude of many Germans, Japanese or Swiss, who may be drawn towards work for its own sake, or on behalf of their organizations and communities. Such a British attitude to work parallels that of the 'gifted amateur' who becomes involved, through innate interest in what he is doing, rather than as a result of professional training.

The cult of the gifted amateur

There is, perhaps, no better known example of 'Britishness', in this recreational context, than the cult of the gifted amateur. One of the earliest and most illustrious cases in point was William Caxton, who brought the printing press to England in 1477:

> Caxton was an early and prominent example of a well known modern type ... the individual-istic Englishman following out his own hobbies ... As a successful merchant he made enough money during 30 years to devote his later life to the literary pursuits he loved.[12]

Caxton provides us with a good example of an individual making the best possible use of the mature phase of his life. Professor Charles Handy refers to that phase as the 'third age',[13] an age of development and recreation:

> Caxton began by translating French books into English. While so engaged, he fell in love with the mystery of printing with movable types. In 1474 he produced abroad two of his own translations, the first books to be printed in our language. Then in 1477 he brought over his press to England, set it up at Westminster, and there during the remaining fourteen years of his life, under royal and noble patronage, he poured out nearly a hundred books. His diligence and success as translator, printer and publisher, did much to lay the foundations of literary English.[14]

In turning his recreation into work and vice versa, William Caxton has had a profound effect on this country's destiny. The same applies to the Reverend Doctor Edmund Cartwright, the inventor of the power loom at the end of the eighteenth century. Here is an excerpt from Cartwright's own correspondence:

> Happening to be at Matlock in the summer of 1784 I fell in company with some gentlemen of Manchester, when the conversation turned on Arkwright's spinning machinery.

One of the company observed that by the time Arkwright's patent had expired, many more mills had been erected, and cotton spun, than there were hands to weave it. Something had to be done about the situation, perhaps involving Arkwright in the invention of a weaving mill. But the Manchester gentlemen agreed that this was impractical:

> ...addressing arguments I was certainly incompetent to answer or even comprehend, being totally ignorant of the subject, I controverted, however, the impracticability of their arguments by commenting that there had lately been exhibited in London an automaton figure that played chess. Full of ideas I employed a carpenter and a smith ...[15]

By the following year Cartwright had taken out a patent on a power loom which he had invented – the clergyman had turned technologist.

Another prominent example of such gifted amateurism is represented in the group of industrialists, scientists, artists and craftsmen who met in Birmingham – at more or less the same period as Cartwright's gentlemen from Manchester – and conspired to change the world. They established a network of connections in their so-called 'Lunar Society', uniquely combining friendship and self-interest. The society included such people as Josiah Wedgwood, James Watt, Benjamin Franklin and Joseph Priestley. And the reason, for example, that Wedgwood initially joined was to pursue his interests in canals rather than in pottery or industry. As far as these 'lunatics' were concerned, their work and recreation were inseparable.

The spirit of creativity

Whereas a love of recreation reflects one fertile source of individual freedom, a spirit of creativity represents the other. Such creative grounds contain, within them, both artistic and scientific originality and innovation. European civilization, as a whole, has made an enormously creative contribution to the development of mankind. Whereas artistic creativity has been exhibited by all nations, across the globe, Europe's uniquely creative contribution has been in the field of science and technology. While grounds for such scientific and technological creativity have stretched across Europe as a whole, a few countries – Britain France, Italy and Germany – have, in the last few hundred years, played the leading part. Of these European countries, Britain's role has been pre-eminent. Why should this have been?

The Celtic tradition

We can trace a line of creative activity, from long before the European Renaissance, stretching back to the Celts in pre-Christian England. In fact it was the Belgic Celts, some 2,500 years ago, who first introduced gold coinage, made pottery, and had ploughs constructed of iron. At the same time they practiced a form of art that involved abstract patterns, free flowing curves, and fantastic reliefs. The Celts who immigrated into Britain produced art of a much higher quality than the Romans or any other invading group. They had beautifully shaped pots, colorful clothes and made exquisite jewellery. They were also musical, possessing flutes, horns and trumpets and the men played a kind of hockey and exercised with swords.

Smith was a Saxon god

Anthony Glyn points out that the British have traditionally had a love of metals – which accounts for the most popular name being Smith. That love dates back not only to the Celts, but also to the Saxons, one of whose gods, Thor, was a smith. The Saxon's great hero, Siegfried, not only conquered and overthrew the existing establishment, but also had to be a smith forging his own sword. Legends like this are deep in the English folk memory. As a result, the Industrial Revolution that began in the North of England, hundreds of years later:

> was not so much an increased production of cotton or wool or railway engines, important though all these became in the industrial world. It was something deeper, an understanding of the importance of the machine in life.[16]

Today, this identification with the world of machines is made visible in many ways. There is the Englishman playing about with the engine of his motorbike or car, on the one hand, and the youngster tinkering with a new computer accessory, on the other. Glyn maintains that it is this combined technical and artistic heritage, stretching back to the Saxons and Celts, that explains our Industrial Revolution. The well-known economic historian, Walt Rostow, naturally has a more sophisticated explanation, to which we now turn.

The great scientific adventure

In his book entitled *How it all Began*,[17] Rostow sets out to explain why the industrial revolution happened, as well as when and where it did. There is no doubt in Rostow's mind that the advance of science and technology was the primary cause, rather than the commercial, demographic, and territorial expansion that was occurring in the seventeenth and eighteenth centuries. It is, as he puts it 'the organized creativity of the human mind' that made all the difference. Rostow traces the origins of the industrial revolution back to developments in European scientific thought, rather than to events in Britain in particular. He describes the way in which a small circle of men sought to discover the laws of heavenly and terrestrial motion.

These sixteenth and seventeenth century scientists knew they were involved in a great adventure. It was a conscious revolution engaging men from Cracow to London, from

Scandinavia to France. The effort was carried forward by a combination of basic principles and practical observations. The meaning of the results was generalized beyond physics and astronomy to anatomy and chemistry. Public authorities were very much in favor of the work that was being done, particularly in countries like Britain, where religion had less of a tight hold on people's hearts and minds, than in, say, Spain or Italy. The question that does remain is why Britain should have led the way, at least towards the industrial, if not the scientific revolution. Here again, Rostow helps us to understand. He describes the three elements that were missing from the ancient world, and which when introduced, converted a slow moving economic expansion into an industrial revolution.

First there was the philosophical impact of Newton's new synthesis. Men were given a new sense of power and confidence that an order of nature was there to be found. Few read Newton's *Principia*, but its triumphant message had the right impact. By changing the way man looked at the world around him, the Newtonian perception increased the supply of inventors and the willingness of entrepreneurs to introduce innovations. The second element built into the scientific revolution, was the two-way linkage between scientists and tool makers. Scientists were willing to learn what they could from the craftsmen. The separation of the man of learning from the craftsman – to be observed from Ancient Greece to medieval Europe – began to disappear. Thirdly, the scientists were not as yet so specialized as to be out of contact with the language, thought and practice of ordinary men. Physicists and chemists such as Franklin and Priestley, were in intimate contact with the leading figures in British industry, like James Watt and Josiah Wedgwood. Through the 'Lunar Society', which I have already mentioned, these people met together as artists and craftsmen, scientists and industrialists, philosophers and engineers. The names of engineers, iron masters, industrial chemists and instrument makers on the list of Fellows of the Royal Society shows how close the relations between science and practice were at the time.

The phenomenon of British inventiveness

While its economy and technology have seemingly declined, during this century, Britain is still seen to be an originator of the very technologies which have seemingly helped to cause that decline. For it was Charles Babbage and Ada Lovelace (Lord Byron's daughter) who were the father and mother of computing. Charles created the seminal hardware and Ada was the first producer of software, in the nineteenth century. Denis Gabor – a Hungarian who emigrated to this country – created holography, which has led in its turn to laser technology. Then Crick at Cambridge (with the American Watson) discovered DNA, which has led to all kinds of developments in biotechnology and genetic engineering.

In none of these three emerging industry groups does Britain have the major companies exploiting the technologies to anywhere near the extent of Japan and America. So what the critics say – and the British love to criticize themselves as well as others – is that we know how to invent but not how to exploit. Our creative vigor takes us halfway there, but not the whole hog. Now this is another of those half-truths that has cost Britain dear because of its negative impact on our national and economic psyche. It is a half-truth for the very reasons that the British are generally outstanding at producing and selling some things and not others. Generally speaking, the more artistically based the product or service – like advertising or television programs – the better the link between production and marketing.

Gaining freedom through order

The themes of quality and diversity, fun and creativity, are now pervading a wide cross-section of industries in which Great Britain is gaining prominence. The City has always offered the modern equivalent of Britain's early Vikings', and later merchant adventurers', scope for imagination and flair. Unfortunately parts of it have become too much of an enclave so that the flair becomes narrowly channelled, and the countervailing traditions backward looking. A way still needs to be found of combining freedom and order, within the City in the ways outlined in this chapter. At the present time, there is too little creativity (freedom) and subtlety (order). We probably know that television, music, theater and pop culture are emerging industries. Interestingly enough, computer software, which may not seem intimately connected with pop music, is often written by the same people who were playing guitars in the sixties. Computers and design come together in the creation of the new flexible manufacturing systems which will gradually replace the old assembly lines in the industrialized countries.

What we are now finding is that the values of the economist and the psychologist are coming together. Whereas the one looks for standardization and simplification, the other wants to cater for the fundamental human need for change, choice and variety. It is the very same polarity that faces the modern manager. The resolving of these polarities comes through quality engineering and the tolerance of difference, on the one hand, combined with the art of recreation and scientific creativity, on the other. So what we are finding is some kind of amalgam between Adam Smith and Karl Marx, on the one hand, and Isaac Newton and E. F. Schumacher on the other. Each one of them attempted to combine freedom and order in a particular way, and in a particular context. Each arose out of, or entered into, the British heritage, at one stage or another, although each had an impact worldwide. Interestingly enough it is in the South, today, and in the developing countries in general, that the debate between capitalism (Adam Smith) and socialism (Karl Marx), and between indigenous roots (Schumacher) and modern technology (Newton) is being conducted, particularly rigorously. Unfortunately, in the developing world, this all too often clouds the real management issue.

South: energy and spirit

The story of Africa

Africa is the home of man. It has the longest inhabited history of all the continents. The great Southern African adventurer, novelist and philosopher, Laurens Van der Post, vividly represents this African perspective in his writings. As a friend of Prince Charles he is also making his influence felt in the North, particularly in Great Britain today.

History presents the story as lived

I had been born with as great a passion for history as for stories – not surprisingly, as both are part of the same indivisible process. History presents the story as lived. The story presents the options and possibilities of life that might have been, and can still be lived. There are moments of crisis when the past is not an inevitability, but presents life with a creative course of new action.

Laurens Van der Post *Venture into the Interior*[18] (1954)

Business is an unfolding story, with intermittent crises, and many a fork along the road of development. The sense, in man and enterprise, of the unrealized potential in life and time, a sense of what though invisible is yet to come, is a source of immense creativity. It enables man, and businessman, to make the purposeful choices along their path. In his seminal work on organizational transformation the American business consultant and lay preacher, Harrison Owen, has introduced myth, ritual and – above all – the unfolding and recurring story into the formative life of an organization.

Myth and legend

Legends and myths attempt to explore the depths of past history in order that we may understand our present society, so that we can go into the future with confidence. Myths help us understand the development of humanity, by demarcating clearly between past present and future. In doing so they assist us in uncovering our innermost beliefs.

George Kahari *The Contemporary African Novel*[19] (1984)

Metaphysical management

It is through the story of its creation, and re-creation, according to Harrison Owen, that the 'spirit' of the organization, is conveyed along its journey. The task of the business visionary is to turn that creative spirit into physical energy, and back again. That act of transformation also forms the substance of metaphysical management. That act is the unique task that the South has yet to accomplish.

> The spiritual conflict in Africa is striving to re-establish the primal unity of man with both the material and the spiritual universe which African man instinctively feels to be true 'being', and which hardly exists anywhere in Africa today.[20]

Commercial enterprises in Africa, such as the one cited in Chapter 26, are only beginning to wake up to that metaphysical challenge. Interestingly enough these enterprises that lend themselves to the role of metaphysical management are inevitably agriculturally based. They are close to mother earth, and to the so-called 'spirit provinces' of the land. Such metaphysical management in fact applied to the organization of the liberation struggle, in Zimbabwe, during the seventies.

The 'spirit' of the ancestors, and the 'energy' of material resources contained within the

The management of liberation

It would be a mistake to imagine that the image of the world to come was based entirely on an imaginary vision of the past. True, the people were promised that they would regain the land in the name of the ancestors, but straightway they would set about making use of all the modern techniques of production and marketing that had, up till then, been denied them. The present world had been rejected because it worked to the peasant's severe disadvantage, but, once this ancestral interregnum was over, the rewards would be better lives lived in comfortable surroundings, better food, better education for their children, better health care...

None-the-less without the powers of the ancestors to transcend the material plane, to triumph over the political sphere, these rewards would always remain out of reach.

David Lan *Guns and Rain*[21] 1985

land – to both of which my fellow Zimbabweans are very close – form a potential and managerial continuum whose two ends need to be linked. The one end corresponds with 'the dream' and the other with 'reality'.

The courage to dream

And Joseph had a dream, and he told it to his brethren, and they hated him yet the more.

Genesis, 37:5

Vision

Visionaries dream and also then turn their dreams into a reality. Yet 'vision', of late, has become an oversold and misused commodity. Because some business managers and academics are searching for an ulterior purpose without knowing how to reach it, they have trivialized vision. In other words, where the person does not find it, he wishes it were there, and so has to fulfil that wish. Warren Bennis and Burt Nanus set the right tone, however, in their recent book on *Leaders*.[22]

By focusing attention on a vision, the leader operates on the emotional and spiritual resources of the organisation, on its values, commitment and aspirations. The manager, by contrast, operates on the physical resources of the organisation, on its capital, human skills, raw materials, and tecnology.

The tone is right, but I am left wondering where both vision and spiritual resources come from, and how they can both be harnessed and developed. Companies, and the people within them, have to summon up the courage to dream. That courage is developed when contact is made with the originating forces in the company. Above all business leaders have to be willing to let go of the scepticism, realism and pragmatism that strangles original vision. They need to allow their 'aboriginal hearts' to be touched and, like Van der Post, to put aside, for the visionary moment, 'the grown up pale faces of my world'.[23]

Chief – Madunha

The Shona chief as I know him is no despot. He cannot evict any of his clan without good reason. He cannot impose rents or tithes on the people. He is in many ways the spiritual representative of the clan. His community can be pictured as a flower with his chief as the central part and his people as the petals linked to the centre.

Michael Gelfand *The Genuine Shona*[24] 1984

The primordial mirror

The 'aboriginal heart' of each and every one of us could only be maintained and enriched if, as Van der Post subsequently learnt from the Swiss psychologist Carl Gustav Jung, man and society kept in constant touch with its 'collective unconscious'. What the American organizational psychologist, Sabena Spencer, has already discovered is that : 'If an organization is in touch with its essence, or source of being, then it has the ability to regenerate itself.'[25] In the collective unconscious of great companies reside the spirit of their countries of origin, of the 'heroes' who founded the businesses and of the 'priests' who guarded their emerging culture. As Deal and Kennedy have written: 'Heroes are symbolic figures whose deeds are out of the ordinary ... Priests are guardians of the culture's values.' Both are in touch with the company's collective unconscious.

What Deal or Kennedy do not reveal is the place that the product or technology holds within the corporate psyche. In order to uncover the true and sustainable corporate culture we have to reach into the 'aboriginal heart' of the product or service. Tracy Kidder gave us a feeling for it in his popular tale, from General Data Corporation, of the launch of a new minicomputer. So much for the spirit of man and organization, that invisible dream world that the metaphysical manager is able to call on. However, spirit divorced from energy is like soul without body, or roots without branches.

Harnessing energy

Not surprisingly I have found in my own place of birth, Zimbabwe, that indigenous approaches to management and organization are most likely to take root within land-agriculture or mining-based enterprises. In fact the closeness to nature is a feature of the South that those of us in the West and North have begun to take to heart ourselves.

Man and nature

The importance of the earth of Africa to my own state of being predisposed me to believe that, however indescribable, there was between man and his nature earth an umbilical cord of life giving imponderables that no circumstance could cut, not even years of exile ... I love my own time too much and would not have chosen to live in any other ...

Yet, if forced to an alternative I would choose to be the first European in Africa free to see, before we laid our blind, violent hands upon it, the vast land glowing from end to end in the blue of its Madonna days like some fabulous art gallery with newly restored and freshly painted bushman canvasses of smooth stone and honey coloured rock.

Laurens Van der Post *Yet Being Someone Other*[26] 1984

The laws of nature

Not surprisingly, therefore, it is a company with strong roots in the South and East, that has formulated its principles of 'real management' (see Chapter 28) based upon natural laws. The Bank of Commerce and Credit, which reflects so strongly the spirit of the South, has grown from virtually nothing to 11,000 people spread over seventy countries, in a matter of fourteen years, because it has understood and applied the fundamental laws of nature. As its President and founder, Agha Hasan Abedi, has said:

> All creeds, all nationalities, all people are governed by the laws of nature. Nature transcends ethnic differences and national boundaries. The laws of nature are universal . . . They are part of the vast unconscious world which governs the more limited conscious world of our perception and reason.[27]

There are four principles, or natural laws, which governed the Bank's thoughts, feelings and actions from the outset:

The totality principle. Nature operates as a dynamic system in its integrated state. All parts of the system are interrelated and interdependent. They interfuse in and through the phenomenon of change, assume their dynamic shape in the form of evolution and live in eternity.

The flow principle. The dynamics of existence are in a state of constant flux. The process of change flows on and on. We live in and through change. We live in the fold of change. Nature is process; nature is change.

The latency principle. No-existence, which is infinite, is the container of existence, which is finite. With due humility, and lack of preconception, man and businessman can remain open to the infinite realm of opportunity.

The integrity principle. The moral, which is equivalent to the laws and principles of nature, governs all that is material. Hence, both must be acknowledged, treated and felt as inseparable. No company can assume its ultimate identity and its pure quality without becoming at one with its moral substance.

Energy and spirit

BCC's interpretation of the 'laws of nature', Jung's idea of the 'collective unconscious' and Van der Post's communion with Africa, all take us back to our origins, and forward *via* our path of originality. In more conventional terms, in the words of two American investigators of high performing organizations:

> The focus of development in the high performing frame of reference is on continuing trans-formation and renewal. This is accomplished through communication which links the positive heritage of the organization with its potential for excellence in the future.[28]

The capacity for such a transformation of energies rests within the psyche of organizations, and of their leaders – who are in touch with their spirit of origination, as well as with their ultimate destination.

Conclusion

Global perspectives

In the same way as the North needs the South, and vice versa, so the West needs the East, as well as the other way around. Already Japan has drawn from Western technology and Africa has adopted European forms of education and organization. However, whereas Japan has relied on its own cultural traditions as a unifying force, many of the developing countries have discarded – or failed to renew – their own, at great economic and social cost. Similarly, as yet, the intelligent North has not yet drawn on the South for inspiration, though the instinctive West is just beginning to draw on the East for its intuition and insight.

Global foundations

Finally, and in relation to the fertility of global business grounds, each quarter has its own contribution to make. (See Fig. 5.)

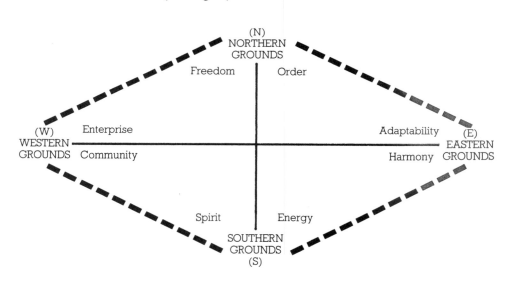

Fig. 5 Global business grounds.

The fertile Northern grounds, then, provide foundations for effectiveness, by efficiently channelling individual freedom through appropriately structured organizational order. The fertile Western grounds provide the foundations for excellence, intuitively holding enterprise and community together. The fertile Eastern grounds provide foundations for quality by subtly balancing commercial adaptability with organizational harmony. The fertile Southern grounds serve to actualize the manager's vision by creatively transforming the spirit of the organization into physical and psychic energy.

I now want to turn from the national and cultural grounds of global business to the alternately hard and soft attributes that underlie them. For behind these alternating features, which the American based management consultants, McKinsey's, have termed 'soft' and 'hard', and the ancient Chinese philosophers have called 'yin' and 'yang', are some very profound and enduring ideas.

References

1. R. Lessem, *The Global Business*, Prentice Hall (1987).
2. B. Nossiter, *A Future that Works*, Andre Deutsch (1977), p. 91.
3. G. M. Trevelyan, *The Social History of Britain*, Penguin (1967), p. 226.
4. B. Nossiter, *op. cit.*, p. 90.
5. P. Toynbee, *The Study of History*, Thames & Hudson (1964).
6. P. Toynbee, *The History of Mankind*, Thames & Hudson (1976).
7. R. J. White, *A Concise History of England*, Cassell (1971), p. 87.
8. A. Bryant, *The Spirit of England*, Collins (1982), p. 112.
9. B. Nossiter, *op cit.*, pp. 88–9.
10. Y. Masuda, *The Information Society*, Futures Publications (1976), p. 112.
11. A. Glyn, *The Blood of a Britishman*, Readers Union (1971).
12. G. M. Trevelyan, *op. cit.*, p. 96.
13. C. Handy, *The Future of Work*, Blackwell (1984).
14. G. M. Trevelyan, *op. cit.*, p. 102.
15. G. M. Trevelyan, *op. cit.*, p. 167.
16. A. Glyn, *op. cit.*, p. 228.
17. W. Rostow, *How It All Began*, Methuen (1975).
18. L. Van der Post, *Venture into the Interior*, Penguin (1954), p. 84.
19. G. Kahari, *The Contemporary African Novel*, unpublished thesis (1984), University of Zimbabwe.
20. H. Owen, *Spirit, Transformation and Development*, Abbott (1987).
21. D. Lan, *Guns and Rain*, Zimbabwe Publishing House (1985), p. 82.
22. W. Bennis and A. Nanus, *Leaders*, Harper & Row (1984), p. 28.
23. L. Van der Post, *The Lost World of the Kalahari*, Penguin (1967), p. 1.
24. M. Gelfand, *The Genuine Shona*, Mambo Press (1984), p. 18.
25. S. Spencer, 'The organization's unconscious', ex *Transforming Work*, J. Adams (ed.), Miles River Press (1985).
26. L. Van der Post, *Yet Being Someone Other*, Pension (1984).
27. A. H. Abedi, Bank of Credit and Commerce company magazine (1982).
28. Ex J. Adams (*see* S. Spencer, *op. cit.*).

4 The soft and hard edges of management

Contents

Key concepts

Once you have fully understood this chapter you should be able to define the following concepts in your own terms:

Competition	Masculinity
Cooperation	Right brain
Femininity	Yang
Left brain	Yin

Objectives

Upon completing this chapter you should be able to do the following:

1. Differentiate between yin and yang, 'feminine' and 'masculine', particularly in the context of management.
2. Compare and contrast the two sides of the brain, assessing the implications for management and organization.
3. Assess the organizational and commercial implications of cooperative and competitive behavior.
4. Comprehend the overall structure of this management text.
5. Identify the 'masculine' and 'feminine' traits within yourself, and assess their implications for management.

Introduction

In the early eighties the well known firm of business consultants, McKinsey's, introduced us to the 'soft', and 'hard' edges of management. Having gone to Japan in search of excellence, the two Americans – Pascale and Athos[1] – discovered that it was their unique blend of soft and hard qualities that enabled the Japanese managers to be successful. They subsequently concluded, as did Peters and Waterman who wrote the book *In Search of Excellence*,[2] that the best American companies follow the same pattern. Their managers combine soft qualities – skills, staff, shared values and style, with hard ones – structure, systems, and strategy. The need to combine soft attributes with hard is of fundamental importance to us, as prospective global managers. To that extent I am at one with my American colleagues. However, for the purposes of this text, the division between soft and hard qualities that they have developed is inadequate. It is *ad hoc*, rather than being rooted in substantive thinking. I have chosen, rather, the Ancient Chinese source of wisdom, as a basis for such division, that is the distinction between 'yin and yang'. In case this particular source of distinction fails to make the point clearly enough, I have drawn – subsequently – on the division between the right and left sides of the brain. This physiological difference has recently captured the imagination of neurologists, psychologists and managers alike, especially over the last ten years. Thirdly, and finally, I have related the soft and hard edges of management to cooperation and competition, respectively.

Yin and yang

The yin and yang of organizations

Nancy Foy wrote a book in 1980 entitled *The Yin and Yang of Organizations*.[3] She is a management educator and communicator who has spent extended periods of time with IBM and Standard Telephones and Cables (STC). As an astute observer of organizational life she has become particularly interested in the managerial complementarity between the so-called yin/soft and yang/hard forces.

Foy presents us with a series of yin–yang opposites, as shown in Table 10.

Table 10 Complementarities

Yin	Yang	Yin	Yang
Feeling	Thinking	Applied knowledge	Knowledge in itself
Relationships	Individuals	Oral tradition	Modern science
Myths	Models	Rituals	Games
Comprehensive	Analytic	Non-disciplinary	Disciplinary
Cooperation	Competition	Pleasure	Accomplishment
Intuition	Action	Diffused awareness	Focussed awareness
Mediator	Inventor	Relaxation	Determination
Consequence	Result	Maintenance	Construction
Community	Hierarchy	Space	Time
Unity	Polarity	Integration	Differentiation
Nourisher	Fertilizer	Spontaneous	Planned

Nancy Foy has endeavored to point out that organizations need to secure a balance between competition and cooperation, between diffused and focussed market awareness, between informal traditions and formal practices – to mention just a few of the important managerial complementarities. Should they not achieve some such balance they will be doomed to fail.

Yin and yang

All geat philosophical (or managerial) disputes can be reduced to an argument between those who are tough minded, rigorous and precise, and like to stress differences and divisions between things, and those tender minded romanticists who like wide generalisations and grand syntheses, and stress the underlying unities.

The first group prefers the idea of particles to waves and discontinuity to continuity, as the ultimate constituents of matter, while the second prefers the concept of waves. The first group also favour structuring organizations according to hierarchies kept in place by rigorous control and discipline, while the second trust in the underlying unity and harmony of all things, and the spontaneous capacity of people to know what is right for themselves.

Alan Watts *The Taboo Against Knowing Who You Are*[4] 1977

Masculine and feminine

Yin–yang theory, which receives some affirmation from both modern physics and analytical psychology, argues that there are two overall principles, the masculine and the feminine, inherent in all phenomena and responsible, by their interactions, for the emergence and dissolution of all things. 'Masculine' and 'feminine' principles do not correspond directly with male and female. A woman may have strong masculine traits and vice versa. Yin and yang describe a world in which people and things, structures and processes, make up different expressions of a continuum, rather than irreconcilable opposites. Management, like humanity at large, can only reveal itself in its essential wholeness when yin and yang are brought into conscious contact with one another.

Changes

Human (or managerial) consciousness has the possibility of finding wholeness if it learns to recognize the principles of development inherent in the changes of Yin and Yang. This involves a gradual evolution, moving cyclically from chaos to order, from undifferentiation to differentiation. It is a development in which an organization and its environment is divided into Yin and Yang by the active, separating energy of Yang, which, in turn, calls forth its polar opposite, the feminine principle. The opposing and yet complementary relationship of the two principles leads to their increasing polarisation, but not, if the laws of change follow their course, to their irreconcilable alienation.

Sukie Colegrave *The Spirit of the Valley*[5] 1979

The so-called laws of change or development will be investigated much more thoroughly in Section D. However, I should emphasize, at this point, that they lead to the progressive evolution of primal, rational, developmental and metaphysical management through cumulative changes in the composition of yin and yang. 'The yin-yang views civilization as a systematic and progressive development from simple, undifferentiated beginnings, towards a complex structure. The task of the sage is to understand the way in which change operates, and to learn to recognize moments of germination, maturity and decay.'[6] Change arises, within an evolving organization and environment, through the interaction of masculine and feminine principles.

The masculine principle behind change

The birth and development of the masculine principle, revolutionizes humanity's experience of itself and of the world. Instead of participating in the rhythms of nature, being contained and regulated by her laws, a drive emerges, drawing upon the assumption that people, not nature, should be primarily responsible for organizing life. Similarly, and by implication, the primal entrepreneur resolves to take charge of his or her own circumstances rather than being controlled by them.

The masculine principle then, in the form in which it developed in traditional China, offered the elite a liberation from their previous bondage to nature. It provided them with a way of understanding the world instead of being enslaved by it, of directing and planning their own lives instead of being the unwitting participants in nature's designs. It also offered them the chance of discovering their own individuality instead of being compelled by the collective impulses of the group. Through the masculine principle, people through the ages have acquired the hitherto unknown possibility of deliberately creating organizations, and whole societies, according to their own conceptions of morality and rectitude, order and justice.

Self-made man

The masculine principle does not only help us to differentiate the world in which we live, to discriminate between the different aspects of man and nature, organization and environment, thereby to classify and to order, it also leads us to an experience of our essential individuality. It gives us the certainty that we stand utterly alone in this world, unsupported by personal relationships. It brings the extraordinary and alarming knowledge that we can look to no one and no thing other than ourselves for directions and answers.

Sukie Colegrave *The Spirit of the Valley*[7] 1979

An awakening of the masculine principle is therefore essential for a person, a manager, an organization or even a nation if each is to acquire a sense of individual identity, and the ability to discriminate. However, if a manager relies too much on either masculine or feminine principle he or she loses it. One principle can only be continually explored and developed in relation to the other.

The feminine principle behind change

An awareness of the feminine principle is valuable to all stages of the development of the masculine. But at the beginning, in the birth of an organization or whole society, its importance is likely to be less significant. For at this early stage the need is to acquire personal independence from the communal whole. However, once sufficient independence from the primal whole has been achieved, individuals, organizations and societies need the complementary influence of the feminine, if they are to avoid despotism, and psychological impoverishment. Whereas the masculine approach to business involves, for example, exploiting opportunities, the feminine approach is different. It involves conceiving an idea, walking around it, lovingly participating in it, and letting it grow quietly from within until it is ready to be born in the world. It is a way of submitting to an evolving process rather than deliberately achieving fame or fortune through an effort of the will.

The feminine is, in fact, a bridging influence. It bridges the individual and the external worlds, one department and another, the conscious and subconscious minds, corporate strategy and corporate culture. In this capacity it acts as an agent of renewal and transformation. Without it we ossify.

Whereas the masculine principle promotes a subject–object relationship which characterizes, for example, the Western approach to systematic quality control, the feminine principle encourages an experience of unity between subject and object. This is a feature of the Japanese approach to quality circles, where subjective involvement with the product rises to the fore.

Men and women

Solitary, disciplined effort to master a skill or to conquer a technical or political problem is a characteristic strength expected of men. Such experience allows men to be 'objective', cool and rational. They have been taught from an early age to shut off their feelings, so that their connections to other people are often weak, as are the bridges between emotional and intellectual hemispheres of their minds.

A woman's life has a different texture. The surface is thickly woven with connections – love and friendship ties, family links, often a hypersensitivity to their own and others' feelings. Those form a web of loyalties that most women put before rules or abstract principles.

Gail Sheahy *Pathfinders*[8] 1983

Masculine and feminine principles

Ultimately, any healthy manager or organization needs to balance masculine with feminine principles, if his or her organization is to develop and prosper. In fact the very emergence of the feminine approach to management – whose salient characteristics are those of recognizing and helping to create relationships between either people or things, of being receptive and recognizing harmony – depends on a prior differentiation by the masculine principle of organizational and commercial activities. We cannot receive, integrate and harmonize – physically, socially or economically – before discovering separate products, people or activities, both in the outside environment and within our own organizations.

Masculine and feminine

The feminine consciousness does not deny the existence of the differentiated world; on the contrary, it could not exist without it. But it does assert that the separation between people and things is not the only reality, that there is another way of seeing, one which perceives the unity between the differences, and focusses on the relationships between things rather than on their separate identities.

Instead of seeing ourselves and our organizations as ways of separating us from the world, the feminine principle sees them as means through which we are joined to the world.

To understand things, a tree for example, we need the masculine consciousness to help us focus on the constituent parts of the tree, its trunk, branches, roots and leaves, to see everything which distinguishes the tree from both ourselves and the rest of nature. We need the feminine to reveal the inner qualities of the tree, its strength, its life force, and to understand the relationship between its parts, how its branches stretch out, gradually tapering off into leaves, until they intermingle and finally disappear in to air.

Explored through the feminine principle, the tree ceases to appear as something separate from both ourselves and from the universe, and becomes an expression of general principles at work throughout the human and natural worlds. Through the feminine principle it is possible to discover and experience the tree in ourselves and ourselves in the tree.

Sukie Colegrave *The Spirit of the Valley*[9] (1979)

It does not take too much of a stretch of the imagination to substitute 'organization' for 'tree' and, thereby, manager for horticulturalist. In such a context we can, I hope, easily see the complementary demands that masculine and feminine principles place upon us. The two sets of attributes are not at all dissimilar from those associated with the two respective sides of the brain.

The two sides of the brain

During the sixties, particularly in the United States of America, extensive research was being undertaken by both neurologists and psychologists into what came to be called 'the two sides of the brain'. What they were discovering was that the right brain, controlling the left side of our body, and the left brain, controlling the right side, yielded very different behavior.

The complementary functioning of the mind

A direct link between yin and yang and the complementary functioning of the human mind was in fact made by the Austrian physicist, Fritjof Capra, who – in the seventies – published his best selling book *The Tao of Physics*.[10] Capra was the first person to make direct links between modern quantum physics and the philosophical traditions of the East.

Rational and intuitive thinking

The rational and the intuitive are complementary modes of functioning of the human mind. Rational thinking is linear, focussed and analytic. It belongs to the realm of the intellect, whose function is to discriminate, measure and categorize. Thus rational knowledge tends to be fragmented.

Intuitive knowledge, on the other hand, is based on a direct, non-intellectual experience of reality, arising in an expanded state of awareness. It tends to be synthesizing, holistic and non linear.

From this it is apparent that rational knowledge is likely to generate self-centred or Yang activity, whereas intuitive wisdom is the basis of ecological, or Yin wisdom.

Fritjof Capra *Mankind at the Turning point*[11] 1981

The psychology of consciousness

By the 1970s these findings had begun to enter the theory and practice of management, particularly via the work on 'managerial thinking' developed by the Australian management educator, Tony Buzzan.[12] However, the leading authority on this emerging so-called psychology of 'consciousness' was the American, Robert Ornstein.

Two modes of knowing

There are two modes of knowing, those of argument and experience. They are complementary to one another; neither is reducible to the other; and their simultaneous working may be incompatible.

One mode is verbal and rational, sequential in operation, orderly; the other is intuitive, diffuse in operation, less logical and neat, a mode we devalue.

Robert Ornstein *The Psychology of Consciousness*[13] 1975

Ornstein compared and contrasted his 'two modes of knowing' and yielded results that largely parallel, those of Nancy Foy (see p. 62).

Table 11 Two modes of consciousness

Left brain	Right brain	Left brain	Right brain
Day	Night	Focal	Diffuse
Intellectual	Sensuous	Creative	Receptive
Active	Sensitive	Masculine	Feminine
Explicit	Tacit	Light	Dark
Sequential	Simultaneous	Verbal	Spatial
Argument	Experience	Time	Eternity
Intellectual	Intuitive	Causal	Acausal

The left side of the brain, then, represented by the right hand, is the 'masculine' and aggressive side that wants to control, to determine what is, to decide what is right. The right side, represented by the left hand, is the 'feminine' and sensitive side that wants to respond, to adapt to what is, and to recognize what is right. (See Table 11.) Entrepreneurs who desire to exploit markets, and hierarchical managers who want to control people and things have highly developed left brains. Managers who run successful cooperatives, and project coordinators who are highly responsive to change, need to have strongly developed right brains. But when power and sensitivity are working in coordination, there is wholeness.

Split brain surgery

Another well-known writer, in the general management field, is the social forecaster Marilyn Ferguson. As an Englishwoman who emigrated to the United States, Ms Ferguson has been a leading advocate of organizational change, in response to the signs of our 'acquarian' times. In her opinion, managers need to take more purposeful account of right brain attitudes in their approach to organizational design.

Personal and social transformation

The right brain 'tunes' information, the left brain 'fits' it. The left deals with the past, matching the experience of this moment to earlier experience, trying to categorize it; the right hemisphere responds to novelty, to the unknown. The left takes snapshots, the right watches movies.

We confine much of our conscious awareness to the aspect of brain function that reduces things to parts. And we sabotage our only strategy for finding meaning because the left brain, in habitually cutting off conflict from the right, also cuts off its ability to see the whole.

Without the benefit of a scalpel we perform split-brain surgery on ourselves. We isolate heart and mind. Cut off from the fantasy, dreams, intuitions and holistic processes of the right brain, the left is sterile. And the right brain, cut off from integration with its organizing partner, keeps cycling its emotional recharge.

Marilyn Ferguson *The Aquarian Conspiracy*[14] 1980

As our organizations and environments become more complex, Ferguson argues, we need whole brain understanding as we never needed it before: 'the right brain to innovate, sense, dream up, and envision; the left to test, analyze, check out, build constructs and support for the new order'.[15] Yin and yang, right brain and left brain, reflect two similar sets of complementary, managerial activities. In the course of this text I shall be representing them as 'soft' and 'hard' approaches. There is one more similar set of opposites, though, and that is 'cooperation' versus 'competition'.

Cooperation and competition

The signs of the times

Until very recently the best companies, at least in Europe and America, sought after cooperative practices, within the enterprise, and competitive advantage without. However, times have changed. In recent years companies like IBM and Olivetti have been stimulating internal competition, as well as cooperation, and external cooperation, as well as competitiveness. Business life is no longer simple. In all walks of life people, organizations and whole societies seek an appropriate balance between competition and cooperation. However, it is much easier to find business texts on competitive strategies than on cooperative ones. 'Aggressive, competitive behavior alone would make life impossible. Even the most ambitious, goal-oriented individuals need sympathetic support, human contact, and times of carefree spontaneity and relaxation.'[16]

The need to balance competition and cooperation has been better documented in biological and ecological studies than in management science. However, one individual who has brought the two together is the Dutchman Roel Van Duyn. Van Duyn was a municipal councillor, in Holland in the sixties, who had a vision of a Utopian society in which competition and cooperation would be in a state of economic, political and social balance. He and his colleagues in fact set up a Dutch 'Freestate' with twelve ministries paralleling the existing government. Homes, crèches, schools and health food shops were established. All over Europe similar groups were set up until the movement withered away in the sober seventies.

Creativity and destructiveness

Van Duyn concluded that there is a special reciprocal relationship between competition and cooperation. On the one hand, he saw this relationship as a form of mutual aid. Competitive aggression fulfills the repellent functions which cooperation, because it attracts, cannot fulfill. So while the one pushes competitors out of the market-place the other attracts customers to the company's products or services. On the other hand, cooperation, through its capacity for organization, can enhance the strength of the self-same competitiveness. 'The urge to cooperate induces zebras to form intimidating groups, and it is this that makes their aggression towards the leopard so effective.'[17]

When 'masculine' competitiveness and 'feminine' cooperation complement one another then, as we can see in Fig. 6,[18] we have creativity. When they overrule one another we have destructiveness. For example, in the pioneering days of the American 'chip' makers internal collaboration and external competition were in a state of healthy balance. Each company was stimulated to produce more for a growth market.

However, with the advent of fierce Japanese competition it was not enough for these

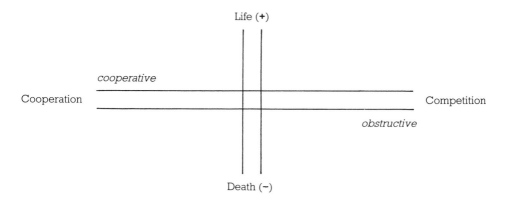

Fig. 6 Cooperation and competition.

same 'chip' makers to compete, individually, against a foe that was accustomed to collaborating with its own government. So, in 1986, the American companies began to collaborate with each other and with their government, externally, as well as their staff working together, internally. A creative tension had been turned into a destructive one, as Japanese competition piled on the agony. Balance between competitive aggression and cooperative intimacy had been lost in the early sixties, hopefully to be regained later. In fact Japanese business as a whole, it has been discovered to America's and to Europe's cost, has achieved a much more creative balance between competition and cooperation (see Chapter 23) than themselves.

Conclusion

The complementary and similar sets of principles of cooperation and competition, left hand and right hand, 'femininity' and 'masculinity', yin and yang, have a very important part to play in this global management text.

Domains of management

For, on the one hand, they form a demarcation line between so-called 'soft' and 'hard' theory. The underlying or root disciplines are set out in Table 12, and the basic areas of management theory in Table 13.[19,20,21,22]

Table 12 Underlying disciplines

Domain	'Soft'	'Hard'
Primal	Anthropology	Economics
Rational	Behavioral science	Administrative science
Developmental	Ecology	Biology
Metaphysical	Mythology	New physics

The precise basis for managerial complementarity changes, as we move from primal to rational to developmental and metaphysical domains of management. The basis for these four domains of theory is set out in the next chapter.

Table 13 Management theory – soft and hard

Domain	Soft	Hard
	A Passion for Excellence	
Primal	Managing people	Managing enterprise
	Management Performance	
	Management skills	Management styles
Rational	Business strategy	Business and society
	Organizational behavior	Organization structure
	The Developing Organization	
Developmental	Industrial design and	Self- and organizational
	organizational harmony	development
	Spirit, Development and Organizational Transformation	
Metaphysical	'Real' management	Vision to action

Global management

On the other hand, diverse parts of the world display varying degrees of 'softness' and 'hardness' in their approaches to management. In general terms the South and the East display their soft edges more fully than the North and the West, and the North and West exhibit their hard edges more fully than the South and East (see Chapters 2 and 3).

In order to acquire a full grasp of management, therefore, we have to expose ourselves to management theory and practice across the globe.

Whole management

The yin–yang symbol of wholeness, as indicated in Fig. 7, reflects the paradoxical nature of softness and hardness. In every hard edge there is at least a touch of softness and in every soft edge there is at least a touch of hardness.

Fig. 7 The symbol of wholeness.

However, to function holistically, a manager needs more than a touch of each. In the next chapter, therefore, I shall explore with you the territory that he must cover, if he is to perform fully.

References

1. Pascale and Athos, *The Art of Japanese Management*, Penguin (1981).
2. T. Peters and B. Waterman, *In Search of Excellence*, Harper & Row (1982).
3. N. Foy, *The Yin and Yang of Organizations*, McIntyre (1980).
4. A. Watts, *The Taboo Against Knowing Who You Are*, Abacus (1977), pp. 130–1.
5. S. Colegrave, *The Spirit of the Valley*, Virago (1979), pp. 69–70.
6. S. Colegrave, *op. cit.*, p. 56.
7. S. Colegrave, *op. cit.*, p. 86.
8. G. Sheahy, *Pathfinders*, Sidgwick & Jackson (1978), p. 181.
9. S. Colegrave, *op. cit.*, p. 111.
10. F. Capra, *The Tao of Physics*, Fontana (1982).
11. F. Capra, *Mankind at the Turning point*, Wildwood House (1981).
12. T. Buzzan, *Use Your Head*, BBC Publications (1974).
13. R. Ornstein, *The Psychology of Consciousness*, Pelican (1975).
14. M. Ferguson, *The Aquarian Conspiracy*, Granada (1980).
15. M. Ferguson, *op. cit.*, pp. 82–3, and 329.
16. F. Capra, *op. cit.*, p. 29.
17. R. Van Duyn, *Message of a Wise Kabouter*, Duckworth (1972), p. 56.
18. R. Van Duyn, *op. cit.*, p. 58.
19. T. Peters and B. Waterman, *A Passion for Excellence*, Random House (1984).
20. P. Drucker, *Management*, Pan (1980).
21. B. Lievegoed, *The Developing Organization*, Celestial Arts (1983).
22. H. Owen, *Spirit, Development and Transformation*, Abbott (1987).

5 Global management principles

Contents

Key concepts

Once you have fully understood the chapter you should be able to define the following concepts in your own terms.

Administrative process   Metaphysical management
Bureaucracy   The new psychology
Developmental management   Organizational transformation
Entrepreneur   Primal management
Group effectiveness   Rational management
Linking pin

Objectives

Upon completing this chapter you should be able to do the following:

1. Trace the evolution of management, from its initial and 'primal' context to its ultimate and 'metaphysical' approach.
2. Identify leading authorities who have contributed to the development of each management domain.
3. Compare and contrast the primal, analytical, developmental and metaphysical approaches to business and management.
4. Assess the relative impact and significance of 'soft' and 'hard' approaches on each of the domains.
5. Gauge which of the domains comes most easily to you, and which poses most difficulty.

Introduction

The managerial revolutions

Management, as Peter Drucker[1] has often reminded us, is in itself a significant innovation. For it has effectively revolutionized the practice of business over the last 100 years. Structures and systems of management and organization have enabled economic, as well as social and political activities, to take place on a scale hitherto deemed quite impossible. Whole industries, livelihoods and products have been created that could never have existed without management. The managerial revolution that has taken place, over the course of the last century, represents what we might call a 'social innovation' of epic proportions. It has, in the same way as the automobile or telecommunications, transformed our lives across the globe. Moreover, just like technological innovation, such a social innovation has linked together, over time, many different people, ideas and circumstances.

Yet today the process of innovation in management thought and activity is gathering pace. While, on the one hand, new light is being cast on the business basics, on the other, the scene is being set for two more fundamental changes. The first fundamental change is being spearheaded by new developments in our lifestyle and in our communications technology, particularly in the industrialized societies. Increasing accent on both individuality and interdependence, both culturally and technologically instigated, is calling on new brands of 'developmental' management. The second major change is being caused by a shift in cultural awareness. Through our rapidly emerging interest in 'corporate culture' and what is being called in America 'organizational transformation', business is becoming a 'metaphysical' as well as a physical reality. Indeed we are reaching down to the most basic management principles, and up to the very spirit of man and organization, at one and the same time. Organizational transformation and metaphysical management is only coming to light, in our day and age, because of the length and breadth of history on which it has been able to draw.

So to begin with, then, let me identify the historical cast of characters who have inadvertently combined forces to transform management. As is the case with any significant innovation, be it the electronic computer or management itself, these responsible characters span, between them, a prolonged period of history, and a very diverse range of fields.

The domains of management

As a business in particular, or management in general, transforms itself, so it passes through successive stages of development. These 'stages' are fundamentally different from 'schools' of management in two ways. Firstly, they mirror the phases of evolution of an individual business. Secondly, they each represent fundamental transformations in overall view.

Because, as I have indicated in Chapter 1, a stage is indicative of, but not equivalent to, a particular form of management, I have termed such forms of management, domains. Within each domain there are, as is evident in successful companies – see Pascale and Athos[2] – both soft and hard manifestations of management thought and practice. Interestingly enough the first such 'domain', which I have termed 'primal' has only come to light very recently. It is focussed on enterprise and people, and draws off anthropology and classical economics. Its guiding light is the youthful Tom Peters, coauthor of *In Search of Excellence* and *A Passion for Excellence*, and its most prolific application is in the United States.

The second domain of 'rational' management is perhaps the best documented, and is otherwise known as analytical or scientific. It focusses on business, management or organizational functions and behaviour, and draws off the administrative and behavioural sciences. Its guiding light is the venerable Peter Drucker, author of *Managing for Results*, as well as many more management tomes, and its most prolific application is in West Germany.

The third domain of 'developmental' management incorporates individuality, interdependence and more. It is oriented towards self-development and business synergy, and draws off developmental biology and social ecology. Its guiding light is the Dutch organizational psychologist, Bernard Lievegoed, author of *The Developing Organization*, and its most prolific application – at least insofar as business synergy is concerned – is in Japan.

Finally, the 'metaphysical' domain covers the most recent, spiritually inspired revolution in management thought and practice. It is oriented towards vision and energy, and draws off traditional wisdom and modern physics. Its guiding light is the American lay preacher and management consultant, Harrison Owen, author of *Spirit, Development and Transformation*. Finally, as yet there is no geographical centre of prolific application, though it may well turn out to be in the South.

Primal management: the instinctive domain

Primal ... Belonging to the first stage of some continuing process; primitive and original; basic and fundamental; not dependent on or derived from something else.

Webster's New International Dictionary

Back to basics: a passion for excellence

People and enterprise

It was Peters and Waterman who initiated a fundamental management rethink in the 1980s.[3] They too perceived that business and management were undergoing a revolution, though one that was somewhat different from the 'organizational transformation' already described.

A passion for excellence

So a revolution is brewing. What kind of revolution? In large measure it is a 'back to basics revolution'. The management systems, schemes, devices and structures promoted during the last quarter century have added up to distractions from the main ideas: the achievement of sustainable growth and equity.

Each such scheme seemed to make sense at the time. Each seemed an appropriate response to growing complexity. But the result was that the basics got lost in a blur of well meaning gibberish that took us further and further from excellent performance in any sphere.

We got so tied up in techniques, devices and programmes that we forgot about people – the people who produce the product or service and the people who consume it.

Peters and Austin *A Passion for Excellence*[4] 1985

One of the reasons that management began to lose its way is that it misconceived its origins. For me the true origins of business management lie not with the bureaucrats in Ancient Egypt or with the military commanders throughout history, but with the gatherers and the hunters in Stone Age communities. These two sets of people were the real forerunners of modern business. They were also closely dependent upon one another.

Soft and hard

In turning management 'back to the basics' Tom Peters has persistently combined the soft (gatherer) and the hard (hunter) sides of business. The one he has identified with 'shared values', and the other with 'entrepreneurship'. These respectively soft and hard elements combine to form primal management's driving force. At each stage of management's progressive transformation we find such soft and hard forces, in varying shapes and forms. For, like man and woman, they need to combine if management is to evolve. They respectively provide the support and the challenge that stimulates growth. Let us see, then, what part the gatherer and the hunter have to play in developing our new management principles.

Cultural anthropology and people management

A sense of place

As the American social ecologist Murray Bookchin,[5] points out, it was woman's foraging activities that first helped awaken in humanity a sense of place, of *oikos*. Moreover, it is from the Greek word *oikos* that the term 'economics' is derived. The gatherer's nurturing sensibility helped create, in fact, not only the original economy and society, but also the very roots of civilization. Her stake in the community was different from that of the predatory hunter. It was more domestic, more pacifying, more caring, more cultivating. For presiding over the gatherer was the figure and symbolism of the Mother Goddess. The hunter too, within a traditional society, was part and parcel of the social fabric. Having collected his spoils he was expected to share them with the rest of the community. His male virtues, of courage, of physical dexterity, and of persistent aggression, were extolled, just so long as he shared the resulting bounties with the rest of the clan.

Wealth, then, was not a personal matter. It was not an individual's personal possession which he or she could will as they pleased. It belonged to the family group and its use was restricted, bound up with marriage and social life and with the spirits of its ancestors.

On people management

Interestingly enough there is a very successful American company today, which draws upon many of these communal principles, albeit in the modern context of free enterprise. Mary Kay Cosmetics is such a business, and its nurturing qualities are not restricted to the cosmetics themselves.

Profit and love

Our belief in caring for people does not conflict with our needs as a corporation to generate a profit. To me p and l does not only mean profit and loss – it also means people and love.
I have always believed that when you put God first, your family second, and your business third, everything will work out.

Mary Kay *On People and Management*[6] (1985)

Kay, as well as Peters and Waterman, have a much more basic, instinctive and spontaneous involvement with people than their 'people-oriented' academic predecessors. They are drawing on an instinctive sense and sensibility. These are more characteristic of 'people management' in primitive communities and everyday households than of 'human relations' in complex organizations and 'liberated' societies. Kay points out, for instance, that a working woman can be as much a breadwinner as her spouse, but that she almost always has to wear a lot of other hats too. She is a wife, a mother, a chef, a laundress, a housecleaner, a chauffeur, a child psychologist and a lover. She therefore has to find time for a multiplicity of nurturing roles, while retaining something of a hunting instinct.

Similarly, and as a direct result, the most important justification for being in business, as far as Kay is concerned, is to serve others. No matter how much profit a company makes, if it does not enrich the lives of others, both within the company and without, it has failed. Finally, Mary Kay Cosmetics is not a company with good human relations in the more sophisticated sense of developmental management. It hunts and it gathers. Each individual is responsible for, and takes a share of, sales and profit. Each therefore operates in a self-employed capacity. However, at the same time, there is a sense of community. When all our people come to understand one another, as Mary Kay describes, a family-like atmosphere remains intact and the customer is better served: 'I often say to my sales support staff, you're not filling an order. You're helping someone who supports three children to make a living.'

Fig. 8 'Gatherer'.

Nurturing, gathering (see Fig. 8) and the symbol of the Mother Goddess therefore typify the gatherer's business activities. Yet a gatherer like Mary Kay needs something of the huntress within her. Market exploitation, commercial survival skills, and the symbol of the Fire God typify the hunter's personal enterprise. It is to the hunter's activities that we now turn.

Classical economics and entrepreneurship

The pursuit of individual gain

The traditional hunter–gatherer societies may have been rich in community spirit, but their lives were materially limited, and each person's individual freedom was heavily constrained. Although the hunter role was well developed; – together with the corresponding qualities of physical stamina, wilful persistence, and raw ingenuity – personal enterprise, yielding individual gain, was heavily circumscribed. It took many hundreds of years before the pursuit of individual gain became acceptable in society. The emergence of capitalism, in the wake of the newly emerging Protestant ethic, gave economic form and religious substance to the pursuit of private enterprise. The classical economists of the eighteenth and nineteenth centuries, in Britain and in France, became the champions of free enterprise. Adam Smith, who wrote *The Wealth of Nations*[7] in 1776, was the leader of this emerging economic band. Ironically, though, for all their belief in the entrepreneur and in free enterprise, these classical economists gave us little insight into the personal qualities of the entrepreneur. The one exception was the Austrian political economist, Joseph Schumpeter, who spent a good deal of his time in America, in the early part of this century.

Entrepreneur and intrapreneur
Schumpeter was also unusual in that, fifty years ago, he saw a place for entrepreneurship inside the major business corporations.

Entrepreneur and enterprise

The carrying out of new combinations we call 'enterprise'; the individuals whose function it is to carry them out we call 'entrepreneurs'.

What motivates the entrepreneur is, first of all, his dream to found a private kingdom ... then there is the will to conquer ... finally there is the joy of creating.

We call entrepreneurs not only those independent businessmen in an exchange economy who are usually so designated, but all who fulfil the function by which we define the concept, even if they are, as is becoming the rule, 'dependent' employees of a company.

Joseph Schumpeter *The Theory of Economic Development*[8] 1934

We see, in Schumpeter's characterization of the entrepreneur, many of the qualities of the hunter. (See Fig. 9.) In fact we would be hard pressed, drawing on classical descriptions of private enterprise, to find the nurturer–gatherer alongside the hunter–entrepreneur. Yet, interestingly enough, the connection between hunter and gatherer was not entirely lost. For although the emergent nineteenth-century entrepreneur set out, relentlessly, to gather his personal and economic spoils, in the background was often a spouse and children who stood to reap the material dividends. The wife or even mistress of the hunter, therefore, played the gatherer role, albeit outside of the business context. This complementarity of hard and soft roles becomes more evident, however, when we return to Tom Peters' management basics: 'The superb business leaders we use as models in this book epitomize paradox. All are as tough as nails and uncompromising about their value systems, but at the same time they care deeply about the respect their people'.

Finally, the re-emergence of the hunter role, contained within a gatherer context, is

Fig. 9 'Hunter'.

well depicted in Gifford Pinchot's concept of 'Intrapreneuring'. Pinchot has devoted himself to the development of entrepreneurs within organizations, using the sorts of basic management approaches that Peters and Waterman have advocated. He has gone so far as to propose the establishment of what he calls 'intracapital' to fund individual, intra-preneurial initiatives. However, for Pinchot as for Peters, the hunter needs a gatherer; the hungry intrapreneur needs a nurturing 'intraprise', that is an 'intrapreneurial' company.

Intrapreneur, Intracapital and Intraprise

The formation of intracapital marks the beginning of a transformation in the role of corporate management. They cease to act as rulers and instead become governors whose task is to create an environment in which manager–intrapreneurs can have freedom while still being guided by an 'invisible hand' to make the decisions that foster the growth and profit-ability of the corporation.

In addition to creating and shaping the internal marketplace, corporate management must put out a clear vision of what the corporation is, and what it is struggling to become. Sharing in the vision, members can overcome pettiness and work together towards common goals without draconian systems of control.

Gifford Pinchot *Intrapreneuring*[9] (1985)

People and enterprise

In taking us back to management basics Tom Peters and Gifford Pinchot, have largely bypassed administrative and developmental management. They have no time for such apparent sophistications. They ignore, substantially, a hundred years of managerial history. They deal with 'tangible' people and things, rather than with 'abstract' structures and systems. Mary Kay, in splendid isolation amongst management writers, puts the gatherer in the foreground, and the hunter – although clearly visible – in the background. People and love are as important to her, if not more so, than profit and loss. Peters and Pinchot, while equally concerned with such management basics as pride and enthusiasm, enterprise and leadership – all highly visible managerial qualities – place the gatherer in the background and the hunter in the foreground.

It is the hunter and the gatherer who play the major part, together, in the early stages of a business' development. Although the hunting, entrepreneurial role is more easily recognized than the gathering one, aggressive and risk taking enterprise without shared enthusiasm and closeness to the customer is bound to fail. As we move beyond the management basics to management science, in its most general sense, the scene changes, as do the cast of leading characters. However, we are still watching the same stage play. It merely unfolds, as does business and management, over time. We begin with basics and end up with metaphysics, via the rational and developmental.

Rational management: the intellectual domain

Rational ... A general principle, law, or warranted assumption that supports a conclusion; the thing that makes some fact intelligible; a sane or sound view or consideration; proper exercize of the intellective faculty with right judgment; the highest faculty of the mind.

Webster's New International Dictionary

Towards rational management: managing for results

As a business develops from youth into adulthood, so the need inevitably arises for more system, structure, and formal management. In fact, in most business texts, it is only at this point that management comes into its own. As the rational manager replaces the primal hunter and gatherer, so the very nature of the organization changes in concept and form. What was informal and instinctive becomes formal and systematized. What was intimate and inclusive becomes impersonal and exclusive. It is for this very reason that Max Weber, the nineteenth century German sociologist, introduced his theory of the 'ideal bureaucracy'. What Weber, and others like him at the time, did, was to apply mental cut and thrust in place of the physical and emotional aggression, that characterized their entrepreneurial predecessors. With the advance of scientific management came, above all else, a mental revolution. Hard analysis supplanted aggressive risk taking. A similarly rational approach transformed a primal, people-orientation into a 'behavioral science'. However, and as we shall see, this behavioral development followed a good fifty years behind the administrative one.

Administrative science

At the turn of the century, as I have already indicated in Chapter 1, administration became a professional discipline in its own right. Business administrators were hired to run ever larger companies, and both processes and systems of administration were required. Max Weber, articulated the 'ideal' administrative system and Henri Fayol, was the first to come up with a comprehensive administrative process.

Bureaucracy

1. A division of labour in which authority and responsibility is clearly defined for each member, and is officially sanctioned.
2. Offices or positions are organized into an hierarchy of authority resulting in a chain of command.
3. All organizational members are to be selected on the basis of technical qualifications through formal examinations or by virtue of training or education.
4. Officials are to be appointed, not elected.
5. Administrators work for fixed salaries and are career officers.
6. The administrative official does not own the administered unit but is a salaried official.
7. The administrator is subject to strict rules, discipline, and controls regarding his official duties.

Max Weber 'The Theory of Social and Economic Organization'[10] 1946

Administrative systems and processes are as impersonal and analytical as primal management is instinctive and personal. (See Fig. 10.) Whereas basic management focusses on personality and community, administrative science places its emphasis on functionality and bureaucracy.

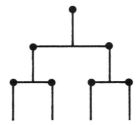

Fig. 10 The structured organization.

The administrative process

To administrate is to plan, organize, command, coordinate and control.
To plan means to study the future and arrange the plan of operations.
To organize means to build up the material and human organization of the business.
To command means to make the staff do their work.
To coordinate means to unite and correlate all activities.
To control means to see that everything is done in accordance with the rules which have been laid down.

Henri Fayol *Industrial and General Administration*[11] 1916

Fayol derived these administrative principles out of a period of prolonged and methodical observation, while acting as an industrial engineer and factory manager in France. Many subsequent elaborations on Fayol's basic theme have emerged, particularly in the 1930s, 1940s and 1950s, under the guise of management principles and processes. None have departed fundamentally from his analytical framework.

Functional and corporate strategy

Subsequent extensions of this process of orientation have yielded management by objectives, as well as business and corporate strategy, each of which have drawn upon a logical and analytical approach to managerial and organizational problem solving. Interestingly enough, unlike the Americans – Kay, Peters and Pinchot – who have been prominent exponents of primal management, it has been two Europeans who have taken the 'hard' analytical lead. Yet there is another side to analytical management. Whereas Fayol and Weber represent the hard edge of the industrial engineer and of the administrative scientist, Elton Mayo and Rensis Likert represent the soft edge of the behavioral sciences. Let me now elaborate.

The administrative–behavioral transition

For administrative scientists at the turn of the century, like Weber and Fayol, aggressive analysis took over from aggressive, primal instincts. To provide managerial cut and thrust, division of function, authority and responsibility, took the place of undivided personal charisma. To provide organizational integration, impersonal bureaucracy and managerial coordination took the place of communally shared values. All that provided the hard, analytical edge. Gradually, though, from the 1920s onwards, a soft edge began to make itself felt. The person most responsible for its emergence, in the early stages, was the Australian Elton Mayo, who spent most of his working life in the United States. Prior to Mayo's so called 'Hawthorne' experiments (see 'The group factor' below), which were initially undertaken in the Western Electric relay room in 1929, teamwork was of no real significance in organizational life. The individual manager faced a mass of workers, within an anonymous setting. There was no real perception of teamwork, that is of group interaction or of interpersonal dynamics at the time.

The group factor

The Hawthorne programme has moved far since its beginning in 1929. Originally designed to study the comfort of workers in their work as a mass of individuals, it has since revealed that the relation of working groups to management is one of the fundamental problems of large scale industry.

It was indeed this study that first enabled us to assert that a major preoccupation of management must be that of organizing teamwork, that is to say, of developing and sustaining cooperation.

So the important fact brought to the attention of our research division was that the ordinary conception of management worker relations, as existing between company officials on the one hand, and an unspecified number of individuals on the other, is utterly mistaken. Management, in any continuously successful plant, is not related to single workers, but always to working groups.

In any department that continues to operate, the workers have – whether aware of it or not – formed themselves into a group with appropriate customs, duties, routines, even rituals; and management succeeds (or fails) in proportion as it is accepted without reservation by the group as authority and leader.

Elton Mayo *The Social Problems of Industrial Civilisation*[12] 1949

Mayo made it very apparent, in his early writings, that the communal setting that characterized primal management had disappeared, in the wake of bureaucratic organization. At the same time he had no desire to see society return to its primitive origins, whereby group life was often brought about through fear and force rather than through voluntary initiatives. What he was acutely aware of, though, was that managers in the second quarter of the nineteenth century had only partially solved the problems of large scale industry. They had succeeded in the application of science and technology to the production process. They had not succeeded, however, in the organization of teamwork, that is in generating sustained cooperation. Yet such sustained cooperation was a prerequisite of adaptive organizations in society.

While Elton Mayo, then, played a major part in introducing the behavioral sciences into management, and in alerting us to the importance of cooperation and teamwork in management, the further development of these behavioral concepts fell to others. While Mayo brought the group factor into the debate, and therefore 'softened' the base of analytical management, it was Rensis Likert who brought more substance into the new argument.

Behavioral science

Organizational behavior

The new, behavioral argument stated, in fact, that it was the interpersonal dynamics of informal organization, rather than the impersonal attributes of formal bureaucracy, that would make or break a manager. Moreover, the crucial factor, within the informal organization, was the small group. Rensis Likert was a behavioral scientist, in the true, analytical tradition. From the mid forties onwards he and many colleagues conducted innumerable programmes of intensive research into the effectiveness of groups within public and private organizations.

Group effectiveness

The properties and performance of the ideal, highly effective group are as follows:
1. The members are skilled in the various leadership and membership roles required for effective interaction.
2. The group has been in existence sufficiently long to have developed a well established, relaxed working relationship.
3. The members of the group are loyal to it and to its leader.
4. The members and leaders have a high degree of confidence and trust in each other.
5. The values and goals of the group are a coincident expression of the values and goals of its members.
6. The members of the group are highly motivated to abide by the major values and achieve the important goals of the group.
7. All the interaction, problem solving and decision making activities of the group take place in a supportive atmosphere.
8. Insofar as group members perform linking functions with other groups, their goals and values are in mutual harmony.

Rensis Likert *New Patterns of Management*[13] 1961

The organizational form that emerges from Mayo's and from Likert's behavioral considerations is softer at the edges than the purely bureaucratic one. There is greater overlap between and amongst levels. An organization will not derive the full benefit from its highly effective groups, according to Likert, unless they are linked to the organization as a whole by equally effective overlapping groups (see Fig. 11).

Fig. 11 The linking pin organization.

Group maintenance, then, and task effectiveness take on the dual focus of managerial style, and behavior.

Managerial behavior

Both Mayo and Likert, by focussing attention on teamwork and organizational behavior, raised some fundamental implications for a manager's style. A wide range of behavioral scientists have since paid attention to the respective 'relationships' and 'task' orientations of managers. The most prominent of these was the American, Douglas McGregor, who in the fifties wrote a book *The Human Side of Enterprise*.[14] In it he compared and contrasted autocratic and participative styles of management, labelling them 'theory X' – autocratic, and 'theory Y' – participative.

Business behavior

Whereas Mayo, Likert and McGregor focussed on the internal organization and its management, from the fifties and sixties onwards increasing emphasis was being placed on the external environment of the business. Peter Drucker in fact took the lead in reviewing business' social responsibilities,[15] and other behavioral scientists, like Jan Dauman at IBM, correlated business survival with social change.

Administrative and behavioral management

In conclusion, the longstanding tradition of 'rational' management stretches back in two different directions, albeit that both are 'scientifically' based. The administrative tradition, which has yielded the bureaucratic form of organization, the functional principles of management, and corporate strategy, is hard edged, and, in Mayo's terms, 'technically' oriented. The behavioral tradition, which has yielded Mayo's group relationships, Likert's 'linking pins' and business' social responsibilities, is more soft edged and 'socially' oriented.

   Both rational approaches, however, place their emphasis on the established and impersonally-managed organization as compared with the new and personally-run enterprise. The primal (new) and rational (established) approaches, in combination, form what I have called elsewhere[16] the 'guts' and the 'brains' of management. That leaves, still to be considered, the 'heart' (developmental) and the 'soul' (metaphysical).

Developmental management: the intuitive domain

> Develop . . . To unfold gradually, to become progressively more manifest; to cause to become visible, to reveal hidden potentialities; to go through a succession of states, each of which is preparatory for the next one; to undergo natural evolution by successive changes from a less to a more perfect or more highly organized state.
>
> *Webster's Third New International Dictionary*

The developing organism

Biology and ecology

Man is a creature of habit. Habits are formed out of past experience, attitudes and behavior, extending over a lifetime. Our current managerial practices are habitually constrained by influences from the past. Free enterprise and communally shared values, functional management and bureaucratic organization, group processes, and inter-departmental linkages, are all part and parcel of our habitual business reality.

Yet at the same time a future is emerging which will be altogether different from the past. To anticipate that future we need to appreciate what I have termed 'developmental' management. The roots of developmental management lie, not in economics or anthropology, nor in engineering or psychology, but in biology and ecology. In his seminal work, *To Grow or to Die*,[17] the American biologist and management consultant, George Land, has applied evolutionary principles to individual, organizational and societal development. The three stages of biological development that Land has proposed mirrors those introduced by Lievegoed in *The Developing Organization*.[18] Moreover, the third and 'mutualistic' stage, has strong ecological overtones, because of its focus on interdependence.

Primal (rational) developmental transitions

For the primal manager the individual focus is on personality and the collective focus is on community. The primal individual draws on his basic drives and instincts. The primal community draws on its blood ties and family feelings. Both focus on the immediate, on the tangible, on the visible. For the 'entrepreneur' the bottom line is profit and loss; for the 'animateur' (see Chapter 30) it is people and love.

For the rational manager individual emphasis is on functionality and the collective focus is on organization. The scientific manager draws continually on his analytical and perceptive abilities. He focusses on concepts and techniques, on structures and on systems that are feasible and practical, logical and flexible. The structured organization draws on its formal rules and procedures, as well as its informal processes and interactions. For the developmental manager, with whom we are now concerned, the emphasis is on shades of individuality, on the one hand, and upon shades of interdependence, on the other. He draws constantly on his awareness of emerging, unfolding potential, and on his capacity to interrelate and to integrate it. He focusses on such potential, both economic and psychological, in association and in motion. Let me now elaborate.

Personal growth and manager self-development

In Great Britain in particular, in the last twenty years, there has been a strong emphasis on so-called 'self-development' in management. Similarly, if only very recently, the focus on individuality of orientation and lifestyle has affected the marketing function, and hence also research and development, as well as general management and organizational behavior. It has been in fact the resurgence of design, in both production and marketing, that has been particularly notable in that respect.

The trouble is, however, that despite this shift in emphasis from enterprise and organization to individual, we have been provided with precious little insight into the different shades of human individuality, and how each can be progressively evolved, grown or 'developed'. Moreover such developmental management has generally been restricted to human resources, and to organization development, rather than spread throughout the business functions. Product, systems, market and business development exist in name, but there is generally little awareness of their developmental essence.

Within the 'human resources' field, the person who has done most to reveal not only the developmental or 'maturation' process, but also the hierarchy of human needs, is the great American humanistic psychologist, Abraham Maslow. He has become particularly well known for his concept of self-actualization,[19] whereby individuals and organizations can realize their potential. The individuation, or maturation process is central to developmental management, as a whole, and will be considered in more detail in Chapter 22. The basic process can be applied to products and to markets as well as to individuals.

Whereas Maslow provided the overall introduction to personal growth and development, it is the American psychiatrist, Daniel Levinson, who has extended our developmental knowledge base through his research into *The Seasons of Man's Life*.[20] In it he identifies the four phases, and transitions from youth and adulthood to midlife and maturity, as crucial factors in our self-development.

Business and organizational synergy

Developmental management involves both recognizing and harnessing the evolutionary potential of people, technologies and businesses. In order to be able to do all of these things the manager needs to appreciate not only individual differences, but also how these differences can be accommodated within an evolving organization. In Europe it was the social philosopher Rudolph Steiner,[21] and in America the management theorist Mary Parker Follett,[22] who both paved the way for such developmental thinking in the early part of this century. Both were true visionaries, who exercised a strong influence on prominent business and societal leaders on both sides of the Atlantic.

It is ironic that we look towards Japan today for examples of orchestrated interdependence between individuals and groups, and also between business and society at large. In fact Mary Parker Follett had all the answers, at least for those of us in Europe and America, if only we would have turned to her for them. She, more than any management philosopher before or since, paved the way for what I have termed developmental management.

The new psychology

What Parker Follet did was to take the concept of the group and to stretch it in two directions. In doing so she took two developmental steps beyond the scientific manager's conception of group functioning. For on the one hand she intensified the significance of individuality, within the group; and on the other hand she extended the significance of the group within business.

Individual–group–individual

The individual

- The importance of the new psychology is that it acknowledges man as the centre and shaper of the universe.

- In his nature all institutions are latent and perforce must be adapted to his nature.

The individual and the group

- A man is ideally free only insofar as he is interpermeated by every other human being.
- Individuality is the capacity for union: the measure of individuality is the depth and breadth of every such union.

The individual, the group and society

- Release man's energies and he, with other free men, will create constantly changing forms, responding sensitively to every need.
- There is of course competition between our big firms, but cooperation is occupying a larger and larger place, relatively.

Mary Parker Follett *The New State*[23] 1929

The picture that I have of business, of management and of organization, based on Parker Follett's new psychology, is hexagonal rather than pyramidical, aesthetic rather than purely functional.

The new corporate architecture
The hexagonal form and potential linkages could apply to individuals, to groups, to departments and to whole businesses, both within and outside any one particular organization. (See Fig. 12.)

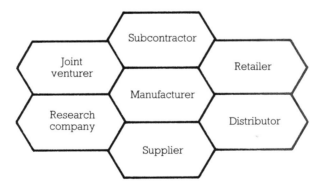

Fig. 12 The new psychology and organization.

Individuality and interdependence
The kind of individuality and interdependence that Parker Follett advocates is not restricted to managerial and organizational behavior. It can also have an impact on the substance of operations, of marketing and of financial management in a way that will be revealed in Chapter 34. Developmental management, then, upgrades primal personality

(hunter; gatherer) and prescribed functionality (production, marketing, finance, personnel) into multifaceted individuality. In Chapter 21 I explore the full managerial implications of this major, developmental phenomenon. It also upgrades close-knit community-based enterprises, and rigidly bounded organization structures, into interdependent business and organizational forms. In this respect it is the Japanese who have taken the lead. The focus of developmental management, then, is on realizing individual, organizational and also business potential through association, and through conscious economic, organizational, social and cultural evolution.

Developmental–metaphysical transition

'Metaphysical' management represents one further and final evolutionary step in management's journey from the days of antiquity into the space age. Emphasis now shifts, again, from primal – personal and communal, to rational – functional and organizational, to developmental – individual and societal, to metaphysical – spiritual and cultural.

Metaphysical management: the domain of inspiration

> Metaphysics ... Underlying reality and its relations; the system of first principles or the philosophy underlying a subject; that which is beyond the physical or the experiential, and is conceived as transcendent, supersensible, or transcendent
>
> *Webster's New International Dictionary*

Spirit and transformation

Ancient world and modern science

When the most recent wave of influential management theorists first introduced us to the term 'corporate culture' few of us realized what momentous managerial dividends this conceptual development would yield. On the one hand, this new focus on culture as 'shared values' represented a return to primal management, to basic instincts and to a communal identity. I shall deal with this primal phenomenon at some length in Chapter 7. On the other hand, and what concerns us at this point, is the 'metaphysical' impact of corporate culture.

This second and metaphysical impact comes once again in two forms, one soft and the other hard. The 'soft' argument relates the 'laws of nature' to the realities of management. The 'hard' argument relates to the role of 'vision' in business creation. For the former I turn to the Bank of Credit and Commerce, and, for the latter, to the world's greatest authority on mythology, Joseph Campbell.[24] To link the two I call on the lay preacher and organizational psychologist, Harrison Owen, and to uncover the roots of metaphysical management I go back to sources of ancient wisdom and forward to modern physics.

Organizational transformation

There is, in fact, nothing particularly new, or even esoteric, about the use of 'spirit' in a managerial context. After all Henri Fayol, the founding father of scientific management, included *esprit de corps* as one of his management fundamentals. We also use, without hesitation, such phrases as 'a lack of spirit' or the 'spirit of enterprise' in our everyday business conversations. What is new is the way in which people like Harrison Owen have focussed on spirit, and its transformation, within public and private organizations. Owen is in fact an anthropologist and a student of religion who has used his background and interests in these areas to provide a metaphysical context for his organizational concepts. In his book *Spirit, Transformation and Development in Organizations*,[25] Owen stresses that it is not his intention to make organizations more spiritual. Rather, he argues, managers should recognize that enterprises are in their essence, 'spirit'. Having recognized this, they should then get on with the business of caring intelligently and purposefully for this most vital of organizational elements. In fact, as he sees it, the real purpose of organizational structure and dynamics is to make explicit, even automatic, the proper flow of spirit.

The way in which you get in touch with the spirit is through the story of the organization, as it has unfolded, and as it is expressed both in itself and through other related stories. When the organization's story is confused, splintered, or isolated, then its spirit will be 'sore', and in need of care or even transformation. How this can be specifically achieved will be considered in Chapter 26, once we have had a chance to take in and digest Owen's argument more fully. Owen is at pains to point out the difference between development, which is associated with an enhancing of existing potential, and transformation, which involves the creation of wholly new potential. On the softer side of metaphysical management is the so-called guardian of the spirit of the organization. He stands closer to development. On the harder side is the visionary. He stands closer to transformation.

Development and transformation

The essence of transformation lies in the odyssey or journey of the human spirit as it moves from one formal manifestation to another. The word 'transformation' says as much, for the central idea is the movement across or through forms.

Butterflies start out as caterpillars. Then when the time is right, the caterpillar spins a cocoon about itself, and after a period, emerges with beautiful colours and wings to fly. That might have been a development, just as the tadpole develops, bit by bit into a frog as its loses its tail and grows its legs.

The reality, however, is different. Once the caterpillar is safely inside it literally dissolves. The caterpillar has gone to its essence, which is then transformed into a butterfly. The only way for the butterfly to get there is to allow the old form to dissolve, thus freeing some essential energy, purpose or Spirit, to achieve the new form.

Harrison Owen, *Spirit, Transformation and Development in Organization*[26] 1987

While the organization, then, is the cradle of the spirit the individual visionary is the one who undertakes the 'spirited' and heroic journey. Agha Hasan Abedi, who created the Bank of Credit and Commerce (BCC), was such a visionary who transformed the spirit of banking, actually within the Indian subcontinent, and, perhaps, prospectively around the world. Drawing on the 'spectral theory' of business and management – initially developed by Kevin Kingsland in India, Great Britain and America – I have related the process of transformation specifically to Abedi's historic journey, and generally to any business enterprise. The journey connects vision to action.

From vision to action: the heroic journey

The vision
In proceeding from vision (spirit) to action (energy) you need first to uncover the historical origins of the company as reflected in the origins of its national culture and economy; the historical roots of its product and technology; the founder's underlying motives and psychology.

The market need or context
You then must relate the company's historically determined origins to emerging economic and cultural trends, thereby discovering the contemporary meaning, significance or context of the heroic journey.

The organizational form and product concept
You then have to structure and conceptualize the union between origination and context, in terms that both relate to the business' foundations and also define its product and organization in practical terms.

The will and commitment
Then harness the will and motivation of people committed to profitable growth, to drive the company forward so that the resources can be acquired to put principles into practice, to fulfill the needs of its people, and to serve the company's mission.

The capacity to adapt
You need to adapt to change, as and when necessary, so that the forces of single minded persistence, clearly principled management, sensitivity to customer needs, and submission to a higher purpose, do not cause rigidity and inflexibility.

Involving the community
The best laid plans are foiled by people. You have to establish a family atmosphere whereby values are shared and people feel they belong together, even though individual flexibility and enterprise is encouraged, and individuals can dream their own dreams within the context of the whole.

Transforming spirit into energy
You have to ensure that spirit is continually transformed into energy; as the true power of vision is realized, the physical resources of the earth are transformed.

'Real' management and the laws of nature

The harder end of metaphysical management, as you can see, provides the visionary impact that is required to transform an enterprise like BCC from a local, and purely commercial force, into an international agency for cultural and economic transformation. The basic and elemental spirit of activity, the way in which it is channelled, structured and directed, is the visionary's responsibility. However, the receiving of this vision can only be achieved through the softer attributes of metaphysical management, that is through the underlying laws of nature. These have been specified by Agha Hasan Abedi, President of BCC, as principles of flow – all is in a state of flux, latency – possibilities are limitless, totality – everything is interconnected, and integrity – the moral governs the material.

Conclusion

An imbalance of domains

I have now introduced you to all four domains of management with which this text will be concerned. They stretch from primal to metaphysical management, crossing the rational and developmental domains along the way. At each point, moreover, there is both a soft and a hard edge to the theory and practice. To date only one domain has been comprehensively covered by the management texts. Rational management, both administrative and behavioral, has been covered in great analytical detail in the literature.

The functions of management, organization and strategy, on the one hand, and the behavior of organizations, managers and businesses in society, on the other, have all received ample consideration. The other three domains of primal, developmental, and metaphysical management have had much less considered attention. It is as if our minds have been well stretched, while our bodies, our hearts and our souls have been ill nourished. There are two major reasons for this. Firstly, theory has been falling behind practice. The emergence in recent years of primal approaches to management is only beginning to be reflected in the academic business literature. Secondly, the concepts we academics have been developing have suffered from cultural bias. Whereas the 'rational' approach is emphatically Western and Northern (America and Europe), the 'developmental' one has a strongly Eastern touch to it. It is only with the emergence of Japan, as an economic force, that we have begun to pay serious attention to developmental management, marketing and business in general. Furthermore the emergence of the 'metaphysical' approach has resulted, at least in part, from a renewed contact with our Southern roots. It is Martin Luther King, the American negro, who will best be remembered for his 'dream', and the Bank of Credit and Commerce has, not surprisingly, developed very firm roots in both Africa and Latin America.

Redressing the balance

As the text unfolds, therefore, I shall try not only to relate, continually, theory and practice, but also to maintain a global perspective. I shall begin, at the beginning, with the emergence of enterprise, and with the social and economic theory that underpins primal management.

References

1. P. Drucker, *Entrepreneurship and Management*, Heinemann (1985).
2. Pascale and Athos, *The Art of Japanese Management*, Penguin (1982).
3. T. Peters and B. Waterman, *In Search of Excellence*, Harper & Row (1982).
4. T. Peters and N. Austin, *A Passion for Excellence*, Random House (1985) p. 36.

5.   M. Bookchin, *The Ecology of Freedom*, Cheshire Books (1982).
6.   M. Kay, *On People Management*, Pan (1985), p. 27.
7.   A. Smith, *The Wealth of Nations*, Penguin (1970), Vols I–III.
8.   J. Schumpeter, *The Theory of Economic Development*, Oxford University Press (1950), p. 84.
9.   G. Pinchot, *Intrapreneuring*, Harper & Row (1985), p. 214.
10. M. Weber, ex Garth and Mills, *Essays in Sociology*, Routledge & Kegan Paul (1943).
11. H. Fayol, *Industrial and General Administration*, Pitman (1948), pp. 43–110.
12. E. Mayo, *The Social Problems of Industrial Civilisation*, Routledge & Kegan Paul (1949), p. 72.
13. R. Likert, *New Patterns of Management*, McGraw-Hill (1961), p. 166.
14. D. McGregor, *The Human Side of Management*, McGraw-Hill (1960).
15. P. Drucker, *Management*, Heinemann (1974), Chapters 24–28.
16. R. Lessem, *The Global Business*, Prentice Hall (1987).
17. G. Land, *To Grow or to Die*, Wiley (1986).
18. B. Lievegoed, *The Developing Organization*, Celestial Arts (1973).
19. A. Maslow, *Motivation and Personality*, Harper & Row (1959).
20. D. Levinson, *The Seasons of Man's Life*, Knopf (1978).
21. R. Steiner, *Toward Social Renewal*, Steiner Press (1945).
22. M. Parker Follett, *The New State*, Peter Smith (1929).
23. M. Parker Follett, *op. cit.,* p. 76.
24. J. Campbell, *The Hero with a Thousand Faces*, Princeton University Press (1949).
25. H. Owen, *Spirit, Transformation and Development in Organizations*, Abbott Publishing (1987).
26. H. Owen, *op. cit.*, p. 74.

Section B
Primal management

Introduction

The domains of management are all-encompassing in that they specifically incorporate entrepreneurship as a management domain. In other words, rather than excluding enterprise from management we include it, but in the specified and so-called primal context.

The business tree

The primal management domain is the first of four that we shall be covering. For each of the four we shall be discovering the main theoretical roots, the core concept, the most visible branch theories, as well as the most prolific, business fruits. Finally, and in each case, we shall be looking for both hard and soft attributes throughout. (See Fig. 13.)

The underlying ground

Primal business management is typically rooted in youthful and immigrant societies, in pioneering or rejuvenated business enterprises, and in youthful and instinctive individual behavior. From a geographical perspective, it is most widespread in the West, particularly within the United States of America. However, pockets of primal business management are in evidence throughout the world, most particularly amongst immigrant Chinese, Indians and Jews in their respective diaspora. Primal business activity thrives, finally, on free enterprise accompanied by a strong family, or community feeling, within the particular organization, ethnic group or nation.

The living characters

Free enterprise is personified by the upgraded hunter, that is the economically oriented entrepreneur; the personification of community feeling has remained latent rather than manifest within business organizations. I have borrowed the term animateur – a person who 'animates' the local community – from the French, and transplanted it into a business context. Finally, the individual who represents an amalgam of the hard entrepreneur and the soft 'animateur' is the 'intrapreneur', personified, as we shall see, by the President of 3M Canada, Tom Myser. He embodies primal management.

The 'primal' tree

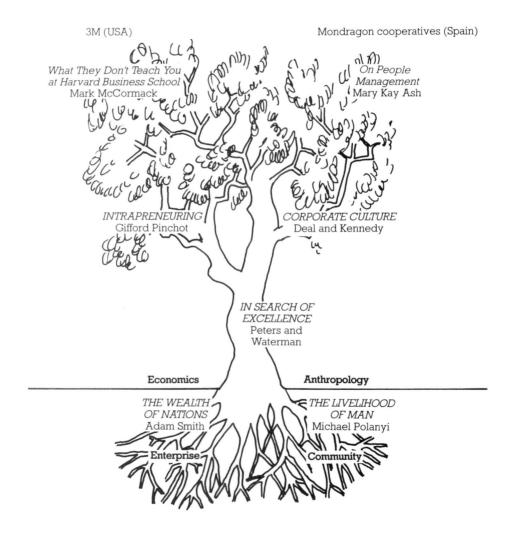

Fig. 13 The primal tree.

The primal roots

Soft Roots

The soft roots of primal management, infiltrating the deeply set cultural sub soil, tap the anthropological origins of hunter–gatherer societies. The primal community, with its close-knit family ties, its strong emphasis on the collective household, and its focus on the hunting band, is characterized by the economic anthropologist, Michael Polanyi,[1] in *The Livelihood of Man*. Polanyi, writing in the sixties, points out that, in pursuing his livelihood, man (and woman) has been communally rather than personally oriented.

Hard roots

The hard roots of primal management, penetrating the shallower economic top soil, tap the free enterprise economics of Adam Smith.[2] When this Scotsman and social philosopher wrote his inquiry into *The wealth of nations* in 1776, he was not only helping to found the discipline of economics, but also legitimizing – for the first time in history – the generalized pursuit of personal self-interest. For Smith, unlike Polanyi, the wealth of nations is acquired by self-seeking individuals rather than collectively bound communities. The roots of primal management, then, are on the one hand, securely and socially established and, on the other, penetratingly, and personally oriented. The hard and personal roots which reach down to contemporary free enterprise, are relatively close to the surface, and therefore easily accessible; the soft, familial ones are embedded more deeply in traditional, community life.

The primal core

A concept of waiting to be born

While the roots of primal management have lain underground for hundreds, if not thousands of years, its visible manifestation had to await the coming of Peters and Waterman.[3] Although, on the one hand, many an anthropoligical text has described the communal and economic activities that characterized traditional societies, no fully fledged concept of communal enterprise has emerged. Similarly, and on the other hand, whereas the entrepreneur was the hero of the classical economists, none of them systematically developed a concept of personal enterprise. There is good reason for this. Because the primal manager is essentially instinctive, whether as an entrepreneur or animateur, it is difficult to conceptualize his behavior. Notable attempts have been made in the early part of the century by the Austrian political economist, Joseph Schumpeter, in his *The Theory of Economic Development*[4] and more recently by the sociological researchers into *Enterprising Man*,[5] Collins, Moore and Unwalla, based at the University of Michigan.

However, neither party was able to develop a concept of management that was sufficiently robust to warrant systematic application. The Americans, Peters and Waterman, though, have developed a set of alternately hard and soft principles, in the eighties, that are readily applicable to management of the primal kind. They have been writing, moreover, at a time when the rational approach to management is under heavy fire.

Primal management comes of age

Peters and Waterman maintain, then, that whether you are starting your own enterprise, or running an existing company, you would do well to search for excellence. In other words, their core concept applies to all comers in business and management. Above all, the two Americans make the plea that we should keep things basic, and simple, and remember that business is fundamentally about people. They much prefer 'gut feeling' to 'cool logic' and basic instinct to sophisticated intellect.

The primal branches

Corporate culture

A whole wave of primal theories have emerged since the early eighties, continuing where Peters and Waterman left off. On the soft side of primal management the new discipline of corporate culture has been born, with another two Americans – Deal and Kennedy[6] – as its arch exponents. In fact corporate culture, in its primal preoccupation with communally shared values, has a sophisticated and metaphysical side to it, as well as a primal one. Of that we shall hear more later (see Chapter 26).

On people management

The emerging literature on primal management is dominated by male authors with the exception of Mary Kay, founder of the Mary Kay Cosmetics company. In her typically earthy, homespun manner, Mary Kay[7] conveys the basic essence of people-management whereby people and love stand their equal ground before profit and loss.

What they don't teach you at Harvard Business School

Using a similarly basic approach to Mary Kay, but concentrating relatively more on 'hunting' rather than 'gathering', the American sports promoter, Mark McCormack, wrote his provocative anti-establishment book in the mid-eighties.[8] Heading his major sections, 'People', 'Sales and negotiation', and 'Running a business', McCormack concentrates on those instinctive elements of managerial behavior, like 'creating impressions' and 'taking the edge' that are easy to acknowledge if not to actually put into effect.

Intrapreneuring

Finally, like 'corporate culture', intrapreneuring, in the eighties, has almost become a discipline unto itself. Its arch exponent is yet another American, Gifford Pinchot,[9] who has introduced us to intracapital, intraprise and intrapreneuring. His preoccupation is with freeing enterprise – intrapreneuring, within the organization – hence intraprise, to match the degree of free enterprise without. The binding force within, therefore, is not the organization's bureaucracy but the intraprise's communally shared values.

The primal fruits

Minnesota Mining and Manufacturing

For both Peters and Waterman, and for Pinchot, the archetypal intrapreneurial and primally excellent company is Minnesota Mining and Manufacturing (3M). Unique amongst large-scale enterprises 3M has been able to engage continuously in new venturing. As a result it has generated thousands of new products, in its general area of coating and bonding technology, by its continuous experimentation (action bias) and closeness to the customer. 3M is a typically Western, and an unusually entrepreneurial large company. While it manages to combine autonomy and entrepreneurship with communally shared values, it is firmly rooted in free enterprise soil.

Mondragon cooperatives

A group of companies that are securely embedded in the communal tradition are the cooperatives of Northern Spain. Unlike other cooperatives around the globe, which were started along ideological grounds, the Mondragon cooperatives were a local outgrowth, emerging out of indigenous economic and social circumstances. They have also drawn, extensively, on the 'tribal' and communal feelings of the local Basque population. In fact, although many traditional communities have been run along collective lines for centuries, only very few have managed, like Mondragon, to build personal enterprise into collective activity, to the extent that the wholesome fruits – both soft and tasty, and also hard and firm – could fully ripen.

The primal manager

Such wholesome primal management combines personal enterprise with a sense of shared values, or communal identification with a sense of personal initiative. The intrapreneur that results, personified by John Myser of 3M, is an amalgam of entrepreneur and animateur (see Chapters 6 and 9 for their separate identities, see also Fig. 14). John Myser who is currently President of 3M Canada, is an archetypal 'intrapreneur'.

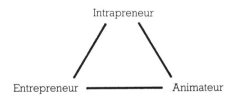

Fig. 14 The primal manager.

Intrapreneur

John Myser,   President, 3M Canada

Background: community and enterprise

Shared values: 'Honey, it feels right'
As a student I ran a garage on the side, to earn my keep – forty hours a week. I graduated in liberal arts and went to work for 3M. 'To do what', my wife asked, 'selling sandpaper?! How are you going to earn a living out of that?' 'I don't know, honey,' I said, 'but it feels right.'

Anyway, I joined the company and they put me on to their training course at St Paul. It involved eleven weeks of classes in the lab, on quality control. Then we were assigned a territory. I went to the State of Oregon as a young salesman. I worked for two divisions out there, over a couple of years: hardware and automotive. I was then promoted to industrial, which carried with it more prestige and responsibility.

I'm a salesman and proud of it

In the early sixties I went on to work on the NASA project. I did work with abrasives, and, though still on the sales side, got very involved with technical aspects. We were developing finishes that didn't react with liquid hydrogen. I talked with all kinds of people who were involved with the Apollo project. I was a salesman, then, and, in a different way, still am today. I'm proud of it. Of course I've always had to learn a lot of technical things.

Autonomy and enterprise

A test of resolve

After a further three years I was given a test of resolve. I was transferred from luscious California to a small, steel mill town in Pennsylvania. In those days a big steel mill could use a million dollars worth of sandpaper in a year. I got involved, once again, with both the sales and the technical aspects. We were trying to demonstrate the worth of new systems to our customers. The proof they were looking for wasn't always technical. Then I moved back to the home office in St Paul, as a sales trainer. My job was to develop the training programme in which I had previously been involved. I had, by now, worked with each of the three major abrasives groupings.

Open house

I carried on as a sales trainer for a couple of years, and then did some marketing work related to the furniture makers. They are, of course, large users of abrasives. When the lab would come out with a new development, we'd arrange for it to be communicated to our customers through seminars or through having an open house.

Simple form

We're a very horizontal company, you see. I go anywhere to talk to anybody. I don't go up the traditional, vertical route. The hell with that. I hate those stilted organization charts. Because we have to deal with so many businesses our communication has to be better than in many other companies. One day I'm talking bionic ears and the next day video tape. I move from digital sound to price points. So, as a salesman, I was in the habit of going back and forth to the lab as if I belonged there. There was an easy interchange, a fairly typical 3M approach.

Opportunity

After this marketing activity, 3M made me a manager for an area of the country, with ten sales reps under me. They put me on to automotive sales for three years. Then I was promoted as National Manager, Automotive. My people were well pleased with that. Soon afterwards I was given the opportunity of starting an Automotive Division. It was a grand opportunity for a young man. We started up our own research lab. My life now depended on the automotive market. We developed our own special products to out-manoeuver our American and foreign competitors.

Action bias: experimentation

We used to sell, for example, to the big steel mills, an adhesive on the back of our abrasives. My gosh, I thought, if we could draw on the steel mill example, and develop an improvement on the competition's product, for our automotive after market. Immediately the lab went to work. They came up with something marvelous, an adhesive product in a roll. We made a dispenser to go with it. Our customers had to pay 50 per cent more for our product, but we knew it was a better one. We went out to about 300 customers as a test market. The reaction that came back was, 'It's okay.' That was terrible. We had to get a better reaction than that to justify a 50 per cent increase! We hadn't done the market test right. We had to be able to show our customers that, with our new product, they could sand down four fenders, rather than just two. We realized our error, as we recovered from our state of shock. In the end we succeeded, and, as a result, increased our market share by 50 per cent. And now we've gone on to a whole new line of abrasives. 'Stick it' has become the generic name for the whole product line.

We run our own show

Four years ago I was asked to go to Canada, and run the subsidiary there. I said I'd take a shot at it. There are four or five super jobs outside the US – Canada, UK, Italy, Germany, France and Japan. These are the big, wholly contained subsidiaries. You do it all yourself. The other eighty countries in which we operate have very small subsidiaries. Here, in Canada, we have everything that you have in a traditional corporation. We even do our own blue sky research. Fortunately London, Ontario, is hard to get to, so we are not pestered by St Paul.

When I took over I got rid of one layer of management. So I have sixteen people reporting to me. Because I have so many I have to allow them to run their own show. If I interfered with so many people I'd foul things up. So that military layer is gone. It's worked out marvelously well. I'm very proud of the result. In 1981 there was a fierce recession in Canada, 50 per cent worse than the US. Our GNP level is only now back to what it was in 1981. It's been a bitch of a four years. That was a gift from God for me! It gave me a chance to streamline things. Now we have 28 per cent fewer 3Mers than we had, when I joined, and yet we do $100 million more business a year. It's spectacular. We've also increased our productivity 14 per cent per annum. The only area where it's difficult to measure increased productivity is in research. But I have been building up our research effort, in Canada, consistently. I wanted the subsidiary to be more self-contained. So I asked our people, from the start, what do you want to do as a company? What have we got that we're particularly good at? We all know that there are research brains outside the US. There are areas where we do things better in Canada than in the USA. For example, the Canadians are very strong in orthopedic medicine. As a result of our reseach and development work we've been able to market a 3M hip replacement all over the world. We've also created a very successful bone growth stimulator. We've deliberately selected areas then, where we feel we can do better than the parent company.

If you fear failure, you don't succeed

When I first arrived in Canada, I found the 3Mers there to be fairly traditional in their approach. They were more concerned about failure than I was, and that can be a deterrent. I remember giving them a speech, mentioning all the failures I'd been associated with! If you fear failure then you can't have a success.

The family feeling

Little items keeping in touch

3M are in all kinds of little businesses in which, if you fail, you fail small. An IBMer might sell a $10 million computer to a customer, and then nothing else for five years. So everything hinges on that sale. They'll fight like tigers for it. It's the survival of the fittest. We, on the other hand, sell sandpaper and tape. Lots of little items keeping in touch with one another ...

I have to communicate with everybody

I have a system. I regularly review the 'Chiefs to Indians Ratio'. I use a lot of cute phrases, you know. I don't care if they're clichés. I have to communicate with everybody. That includes people inside and out. We have this guy Robin. I'm his 'godfather'. That means I've been keeping a watchful eye over him, so he doesn't get lost in the system. He's a Canadian who had spent years in Marseilles as a diver. He'd become aware of the growths eating away at underwater structures, particularly oil rigs. After a while he got tired of chasing girls in the South of France and went to work on nonwoven webs, to clean floors. He began to think to himself, 'if Scotchbrite can clean pans, why not ships and oil rigs'. He became a driven man. My secretary, who actually runs 3M Canada, told me one day that Robin wanted to see me, to tell me about his idea. 'Come and dive with me in Toronto harbor', he said. I had just joined 3M Canada, and he wanted to ensure that the new guy in the block was converted to his idea. He was making pads and Scotchbrite brushes to clean the undersides of oil rigs. Soon he outgrew what we could do in London, Ontario. He moved across to the States, and has since put a marvelous business together. As his godfather, I'm willing to take him back at any time if it becomes necessary or desirable. Robin's always sending me information about what he's doing. I couldn't forget him even if I wanted to.

We're niche players

We also keep in very close touch with our customer. When I arrived I asked everyone the question, 'are you doing work that the customer – inside or outside – is willing to pay for?' We started this exercise three years ago, finding out exactly what the customer wants. 'Get off your derriere', I said, 'and go ask your customer what he wants.' We don't usually get involved in price wars, and battle situations. We're niche players. One thousand creative people develop five hundred different niches for themselves. Our strength is our niche. Because we're niche players we have to get to know our customers intimately. We make a little and sell a little. Then we come back and tinker some more. We're not much into large-scale market analysis, and we don't fancy all out market warfare. We only take on allcomers when we're competing on home grounds – creativity, uniqueness, innovation. And my home territory, for the moment, is Canada.

Together we stand

We're a strange mixture at 3M. We'll never fire people if they become redundant. We find another place for them elsewhere, and train them up, as long as they are willing to move. At the same time, I love a scrap. I'd be willing to take on anyone, if it was necessary. When the need arises we close ranks, like a commando group. Together we must be greater than each one of us apart. That applies both to our people and to our products. One of the things I'm proudest of is the 'Lunchtime Learning' programme I've started in 3M Canada. People come along to learn about anything and everything. You can even get a 3M degree! We're that kind of company.

London, England 1987

John Myser started out in St Paul and hopes to return there one day. He remains proud to be a salesman, while taking equal pride in his technical proficiency. He loves running his own show, but places high priority on communication with others. He is independent minded, but very much a part of the 3M family. He welcomes failure, albeit in a small way, in order to succeed. These inherent contradictions are all part of the 3M way. They are also very much the American way. They make up the intrapreneur – independent, but sharing values.

Conclusion

You will now be introduced more fully to primal management, that is its roots – in anthropology and economics (Chapter 6), its core – the passion for excellence (Chapter 7), its branches – intrapreneuring and corporate culture (Chapters 8, 9), its fruits – 3M and the Mondragon cooperatives (Chapter 10). All together represent the first and youthful management domain.

We shall explore its living characteristics, then, in the five chapters that follow. Thereafter we shall turn from youth to adulthood, from instinct to intellect, from primal to rational management.

References

1. M. Polanyi, *The Livelihood of Man*, Academic Press (1967).
2. A. Smith, *An Inquiry into the Wealth of Nations*, Penguin (1970).
3. T. Peters and B. Waterman, *In Search of Excellence*, Harper & Row (1982).
4. J. Schumpeter, *The Theory of Economic Development*, Oxford University Press (1951).
5. O. Collins, D. Moore and T. Unwalla, *Enterprising Man*, Michigan University (1964).
6. T. Deal and A. Kennedy, *Corporate Cultures*, Addison Wesley (1982).
7. M. Kay, *On People Management*, Pan (1985).
8. M. McCormack, *What They Don't Teach You at Harvard Business School*, Fontana (1986).
9. G. Pinchot, *Intrapreneuring*, Harper & Row (1985).

6 Economics and
anthropology

Contents

Key concepts

Once you have fully understood the chapter you should be able
to define the following concepts in your own words:

Agents of production	Matricental community
Capitalism	*Oikos*
Enterprise	Personal gain
Entrepreneurial attributes	Self-interest
Invisible hand	Substantive economics
Market-place	

Objectives

Upon completing this chapter you should be able to do the following:

1. Trace the development of primal management from its archaic origins.
2. Compare and contrast the 'substantive' and 'economizing' approaches to economics.
3. Articulate the role of manager as hunter–entrepreneur, and as gatherer– 'animateur'.
4. Understand the character and attributes of the classical entrepreneur.

Introduction

The market economy and cultural anthropology

The primal roots of management, relatively close to the surface, lie in economics, and in Adam Smith's 'market economy'. Through the 'market', resources are allocated and controlled. Deeper down, within the historical soil, the primal roots reach cultural anthropology, inside primordial, Stone Age communities. Through 'culture' physical and human nature is cultivated and values are exchanged and shared. The human being also evolves a sense of place.

Oikos

Hundreds of thousands of years ago our ancestors, the ape men, lived out in the wild as nomads, barely able to communicate with their fellows, or to settle in one place. Then, some 10,000 years ago, Neolithic men and women began to settle in one home, one place, one *oikos*. At this late dawn of history, a village society had emerged in which life seemed to be unified by a communal disposition towards work, and its products. Nomadic bands of hunter–gatherers had begun to develop a crude system of horticulture, and had settled down in small villages, where they engaged in mixed farming.

Although both hunter and gatherer had their parts to play, the one killing and trapping animals and the other cultivating the land, social life began to acquire distinctly 'matricental' qualities. The first settled communities, then, under their primal, Neolithic management, began to shift their prime focus from the male hunter to the female food gatherer. Woman's foraging activities helped awaken in humanity an acute sense of place, of *oikos*, to use the Greek term. Her stake in society was different from that of the male. It was more domestic, more pacifying and more caring. The primal roots of management are to be found, therefore, not in the armies and churches of antiquity, but in the first settled villages, in our original *oikos*. The modern term 'economics' owes its origins to this Greek word for place.

Economic and cultural transformation

The hunter becomes an entrepreneur

In fact, it was not until the seventeenth and eighteenth centuries, that economics was transformed, and gradually lost its homely connection. It was at this point that primal management took a strong turn towards the hunter, and gave birth to the modern 'entrepreneur'. The entrepreneur, and his business enterprise, visibly evolved from primal, hunting origins. The entrepreneurial tradition has lived on since the eighteenth century, and has even gained renewed force, recently, within business and the community. In the eighties, for the first time, it was brought into the conventional managerial fold, and even given a new title, 'intrapreneurship'. The original 'hunting' image, stretching back to Neolithic times, still retains much of its primal force and identity.

The gatherer reappears in Marxian guise

The communal tradition, on the other hand, has undergone an ironic transformation. The gatherer has been thrust out of classical economics, despite the original *oikos*. She reappears, in the nineteenth century, in Marxian guise. By this point, of course, the gatherer is sitting outside of, and in opposition to, business, rather than comfortably within it. In the twentieth century this results in both Russian and Chinese revolutions.

The stage is then set for a conflict between 'capitalism' and 'socialism' that eclipses the gatherer role within business. Therefore when the 'behavioral sciences' are introduced into management they lack the basic, instinctive thrust that entrepreneurship carries. Inevitably, as we shall see, 'human relations' gets pushed into the commercial sidelines.

However, we are now jumping the gun. Let me return to anthropology and to economics, from whence management came.

The gatherer's role and evolution

Substantive economics

Karl Polanyi[1] was an unusual mix of anthropologist and economist. Moreover he took a particular interest in the way economics became transformed over the course of thousands of years.

Survival and nurturance

Economics, for Polanyi, had two meanings. The first, 'formal' meaning, related to the 'economizing' function, that is to the allocation of scarce resources. It ties in with the manager's survival role. The second, 'substantive' meaning, pointed to the elemental fact that human beings, like all other living creatures, cannot exist for any length of time without a physical and social environment that sustains them. It ties in with the manager as nurturer and communicator. It is the second, often neglected definition, that brings the gatherer into the foreground. This substantive meaning is derived from man's dependence for his livelihood upon nature and upon his fellows. It draws from primal origins within matricentric, Neolithic communities.

The American social ecologist, Murray Bookchin, characterizes such horticultural communities as 'procreative in their relationship with the natural world, touching the earth and changing it, but with a grace, delicacy, and feeling that may be regarded as nature's own harvest'.[2] The social and economic imagery of the time, therefore, shifted from the predator to the procreator, from the camp fire to the domestic hearth, and from cultural traits associated with father to those associated with mother. The role of 'gatherer' as collector, grower, carrier and maker of useful things, superceded that of hunter. In contemporary terms, shared values surpass autonomy and entrepreneurship as a guiding, primal ethic.

Subsistence communities

Of course the substantive economy of 10,000 years ago still exists today, in so called 'subsistence' communities. One such community which I happen to know well has been formed, over the centuries, by the Shona peoples of Zimbabwe. While, as the country develops, traditional and modern forms become increasingly juxtaposed, a 'substantive' economy still exists within substantial parts of the society.

Matricental community

Wealth is not a personal matter for the Shona. It is not a man's own possession which he can will as he pleases. It belongs to the family group and its use is restricted and bound up with marriage and family life. Shona villagers extol the virtues of solidarity, fraternity and equality.

The chief, his councillors and his headmen, are thus expected to set an example by not living differently from the rest of the people. He must avoid creating the impression that he is superior to others.

In his traditional background, therefore, no Shona man or woman works alone or independently; all are geared towards dependence. He has to learn that an individual is part of a group, of a society that depends for its smooth working on the control of its wants. Without such self-abnegation there would be insufficient food for the whole community.

Michael Gelfand *Growing Up Shona*[3] 1979

In a traditional community, then, the economic process is imbedded in the extended 'kinship' relations. The communal setting formalizes the situation, and the shared values, out of which organized economic activities spring. What there is of production and distribution of goods and services is therefore imbedded within the overall communal and 'corporate culture'.

The economic watershed

Self-sufficiency

The substantive view of economics, as imbedded within the norms and values of the community at large, continued to be held for thousands of years. Aristotle, in ancient Greece, saw the role of barter in society to be that of returning society to self-sufficiency rather than that of securing profit or gain. He saw the need to set rates of exchange, through law and custom, in such a way that the natural friendliness that prevails amongst members of a community, is maintained. At the same time he likened the labor process not to a form of production, but to one of reproduction, not to an act of fabrication, but to one of procreation.

Reciprocity

In feudal times, in Western Europe, the famous open field system was indeed organized around individually formed, narrow strips. Yet strip farming necessarily involved such close coordination of planting and harvesting between cultivators of adjacent strips that the peasantry normally shared its ploughs, draft animals and implements. The reciprocity involved reinforced archaic communal traditions, and, with them, the gatherer's role. In fourteenth-century England technology was still deeply imbedded in society. Every village had its masons, carpenters, spinners, smiths and millers, each of whom was bound to his fellow craftsmen through a guild. Home and occupation were still closely inter-twined, as were family and working life. A self-contained economic world had not yet lifted itself outside of the social context. The very idea of personal gain was foreign to social and religious thought, at least for most people, during the Middle Ages.

Whereas, then, the concept of personal gain was blasphemous, the broader notion that a general struggle for gain might actually bind together a community, would have been held as little short of madness. There was a reason for this supposed blindness. Land, labor and capital – the basic agents of production which the market system allocates – did not yet exist. They did not enter the gatherer's vocabulary. Land, labor and capital in the sense of soil, human beings, and tools are of course coexistent with society itself. But, these same entities as impersonal, dehumanized, agents of production had not yet been conceived of as such.

Self-interest

Over the course of the seventeenth and eighteenth centuries all that morality changed, paving the way for the transformation of the hunter of old into the new entrepreneur. The gatherer was left very much behind. She became, until only very recently, the proverbial housewife.

The economic revolution

What forces could have been sufficiently powerful to smash a comfortable and established world and institute in its place this new unwanted society?

There was no single massive cause. The new way of life grew inside the old like a butterfly inside a chrysalis, and when the stir was strong enough it burst the old structure asunder. It was not great events, single adventures, individual laws or powerful personalities which brought about the economic revolution. It was a process of internal growth.

First there was the gradual emergence of national political units in Europe, the isolated existence of early Feudalism giving way to centralized monarchies. With the growth of monarchies came the growth of national spirit; in turn this meant royal patronage for favoured industries.

A second great current of change was to be found in the emergence of Protestantism. The Protestant leaders paved the way for an amalgamation of spiritual and temporal life. Acquisitiveness became a recognized virtue, not immediately for one's private enjoyment, but for the greater glory of God. From here it was only a step to the identification of riches with spiritual excellence, and of rich men with saintly ones. Perhaps most important of all in the pervasiveness of its effect was a rise in scientific curiosity. The precapitalist era saw the birth of the printing press, the paper mill, the windmill, the map and a host of other inventions. Experimentation and innovation were looked on for the first time with a fresh eye.

Robert Heilbronner *The Worldly Philosophers*[4] 1969

The role and evolution of the entrepreneur

Self-interest in the market-place

Whereas the role of gatherer had been left behind in the economic history books, by the eighteenth century, the hunter of old was gaining a new lease of life. With the birth of 'economic man' came the entrepreneur, hunting for economic and financial, rather than for natural and physical, gain. Whereas the Neolithic hunter had made his 'killings' on the open plain, the new entrepreneur made his particular ones on the open market! The problem of survival, in the eighteenth century, was to be solved not by groups of men of physical prowess, bound by community and custom, but by the free action of profit seeking individuals bound together only by the market. Moreover, the idea of personal gain that underpinned it became so firmly rooted that it was soon assumed to be an omnipresent attitude. The idea, though, needed a binding philosophy. That philosophy came, in 1776, in the form of Adam Smith's *Inquiry into the Wealth of Nations*.[5] Dr Smith, a Scot and Professor of Moral Philosophy, a slight man who had more than a slight tendency to be absent minded, turned traditional society on its head. Instead of focussing on the community, within which the individual is contained, Smith focussed on the individual, around whom society revolves.

Adam Smith concluded that through his famous and 'invisible hand' the private interests and passions of men are led in the direction 'which is most agreeable to the interests of society'. The 'gatherer' has therefore become 'invisible'; her role has been overtaken by that of the impersonal market. She becomes a non-entity. The entrepreneur's role gathers apace. Adam Smith demonstrates to us that the drive of 'individual self-interest', within an environment of similarly motivated individuals, will result in healthy competition. He then further illustrates how competition will result in the provision of those goods that society wants, in the quantities that society desires, and at the prices that society is prepared to pay. 'It is not from the benevolence of the butcher, the brewer or the baker that we expect our dinner', says Smith, 'but from their regard to their self interest. We address ourselves, not to their humanity, but to their self-love, and never talk to them of our necessities, but of their advantages'.

Self-interest therefore replaces social interest as the primal force. A primal motive is retained, through its powerfully instinctive nature, but the direction of such a motive is fundamentally changed. The directive and controlling side of primal management, instinctively expressed, takes over from the communicative and nurturing one. This imbalance, over time, is destined to lead towards the 'ugly face of capitalism'. Yet self-interest is only half of Smith's picture. The other half is represented by competition. For each man, out to do his best for himself with no thought of social cost, is faced with a flock of similarly motivated individuals who are in exactly in the same boat. Thus a man who permits his self-interest to run away with itself will find that competitors have slipped in to take his trade away. The trouble with Smith's argument, of course, is that he relies on one hunter to scare the other away. There is no gatherer in place to create a balance. The result, historically speaking, has been the rise of socialism, of communism, and of workers' movements around the globe, each of which has attempted to alter the 'capitalist' imbalance. The problem is that they have become imbalanced in their own turn.

The emergence of the entrepreneur

The art of primal management, then, as we shall soon see, is to maintain an effective balance between hunting and gathering. In other words, both enterprise and community must have their proper place. Ironically, although Adam Smith introduced us to the entrepreneur as the creator of the *Wealth of Nations*, neither Smith nor his successors amongst the classical economists, gave us much insight into this entrepreneur's character. In fact the first of the political economists to do so properly was Joseph Schumpeter.

Schumpeter was an Austrian, born in the second half of the nineteenth century, who spent much of his life in America. In *The Theory of Economic Development* Schumpeter portrayed the entrepreneur as a man of courage and instinct, a truly primal hero. For it was the entrepreneur's will and intuition rather than his formalized knowledge and skill that made him successful in his business pursuits. More specifically, Schumpeter identified three leading attributes of enterprising man. These three attributes incorporated the desire for a private kingdom, a will to conquer, and joyful creativity. Incidentally it is worth noting that, historically at least, entrepreneurship has been identified with the male species rather than the female.

Attributes of entrepreneurship

First of all there is the dream and the will to found a private kingdom. What may be attained by industrial or commercial success is the nearest approach to medieval lordship possible to modern man. Its fascination is specially strong for those people who have no other chance of achieving social distinction.

Then there is the impulse to conquer: the impulse to fight, to prove oneself superior to others, to succeed for the sake, not of the fruits of success, but for success itself.

Finally there is the joy of creating, of getting things done, or simply of exercising one's energy and ingenuity. This set of motives is the most directly anti-hedonist of the three.

Joseph Schumpeter *The Theory of Economic Development*[6] 1954

In his theory of economic development Schumpeter not only saw the entrepreneur to be an innovative and disruptive force, but also acknowledged that such a person played an important part within a large organization as well as in a small one. Schumpeter therefore sowed early seeds for the subsequent emergence of the 'intrapreneur'. Finally, Joseph Schumpeter equated enterprise with development, both under the guise of the carrying out of new combinations. These could involve:

- The introduction of a new good, that is one with which consumers are not yet familiar, or of a new quality of good.
- The introduction of a new method of production, that is one not yet tested by experience in the branch of manufacture concerned.

- The opening of a new market.
- The conquest of a new source of supply of raw materials or half manufactured goods.
- The carrying out of a new form of industrial organization.

Conclusion

The new primal wave

In the fifty years between the time that Schumpeter was writing, and the present day, primal management has been largely eclipsed by, particularly, rational management in some guise or another. However in the 1980s the search for primal 'excellence', in a contemporary context, began in earnest. *In Search of Excellence* by Peters and Waterman is in fact a modern updating of primal management. As we shall see, in Chapter 7, the two Americans have resurrected both hunter and gatherer in modern garb, and given their respective qualities equal weight and influence.

The need for character balance

Despite their efforts, though, we still find ourselves bereft of character balance at this primal stage. For while the entrepreneur or intrapreneur is alive and well, his 'gatherer' counterpart remains characterless. She has 'soft' qualities, but has no name to call her own. In my own work I have borrowed from the French and come up with the word 'animateur' to give the gatherer of old, modern substance. The 'animateur' is the person who brings life to a community, who fosters group spirit, and who animates people in a communal setting. She shares with the entrepreneur his enthusiasm and flair; where they differ is in their relative individualism and competitiveness.

Primal management has recently come into its own so as to ward off the prospects of 'paralysis by analysis'. It also serves as a reminder that basic human qualities, both soft and hard, remain vitally important in business in particular, and have served mankind, in general, for many thousands of years. What we must not forget as we go out 'in search of excellence' is that the soft and communal values are as important as the hard and individual ones, and that primal management initiates, rather than culminates in the managerial debate. While all managers – primal, rational, developmental, and metaphysical – control and direct, on the one hand, and communicate and cultivate, on the other, the primal species do so in a particular way. Their approach is basic, instinctive, immediate, as we shall see when we turn to Peters and Waterman, and attend to their 'excellent' primal thesis.

References

1. K. Polanyi, *The Livelihood of Man*, Academic Press (1977).
2. M. Bookchin, *The Ecology of Freedom*, Cheshire Books (1982), p. 62.
3. M. Gelfand, *Growing Up Shona*, Mambo Press, Zimbabwe (1979), p. 80.
4. R. Heilbronner, *The Worldly Philosophers*, Allen Lane (1969), p. 64.
5. A. Smith, *An Inquiry into the Wealth of Nations*, Penguin (1970), Vols. I–III.
6. J. Schumpeter, *The Theory of Economic Development*, Oxford University Press (1954), p. 86.

7 A passion for excellence

Contents

Key concepts

Once you have fully understood the chapter you should be able to define the following concepts in your own words:

Adhocracy	Loose/tight organization
Champion	MBWA
Championing systems	Organizational fluidity
Close to the customer	Productivity through people
Coach and coaching	Seven Ss
Experimental organization	Shared values
Hard and soft attributes	Three pillar structure

Objectives

Upon completing this chapter you should be able to do the following:

1. Outline the core of primal management, as reflected in *The Search for Excellence* and *A Passion for Excellence*.
2. Compare and contrast the soft and hard attributes therein.
3. Comment on the significance of the 'back to basics' movement in the evolution of management.
4. Describe, in some detail, each of the eight particular attributes characterizing the seventy-five excellent organizations.
5. Comment on the unique approach to people, and to leadership, adopted by Tom Peters and his colleagues.

Introduction

In the 1980s, that is over the course of the past five years, management has undergone a regression, and a progression. For on the one hand management has 'regressed' back to its primal origins; on the other hand it has progressed through, and beyond, its supposedly analytical straight-jacket. The prime instigator of this 'back to basics' movement has been Tom Peters, a highly energetic and dynamic American based in California. Going out *In Search of Excellence*, with his McKinsey colleague, Bob Waterman, Peters established a new wave of management thinking that very quickly became vogue in both Europe and America. Peters' 'new' wave represented, at one and the same time, a return to primal, hunter–gatherer instincts and a reinstatement of the American enterprising–communal spirit. The personalized, hunter instinct, resurrected in the form of 'winning', gained precedence in Peters' initial search for excellence. 'The message that comes through so poignantly in the studies we reviewed is that we [Americans] like to think of ourselves as winners. The lesson that the excellent companies have to teach us is that there is no reason why we can't design systems that continually reinforce this notion.'[1]

The communal, gatherer instinct, at first resurrected in the form of 'shared values', ultimately secured the upper hand in his second book, *A Passion for Excellence*.

> Let us suppose that we were asked for one all purpose bit of advice for management, one truth that we were able to distill from the excellent company research. We might be tempted to reply, figure out your value system, decide what the company stands for. What does your enterprise do that gives everyone most pride?[2]

What Peters has done of course, in his pursuit of excellence, is to figure out his country's primal, or instinctive value system. He has therefore rediscovered what America basically stands for, including the approach to management and enterprise that gives Americans most pride. For that rediscovery we have the Japanese to thank, for edging American business out of what Peters would call an evolutionary and analytical, cul de sac. In other words, the Japanese threat forced American business, and its management, to rethink its whole approach. The rational orientation that it had adopted, largely under the influence of such Central Europeans as Peter Drucker, was being called into question. Something new was now being put in its place, something much more American in scope and form.

Let me now elaborate in more detail, on 'excellence', its origins and development, thereby revealing the core of what I have termed primal management.

In search of excellence

Soft and hard approaches to management

The American search for a new approach to management was spurred on by the accelerating Japanese competition, in the mid-seventies. At the time the rational and scientific managerial approach – to which I alluded in Chapter 5 – held sway. The search was instigated by McKinsey's, the highly reputable American business consultants, and by Richard Pascale and Anthony Athos. Pascale and Athos, who subsequently wrote *The Art of Japanese Management*,[3] concluded that the Japanese had managed to combine so-called soft and hard approaches to management more successfully than most American companies had done.

They subsequently developed the 'seven Ss' framework, shown in Fig. 15, which incorporated four soft, as well as three hard elements. Strategy, structure and systems comprised the 'cold triangle', so revered by business schools, and rationally oriented managers. Skills, staff, style and – most importantly – shared values, made up the 'warm' and softer side. Japanese companies, it appeared, were uniquely adept at both.

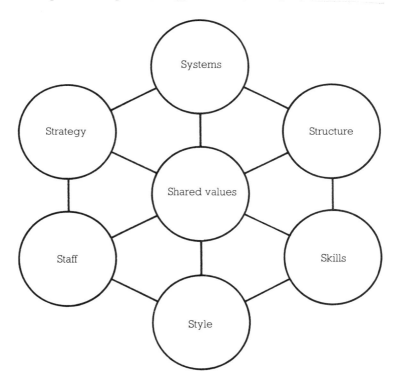

Fig. 15 The seven Ss of management.

However, Pascale and Athos then discovered, that the best American companies, like their Japanese counterparts, combined soft and hard, warm and cold attributes. Peters and Waterman, focussing on America rather than Japan, continued on from where Pascale and Athos left off, placing less emphasis on conceptual sophistication and more on finding basic, home truths.

Back to basics

The seven Ss framework, as far as Peters and Waterman were concerned, enabled them to say: 'All that stuff you have been dismissing for so long as the intractable, irrational, intuitive and informal organization can be managed ... Not only are you foolish to ignore it, but here's a way to think about it.'[4]

However, the two Americans still felt at the time that McKinsey's had only scratched the surface of, particularly, the softer sides of management. More work needed to be done. So they chose, in 1979, seventy-five highly regarded American companies, and went out in search of reasons for their excellence in performance and reputation. It is important to bear in mind, moreover, that Peters and Waterman, prior to their detailed research, were skeptical of the real contribution that rational management, in isolation, was likely to make to business success. Nevertheless, Tom Peters and Bob Waterman claim that their ultimate findings were 'a pleasant surprise'. For their research showed,

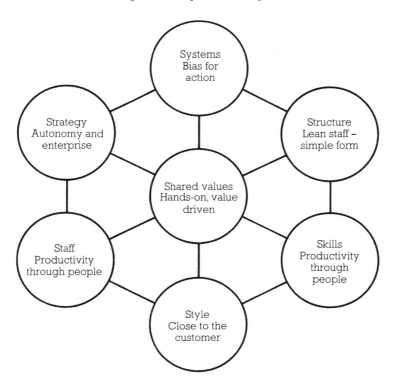

Fig. 16 Primal attributes.

'more clearly than could have been hoped for, that the excellent companies were, above all, brilliant on the basics. Tools didn't substitute for thinking. Intellect didn't overpower wisdom. Analysis didn't impede action. Rather these companies worked hard to keep things simple in a complex world'.[5] We can now investigate what the companies did, and how.

The primal core

Peters and Waterman have identified a set of core attributes that characterize their excellent companies. It is these basic attributes which have displaced the conventional and analytical wisdom, amongst many a 'progressive' manager in America and Europe in the eighties. As we can see, from Fig. 16, their characteristics (e.g. 'Bias for action') – both soft and hard – are much more basic, or primal in language and tone than those of Pascale and Athos (e.g. 'Systems').

The so-called 'hard and cold triangle' – strategy, system and structure – amongst the seven Ss, has been displaced by more distinctly American, more basic and tangible, as well as more primal and entrepreneurial virtues:

- Strategy – autonomy and entrepreneurship; stick to the knitting.
- Systems – bias for action.
- Structure – lean staff/simple form; loose-tight organization.

Similarly the soft and 'warm' attributes, staff and skills, style and superordinate goals – have also been suitably displaced:

- Staff and skills – productivity through people.
- Style – close to the customer.
- Superordinate goals – shared values.

Autonomy and entrepreneurship

The central character in the pursuit of excellence is the winner, the champion, or the individual that Gifford Pinchot has since termed the intrapreneur. This 'primal manager' displaces his analytical counterpart as the business' linchpin. The primal, instinctively driven champion thus replaces the rational, analytically oriented strategist as the business' driving force. I shall now investigate, through Peters and Waterman, the personality of the primal manager, or 'champion', and the systems and attitudes required to support him. We can then turn to the role and importance of 'sticking to the knitting', within a strategic and overall corporate context.

The champion

The champion carries those qualities of presence, immediacy, heroism, and ingenuity that can be associated with the primal hunter and entrepreneur. He merely transfers these attributes from his traditional hunting ground into an organizational context, albeit a favorable one like 3M in America, where his approach is welcomed rather than ridiculed or ignored. More specifically then:

- All the activity and apparent confusion Peters and Waterman observed within their excellent companies revolved around 'fired up champions', and around making sure that the potential innovator, or champion, comes forward, grows, and flourishes – even to the extent of indulging in a little madness.
- The champion is not a blue sky dreamer, or an intellectual giant. The champion might even have pinched somebody else's idea. But, above all, he is the pragmatic one who grabs on to a theoretical construct if necessary and bullheadedly pushes it to fruition.

Championing systems

Your average company is unable to cope with the irrationality, the egotism and the impatience of your characteristic champion. So he never gets hired, or if he does pass through the recruitment barrier, he is made to feel uncomfortable for ever after. The excellent and innovative companies, by way of contrast, have the appropriate support systems for this entrepreneurial character:

- Three primary roles are required, to foster innovation. There is firstly the product champion himself, cranky and fanatical. He is supported by an 'executive champion' and a 'godfather'. The executive has been through the lengthy process of husbanding, and has learnt how to shield an embryonic product from organizational negativity. The godfather is typically an ageing leader who provides a role model for championing.
- Champions are pioneers, and pioneers get shot at. The companies that get the most from champions have rich support networks for them. In particular their systems are designed to 'leak' so that scrounging champions can get something done.
- Whereas rational managers sort things out by rules and procedures, primal ones use internal competition as a basis for selection. In other words, the fittest, rather than the most reasonable, survive.
- In excellent companies there are two attributes of communciation that seem to foster innovation and enterprise – informality and intensity, both of which encourage both looseness (freewheeling) and tightness (peer pressure).

Tolerating failure

Finally, a special feature of the success-oriented, positive, and innovating environment is a substantial tolerance for failure:

- Specifically, champions do not automatically emerge. They emerge because history and numerous supports encourage them to, nurture them through trying times, celebrate their successes, and nurse them through occasional failures.
- At 3M, by way of example, if you want to stop the development of a new product, the burden of proof is on the one who wants to stop the project, not on the one who proposes it.

In the final analysis, though, Peters and Waterman argue that autonomy and entrepreneurship involve, as at 3M, a whole combination of interrelated features, rather than several separate and discrete ones.

How 3M innovate

Sure, the champion, the executive champion, and the venture team are at the heart of the process. But they succeed, when they do succeed, only because heroes abound; the value system focusses on scrounging; it's okay to fail; there's an orientation towards nichemanship and close contact with the customer.

There's a well understood process of taking small manageable steps; intense, informal communications are the norm; the physical setting provides plenty of sites for innovation; the organizational structure is highly accommodating of 3M style innovation; and the absence of planning and paperwork is conspicuous, as is the internal competition.

Peters and Waterman *In Search of Excellence*[6] 1982

Stick to the knitting

Peters and Waterman want as little as possible to do with such sophisticated analytical devices as 'corporate strategy'. For them it is the individual who drives the organization and shared values that make it cohere. It is as simple as that. They reduce 'business strategy', therefore, to its simplest terms. Companies, they say, must 'stick to the knitting'. While individuals should be encouraged to champion a wide range of ideas, the organization itself should be circumspect. In other words, businesses which branch out to only a limited extent, and thus 'stick very close to their knitting', out-perform others. 3M, which has diversified around a single knowledge base, coating and bonding technology, is a good case in point.

The important point, of which the primal manager should be aware, is that when he strays far afield, he loses his 'feel'. Such management feel can be trusted, whereas a business concept, abstract and abstruse, is inevitably suspect.

Bias for action

In the same way as abstract business concepts are suspect, learning divorced from action is unreal. The best systems, as far as Peters and Waterman are concerned, are those which are always moving, and always changing. Just like the hunter and his prey, they are seldom still. A bias for action involves organizational fluidity as well as constant techno-logical, commercial and social experimentation.

Organizational fluidity

- In rapidly changing times bureaucracy, and its static procedures, are insufficient. An 'adhocracy' is needed, that is an organizational mechanism to deal with all the new and emerging issues that fall in between the bureaucratic cracks that lie across its unchanging divisions.
- 'Chunking' means breaking things up to facilitate organizational fluidity and to encourage action. The resulting, action oriented bits and pieces come in many guises, as teams, as quality circles, as task forces, as project groups. Such small and temporary groups are the building blocks of excellent companies. Yet they hardly appear at all in the formal organization charts.
- Temporary task forces of this kind usually have ten or less people attached to them;

their duration is limited; membership is always voluntary; documentation is informal and scant.

Experimenting organizations

'Do it, fix it, try it' is the favourite axiom of Peters and Waterman. Getting on with things, especially in the face of complexity, simply comes down to doing something. Primal management is therefore involved, unstintingly, in a process of basic – if not scientific – experimentation.

- The most important and visible outcropping of the action bias in the excellent companies is their willingness to try things out, to experiment.
- Sheer numbers of experiments are critical ingredients for success through experiment-ation. The critical difference between successful and unsuccessful oil exploration companies, in the opinion of Peters and Waterman, is the sheer volume of drilling each has accomplished.
- Experimentation acts as a form of cheap learning for most of the excellent companies, usually proving less costly – and more useful – than sophisticated planning or market research.
- Management therefore has to be tolerant of leaky systems, it has to accept mistakes, support bootlegging, and roll with unexpected changes.
- Fluidity, chunking and experimentation are facilitated by simplified systems. Proctor and Gamble, for example, are famous for their one-page-only memoranda.

In summary, and according to our two Americans: 'There is no more important trait amongst excellent companies than an action orientation. Ready. Fire. Aim. Learn from your tries. That's enough'.

Simple form/lean staff

Peters and Waterman show positive disinterest in organizational form, particularly if it smacks of complexity. As far as they are concerned the less formal the organization, and the simpler the structure, the better. In that sense they reflect, to a tee, the attitudes and behavior of an entrepreneur.

- In the excellent companies, small in almost every case is beautiful. In the small unit its motivated and highly productive employee, in communication and in competition with his peers, out-produces the worker in big facilities time and again. Small, quality, excitement and autonomy belong to the same side of the coin.
- The point about smallness is that it induces manageability and, above all, commit-ment. More importantly, if the divisions are small enough, the individual still counts, and can stand out.
- Virtually all the growth, in the excellent companies, has been internally generated – starting small – and home grown. The few acquisitions followed a simple rule. They have been small businesses that could be readily assimilated, and, if there is subsequent failure, the company could write or sell off the acquisition without incurring heavy financial damage.
- The 'structure of the eighties' responds to the need for efficiency around the basics by

retaining a lean, but stable, form; responds to the need for innovation it will require by an entrepreneurial focus; responds to the need to avoid calcification by a habit-breaking structure. The composite and resulting form contains 'three pillars' of structure and strategy. (See Fig. 17.)

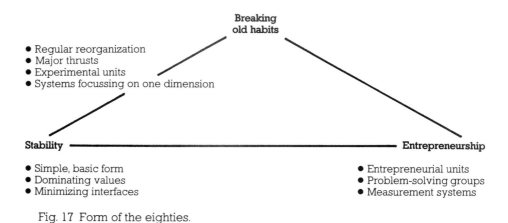

Fig. 17 Form of the eighties.

Hands-on/value-driven

Peters and Waterman were much more interested in 'shared values', as a means of coordinating individual activity, than in organizational structures. They were particularly struck, during their researches, by the attention paid, in excellent companies, to 'corporate culture'. Shared values, within such a cohesive culture, formed the glue that bound individuals together.

Clarifying the value system, therefore, and breathing life into it, are the greatest contributions a leader can make. Moreover the sort of values an excellent company might espouse are narrow in scope, including just a few basic values and beliefs, that is a belief in:

- Being the best.
- The nuts and bolts of doing the job well.
- The importance of people as individuals.
- Superior quality and service.
- Most members of the organization being able to innovate.
- The importance of informality to enhance contact.
- The explicit importance of economic growth and profit.

Once again Peters and Waterman affirm their orientation towards basic, visible, American values. In focussing on 'hands-on, value-driven' leadership, they also reflect the importance of personifying such values up front. Values and beliefs are not relegated to mere statements of intent. They must be reflected, and exemplified, in everyday behavior. This will become even clearer when we turn to *A Passion for Excellence*. Before we do so, however, we need to investigate those two crucial and soft attributes of primal management: people orientation and closeness to the customer.

Productivity through people

Peters and Waterman's book came to light some fifty years after the first social scientists had begun to focus on 'people in organizations'. However, by the 1980s, 'human relations' in business enterprises had become first 'personnel' and subsequently 'human resources management'. Analytical managers had taken over where their less formal predecessors had left off. True to overall form, then, our two Americans were going back to basics, and treating people as people!

- Treat people as people. Treat them as partners; treat them with dignity; treat them with respect. Treat them – not capital spending and automation – as the primary source of productivity gains.
- Respect the individual. Give people control over their destinies. Turn the average Joe and Jane into winners. Accentuate the positive. Insist that people stick out.
- Measure performance regularly, and purposefully, through peer review rather than through complicated and formalized control systems. Participate with the individual in setting high performance standards.
- True people orientation requires a language to go with it. Words and phrases like family feeling, open door, and management by wandering around show people in the organization that the orientation is bone deep.
- View the business as an extended family. Companies like 3M have become a sort of community centre for employees, as opposed to just a place of work.
- Avoid any rigidly followed chain of command. Make informality the norm. Ensure that top management is constantly in touch with all employees. Open doors, open plan, and open workspaces all contribute to such informality.
- Socialize incoming managers. Teach people the corporate values through role models, through heroes, and through perennial stories. Hewlett Packard even systematically collects 'HP Way stories' via a suggestion box, to revitalize the existing stock of corporate tales.
- Share information widely so that people know quickly whether or not a job is getting done, and who's doing it well or poorly. Peer comparison rather than the chain of command becomes the basis for such information and evaluation.

So excellent companies, according to Peters and Waterman, have a deeply ingrained philosophy that says, in effect, respect the individual, make people winners, let them stand out, treat people as adults. Thus the primal manager's attitude to people is distinctive. He is concerned with both the person and the task, in the context of individual and commercial achievement. Moreover his attitude to people inside the company is very similar to his orientation towards those without.

Close to the customer

A distinguishing feature of the primal manager, and one which links him closely to the entrepreneur, is his closeness to both his customers and to his employees. It is as if both emerge out of the same mind set. Closeness to the customer, as far as the excellent companies are concerned, involves an obsession with four things: service, quality, nichemanship and listening.

- The obsession with service, according to Peters and Waterman, lies at the heart of excellent company attitudes and operations. Whether they are involved with metal binding, high technology or hamburgers, all these enterprises have defined themselves as service businesses, in which all of their staff become involved.
- The real barriers to market entry lie not in the costs of investment in plant and equipment but in the investment cost of developing and maintaining quality. This quality barrier, the search for excellence revealed, is the critical one, that is, the people-capital tied up in iron-clad traditions of service, reliability and quality.
- Nichemanship involves learning about a particular sector of the market, test marketing and solving problems for the potential buyers within it, getting in early and stretching the price to reflect the newly added value to the customer, and being prepared to get out when the niche becomes saturated.
- Finally, the excellent companies are not only better on service, quality, reliability and finding a niche, they are also better listeners. That is the other half of the close to the customer equation. The fact that these companies are so strong on quality and service comes, in large measure, from paying attention to what the customer wants. They listen, they invite their customers into the company, they become partners with them.

The search and the passion

In their search for excellence Peters and Waterman came up with a powerful array of soft and hard attributes that characterized the best-run American companies. These attributes were all basic, colloquial, primal to business in America. They were more like instinctive home truths than sophisticated business concepts. As such they took American business by storm, instilling it with a new sense of vigor and pride at a time when its fortunes were waning. Drawing on the hunting instincts of action and competition, and the gathering instincts of community and intimacy, Peters and Waterman regressed to business basics. The 'hard' drive to act and to win ('ready, fire, aim!') led the way, but was closely followed by the 'soft' attachment to people and to shared values.

In his second book, *A Passion for Excellence*, Tom Peters reversed the priorities. The soft attachment to people, albeit in a primal sense, took precedence over the hard desire to win. Not surprisingly Peters' coauthor, on this occasion, was a woman, Nancy Austin. Moreover, in this second book, the primal nature of their management orientation, as they grew in conviction and in confidence, became even more apparent. Indeed primal management, dressed up as 'excellence', developed into a veritable passion.

A passion for excellence

Peters and Waterman had set out, in the early eighties, to simplify management, to attune it more closely to American entrepreneurial and communal values, and to counterbalance the business sophistication of the Japanese. The response, from practising managers in Europe and America, to this drive for simplicity and for homespun, instinctive truths was overwhelming. In fact, Tom Peters concluded, as a result of such extraordinarily positive reaction, to simplify even further. Instead of eight fundamental attributes, he now reduced them to only two, irrespective of the size or the orientation of the institution.

These two were also coordinated by a new form of leadership, and a new form of show business!

Business made simple

In the public or private sector, in big business or small, we observe that there are only two ways to create and sustain superior performance over the long haul. First, take exceptional care over your customer *via* superior service and quality. Secondly, constantly innovate. That's it. Obviously, the two courses of action do not constitute all that's needed. Sound financial controls are essential. Solid planning is not a luxury but a necessity. Nonetheless these factors are seldom, if ever, the basis for lasting distinction. That is, financial control is vital, but one does not sell financial control, one sells a quality product or service.

Peters and Austin *A Passion for Excellence*[7] 1985

In fact, as we shall see, Peters almost reduces business and management to one attribute, and that is 'people', as innovation becomes absorbed by and through them. It all begins, though, with a new approach to leadership that is required to link up people and innovation. This approach draws on two main elements: management by walkabout – the technology of the obvious, and an enriched concept of coaching.

MBWA: the technology of the obvious

The picture of the passionate and excellent organization is indeed a primal, and a simple one. Leadership, at the center, is epitomized by MBWA – 'Management by Walk About'. (See Fig. 18.) It is as tangible, as visible, and as immediate as that. Peters and Austin have no time, for example, for sophisticated concepts of situational, action centered, or transformational leadership.

> MBWA is being in touch with customers, suppliers, your people. It facilitates innovation. and makes possible the teaching of values to every member of an organization. All this can be accomplished only through means that are visible and tangible.[8]

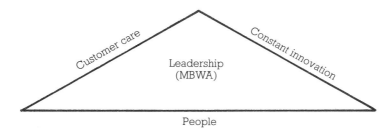

Fig. 18 The simple scheme.

Leadership, in effect, becomes a form of show business. It involves enthusiasm, cheerleading, love, trust, verve, passion, obsession, the use of symbols as well as out and out drama. In fact, as far as Peters and Austin are concerned, the whole of business is show business.

MBWA: show business

MBWA has become for us shorthand for bringing business – customers, suppliers, employees – to life, somehow, for all hands.

A Texas bank is following this lead. Here are both the logic and the technique. A bank doesn't 'lend money'; rather it lends money so that others can productively employ it, for example, in building factories and restaurants.

This particular bank's innovative programme involved bringing the customer to life for the operations people by shooting live footage of the new construction financed by the bank, and then showing it to all those distant from day to day contact with customers.

Peters and Austin *Passion for Excellence*[9] 1985

For the last twenty-five years, as Peters and Austin lament, we have carried around with us a model of a manager as referee, devil's advocate, dispassionate analyst, professional problem solver or naysayer. The alternative that they propose is the manager as cheer-leader and enthusiast, as nurturer of champions and founder of heroes, as wanderer and dramatist, and as facilitator and coach.

The manager as coach

As we can now see, the passion for excellence brings out the soft sides of primal manage-ment more visibly than the hard. This is exemplified by the leader's role as 'coach'. In fact, alongside his role as show businessman, the leader is seen to be more of a coach than anything else, and yet a coach with a primal difference! The roles of coach and showman reinforce one another in this primal context. For coaches are people who find and nurture champions, who dramatize company goals and direction, and who spread irresistible enthusiasm. They are gatherers supreme, who wander about and tell exciting stories, and who encourage, teach, listen and facilitate. Moreover, you know that they take the coaching seriously because they live their role visibly and dramatically. – 'They walk the talk.' A good coach is a good educator, a good counsellor, and an effective sponsor. Let us identify the characteristics of each, in turn.

The good educator:
- Articulates consistent performance expectations and objectives.
- Finds a 'learning lab' in task forces and low-risk projects.
- Gives balanced, believable, timely feedback.
- Provides access to the information people need to be full partners in the organ-ization.
- Explains, most effectively by storytelling, the difference between acceptable and unacceptable performance.
- Transmits values with integrity.

The good counsellor:
- Is easy to talk to.
- Listens well.
- Is receptive to the ideas of others.

- Helps people solve problems but does not overcontrol.
- Shows sympathy when discussing problems.
- Is receptive to feelings.
- Can keep a confidence.
- Is receptive in recognizing when help is needed.
- Builds esteem and self-confidence.
- Wants people to do well.

The good sponsor:
- Treats people as colleagues.
- Is on the lookout for opportunities to help people to learn.
- Makes company norms and philosophy explicit and understandable.
- Regularly discusses an individual's career plans with him.
- Is not threatened by other people with exceptional ability.
- Desperately and passionately wants people to succeed.

Finally a good coach – educator/counsellor/sponsor – is also a showman, a walkabout, a dramatist and a storyteller. He fits more closely, as Peters and Austin portray him, the image of an American football coach than that of an analytical psychologist or thoughtful facilitator. He is, therefore, soft-centered but goes hard at it!

The good coach

Fine performance comes from people at all levels who pay close attention to the environment, communicate unshakeable core values, and patiently develop the skills that will enable them to make sustained contributions to their organizations. In a word, it recasts the detached, analytical manager as the dedicated, enthusiastic coach.

Coaching is face to face leadership that pulls together people with diverse backgrounds, talents, experiences, and interests, and encourages them to step up to responsibility and continued achievement, and treats them as full partners and contributors.

Coaching is not about memorizing techniques or devising the perfect game plan. It is about really paying attention to people – really believing them, really caring about them, really involving them.

At heart, then, coaching involves caring enough about people to build a personal relationship with them. That's easy to say and tough to do. For relationships depend on contact. No contact, no relationship. The best coaches know this. They lavish time and attention that others never quite get round to spending on a consistent basis, on people.

Participating directly, coaching or being coached, seeing with your own eyes and hearing with your own ears, is simply the only thing that yields the unfiltered, richly detailed impressions that tell you how things are really going. It gives you the minute to minute opportunities to take another couple of steps towards building trust. It is the awesome power of personal attention, and it is communicated in only one way, physical presence.

In the course of managing by walkabout, and direct coaching, nothing you say reveals what a company really cares about more than its stories and legends, that is its folk wisdom. Leaders use stories to pursuade, and to symbolize day to day actions. There's simply nothing better than a story to tell people what they really want to know about 'how things work around here'.

Stories engage. They help put current decisions and events into an overall framework that is really understood, and they embellish a company philosophy in a new way. The common memory created by swapping tales imparts a sense of tradition and continuity, and sparks interest as nothing else can. Listening to company stories is the surest way to determining real priorities and who symbolizes them.

Peters and Austin *A Passion for Excellence*[10] 1985

The primal leader then is dedicated, caring, easily contactable on a face to face basis, is physically present day to day, and engages in ongoing symbolic storytelling. He is a coach and a friend rather than a commander and a superior. He is above all else a people person and, for Austin and Peters, it is people with passion who make business go round.

Customer care

People with passion are to be found within the organization, as employees, and outside it, as suppliers, distributors and, most especially, as customers. Peters and Austin place so much emphasis on being close to the customer that they even give the impression that innovation is an aspect of customer care. As far as they are concerned, the number one managerial productivity problem in America is, quite simply, an 'out of touchness' with people and with customers. Being in touch, then, is not a matter of improved computer printouts, but rather tangible, visceral ways of being informed. It means 'a remarkably successful thirty-year veteran geologist–entrepreneur sinking his toes in the sand of a transgressive overlap'[11], instead of his depending on a computer's interpretation of sophisticated geological surveys. Being in touch also involves people and customers rather than 'personnel' or 'markets'. A market, as Peters and Austin observe, has never been seen to pay a bill. Customers do that!

The two Americans go further, drawing on their primal and sensual orientation, and raise the question, 'Does your company smell of customers?' Businesses with that particular smell have distinctive characteristics.

The 'smell' of customers

- Company bulletins, annual reports, and all other printed matter feature stories about working with customers.
- A disproportionate share of sales people are promoted to general management.
- Customer support people are showered with attention.
- The importance of customers pervades every function in the organization.
- There is a special language (friendly/respectful) associated with customers.
- Visits with customers are exchanged regularly, at all levels.
- Customer support stories are prolific and inevitably personalised, about particular people and circumstances.
- Devices abound for customer listening, including regular surveys, formal and informal customer feedback.
- Foulups with customers, big or small, are not tolerated.
- Promises to customers are kept, regardless of cost and overtime.
- Quality and reliability is an obsession throughout the company.
- The product is prominently and excessively displayed.
- Operations people are deeply involved with customer activities, especially with joint problem solving.

- Managers at all levels spend time manning the reception, working at the loading desk, performing customer support tasks.
- There is an explicit philosophy statement that deals with 'the way we perceive and treat customers'.

Peters and Austin *A Passion for Excellence*[12] 1985

Constant innovation

Such is Peters' and Austin's gut level concern for people in organizations that innovation, although identified as the second major attribute of excellent companies, is almost subsumed under customer care. For the key to innovation, as far as they are concerned, lies not with any far-reaching technical inventiveness, but with a process of 'naive listening'. If customer and supplier listen to one another, if the different departments within a company hear each other out, if technologist and salesman keep in constant contact, innovations are bound to emerge.

More specifically, the excellent company is bound to respond positively to the following questions:

- Are all customers 'hounded' for new ideas?
- Is there a specific and regular mechanism for salespersons to solicit customer ideas?
- Are awards given for the best idea generated?
- Are the designer–innovators treated as all round business people and team members?
- Are the 'idea' people – engineers, buyers, brand managers – forced to visit customers?

The innovative company is also the adaptive one. It is adaptive not because of its complex feedback loops or sophisticated learning systems, but because the organization keeps in touch with the outside world, via 'living data'. People and leadership, customers and innovation – in their passion for excellence – adapt to change not via great paper plans but through constant contact with, and reaction to, people, on the part of every person in the organization.

Conclusion

Peters, Waterman and Austin during the first half of the 1980s, have established the core of what I have termed 'primal management' and what they call 'back to basics'. Although they are by no means the first to adopt this raw, immediate, tangible approach to the management of people and things, they have certainly been the most comprehensive in their primal approach. *In Search for Excellence*, and the eight basic attributes that emerged from it, brought management back, very thoroughly, to basics. Rational and scientific management was virtually thrown out the window and any fine differences between small or large, young or old, public or private organizations, were largely dismissed. Enterprise, under the guise of autonomy and entrepreneurship, and community, reflected in shared values, reinstated the American Dream within a corporate context.

A Passion for Excellence, although longer and somewhat less readable than its predecessor, in fact represented a distillation of Peters' previous work. What emerges is fundamentally two, and only two things. Successful companies constantly innovate by caring for their customers, and are led by active individuals who are also natural coaches. Moreover people are people, not personnel, customers are customers, not markets, and quality, which unites the two, is homespun America. Quality is not a technique. It is about care, passion, eye contact and gut reaction. Having established the core of primal management, then, we can proceed to investigate the branches. The 'soft' ones that have emerged are Deal and Kennedy's *Corporate Cultures*[13] and Mary Kay's *On People Management*;[14] the hard ones are Mark McCormack's *What They Don't Teach You at Harvard Business School*,[15] and Gifford Pinchot's *Intrapreneuring*.[16] These we examine in the next two chapters.

References

1. T. Peters and B. Waterman *In Search of Excellence*, Harper & Row (1982).
2. T. Peters and N. Austin, *A Passion for Excellence*, Collins (1985).
3. Pascale and Athos, *The Art of Japanese Management*, Penguin (1983).
4. T. Peters and B. Waterman, *op. cit.*, p. 11.
5. T. Peters and B. Waterman, *op. cit.*, pp. 44–51.
6. T. Peters and B. Waterman, *op. cit.*, p. 234.
7. T. Peters and N. Austin, *op. cit.*, p. 4.
8. T. Peters and N. Austin, *op. cit.*, p. 8.
9. T. Peters and N. Austin, *op. cit.*, p. 205.
10. T. Peters and N. Austin, *op. cit.*, pp. 324–77.
11. G. Gilder, *The Spirit of Enterprise*, Penguin (1986), p. 112.
12. T. Peters and N. Austin, *op. cit.*, p. 107.
13. T. Deal and A. Kennedy, *Corporate Cultures*, Addison Wesley (1985).
14. M. Kay, *On People Management*, Pan (1984).
15. M. McCormack, *What They Don't Teach You at Harvard Business School*, Collins (1985).
16. G. Pinchot, *Intrapreneuring*, Harper & Row, (1985).

8 Enterprise

Contents

Key concepts

Once you have fully understood this chapter you should be able to define the following concepts in your own words:

Achiever	Innovation process
Entrepreneur	Machiavellian manager
Entrepreneurial management	Marginal man
Expander	Marketability
Gamesman	Negotiation
Getting ahead	Pioneer
Good timing	Product champion
Intracapital	Strategems
Intrapreneur	Systematic innovation
Intraprise	Wheeler dealer

Objectives

Upon completing this chapter you should be able to do the following:
1. Compare and contrast enterprise and intraprise.
2. Trace the development of the theory of entrepreneurship over the past fifty years.
3. Outline the essential content of *What They Don't Teach You at Harvard Business School.*
4. Trace the development of entrepreneurial management, in the business literature, over the last twenty years.
5. Outline the essence of 'intrapreneuring'.

Introduction

The hard and soft branches of primal management lead off in opposing, albeit complementary, directions. The tough branches project themselves through autonomy and entrepreneurship. They are hard and wiry, thrusting and resilient. The tender ones project themselves through people and culture. They are soft and pliable, sensitive and rounded. In this chapter we are concerned with enterprise – the hard branches – and with the way in which it has been channelled through business life. I shall deal with entrepreneurial theory first, and then move on to a specific and contemporary exposition of it: *What They Don't Teach You At Harvard Business School.* I shall then cover the general theory of entrepreneurial management, before focussing on the very important topic, in the primal context, of 'intrapreneuring'.

Origins of enterprise

Whereas this text focusses on managers, the originators of contemporary business have been, and still are, entrepreneurs. Long before the Industrial Revolution, traders bought in one country, sold in another, and sometimes even built up commercial empires. Moreover, they followed their hunter predecessors in venturing out into the unknown.

The actual term 'entrepreneur' is derived from the French: it originally represented an active person who got things done in any walk of life. Sixteenth-century French writers referred to Trojan warriors as entrepreneurs, hardy and usurping, intent on risking their lives and fortunes. Other French writers and philosophers linked entrepreneurship with land cultivation. It was only in the seventeenth century that the term began to be applied in the economic context.

Classical economic theory, as it emerged in the eighteenth and nineteenth centuries, located the entrepreneur at the center of its micro-economy. As the risk taker, the entrepreneur assembled together the factors of production, and – supported by the new Protestant ethic – was motivated to maximize profit and to create wealth. In more recent times the entrepreneur, has been seen as a risk taker, taking chances; an achiever, securing results; a wheeler dealer, doing deals; a powermonger, influencing people; a marginal man, securing an edge; and a pioneer, venturing into the unknown.

The resurgence of the entrepreneur

During the 1980s the spirit of enterprise has undergone a major resurgence throughout the globe. From America to the Republic of China, and from Europe to Africa, the emergence of the indigenous entrepreneur has been very marked. This has had an inevitable influence on management as a whole, culminating in the rise of the so-called 'intrapreneur'. Before we look in this intrapeneurial direction, though, let me introduce you to the theory of entrepreneurship, *per se*, starting with the classical economists and with risk.

A risk taker – taking chances

The classical economists of the nineteenth century did the entrepreneur both a service and a disservice. On the one hand they brought him on to center stage, as the originator and orchestrator of enterprise. Yet, on the other hand, they rendered him impersonal and characterless. Whereas the literature on analytical management abounds, that on entrepreneurship – anecdotal and biographical material aside – is extraordinarily scarce. The only nineteenth-century economist to provide us with any insight into the entrepreneur is the formidable Austrian we met in Chapter 5, Joseph Schumpeter. He portrayed entrepreneurship as a positive and disruptive force, keeping everyone on his toes, and constantly breaking up the old order by introducing new ideas and products.

Entrepreneur as risk taker

The social function of the entrepreneur is not only to introduce something new into economic development, to invent, to discover, and to diversify products, but also to spread new methods of organization and manufacture, and to adopt and popularize the inventions of others.

He does not confine himself to the efficient management of the existing economic system according to traditional rules, but at each moment, by his initiative and bold faith in the future, he threatens the habits of customers and therefore the sources of profits of his more conservative competitors.

Joseph Schumpeter *The Theory of Economic Development*[1] 1961

Schumpeter was writing in the early part of this century, and it was not until the fifties that further, intensive work on entrepreneurship was undertaken. The focus then shifted from risk taking to achievement.

An achiever – securing results

David McClelland is an American psychologist who has spent many years studying the need for achievement in different societies. He has done this, in fact, by analyzing the content of each culture's traditional children's stories. In the last twenty years he has run extensive programmes, particularly in America and in India, to recognize and enhance this achievement orientation, thereby – according to his reckoning – raising entrepreneurial activity in each country.

Entrepreneur as achiever

The achievement-oriented person is attracted to tasks that involve skill. Unlike the gambler, he prefers moderate risks, and he tends to be realistic. He likes to do a job well, for its own sake, and he plans and directs his energies accordingly. He is a persistent problem solver, and obstacle remover, patient, determined and competitive.

When there is a job that needs help he draws on experts. He has a lesser need for closure, and for black and white solutions, than the person who is not achievement oriented. He has good, practical intelligence, is able to think clearly under stress, has good product knowledge, and an ability to perceive and exploit power.

David McClelland *The Achieving Society*[2] 1961

Whereas Schumpeter was an economist and McLelland is a psychologist the next prominent source of entrepreneurial wisdom was a group of sociologists.

A wheeler dealer – doing deals

In the early sixties Collins, Moore and Unwalla, based at Michigan State University, undertook an intensive study of 200 American entrepreneurs. They came to the conclusion that they were indeed a distinctive breed, very different from the classical, organization man.

Entrepreneur as wheeler dealer

The business hierarch climbed to success in an established social and authority structure. His tools were occupational proficiency and social skill. He rose because he had a positive attitude towards authority. Having arrived, he perceives his role as one of social leadership within an established organization.

The enterprising man ... built his own structure ... not hierarchical and bureaucratic, but rather a system of exchange and transaction, one that he put together by making deals. He does not perceive his role as one of leadership so much as one of being a key figure in a transactional system.

Collins, Moore and Unwalla *Enterprising Man*[3] 1964

As academic sociologists the Michigan researchers refer to a 'transactional system' as opposed to a more primal market-place in which the fabric of business life is woven by wheels and deals. They do, however, emphasize that the 'school for enterprise' is not any formalised career or training programme, but a process of drifting, dealing and apprenticeship. Through drifting, first, from job to job, enterprising man picks up basic, often technical skills. By gaining early practice in negotiation, and in doing deals, he prepares himself for future business transactions, and by being apprenticed to a 'master-entrepreneur' he is set an appropriate example.

Marginal man – securing an edge

As sociologists, Collins and his colleagues place great emphasis on the 'marginal', status of the classical entrepreneur, positioned at the edges of society. Traditionally it is such minority groups as the Jews in the diaspora, the Chinese abroad, the Ugandan Asians in Britain, or the Cubans in North America, who have occupied such a status. Today, in some cases, it is the emancipated woman and the redundant executive, who see themselves in such a marginal light.

Entrepreneur as marginal man

A business enterprise is a system of exchange and transaction that has no end in any linear sense. Accordingly, the lack of problem resolution among the entrepreneurs may fit their world. Perceiving the world in terms of irreconcilable dichotomies may be a very realistic assessment of the negotiational, transactional environment in which they live.

Collins, Moore and Unwalla *Enterprising Man*[4] 1964

Again the sociologist's academic language may conceal the gut level motives that drive the entrepreneur on and on, in order to make his own mark. He knows full well that he will never become an accepted part of the establishment, and therefore he has to make his own way. That is his commercial strength and, in Collins' terms, his psychological weakness. Yet the one feeds off the other. This 'irreconcilable dichotomy' is also a source of power.

Being powerful – influencing people

Power is something dear to the heart of the entrepreneur, though it is not a subject the established management literature deals with very well. In fact, I have drawn on what might be called the management fringe, to be able to make the 'power point'. Michael Korda is a publisher and businessman who wrote an intriguing little book, in the seventies, on power in business. From the outset, he emphasizes, it is important to develop a style of power based on one's personality and desires. Power is not good nor bad in itself; it depends on how it is used. Power, moreover, is not static, but must be sought, defended, increased and protected. The person who knows how to use power subtly and appropriately, as far as Korda is concerned, is the so-called 'expander'. Unlike the 'ladderer' who confines himself to conventional forms of vertical or horizontal movement, the expander creates his own power base.

Entrepreneur as 'expander'

Instead of moving upward he expands outward, flowing like lava, gradually enveloping enough people and functions, so that he has to be upgraded to regularise his acquisitions. These are made, as it were, by reaching out arms, like an amoeba, and then filling in the spaces.

Even when he acquires the power he seeks, he is careful not to establish a fixed hierarchy to replace the one he might have destroyed. You can't knock the expander off his perch because he has none. The moment he begins to spread out like the tide, he floats away!

Michael Korda *Power*[5] 1975

A pioneer – discovering new frontiers

Finally, like the 'expander' and unlike the 'ladderer' the entrepreneur can be seen to be an explorer, venturing into the unknown, crossing into new frontiers, tapping new sources of energy. In that context he is constantly reliving and recreating the American dream, linking – as it were – primal matter with metaphysical spirit. George Gilder, in his recent book *'The Spirit of Enterprise'* has succeeded in bringing matter and spirit together very well. I shall be dealing more extensively with the metaphysical ramifications in Chapter 26.

Entrepreneur as pioneer

Here at Sun Valley I've been trying in vain to keep up with a rugged citizen of Idaho. His name is Jack Simplot, from Boise. Built like a Notre Dame fullback, he is one of the outstanding personalities of the West, head of an empire that includes tens of thousands of acres of cattle ranches, gold and uranium mines.

The world of Jack Simplot and other entrepreneurs is registered, not in econometric printouts or elegant prose, but in actions and attitudes, intuitions and tacit beliefs that seem to reflect a different time and a different land: less the new world of great powers and cartels than the struggles of men and nature of the old frontier.

George Gilder *The Spirit of Enterprise*[6] 1985

George Gilder returns us to primal base with a jolt. We are back to the old American frontier, if not to the frontiers of our very civilization, where and when the struggle between man and nature was just beginning. And yet, at the same time, Gilder is very much a contemporary analyst of the business scene. He is appealing to corporate America as well as to the small businessman and woman. I now want to turn to Mark McCormack who has joined hands with Gilder in returning to primal enterprise, but who has also upgraded it, to reflect the contemporary management wave. McCormack's very popular book was appropriately titled *What They Don't Teach You at Harvard Business School*.

What they don't teach you at Harvard Business School

Mark McCormack, American businessman and sports promoter supreme, followed *In Search of Excellence*, with a book that was instantly snapped up by both business students and practitioners. Its title, *What They Don't Teach You at Harvard Business School*, revealed McCormack's primal, 'street smart' orientation:

> The best lesson anyone can learn from business school is an awareness of what it can't teach you – all the ins and outs of everyday business life ... What this book is really about is street smarts – the ability to make active, positive use of your instincts, insights and perceptions.[7]

His book is divided into three sections – 'People'; 'Sales and negotiations', and 'Running a business'. It is intended, moreover, for primal managers of businesses small or large.

People sense

As far as McCormack is concerned, being street smart implies, above all, an applied people sense. Such 'sensitivity' involves not so much the gatherer's empathy or compassion but more the hunter's 'fine tuned people sense', and an awareness of how to apply it, so as to get the most out of others. To get the most out of people, in business situations, you need to be able to read people, create good impressions, take the edge and get ahead.

Reading people

People-reading is a matter of opening up your senses to what is really going on and converting this insight into tangible evidence that can be used to your advantage.

Use your insight. Insight demands opening up your senses, simply by watching and listening, keeping your eyes peeled and your ears open and keeping your mouth shut.

Observe aggressively. Observation is an aggressive act. People are constantly involved in revealing themselves in ways that will go unnoticed unless you are aggressively involved in noticing them. The statements people make about themselves, and the signals they give, are both conscious and unconscious. Both are revealed in what they say, the body language they use – including posture, gesture and eye contact – and the way they dress. Aggressive observation means taking all these things in, and going for the big picture.

Touch the person's ego. A person's ego, even an overbearing one, may be your strongest ally. If you can read ego, understand its impact on business events, then control it by either stroking it, poking it or minimizing its damage, you can be at the winning end of many a deal. Finally, and at the same time, you need to be aware of your own ego, and how it may slant your reaction to others.

Be discreet. Discretion is the better part of reading people. You do not owe anyone an insight into yourself for every insight you have from him. You can only use what you have learnt about the other person, McCormack suggests, if he has learnt less about you.

Be detached. If you can force yourself to stand back from any business situation, particularly one that is heating up, your powers of observation will automatically increase. Acting rather than reacting allows you to use what you have learned. This leads you on to the impression you make.

Creating a good impression

How people relate to you in business is based on the conscious and unconscious statements you make about yourself. The way you act, the way you dress, the way you phrase a letter, the way you talk to others, the way you present yourself, all affect people's 'reading' of you.

Play off preconceptions. Consider doing the opposite of what someone expects. If someone expects toughness, it is amazing what a simple, self-effacing remark will do. If someone expects a hard line, an immediate if insignificant concession is a good way to begin, or vice versa.

Dress as though you mean business. The way you dress forms a strong and immediate impression about who you are. In general, McCormack advises, it makes more sense to dress conservatively. For the more conservative your dress the harder you are to read.

Letters as emissaries. Correspondence – both internal and external – is one of the most frequent opportunities you have for presenting yourself to the business community. Be a stickler about written communication that goes out under your name. Combine a personalized approach with total accuracy and complete readability.

Make friends. You do not have to be best buddies with everyone with whom you do business. But call people up occasionally, find out what they are doing, express an interest in them. All things being equal, people will prefer to buy from a friend.

Be your best self. If you consistently present your 'up-front-warts-and-all' self, you are not going to be very effective. The key is to come across as your best self by playing a role that features your strongest business qualities and hides your worst. This should also enable you to 'take the edge'.

Taking the edge

Taking the edge is the gamesmanship of business. It is taking everything you know about others and everything you have allowed them to know about yourself, and using this information to tilt a business situation to your advantage. In the beginning it is a matter of doing your homework, knowing the players and all knowable aspects of the game. In the end it is knowing how to play the game itself.

Take a look at the facts. You cannot take an edge until you have first taken a look at the facts. Facts alone will not guarantee you an edge but they can protect you from handing it over to someone else.

Know the players. The whole point about reading people, understanding their ego, and discovering soft spots, is to use this information to advantage, by exposing what you know about someone at the right time, in the right place.

Think on your feet. The need to be opportunistic, to think on your feet, again underscores the importance of tuning in to people – of hearing not only what they say but the underlying meaning as well. This alone can tell you whether taking an edge requires an instant reaction or not.

Getting lucky. You need to be able to not only attract luck, but also to take advantage of it. Both require being out and about, recognizing a lucky break when you come across one. People who are 'naturally lucky' see a crack and turn it into a crevice.

Turning crises into opportunities. People tend to deal with crises only in terms of their potential for disaster. Yet, in a crisis, people are more on edge and agitated then they might otherwise be. Their vulnerability can therefore be turned into a great advantage. Do not react to a crisis, then, but give yourself time to analyze the potential for opportunity before you respond. That is how you get ahead in business and in life.

Getting ahead

People who merely work up to their capabilities don't become stars. Those who are stars combine their capabilities with other things – know how, people-sense, and understanding of how the game is played.

Know the rules. Rule one – the fittest survive. There are only so many presidencies to go around. Rule two – your peers are your natural allies. If you alienate your peers you will not need any corporate enemies! Rule three – there is always a system. You have to work through it, or else around it.

Pick your spots. Your effectiveness in a company is directly proportionate to your ability to lever yourself. How can you make the most impact in the least amount of time?

Avoid standing still. One of the sure signs of incipient boredom is knowing your job too well. Never allow this to happen. Redefine your job all the time, take on new tasks, constantly create new challenges for yourself.

Project yourself beyond your job. The jobs most people occupy have existed before them and will continue after they have left. The job is constant. What you do by going beyond it is what gets noticed.

Perform to your limit. You get ahead if you have an unfulfilled need, and are driven to perform a task well, no matter how mundane it may be. You bring to any job an attitude which transforms the work into something greater. In that way, inevitably, you sell yourself to your masters.

Negotiating with people

Avoid showdowns

The point of negotiation is to reach an agreement that is mutually advantageous to both parties. To make it a contest of egos can only work against you.

Negotiate backwards

Try to work out in advance where the other person would like to end up – at what point he will do the deal and still feel that he is coming away with something.

Trade places

Put yourself in the other person's shoes. Run through a series of questions and answer them as though you were he. This can help you envisage where you are going to end up.

Control emotion

Whoever controls the emotional content of the negotiation is almost always going to walk away with the bigger winning. Anger can be an effective negotiating tool, but only as a calculated act, never as a reaction.

Keep your time frame to yourself

Finally, time itself – or the passing of it – can be one of your most valuable negotiation allies. Anxiety, and the desire to get a deal done, breeds frenetic behavior. There is a natural tendency to speed up the negotiation process. Force yourself to resist that urge and take advantage of it in others.

Negotiate to build up strength

In the final analysis, you want to ensure that you get as much as you can from a negotiation, but make sure that you get something. Tough negotiators may find that for every deal they ram down someone's throat they lose the next two. They fail, therefore, to run a successful, ongoing business – first in starting a business, and then in staying in one.

Mark McCormack *What They Don't Teach You at Harvard Business School*[8] 1986

As an negotiator, then, you need to be tough and resilient. The same goes for the intrapreneur, and for the entrepreneurial manager who we shall now meet.

The rise of the intrapreneur

The literature on entrepreneurship, interesting as it may sound, has only marginally affected the mainstream of managerial thinking. In fact the new wave of primal management stems, not from *The Theory of Economic Development* or from *Enterprising Man*, but rather from *Management and Machiavelli*.[9] What I shall now do is trace the development of entrepreneurial management, from management and Machiavelli to today's so-called intrapreneur. I then want to focus in some detail on this intrapreneurial phenomenon.

Machiavellian management

Anthony Jay, the British journalist and author, caused something of a storm in 1970 when he published his book *Management and Machiavelli*. Jay was of the opinion that organizations, and their management, should be understood as an objective phenomenon and not as an idealized form. Machiavelli, unscrupulous as his political approach may have been, was being realistic for his time (sixteenth century), in the corrupt Italian principality in which he worked and wrote.[10] It was important, for Jay as for Machiavelli, not to look for proof that industry, or politics, is honourable or dishonourable, but only for patterns of success or failure, growth or decay, harmony or strife, and for the forces that produce one or the other. Jay made use of analogies from politics and warfare, and from games of conflict. Like warfare, both ancient and modern, he saw commerce in terms of the securing of territory (market share) with swords or muskets (samples or specifications). While it might have appeared out of character in the more analytical world of the managed seventies, Jay's primal language accurately reflects the tough and competitive world of the entrepreneurial eighties.

Machiavellian management

The real pleasure of power is the pleasure of freedom, and it goes back to one of man's most primitive needs, the need to control his environment. You get no great sense of freedom if you are liable at any time to starve or freeze, or be devoured by wolves, or speared by a neighbouring tribe.

So you set about securing a supply of food, shelter, warmth and defensive weapons. Gradually you increase control, and one of the most important ways you increase it is by organization, by making your tribe the biggest and strongest in the area.

Your life is still regulated by the actions and decisions of others, but now a part of it is regulated by your own choice and your own decisions.

Anthony Jay *Management and Machiavelli*[11] 1970

Jay set off along a path that, until recently at least, only very few management writers have followed. Robert Heller, in Britain, with his *Naked Manager*[12] and Robert Townsend, in America, have been notable exceptions.

The manager as gamesman

It was actually Robert Townsend, President of the Avis car hire firm, who in his bestselling book, *Up the Organisation*, publically signalled a new, management trend. He claimed in fact, in the introduction to his book: 'If you're not in business for fun or profits, what the hell are you doing there.'[13] Townsend was reflecting the affluent sixties and early seventies, in his switch from survival and profitability, as the sole and material reason for business' existence, to fun and gamesmanship as its new, personalized reason for being. It was as if the fun of 'the hunt' had taken over from its more instrumental purpose. The game, and the desire to win, was becoming more important than the battle, and the need to survive. Maccoby went a step further, dedicating his book to his so-called 'Gamesman'. In this book, based on in-depth interviews with American senior managers, he compares and contrasts the old 'jungle fighter' or Machiavellian manager with the new 'gamesman'. While both respond to primal instinct rather than to methodical analysis the one is more of a contemporary character than the other.

Manager as gamesman

The jungle fighter's goal is power. He experiences life and work as a jungle (not a game), where it is eat or be eaten, and the winners destroy the losers. The gamesman, on the other hand, is the new man. His main interest is in challenge, in competitive activity where he can prove himself the winner ... he likes to take risks and to motivate others to push themselves beyond their normal pace. He responds to work and life as a game.

The contest hypes him up and he communicates his enthusiasm thus energizing others. He enjoys new ideas, new techniques, fresh approaches, and short cuts. His talk and his thinking are tense, dynamic, sometimes playful and come in quick flashes. His main goal in life is to be a winner.

Michael Maccoby *The Gamesman*[14] 1977

Interestingly enough Maccoby introduces us to two other managerial characters, other than the jungle fighter and gamesman. The one is the 'craftsman', who represents the soft side of primal management, and the other is 'organization man', the analytical manager at work. Yet Maccoby's gamesman, and related typology, has been eclipsed, in more recent years, by the focus on winners and on 'champions', in the 'excellent' Peters and Waterman context.

The manager as champion

Although 'champions' came to particular light through the course of the search for excellence, they had formed part of the managerial vocabulary for many years. The trouble is that they had been locked away in an analytical cupboard, as part of the extensively documented, but highly structured view of the innovation process. The American management analyst Lowell Steele, for example, writing in 1975 before 'champions' had entered Peters' hall of fame, was saying: 'We must continue to encourage and reward the individual inventor–entrepreneur, but we dare not ignore the much more difficult problem of maintaining the viability of the large corporation, a viability that is fostered by achieving skill in innovation.'[15]

Compare and contrast Steele's approach with the more recent one taken by two British commentators on the innovation process, Rothwell and Zegveld, based at the University of Sussex, and writing (post Peters) in the 1980s:

> The champion must be a man willing to put himself on the line for an idea of doubtful success. He is willing to fail but he is capable of using every means of informal pressure to succeed. It is characteristic of such champions that they identify with the idea as their own, and with its promotion as a cause, that goes far beyond the requirements of a job.[16]

The two Britons then locate the instinctive champion within the logically ordered innovation process, where our primal champion is again in danger of becoming lost in between the analytical undergrowth.

The product champion and the innovation process

There are eight critical functions that, in logical order, make up the complete innovation process:

1. The creative scientist or inventor – his primary role is to create new ideas.
2. The entrepreneur or product champion seeks organizational support for an idea and convinces management of its worth, thereby moving it through the organization.
3. The sponsor shows the champion the organizational ropes, helping him raise funds, and gain 'political' support.
4. The project manager plays the part of administrator, wielding the different functions into a continuous innovation process.
5. The technological gatekeeper communicates outside of the immediate project and organizational circle, interacting with other technically based groups within the company and without.
6. The production engineer advises the R&D personnel on the limitations and possibilities of the production process.
7. The marketeer continually feeds in information concerning user needs and market changes, ensuring that the customer remains a key point of focus.
8. The controller allocates sufficient funds to the project to enable it to progress.

Rothwell and Zegveld *Innovation and the Small Firm*[17] 1983

The last word on innovation and entrepreneurship comes, however, not from Great Britain but from Peter Drucker in America. Although Drucker, as we shall see in Chapter 12, is in fact the doyen of analytical management, he has always retained a foothold, however slight, in the primal and entrepreneurial camp.

The entrepreneurial manager

From the outset, that is already in the fifties, Peter Drucker established that management was an amalgam of entrepreneurial strategy and administrative structure. The entrepreneurial side of the business coin reflected the two, revenue-generating functions of 'marketing' and 'innovation'. The task of the entrepreneurial manager was to convert society's needs into opportunities for profitable business. Drucker, however, never actually referred to 'entrepreneurial management'. For him the two aspects – entrepreneurial and managerial – were so closely interwoven that there was no need to labor the separate point of each. It was Charles Dailey, then, in the early seventies, who produced the first serious book on entrepreneurial management.

Entrepreneurial management

The entrepreneur speaks a language which enables him to compare the 'ought' and the 'is', because his role is to bring the desirable future into being. This, in turn, requires him to speak a language which refers to the environment as well as to the organization. Only environmental response can tell him what is desirable in relation to sales, votes or cures....

Charles Dailey *Entrepreneurial Management*[18] 1971

Dailey's book emerged in reaction to the seemingly introverted attitude of the analytical managers, but it preceded the deluge of primal approaches that were to appear in the eighties. His, approach, like Peter Drucker's before him and Ralph Horwitz' afterwards, was still tainted with an analytical overlay. Ralph Horwitz was a businessman and publisher who wrote another book on *Entrepreneurial Management* in the late seventies.

Horwitz makes his case most succinctly: 'Business is constituted by an evolving buyer–seller relationship, entrepreneurially managed. The entrepreneurial element is predominantly originative of activity, and the managerial element is predominantly proceduralising.[19]

Relatively few students or practitioners of management took notice of either Dailey or Horwitz. When, however, Drucker reappeared with his thoughts on 'Entrepreneurship and Innovation' the business world had to take note. Ironically, while Drucker has picked up the entrepreneurial theme, and does so very strongly, he reacts against Peters' primal approach, rather than being in sympathy with it. In other words he welcomes the resurgence of entrepreneurship in America, but insists that it is a developed science rather than an improvized art.

'Entrepreneurship is risky,' he says, 'mainly because so few of the so called entrepreneurs know what they are doing. They lack the methodology. They violate the elementary and well known rules. Entrepreneurship needs to be managed. Above all it needs to be based on purposeful innovation.'[20]

Drucker therefore takes entrepreneurship out of its basic, primal, instinctive court, and into the powerful domain of analytical management. As such it should not concern us here, but I cannot resist a little taste of the analytical management to come.

Systematic innovation

The discipline of innovation, that is the knowledge base of entrepreneurship, is a diagnostic tool, a systematic examination of the areas of change that typically offer entrepreneurial opportunities. Specifically, systematic innovation means monitoring seven sources for innovative opportunity.

1. The first four lie within the enterprise:
   - The unexpected – the unexpected success, the unexpected failure, the unexpected outside event.
   - The incongruity – between reality as it actually is and reality as it is assumed to be.
   - Innovation based on process need.
   - Changes in market or industry structure that catch everyone, except the opportunist entrepreneur, unawares.
2. The second set of sources involve changes outside the enterprise or industry:
   - Demographics (population changes).
   - Changes in perception, mood, meaning.
   - New knowledge, both scientific and nonscientific.

Peter Drucker *Innovation and Entrepreneurship*[21] 1984

For all Drucker's analytical protestations it is his primal countryman, Gifford Pinchot, who has gained the upper hand recently, as far as corporate entrepreneurship is concerned. Pinchot has taken on from where the hard edges of Peters and Waterman have left off, and has developed the concept of 'intrapreneuring'.

Intrapreneuring

The coming entrepreneurial revolution

The origins of intrapreneurship actually lie with the British economist and business journalist, Norman Macrae, who in 1976 predicted the 'coming entrepreneurial revolution'.[22]

Macrae's particular emphasis was on changing technology and expectations, coupled with the demands of efficient and competitive enterprise. This led him to conclude that:

- Management in each progressive firm should define the modules of work that it wants to be done, and then invite bids from individuals or from groups of friends within the company.
- New ventures will need to be created within or alongside corporations to accommodate the more artistic and maverick amongst its members.
- Incentives to make workers happy will have to become much more individual and be geared to allowing each human to choose his lifestyle – because choosing one's lifestyle is what freedom in future must mainly mean.
- People will move to areas with the domestic lifestyle they like, and telecommute to offices with the workstyles they want. Sensible people will want different lifestyles and sometimes different workstyles at different periods of their lives.

Gifford Pinchot has taken Macrae's concept and adapted it for an American business audience.

What is an intrapreneur?

For Pinchot then, who introduced 'intrapreneuring' to corporations in 1984, the starting point is the selection of intrapreneurial people who are capable of turning ideas into action: 'Self-selection is the first great divide between treating people as mere employees and treating them as intrapreneurs. Some companies paternalistically plan job assignments as if they were a religious act. But intrapreneurs don't fit this mould. They passionately appoint themselves executors of their ideas and then find ways to get the corporation to give them the tools to do so.'[23] Such self-selected intrapreneurs are likely to obey the ten intrapreneurial commandments set out below:[24]

1. Come to work each day willing to be fired.
2. Circumvent any orders aimed at stopping your dream.
3. Do any job needed to make your project work, regardless of your job description.
4. Find people to help you.
5. Follow your intuition about the people you choose and work only with the best.
6. Work underground as long as you can – publicity triggers the corporate immune system.
7. Never bet on a race unless you are running it.
8. Remember it is easier to ask for forgiveness than for permission.
9. Be true to your goals, but be realistic about the way to achieve them.
10. Humor your sponsors.

From idea to action

By this time you should have a snapshot picture of the intrapreneur. The picture thus far, however, is a static one. By considering the intrapreneur's movements, from idea to action, we turn the snapshot into a moving film. Most of the peculiarities of the intrapreneurial personality, according to Pinchot, can be understood by considering the pressures of combining in one person both a strong ideas man and an insatiable doer. Such a person cannot rest until his idea is physically realized. This restlessness not only explains his drive but also his intolerance of being told what to do or how to do it. While he is open to information and other people's ideas, he has all the orders he can stand from his own internal imperatives. In taking an idea through from idea to action, the intrapreneur is likely to pass through a series of cumulative phases, including:

- A solo phase during which the vision is being formulated.
- A network phase, during which he begins to share his idea with trusted friends and customers, who, having given of themselves, may subsequently become allies.
- The 'bootleg' phase, when an informal team is formed around the idea.
- The formal phase, when an official project team is set up to carry the idea forward.

Intrapreneur and intraprise

Unlike the independent entrepreneur, the corporate intrapreneur depends on the support of the company, in order to turn his idea into action. That is why his idea has to fit the needs of the 'intraprise' as well as those of the market-place. An idea, therefore, has the greatest chance of success when there is a good fit between it and the intrapreneur, the market-place and the company.

Intraprise and intracapital

Pinchot uses the term intraprise, rather than organization, very deliberately. For he points out that whereas America's economy at large is run along free enterprise principles, individual corporations, internally, are run like bureaucratic, socialist states. What he is trying to do is to create a free enterprise system within as well as without. If the driver of this new corporation is the intrapreneur the new vehicle that Pinchot introduces to drive the intraprise forward is 'intracapital'. For example in 3M, which has now introduced intracapital into its research and development activities, individuals are eligible to receive up to $50,000 for approved projects.

Effective as it may be as a reward, and cost effective as it might become as a means of investing in innovation, intracapital can be seen most fundamentally, Pinchot argues, as a principle of freedom. In economic life, capital is a powerful form of freedom. Because intracapital provides the kind of 'freedom' that is renewable only on the basis of more success, it supposedly 'grabs deep' and motivates the person to greater care and frugality. No system of budgetary reviews and approval by seniors could be half as tight, Pinchot maintains, as spending 'one's own irreplaceable freedom'.

The formation of intracapital, then, marks the beginning of a transformation in the role of corporate management. They cease to act as rulers and instead become governors.

Their task now is to create an environment in which manager – intrapreneurs can have freedom, while still being guided by an 'invisible hand' to make the decisions that foster the growth and development of the corporation.

The visible invisible hand

What then is this 'invisible' hand that guides intrapreneurs to freedom? It turns out, in fact, that unlike the market-place which is self-adjusting in some almost invisible way, the company needs to support the cause of intrapreneurial freedom visibly. In other words, it does not just happen of its own accord. Conventional career paths do not lead in the direction of freedom that genuine intrapreneurs seek. Formal promotion systems are much too rigid to cater for the natural, and often indirect, course of business development. Traditional reward systems are also too restrictive to compensate for the risks involved.

Role evolution, then, is more in tune with intrapreneurship than with normal management development, whereby individuals follow the natural curves of living businesses rather than the unnatural lines of family trees. To make such role-evolution work requires active encouragement of intrapreneurial self-selection and visible sponsorship of such intrapreneurs.

Conclusion

Gifford Pinchot on one side of the Atlantic, like Macrae on the other, sees the corporation of the future in terms of confederations of entrepreneurs and intrapreneurs. These confederations need to be tied together to gain economies of scale in marketing and communications, while smaller and more intrapreneurial units design and manufacture goods. McCormack in America, like Jay in Britain, sees the primal manager as concerned with the basics of business and adopting ingenuity and instinct rather than science and analytical method. Deal and Kennedy, in their best selling book on *Corporate Cultures*[25], combine all these views to say the following about organizations of the future:

- They will have small, task focussed units.
- Each with economic and managerial control over its own destiny.
- Interconnected with large entities through benign computer and telecommunication links and
- Bonded into larger companies through strong cultural ties.

Having discussed entrepreneurism and intrapreneurism, the basic forces that cut and thrust, I want to move on to the primal forces that bind and connect, corporate culture and people management.

References

1. J. Schumpeter, *The Theory of Economic Development*, Cambridge University Press (1961).
2. D. McClelland, *The Achieving Society*, van Nostrand (1961), p. 265.
3. Collins, *et al.*, *Enterprising Man*, Michigan State University (1964), p. 79.
4. Collins, *et al.*, *op. cit.*, p. 18.

5. M. Korda, *Power*, Coronet (1975), p. 87.
6. G. Gilder, *The Spirit of Enterprise*, Penguin (1985), p. 24.
7. M. McCormack, *What They Don't Teach You at Harvard Business School*, Collins (1985).
8. M. McCormack, *op. cit.*
9. A. Jay, *Management and Machiavelli*, Penguin (1970).
10. N. Machiavelli, *The Prince*, Penguin [George Bull translation] (1961).
11. A. Jay *op. cit.*
12. R. Heller, *The Naked Manager*, Barrie & Jenkins (1972).
13. R. Townsend, *Up the Organisation*, Michael Joseph (1970).
14. M. Maccoby, *The Gamesman*, Torch Books (1977), p. 84.
15. L. Steele, *Innovation in Big Business*, Elsevier (1975), p. 117.
16. Rothwell and Zegveld, *Innovation and the Small Firm*, Frances Pinter (1983), p. 62.
17. Rothwell and Zegveld, *op. cit.*, p. 11.
18. C. Dailey, *Entrepreneurial Management*, (1971), p. 54.
19. R. Horwitz, *Entrepreneurial Management*, Westhall Books (1972), p. 62.
20. P. Drucker, *Innovation and Entrepreneurship*, Heinemann (1985), p. 88.
21. P. Drucker, *op. cit.*, p. 114.
22. N. Macrae, 'The Coming Entrepreneurial Revolution', *The Economist* (December, 1976).
23. G. Pinchot, *Intrapreneuring*, Harper & Row, (1984), p. 212.
24. G. Pinchot, *op. cit.,* p. 94.
25. T. Deal and A. Kennedy, *Corporate Cultures*, Addison Wesley (1981), p. 234.

9 People

Contents

Key concepts

Once you have fully understood this chapter you should be able to define the following concepts in your own words:

Animateur	P&L
Corporate myths	Priests
Cultural roles	Primal group
Cultural orientation	Rituals
Family business	Shared values
Golden rule	Storytellers
Heroes	Symbolic manager
Levelling force	*Uchi*

Objectives

Upon completing this chapter you should be able to do the following:

1. Trace the origins of the soft side of primal management from the household and community in traditional cultures.
2. Relate key, soft features of contemporary Japanese business organization to primal origins.
3. Trace the origins and development of the animateur in business and management.
4. Outline Mary Kay's essential approach to people management.
5. Outline the essential features of Deal and Kennedy's approach to corporate culture.

Introduction

Primal imbalance

The soft side of primal management has been relegated to second place in the development of business enterprise. In the last 200 years the image of the buccaneering entrepreneur, the hunter, has obliterated that of his nurturing counterpart, the gatherer. Whereas a subsequent balance has been achieved within analytical management, that is between technical (administrative) and social (behavioral) approaches, not until very recently has the instinctive, primal orientation – thanks to Peters and Austin – begun to balance out.

The first reason for this two-hundred-year imbalance has been the commercial dominance of Europe and then America in the world. The Western 'business' culture has elevated toughness, both instinctively (competitive battles) and analytically (competitive strategies). It is only with the emergence of Japan, from the East, that the desirability of a more subtle balance between soft and hard in business has become more apparent. A second reason has been the relative absence of women in business, both as writers and practitioners. Whereas in developing countries, like Nigeria for example, women have always been a strong commercial force, this has not been the case in the industrialised world. So toughness, in both theory and practice, has dominated tenderness. Thirdly, and also arising out of the second point, the 'hard' theory of the 'firm' has eclipsed the 'softer' concept of the 'household', in business and economics. While the word economics was derived from the Greek *oikos* – meaning household – that original derivation has been lost.

Resurrecting 'household' management

In this chapter I therefore want to resurrect 'household management' as a soft and formative influence on business that has been neglected to our cost. In doing so I also hope to provide a meaningful context, that is the home, for all those young students of business and management who insist that they have no 'relevant' management experience on which to draw. I shall firstly draw on African and Japanese examples of household management and its business applications, and then move on to a modern American adaptation, that is Mary Kay Cosmetics. Thereafter, I shall introduce you to the tender hearted 'animateur', to be set alongside the tough-minded entrepreneur.

Management and household

The discipline of management, from a Western perspective, is seen to originate from large-scale and impersonal religious, military and political administrations. The small-scale and intimate organization of household and community has therefore been left behind. Even the development of 'human relations', in management theory, arises from research into factory rather than into household conditions. The thereby neglected soft side of management originates from the household, that is from the primal '*oikos*' or economy. In fact the relationship between household management and business administration has recently become much more evident, because of the increasing number of women entering management positions. Unlike men, many of them draw more consciously on their home-making skills, for general management purposes.

The connections, however, within an industrialised society, are still few and far between. More ample evidence can be obtained from developing countries, undergoing modernization, yet still in touch with their primal roots. A case in point is Nigeria, particularly insofar as their market women are concerned.

The market women of Nigeria

Susanne Gutierrez is a Mexican American who married a Nigerian and decided to undertake her doctoral research into the market women of West Africa. She was fascinated by the way the women, whatever their ethnic background or geographical location in Nigeria, had managed to retain their communal identity within a modern business context.

The market-place

There is a clear reflection of European commercial and philosophical influences – in the emerging impersonal, formal and specialized attitude – in today's African institutions. In the market place, however, women are able to transcend these influences and bring to their daily lives the historical African sense of family and community.

Regardless of the sophistication of the surrounding community, no matter how urbanized and industrialized it may have become, the market-place prevails as a center of trade and communication, whether the traders are dealing in cement, tomatoes, or television sets.

Suzanne Gutierrez *The Market Women in Nigeria*[1] 1986

In researching the ways in which these market women managed their businesses, Gutierrez – who had herself lived within a traditional Nigerian household – was struck by the way in which they drew on the skills they had acquired as children, such as supervision, cooperation, self-assertion, organization and communication. In a traditional Nigerian family, in any one of the main tribal groupings, the woman was the strong force who held the family together. As a teenager she would take responsibility for the younger children in the family. Subsequently her supervisory responsibility would be increased, outside of the immediate family context.

The cultivation of food crops and trade within the market-place become added responsibilities for the older teenage girl. These girls are taught to trade from a young age, not in isolation but in groups. When they become the supervisor of a group in the market-place, they are, therefore, in a position to consolidate on skills which they have acquired as children. Within a traditional society cooperation in the family and community ensures not only the continuance of both but also their economic stability. The 'Yoruba' women, for example, who are the most independent and aggressive in business, still cling to cooperative practices amongst one another. Such collaboration amongst staff as well as between fellow traders is a feature of the market women.

The market-place is an extension of the home environment in that women are encouraged to assert themselves in roles that serve the interests of the whole – community or market-place. In the communal context they would be involved in soliciting help from other people for crop production or family rituals. Similar powers of empathy and persuasion are required in the market context, in staffing, in selling and in supervisory functions. In the market-place, where competition is especially severe in the urban areas, women experience every day the importance of a planned and structured approach to business. The inference is that without such a methodical approach to such commercial functions as pricing, distribution and inventory control, their economic standing and family units might be jeopardized. Should their businesses fail, they would run the risk of losing face in their immediate family, and within the community at large. The market women have had to rely on their verbal skills since childhood. The importance of their oral history, their richness in cultural expression and oratory, has contributed to their self-assurance in face to face communication. Furthermore, the close connections which make or break the extended family will have drawn out skills of diplomacy amongst the women that enhance their business communications.

The levelling force of the market-place

For the entrepreneur with the 'hunter' instinct, the market – on a local or international scale – is a place in which to wheel and deal, to out-maneuver the competition, and to secure economic gains that are sufficiently large to compensate for the risk and uncertainty involved. For the animateur, with the 'gatherer' instinct, the market necessarily involves all of these tough-minded activities, but they are secondary rather than primary. What is primary, according to Gutierrez, is the 'levelling force' of the market-place.

The levelling force

While tradition and tribal values dictate some degree of differences, the market-place is a leveller amongst Nigerian women. In other words, no matter how she sees herself in terms of family, culture and tribal influence, the market woman enters into a new equality, a new sense of sisterhood within the market-place.

Alongside her roles as wife and mother, the Nigerian woman of the market-place assumes the role of businesswoman. It becomes a safe place, in which to assert herself. The marketplace serves as a common ground for women to act as one driving force in society. That one common ground, more than anything else, is a leveller.

Suzanne Gutierrez *The Market Women in Nigeria*[2] 1986

The Japanese company and household

The levelling influence of the Nigerian market-place is not too far removed from the similar influence of a large Japanese company, although the scope for any individual impact is substantially downgraded in Japan. There is no doubt, however, that the shape and form of the Japanese household has had enormous influence on company-based management and organization.

The primary circle

The primary circle is first the family, then the school, and finally the company. In fact Japanese often use the same word, *uchi*, to refer to their homes and company – the two are synonymous by being the primary circle.

George Fields *From Bonsai to Levis*[3] 1983

Cooperation between a man and his wife means that the one makes up and takes responsibility for the other. Similarly a pair of workers offers the most primitive and appropriate vehicle for training. Of course, for the system to be effective, the pair must be composed of two individuals with different characteristics. An organizational cell, similarly, is made up of pairs of this kind, which leads to well developed teamwork.

Shigeru Kobayashi *Creative Management*[4] 1974

In Japanese, the word for company, *kaisha*, has strong connotations of 'community'. In referring to their place of employment, the Japanese typically use the term '*uchi*', in my house, and '*kaisha*', in my community. The Japanese way, moreover, is to promote the man who gets along with everybody, is good at maintaining harmony, and can be expected to be concerned with the welfare of all.

Boye De Mente *The Japanese Way of Doing Business*[5] 1981

Through force of circumstance both the market women of Nigeria and the business institutions of Japan have evolved ways of organizing which draw heavily upon a rich heritage of household and community roles and functions. In Japan, in particular, this has taken place because such womanly activities have been observed, and articulated so that they could subsequently be transferred from a domestic to a corporate context. By way of contrast, business organizations in Europe and America have underplayed and undermined the home and community heritage, reducing its application to the limiting roles of 'boss' and 'secretary', and the limiting functions of manager and assistant. No wonder, therefore, Peters and Austin have elevated the roles of, for example, receptionist and dispatch clerk, in their primal organization. However they have not gone as far as Mary Kay in creating an entire business and organization that draws on household virtues. In doing just that Mary Kay has developed a theory and practice of primal, 'people management'. This can be compared and contrasted against the more analytically based management of 'personnel' or 'human resources'. What emerges, above all in the primal context, is a role of 'balancer' between profit and love, between home and work, between cooperation and competition, between equality and individuality, and between oneself and another. We can see this vividly in Kay.

On people management

Mary Kay Cosmetics, in some twenty years, has grown into a multi-million dollar business involving 200,000 saleswomen, working in a self-employed capacity through the company. In the 1980s the founder, Mary Kay, exposed her business philosophy and practices in a book that was at first entitled *Mary Kay* and, subsequently, *On People Management*. Her book reveals an approach to business and to management that draws on some of the tenets of the market women in Nigeria, albeit unwittingly, and applies them to an American, corporate context. The result is the only comprehensive exposition on 'primal management', from a gatherer's perspective, but also incorporating a hunting instinct.

Profit and love

Mary Kay set up in business not only to achieve success herself but also – and at least as importantly – to help other women do so. Her dual motivation was profit and love.

'P & L'

When a man starts a business, he usually establishes monetary goals such as 'We're going to do a hundred thousand dollars the first year'. I'm often asked what my financial objectives were when we first started Mary Kay Cosmetics. Well, I didn't have any. My objective was to give women the opportunity to do anything they were smart enough to do. To me P & L meant people and love.

Mary Kay *On People Management*[6] 1984

As far as Mary Kay is concerned the most valuable assets of the company are her people, rather than whatever might be found in the company balance sheets. No matter how much profit the company makes, therefore, if it does not enrich the lives of the people, it has failed. Mary Kay's true wealth is therefore reflected in the thousands of women who have become materially, socially and psychologically enriched by their involvement in the company. 'When I come into the office, everybody is happy and smiling. It's like coming into the sunshine. I feel good all over. We want everyone who comes into contact with us to feel our warmth'.

Home and work

However enriched a woman might become through her involvement with Mary Kay, that enrichment is never fundamental to her being. As a gatherer, by motive and instinct, Mary Kay recognizes that family comes before career or business, as a primary source of motivation for her women. In fact, she argues, when the family–work priority is reversed everything is liable to go wrong. Inevitably, then, a woman must wear several hats. She may be just as much the breadwinner as her husband, and yet will still retain the roles of 'wife, mother, chef, laundress, chauffeur, child psychologist, social director and lover'. She has to find time, therefore, for everything.

Similarly, Mary Kay support staff are made aware of the extent to which their sales personnel depend on them. 'I often tell them, you're not just filling an order, you're helping someone who supports three children to make a living'. Finally Mary Kay herself has the kind of paired relationship with her son, Richard, that Kobayashi alluded to in the Japanese context: 'From the beginning, Richard was a godsend. He ran the corporate business, from manufacturing to finance, leaving me free to spend my full time and energy directing and motivating the sales organization'. In fact this kind of symbiotic relationship, usually between wife and husband, characterizes such successful international businesses as Laura Ashley in fabrics, and Bodyshop in cosmetics.

Competition and cooperation

The ultimate award given to a sales person at Mary Kay is a large, diamond studded bumble bee. According to company folklore, 'We think the bumblebee is a perfect symbol because, as aerodynamic engineers "proved" many years ago, the bumblebee cannot fly. Its wings are too weak and its body too heavy. Fortunately the bumblebee doesn't know that and goes right on flying. At Mary Kay Cosmetics we teach people how to spread their wings and fly on their own. We cannot think of a better way to help people.'[7]

The combined imagery of helplessness and self-help is very powerful, both softening and reinforcing the American Dream. Mary Kay argues that a woman loves to gain recognition by competing with herself rather than against others. 'A long time ago I realized that the wrong kind of competitiveness can create a destructive atmosphere in a company. Whereas Andrew Carnegie once said that the first man gets the oyster and the second man gets the shell, at Mary Kay everyone has the opportunity to get the oyster, the shell, and the pearl.'

This philosophy of competitiveness, within oneself, and cooperation, with others, pervades the whole company.

The golden rule

It's a philosophy based on giving and it is applied in every aspect of our business. At our beauty shows we do not like a beauty consultant to think 'How much can I sell these women?' Instead we stress, 'What can I do to make these women here today feel better about themselves? How can I help them have a better self image?'

We know that if a woman feels pretty on the outside, she becomes prettier on the inside too. She'll go home a better wife, a better mother, and a better member of the community.'

Mary Kay *On People Management*[8] 1984

The golden rule not only reiterates those shared Mary Kay values which stress cooperation with the customer, but it emphasizes the primal orientation of the company, on tangible, visible appearances. 'Feeling good on the outside makes you feel good on the inside.'

Equality and individuality

In Mary Kay, the approach to managing people combines a special breed of equality with a particular brand of individuality. To reinforce the notion of equality, there are few middle management positions built into the organization. In order to grow and progress the women expand outward rather than upward. The sales force therefore know that they are not competing with one another for a spot on the 'managerial pecking order'. Therefore contributions of each individual are of an equal value, rather than being ranked according to seniority.

So each individual sales person can expand and progress without moving up the traditional corporate ladder. Approximately 200,000 beauty consultants operate as independent retail businesses, dealing directly with their customers. Each consultant defines her own goals, productivity targets and subsequent rewards. Everyone is treated as special. This is where individuality comes in. Even so, such individuality is not purely self-centered. 'Each of us', says Mary Kay, 'wants to feel good about herself, but to me it is just as important to make others feel the same way. Whenever I meet someone I try to imagine him wearing an individual sign saying make me feel important'.

Self and other

The company structure, therefore, requires each person to help others in order to be successful. In other words, those who succeed are the women who help others to grow. Every director's success is in fact based on the achievements of the women that she supervises. If she tries to convey an image of superiority to these women, thus undermining the person's confidence, her attempt to succeed will backfire. 'Eventually such a person's pomposity will herald her downfall'.

From a bud to a rose

For me, the most meaningful thing about the growth of Mary Kay Cosmetics has been seeing so many women achieve. All of us here thrive on helping instil in other women the 'You can do it' spirit.

>So many women just don't know how great they really are. They come to us all vague on the outside and vague on the inside. It's so rewarding to watch them develop and grow.
>
>A woman often comes in like a tight little rosebud; sometimes she appears at my door too inhibited to even tell me who she is. And the same woman coming back after six months of praise and encouragement is hardly recognizable. She has changed from a tight little bud into a beautiful rose, poised and confident.
>
>Mary Kay *On People Management*[9] 1984

Mary Kay has played a unique part in the evolution of management theory, introducing a soft primal perspective where nothing comprehensive existed before. However, she has not quite been operating in the wilderness. There have been other formative forces at work, which have culminated in the development of a new management discipline, that of 'corporate culture'. Let me now elaborate.

The rise of the animateur

As I already indicated in Chapter 6, whereas the hunter has his direct equivalent in primal management, that is the entrepreneur or intapreneur, the gatherer role has not been updated and upgraded. While Mary Kay has adopted a unique approach to people management she has not identified a newly defined role for herself. I have therefore borrowed a term from the French (who also gave us 'entrepreneur'), that is the 'animateur'.

The animateur, unlike the entrepreneur, views her people as family rather than as human resources or employees; she animates her staff rather than dictating to them; she enthuses others rather than driving or motivating them; she uses myth, ritual and shared values as a binding force rather than loyalty to herself or to her company; and her own loyalty is to the group and to the community rather than to the individual or to the organization. Naturally, you will find many an entrepreneur who has strong animateurial tendencies, and vice versa, but we need to separate the two primal outlooks, and their theoretical foundations, before we can usefully bring them back together again.

The primal group

Elton Mayo, the American social scientist to whom we were introduced in Chapter 5, wrote an elegant treatise – in the 1940s – entitled *The Social Problem of an Industrial Civilization*. In doing so he became one of the forerunners of the 'Human Relations' movement. The movement developed as a reaction against the so-called 'scientific management' of the day. Mayo set himself up in opposition to what he called the 'rabble hypothesis'. The hypothesis went like this – natural society consists of a horde of unorganized individuals; every individual acts in a manner calculated to secure his own self-interest. Mayo countered with his own view that effective cooperation was the key to all human activity. In fact, perhaps even unwittingly, Mayo stood on very important primal ground, stretching back into history, and across into different cultures. For the instinctive group consciousness he draws upon is as characteristic of Africans in traditional communities, as it is of the Japanese in their contemporary business enterprises.

I participate, therefore I am

Any attempt to look upon the world through African eyes must involve an adventure of the imagination whereby we abandon our image of man whose complex identity is encased within the shell of his physical being, and allow ourselves instead to visualize a centrifugal selfhood, equally complex, interpermeating other selves in a relationship in which subject and object are no longer distinguishable. 'I think, therefore I am' is replaced by, 'I participate, therefore I am'.

John Taylor *The Primal Vision*[10] 1963

We may look upon the cultural life of the Shona peoples of Zimbabwe as revolving around the family – a kinship or brotherhood. The ideal is the good man, a person who is kind, humble, and ready to help and share with the rest of his kin, one who conforms to the social code of behaviour, respects others and is not greedy.

Michel Gelfand *African Crucible*[11] 1979

The group instinct in Japanese society is not significantly different from that in Africa, albeit that the Japanese have managed to turn that identity to substantial commercial advantage. Chie Nakane, one of the few indigenous Japanese to analyze her own culture, for Western as well as home consumption, has some very interesting and relevant things to say.

Culture and informality

It is in informal systems rather than in overt cultural elements that persistent factors are to be found. The informal systems, the driving force of Japanese activities, are a native Japanese brew. In the course of modernization Japan imported many Western cultural elements, but these were partial and segmentary. It is like a changing language with its basic indigenous structure of grammar, which has accumulated a heavy overlay of borrowed vocabulary; while the outlook of Japanese society has suffered drastic changes over the past one hundred years, the basic social grammar has hardly been affected.

Japan has no native concept of 'organization' or 'network' abstracted or divorced from actual man. Organization is perceived as a kind of succession of direct and concrete relationships between man and man. Tangibility, the essential element in 'organization' for the Japanese, may well have also some bearing on Japanese religious concepts. Japanese culture has no conception of a God existing abstractly, completely separate from the human world. Similarly the Japanese language has no term for 'leadership' as existing separate from the group.

Chie Nakane *Japanese Society*[12] 1970

The view of individual, group, organization and society adopted by these traditional cultures, has not been reflected in the conventional management wisdom. In fact, the normal 'family business', as we know it in the West, is pretty far removed from it. It has therefore taken a primal 'animateur', like Mary Kay, to bring these views into managerial light. Similarly, it has taken a new discipline – 'corporate culture' – to shed new light on these old communal values. One of the main reasons that the primal group has not, until recently, come to light, is the imbalanced nature of conventionally based family business – in which the entrepreneur male role has usually predominated over the animateurial female one.

Animateur: outside the family business

Family businesses are part and parcel of our economic heritage, wherever we may live around the globe. However, at least in the West over the past two hundred years, such businesses have been cast in rather imbalanced terms. Characteristically the male entrepreneur, and possibly his sons, have occupied the starring role or roles, while his wife, and possibly daughters, have made up the supporting cast.

The hard role for 'Momma'

While Dad was plowing through the early years thinking about little other than the particular bushfire he was stamping out at any given moment, you can bet Momma had plenty of time to think about a lot of things. She had to watch from the sidelines as he drained the bank account, mortgaged the house, and borrowed on the insurance so that he could throw it into something she really didn't understand. She didn't feel proud of her hero so much as she felt terrified.

The hero needs talent and guts to survive. That's sure. But he also needs an understanding spouse. Without that understanding, he probably would have thrown in the towel ... The help he really needs is to have someone to talk to, someone with whom he can share his worries, his doubts and his risks.

Leon Danco *Inside the Family Business*[13] 1980

Times have changed, even since the period in which Leon Danco was writing, and many more businesses are being started by women, or are genuine partnerships between husband and wife. Nevertheless, the traditional division of labor between hunter–entrepreneur in business, and nurturer–animateur in the home, often remains. As a result the 'family' business itself is imbalanced. At the same time, if a family business does develop into a large-scale organization, while retaining both its family-based heritage and its traditionally based division between roles, there will be interesting consequences. Typical examples in Europe and America of such companies are Marks & Spencer and IBM.

In both cases employees will feel that strong sense of belonging, as if to a family. This will be reinforced by the shared values, inherited and updated, from the original founding fathers. These founder–entrepreneurs, having been nurtured at home, transferred some of that nurturing quality into their businesses. Life-long employment, social welfare programmes, and homely relationships amongst staff and between staff and customers, have probably resulted. This is good for the people and good for the business.

However, the role of animateur remains hidden, just like the original woman at home. Unlike the case of Mary Kay, the primal virtues of the hunter–entrepreneur remain dominant. The differences, as well as the similarities, between familial and commercial values – perhaps inevitably – remain visible for all to see. The management of human resources, and the existence of employees, remains a corporate reality. Where the animateur does occupy pride of place we do see a genuine difference. The largest translations and interpreting company in the world, Interlingua, was started in Britain by a Czech refugee (from the invading Nazis) Nelli Eichner. Together with her husband Fred, who took up the role of entrepreneur and innovator, they built up a flourishing business after the war, based in rural Britain (see the case study on pp. 612–16).

However, although at one stage there were thirty different nations – a veritable family of nations – lodged on one site, Interlingua has never become a big business. It has retained its family proportions, as did Nelli Eichner herself: 'Interlingua became one family, one group of people who pulled together for the common good.'[14] Whereas Fred Eichner's dream was a lofty one, to eliminate misunderstanding in the world at large, through generating mutual awareness for the multiple languages of man, Nelli's was more parochial, and animateurial!

Animateur as animator

Nelli Eichner had no end of stories to tell. Here is just one of them.

> Once we had to carry out a very urgent translation for a chocolate manufacturer. It was finished by midnight. I apologized to our client that some of the typing mistakes were due to the fact that my little daughter had stayed up half the night to help type out the telex. No, the client was not at all cross. He sent, to my children's huge delight, a huge parcel full of the most delicious chocolates.[15]

The animateur brings an organization to life via stories. In fact, for someone like Nelli Eichner, to know these stories is to know her company in a way that balance sheets and organization charts can never impart. That is something which John Morris, a British anthropologist who found his way into management education, understands only too well. For he has divided business and social activity into drama, routine and ritual.[16] Dramatic experience and activity is novel, significant, and characterized by uncertainty.

In comparison with drama, rituals provide a safer, more familiar world. They also serve to re-enact the central formative myth of the organization. When the Eichners sat down, every Friday evening, to have their family councils, not only did they reinforce their Jewish faith, but they re-enacted their family involvement in the business. In similar vein, Japanese workers' ritual morning exercises reinforce their commitment to the organization. According to Morris, man lives by drama, remembers by ritual, and survives through routine. In that context, the entrepreneur provides the drama, the animateur relives and revivifies it through storytelling, and the administrator records and 'routinizes' its detailed implications, and ramifications.

Animateur: sharing values

At Interlingua, two things bring most pride to the company. The first is the involvement of the whole Eichner family, including, at one stage, the young children, in the business. The second is the shared love of languages. I have found it a particular characteristic of women in business, from whom most of our natural animateurs originate, that their product or service, and the people with and for whom it has been created, are inextricably intertwined. To put it another way, women are seldom willing or able to go into business, like the classical entrepreneur, purely to survive, or to make money. Shared values, for the true animateur, therefore encompass the product, or service, as well as the people. For example, Anita Roddick, who founded the fast growing, internationally based Body-shop, producing and marketing naturally based cosmetics, has created and shared values which transcend either people or product.

Sharing values

As far as the cosmetics industry is concerned we have broken just about every rule in the book. We've never marketed hope. We've never packaged. We've never advertised. We're not controlled by design groups. We're the only company who offer a choice of mud, herbal and conventional shampoos.

Our herbalists will come out of the laboratories to talk to the customers and the assistants are trained on how the products are made and on their suitability for the individual's needs. I continue to develop new products via my travels to developing countries.

Whether in India or Malaysia, Peru or Papua New Guinea, I give a lecture on cosmetics in a hall or market-place, and then turn the session inside out and get information from my audience. All our products are natural and earthy. People came back for them again and again.

Anita Roddick *Bodyshop*[17] 1986

For Anita Roddick, operating from Britain, her shared values cover creativity, individuality, and recreation, all in the context of an international community. The values being shared are distinctly British ones. For Peters and Waterman, shared values center upon winning, growing, being the best, and on believing in individuals, in innovation and in informality. The values being shared are distinctly American ones. In a Japanese context, like that of Matsushita, the values that predominate are: 'National service through industry; fairness; harmony and cooperation; struggle for betterment; courtesy and humility; adjustment and assimilation; and gratitude.'[18] In other words, the values being shared will depend on the national and cultural context in which the individual business is set. However, the animateur's role remains more or less constant.

The animateur in the community

Animation, in its broader, communal context, emerged as a movement, not in business but in community work, in the sixties and seventies: 'Animation is everything which facilitates access to a more creative life for individuals and groups, and which increases capacities for communication and adjustment, and the ability to participate in community and social life.'[19]

The job of the so-called animateur, in a French communal setting was, therefore, to:

- Multiply occasions for group life, and to combat any tendency for the individual to isolate himself.
- Foster a community consciousness, an informed social and political awareness, and a readiness and ability to participate in decision making.
- Widen the horizons, enlarge the range of experience, and raise the expectations of people.

These are all things we could well imagine Nelli Eichner promoting at Interlingua. In order to be able to function in that way the animateur needs not only to live and breathe her organization's culture, but also to know how to bring people out of themselves in a natural, and unselfconscious manner. Such innate skills, which were relegated in the traditional family business to the home, now comprise the heart of primal management.

They are alo second nature to a traditional community, in which the animateur holds pride of place. Recently they have become reinstated, within the context of 'corporate culture'.

Corporate cultures

Although 'culture' has recently become a buzzword in management circles, very few academics or consultants have had anything comprehensive, and thereby very useful, to say about it. Two notable exceptions, both American, have been Deal and Kennedy and Harrison Owen. Whereas the first two have picked up the primal implications of culture, Owen has focussed on the metaphysical ones (see Chapter 26). Deal and Kennedy tackle corporate culture from three major perspectives: cultural context, cultural roles, and, finally, cultural orientation.

Cultural context

In focussing on 'corporate culture', Deal and Kennedy are not concerned with comparative cultures, around the globe, but with the 'symbolic' role that managers play within organizations.

'Symbolic' versus rational managers

A day in the life of any modern manager is chock full of little things that don't matter, little things that matter some and big things that matter a lot. We call the first trivia, the second events, the third dramas. One of the chief skills of a 'symbolic' manager is to distinguish among the three.

To dramatize trivia is to look like a fool. To overcome drama is to become a victim or a villain. Symbolic managers never overlook an opportunity to reinforce, dramatize or involve the central values of a culture.

Deal and Kennedy *Corporate Cultures*[20] 1984

For Interlingua, for example, the central values of the culture revolved around family, including those of the 'family of man'. Nelli Eichner never missed an opportunity for one or other of the thirty different cultures represented at head office to present their national food or costume to the others assembled there. Successful companies, for Deal and Kennedy – as for Peters, Waterman and Austin – keep their shared values on regular display, so that they can be seen, heard, touched, felt, tested or smelt! These values have to be tangible rather than intangible, and thus primal rather than metaphysical.

Shared values

Values are the bedrock of any corporate culture. As the essence of a company's philosophy for achieving success, values provide a sense of common direction for all employees and guidelines for their day-to-day behavior. These formulas for success determine (and occasionally arise from) the types of corporate heroes, and the myths, rituals and ceremonies of the culture. The values may be grand in scope ('Progress is our most important product') or narrowly focussed ('Underwriting excellence'). They can capture the imagination ('The first Irish multinational'). They can tell people how to work together ('It takes two to tandem').

Deal and Kennedy *Corporate Cultures*[21] 1984

In the final analysis shared values are effectively generated and shared when:

- They stand for something – that is they incorporate a clear and explicit philosophy about how the company aims to conduct its business.
- Management plays a great deal of attention to shaping and fine tuning these values to conform to the economic and business environment of the company, and to communicate them to the organization.
- These values are known and shared by all the people who work for the company.

This is all unlikely to take place, however, if a suitable cast of cultural characters is not recognized and developed inside the company.

Cultural roles

Drawing on their anthropological background, Deal and Kennedy have identified a series of cultural roles within a business, each of which may play an important part in the company's ultimate success. The key roles are those of the 'hero', the 'priest' and the 'storyteller'. Subsidiary ones include those of whisperer, gossip and spy.

Heroes

There are three different kinds of hero. The 'born hero' is the great man who created the whole business, or at least a substantial part of it. In adding his personal sense of values to the world his influence remains pervasive. The 'compass hero' serves as a role model. If a company wants to change in a particular direction, for example to become more entrepreneurial or market-oriented, then it can choose compass heroes who reflect that special focus.

'Outlaws', according to Deal and Kennedy, are highly valued in a strong culture company. Such mavericks are characteristically placed in creative jobs in research, in sales, or in organization development. In a weak culture, such outlaws tend to turn against such maverick values and become 'whistle blowers'.

Priests

Like the Church, a company with a strong corporate culture also needs its priests, that is the guardians of the culture's central values. They always have time to listen to a cultural or moral dilemma and will often be expected to come out with a solution. To become a 'priest' within a company requires a seriousness and a maturity that transcends simple age. Priests seldom worry about mere details. Their concern is with the big company picture, or central story, which will be represented in myth and allegory rather than in 'straight language'.

Storytellers

For the company, 'storytellers' maintain cohesion and provide guidelines for everyone to follow. The story is the most powerful way to convey information and to shape behavior.

The beauty of a story is that just by remembering the punch line you can remember the whole occasion.

Minor cultural characters

'Gossips' are the troubadours of the culture. They will know the names, dates, salaries, and events that everyone wants to hear about. The storyteller creates the legends of the company and its heroes, but the gossip helps the process to flourish by embellishing the story in an entertaining way. 'Whisperers', according to Deal and Kennedy, are often powers behind the throne, the influential people without portfolios. They must firstly be able to read their superior's mind quickly and clearly, and secondly have a vast network of contacts to call upon. Similarly 'spies' have access to a wide network of stories and contacts, thereby keeping the boss informed. However, they lack the whisperer's influence.

The full cast of characters between them – heroes, priests, storytellers and the minor players in the wings – personify the corporate culture. Their roles are as important as those of the more easily recognized business functionaries in making a company succeed. However, you need to be in sympathy with 'symbolic management' if you are to make proper use of them.

Cultural orientation

The shared values within a particular company, as well as its prevailing cast of cultural characters, will influence the kind of cultural orientation that pervades. In fact Deal and Kennedy identify four different cultural orientations within American companies. Each one brings with it different structural features. (See Table 14.)

Table 14 Cultural orientation

Culture	Structure	Characteristics
'Bet your company' culture	Hierarchical	Oriented towards roles, structures, rules and procedures, job descriptions
'Macho' culture	Centralized	Individualistic, risk taking, winning, starring, powerful
'Process' culture	Flexible	Scientific, problem and project oriented, experimental
'Work hard/play hard' culture	Lean form	Action oriented, 'try it' and 'fix it', speedy

Corporate culture, then, involves a particular context (shared values and rituals), a specialized set of roles (heroes, priests, storytellers), and a distinctive cultural orientation (bet your company, macho, process, or work hard/play hard). Deal and Kennedy have taken the culture and roles of a traditional community and woven them into a corporate context. They have not, however, made the traditional household and communal context explicit.

Conclusion

The fact that economics, and also management, originated in the household, within the community, has until recently been ignored by the conventional wisdom. However, the advent of Japanese management together with the emergence of women in business, has altered our historical perspective. We can now make meaningful connections between, for example, market women in Nigeria and Mary Kay Cosmetics in America. Traditionally a woman in the home, thereby in the community, has exercised a levelling influence, balancing profit and love, work and home, self and other. In a more active sense her role might be perceived as that of an 'animateur', animating the individual through the primal group, or, in Mary Kay's everyday terms, bringing warmth and happiness to everyone.

The new and recent wave of interest in 'corporate culture' draws upon this skill of 'animation', as a levelling influence, and as a means of sharing values. The kind of storytelling we can now associate with Nelli Eichner, of Interlingua, provides an animated means whereby her company's values live on. Indeed without the animateur Peters' and Austin's 'passion for excellence' will soon dry up. Entrepreneur and animateur, then, are the pair who, between them, support the primal base of the company's operations. In other words, they provide that blend of tough persistence and tender care that form the most tangible, and visible evidence of a successful business. They bring us 'back to the basics'. A company in which entrepreneur and animateur thrive is 3M – Minnesota Mining and Manufacturing Company – in America. So it is from 3M that we shall draw our 'primal fruits'.

References

1. S. Gutierrez, *The Market Women in Nigeria*, PhD thesis, City University London (1986), p. 188.
2. S. Gutierrez, *op. cit.*, p. 193.
3. G. Fields, *From Bonsai to Levis*, Mentor (1983), p. 85.
4. S. Kobayashi, *Creative Management*, AMA (1974), p. 184.
5. B. De Mente, *The Japanese Way of Doing Business*, Prentice Hall (1981), p. 64.
6. M. Kay, *On People Management*, Pan (1984), p. 23.
7. M. Kay, *op. cit.*, p. 97.
8. M. Kay, *op. cit.*, p. 3.
9. M. Kay, *op. cit.*, p. 2.
10. J. Taylor, *The Primal Vision*, SCM Press (1963), p. 11.
11. M. Gelfand, *African Crucible*, Mambo Press (1979), p. 7.
12. C. Nakane, *Japanese Society*, Weidenfeld & Nicolson (1970), pp. 139 and 149.
13. L. Danco, *Inside the Family Business*, Center for Family Business, (1980), p. 33.
14. N. Eichner, 'Animating People', ex R. Lessem, *Enterprise Development*, Gower (1986), p. 135.
15. N. Eichner, *op. cit.*, p. 129.
16. J. Morris, 'Three Aspects of the Person in Social Life', ex J. Ruddock, *Six Approaches to the Person*, Routledge & Kegan Paul (1972), pp. 70–92.
17. A. Roddick, 'Making Things Happen', ex R. Lessem, *Enterprise Development*, Gower (1986), p. 151.
18. Pascale and Athos, *The Art of Japanese Management*, Penguin (1983), p. 51.
19. J. Simpson, *Cultural Democracy*, Council for Europe, p. 17.
20. T. Deal and A. Kennedy, *Corporate Cultures*, Addison Wesley (1984), p. 13.
21. T. Deal and A. Kennedy, *op. cit.*, p. 27.

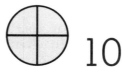

10 Personal and cooperative enterprise

Contents

Key concepts

Once you have fully understood the chapter you should be able
to define the following concepts in your own words:

Cooperative enterprise	Nichemanship
Kibbutz	People's commune
Management buy out	Role evolution
Networker	Takeover fever
New venture	

Objectives

Upon completing this chapter you should be able to do the following:

1. Outline key 'primal' trends, covering the historical development of cooperative enterprise, and more recent developments in personal enterprise.
2. Account for the success of the Mondragon group of cooperatives, paying particular attention to the balance between personality and cooperation.
3. Tell the story of 3M, drawing out the forces of personal initiative and community feeling that have fostered its growth and development.
4. Trace the development of primal management in 3M, from its early and instinctive days, to more recent times, in which the evolution of the organization has become more conscious.
5. Assess how you would personally fare within a 3M-type organization, on the one hand, and in an Israeli kibbutz, on the other.

Introduction

In this chapter, on the fruits of primal management, I want to widen the application of our primal analysis. On the one hand I want to investigate the resurgence of personal enterprise, in the context of business' development on the 1980s, particularly in Western Europe and in America. On the other hand I want to retrace steps, and to place the resurgence of cooperative attitudes and outlook – shared values – in the context of cooperative enterprises that have emerged around the globe. For the first investigation I shall focus on mainland China and Israel generally, and on the Mondragon group of cooperatives in northern Spain, in particular. For the second analysis I shall focus on Britain and the United States generally, and on Minnesota Mining and Manufacturing Company (3M) in particular. I shall begin with a general review of cooperatives, and then personal enterprise, before moving on to the specific companies.

Cooperative enterprise

Emergent cooperatives in the United States and in Britain

The cooperative enterprise is to the gatherer what the personal enterprise is to the hunter.

United States

Cooperation – working together to achieve a common end – is a practice that has existed in the United States of America, for example, since the days of the first colonists. The Pilgrim Fathers in 1620 banded together on a cooperative basis. Cooperative business enterprise, however, even in its most elementary forms, did not begin until the early 1800s.

Cooperative enterprise: definition

A cooperative enterprise is one which belongs to the people who use its service, the control of which rests with all its members, and the gains of which are distributed to the members in proportion to the use they made of its services.

Martin Abrahamsen *Cooperative Business Enterprise*[1] 1976

In agriculture, associated groups of dairy and pig farmers in the 1800s organized cooperatives to manufacture cheese and to slaughter and transport hogs for market. By 1860, moreover, about 100 rural, mutual fire assurance companies were in operation. In the urban community, by 1830, much interest in cooperative workshops had risen amongst furniture makers, weavers, tailors and saddlers. Building and loan associations were founded in the 1950s to combat the high cost of housing. They adopted as their motto 'Do your own landlording'. Over 150 years such cooperatives have developed in America to the extent that they now provide a wide range of services and handle a large variety of products. They have grown from small, local associations to large-scale organizations. By far the most important of these today, however, are the agricultural ones.

Great Britain
The predominance of agricultural cooperatives also characterizes Western Europe where, in France and Italy in particular, a longstanding tradition of cooperatively based farming has existed. Britain has lagged comparatively, in this respect, but recently has experienced a resurgence in cooperative enterprise as a whole.

Workers' cooperatives in Britain

As recently as 1976 there were some 47 worker co-operatives (as opposed to consumer co-operatives) in the United Kingdom. By the end of 1982 nearly 500 were listed in the Directory of the Co-operative Development Agency. Currently the number is increasing by some five a week.

The growth has been admittedly from a very low base, the number of employees belonging to organizations supporting the main co-operative movement being only 10,000, as compared with 200,000 in Italy.

Michael Young *Revolution from Within*[2] 1983

In spite of recent growth and development, in Britain at least, cooperative enterprise in Western Europe and America is dwarfed by conventional and personally based enterprise. This has not been the case in China, at least for the past forty years.

Cooperative enterprise across the globe

The Chinese cooperatives
It is agricultural enterprises, around the world, which lend themselves, particularly, to cooperative management. In fact cooperatives, as an emerging business phenomenon, are much less a feature of the American and Western European landscape, and much more one associated with the developing countries. For in countries where individualism is not strongly rooted – in other words, where the hunting band has not been manifestly transformed into individual enterprise – the cooperative or communal ethic can more easily take root within traditional communities. I have certainly seen evidence of this in my own country of origin, Zimbabwe.

Communal traditions

Shona villagers in Zimbabwe extol the virtues of solidarity, fraternity and equality. In their traditional environment they are firmly wedded to the way of life and to the virtues approved of by their ancestral spirits . . . The Shona have a deep seated loyalty to their kin. They place great stress on harmony and tranquility.

Michael Gelfand *The Genuine Shona*[3] 1983

The most wide ranging application of cooperative principles to business practice has, of course, taken place in Communist China. Moreover, unlike in Eastern Europe where there is often an unhappy blend of indigenous culture and exogenous ideology, in China there has been more of an ongoing attempt to align political ideology with local needs and circumstances. The establishment of a collectively based system of agriculture, took place in modern China during the ten year period 1949 to 1959. The transition from a feudal economy to a cooperative one came about in four stages.

The first step towards collectivization was the formation of mutual-aid teams. By grouping some six to ten households into such teams labor, animals and farm implements could be pooled. At the end of 1952 eight million mutual-aid teams were established. However, the units were not large enough to cope with national disasters nor with large-scale purchasing schemes and agricultural projects. To overcome these problems element-ary cooperatives were established in 1953. While two thirds of the total income was distributed on the basis of individual effort, the other third was distributed collectively. By 1955, about one third of peasant households had been formed into about 633,000 elementary producer's cooperatives. The third stage in China's rural development was that of advanced producers' cooperatives through which the entire income was collectively distributed. These were formed by amalgamating from ten to twenty elementary cooperatives. The fourth and final stage of cooperative development involved the formation of the people's communes.

People's communes

A Chinese commune is not a large agricultural cooperative but a composite unit of local government that encompasses the whole range of economic, social, administrative and political functions for the rural community. Its essential purpose is to organize and mobilize the rural population, to develop their land and other resources to meet their essential needs on the principle of self reliance while at the same time reducing social inequalities and creating a rural society based on justice and equality.

Sartaj Aziz *Rural Development*[4] 1978

The people's commune, then, has not merely resulted from an attempt to impose a Maoist philosophy upon China's economic and political development. It is also a primal response to physical and social need, drawn out of the communal heritage – embracing values of solidarity, fraternity and equality – of the Chinese peasant people. Yet, as we all know today, the Chinese government is now injecting more individualized incentives and Westernized technology into agricultural and industrial enterprise. Nations, like busi-nesses, need to undergo evolutionary phases of development. Moreover, communal and gatherer values divorced from their individual and hunting counterparts are found to result in imbalance.

The Israeli kibbutz

Whereas the Chinese commune represents the most prolific example of cooperative enterprise, the Israeli kibbutz represents the best known such example in the West. Kibbutzim were first set up by immigrants into what was then Palestine, at the turn of the century. They were, and still are, based on the collective ownership of resources, and the equal sharing of work and produce amongst its members. Having started out in agriculture, the so-called kibbutzniks diversified into light industry. At the same time they played an important part in defending precarious national borders. Members are provided with a small house but they have their food in a communal dining room and, in most kibbutzim, children live together in nurseries and in special children's quarters. Each member works on the farms, in the light industries, and in the communal facilities according to a centralized work schedule. No wages are paid, but members are provided with goods and services that they need.

> The kubbutz is based on voluntarism, informality, and face to face interaction . . . Kibbutz values stress the oneness of the individual and the community and encourage the total indentification of the individual with the collectivity.[5]

Ironically the kibbutz movement in Israel today is struggling in the face of waning social idealism and growing individual self-interest. Like the Chinese commune it is inevitably subject to the forces of evolutionary change. Having spent extended periods of time on kibbutzim myself I am certainly aware of the extent to which they can inhibit individual self-expression.

Both Chinese agricultural cooperatives and the kibbutzim have historically been noted for their success, but in recent times have come under increasing criticism. Whereas the kibbutzim are struggling to hang on to their membership the Chinese cooperatives are now being opened up to more personal enterprises. By comparison, then, the Mondragon group – in northern Spain – remains a shining cooperative light.

The Mondragon group

Perhaps the most visibly successful of all cooperative enterprises around the world, at least in a modern industrial context, is the Mondragon cooperative movement in the Spanish Basque country. Today some 55,000 people are employed in a wide range of flourishing industrial enterprises.

Aims and origins

The Mondragon cooperative experiment was initiated by a Basque priest, Father Arizmendi, who first set out in 1941 to be an advisor to young people. The Basque nation, of which he was a committed part had a strongly nationalistic streak to it and had vigorously opposed General Franco during the civil war. It also had a tradition of metalworking, of voyages of discovery, of social as well as social militancy, and of staunch catholicism. Arizmendi's first priority, as he saw it in the forties, was to establish a technical school for young people. He immediately enlisted the local community's support, as he continued to do for all of his subsequent initiatives. In fact he soon realized that technical education, without industries in which to subsequently apply it, would leave the young people frustrated. So he encouraged five of the graduates of the initial technical school to set up the first of the Mondragon cooperatives.

The Mondragon group

A small part of the starting capital needed to buy up a bankrupt business came from the savings of the five founders. The remainder was raised from the Mondragon community and in particular through friends and contacts in drinking clubs – *chiquitoes* – which are a strong feature of Basque cultural life. These clubs are quite small and encourage lasting relationships of high trust and solidarity amongst members.

Of course it would be absurd to imply that these convivial clubs were more important than, say, the links that had been established between the technical school and the community. Yet they can, I think, be seen as a symbol of the mutual Basque solidarity which has been a key element in the success of the cooperatives from the start.

Robert Oakeshott *The Case for Workers' Cooperatives* [6] 1978

While the five initial founders set up their operation to manufacture stoves, in the mid-fifties, Father Arizmendi was busy setting up a cooperative bank.

One of the most powerful arguments that Arizmendi had used in urging that the bank be set up was that the isolation of individual cooperatives involved the most formidable risks to which their members should not be exposed. Another had been that the potential for cooperative enterprise would never be adequately developed if the task of encouraging and midwifing new initiatives was left to the individual enterprises themselves.[7]

Cooperative development

Fifty-six new industrial cooperatives came into existence, within the Mondragon group, between 1961 and 1976, together with five agricultural ones.

Mondragon's success factors

- Ultimate control rests firmly and democratically with the general assembly of the entire workforce. No outsiders may be members; and no workers may not be members.
- Each worker–member must purchase a significant stake in the enterprise. The value of the stake will rise or fall, depending on the fortunes of the enterprise.
- A significant proportion of the co-op's capital is and remains collectively owned and indivisible. This is the condition which makes possible the indefinite survival of the enterprise.
- The first initiative for the setting up of a new co-op comes from a group of ordinary people, and it is a necessary condition that the group should share in a positive decision to launch it. This ensures joint commitment from the start.
- Wage and salary differentials are fixed to take account of the needs for enterprise solidarity as well as market constraints. This is the condition which ensures vertical solidarity within the enterprise.
- The separate executive functions of management are clearly defined and management,

though appointed by and answerable to the co-op's elected representatives, normally enjoy security of tenure for four years.
- The isolated individual co-ops have continuous access to a full range of highly professional advice, as well as to a continuous supply of newly skilled and high-level manpower.
- The co-ops have access to capital for expansion, and to tide over hard times.
- The co-ops, partly through their support for local social and educational projects, enjoy strong backing from the community.
- Though the independence of the individual co-ops is jealously guarded they are essentially integrated into a group.

Robert Oakeshott *The Case for Workers' Cooperatives*[8] 1978

Overall, as we can see, the Mondragon Group has been able to combine the positive features of individual and cooperative enterprise, given the context of a fiercely patriotic, and technically astute, Basque nation. Moreover, Father Arizmendi and his successors have succeeded in linking a primal community instinct with a managerial rationality. Interestingly enough – as we shall now see – the same might be said of 3M. However, while Mondragon has accommodated an independent spirit within a cooperative ethos, Minnesota Mining and Manufacturing houses a cooperative spirit within an independent enterprise. We shall be investigating 3M in depth, on pp. 170–8. Before we do that, however, let me review the general features in today's business environment which are reinforcing the tough and competitive side of primal enterprise.

Competitive enterprise

Even more visibly in evidence than these cooperative enterprises, in today's tough business world, is the new spirit of competitiveness and personal enterprise that has emerged. It is reflected in three major ways, in the resurgence of entrepreneurship, in an increasingly acquisitive streak, and in the emergence of 'intrapreneurship' within big business. I shall consider each in turn.

New enterprise

The resurgence of entrepreneurship, over the past ten years has been nothing short of remarkable. In Russia and China, in India and Indonesia, in Africa and Australia, as well as in Europe and America, indigenous entrepreneurs are now being sought after, and appraised, just as if they were golddust.

Since the mid seventies, such slogans as 'the no-growth economy', the 'de-industrialization of America', and a long-term 'Kondratieff stagnation of the economy' have become popular and have been invoked as axioms. Yet the facts and figures belie every one of these slogans. What is happening in the US is something quite different: a profound shift from a 'managerial' to an 'entrepreneurial' economy ... According to *The Economist*, 600,000 new businesses are being started in the United States every year now – about seven times as many as were started in each of the boom years of the fifties and sixties.[9]

The acquisitive streak

Whereas in the 1970s small was beautiful, in the eighties aggressive entrepreneurship has by no means been restricted to small enterprises. An extraordinary wave of mergers and takeovers has ensued, in America, in Europe and even in Japan. In Britain, for example, the value of takeover bids, in the space of just two years between 1983 and 1985, had grown from £2.3 to £7.1. There has been no mistaking the primal, acquisitive drive which has been overtaking both the habitual conglomerates, like Hanson Trust, and the new corporate raiders, like the ill-fated Ivan Boesky.

Takeover fever

It has not just been the number of takeovers or their size which has revealed how different the corporate world has become. It has also been the intensity with which the attacks have been mounted and resisted, and the way in which a handful of professional predators have made the headlines.

It has additionally been the fact that many companies have continued to grasp for growth by acquisition while surrounded with evidence from their own, or from competitors' recent experience, that acquisitions frequently cause more headaches than cure. In short there has been incontrovertible evidence that a fever has gripped the business community which made captains of industry lust to collect any corporate entity within sight, whether corporate logic supported it or not.

Christine Moir *The Acquisitive Streak*[10] 1986

Intrapreneurs

While entrepreneurs and takeovers have been making the media headlines, the rise of the 'intrapreneur', within the large corporations, has been quite marked. Such intrapreneurship is most visibly reflected in 'new ventures', in 'management buyouts', or in a new form of 'networking'.

Firstly, so-called new ventures, which seemed to go through the doldrums in the seventies, have once again returned to the forefront. The IBM 'PC' is perhaps the best publicized of such ventures, arising out of new business units within a large company. New ventures – as we shall see with 3M – are a form of internal, organic business creation within a company, as opposed to acquisitions, which bring in new companies from outside.

Secondly, in both America and in Europe, there has been a massive increase in the rate of 'management buyouts', whereby a management team, from within the company, take over ownership and control over a part, or a whole, of the enterprise. This particular, primal trend totally counteracts the managerial revolution of the past 100 years, whereby ownership has become separated from control.

Thirdly, and for example, in Rank Xerox International there has emerged a new breed of so called 'Networkers' – usually knowledge workers – who have spun off their separate and freelance businesses, while retaining commercial and social links with their parent company.

Let me now investigate, in depth, one powerful manifestation of such primal fruit, one that combines toughness and tenderness in a highly visible way.

Primal enterprise and community

For me to choose one major company that best represented the primal spirit was not difficult. For I wanted to select a well-known business corporation that lived and breathed the spirit of community and enterprise. That narrowed down the choice considerably. Even IBM, for example, that wonder of the business world, is more representative of channelled corporatism than of free enterprise. Other candidates, like Hewlett Packard, had not quite stood the test of time, and mature corporations like General Motors and Exxon still manifest too strongly the symptoms of an analytically managed organization. So 3M (Minnesota Mining and Manufacturing) had to be my choice. After all it had received no less than 123 separate mentions in *Search for Excellence* by Peters and Waterman.

I first came across Minnesota Mining and Manufacturing (3M) when running courses in Great Britain on new venturing. Little did I realise at the time that this company, conveniently situated in America's mid-west, had a unique and quite fascinating history. Before flying over to visit 3M for the first time, in the summer of 1985 I read, with very great interest, Virginia Huck's *The 3M Story*.[11]

Let me now share with you the 'primal fruits' of personal enterprise, by describing the birth, growth and development of Minnesota Mining and Manufacturing.

The story of 3M

The birth of primal management

Making and letting things happen

Founded in 1902, with a purpose to mine, our originators had in mind the sale of a mineral to manufacturers of grinding wheels. Our founders were a butcher, a railway man, a lawyer.... Their first product was an absolute disaster...'

Lewis Lehr, Chairman and Chief Executive, 3M[12] 1986

I shall never forget the chuckle in President Lehr's voice as he started to tell me his company's story. The early and continuing mishaps taught 3Mers forever after to expect the unexpected, and not to despair, but to turn problems into opportunities.

The men who founded the company launched their venture on a misconception. They believed that they were the owners of a raw material, corundum, of industrial value. They had only to exploit it with wisdom and vigor to reap a reward similar to that which had come to many American prospectors before them. These men of courage and optimism could not have been more mistaken. Minnesota Mining and Manufacturing made its first sale of this auspicious mineral, extracted at great cost to them, in the second week of March 1904. It turned out to be the last. By the end of the year, 3M stock had fallen to an all-time low on the bar room exchange. But their founders were determined not to give up.

Involving the community within and without
Fortunately their employees felt the same way. Everyone offered some personal sacrifice to keep the company going. Then the general freight agent for the Chicago, St Paul, Minneapolis and Omaha railway stepped in. Edgar B. Ober had been actively interested

in 3M ever since his investment of $5000 in 1903. He felt that the only way to get a return on Crystal Bay corundum was to manufacture sandpaper and abrasive wheels. Ober had limited funds himself, but he managed to interest his friend Lucius Pond Ordway in the proposition. Ordway was not only a man of means but a civic leader in St Paul. The deal between the two men and 3M was signed in May, 1905. It effectively gave them control over the company. Even then they still remained unaware that the mineral on which their business was still based, remained worthless. For years they were to travel down the same road of failure that their founders had followed before them. Yet, though few realized it at the time, the abrasives industry itself was on the verge of a massive expansion.

The creation of 3M involved a strong combination of entrepreneurial risk taking and animated, community spirit. The company's founders persevered relentlessly, in the face of unremitting adversity. At the same time, it was the involvement of a group of individuals, ultimately backed by the civic leader himself, that sustained the operation during its early years. In other words, no single entrepreneur called the shots!

The expansion of primal management

Laying firm business foundations
Eventually 3M came to realize that the Crystal Bay corundum was quite useless. So they started importing the mineral from Spain, to supply their newly built sandpaper factory. On one of the early ships carrying the stuff over, believe it or not, a huge bottle of olive oil broke and seeped into the Spanish mineral, ruining it. Again they almost went broke.

Out of that experience was born the idea of 3M having its own research laboratory. Not many companies had one at the time. So 3M put together some technical people who were interested in fiddling around with things. Because they were dealing with sandpaper they called on the automotive industry. One of the technicians noticed that the auto workers were trying to mask paints with old surgical tape and newspaper. So he hatched the idea of sticky tape. That was the origin of 3M's Scotch tape. It also set a precedent, whereby 3M researchers were to remain always close to the customer.

Developing products *via* markets
In fact the company's most famous 'Scotch' brand trademark is believed to have had its origin with an angry auto body painter in the mid 1920s who, having trouble with the adhesion of an early roll of masking tape, told a salesman: 'Take this tape back to your stingy Scotch bosses and tell them to put more adhesive on it'. It was early in 1929 when an inventor by the name of Drew began to experiment with a sealing tape, using Dupont's new moisture proof, transparent cellophane. His 1929 tape was not marketable, but it was the embryo of a product which was to prove more spectacular than anyone could imagine.

Drew had begun work on the tape because he was trying to solve a packaging problem for a St Paul manufacturer. At first all the attempts that he and his lab made to solve the problem were unsuccessful. The tape had to have a proper balance of adhesiveness, cohesiveness, stretchiness and elasticity. Finally, after many trials and tribulations, on 8 September, 1930 a roll met these requirements.

Almost daily, thereafter, new ideas for using the tape popped up, from the public and 3M salesmen. Laundries, ribbon manufacturers – everyone wanted the tape after they had heard about it.

In those early years, Drew recognized the potential, even if only subconciously, of a product that was to become a household name. Once the product saw daylight, then an extraordinary community of interests emerged, as the diverse customers that had come to know 3M, got in on the act. Scotch Tape became a shared development, to an even greater extent than it had originally been. A widely spreading mutual interest group of producers and consumers accelerated its further evolution.

Grass roots selling

The reference to 'Scotch bosses' takes the story on to the legendary William L. McKnight, who joined the company in 1907, as assistant book-keeper, for the princely sum of $11.55 a week. 3M continued to founder in those early years, but McKnight's influence grew. In return for his display of ability, loyalty and hard work, he was appointed office manager, in spite of his complete lack of sales background. McKnight also called for more coordination between salesmen and the factory, finally arguing that quality and uniformity, sadly lacking in 3M products, would be achieved only if a general manager were named to supervise both production and sales and bring them closer together. Ober agreed and selected McKnight for the job. On 11 August 1916, having survived precariously for fourteen accident-prone but perseverent years, President Ordway announced to his fellow management and friends: 'Gentlemen this is the day we have been waiting for, the day some of us doubted would ever come. We're out of debt, and the future looks good. For the first time, we'll have enough left after expenses to pay a dividend.'[13]

McKnight trained his salesmen to do what he had learned could be done, get into work areas, find what kind of abrasive materials were best suited for customer needs, demonstrate 3M products and report problems precisely to the factory with samples of poor quality sandpaper.

Cultivating the art of nichemanship

3M's newly found though modest prosperity was mainly due to the development of 3Mite, a new abrasive cloth made with aluminium oxide, used for cutting metal by manufacturing engaged in the war effort. The product had been developed by 3M in close collaboration with the automative industry.

However the real breakthrough was still to come in January 1920. A certain Mr Francis Okie wrote in to 3M, requesting 'every mineral grit size you use in manufacturing sandpaper'. Instead of dismissing the request, McKnight responded. His response changed the course of 3M history. An agreement was drawn up between 3M and Okie, in February 1921, to develop and manufacture Wetordry, their first waterproof sandpaper – a product that industry needed and for which 3M could set its own price. Wetordry effectively led to a quadrupling of the company's sales.

But success, inevitably for 3M, did not come immediately. The market which Ober and

McKnight had envisioned for waterproof sandpaper failed to materialize. So eventually, instead of selling the product to the furniture finishers, 3M's salesmen discovered a market, once more, in the automotive industry. In these early years a pattern was established which 3M was set to follow through to the 1980s. The company became what John Myser, President of 3M Canada, calls a 'niche player'. Technologies, products, people and businesses evolved through a combination of insight, persistence and chance.

> When you go back to our beginnings, we started out making sandpaper. We put glue on to it, and dropped on pieces of grit. If the glue doesn't dry you have tape. Put on glass beads and you recreate reflective sheeting. Add in magnetic oxide and you get recording tape. What we know about is coating things. It all sort of flows. All our products are related – in the family.[14]

Chance follows not only the brave, but also a distinct pattern of physical and human relationships. To put it at its most basic, 3M are good at putting two and two together and coming up with five, whether it is to do with new technologies or business opportunities. Mary Kay would put it down to 'people and love'.

Things and people combine in 3M because they are in regular contact, are open to the unpredictable, and are willing to cross boundaries. 3Mers are constantly looking for the niche that falls between and across the straight lines within which most competitors are working. They are venturesome enough to cross over into unknown territory, and familiar enough with each other, and with their customers, to want to keep products and relationships within the family.

The development of primal management

Research: generating and testing

Richard P. Carlton, who was destined, as was McKnight, to become President of 3M, joined the laboratory staff in October, 1921. He had the distinction of being the first technical man in the company with a degree from an accredited college. His first accomplishment was to switch the laboratory program on to a more technical track by supplanting trial and error methods of quality control with more specific scientific standards.

> The day of rule of thumb method has passed in the 3M organization. The laboratory of the modern industrial plant must have something more than the men and equipment to control the work. It must possess a two fisted generating and testing department for ideas. This work, dressed in its best Sunday clothes, is research.[15]

After setting the laboratory on the right course, Carlton gradually began coordinating the activities of research, engineering and manufacturing, and directing the technical development of new ideas from the dream stage to that of commercial success. He was subsequently promoted to assistant general manager in charge of factory administration and then to director of manufacturing. Like in the case of McKnight before him, Carlton's role evolved, following his developing competence. In many ways the roles were cast to fit the man rather than vice versa. For Carlton was more than an organization man. In fact he made some of his most important contributions through the development of his own product ideas. Carlton was an inventor as well as someone able to do generate creative thinking in others, drawing out men's ideas and nurturing them to maturity. No one knew better than he that in a sympathetic atmosphere one idea fosters another.

The instigation of organization and method, therefore, was never entirely separated from either the spirit of challenge and adventure, or from the urge to communicate and cooperate. For that reason the development of new products continued to follow the 3M pattern of technical ingenuity, empathy with the customer, dogged perseverence and acknowledgement of serendipity. In the thirties and forties all this was subject to some greater degree of formalization than hitherto.

Development: autonomy and integration

In 1937, management sat around a table and asked themselves, as the United States was emerging out of the recession, how best to secure continued growth. They concluded that within research lay the key. They decided, first, to establish a Central Research Laboratory to supplement the activities of divisional research. Three years later a New Products Department was organized, and in 1943 a Products Fabrication Laboratory. So the steps in innovation, from idea generation to implementation, now had been given organizational recognition. In 1944, a major departure was made in 3M's organizational structure, when the Detroit automotive department was given near autonomous status, the first such status given to any division. This was the company's first experiment with a vertical type organization. Yet even this formalized structure, in the words of William McKnight, carried its particular 3M stamp.

> As our business grows, it becomes increasingly necessary for those in managerial positions to delegate responsibility, and to encourage men to whom responsibility is delegated to exercize their own initiative. This requires considerable tolerance. Those men to whom we delegate authority and responsibility, if they are good men, are going to have ideas of their own and are going to want to do their jobs in their own way. These characteristics should be encouraged as long as their way conforms to our business policies and our general pattern of operation.[16]

In organizing for innovation McKnight payed equal attention to the soft and hard sides of management. On the one hand he emphasized tolerance and diversity; on the other hand he focussed upon responsibility and conformity. Moreover, this pattern of business development, which he now articulated, was to become 3M's hallmark. A unique interplay between individual enterprise and community orientation is mediated through a shared concern for product and market development. This interplay of hunting and gathering – personal initiative and group support – lies at the heart of the company's successful new venturing.

Implementation: personal initiative and group support

McKnight's statement of intent has been borne out in practice again and again within the company, for example by its last chief executive, Lew Lehr:

> I was educated as a chemical engineer. I came to work for 3M, and went to night school, at the same time, to study law. I got so busy at work that I couldn't pursue my studies. I became a law school drop-out.
>
> About the same time a group of surgeons asked us to develop a special product for them. I 'signed on' and became the manager of a small laboratory based operation. I grew together with it. It ultimately became a Division, and then a Group. Within the Group were hospital products, including stethoscopes, masks and binding tapes; from there it expanded into

dental products, pharmaceuticals and veterinary supplies. I was made Group Vice President in 1972 and Vice President of a larger Group two years later.

In 3M we haven't had a lot of CEOs. My predecessor started out in one of our four factories as a superintendent. He moved into new products in office equipment. His predecessor had been involved in reflective sheeting. He followed it up, out of the lab, and moved on from there. His predecessor, in turn, followed the same kind of route. There's a flavor here of people becoming involved with new products, and moving on from there. I don't know which came first, the chicken or the egg, that is the enterprising individual or new product development.[17]

Within a division, something new develops and a group of people feel 'we've got something'. But it doesn't quite relate to the division's current activity. So 3M says, 'let's assign someone to head this BDU unit'. The unit will include technical, sales and marketing personnel, as well as staff support. At this early stage everyone involved will still be holding other jobs. But they set themselves up as a team. As a prototype product emerges they don't look towards a full manufacturing facility. They form themselves into a Business Development Unit (BDU) and then they ask themselves 'Is there somebody's plant, in the company, where we can get ourselves a little corner?' These BDU teams are responsible for getting a product developed. Every year some 15–30 of them are recognized, once their turnover has reached $2 million. As the business develops a full time leader, a 'spokesman' is appointed. It then becomes a 'project'. As a 'project' grows it becomes a 'department'. As a 'department' grows it becomes a 'division'.

3M is a company where there is a low turnover of people. They stay. Involved. It is not one track. Besides the path of development already described, there's a parallel approach. People move from one division to another, from one country to the other. Donn Osmon, for example, started as a salesman. He moved into marketing, in a particular division. Then he became MD of our UK operation. Now he's back at headquarters as Vice President of Marketing and Public Affairs. He had the experience of a specific job, followed by company wide experience in the UK.

Both kinds of movement, following product and market evolution or boundary crossing the organization, prevents inbreeding within a particular part of the business. They give people a breadth of background. People get exposed to different kinds of operation. They learn. They carry ideas back and forth. New products and businesses are created. It is a way of life for 3M. It also spearheaded the next step in the company's evolution.

Beyond primal management

Global identity and integrity

It was McKnight, in fact, who also pioneered the development of a European, if not initially global perspective. From the moment 3M bought a new patent, and developed Wetordry, he began thinking about the British and European market. It was not until the 1950s though, with Carlton in the Presidential seat, that 3M organized an International Division. So, by the end of that decade, 3M's organizational foundations had been firmly laid. There was just one further, and major development, to come.

Until the early fifties 3M was a middle-sized, regionally based company, in St Paul, Minnesota. At that time William McKnight, who laid the foundations for 3M's success, saw that the company's future lay in developing overseas. He started out with very clear guidelines, to be a good corporate citizen in other countries. 3M's global development has come a long way since McKnight's early initiatives. Today more than one third of the company's turnover is generated outside of the United States of America, in Europe, Latin America, Asia and Africa. Its primal intent, to promote enterprise and community, now stretches across a global stage. This is spelled out in the company's corporate principles.

> The first principle is the promotion of entrepreneurship and insistence upon freedom in the workplace to pursue innovative ideas. Second is the adherence to uncompromising honesty and integrity. Third is the preservation of individual identity in an organisational structure which embraces widely diverse businesses and operates in different political and economic systems throughout the world.[18]

Planned action and reflection

Over the period, then, between McKnight's reorganization in 1948 and 1981, the company grew and developed, uninterruptedly, according to the above-mentioned pattern. Divisions proliferated happily until 1980 when it was realized that it had become necessary to regroup under four major sectors: Electronic and Information Technologies, Graphic Technologies, Industrial and Commercial and Life Sciences. 3M had come a long way from adhesive and yet remained closely in touch with bonding and coating technologies. It remained close to home.

However, and interestingly for the first time in its history, 3M in the eighties took an introspective look at its approach to business development. To a large extent, until then, it had just evolved, seemingly naturally, primally and thus almost instinctively. So it institutionalized strategic planning. The company also began to feel that innovation might have to be more consciously promoted. 'It's too easy', Lew Lehr told me, 'to become complacent. There's been a lot of publicity recently on how innovative we are. Also, we live in a rapidly changing world. Unless you're out there driving you'll be left behind. So we decided we ought to have an audit. Do we have the right attitudes towards innovation?

We discovered that we looked to the labs for innovation, rather than on the company as a whole. So we set up a task force to get everyone involved. It was really an extension of what we were doing before, with quality circles, encouraging everyone to be open and creative. We have to learn how to manage innovation. We will need another two years of awareness building before we shall be able to establish clear priorities. We shall have to spread our innovativeness internationally. We will need to improve our ability to market and distribute on a worldwide basis. We will need to be even more innovative in order to become a global market leader. Research in space will also offer us great opportunities.[19]

Exploring outer space

3M's involvement with space research did not emerge as a carefully planned strategic step. NASA was pushing for industry to get involved, and 3M thought maybe there might be something in it. Chris Chow, a Chinese American, was one of the team leaders in the new research project.

I want to be up there

I was a member of the physical science team at the time. We were working on a programme on the growth of organic crystals. We realized that a zero gravity space environment could enable us to grow much better crystals. NASA was also very receptive.

We didn't negotiate for one experience in space, but for two. Also management was of the opinion that it would take three or four years to get our first experiment ready. We said we would do it in one.

The whole thing evolved like a spiral.

Space research is not new. It's been with us for some years now. But the timing is right for us at 3M now. Space research is a national initiative and we want to be the first, that is our company, to commercialize the application.

If we merely rely on government nobody will stay up there in space. The profit motive will lift human beings, enabling them to enter a new plateau in our civilization. Space research will have a crucial role to play in the future of energy and resources. There are a couple of points in space where there's a stable equilibrium that acts as a power source. The calculations are there. There's no question in my mind.

3M is striving for two things. First, to manufacture up in space, if there is a sufficient return. Second, we want to gain sufficient knowledge to benefit people on earth. The knowledge we gain will be useful to a broad range of product lines.

I want to be up there. When you see that vision you get really excited about it. Boy, that would be wonderful.

Chris Chow *3M Space Lab*[20] 1986

3M's exploration, into outer space, has come at the same time as its more conscious exploration of the 'inner space' of its organizational and business development. This all heralds a new era of primal development, in which the instinctive urge to hunt and to gather is transformed into a more conscious, and purposeful desire to extend its physical and social operating domains.

Personal enterprise and cooperative activity

Throughout its development 3M has combined tough-minded personal enterprise with tender-hearted group support – both within and outside the company – initially as an instinct rather than as a consciously worked out strategy. 3M has been making and letting things happen, involving the community inside and out, and developing products via markets. In also combining individual autonomy with group integration, and exploring inner as well as outer space, it has alternated between soft and hard business approaches. In the process primal management, while retaining its operational core, has evolved.

In fact by now, in the late eighties, 3M has become a focal point for new venturing around the world. In that sense its basic hunting, and pioneering instinct has evolved far beyond the physical realms of mining and manufacturing. Instinct has become transformed into a conscious pursuit of excellence, drawing on revitalized organizational structures and purposes. Similarly, the family circle of the early days, while still ever present, has evolved into a community of '3Mers' now spread around the globe.

Community center for employees

If you look at the entrepreneurship of American industry it's wonderful. On the other hand, if you look at the paternalism and discipline of the Japanese companies, it's wonderful too ... There are certain companies that have evolved into a blend of these two, and 3M is one of them ... Companies like 3M have become a sort of community center for employees, as opposed to just a place to work. We have employee clubs, intramural sports, travel clubs, and a choral group. This has happened because the community in which people live has become so mobile it is no longer an outlet for the individual. The schools are no longer a social center for the family. The churches have lost their drawing power as social–family centers. With the breakdown of these traditional structures certain companies have filled the void. They have become sort of mother institutions, but have maintained their spirit of entrepreneurship at the same time.

Lew Lehr Chairman, 3M[21] 1982

Conclusion

As we can see, the soft primal instincts are still there at the core of 3M, as are indeed the hard ones, but they have been extended by Lew Lehr, now consciously. At the same time, no matter how strong the shared values within 3M, personal enterprise – championing, winning, competing – lies at the core of the company's being. By way of contrast, within successful cooperatives like the Mondragon group, no matter how strong the urge to compete in the market-place, cooperative enterprise – communion, sharing, cooperating – lies at the core of the organization's being. Finally, and at this primal level, it is important to emphasize that both competitive and the cooperative behavior patterns are instinctive and innate rather than consciously contrived. Whenever competitive or cooperative enterprise is foisted on to a country or a company, without either tapping indigenous fertile soils or consciously fertilizing existing ones, it is bound to fail.

At this level of primal management we are more concerned with tapping innate and indigenous behavior than with consciously cultivating developmental forms of business activity. I shall be attempting the latter, in fact, in Section D. But before I do that we have a lot of ground to cover. We need to investigate first analytical and then developmental and metaphysical management. In each case we shall proceed from their roots to their core, and then further upwards. I start, then, with the rational or scientific roots.

References

1.   M. Abrahamsen, *Cooperative Business Enterprise*, McGraw-Hill (1976), p. 2.
2.   M. Young, *Revolution from Within*, Weidenfeld & Nicolson (1983), p. 47.
3.   M. Gelfand, *The Genuine Shona*, Mambo Press, Zimbabwe (1983), p. 73.
4.   S. Aziz, *Rural Development*, Macmillan (1978), p. 17.
5.   S. Aziz, *op. cit.*, p. 83.
6.   R. Oakeshott, *The Case for Workers' Cooperatives*, Routledge & Kegan Paul (1978).
7.   R. Oakeshott, *op. cit.*, 1978, p. 170.
8.   R. Oakeshott, *op. cit.*, 1978, p. 171.

9. P. Drucker, *Innovation and Entrepreneurship*, Heinemann (1985), pp. 1–13.
10. C. Moir, *The Acquisitive Streak*, Hutchinson (1986), p. 8.
11. V. Huck, *The 3M Story*, Appleton Century Croft (1955), p. vii.
12. L. Lehr, Personal interview (Summer 1986).
13. V. Huck, *op. cit.,* p. 80.
14. T. Myser, Personal interview (Summer 1985).
15. R. Carlton, *Manual of Technical Information*, 3M (1925).
16. W. McKnight, *The 3M Story*, 3M (1981), p. 17.
17. L. Lehr, Personal interview (Summer 1986).
18. 3M, 'Corporate Principles', company leaflet.
19. L. Lehr, *op. cit.*
20. C. Chow, Personal interview, (Summer 1986).
21. L. Lehr, ex Peters and Waterman, (1982), p. 261.

Section C
Rational management

Introduction

The underlying ground

Whereas primal management is typically rooted in youthful and immigrant societies, rational management characteristically draws on a more established, and, if you like, adult society. Such an established, and rationally managed organization, then, demands intelligent and responsible behavior from its managers. From a geographical perspective, such 'adult' managerial behavior is most widespread in the North, especially in West Germany, but typically throughout Western Europe. At the same time, there are elements of such rational management spread throughout the world, especially in developed economies such as those in America and Japan, where large-scale enterprise predominates. Rational management activity thrives, finally, on a balance of organizational order and individual freedom, both of which are impersonally rather than personally based. (See Fig. 19.)

The living characters

Whereas primal management is appropriate at the first stage of a business' development (e.g. Steve Jobs of Apple Computers), rational management is more suited to the second (e.g. John Sculley, who took over from Jobs). Organizational order, at this second stage, is personified by the business executive; individual freedom, in turn, is personified by the change agent. Whereas the typical executive thrives on the vertical hierarchy of command, the agent of change prefers the more horizontal network of relationships. Whereas the one is inclined to regulate others the other prefers self-regulation. Finally, the individual who represents a combination of the 'hard' executive and the 'soft' change agent, is the manager of change. She is personified, in this text, by the managing director of F International, Hilary Cropper. She embodies rational management.

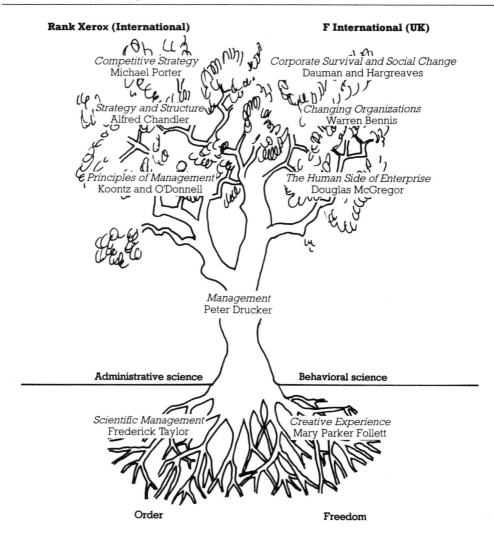

Rank Xerox (International)   **F International (UK)**

Competitive Strategy   *Corporate Survival and Social Change*
Michael Porter   Dauman and Hargreaves

Strategy and Structure   *Changing Organizations*
Alfred Chandler   Warren Bennis

Principles of Management   *The Human Side of Enterprise*
Koontz and O'Donnell   Douglas McGregor

Management
Peter Drucker

Administrative science   **Behavioral science**

Scientific Management   *Creative Experience*
Frederick Taylor   Mary Parker Follett

Order   Freedom

Fig. 19 The rational tree.

The rational roots

Hard roots

The hard roots of rational management reach tenuously down to the bureaucracies of Ancient China, Egypt and Rome – into their civilian, military and church administrations. More substantively within business they originate from the first truly large-scale industrial organizations, that is the American railroads, and from the writings of three of the first administrative scientists at the turn of the century. Such administrative science was greatly influenced by engineers, on the one hand, and by classical and Newtonian science, on the other. One such engineer was the American, Frederick Taylor,[1] who committed his whole adult life, in the early part of this century, to a scientifically based examination of work, its organization and management. Taylor's prime emphasis was on the physical nature of work, and how it could be more rationally ordered.

Taylor's drive for managerial order was accompanied by an equally dedicated drive for organizational order, in the name of bureaucracy. The German sociologist, Max Weber,[2] was the first person to systematically apply the depersonalized rules of bureaucratic order to the highly personalized world of primal business, in the late nineteenth century. Weber's mission, like Taylor's, was to apply rational organization to irrational, and often both brutal and inefficient, enterprise. Finally, and perhaps most importantly, the rational roots of management reach down to Henri Fayol[3] in the 1920s, a French engineer and industrial administrator who combined Taylor's principles of scientific management with Weber's bureaucratic organization. Fayol's book *Industrial and General Administration* was the first to analyze systematically not only the different functions of business but also the principles of management which have become so commonplace in large-scale organizations today.

Soft roots

Taylor, Weber and Fayol tried to impose organizational order and objective reason, on institutional whim and personal irrationality. They were, as a result, replacing warm instinct with cool reason. All three were tough-minded analysts, converting primal and instinctive cut and thrust into the rational and intellectual equivalent. Mary Parker Follett,[4] an American who spent much of her time in Great Britain, and Elton Mayo,[5] an Australian who spent much of his time in America, were both similar and different in this approach. As behavioral scientists they shared a commitment to the powers of dispassionate reason in solving technical and social problems. Where they differed from their tough-minded counterparts was in their concern for the individual, within the organization.

In his now famous 'Hawthorne' studies into the behavior of manual workers at Western Electric in the USA, Elton Mayo uncovered the power of the group as a cohesive social force. Unlike Frederick Taylor, who believed that people in groups were a 'disorganized rabble', Mayo observed that such working groups could be mutually supportive of one another. As a social psychologist, moreover, and not an engineer, he felt himself trained to predict and control such social attitudes and behavior, scientifically. Mary Parker Follett, as a political and social scientist in the 1920s, went a step further than Mayo. As a passionate believer in both science and democracy, she advocated the true 'democratization' of organizational life via the group. For her the small group was the vehicle through which the person could express himself, as an individual, within the context of an organization. For her the freedom of individual expression and association was primary; organizational order was therefore secondary, and the group mediated between the two.

Finally, for Parker Follett as an objective scientist, 'the law of the situation' displaced hierarchically based 'law and order' as a guiding principle for rational management. In other words, the objective circumstances of a particular situation should rule over conduct rather than the personal whims of a superior, or the impersonal rules of a bureaucracy. In this respect she considerably influenced Drucker, who has established, over forty years, the core of rational management.

The rational core

Primal–rational balance

Peter Drucker is an Austrian, by birth, who emigrated to the United States to escape from the Nazis. As a European intellectual Drucker has retained a fundamental belief in the powers of reason. As an American, by naturalization, he is a passionate believer in free enterprise. As a European–American he has been the intellectual force behind the evolution of small-scale business enterprise into large-scale, rationally managed organization. Because Drucker's approach to management[6] is, on the one hand, deeply rooted in the rational tradition and, on the other, broadly commited to primal enterprise, he has always managed to retain a fine balance between the two. While his theoretical outlook is essentially rational, poised between order and freedom, Drucker is strongly aware of the primal context in which free enterprise is set, between community and enterprise. As a result, for example, he sees marketing and innovation – his management fundamentals – as rational, and codifiable outgrowths of primal entrepreneurship. Moreover, he views sociable responsibility, or 'accountable enterprise', as again a natural and rationally based extension of community spirit.

Business, management and organization

Whereas for Drucker, then, accountable enterprise embodies the forces of order and of continuity, marketing and innovation embody the forces of freedom and of change. This applies not only to management but also to business and organization theory. For Drucker, in a way that is unique amongst the rational theorists, has managed to straddle not only the administrative (functional management) and behavioral sciences (behavioral management), but also the usually segregated areas of business, management and organization. As a result he has managed to balance the forces of order and freedom in at least three different respects. In respect to the functions and behavior of business he compares and contrasts what he terms the more 'entrepreneurial' (free) functions – innovation and marketing, with the more 'administrative' (order) ones – operations, finance and personnel.

In relation to the functions and behavior of management he again compares and contrasts the 'harder' aspects of measurement and control – related to planning and organization, with the 'softer' attributes of self-control, related to motivation, communication and management development. In the first case he draws on the legacy of Taylor, Weber and Fayol, and in the second, he draws on the seminal work of Elton Mayo and Mary Parker Follett. Finally, in relation to the functioning of organizations, Drucker is strongly in favor of the 'federally decentralized form', which stands halfway between the stable, centralized and functional (ordered) structure and the more fluid (free) task-based one.

Administrative and behavioral science

Drucker, then, has drawn together the major threads of rational management, into a solid core of balanced theory, also closely related to practice. Now in his seventies he believes, as Drucker always has done, that management is a science in the broadest – administrative and behavioral – sense. In other words there is little place for instinct or intuition in his scheme of things. The same goes for the major branches of rational management, rooted as they are in both administrative and behavioral sciences.

The rational branches

Hard branches

Management functions

There is a clear line of development from Henri Fayol in the twenties and thirties, who first delineated the management functions of planning, organizing, command and control, through Drucker and others in the forties and fifties, to Koontz and O'Donnell[7] in the sixties and seventies.

Koontz and O'Donnell, who have written perhaps the best known text on *The Principles of Management*, have divided the management functions into planning, organizing, directing, staffing and control, while adding coordination as the major integrative function. Scores of management texts have in fact since been written, based on this analytical framework, or at least on minor variations to this basic theme. There have been two major analytical variations to this functional approach to categorizing the functions of management. The first, based upon managerial decision making and problem solving, was initiated by the American management scientist, Herbert Simon,[8] in the fifties. It has since been elaborated into a basic methodology which, instead of basing itself upon management functions, rests on a decision making process that involves problem definition, generation of alternative solutions, evaluation of these solutions, and implementation of the chosen one.

This rational decision making approach, as we shall see, has close links with corporate strategy formulation. The second major, and analytical variation, however, is based on the codification of actual managerial work. For whereas Koontz and O'Donnell's 'principles' are an idealized form of rational management, the Canadian Henry Mintzberg[9] has played a leading part in codifying what managers actually do. He concluded that managers divide their time between three kinds of major activity and role: decision making (entrepreneur, disturbance handler, resource allocator and negotiator); informational (monitor, disseminator and spokesman); and interpersonal (figurehead, liaison and leader). So management functions have been analyzed according to idealized principles, rational problem solving activities, and the actual work that managers do. What about organizational functions?

Organizational functions

Many a book has been devoted to the analysis of organizational structures and functions. A seminal work in this area is that of Alfred Chandler,[10] Professor of Economic History at Harvard, who analyzed the structure and functioning of such major American corporations in the fifties, as General Motors and Dupont. His overall conclusion was that structure, in the fully functioning organization, follows strategy. Perhaps the best known taxonomy of organizations, together with their structures and functions, is that developed in the UK by Professor Charles Handy.[11] Handy compares and contrasts four types of organization, based respectively on power (entrepreneurial), role (bureaucratic), task (matrix), and person (individualistic).

Business functions

The third and major form of managerial analysis is that of business functions. Interestingly enough there is very little work, in the management literature, on the functions of business in combination, in contrast to the prolific academic writing on individual business functions, that is operations, marketing, finance and accounting, and human resource management.

The work that there is on the functioning of the business as a whole comes under business policy/strategy/planning. Peter Drucker, in many ways, was the founding father of such business strategy and planning, and his leading successor was Igor Ansoff. It was Ansoff,[12] in the sixties, who charted a highly rational path for what he called 'corporate strategy'. Pursuing a problem-solving approach he likened strategy formulation with, firstly, an assessment of the threats and opportunities facing the company (problem definition); secondly, with the formulation of alternative strategies (generating alternatives); and, thirdly, with the choice and implementation of a strategy (implementating the solution).

Ansoff's highly rational approach, elaborated upon by George Steiner[13] at the University of California, has since been superseded. Michael Porter,[14] at Harvard, whose approach to 'competitive strategy' is a mix of primal and rational, has become more popular in the eighties, because of the aggressively competitive overtones of his approach. Porter, like Kotler[15] at MIT, focusses on industrial competition, taking his key variables to be the bargaining power of suppliers, the threat of new entrants to the industry, the bargaining power of buyers, and the threat of substitute products. Though the tone and flavor of Porter's strategic analysis is very different from Ansoff's, he retains the intellectual thoroughness of the rational approach. So much for the hard branches of rational management, representing the tough-minded analysts of managerial, organizational and business functioning. What, then, of their tender-minded counterparts?

Soft branches

Management style and behavior

Management style

Whereas the managerial 'functionalists' have been primarily concerned with management skills, the behaviorists have been more interested in management 'style'. In 1960, the American social psychologist, Douglas McGregor,[16] introduced the management world to 'theory X', which he associated with autocratic, task-centered behavior, and to 'theory Y', which he linked with a democratic, relationships-centered approach. Bill Reddin,[17] in the UK, took the concept of management style one step further by adding a third dimension to 'production' and 'people', that of managerial effectiveness.

Reddin maintained that a desired style, whether task or relationship centered, depended on the situation at hand. His work, in the late sixties, heralded a new era of so-called contingency. At the same time, and in the early seventies, the subject area of learning style became of great interest to managers.

Learning style

David Kolb,[18] a psychologist at MIT, introduced managers to the learning cycle, and differentiated them according to their learning style, whether concrete or abstract, active or reflective. In Great Britain, Professor Reg Revans[19] compared the scientific method to the process of managerial learning, and introduced the methodology of action learning to managers. Finally, in Britain, Edward De Bono[20] became renowned for his work on lateral thinking for managers, through which he began to wean them away from so-called vertical thinking.

Organizational behavior

'Human relations'

The most prolific application of the behavioral sciences, for the purposes of this text, has been in the area of organizational behavior. Following in the footsteps of Douglas McGregor, Burns and Stalker[21] in Britain compared and contrasted mechanistic (theory 'X') and organic (theory 'Y') approaches not to management style but to human relations in organizations. Prior even to Burns and Stalker's analysis, Chris Argyris,[22] the organizational psychologist at Yale, had focussed his attention on how to integrate the needs of the individual with those of the organization. His hypothesis, in the fifties, was that there was a lack of congruency between the needs of the healthy individual and those of the formal organization. As a direct result, and in the sixties, Rensis Likert,[23] at the University of Michigan, initiated a major research project into the workings of the human organization, in general, and into effective groups, in particular. In such groups, he found for example, all interaction and problem solving takes place in a supportive atmosphere.

Organization development

The work of Mayo and Parker Follett, on the one hand, and of Burns and Stalker, Argyris and Likert, on the other, was picked up in the seventies by students of organization development. They considered that a healthy organization needed to interact 'proactively' with its internal and external environment. Its leading exponent in America was Warren Bennis, and in Britain it has been Charles Handy.

Bennis[24] compared and contrasted bureaucratic and democratic structures and processes in the context of the changing organization. Wereas the former was organized around functional specialization, the latter was structured around problems to be solved. Bennis' ideas, therefore, followed from Parker Follett and her 'law of the situation'. Charles Handy[25] went a step fruther and postulated the development of a dispersed organization created for professionals who seek independence and autonomy, prefer networks to hierarchies, and flexible time contracts to permanent, full-time employment.

Business behavior

Business and society

Whereas management and organizational behavior have come under close scrutiny from the behavioral scientists, business behavior – as opposed to the more hard nosed business functions and strategy – has received much less attention.

Such attention as there is has been given to the role of business in society, in interaction with its so called 'stake holders'. In fact from the sixties onwards, and following a lead set by Peter Drucker, business was conceived of as accountable to customers, employees and even to whole communities, as well as to its shareholders. Jan Dauman and John Hargreaves[26] both of IBM, in one of the more succinct texts on this subject, referred to three levels of corporate response: basic or legal, organizational or accountable, and social or moral. Whereas, in relation – for example – to pollution control, a company may merely pay heed (basic response) to the letter of the law, it may alternatively respond (accountable response) to the spirit of the law, or even decide to become the leading company (moral response) in its industry with respect to environmental concern. Dauman and Hargreaves went on to describe ways in which companies could successfully manage this business – society interface, incorporating techniques of environmental monitoring and of social auditing. Each involved means of measuring and accounting for a company's social performance.

The business behavior field

Whereas several academics took an interest in the interface between business and society, only one attempted to develop a sophisticated concept of such business behavior. Albert Low,[27] a practicing Canadian manager, viewed a business as a set of interacting forces contained within a 'force field'. Influenced by the systems theorists, in the West, and by Zen Buddhist philosophies from the East, Low set business within a field of interacting causes and effects. The separate forces in that behavior field were the employee, the customer, and the shareholder, and the integrative force was the product. The resulting approach Low termed 'management by idea'.

The rational fruits

The most visible fruits of rational management are the functionally based, bureaucratic structures that are symbolic of the conventionally managed organization. In some respects Rank Xerox International, having grown from a pioneering enterprise into a rationally managed institution, was no exception.

What is exceptional about the company, though, is that in recent years it has conceptualized the split between continuity and network personnel. Whereas the former, who are still by far the majority, are contained within the conventional and hierarchical structures, the latter network from outside the organization, basing their activities at home or within small business premises. As professionals they are free to offer their services both within the organization and without.

The rational manager

The wholesome, rational manager combines order with freedom, stability with change. In fact he or she is a manager of change, as is Hilary Cropper, the managing director of F International in the UK.

Individual and organization

Hilary Cropper   Managing Director, F International (UK)

I've been in F International now for less than a year. The organization is very strong. It's a sure foothold from which to leap to other things. I must preserve the strengths, the culture, the motivation of individuals to express their individual worth and to cooperate with others.

In 1988 we will be adding new people to the organization and installing a 'management culture'. We've got to watch the market trends. We have to outmaneuver our competition! We need to keep our eyes and ears open and to tap our native intelligence. That means each individual contribution and innovation matters even more.

Berkhamsted, England 1986

References

1. F. Taylor, *Scientific Management*, Harper & Row (1947).
2. M. Weber, *Economy and Society: An Outline of Interpretive Sociology*, Bedminster Press, (1968).
3. H. Fayol, (trs. J. Coubrough), *Industrial and General Administration*, International Management Institute (1930).
4. M. Parker Follett, *The New State*, Peter Smith, (1929).
5. E. Mayo, *The Human Problems of Industrial Civilisation*, Routledge & Kegan Paul (1949).
6. P. Drucker, *Management*, Pan (1980).
7. H. Koontz and C. O'Donnell, *Principles of Management*, McGraw-Hill (1968).
8. H. Simon, *The New Science of Management Decision*, (revized edn), Prentice Hall (1977).
9. H. Mintzberg, *The Nature of Managerial Work*, Prentice Hall (1973).
10. A. Chandler, *Strategy and Structure*, MIT Press (1962).
11. C. Handy, *Understanding Organisations*, Penguin (1976).
12. I. Ansoff, *Corporate Strategy,* McGraw-Hill (1964).
13. G. Steiner, *Top Management Planning*, Macmillan (1969).
14. M. Porter, *Competitive Strategy*, Macmillan (1984).
15. Kotler *et al.*, *The New Competition*, Prentice Hall (1985).
16. D. McGregor, *The Human Side of Enterprise*, McGraw-Hill (1960).
17. W. Reddin, *Managerial Effectiveness*, McGraw-Hill (1972).
18. D. Kolb, *Organization Psychology: An Experimental Approach*, Prentice Hall (1979).
19. R. Revans, *Action Learning*, Blond Briggs (1980).
20. E. De Bono, *Lateral Thinking for Managers*, McGraw-Hill (1971).
21. T. Burns and G. Stalker, *The Management of Innovation*, Tavistock (1961).
22. C. Argyris, *Integrating the Individual and the Organization*, Wiley (1964).
23. R. Likert, *The Human Organization*, McGraw-Hill (1967).
24. W. Bennis, *The Changing Organization*, McGraw-Hill (1969).
25. C. Handy, *The Gods of Management*, Sovereign (1976).
26. J. Dauman and J. Hargreaves, *Business Survival and Social Change*, Associated Business Press (1975).
27. A. Low, *Zen and Creative Management*, Doubleday (1976).

11 Administrative and behavioral science

Contents

Key Concepts

Once you have fully understood the chapter you should be able to define the following concepts in your own terms:

Efficiency
Group process
Heterogeneity
Individual ethic
Integration
Law of the situation
New psychology

Principles of scientific
management
Rabble hypothesis
Social ethic
Social scientific method
Visible hand

Objectives

Upon completing this chapter you should be able to do the following:

1. Compare and contrast the analytical and primal approaches to management.
2. Outline, in essence, Taylor's approach to 'scientific' management.
3. Place Taylor's approach in its historical context.
4. Outline, in essence, Follett's approach to management, including the role of the group process in organizational life.
5. Locate both Mayo's and Follet's approach in their historical and scientific contexts.

Introduction

The ancient management heritage

The roots of management reach down to the primal hunter–gatherer communities. Management, of this basic kind, is still to be found in trading communities, in the developing world, and in contemporary households around the globe. It also characterizes the newly emerging business enterprise, created by both the animateur and entrepreneur.

The problem, of course, with primal management, is that it is generally implicit rather than explicit, subconscious rather than conscious, felt and acted upon rather than thought out, and based on oral rather than literary traditions. Despite the primacy of its existence, therefore, it fails to become recognized by the conventional, literary based wisdom. Conventional management texts, then, locate the origins of management in other, more 'civilized' quarters. In most cases its origins are drawn from the civil, religious and military administrators of ancient civilizations – chiefly in China, Babylon, Egypt, and Rome.

> The oldest known military treatise is the product of the Chinese general Sun Tzu, around the sixth century BC. He wrote of marshalling the army into subdivisions, or gradations of ranks amongst officers, and of using gongs, flags, and signal fires for communications. In Ancient Mesopotamia, flourishing around 3000 BC, the temples developed an early concept of a corporation, or a group of temples under a common body of management ...
>
> The 'rule of ten' in the span of management is an Ancient Egyptian practice. Excavations also revealed distinct dress for managers and workers ... The Romans had a genius for order, and the military autocracy ran the empire with an iron hand ... the Catholic church leaders, in the early middle ages, perceived the need to specify policies, procedures, doctrine and authority to its minions.[1]

The scientific origins of management

Management, as a rationally based science, has much more recent origins, and it is with these roots that we shall be more concerned here. Because this more recent management heritage is firmly linked with business enterprise it is more accessible to us, today, and provides more digestible food for thought. These more contemporary and scientifically based roots, then, draw from two major sources. The first one, now strongly entrenched within business, taps into the physical sciences, especially engineering in the latter part of the nineteenth century. The second, and the more shallow rooted within business, taps into the social sciences, particularly in the early part of the twentieth century.

In this chapter, therefore, I want to draw on the two traditions, one focussed on the physical sciences and the other on the social. The two key figures that will be represented are both American, one – Frederick Taylor – an industrial engineer at the turn of the century, and the other – Mary Parker Follett – a social philosopher who was most influential during the thirties.

The physical–social balance

Each of these two historical figures were very formidable and – in their time – influential characters. However, the subsequent influence of Taylor has been much greater than that of Follett. The reason for this, at least in Europe and Japan, is that the 'hard' side of rational management has pervaded the entirety of business, whereas the 'soft' and integrative side has either been restricted to the 'personnel' function, or else submerged within a poorly conceptualized 'general management'.

As we shall see, in Chapter 23, this imbalance in the conduct of business, in the Western hemisphere, has been one of the main reasons why Europe and America have lost out to the Japanese in the global market-place. For in Japan management has more successfully blended soft and hard qualities in finance and marketing, as well as in personnel and organization. In the interests of overall balance, I shall give equal historical weight to the social as to the physical roots of rational management.

The 'hunter' and 'gatherer', are now upgraded into the 'hierarch' and the 'networker'. For both, thought and reason take precedence over feeling and instinct. However, whereas the former is particularly good at dividing things – analytical cut and thrust, the latter is especially adept at putting them together – integrative appreciation and coordination. Similarly, whereas the 'hierarch' is oriented towards order and organization, into which the individual must be fitted, the 'networker' is geared towards cohesive interpersonal relationships, around which the organization must be fitted. For the business 'administrator', the organization rationally serves the impersonal individual interests of the employee, the customer, and the shareholder. For the organizational 'facilitator' the organization serves the social needs of a diversity of parties, each with their own particular group interests.

'Super value systems'

The individualistic and the social ethic are like 'super value systems' for management. The individualistic ethic is rooted on liberalism, the Protestant ethic, and the American frontier.

The social ethic has grown as a dominant current in social thought during the twentieth century because of increased human interdependence. Interdependency requires a social philosophy directed towards collaboration and solidarity rather than competition and conflict.

The reference point of the social ethic is the collective nature of man. The social ethic affirms the value of human collaboration and social solidarity. Individual satisfactions are seen to result from participation in a social environment. In contrast the individualistic ethic starts with the person as the ultimate source of individual and social values. The 'atomistic' person, acting intelligently in pursuit of his own self-interest, will eventually contribute the most to the good of the group.

Mitchell and Scott *Organization Theory*[2] 1972

Let me consider, now, the emergence of each tradition in turn. In the seven chapters that follow this one I shall then identify the core and branches of analytical management, both administrative and behavioral, that have developed in more recent times.

The physical–scientific tradition

The visible hand

Before introducing you to the founding father of so-called scientific management, I want – via the eminent business historian, Alfred Chandler – to describe to you the economic and industrial conditions under which Frederick Taylor rose to prominence. The market forces through which primal enterprise emerged in the eighteenth and nineteenth centuries had been benevolently guided, or so it seemed to Adam Smith, by a remarkably 'invisible hand'. Of course, for the rational and scientific mind, such invisibility is anathema. Smith's theory lacked scientific and demonstrable proof. Alfred Chandler the contemporary apostle of the analytically managed organization, has referred to the 'visible hand' that made its appearance, in America, in the late nineteenth century.

The visible hand

... modern business enterprise took the place of market mechanisms in coordinating the activities of the economy and allocating its resources. In many sectors of the economy the visible hand of management replaced what Adam Smith referred to as the invisible hand of market forces. The market remained the generator of demand for goods and services, but modern business enterprise took over the functions of coordinating flows of goods through existing processes of production and distribution, and of allocating funds and personnel for the future. As modern business enterprise acquired functions hitherto carried out by the market, it became the most powerful institution in the American economy and its managers the most influential group of economic decision makers.

Alfred Chandler *The Visible Hand*[3] 1977

The new captains of industry

As large-scale enterprise began to take over from small-scale production and distribution in the latter part of the nineteenth century, the newly qualified engineers were on hand, to take on the mantle as the critical actors in industrialization. Their self-image was one of men who made things work, who avoided any waste of time, capital and labor. They also saw themselves as the mediators in the struggle between capital and labor, and were convinced that the best of their profession, men who combined a scientific with a business orientation, were the ideal captains of industry. As engineers, finally, they were heavily affected by their 'mechanistic' view of people and life.

Daniel McCallum, one of the first such engineers to write on management matters[4] in the mid-nineteenth century, was railroad superintendent of the Erie Line. His mechanistic view of a living organism was indicative of the engineer's approach:

> McCallum developed a formal organization chart. The chart took the form of a tree [see Fig. 20] and depicted the lines of authority and responsibility, the division of labor amongst operating units, and the reporting lines for communication and control.

Fig. 20 Formal organization tree.

The roots of the tree represented the board of directors and the president; the branches were the five operating divisions plus the staff service departments; the leaves were the various local freight and ticket forwarding offices, subordinate offices, and so on. Adherence to formal lines of authority was to be absolute.[5]

The emerging science of management

McCallum reflected the prevailing managerial wisdom of the day. Indeed, because management relied heavily on the engineer's advice, in the new factories and railroads, it is not coincidental that their associations were the first to examine and write about management problems. The American Society of Mechanical Engineers was founded in 1880 and became the first active proponent, in that country, of the search for systematic, scientific management. Of course, in Western Europe, and most particularly in France, this search had begun – admittedly somewhat haphazardly – some 200 years before. In the early part of the twentieth century this scientific work was to culminate, as we shall see in Chapter 13, in the substantive insights of that great Frenchman, Henri Fayol.

The evolution of management science in France

- At the call of a minister of France's Louis XIV, in the second half of the seventeenth century, physicists and engineers made the first experimental researches into 'human work'. A short time afterwards the French Academy of Sciences invited all its scientists to study the activities of the workman in their workshops, with a view to improving their workrate.
- De La Hire (1640–1718) investigated the relationship between the physical strength of the worker and his weight and concluded that sloping boards were the most rational and effective way to elevate heavy loads.
- Amontons (1663–1705) conducted experiments on the comparative work rate of men and horses, and methodically collected data on both, on a daily basis.
- In a book entitled *Architecture Hydraulique* (Paris, 1750), Belidor, a military engineer, studied the problems and opportunities in separating planning from performance, in the course of preparing for a military campaign.
- Dublin, a Professor of Mechanics, noted in 1829 that 'whereas a huge effort toward perfecting machinery had been made, very little had been done towards perfecting workmen'. He therefore initiated a campaign for rational methods of work analysis in industry.

H. A. Hopf *Historical Perspectives in Management*[6] 1949

Scientific management in perspective

Frederick Taylor joined the American Society of Mechanical Engineers in 1880, against this backdrop of early scientific investigation into work and organization. Daniel Wren has put Taylor's scientific management in perspective:

> On the technique side, Taylor's scientific approach sought to analyse existing practices, study them for standardization and improvement, and rationalize resource utilization. On the human side, Taylor sought to attain the highest degree of individual performance improvement, and financial reward, through such visible and determinable measures as fatigue reduction, scientific selection, matching men's abilities to jobs, and incentive schemes.[7]

Efficiency and productivity

The concept of increased productivity became the lodestar of modern work in the late nineteenth century, replacing such concepts as morality, expiation of sin, individual self realization, aesthetic fulfilment, and community wellbeing that, singly or together, defined and guided work in other epoches.

Efficiency, with which Taylor's name is primarily associated, has come to mean that particular 'efficiency' which can be expressed in measurable, quantifiable terms.

Sudhir Kakar *Frederick Taylor*[8] MIT Press 1970

This intention was borne out by a speech Taylor gave to the American Society of Mechanical Engineers, at the turn of the century.

Material increase

I do welcome the opportunity of speaking upon the far broader subject, of which the art of cutting metals and the proper use of machines is but one of the small elements, namely, the great opportunity as well as the duty, which lies before us as engineers of taking such steps as will result in a very material increase of output if every man and every machine in their manufacturing establishments is significantly upgraded.

It gives us the opportunity at this time to give the men what they want most – higher wages, shorter hours, better working conditions; and, on the other hand, to give the companies what they need most – a lower labour cost, so that they may be able more successfully to compete at home and abroad.

Frederick Taylor *On the Art of Cutting Metals*[9] 1908

Principles of scientific management

In a nutshell, then, Taylor's principles of scientific management were directed at increasing productivity, for the benefit of both worker and management, by:

- Breaking the work process into the smallest possible components.
- Fitting jobs into structures that clearly emphasize the duties and boundaries of each job, rather than its part in the total.
- Wherever possible using individual, financial incentives, thereby gearing pay to output.
- Subtracting skill and responsibility from the job to make them functions of management.

Taylor's scientific management principles were derived out of many years of his own meticulous observations of the work process, of the interface between man and machine, and of the interaction between management and worker. His structured observations led him to make two major conclusions about the process of analytical management.

First, the manager's job was to provide planned and authoritative direction, including training, while the worker's responsibility – in his own best interests – was to follow the lead he had been individually given.

Providing managerial direction

The efficient teacher gives a class definite tasks to learn ... In that respect, all of us are grown up children, and it is equally true that the average workman will work with the greatest satisfaction, both to himself and to his employer, when he is given each day a definite task which he is to perform in a given time.

This also furnishes the workman with a clearcut standard, by which he can throughout the day measure his own progress, and the accomplishment of which affords him the greatest satisfaction.

Frederick Taylor *Principles of Scientific Management*[10] 1911

Secondly, Taylor concluded, individual responsibilities and relationships were much more productive than group ones. It is in that respect that he set himself clearly apart from those social scientists who were to follow him in their own different approach to analytical management.

'Rabble hypothesis'

A careful analysis has demonstrated the fact that when workmen are herded together in gangs, each man becomes far less efficient than when his personal ambition is stimulated, that when they work in gangs their individual efficiency falls almost invariably down to or below the level of the worst men in the gang; and that they are all pulled down instead of being elevated by being herded together.

Frederick Taylor *Principles of Scientific Management*[11] 1911

Scientific management: administrative and behavioral science

In fact it is in direct reaction to this so called 'rabble hypothesis', of Frederick Taylor's that Elton Mayo, the first and most prominent of the emerging behavioral scientists, nailed his colors to the new behavioral mast. We shall see what he had to say very shortly.

Before we move on to that other, social side of the analytical manager's coin, though, we need to make some concluding comments – on the 'scientific manager's' behalf. We have deliberately focussed on Frederick Taylor, at this point, because he has presented the hard side of 'scientific' management in its purest form. As you shall see when we come to consider Henri Fayol, in Chapter 13, and more particularly Drucker, in Chapter 12, there is a greater breadth to the hard, analytical argument than has been so far indicated. At this stage the argument has been deliberately sharpened to provide clarity of focus. In fact, when we investigate Mary Parker Follet's approach, you will find yourself considering an extreme end of the behavioral position. The reasons for doing this are again the same, to sharpen, this time, the 'soft' analytical focus. However, before being immediately exposing Follet's position, you need to provide something of a social context.

The behavioral–scientific tradition

The call for a New Deal

Within its organizational and cultural context, 'scientific' management, at the turn of the century, found its basis – as the gospel of efficiency – in the economic necessities of running a large-scale business. It also secured social sanction through the belief in free and unfettered enterprise, and political sanction, in Europe and America, through the widespread concern for national productivity in a competitive market-place. The 1930s era of 'social man' was an age, on the other hand, in which individual hopes had become dashed on the reefs of economic misfortune, and during which political beliefs were undergoing dramatic shifts. While in Europe the new socialist parties were being formed, or consolidated, in America a 'New Deal' was soon to announce itself. The trigger for it was, of course, the Great Depression.

Psychological depression – the Great Crash

The Great Crash of 1929 found the winter of its discontent in earlier days. The 1920s saw a wave of business consolidations. American productive capacity began to outrun its ability to consume. A scramble for size to gain efficiencies of scale led to more consolidations.

The public wanted a piece of this dynamic growth. An orgy of speculation led to Black Friday, 24 October, 1929. On that day the stock market fell 40 points, and wiped out $30 billion worth of inflated stock values. By 1933, 30% of the nation's workers were without jobs. Gone were the optimism of prosperity and promise; the old guideposts had apparently failed as 'rags to riches' became the midnight pumpkin. Perhaps it was not the economic depression but the psychological one which left the lasting imprint on our forefathers.

Daniel Wren *The Evolution of Management Thought*[12] 1979

In 1933 the Harvard professor and social psychologist, Elton Mayo, published a book appropriately entitled *The Human Problems of an Industrial Civilisation*.[13] In it he vehemently rejected Taylor's 'rabble hypothesis' (see p. 197). Rather, he lamented the passing of that form of social solidarity that characterized traditional societies.

The factory system and the process of industrialization, he said, had destroyed this community feeling through its widespread division of labor. Increased social and physical mobility and the growth of organizations had led towards ever increased impersonality. The result was growing rootlessness and loss of identity, and of increasing social discontinuity. In essence, social invention to keep up with industrial changes had not kept up with the technical inventions.

The emergence of the social sciences

Mayo's solution, that is his social invention, was not to abandon a scientific approach to management, but to turn it in a new direction. In fact, Mayo had himself drawn on a scientific tradition, not rooted in physical science or engineering, but in the emerging discipline of 'sociology'. There were three giants of sociological theory, emerging in Europe during the latter part of the nineteenth century. Max Weber, of whom we shall hear more in Chapter 15, was German; Emile Durkheim French, and Vilfred Pareto Italian.

Durkheim divided society into two primary types, 'mechanical' and 'organic'. This typology was destined to recur at regular intervals in the evolution of management thought. Durkheim identified Adam Smith's approach, which drew on abstract market mechanisms, as mechanistic. His own approach, as a sociologist – who substituted the group for the individual as a source of values – was organic. Mayo took on where Durkheim left off, always adopting a thoroughly scientific approach to his work. In fact his best known, and epoch making Hawthorne experiments, previously alluded to in Chapter 5, were set up in a thoroughly scientific manner. In that methodological context Mayo quotes, with obvious approval, a medical scientist of his immediate acquaintance.

Social scientific method

In the complex business of living, as in medicine, both theory and practice are necessary conditions of understanding. First is needed, persistent, intelligent, responsible, unremitting labour in the sick room, not in the library.

Second is required accurate observation of things and events, guided by judgement borne of familiarity and experience of the salient and recurrent phenomena, and their classification and methodical exploitation.

Third, is needed the construction of a theory, not a philosophical theory, but a useful walking stick to help on the way.

All this may be summed up in this way. A physician (or a social scientist) must have, first, intimate, habitual, intuitive familiarity with things; secondly, systematic knowledge of things; and thirdly, an effective way of thinking about things.

Lawrence Henderson *Fatigue of Workers*[14] 1941

As a result of his systematic research at the Western Electric relay room (the Hawthorne experiments) Mayo concluded that the group rather than the individual was the fundamental building block of organizational life. 'Management in any continuously successful plant', Mayo affirmed, 'is not related to single workers, but always to working groups.'[15]

The 'new administrator', that Mayo subsequently sought out, would be able to restore opportunities for human collaboration in work and in life, by recognizing and then fulfilling people's need for social solidarity. Unlike the 'primal animateur', however, such a contemporary 'facilitator' would be trained for his or her role – particularly in listening and counselling skills – and, in their own managerial turn, would act as a skilled social scientist. For all his pioneering insight, however, Mayo was not the person to fully develop the role and operating context of this new, group oriented administrator. That was left to his colleague at Harvard, Mary Parker Follett, one of the very few women to make their historical mark on management theory.

The new psychology

Mary Parker Follett, who rose to pre-eminence in America in the twenties and thirties, started out in life as a political scientist. As a democrat, in the truest sense, she wanted to bring a 'new psychology of individuality in community' into public awareness. Given the breadth and the depth of her perspective, Follett will reappear in this book in the context of developmental and metaphysical management. As a business and management analyst, Follett – like Elton Mayo – focussed on the power of the group. Her analysis is much more far-reaching than Mayo's. In fact it is so penetrating, and indeed radical for the time, that it has been substantially lost, even by management posterity to this day.

The new psychology

By the 'new psychology' I mean partly that group psychology which is receiving more attention and gaining more influence every day, and partly I mean simply that feeling out for a new conception of modes of association which we do see in law, economics, ethics, politics, and indeed in every department of thought. It is a short way of saying that we are now looking at things not as entities but in relation.

Mary Parker Follett *The New State*[16] 1929

Immediately we can see the broad sweep of Follett's analysis, and synthesis. She is combining psychological, social and political insight all into one, grand synthesis. She is playing the role of a 'gatherer', but from a conscious and analytical rather than from a subconscious and instinctive perspective. She also extends her reference point, with no great difficulty, from a social to a commercial context:

> The business world is never again to be directed by individual intelligences, but by intelligences interacting and ceaselessly influencing one another. Every mental act of the big businessman is entirely different from the mental acts of the man of his predecessors, continuing to manage their own competitive businesses. There is of course competition between our large firms, but the cooperation between them is coming to occupy a larger and larger relative place.[17]

These might appear to be, especially in the twenties, words of a romantic idealist. However, what is noteworthy is the real influence Parker Follett had on practicing businessmen and community leaders of her day. She had a particular affinity, in fact, with a group of business leaders and management consultants in Great Britain, of whom Seebohm Rowntree, a captain of industry, and Lyndall Urwick, a leading business consultant, were the most prominent. Her analysis was certainly a compelling one, coming, as it did, in the trouble-torn years between the wars, and just before the Great Depression. As always, she combined economics and politics with psychology and sociology.

Group life

Our political life is stagnating, capital and labour are virtually at war, the nations of Europe are at each other's throats – because we have not yet learnt to live together. The twentieth century must find a new principle of association. Crowd philosophy, crowd patriotism, crowd government must go. The herd is no longer sufficient to enfold us. Group organization is to be the new method in politics, the basis of our future industrial system, the foundation of international order. Group organization will create the new world we are blindly feeling after, for creative force comes from the group, creative power is evolved through the activity of group life.

Mary Parker Follett *The New State*[18] 1929

The great American psychologist William James was a contemporary of Parker Follett's. While he maintained that man is a complex of 'many selves in one', she saw society as a complex of groups, all of which together made up a social whole. Within the group process was contained the secret of collective life, the key to democracy, the master lesson for every individual to learn, and the chief hope for the political, social and international life of the future. What, more specifically then, is this extraordinary group process, in which Mary Parker Follett had so much faith?

The group process

The key to unlock Follett's group process is the human craving for totality, or for wholeness. Democracy, for her, is not a spreading out and an extension of suffrage. That is merely its external aspect. It is rather a drawing together. 'It is the imperative call for the lacking part of the self'. Democracy is the finding, then, of the one will to which the will of every single man and woman must contribute. 'We have an instinct for democracy because we have an instinct for wholeness'.

The human being, then, craves totality. This craving is in fact the motor of social progress. The process of getting and growing is not one of adding more and more to ourselves, but one of offering more and more of ourselves. For Parker Follett, contribution, not appropriation, is the law of growth. What our special contribution is, as an individual, is for us each to discover. The definition of individuality must therefore be, finding one's place on the whole. 'One's place' gives you the individual; 'the whole' gives you the society. The connecting agency is the small, adaptable group. If I fail to make my individual contribution to the group, the whole of society suffers.

In the twenties, Parker Follett wrote, 'the individual is being submerged, smothered, choked by the crowd fallacy, the herd theory. Free him from these, release his energies, and he will work out, together with all other free men and women, quick, flexible, constantly changing group forms, which shall respond sensitively to every need'.

Creativity in unity

Imitation is for the shirkers, like mindedness for the comfort lovers, unifying for the creators ... The unifying now demanded of us is that which is brought about by the enlargement of each by the inflowing of every other. Then I go forth a new creature.

But to where do I go forth? Always to a new group, to a new 'society'. There is no end to the process. A new being springs forth from every fresh contact. My nature opens up to a thousand influences. I feel continuous new births.

Mary Parker Follett *The New State*[19] 1929

Integration not compromise

What Parker Follett had to say had very direct implications, not only at a philosophical level, but also at a practical business level. In fact the whole of 'industrial relations', as conventionally practiced, cut completely across her convictions, and her understanding of constructive human behavior.

As far as Follett is concerned, whoever advocates compromise – which is the stuff of everyday negotiations – abandons the individual. The individual has to give up part of himself in order that some action might take place. The integrity of the individual can only be preserved through integration. If you believe in compromise you see the individual as static. So what is integration? Integration is a qualitative adjustment whereas compromise is a quantitative one. In the first case there is a change in the ideas and their action tendencies; in the second there is mere barter of opposed 'rights of way'. In a compromise situation the underlying conflict continues.

Compromise, then, is on the same plane as fighting. Integration, on the other hand, involves, first, the discovery of difference, and, second, the unifying of apparent opposites. After all, we attain unity only through variety. Differences must be integrated rather than annihilated or absorbed. Every difference that is swept up into a bigger conception feeds and enriches society; every difference which is ignored feeds on society – or on a business – and eventually corrupts it. Heterogeneity, not homogeneity, makes for unity. The higher the degree of business or social organization, the more it is based on a wide variety across its members.

Friendship and sympathy

The deep and lasting friendship is one capable of recognizing and dealing with all the fundamental differences that must exist between any two individuals, one capable therefore of such an enrichment of our personalities that together we shall mount to new heights of understanding and endeavor. Pleasant little glows of feeling can never be fanned into the fire which becomes the driving force of progress.

Sympathy is a whole feeling; it is a recognition of oneness. Suppose six manufacturers meet to discuss some form of union. What these men need most is not altruistic feelings, but a consciousness of themselves as a new unit, and a realization of the needs of that unit. True sympathy, therefore, is not a vague sentiment they bring with them. It springs from their very meeting, to become, in its turn, a vital factor in the meeting.

Mary Parker Follett *The Creative Experience*[20] 1926

The law of the situation

Amongst all this wealth of group analysis and integration, only a very small amount has been picked up and assimilated by management posterity. I find this extraordinary, especially given Parker Follett's powers of communication during her lifetime, which Lyndall Urwick[21] considered to be exceptional. She was apparently able to communicate easily with businessman and politician, psychologist and community worker alike. Follett evidently practiced what she preached.

In fact when I began my career as a management educator, I can clearly remember my senior colleagues mentioning Follett in passing, with an intriguing mixture of superficiality and awe. The one crucial aspect of her thinking which was picked up by Drucker (see p. 209), and is documented by Wren, is her 'law of the situation'.

The law of the situation

In all forms of life, from interpersonal relations to the handling of interpersonal disputes, 'power over' has to be reduced, and obedience has to be shifted to the law of the situation. The basis for such integration is what Parker Follett called a 'circular response'.

By this she meant a process based on the opportunity for each party to influence the other, and through open interaction, over a period of time, 'power with' could be obtained.

For labour and management it would come through an open disclosure of costs, prices and market situations. In international diplomacy it would involve open disclosure, rather than a withholding of the facts.

Parker Follett thought that 'final authority' was in fact an illusion, based on a false premise of power; authority accrued in the situation, not in the person or his position. Responsibility was inherent in the job or function, and was cumulative in the sense that it entailed a seam of responsibilities in a system of cross relationships.

Daniel Wren *The Evolution of Management Thought*[22] 1979

Peter Drucker, as we shall see, and Daniel Wren, as we have seen, have distilled out one, and only one of the essences of Follett's penetrating analysis, and that is 'the law of the situation'. For Drucker it accorded very well with his own position, which is that task (analytically derived) rather than personality (primally projected) should rule the management roost.

Conclusion

The two-way stretch

In tapping the roots of rational management, I have been necessarily selective. For the entirety of the acknowledged management tradition lies within this rational realm. Management historians, like Daniel Wren, have devoted entire books to the subject, whereas I have restricted myself to a chapter. I shall, however, continue to draw on historical threads, particularly when covering some of the branches of analytical management

At the same time I have purposefully attempted to cover the two, purest extremes of analytical management. All to often, in management texts, a cluster of historical streams are presented, with inadequate reference to their very fundamental differences. On the one hand, for example, Frederick Taylor is portrayed as much more of a humanist than one might have imagined; on the other hand, Mary Parker Follett's seminal work is by-passed or substantially watered down. Equally undesirable is the tendency to stereotype management thinkers according to one's ideological preferences. In my view both Taylor, and the other 'hard' analysts (like Fayol and Chandler), and Follett, and the other 'soft' analysts (like Mayo and Barnard), have had vital roles to play in the evolution of management thought and practice.

Where I agree, absolutely, with Parker Follett, is that if we try to hide the real differences, or select one side rather than another for ideological reasons, we will make poor theorists and bad practitioners. In fact, I would argue that the recurring, and usually sterile debate over generalist versus specialist management, within business schools and without, is plagued by a lack of clear differences, and comparative clarity in that respect.

We management educators are usually unwilling, or unable to provide the generalist with the kind of integrative framework he needs, and that Parker Follett has developed. As a result we have nothing that genuinely contrasts with the more narrowly based, but more penetratingly analytical frameworks used by the specialist. In the same way, if we put the primal operators on a pedestal as Peters and Waterman have done, or alternatively the analytical managers – as we shall see with Drucker, both will inevitably fall off. One without the other, like the soft qualities without the hard, will lose its balance.

The rational way forward

Let me now introduce you to Drucker, who has had such an all-pervasive influence on rational management, and has achieved as unique a balance between the hard and soft approaches as anyone.

After we have had a chance to digest Drucker's analytical core, I shall then move on to the vital management branches, starting off with Fayol and his 'management skills'. We shall also be drawing on Fayol, when considering planning and 'strategy'. In finally moving over to a third 'structural' branch I shall have the opportunity of introducing you to Weber, who has so far only received a passing mention.

References

1. D. Wren, *The Evolution of Management Thought*, Wiley (1979), pp. 21–5.
2. T. R. Mitchell and W. G. Scott, *Organization Theory*, Irwin Dorsey (1972), pp. 18–19.
3. A. Chandler, *The Visible Hand*, Belknap Press (1977), p. 1.
4. D. McCallum, 'Superintendent's report', 25 March 1856, in Annual Report for the New York & Erie Railroad Co. (1855).
5. D. Wren, *op. cit.,* p. 96.
6. H. A. Hopf, *Historical Perspectives in Management*, Hopf Institute of Management (1949), p. 11.
7. D. Wren, *op. cit.,* p. 157.
8. S. Kakar, *Frederick Taylor: A study in Personality and Innovation*, MIT Press (1970), p. 19.
9. F. Taylor, *On the Art of Cutting Metals*, Speech to ASME (1908).
10. F. Taylor, *Principles of Scientific Management*, p. 39 Harper Bros. (1911), p. 39.
11. F. Taylor, *op. cit.,* p. 73.
12. D. Wren, *op. cit.,* p. 412.
13. E. Mayo, *The Human Problems of an Industrial Civilisation*, Routledge & Kegan Paul (1949), p. 18.
14. L. Henderson, *Fatigue of Workers*, Reinhold Publishing (1941) pp. 12–13.
15. E. Mayo, *op. cit.,* p. 32.
16. M. Parker Follett, *The New State*, Longman & Green (1929), p. 3.
17. M. Parker Follett, *op. cit.,* p. 112.
18. M. Parker Follett, *op. cit.,* p. 3.
19. M. Parker Follett, *op. cit.*
20. M. Parker Follett, *The Creative Experience*, Peter Smith (1926), p. 41.
21. L. Urwick (ed.), *Dynamic Administration*, Pitman (1941).
22. D. Wren, *op. cit.,* p. 330 (1979).

12 Managing for results

Contents

Key concepts

Once you have fully understood the chapter you should be able to define the following concepts in your own words:

Accountable enterprise	Business purpose
Budgetary control	Communication
Business ethics	Control
Business foundations	Controls

Entrepreneurial foundations	Objectives: nature
Federal decentralization	Objectives: scope
Formal organizational specs	Organizing
Functional structure	Self-control
Innovative organization	Strategic planning
Integrity in management	Systems structure
Management by objectives	Team structure
Motivation	Top management functions

Objectives

Upon completing this chapter you should be able to do the following:

1. Compare and contrast the respective 'cores' of the primal and analytical approaches to management.
2. Outline, in essence, Drucker's analysis of the individual manager, including his required skills and character.
3. Describe Drucker's approach to business and management, including the business' foundations, the nature and scope of objectives, and strategic planning.
4. Analyze Drucker's approach to managerial organization, including the five operational designs specified, and his assessment of innovative organizations and top management.
5. Assess your own personal response to analytical management, including its impact on yourself as a potential manager.

Introduction

Managerial background

Peter Drucker, if not the founding father of analytical management, is certainly its best-known advocate. Indeed he has done more than anyone else, before or after him, to bring together the diverse strands of analytically based management. Drucker was born in Austria, at the turn of the century, and spent his early, and formative years in that country. At the time Austria was in a state of intellectual ferment. The great political economist, Joseph Schumpeter, and the clinical and social psychologists, Sigmund Freud and Rudolph Steiner, were in Vienna at the time. In those fertile central European conditions, Drucker acquired his profound analytical aptitude, first as an economist, and subsequently as a management theorist. Moreover, having emigrated to the United States of America, in order to escape from the Nazis, he began to soak in the all-pervasive spirit of American free enterprise.

In the thirty-year period, from the 1950s to the 1980s, Drucker became the undisputed management guru in America, if not around the world, at least as far as the practicing manager was concerned. It is only in the last few years, as what I have termed 'primal' management has begun to reassert itself, that Drucker has taken somewhat more of a backseat. Ironically, and unlike Peters and Waterman, Peter Drucker has always retained something of a European, and analytical aloofness from primal American values. In that sense he has drawn on his predecessors, Fayol and Weber, and carried the European scientific tradition into the USA. In combining a Northern scientific outlook with a Western spirit of enterprise Drucker, as a prolific management writer and consultant, has done more than anyone also to establish analytical management within business enterprise.

Management in context

As far as Drucker is concerned, 'management' is probably the most important innovation of this century. For, at this stage of society's development, most significant tasks – be they commercial, political, educational, medical or cultural – have to be performed in and through organizations. Moreover, each such organization is entrusted to 'managers' who practice 'management'. Of course most large organizations start off as small enterprises. At that small stage they hardly require management. But soon enough, as the enterprise grows quantitatively, it will require a new 'quality', and that is management. Such management is required once a degree of organizational complexity has been reached, whereby a variety of tasks have to be performed in cooperation, synchronization, and communication.

Management perspectives

Unlike any other management theorist, Drucker has applied sufficient breadth of analysis to cover, equally well in each case, the three fundamental management perspectives. These consist of the manager as an individual, the business in which he is engaged, and the organization that he runs. (See Fig. 21.)

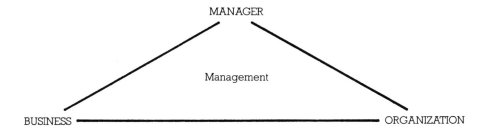

Fig. 21 Management perspectives.

I shall now deal with each perspective in turn, drawing out the essence of Drucker's core contribution. Having done so, I can then investigate with you the analytical branches which have since emerged. Specifically, in fact, they fall under the hard (left-hand side) and soft (right-hand side) categories outlined in Fig. 22.

The individual manager

What a manager does can be analysed systematically. What a manager has to be able to do

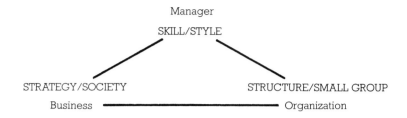

Fig. 22 Analytical branches.

can be learned. But there is one qualification that the manager cannot acquire but must bring to the task. It is not genius: it is character.[1]

Peter Drucker has been broad enough in his analytical approach to cover both the harder – administrative, and the softer – behavioral aspects of management. He also has insight enough to recognize that analytical skills, divorced from integrity of character, will be of limited use and application. I shall start by considering 'skills', and then move on to management 'style' and character.

Management skills

Management skills comprise that part of the individual manager's job that can be systematically analyzed, and, according to Drucker, can be formally learnt, that is 'by anyone with normal intelligence'. Management, for him and his analytical predecessors and successors, is definitely not just a matter of hunch, experience and native ability. It involves four definable skills – objective setting, organizing, motivating and communicating, and measuring – which I shall now consider in turn. The fifth skill, that of developing people, is of a different order, and I shall therefore link it with management style.

Planning and objective setting

The first definable skill, as far as the individual manager is concerned, is that of management by objectives coupled with the exercise of self-control. A manager, in the first place, sets objectives. He determines what the objectives should be. He determines what the goal in each area of objective should be. He decides what has to be done to reach these objectives. He makes the objectives effective by communicating them to the people whose performance is needed to attain them.

Each manager, from the chief executive down to the production foreman or sales supervisor, needs clearly spelled out objectives. Otherwise Drucker guarantees confusion. These objectives should lay out what performance each managerial unit is supposed to achieve. They should also lay out what contribution a manager and his unit are expected make to help other units achieve their objectives, as well as vice versa. In other words, right from the start the emphasis should be on teamwork and on team performance. However, even if management by objectives (MBO) were not necessary to give the enterprise the unity of effort and direction of a management team, it would be necessary to make possible management by self-control. In other words, the greatest advantage of MBO is that it makes it possible for managers to control their own performance. The goals they set themselves, moreover, must be circumscribed by the contribution they have to make to the larger whole of which they are part.

MBO and self-control thus makes the interest of the enterprise the aim of every manager. It substitutes for control from outside the stricter, more exacting and more effective control from inside. It motivates managers to action, not because somebody tells them to do something, but because the objective task demands it. They act not because somebody wants them to but because they themselves decide they have to. They act, in effect, as free men and women. What Drucker has done, in fact, is to combine the separate strands, originally woven by Henri Fayol, on the one hand, and by Mary Parker Follett, on the other. Whereas Fayol focussed on organizational goals – hence 'management by objectives', Follett emphasized individual self-determination – hence 'self-control'.

The second of Drucker's management skills, in logical order, is that of organization.

Organizing

The skill of organizing involves an ability to analyze, to design, to describe, to authorize, and to relate the manager's job, up and down the line, efficiently and effectively.

Analyzing the job thoroughly

Whereas a manager must start by setting objectives – whether in the context of physical operations, financial or sales targets, or personnel programmes – he needs, thereafter, to organize himself and others. He must analyze the activities, decisions, and relationships which need to be followed through. He needs to classify his work, dividing it into manageable activities. He then must group such activities into an organization structure. Thereafter, he selects people for the management of these activities and for the jobs to be done. The activities that have to be performed and the contributions that have to be made to attain the company's objectives should always determine what managerial jobs are needed. Since a manager is someone who takes responsibility for, and contributes to, the final results of the enterprise, the job should always embody the maximum challenge, carry the maximum responsibility, and make the maximum contribution.

Designing the job appropriately

The three most common mistakes that impair the effectiveness of managerial organization, and their corresponding remedies, are:

- The 'too small' job, designed so small that the manager cannot grow.
- Managerial jobs should therefore be designed to allow a person to grow, to learn, and to develop for many years to come. All managerial jobs should be designed to provide satisfaction through performance.
- The 'non-job', that is the typical 'assistant to'.

A manager must have specific objectives and a specified purpose and function. A manager must be able to make a contribution that can be identified. He must be accountable.

As a rule a manager should be both a manager and an individual career professional. In other words, he should have responsibility for a specific function or job of his own.

Describing the job broadly

The position guide and job description are, so to speak, the mission statement of a managerial job. They correspond to the definition of 'what is our business and what should it be' for the enterprise as a whole. The assignments are the objectives and goals. They need, therefore, a deadline, a clear statement of who is accountable and a built-in measurement by feedback from results. It is the mark of a performing manager that these assignments always exceed the scope of the job as outlined in the job description. A job description usually represents what has already been done; what needs to be done to make the future always exceeds and goes beyond what has been done in the past.

Allocating sufficient authority on the job

Top management decides what activities and tasks the enterprise requires. The analysis begins with the desired end product: the objectives of business performance and business results. From these the analysis determines step by step what work has to be performed. But in organizing the manager's job we have to work from the bottom up. We have to begin with the activities on the 'firing line' – the jobs responsible for the actual output of goods and services, for the final sale to the customer, for the production of blueprints and engineering drawings.

The managers on the firing line have the basic management jobs – the ones on whose performance everything else ultimately rests. Seen this way, the jobs of higher management are aimed at helping the firing line managers do their job. Viewed structurally and organically, it is the firing line managers in whom all authority and responsibility center; only what they cannot do themselves passes up to higher management.

Providing formal and informal job relationships

The manager's relationships to superiors and subordinates are two-way ones. Both are formal and informal relationships of authority as well as of information. Both are relationships of mutual dependence. The vision of a manager should always be upwards, to his superiors, and towards the enterprise as a whole. Objectives should always focus upwards, contributing to the success of the whole enterprise. But the manager's responsibility runs downwards as well, to his team. In other words the manager has specific responsibilities to his subordinates. He has first to make sure that they know and understand what is demanded of them. He has to help them set their own objectives. Then he has to help them to reach those objectives. He is responsible for helping them get the tools, the staff and the information they need.

Organizing the job as a whole

In the final analysis, Drucker tells us, a manager's job should always be based on a necessary task. It should be a real job that makes a visible contribution to the objectives of the entire enterprise. It should have the broadest scope and responsibility possible. Finally, managers should be directed and controlled by the objectives of performance rather than by their superior.

Motivating and communicating

Having set objectives, and organized for their accomplishment, the manager then has the integrative task of motivating, and communicating with, the people below and around him.

Work and motivation

The basic fact – unpleasant but escapable – is that the traditional approach to managing, the 'carrot-and-stick' no longer works. Save in exceptional cases, the big stick, the horrible fear of hunger and starvation that drove workers yesterday, is no longer available to workers in developed countries. Similarly, the rising level of material expectations makes the carrot of material rewards, for Drucker, less and less effective.

Traditional approaches to managing assume the existence of a 'master'. But in a society of organizations there are no masters. The manager is a superior, but he is also a fellow employee, a fellow servant of the company. Managers must therefore accept that it is their job not to control others, but to make work and worker achieve, so as to attain efficient and effective performance. The focus must be on the job, rather than on the person. If the job itself is not achieving, nothing else will provide achievement.

To enable workers to achieve, they must be able to take responsibility for their jobs. This requires productive work, feedback information, and continuous learning. Productive work is dependent on the proper tools for working, and on an appropriate work structure. Responsible work requires self-control. That in turn requires continuous information on performance against standards. Information is the worker's tool for measuring and directing himself. It is also a source of ongoing learning.

Managerial communications

There are, for Drucker, four fundamental attributes of communications. One is information; the others are perception, expectation, and intention. Communication, in management, has become of central concern. Integration of people and activity cannot take place without it. I shall therefore consider each aspect of communication in turn.

Communication is perception. There is no sound unless someone receives it. Unless there is someone who hears there is no communication. Thus the communicator cannot communicate. He can only make it possible for someone else to perceive. In other words, one can only communicate in the recipient's language or terms. Moreover, these terms have to be experience-based.

Communication is expectation. As a rule people perceive what they expect to perceive. The unexpected is therefore usually ignored or misunderstood. The human being, Drucker tells us, vigorously resists any attempt to make it 'change its mind', that is to perceive what it did not expect. As a result, in management, before we can communicate we must know what the recipient expects to see and hear.

Communication makes demands. Communication is always 'propaganda'. The sender always wants to get something across. In other words, communication inevitably makes demands on the recipient, to become somebody, to do or believe something. It always appeals to motivation. If a communication fits in with the aspirations, values and purposes of the other person, it is powerful. If it goes against them, it is unlikely to be received at all.

Communication and information are different. Communication is perception; information is logic. Whereas information is impersonal, communication is interpersonal. Information is valid and reliable when freed of emotions and perceptions. Communication is inappropriate and ineffective if it ignores the other person's subjective beliefs and values. In other words, the efficient dissemination of information is dependent upon the pre-establishment of communication.

As a result of these communication attributes communication downwards is bound to fail. All one can communicate downwards are commands. One cannot communicate anything downwards connected with information, let alone with motivation. This requires communication upwards from those who perceive to those who want to reach their perception. Management by objectives is thus a prerequisite for functioning communication. It requires the subordination to think through and present to the superior his own conclusions as to what major contribution to the organization he should be expected to make. What the subordinate comes up with is rarely what the superior expects. Indeed the first aim of the exercise is to bring out the divergence in expectations, with a view to then working out a means of reconciliation. In the final analysis, communication requires shared experience.

Measuring and controlling

Drucker pays a great deal of attention to 'measurement and control', as a vital part of the manager's toolkit. He divides this area of skill into three distinct parts: controls specifically, control in general, and the distinctive process of budgeting.

Drucker begins by comparing and contrasting 'controls' with 'control'.

If we deal with a human being in a social institution, he argues, controls must become personal motivation that leads to control. A translation is required before the information yielded by the controls can become grounds for action – the translation of one kind of information into another, which Drucker calls 'perception'.

In other words, in the task of management 'controls' are merely a means to an end. The end is 'control'. Controls deal with facts, that is events of the past. Control deals with expectations, that is, with the future. Controls are analytical, concerned with what was and is. Control is normative of and concerned with what ought to be. Both control and controls need to be mediated through perception.

Controls

There are three major characteristics of controls in business:

1. Controls can be neither objective or neutral. Controls in a business situation acquire value by the fact that they are singled out for attention. This means that the basic question is not 'How do we control?' but 'What do we measure in our control system?'
2. Controls need to focus on results. Everything inside a business, including its operational, its marketing, its finance and personnel functions, only create costs. Results are entrepreneurial, and exist only on the outside, in the economy, in society and with the customer. If modern controls are to make a contribution it would be, above all, here.
3. Controls are needed for measurable and non-measurable events. The measurable

events are things that happened. There are no facts about the future. Measurable events are primarily inside events rather than outside ones. The things which determine that the buggy whip industry disappeared and that IBM became a big business cannot be measured. Maintaining a balance between the measurable and the unmeasurable is therefore a matter of continuing managerial judgement.

To give the manager control, controls must satisfy seven specifications:

- Controls must be economical. The less effort needed to gain control, the better the control design. The fewer controls needed, the more effective they will be.
- Controls must be meaningful. They should, in other words, be based on a company's definition of what its business is, what it will be, and what it should be. Controls should always be related to key objectives, and to the priorities within them.
- Controls must be appropriate to the character and nature of the phenomenon being measured. For example, absolute sales levels not related to product mix and to the relative profitability of each product, gives no control whatsoever.
- Controls must be congruent with the event measured. A measurement does not become more accurate, for example, by being worked out to the sixth decimal, when the phenomenon is only capable of being verified within a range of 50 per cent.
- Controls must be timely. Frequent measurements and rapid reporting back do not necessarily give better control. For example, the attempt to measure the progress of research at frequent intervals can only be misleading.
- Controls must be simple. Complicated controls do not work. They confuse. They misdirect attention away from what is being controlled, and towards the mechanics of control.
- Controls, finally, must be operational. They must be focussed on action. Action rather than information is their purpose. Therefore controls must always reach the person who is capable of taking the resulting action.

Control

In the final analysis, controls are only a means. The end is control.

A social institution, like a business enterprise, is comprised of persons, each with his purpose, ambitions, ideas and needs. A system of controls which is not in conformity with this ultimate control of the organization – which lies in its people's decisions – will be at best ineffectual. At worst it will cause neverending conflict and will push the organization out of control.

Budgetary control

Next to double-entry book keeping and the copying machine, Drucker tells us, budgets are the most commonly used management tools. For the budget is the best tool for ensuring that key resources, especially the performance of people, are assigned to priorities and results. The starting point for the budgeting process, especially in a business, should always be expected results. Only when the expected results have been thought through carefully, should one ask, 'what efforts does this require?'.

Budgets are expressed in monetary terms. But monetary terms should be seen as symbolic expression – a kind of shorthand – for the actual efforts needed. They should ultimately be based on 'real values', that is for example, on raw material needed, on work required, on manufacturing capacity warranted. Budgets, in other words, should always be used as a tool to think through the desired relationship between desired results and the available means. If they are looked at simply as a statement of cost, they soon cease to be the manager's tool for planning and control. Instead they may degenerate into a straight-jacket that controls the manager and inhibits the correct action. The budget cuts across the entire organization, whether a whole company, a division, or a department. It presents, for each time period, a portrayal – or at least at X-ray – of the entire organiza-tion, and indicates where control is needed.

Businesses typically look upon the budget as an early warning system for danger and lack of performance, and this is an important function. But performance against budget should also be seen as an early warning system for opportunities, that is, for performance that is better than expected. Finally, in addition to being the manager's planning tool, budgeting is also one of the most effective tools for communication and integration. Budgeting always tries to present a picture of each part of the business. But it should also show how each part relates to the whole. The budget for the whole business, therefore, is a sum of all the parts. Property used, the budgeting process should therefore induce effective upwards and sideways communications.

Management skills as a whole

Setting objectives, organizing, motivating and communicating, and measuring are formal, classifying categories. Only a manager's experience, Drucker argues, can bring them to life, and make them concrete and meaningful. But because they are formal, they apply to every manager and to everything he does as a manager. This is the essence of Drucker's analytical approach. The categories can thus be used by all managers to appraise their own skill and performance and to work systematically in improving themselves and their performance.

Every one of these categories can be divided into sub-categories. Moreover, each one requires different qualities and qualifications. Setting objectives, for example, is a problem of balances: between past and future, between ends and means, between what is actual and desirable. It clearly requires analytical and synthesizing abilities. Organizing, too, requires analytical ability. For it demands the most economical use of scarce resources. But it deals with human beings, and – as we shall soon see – demands integrity, as well as human perception and insight.

The skill needed for motivation and communication is primarily social. Instead of analysis, integration and synthesis are required. Measurement requires, first and fore-most, analytical ability. But it also demands that measurement be used to make self-control possible rather than be abused to control people from above, that is to dominate them.

So, as we can see, Drucker is at constant pains to retain a balance between the soft and hard attributes of his analytical management. While 'measurement', for example, is primarily analytical, and 'motivation and communication' are fundamentally social, the former cannot be isolated from people and the latter from hard-headed analysis.

Being able to set objectives does not make a manager, any more than the ability to tie a small knot in a confined space makes a surgeon. But without the ability to set objectives a person cannot be an adequate manager, just as no one can do good surgery without tying small knots. And as a surgeon becomes a better surgeon by improving the knot-tying skill, so a manager becomes a better manager by improving skill and performance in all categories of work.[2]

Management style and character

The fifth and final skill that managers need to acquire, according to Drucker, is that of developing people. However, because of the particular nature of this skill, I have chosen to integrate it with management style and character. As such it contains the softest edge of Drucker's thinking.

The manager's resource: people

The manager works with a specific resource, that is 'people'. The human being, for Drucker, is a unique resource requiring peculiar qualities for whoever attempts to work with it. Note that, whereas for Peters, and Waterman and Austin customers and employees are combined together as just 'people', for Drucker they are one analytical step removed. While being unique entities they are, nevertheless, abstracted as 'resources'. Working with the human being, Drucker tells us, always means developing him or her. Moreover the direction which this development takes decides whether the human being – both as a person and as a resource – will become more productive. When all is said and done, this ability to develop people requires integrity of character.

Integrity: the touchstone

The final proof of the sincerity and seriousness of management is uncompromising emphasis on integrity of character. This, above all, has to be reflected in management's people-related skills and attitudes. For it is integrity of character through which leadership is exercized. Such integrity of character is not something, in Drucker's opinion, that managers can acquire. If they do not bring it to the job they will never have it. Character and leadership is not mere personal magnetism. Rather it involves such specifics as lifting another person's vision to higher sights, and the building up of another personality beyond its normal limitations. Leaders with integrity conform to strict principles of conduct and responsibility, attain high personal standards of performance, and respect other individuals and their work. In the final analysis, Drucker says, the purpose of organization is to enable ordinary human beings to do extraordinary things. The test of an organization is the spirit of performance. This requires above all the realization that integrity is the one absolute requirement of managers.

Developing management and managers

If character and integrity, then, are innate, what can and should be developed? Managers, according to Drucker, must acquire today the skills that are required tomorrow. Managers also need an opportunity to reflect on the meaning of their own experience and – above all – they need an opportunity to reflect on themselves and to learn to make their strengths count.

Management development is therefore not merely a matter of going on courses. Managers are action-focussed. They are not philosophers and should not be. Unless they can put into action right away what they have learnt a course will not 'take'. It will remain information and never become knowledge. The starting point for any management development effort is the performance appraisal. Such an appraisal should always be a joint effort. It should be based on the performance objectives which the managers set for themselves in conjunction with their superiors. It should start with their performance against those objectives. It should never start, Drucker insists, with their mere potential. The appraisal should lead to a recognition of the manager's strengths and of the factors which prevent him from making those strengths fully effective. Those factors resting within the individual, and which can be remedied through the acquisition of new skills, need to be identified. Subsequent development can be realized primarily through new experience. It is necessary for the spirit, the vision and the performance of today's managers that they be expected to develop those who will manage tomorrow. Indeed, no one can develop himself unless he works on the development of others. The context in which that development takes place, at least in most instances for Drucker, is that of the business enterprise.

Business and management

Unlike many management theorists both before and after him, Peter Drucker retained a close connection with the business context that underpinned his management concepts. Business and managerial performance were therefore never kept far apart. Out of this business context Drucker's thinking has since been extended, and adapted, in two main directions. The major thrust has been in the hard areas of corporate planning and 'business strategy'; a minor, but clearly visible thrust, has been in the area of 'business and society'. I shall consider each in turn.

Business strategy

In his consideration of business strategy, four aspects concerned Drucker most:

- What a business is.
- The purpose and mission of a business.
- The power and purpose of business objectives.
- The nature and significance of strategic planning.

What is a business?

Business foundations

A business enterpise, for Drucker, is created and managed by people and not by forces. In this way Peter Drucker immediately sets himself apart from the classical economists, and from their theory of the firm. Economic forces, he says, set limits to what management can do. But they do not themselves determine what a business is or what it does. The prevailing economic theory of business enterprise, moreover, is based on profit maximization. Yet, for Drucker, profit is not the purpose of, but the limiting factor on, business enterprise. Profit is not the cause, explanation, or rationale of business decisions, but the test of their validity.

The purpose behind a business, then, lies not in any profit motive held by an individual, but in society, in the creation of a customer. It is the customer who determines what a business is. It is the customer, Drucker argues, whose willingness to pay for a good or for a service converts economic resources into wealth. In effect Drucker succeeds in depersonalizing business, and decoupling it from individual and entrepreneurial desire, or profit motive. In his scheme of analysis:

> Customers are the foundation of a business and keep it in existence. They alone give employment. To supply the wants and needs of a customer, society entrusts wealth producing resources to the business enterprise.[3]

The entrepreneurial functions

Because its purpose is to create a customer – which is its entrepreneurial reason for being – the business enterprise has just two basic functions, marketing and innovation. Marketing and innovation produce results; all the rest are costs.

Marketing is the distinguishing, unique function of the business, the funtion which sets it apart from other organizations. Marketing is so basic that it cannot be considered a separate skill or work within the business. Marketing requires specific work, but that work is central to the whole company. It is the entire business seen from the point of view of its final result, that is, from the customer's point of view. Concern and responsibility for marketing must permeate all areas of the firm.

The second basic, and entrepreneurial function is innovation, which Drucker defines as 'the provision of different economic satisfactions'. A business enterprise, he argues, can exist only in an economy that considers change both natural and acceptable. Business then becomes the specific organ of growth, expansion and change. So it is not enough for the business to provide just any goods and services. It must provide ever better and more economic ones – managers must convert society's needs into new opportunities for profitable business.

Productive administration

The enterprise must use wealth producing resources, efficiently and effectively, to discharge its purpose of creating a customer. This is the administrative function of business. The resulting productivity means balancing all factors of production in order to give the greatest output for the least effort. The greatest opportunities for increasing productivity are to be found in knowledge work and especially, according to Drucker, in management itself. Productivity is affected by knowledge, by time, by product and process mix, and by the balance amongst different management activities. There is great need for productive, administrative performance. But it follows the entrepreneurial objectives, in the same way as structure follows strategy. So the more that management creates economic conditions or changes them the more it manages the business. That leads us on to business purpose and mission.

Business purpose and mission

As should by now have become apparent, not intuition but – for Drucker – a clear, simple and penetrating theory of the business characterizes the truly successful entrepreneur. Such a person will not only amass a large fortune but will also build an organization that can endure and grow.

The individual entrepreneur, that is the kind that Peters or McCormack are likely to admire, does not need to analyze concepts and explain a theory of business to others. He is thinker, analyst and executioner rapped up in one. Business enterprise, however, requires that the theory of the business be spelled out. 'What is our business, and what should it be?' needs to be asked. The answer to the question, 'What is our business?', is therefore the first responsibility of top management. It should be a genuine decision, based on divergent views and assumptions of what the business is. The first and crucial question, in defining the business, must be 'who is the customer?'. The customer never buys a product. He buys value. The second question should therefore be, 'what does the customer consider to be value?'. Only a clear, resulting definition of the mission and purpose of the business makes possible clear and realistic business objectives. Such a definition is the foundation for priorities, strategies, plans and work assignments. It is the starting point for the design of managerial jobs. Strategy determines what the key activities are in the business, following after the objectives.

The nature and scope of objectives

The nature of objectives

Objectives must be derived from 'what our business is, what it will be, and what it should be'. Such objectives are not abstractions. They are the action commitments through which the mission of a business is carried out, and the standards against which performance is measured.

Objectives must be operational. They must be capable of being converted into specific targets and specific assignments. They must lend themselves to becoming the basis, as well as the source of motivation, for work and achievement.

Objectives must enable the concentration of resources and efforts. They must enable management to select the fundamentals from amongst the goals of a business so that the key resources of people, money and physical facilities can be concentrated. They must therefore facilitate selectivity. There must be multiple objectives rather than a single one. To manage a business is to balance a variety of needs and goals. This requires a multiplicity of objectives.

The scope of objectives

Objectives are needed in all areas on which the survival of the business depends:

- A business must first be able to create a customer. There is, therefore, need for a marketing objective.
- Businesses must be able to innovate, or else their else their competitors will make them obsolete. There is need for an innovation objective.
- All business depends on three factors of production – human resources, capital resources and physical facilities. There must, therefore, be objectives for their supply, their employment, and their development. The resources must be employed productively and their productivity has to grow if the business is to survive. So there is need for productivity objectives.
- Business exists in society and community and, therefore, has to take responsibility for

its impact on the environment. As a result objectives covering the social dimensions of business are needed.

- Finally, there is the need for profit, otherwise none of the other objectives can be attained. They all require cost. Such costs can only be financed out of the profits of the business. They all entail risks; they therefore require a profit to cover the risk of potential losses. Profit is not an objective but it is a requirement that has to be objectively determined in respect to the individual business, its strategy, its needs, and its risks.

Objectives have therefore to be set in eight key areas: marketing, innovation, human organization, financial resources, physical resources, productivity, social responsibility and profit requirements.

> Objectives in these key areas enable us to do five things: to organize and explain the whole range of business phenomena in a small number of general statements; to test these statements in actual experience; to predict behavior; to test the soundness of decisions while they still being made; and to let managers on all levels analyze their own experience and improve their performance.[4]

Strategic planning

The setting of objectives is in fact part of a more extensive planning process. The business discipline of 'strategic planning', which became so popular in the sixties and seventies, was – like so many other things in management – inaugurated by Drucker in the fifties.

Strategic planning defined

Strategic planning, for Drucker, is not simply a technique, such as a particular method of forecasting. It has much broader scope and implications. In fact he regards it as the 'entrepreneurial' side of management, in that it is intimately concerned with risk.[5]

> While it is futile to try to eliminate risk, and questionable to try to minimize it, it is essential that the risks taken be the right ones. The end result of successful strategic planning must be capacity to take a greater risk, for this is the only way to improve entrepreneurial performance.
>
> To extend this capacity, however, we must understand the risks we take. We must be able to choose rationally amongst risk taking courses of action rather than plunge into uncertainty on the basis of hunch, hearsay or experience.
>
> We can now attempt to define what strategic planning is. It is the continuous process of making present risk-taking decisions systematically and with the greatest knowledge of their futurity; organizing systematically the efforts needed to carry out these decisions; and measuring the results of these decisions against expectations through organized, systematic feedback.[6]

As we can see Drucker views planning as a systematizing and rationalizing device, but one used to enhance our ability to deal with risk rather than to lessen our inclination to take such risks. Strategic planning, in his eyes, is an entrepreneurial function because it deals with risk, but rationally rather than intuitively. As a result entrepreneurship, in itself, becomes systematized, in the way it is described in Drucker's most recent book on entrepreneurship and innovation.

Sloughing off yesterday
Planning starts with the objectives of the business. In each area of objectives, the question needs to be asked, 'What do we have to do now to attain our objectives tomorrow?' The first thing to do to attain tomorrow, says Drucker in true entrepreneurial vein, is to 'slough off yesterday'. Most plans concern themselves with the new – new products, new processes, new markets. But the key to doing something different tomorrow is getting rid of the no longer productive, the obsolescent, the obsolete.

What new things do we have to do – when?
The next step in the planning process is to ask, 'What new and different things do we have to do, and when?'. We need to look for new and different ways to attain objectives rather than believing that doing more of the same will suffice. Furthermore, we need to think through the time dimensions, and ask, 'When do we have to start work to get results when we need them?'.

Everything degenerates into work
The best plan is only a good intention unless it leads into work. What makes a plan capable of producing results is the commitment of key people to work on specific tasks. The test of a plan is whether management actually commits resources to action which will bring results in the future. Unless such commitment is made, there are only promises and hopes, but no plan. The end result of planning should be not knowledge but strategy. Its aim is action now.

Planning as a whole
Strategic planning, then, prepares today's business for the future. It asks: What should our business be? What do we have to do today to deserve the future? Strategic planning requires risk taking decisions. It requires an organized process of abandoning yesterday. It requires that the work to be done to produce the desired future be clearly defined and assigned. The aim of strategic planning, as has been said, is action now. Finally Drucker, in his habitually intriguing way, stresses that strategic planning does not substitute facts for judgement. 'It does not even lessen the importance and role of managerial ability, courage, experience, intuition, or even hunch . . .'. These primal qualities he leaves as the 'givens' of any managerial situation. It is the analytical qualities alone that can be acquired and developed, to leave more room for whatever leadership qualities might already be there. Such qualities of leadership, judgement and vision are amply required when we turn to the social responsibilities of business.

Business and society

Social impacts and responsibilities
Aside from introducing the business world to strategic planning, Drucker was one of the first management consultants to address the social responsibilities of business. He argued that such responsibilities were not marginal, soft 'add ons' to the performance of a business, but were an integral part of its strategic functioning, as an organ of society.

Managements of all institutions are responsible for their by products, that is, the impacts of their legitimate activities on people and on the physical and social environment. They are increasingly expected to anticipate and to resolve social problems.

They need to think through and develop new policies for the relationship of business and government, which is rapidly outgrowing traditional theories and habits. What are the tasks? What are the opportunities? What are the limitations? And what are the ethics of leadership for the manager who is a leader but not a master?[7]

In the final analysis, Drucker argues, because business is responsible for its impacts, it should minimize them. The fewer impacts a business institution has outside of its own specific purpose and mission, the better it controls itself, the more responsibly it acts and the more acceptable a citizen, neighbor and contributor it is.

Interestingly enough, then, whereas society at large is virtually non-existent for the primal manager in his 'free enterprise', for his analytical counterpart it is both a constraint and an opportunity. Society definitively exists, though outside of himself and his enterprise. Therefore it is something towards which he needs to be accountable.

Accountable enterprise

More specifically, Drucker argues that 'accountable enterprise' might be a better slogan than the 'now overused free enterprise'. Such accountable enterprises need to operate under four particular guidelines.

1. The economic organizations of society – business and their managers – require autonomy and accountability in the interests of the economy; for the sake of strong and effective government; and in the interests of society.

   One cannot be accountable, Drucker emphasizes, for what one has no authority over and cannot control. Business enterprises and their managements need to be under performance test or they cease to perform. They have to be able to allocate society's and the economy's resources in a rational mananer against objective criteria, or resources will be misallocated.

2. Society also needs a healthy and functioning government, especially the complex and interdependent society ours has become. The fatter government becomes the flabbier and weaker it actually is.

   Business and business management cannot restore government to health. This is a political job. But they can at least avoid damaging government performance in any respect. In this area their responsibility is *primum non nocere* – not knowingly to do damage. In fact this is the moral and ethical code – 'Above all not knowingly to harm' – that management should adhere to in all its activities.

3. The twin needs for economic autonomy and effective government come together in one major problem of the business–government relationship. The multinational, perhaps the most fruitful social innovation of this century, is also a problem. What is needed is to work out a relationship that safeguards both a true world economy and the political sovereignty of national governments, in peaceful coexistence.

4. The need to think through the business–government relationship is not really the result of a crisis of business. It is the result, according to Drucker, of a serious crisis of government. Yet business managers will have to look upon the relationship to government and society as their task. They cannot wait, Drucker says, for the political

scientists or for the theoretical economist. A purely negative attitude that fights 'their encroachment' is not going to be effective. Positive, affirmative action is needed.

The ethics of responsibility

In this tension between the private functioning of the manager, the necessary autonomy of the institution and its accountability to its own mission and purpose, and the manager's public character, lies the specific responsibility of Drucker's 'society of organizations'. The managers of our modern institutions – business, schools, hospital and government agencies – are the leadership groups in contemporary society. As such they need an ethic, a commitment, a code. The right one, at least for Drucker, is one developed more than two thousand years ago for the physician, and that is 'not knowingly to do harm'.

It is interesting to note, finally, that 'business ethics' are unique to the rational manager. His primal counterpart is solely concerned with caring for people, personally and immediately, as staff or as customers and suppliers. For the developmental manager, social and economic considerations are so intertwined they cannot be separated. For the metaphysical manager, of course, the whole of business is an ethical enterprise, or not – as the case may be. Business ethics cannot be analyzed out for separate treatment. But we are jumping the gun. We still need to investigate one more area of analytical management, as conceptualized by Drucker. This is the specific area of 'managerial organization'.

Managerial organization

The individual manager comprises one analytical part of the managerial whole ; business and management comprises the second; finally we have 'managerial organization'.

The investigation of the individual manager has led to voluminous literature on management 'skills' and 'style'. The study of business and management has yielded a proliferation of material on business and corporate strategy and planning, and more limited coverage of corporate and social responsibility. The investigation of managerial organization has led to prolific analyses of both organization structures and of people in groups. Drucker has placed relatively more emphasis, in his study of managerial organization, on structure.

> Organization structure is the oldest and most thoroughly studied area in management. But we face new needs in organization that the well known and well tested structural design of 'functional' and 'decentralized' organization cannot adequately satisfy.
> New structural designs are emerging: the task force team; simulated decentralization; the systems structure. We have learned that organization does not start with structure but with building blocks. There is no one right or universal design; each enterprise needs to design around the key activities appropriate to its mission and strategies.
> Three different kinds of work – operating, innovative and top management – have to be accommodated under the same organizational roof. Organization structure needs to be both task-focussed and person-focussed and to have both an authority and a responsibility axis.[8]

Drucker has divided his analysis of managerial organization into five areas: structures and strategies; work and task-focussed design; result and relations-focussed design; the innovative organization; and, finally, top management and the board. These all serve to highlight his structural (hard), as opposed to behavioral (soft) orientation.

Structures and strategies

Organization studies leading to reorganizing companies, divisions, and functions have been one of the more spectacular 'growth industries' of the last two decades. Since the Frenchman, Henri Fayol, first introduced us to the subject of organization design in business management, we have learnt three crucial lessons.

What we have learnt

1. Organization structure will not just evolve. The only things that develop spontaneously in an organization are disorder, friction, and malperformance. Organization design thus requires thinking, analysis, and a systematic approach.
2. The first step is not designing an organization structure. That is the last step. The first step is identifying and organizing the building blocks of the organization, that is, the activities that have to be built into the final structure and that carry the 'structural load' of the organization.
3. Structure follows strategy. Organization is not mechanical. It is not assembly. It cannot be prefabricated. Organization is unique to each individual business or institution. Structure, to be effective, must follow strategy.

Structure is a means for attaining the objectives and goals of an institution. Any work on structure must therefore start with strategy – 'What is our business, what should it be, what will it be?' Strategy determines the key activities. Effective structure is the design that makes these key activities capable of functioning and of performance. So much for what we have learnt. Now what about the things that Drucker maintains we have to unlearn? There are again three of them.

What we need to unlearn

1. The conflict between task and person focus is a sham. Structure and job design have to be task-focussed. But specific assignments have to fit both the person and the needs of the situation. Work is objective and impersonal; the job itself is done by a person.
2. The conflict between hierarchical and free-form organization is another sham. According to Drucker, it is not true to say that hierarchy represents regimentation and free-form organization provides freedom. In fact the more flexible an organization the stronger the individuals need to be and the more load they have to carry.

     Morever, a formal hierarchy protects individuals from the exercise of arbitrary authority over them. Sound organization therefore requires both a durable hierarchical structure and also the free forms through which task forces and project teams can be established.
3. There is no one right form of organization – whether functional, federal or geographical. Different kinds of work require different structures. There are, essentially, three kinds of work.

Three kinds of work

There is first operating work, the work of managing what is already in existence and known, building it, exploiting its potential, taking care of its problems. There is always top management work, with its particular tasks and requirements. Finally, there is innovative work.

None of the available design principles, as we shall see later, can be used to organize all three. Yet each needs to be organized. Moreover, they all need to be integrated into one organization. Let us see how this is done.

Formal specifications

Whatever form of organizational design is adopted needs to conform, as far as Drucker is concerned, to seven formal specifications:

1. Clarity of organization. All managerial components, and all individuals within the organization, need to know where they belong, where they stand, where they have to go for what. The lack of such clarity creates fiction, wastes time, causes frustration, and unnecessarily delays decision making.
2. Economy of effort. Closely related to clarity is the requirement of economy. One should be able to control, to supervise, and to coax people to perform with minimum effort. Organization structure should make self-control possible and should encourage self-motivation.
3. Direction of vision. Organization structure should direct the vision of individuals and of managerial units towards performance rather than towards efforts. Performance is the end that all activities serve.
4. Understanding the task. An organization should enable all individuals to understand their own tasks. At the same time, an organization should enable everyone to understand the common task, the task of the entire organization.
5. Strengthening decision making. Decisions have to be made, at the right level and on the right issues, and have to be converted into work and accomplishment. An organization design needs to be tested, therefore, as to whether it impedes or increases the speed and reliability of decision making.
6. Attaining stability and adaptability. An organization needs stability. It must be able to do its work even though the world around it is in turmoil. It needs to be able to plan for its own future and continuity. But stability is not rigidity. On the contrary, organization structure requires adaptability. Only if it can adapt will it survive.
7. Perpetuation and self-renewal. Finally, an organization needs to be able to perpetuate itself. It needs to be able to provide for its self-renewal. It must therefore be able to produce tomorrow's leaders from within, and must also be accessible to new ideas.

Business operations

The 'organization architect', for Drucker, has five distinct ways of organizing activities open to him – with a view to meeting the formal specifications just outlined. Two of them are the traditional approaches to 'work and task-focussed design'. The three less traditional forms he identifies as 'result and relation-focussed designs'.

Work- and task-focussed design
The two traditionally based organizational designs are first, functionally and second, team based.

The functional structure

Functional design – conventionally based on production, marketing, finance and personnel functions – has the great advantage of clarity. Everybody has a home. Everyone understands his or her task. It is an organization of high stability. But the price paid for clarity and stability is that it is difficult for people to understand the task of the whole, and to relate their work to it. While stable, the structure is rigid and resists adaptation. In the final analysis, therefore, the functional structure is most suited to operational work and least suited to either top management or innovative activity.

Teamwork

A team is a number of people – usually only a few – with different backgrounds, skills and knowledge and drawn from various areas of the organization who work together on a specific and defined task. The mission of a team is a specific task, hunting expedition or product development. Performance responsibility rests with the whole team, although the team will invariably have its own leader.

More specifically, teams need a particular or continuing mission; they need a sharply-defined objective; they need leadership, although the authority is necessarily task-derived and task-focussed; finally, empathy and rapport is required. The team has obvious strengths. Everyone knows the work of the whole and holds himself responsible for it. It is highly receptive to new ideas, and is extremely adaptive. There are equally obvious shortcomings. There is clarity only if the team leader provides it. It has little stability. Much of the energy of members goes into maintaining cohesiveness.

Team and function

Functional organization and teamwork are both organized around the logic of work and task. Both also have a longstanding history. Functional organization has existed for thousands of years in government, in the church and in the military. Teams, as hunting bands, have existed for even longer. Although these two design principles may be seen to conflict, they are essentially complementary, especially for knowledge-based work, which is often organized on so-called 'matrix' lines. In other words a project team is established whereby each member has a dual loyalty – first to his team, and second, to his professional function. The other three of Drucker's five organizational designs are result- and relation-focussed.

Result- and relation-focussed design

There are three forms of organization in this category. Each has more recent origins than their two predecessors.

Federal decentralization

'Federal decentralization' is Drucker's favorite organizational form. Here is the reason why. Functional and team organization start with work and task. They assume that results are the sum total of the efforts. 'If only efforts are organized properly, the right results will follow' is the underlying premise. Federal decentralization, by way of contrast, starts out with the question, 'What results do we aim for?' It tries to set up the right business first, that is, the unit that will have the best capacity for results and especially for results in the market-place. Then the question is asked 'What work, what efforts, what key activities have to be set up and organized?'

In federal decentralization, a company is organized in a number of self-governing businesses. Each unit is responsible for its own performance, its own results, and its own contribution to the total company. Moreover, the autonomous businesses of a decentralized structure are designed to be large enough to put the strengths of a functional structure to work and yet small enough to neutralize its weaknesses. Federal decentralization has great clarity and considerable economy. It makes it easy for all members of the autonomous business to understand their own tasks as well as that of the whole business. It has high stability and yet is adaptable. It focusses the vision and efforts of managers directly on business performance and results. Moreover, managers are close enough to results to get immediate feedback, which facilitates management by self-control. Above all, the autonomous units prepare managers for top management posts.

Simulated decentralization

Whenever a unit can be set up as a business, Drucker argues, no design principle can match federal decentralization. There are a great number of companies, though, that cannot be divided up into many genuine businesses, each with a visibly separate market. Yet they have clearly outgrown the limits of size and complexity of the functional, or the team structure. These companies increasingly turn to 'simulated decentralization' as a solution. Units are formed which are not, strictly speaking, autonomous businesses with their own distinct market-places, but they are set up as if they were. They have their own management and they sell to one another using internal 'transfer prices'. But simulated decentralization should only be used as a last resort. If a functional structure is lean enough to work economically and adaptively it should be retained as such. There is, furthermore, a third variety of 'results and relation focussed design'.

The systems structure

Whereas federal decentralization is organized around results the 'systems structure' is formed around relationships.

Systems organization is an extension of the team design principle. But instead of a team consisting of individuals, the systems organization builds the team out of a wide variety of organizations. They may be government agencies, private businesses or universities. The different parties may be joined together for a specific, time defined task or on a permanent basis. Japanese companies, for example, seldom own their suppliers. Yet the suppliers they use are quite obviously integrated into their closely interwoven business system. Similarly the company usually depends on a 'trading company' that is both independent and integrated with its own operation.

The Chase Manhattan Bank, as another example, decided not to rely on wholly-owned branches abroad. Instead it has expanded internationally by acquiring minority interests in foreign-owned banks. We shall be able to see, in the section on developmental management, that this form of systems structure has recently been expanding at a very rapid rate.

At this stage the structure necessarily lacks clarity and stability. However, the system is eminently flexible and receptive to new ideas. Drucker also argues that the structure lacks economy in that it is heavily reliant on the personal relationships established by key parties within the adjacent organizations.

> The systems structure will never be a preferred form of organization; it is fiendishly difficult. But it is an important structure, and one that the organization designer needs to know and needs to understand – if only to know that it should not be used where other, simpler and easier structures will do the job.[9]

Composite organization design

So much for Drucker's four or five organizational designs – based on team or function, autonomous business units, or a system of interdependent relationships.

The functional organization, whether it be based on business function, geographical region, or even product line, is the classical form which still predominates in large organizations today. The team, project based or so called matrix form is becoming increasingly popular, though, in the newer and more rapidly growing industries.

Federal decentralization, whether simulated or real, is very much the kind of thing that warms the primal hearts of Peters and Waterman. It is a more analytical way of fostering 'autonomy and entrepreneurship'. The joker in the pack, in fact, is the systems structure of joint ventures. I shall have much more to say about it, and its related forms, in Section D.

The innovative organization

All five organization designs, that we have been considering up to now, refer to the basic operating business of a business enterprise. Drucker pays special and additional attention, first to the organization of innovation, and second, to the organization of management at the top.

The innovative organization, like 3M in America and – to some extent – ICI in Britain, somehow builds an innovative spirit into its culture, and even creates a habit of innovation. Drucker has identified six characteristics of such innovative organizations:

- They know what innovation means.
- They understand the dynamics of innovation.
- They know that innovation requires particular kinds of goals and measurements.
- Top management has a definitive attitude.
- The innovative organization is structured differently.
- They will be central to the last quarter of the twentieth century.

The meaning of innovation

Innovative organizations know that innovation is not science or technology but value. They know that innovation is not something that takes place inside the organization, but is a change outside. The measure of innovation is impact on the environment. Innovation must always be market-focussed.

The dynamics of innovation

Innovating companies know that innovation happens neither by chance nor according to some predetermined timetable. It follows the laws of probability. They know how to spot the areas where innovative activity is likely to enjoy success. These areas were spelled out in more detail in Chapter 8.

Innovative strategy

Like all business strategies, an innovative strategy, for Drucker, begins with the question 'What is our business, and what should it be?' But the ruling assumption of an innovative strategy is that whatever exists is ageing. Whereas the governing device for an ongoing business is 'better and more', that for an innovative strategy has to be 'new and different'.

Measurement and budgets

Nothing is more inconsistent with successful innovation than a goal of '5 per cent growth in profits' every year. Innovations for the first three or five years – some for longer – show no profit at all. Then their growth rate for five to ten years should be closer to 40 per cent.

The innovative attitude

The innovative organization builds a kind of nervous system next to the bony skeleton of the formal structure. Where the traditional organization is focussed on the logic of work, there is an additional relationship focussed on the dynamics of ideas. Top management make it their business to sit down with younger ones and ask, 'what opportunities do you see?'

Structure for innovation

The search for innovation needs to be organized separately and outside of the ongoing managerial business. At the same time innovative organizations realize that innovation needs to be organized like a business rather than as a function. The design principle of innovation is the team, with a project or business leader, set up outside existing structures as an autonomous unit.

Innovation as a whole

There is every indication, according to Drucker, that the innovative organization will have to be developed into a central institution for the last quarter of the twentieth century. This has important implications for top management, to whom we now turn.

Top management and the board

> No business can do better than its top management will permit; the bottleneck is, after all, always at the top of the bottle. Of all the jobs in the enterprise the top-management is the most difficult one to organize. But it is also the most important.[10]

Every building block of organization is defined by a specific contribution. The one exception is top management. Its job is multidimensional. There is no one top management task; there are only top management tasks.
There are six such tasks:

- There is, first, the task of thinking through the mission of the business, that is, of asking the question 'what is our business, and what should it be?' This leads to setting objectives, developing strategies and plans, and to making today's decisions for tomorrow's results.

- There is need for standard setting, for example setting standards for what we have called the conscience functions. There is need, then, for an organ concerned with vision and values in the key areas.
- There is the responsibility to build and maintain the human organization. There is need for work on developing the human resources for tomorrow, and especially for work on providing tomorrow's top management.
- Equally important are major relations that only the people at the top can maintain. These may be relations with customers or major suppliers, with government or banking institutions. They are relations that can only be made by someone who represents the entire business, speaks for it, stands for it, commits it.
- There are countless ceremonial functions that must be performed by top management, including civic events, formal dinners, and ritual farewells and celebrations.
- Finally, there is a need for a 'stand by' for major crises, for somebody who is available to take over when things go seriously wrong. Then it is the wisest, the most prominent people in the organization who have to 'roll up their sleeves and go to work'.

Conclusion

Drucker is a profound management philosopher as well as an incisive management analyst. Such books as *The Concept of the Corporation*,[11] written in the fifties, and *Management in Turbulent Times*,[12] published in the seventies, are just two particularly well-known examples of his prolific, literary output. More than any of the management theorists, over the last thirty years, Drucker has shaped the thinking of practicing managers in the industrialized world.

Aside from his more philosophical work, and his weighty tome *Management: Tasks, Responsibilities and Practices*, Drucker has also written the two more readable books, *Managing for Results*[13] and *The Practice of Management*.[14] Moreover, Drucker's conceptual grasp has been broad enough to accommodate the full range of managerial (skills and style), business (strategy and responsibility) and organizational (structure and dynamics) attributes. He has also retained, for most of the time, a continuing balance between the structural and the behavioral aspects of management. Poised neatly in between Fayol and Weber, on the one hand, and Follett and Mayo, on the other, he alternates between hardness and softness, top down and bottom up, management controls and self-control, freedom and order.

Moreover, Drucker has been a seminal influence in the development of management by objectives for the individual manager; of business strategy and planning, for the business corporation; and of entrepreneurship and autonomy, for the managed organization. However, for all his expansive analytical strengths, Drucker has denied his own instinctive and developmental traits. Although he makes frequent reference to instinct and intuition he inevitably distrusts these primal qualities. Drucker's tried and tested entrepreneur is made of much more analytical stuff than Peters and Waterman's.

Similarly, although Drucker is very much in favor of developing people and products, the kind of insight and foresight that goes with the truly 'developmental manager' lies beyond Drucker's ken. He is ultimately too much of a business realist to become involved with the invisible realms of latent human potential, or with the mystical domains of corporate myth and ritual. He is also too much of a refined analyst to take on board the rawness, and unruliness, of Peters' and Austin's 'passion for excellence'. Drucker distrusts emotion. He is much more at home in the worlds of thought and action than in the world of pure feeling.

Drucker is a man of the North (Central Europe) rather than of the South (Africa or Latin America) or East (Japan, India or China). Even his relationship with the West is a somewhat uneasy one. He is an outsider looking into America, rather than a Tom Peters, a Mary Kay or a Mark McCormack working from the inside out. As such he has helped his adopted country to create its vast business organizations, but has withheld himself from the primal power and influence of the United States. He respect entrepreneurs, but he does not love them. In that sense he is not unlike the complete cast of rational characters you will now be meeting. I shall start with those who have played a leading role in establishing management skills.

References

1. P. Drucker, *Management: Tasks, Responsibilities and Practices*, Pan (1979), p. 23.
2. P. Drucker, *op. cit.*, p. 22.
3. P. Drucker, *op. cit.*, p. 57.
4. P. Drucker, *op. cit.*, p. 92.
5. P. Drucker, *op. cit.*, p. 120.
6. P. Drucker, *Entrepreneurship and Innovation*, Heinemann (1985).
7. P. Drucker, *op. cit.*, (1979), p. 259.
8. P. Drucker, *op. cit.*, (1979), p. 439.
9. P. Drucker, *op. cit.*, (1979), p. 500.
10. P. Drucker, *op. cit.*, (1979), p. 522.
11. P. Drucker, *The Concept of the Corporation*, Crowell (1972).
12. P. Drucker, *Management in Turbulent Times*, Heinemann (1980).
13. P. Drucker, *Managing for Results*, Heinemann (1964).
14. P. Drucker, *The Practice of Management*, Heinemann (1967).

13 Management skills

Contents

Key concepts

Once you have fully understood the chapter you should be able
to define the following concepts in your own words:

Administrative theory
Communication
Controlling
Control process
Decisional roles
Departmentation
Directing
Fayol's management
    principles
Industrial functions
Informational roles
Interpersonal roles
Leadership

Line and staff
Management appraisal
Management audit
Managerial problem solving
Operation research (OR)
Organizing
Planning
Planning premises
Policy-making
POSDCORP
Span of management
Staffing

Objectives

Upon completing this chapter you should be able to do the following:

1. Trace the evolution of management principles.
2. Outline the essential elements of planning, organizing, staffing, directing, and control.
3. Describe the methodical process of managerial problem solving.
4. Analyze managerial work.
5. Undergo, systematically, the functions of management, in carrying out a basic managerial task.

Introduction

The scope of management skills

The first of the hard branches of rational management is that of managerial skill. It is in fact the most enduring of all aspects of management, the most tried and tested of the manager's attributes. It is also the framework within which most conventional management theory has been placed. The best-known approach to categorizing the individual manager's skills is the 'operational school', alternatively entitled the 'functional', 'principles', 'processes' or 'activities' school of management. It is this operational method of simple categorization with which we shall be most concerned here. In its crudest form, it involves a division between planning, organizing, directing and controlling.

The two academics whose work I shall be calling upon, in particular, are those venerable Americans, Harold Koontz and Cyril O'Donnell. Their book *The Principles of Management*,[1] first published in 1955, is now in its eighth edition, and is almost as popular as it has ever been. The two next most common classification schemes that will also be included in this chapter are 'managerial decision making', with whom the name Herbert Simon is particularly associated, and 'managerial work', which has been popularized by Henry Mintzberg. This does not, however, complete the managerial picture.

Patterns of managerial analysis

In *The Principles of Management* Koontz and O'Donnell have placed those 'hard' and depersonalized skills, within a broader context of management. That broader context, incidentally, also encompasses the 'soft' and more personalized skills, or 'styles', which I cover in Chapter 10.

While Koontz and O'Donnell see themselves as part and parcel of a specific management tradition, that is the 'operational school' started by Henri Fayol, they position themselves within a broader, and more contemporary theoretical context. As a result their operational principles have become progressively enriched in content, even if they retain their fundamental form. Specifically, as shown in Fig. 23,[1] they identify five major influences, or 'schools', surrounding their own.

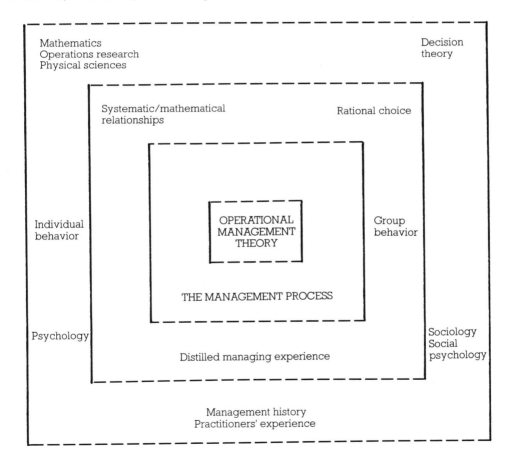

Fig. 23 Patterns of management analysis.

The 'decision making' schools, both quantitatively and qualitatively based, as well as the 'empirical' school, concerned with managerial work, fall into this chapter on management skill. The behavioral schools, both individually and group-oriented, fall into the next chapter on management and learning style. Their own 'operational' or 'process' school will be of prime concern here.

The evolution of management

Principles of scientific management

The notion that a set of rules, principles, or activities could be prescribed for management – thereby rendering it a precise skill – was first advanced by the noted Frederick Taylor. In 1911, in America, he produced his 'cornerstone of scientific management':

The origins of scientific management

First: To point out . . . the great loss which the whole country is suffering through inefficiency in almost all of our daily acts.

Second: To try to convince the reader that the remedy for this inefficiency lies in systematic management, rather than in searching for some unusual or extraordinary man.

Third: To prove that the best management is a true science, resting upon clearly defined laws, rules and principles, as a foundation. And further to show that the fundamental principles of scientific management are applicable to all kinds of human activities, from our simplest individual acts to the work of our great corporations.

Frederick Taylor *The Principles of Scientific Management*[2] 1911

Science is systematized in the sense that relationships between variables and limits have been ascertained and underlying principles discovered. Most of Taylor's 'scientific' activity involved him in discovering, through systematic observation and experimentation, precise connections between manual labor and economic efficiency. The initial development of broader management principles was not so much the work of Taylor – despite his professed intentions – as that of the Frenchman, Henri Fayol.

General and industrial administration

Fayol was the industrial engineer who, during the first quarter of this century, devoted his life to codifying the principles and practices of business administration, of organizational structure and dynamics, and of general management. In fact he virtually established the working agenda that Drucker subsequently followed. Henri Fayol began by identifying the six groups of activities that he found in all industrial undertakings, thus anticipating the development of the major business functions. Secondly he identified thirteen general principles of management and organization. Finally, and most pertinent to this chapter, he formulated specific and general management skills. I shall now outline Fayol's three sets of contributions in turn, starting with industrial functions.

Industrial functions

All activities to which industrial undertakings give rise, according to Fayol,[3] can be divided into:

- Technical activities, specifically as production, manufacturing and the adaptation of products and operations.
- Commercial activities, including buying, selling and exchange.
- Financial activities, including the search for capital and its optimal use.
- Accounting activities, specifically stock taking, costing, compiling general statistics and producing a balance sheet and profit and loss account.
- Security activities, involving the protection of property and persons.
- Managerial activities, including planning, organization, command, coordination and control.

It is interesting to note that, aside from 'human resources', which he subsumed under 'security of property and persons', Fayol, in the twenties, anticipated all the modern industrial functions. He also developed thirteen principles of administration.

Administrative theory

Although Fayol's findings might appear as commonplace today, at the time they represented a real breakthrough in business thinking. In the early part of the century, as often for the very small businessman today, each manager followed his own methods, principles and personal theories, but nobody had yet formulated a general framework of administrative theory. Fayol built up his case for a general theory, that is a systematic grouping of interrelated principles, on the basis of his observations that:

- Management was a separate activity applicable to all types of undertakings.
- Managerial ability was sorely needed as one moved up the managerial hierarchy.
- Management was a discipline, in its own right, which could be formally structured and disseminated.

He then formulated his thirteen specific principles,[4] which, combined together, constituted his administrative theory. These involved the following:

1. Division of work – the idea of specialization of labor, and of the advantages which accrued in reducing waste, increasing output and easing the task of on the job training.
2. Authority – the right to give orders and the power to exact obedience.
3. Discipline – based on obedience and respect held by the employee towards the firm.
4. Unity of command – for any action whatsoever, an employee should receive orders from only one superior.
5. Unity of direction – involving a sound organization structure, and was essential to a unity of action, a coordination of strength, and a focussing of effort.
6. Centralization – varying according to different organizational needs and circumstances. The objective, in all cases however, was to pursue to the optimum the utilization of all the firm's people and facilities.
7. Subordination of individual interests to the general interest – involving the abolishing of ignorance, laziness, selfishness, ambition and of all human passions which cause conflict, when the interests of the individual prevail over those of the group.
8. Remuneration of personnel – strictly economic remuneration, including wages, piece

rates, bonuses, and profit sharing, in order to make personnel more valuable and also to inspire keenness.

9. The scalar chain – showing the routing of the line of authority and the channels for the transmission of formal communications.

10. Order – insuring a place for everything and everything in its place. It applied to materials and to shop cleanliness as well as to personnel.

11. Equity – resulting from a kindness and justice and providing a principle of employee relations.

12. Stability of tenure – providing for orderly personnel planning and provisions to replace the human resource.

13. *Esprit de corps* – stressing, finally, the building of harmony and unity. 'Dividing enemy forces to weaken them is clever, but devising one's own team is a grave sin against the business'.[5]

Even more relevant to management skill than Fayol's administrative theory are the principles of management that he formulated. In fact they paved the way, over the next fifty years, for the innumerable writers who would follow in his suit, developing variations, and elaborations, on his basic theme.

Principles of management
Using systematic powers of observation and analysis, then, Fayol came up with his principles of management, which have since served as the foundations for all subsequent categorizations of the manager's functions. Moreover, they have stood the test of time somewhat better than his organizational principles, which were very much a product of his time.

Fayol's management principles

- To manage is to forecast and to plan, to organize, to command, to coordinate and to control.
- To forecast and to plan is to foresee, to provide means of examining the future, and to draw up a specific plan of action.
- To organize means building up the dual structure, material and human, of the organization.
- To command means maintaining activity among the personnel.
- To coordinate means binding together, unifying and harmonizing all activity and effort.
- To control means seeing that everything occurs in conformity with established rules and commands.

Henri Fayol *General and Industrial Administration*[6] 1949

The first management analyst to develop Fayol's basic principles was the American, Luther Gulick.

The evolution of management principles

POSDCORB
Amplifying Fayol's version of the management process in the thirties, Luther Gulick –

Director of the Institute of Public Administration at Columbia University in New York –
developed his famous 'POSDCORB'.[7] POSDCORB represented his view of the
functions of the executive:

P lanning – working out in broad outline the things that need to be done, and the
methods for doing them to accomplish the purposes set for the enterprise.

O rganizing – establishing the formal structure of authority through which work subdivisions are arranged, defined and coordinated for a defined objective.

S taffing – involving the whole personnel function of recruiting staff, training them, and
maintaining favorable conditions of work.

D irecting – encompassing the continuous task of making decisions and embodying them
in specific and general orders and instructions, as well as serving as the leader of the
enterprise.

C oordination – the all important duty of interrelating the various parts of the work.

R eporting – keeping himself, and those to whom the executive is responsible, informed
as to what is going on, through records, research and inspection.

B udgeting – involving financial planning, accounting and control.

George Terry, in America, wrote the first text on management principles.[8] Meanwhile,
while Gulick and Terry were enriching the principles of management, another important
and rational development was in progress.

The emergence of decision theory

The development of operations research

Underlying the advance of management theory, in the first half of the nineteenth century,
was an ever-growing belief in the powers of scientifically based rationality. In its ultimate
form this rationality was represented quantitatively rather than qualitatively.

The quest for quantification

In the search for order and predictability, the scientific method has donated a rational
approach to problem solving through the statement of hypotheses, the accommodation of
data, the identification of alternatives, and the testing, verification and selection of a path of
action based on the facts.

Daniel Wren *The Evolution of Management Thought*[9] 1979

The Second World War had brought about a union of managers, government officials
and scientists in an effort to bring order and rationality into the global logistics of
war. The British formed the first operations research (OR) teams of various specialists in
order to bring their knowledge to bear upon the problems of radar systems, anti-aircraft
gunnery, and so forth.

After the war industrial organizations began to realize that the OR methods were
applicable to problems of a non-military nature. The Operations Research Society of
America was founded in 1952. The sorts of areas that mathematical and statistical
methods were applied to were problems of inventory control, production scheduling,

quality control, and capital acquisition. Production and operations management in particular, in the fifties and sixties, became heavily oriented towards mathematics and statistics. At its base was the scientific method of problem solving; the body was composed of specific techniques for quantifying variables and relationships; and its apex was the notion of a model which represented the variables and their relationships for the purposes of prediction and control. Techniques such as statistical sampling – in both market research and quality control – as well as 'linear programming', 'game theory', 'decision trees' and 'simulation' devices were developed. With the advance of electronic computing, models that 'simulate' the behavior of firms, markets and of whole economies became particularly popular – for once you can stimulate something you are in a better position to control it.

The development of decision theory

Along with the development of the quantitatively based, analytical techniques, serious attempts were being made, in the forties and fifties, to bring the OR tools into an overall framework. The outcome of these efforts was the formation of a school of 'decision theorists', who sought to combine the economic concepts of utility and choice with the more modern quantitative tools. The leader of that school was the American economist Herbert Simon.

Simon was particularly concerned with decision making from the standpoint of the logic and psychology of human choice. His central theme was that to study an organization one had to study the complex network of decision processes, which were all directed towards influencing human behavior.[10] By studying the distribution and allocation of decision-making functions, one could comprehend the influences on human behavior, the human choices with regard to organizational inducements, and the establishment of an effective and meaningful equilibrium between freedom offered the individual to make the decision on the job, and the necessity for the organization to impose restrictions on individual freedom.

At a more basic level Simon also paid a lot of attention to studying the basic nature of decision making, from the point of view of the individual decision maker. He distinguished[11] between 'non-programmed decisions', made in accordance with some habit, rule or procedure and 'unprogrammed decisions'. Routine, programmed decisions were not necessarily simple ones, but, like with inventory control, they were susceptible to quantification. Non-programmed decisions, on the other hand, tended to be unique, and qualitative in nature. This qualititative form of managerial decision making, or problem solving, has occupied the time and attention of innumerable management consultants and academics to the present day.

Managerial problem solving

Keith Jackson is an unusual mix of engineer and occupational psychologist who spent the early part of his career researching the skills of airline pilots. He subsequently took up an academic post in the UK, specializing in the area of managerial problem solving. Like corporate strategy and long-range planning this was a subject of great interest to theorists and practitioners alike, in the sixties and seventies.

What managerial problem solving and long-range planning have in common is a methodical approach to management and to business. In fact, at the very foundations of such a methodical approach is the principle that careful planning improves the chances of successful action.

Table 15 The whole problem-solving process

Stages	Phases
1. Formulation	Detection; identification; definition
2. Interpretation	Analysis; description
3. Constructing courses of action	Establishing criteria; generating ideas
4. Decision making	Evaluation; choice; commitment
5. Implementation	Plan; action; control

The methodical approach is brought to bear by dividing the work of problem solving into stages, and by concentrating on one stage at a time. It starts with a formulation of the problem. (See Table 15.)

Formulating the problem
The first stage is really, for Jackson,[12] three stages rolled into one. For before doing anything about looking for a solution to the problem, you have to detect that it exists; identify the problematic aspects of the situation; and then define the problem accurately.

Defining the problem is the most important step – for the analytical problem solver – in solving it. For if you start work on a problem without being absolutely clear what it is, you are bound to waste time and effort on enquiries and activities which are not necessary to the solving of the real problem. The fact that in any problem there is an objective that is sought and an obstacle that prevents someone from reaching the objective, provides you with an effective formula for stating the definition of all problems. Simply to state what the objective and the obstacle are – that is having recognized them both – is sufficient definition for any problem.

Interpreting the problem
The chances of finding a satisfactory solution to a problem are highest when the person solving it understands the problem thoroughly. The second stage, therefore, is devoted to developing an understanding of the problem

For a problem solver to have an understanding of the problem it is first necessary for the essential facts to be put in his mind. Next they must be brought into proper relationship with each other. Only then will it be possible for his mind to make effective use of the information and produce a good solution.

Constructing courses of action
The third stage of problem solving includes both collecting ideas from various outside sources, and also generating ideas of one's own in order to build up one or more possible courses of action. It should begin near where the second stage ends, at a point where an appreciable understanding of the problem situation has been attained.

Decision making

In real life few problems are found to have only one possible solution. The usual state of affairs is that several quite different promising courses of action can be identified, and it then becomes necessary to make a choice between them. The 'decision making' stage, for Jackson, is the one in which a choice is made. Decision making entails evaluating the proposed courses of action against the relevant criteria. The process often has to take account of uncertainty about the outcome of events that have not yet occurred, and it relies on the ability to make sound judgements of the relative merits of the various possible outcomes. The decision making stage is completed when the preferred course of action has been chosen and a firm commitment has been made to carrying it out.

Implementation

The final stage of problem solving is the implementation of the chosen course of action. All the work done in the previous stages may be wasted unless the chosen course is carried out properly. The implementation stage includes all the ways and means of ensuring that this is done. The basis of implementation is detailed and thorough planning, by which one can ensure that the necessary resources are obtained and that a programme of action is drawn up. It must be arranged that all concerned have the information and skill required to do the job properly and are properly led and managed. The plan must be flexible, to take account of further obstacles that may appear, and should have built in control points and procedures. To implement a course of action for solving a problem is to take the necessary steps to get from the current state of affairs in which the problem exists to another state where the objective has been reached. The process of implementation, of course, reintroduces us to management as a whole.

Managerial work

The manager's job

In the same way as Simon in America, and Jackson in Britain, have attempted to ground the abstracted principles of management in everyday reality, so Henry Mintzberg has tried to achieve the same thing, but via a different route. Instead of specifically focussing on decision making and problem solving, in order to ground management theory, he observed and subsequently categorized the totality of the work that managers actually do.

In actual fact Mintzberg was not the first management researcher to categorize managerial work. It is only that he has developed the most appealing conceptual

Table 16 Managerial work

Roles	Sub-roles
Decisional roles	Entrepreneur; disturbance handler; resource allocator; negotiator
Informational roles	Monitor; disseminator: spokesman
Interpersonal roles	Figurehead; leader; liaison

framework. Indeed Koontz and O'Donnell refer to a whole 'empirical school', of which Carlson[13] in Sweden and Steiner in Britain[14] are the best-known representatives. Mintzberg, in the early seventies, made an extensive survey of existing research on the subject of what managers, at all levels, actually do with their time. He integrated his findings with the results of his own intensive research into the activities of a small group of chief executives. The results of his analyses are set out in Table 16.

Decisional roles

Rather than seeing decision making as central to the manager's work, Mintzberg sees it as one of three equally important categories of work. Moreover, he divides 'decision making' roles into four distinct types. Each is involved with the making of decisions from a different angle and within a different context.

Entrepreneur. The 'entrepreneurial' role, for Mintzberg, involves the most managerial initiative. As entrepreneur the manager improves and develops the work of his unit, for example by deciding upon new methods of work or organization. In other words, as entrepreneur, he initiates change himself. Another term for such a role is that of change agent, or of a 'proactive' decision maker.

Disturbance handler. In the role of 'disturbance handler', on the other hand, the manager merely responds to circumstances beyond his control, such as a sudden strike, a breach of contract, or a bad debt. Such 'disturbances' are an inevitable, if not a highly desirable part of a manager's job. They usually call upon powers of instant decision making.

Resource allocator. As a 'resource allocator' a manager is responsible for deciding who and to whom the resources of the organization and of the manager's own time will be allocated. In this role the manager usually makes pre-planned decisions as opposed to proactive or reactive ones. In addition he screens the decisions of others, where necessary, before they are put into effect.

Negotiator. The fourth and final decisional role is that of 'negotiator'. A sales manager negotiates a new contract, a purchasing officer negotiates a new discount structure, or a chief executive negotiates the terms of a collaborative research project with another company. Managers spend a great deal of time making decisions, in the context of negotiations, because they have the information, the contacts and the authority to do so. The decisions involved are both pre-planned and improvised, depending on need and circumstances.

Informational roles

For Mintzberg it is the communicating and receiving of information, rather than the making of decisions, which is central to managerial work. He also stresses that it is the informal rather than the formal aspects of communication which are most called upon, especially at the higher level of management. There are three 'informational' roles in all, starting with that of 'monitor'.

Monitor. As monitor, the manager constantly seeks out information that can be used to advantage. Subordinates and immediate superiors are questioned, and unsolicited information is also collected, mainly through the manager's personal contacts. The monitor role thus enables the manager to be the best informed member of his immediate group.

Disseminator. As disseminator the manager distributes to those immediately above and below him, useful information that would otherwise be inaccessible to them. More often than not the information is disseminated from person to person, individually or in group meetings, rather than through formal and impersonal channels. It is generally information of an everyday nature rather than the more irregular communications that become part of his 'spokesman' role.

Spokesman. Finally, as a spokesman, the manager transmits some of the information he has collected outside of his unit, or even outside of his organization. Keeping people in high places informed, both within and without the enterprise, is part and parcel of this role. Speeches and reports to official bodies, like trade associations, consumer groups, and government regulatory agencies, is part of the spokesman's responsibility.

Interpersonal roles

Three interpersonal roles help the manager keep the organization running smoothly. Although both the decisional and the informational roles involve dealing with people, the interpersonal aspect in both cases is secondary rather than primary. In his 'liaison' role, in the role of 'figurehead', and as 'leader', the manager puts interpersonal relations first.

Liaison. In his liaison role, then, the manager deals with people other than his immediate peers, superiors and subordinates. He makes, and responds to, contacts from other departments, other divisions, and even other organizations – such as suppliers, distributors or educational and research establishments. As a liason person, moreover, his effectiveness depends primarily on his interpersonal abilities rather than upon his capacity to make quick decisions or process information efficiently.

Figurehead. As a head of a unit the manager sometimes acts as a 'figurehead' by performing ceremonial duties. These may involve welcoming a new member of staff, attending a subordinate's wedding, or addressing a sales conference. In each case more is involved than acting as a spokesman on a particular issue. For in this figurehead role the manager is representing the organization, or his particular unit, as a whole.

Leader. The all important 'leader' role is more pervasive than either of the other two. It is a role that the manager, in dealing with people inside and out, needs to carry with him wherever he goes. As leader it is his function to empathize with others, and to respond to their needs, and also to project the values and beliefs of his organization upon them, so that they become duly motivated and inspired.

Managerial work as a whole

The three sets of decisional, information, and interpersonal roles then – at least as Mintzberg sees them[15] – are actual rather than 'idealized' management activities. Mintzberg, like all other members of the empirical school, are interested in what managers actually do. Unlike the decision theory school, which takes a prime interest in decision making and problem solving, and the operational (or process school), which has established a management ideal, the empiricists are pragmatic. They have taken an interest in what actually happens.

The trouble is, of course, as Peters and Waterman would be the first to emphasize, that these empiricists are also biased. They ignore the 'primal' aspects of management because they are not looking in that direction. They refer, for example, to 'interpersonal processes' rather than to 'people'. They also relegate entrepreneurship to only a small part of a further part of the managerial whole. There is no such thing, then, as objective, impartial, empirical observation. Mintzberg is therefore presenting just another view of management, albeit a very useful one. He helps us to see beyond that strongly entrenched and conventional wisdom that Fayol established in the 1920s.

It is to that conventional wisdom that I now wish to turn. Because it still does have an enormously important influence on the theory and practice of management I want to give this 'operational', 'process', or 'principles' school full consideration. In order to do so I need to call on the redoubtable pair, Koontz and O'Donnell, for their in-depth analysis of managerial principles, or functions.

The analysis of management functions

The need for principles of management

Harold Koontz and Cyril O'Donnell, as Professors at the University of California's Graduate School of Business Administration, set about – in the fifties – providing a conceptual framework for the 'orderly presentation of fundamental knowledge in management'.

The need for such a framework of principles, as they saw it, was fourfold:

- To increase efficiency – when management principles can be developed, proved, and used, they say, managerial efficiency inevitably improves. The conscientious manager becomes more effective when he uses established guidelines to help solve his problems, without having to engage in risky trial and error.
- To train management – principles act as a checklist on the elements of management. Without such principles the training of managers becomes a haphazard, hit and miss activity.
- To improve knowledge – the need for tested knowledge of organized management, Koontz and O'Donnell argue, is great, and anything which makes management research more pointed will help improve management practice.
- To attain social goals – in a broad sense, management coordinates the efforts of people so that individual objectives become translated into social attainments. 'Development of management principles, by increasing efficiency in the use of human as well as

material resources, would unquestionably have a revolutionary impact on the cultural level of society.'[16]

The functions of the manager

Koontz and O'Donnell, in arriving at their functional classification, firstly distinguish between business and management functions. Whereas the functions of production, marketing, finance and accounting differ from one enterprise to another, those of the manager are common to all.

Management functions are grouped around the activities of planning, organizing, staffing, directing and control. Each have their particular subdivisions which I shall now review.

Planning

Planning consists of setting objectives, establishing key premises or assumptions, setting policies, making strategic decisions, and acting on the plans and decisions.

Objectives

The identification of objectives is the first step in planning. 'Objectives' are variously referred to as purposes, missions, goals, or targets. 'Purpose' or 'mission' might be used to convey such ultimate ends as the basic reason for the enterprise's being. 'Goals' or 'targets' reflect more specific qualitative, or especially quantitative, performance expectations. Objectives must be set for the enterprise as a whole and for each of its sub-divisions. They need to be prescribed for both the short and for the long term, and achievement has to be regularly monitored against expectation. Finally, objectives must be planned and communicated throughout the organization.

Premises

Planning 'premises' are assumptions regarding the quantity and quality of those key elements, in the firm's internal and external environments, that affect the manager's plans and forecasts. Externally these are reflected in the general business environment – economical, political, technological and social; in the product market, that is in the factors influencing the demand for the firm's product; and in the factor market, that is in the factors influencing the nature and extent of the supply of physical and human resources.

Premises internal to the firm include the sales forecast, capital investment in plant and equipment, major policies and programmes already in force, as well as the values and attitudes of key people in the company.

Policy making

Policies are guides to thinking in decision making. They reflect and interpret objectives, channel decisions to contribute to objectives, and thereby establish the framework for planning programmes. They thus establish limits to plans, as planning premises provide the operational background to them. Major policies beget minor ones. Thus a policy might be as broad as that of financing growth through internally generated profits, and as narrow as the derived policy of accounting separately for each particular unit's imputed profitability.

Decision making

Decision making – the actual selection from among alternatives of a course of action – is at the core of planning. Assuming known goals and clear planning premises, the first step in decision making is the development of alternatives. Once appropriate alternatives have been isolated, the next step is to evaluate them and select the one that will best contribute to the firm's goal. That process of evaluation and selection will be based on experience, on experimentation, or on further research and analysis.

Planning in action

When a plan is complete – with proper assignments made and understood – and it enters the phase in which the manager checks on actual execution, the planning function shifts into control. However, in practice these two functions inevitably blend into a whole. The shift to control may be imperceptible, as exemplified in budgeting. Making a budget is planning, whereas administering it is control. Inevitably, the coordination of the entire planning process down the line must precede proper execution.

Organizing

Whatever is planned needs to be organized, if it is to take effect. Organization encompasses the span of management, basic departmentation, the assignment of activities, line and staff functioning, the decentralization of authority, and making organizing effective.

Span of magement

The principle of span of management asserts that there is a limit in each managerial position to the number of people an individual can effectively manage. However, the exact number will vary from case to case, depending on the person managing, the persons being managed, and the tasks in which they are engaged. The basic principle, according to Koontz and O'Donnell, does exist, has not been superseded, and is useful in guiding managers toward managing the right number of subordinates in the rightly proportioned organization.

Basic departmentation

The limitation on the number of subordinates that can be directly managed would restrict the size of companies if it were not for the device of 'departmentation'. Grouping activities and employees into departments makes it possible to expand organization to an indefinite degree. The basis for departmentation varies. It may be according to function, territory, product, or customer, as well as by sub-departments in each of these areas. For example, marketing (functional) may be subdivided into publicity and sales. The wider the spread of business – functionally, geographically, product- or customer-wise – the stronger the case for departmentation in that area.

Assignment of activities

In order to accomplish goals, carry out plans, and make it possible for people to work together, an intentional structure of roles and activities must be designated and maintained. Activities must be grouped logically and assigned to appropriate departments. An activity may be defined in terms of what people do that is essential to the realization of the enterprise objective, or of one particular part of the enterprise.

Line and staff relationships
Authority relationships, whether perpendicular or horizontal, are the factors – for Koontz and O'Donnell – that breathe life into the organization, as well as harness departmental activities, and bring coordination to the enterprise. In 'line' authority, one finds a superior and a subordinate with a line of authority running from the former to the latter. The nature of the staff relationship, however, whether it be in public relations or corporate planning, is advisory.

Decentralization of authority
Top managers increasingly realize that the functions of managing extend through the organization to the foreman level and that they must decentralize authority accordingly. Moreover, if one is to learn to manage, one must experience managing.

At the same time, extensive decentralization, Koontz and O'Donnell emphasize, is not to be followed blindly. In many organizations, they say, the size and complexity of operations militate against it. But the principal problem of decentralization is loss of control. No enterprise can decentralize to the extent that its existence is threatened and the achievement of its goals is frustrated. Selective centralization of such vital areas as financing, major capital expenditures, overall budgeting, new product planning, and personnel planning and policy making is highly desirable.

Making organizing effective
Application of logic to organization indicates the following sequential steps, in making organizing effective:

1. Establishing of enterprise objectives.
2. Formulation of derivative objectives, policies and plans.
3. Determination of activities necessary to accomplish these.
4. Enumeration and classification of these activities.
5. Grouping these activities in the light of human and material resources available, and the best way of using them.
6. Delegating to the head of each grouping the authority necessary to perform the activities.
7. Tying these groupings together horizontally and vertically, through authority relationships and information systems.

Staffing
Staffing, as a management function, includes the selection, appraisal, training and development of managers. Though something of an odd man out – when compared with the sequential functions of planning, organizing, directing and controlling – it is nevertheless an important part of management. The clearer the definition of management roles and their translation into human requirements, and the better incumbents are evaluated and trained, the more the quality of personnel can be assured.

Selecting managers

Selection of managers, at all levels of the company, may be made from within or without the company. This basis for selection is subject to both personnel policy, and availability of personnel. Some of the most important managerial qualities sought after, with a view to recruiting, are general intelligence and analytical ability, an ability to motivate and communicate, the desire to manage at an appropriate level, and basic integrity. These qualities can be gaged through testing, through personal interviewing, and through the routine appraisal of current and potential managers.

Appraising managers

Management appraisal involves an assessment of the actual and potential effectiveness of incumbent managers. Most companies provide for an annual or semi-annual formal appraisal and review. Periodic, informal assessments are a useful addendum.

A particularly popular approach to management appraisal is that of management by objectives (MBO), as – for example – advocated by Peter Drucker. It embraces the practice of setting mutually agreed goals, that is between superior and subordinate, and regularly monitoring progress against them. The results of formal appraisals, whether or not MBO is involved, predetermine the promotion prospects of managers at all levels of a company. They are also a very useful tool in their training and development.

Training and developing managers

Koontz and O'Donnell use 'manager development' to refer to the progress a manager makes in learning how to manage, and 'managerial training' to refer to the programme devised by top management to facilitate this learning process. Thus, the firm is seen as providing training; the manager, as developing efficiency by way of his training. The practice of management training may be on or off the job, it may involve formal schooling or be experientially based, it may involve one or all of the management functions, and it may be undertaken individually, or in groups. Finally, training and development, combined, may involve job rotation, planned career progression, and the creation of 'assistant to ...' positions, as well as actual training programmes on the one hand, and formal mentoring or coaching on the other.

Directing

To direct subordinates, in Koontz and O'Donnel's terms, a manager must motivate, communicate and lead. Faulty directing can completely nullify all the work that has gone into organizing and staffing the enterprise, and it can make the attainment of objectives called for by plans impossible.

Motivation

A sound motivational system for management is likely to be based on sociological principles, the practices of enterprise, and convictions concerning the ends of man. Managers must attempt to understand their subordinates in order to select intelligently effective elements of a motivational system to be applied to each individual.

One way of understanding people is through an 'hierarchy of needs' (see Chapter 22), with basic physical needs at the lower end of the hierarchy, and social and psychological ones higher up. Firms whose reward systems are purely geared towards financial remuneration might only satisfy the lower order needs. A sound motivational system, for Koontz and O'Donnell, will therefore not only provide adequate financial rewards but also opportunities for growth in stature and responsibility. Moreover, through also 'doing unto others as you would have them do to you', morale can be maintained at a high level.

Communication

Although communication pervades all management functions it is particularly important in the context of directing. Good communication might be defined as 'the interchange of thought or information to bring about mutual understanding and confidence, as well as good human relations'. Communication is the means whereby organized activity is unified. It is also the means whereby behavior is modified, change is effected and goals are achieved. In its broadest sense, according to Koontz and O'Donnell, the purpose of communication within the enterprise is to effect change – to influence action in the direction of the corporation's overall interests.

Finally, there are – so Koontz and O'Donnell tell us – four principles for establishing good communication:

1. The principle of 'clarity'. Communicate in commonly understood language.
2. The principle of attention. Give full attention to receiving communications.
3. The principle of integrity. Make communications support organizational objectives.
4. The principle of 'strategic use of informal information'. Use informal information constructively as a means of communication.

Leadership

Leadership is that skill of a manager which enables him to persuade subordinates to apply themselves with zeal and confidence. Leadership also means shaping the 'character' of the organization so that the execution of policy will be achieved to the 'spirit' as well as to the 'letter'.

Leadership functions may be classified as directing, responding and representing. Whereas directing is of the essence of leadership, the good leader is responsive to his subordinates' felt and expressed needs, and represents them effectively to his superiors, and to the outside world. Finally, a leader has special traits – especially self-knowledge, empathy towards others, and objectivity towards situations. In fact it is impossible to be objective without self-knowledge, and it is impossible to inspire people, to follow your lead, without empathy for them and their situations.

Controlling

The final management function involves controlling. It implies measurement of accomplishment against plan, and the correction of deviations to assure attainment of objectives. Once a plan becomes operational, control is necessary to measure progress, to uncover deviations from plan, and to indicate corrective action. Control is thus the function whereby every manager, from chief executive to sales supervisor, makes sure that what is done is what is intended.

The basic control process

Specifically, then, the basic control process – whereever it is found and whatever it controls – involves three steps:

1. Establishing standards.
2. Measuring performance against these standards.
3. Correcting deviations from standards and plans.

Standards represent the expression of planning goals in such terms that the actual accomplishment of assigned duties can be measured against them. The measurement of performance against standard should ideally be on a future basis, so that deviations may be detected in advance of their actual occurrence, and corrective action taken. Such corrective action is the point at which control merges with the other management functions.

Finally, for Koontz and O'Donnell, there are ten requirements of effective controls: they must reflect the nature and needs of the activity; they should report deviations promptly; they must be forward looking; they should point up exceptions at critical points; they should be objective; they must be flexible; they should reflect the organizational pattern; they should be economical; they must be understandable; finally, they should indicate where corrective action is required.

Control techniques

Although the basic nature and purpose of management control does not change, new tools, in recent years, have extended the range and focus of control procedures and processes. Electronic computing and telecommunications, in particular, have enabled data to be processed at a speed and in volumes, previously considered impossible. Moreover the advance of desk top and personal computing has reinforced the prospects of real time, on line control.

With the increasing use of the computer a great deal of attention has been given to the development of information systems. This is a recognition of the fact that many items of input data may be useful for a number of different outputs. Such information has had particular impact, recently, in retailing, where information systems connecting points of sale with warehouses are ever expanding, as well as becoming more refined.

Control of overall performance

Control techniques and systems must be tailored to the areas they are designed to measure and correct. Most controls are designed for specific things, including: policies, wages and salaries, employee selection and training, research and development, product quality, costs, pricing, capital expenditures and cash flow. A widely used control of overall performance takes the form of a summary of budgets. A budget summary, being a resumé of all the individual budgets of the company, reflects company plans so that sales volume, costs, profits, utilization of capital and return on investment might be seen in their proper relationship. One of the most successfully used control methods, in fact, is that of measuring both the absolute and relative success of a company unit by the ratio of earnings to investment of capital. This tool, therefore, does not look at profit as an absolute, but as a return on capital employed in the business.

Control of management quality

At the base of control is the fact that the outcome of plans is influenced by people. Any hope of abolishing unsatisfactory results lies in changing the future actions of the responsible person, through additional training, modification of procedures or new policy. This is the crux of controlling the quality of management.

There are two ways of seeing that the person responsible modifies future action. The normal procedure is to trace the cause of an unsatisfactory result back to the person responsible for it and get him to correct his practices. This Koontz and O'Donnell call 'indirect control'. The alternative is to develop better managers who will skillfully apply principles and thus eliminate undesirable results caused by poor management. This is called 'direct control'.

The desirability of direct control, in the context of the broader aim of controlling management quality, rests on what Koontz and O'Donnell consider to be four valid assumptions:

1. That qualified managers make a minimum of errors.
2. That managerial performance can be measured.
3. That management principles are useful diagnostic tools in measuring management performance.
4. That the application of management principles can be evaluated.

In other words, the principles outlined in Koontz and O'Donnell's analysis of management functions, may – in their view – be used as standards in objective quality control of managers. By framing these principles in the form of objective questions, the questioner can establish whether managers are operating essentially in accordance with principles.

Management audit

Planning

A high degree of exactitude can be reached by a superior who wishes to determine the planning ability of a subordinate, because planning is a logical process, calling for clear definition of objectives, thorough understanding of planning premises and careful analysis of alternatives.

Organizing

To determine the organizing skills of subordinates, a superior will methodically check grouping of activities and authority delegations to see how much they contribute to departmental goals. The clarity, completeness, and timeliness of activity assignments and authority delegations can also be gauged.

Staffing

The superior wishing to assess the staffing ability of his subordinates will first examine the job profile or description for each person reporting to the subordinate to see whether it is up to date and whether the specifications are clear and pertinent. He will also assess the suitability and promotability of personnel selected for posts, and the extent to which they have been developed while on the job.

Directing

Determining the ability of the manager to direct involves an assessment of his skill in guiding his subordinates, his ability to communicate within and without his department, and his skill in motivating his personnel to work zealously, and with pride.

Controlling

The superior, in managing a subordinate's ability to control, will check the standards used to measure results of planned activity. Significant standards, properly located, which avoid overlapping and obsolescence, will reflect good judgment. The superior will also examine his subordinate's attention to the review and revision of such standards.

Koontz and O'Donnell *The Principles of Management*[17] 1968

Conclusion

The essence of good management, for Koontz and O'Donnell, is coordination. It is the 'meta function' that ultimately controls, and thereby links together, all the five separate functions of planning, organizing, staffing, directing and controlling. The essence of coordination, though, eludes Koontz and O'Donnell, because they are too good at analysis!

Managerial coordination

It is the manager's responsibility to achieve coordination. He achieves it in two ways. First, he assures that the environment facilitates coordination by creating an appropriate organization structure, selecting skillful subordinates and training and supervising them effectively, providing and explaining the integrated plans and programs that subordinates will carry out, and establishing means to determine whether plans are being carried out properly and programs are on schedule.

Second, he makes certain that his subordinates understand the principles of coordination and the importance of acting upon them.

Koontz and O'Donnell *The Principles of Management*[18] 1968

Unfortunately, for all their brilliance in analysis, neither Taylor or Fayol, nor Simon or Mintzberg, nor Koontz or O'Donnell, were particularly adept at synthesis. In other words they were all much better at dividing things up than at bringing them together. For that very reason, as I have already emphasized in Chapter 5, they missed the essential message that Mary Parker Follett – the only one of two early management theorists capable of genuine synthesis – had conveyed.

The other great synthesizer, to whom we shall now turn in Chapter 18, is Chester Barnard. In fact, in turning from the 'hard' branch of management 'skill' to the softer branch of management and learning 'style', we switch from a pre-emphasis towards analysis and classification to an orientation towards synthesis, and integration.

References

1. H. Koontz and C. O'Donnell *The Principles of Management*, McGraw-Hill (1968), p. 35.
2. F. Taylor, *The Principles of Scientific Management*, Harper Bros (1911), p. 7.

3. H. Fayol, *General and Industrial Administration*, Pitmans (1949), p. 4.
4. D. Wren, *The Evolution of Management Thought*, Wiley (1979), pp. 237–238.
5. H. Fayol, *op. cit.*, p. 40.
6. H. Fayol, *op. cit.*, pp. 5–6.
7. L. Gulick and C. Urwick (eds), *Papers on the Science of Administration*, Columbia University (1937), p. 13.
8. G. Terry, *Principles of Management*, Irwin (1953).
9. D. Wren, *op. cit.*, p. 509.
10. H. Simon, *Administrative Behaviour*, Macmillan (1945).
11. H. Simon *The New Science of Management Decision* (revised edn), Prentice Hall (1977).
12. K. Jackson, *The Art of Solving Problems*, Heinemann (1975).
13. C. Carlson, *Executive Behaviour*, Strombergs (1951).
14. R. Steiner, *Managers and Their Jobs*, Macmillan (1967).
15. H. Mintzberg, *Managerial Work*, McGraw-Hill (1973).
16. H. Koontz and C. O'Donnell, *op. cit.* (1968), p. 15.
17. H. Koontz and C. O'Donnell, *op. cit.* (1968), pp. 720–23.
18. H. Koontz and C. O'Donnell, *op. cit.* (1968), p. 53.

14 Management style

Contents

Key concepts

Once you have fully understood the chapter you should be able to define the following concepts in your own terms:

Action learning	Lateral thinking
Accommodative style	Learning cycle
Apprehension function	Learning functions
Assimilative style	Learning styles
Autocratic manager	Management science
Benevolent autocrat	Management styles
Bureaucratic manager	Missionary manager
Comprehension function	Motivating factors
Compromiser manager	Motivation/hygiene theory
Contingency theory of	'P' and 'Q'
leadership	Related manager
Convergent style	Relationships orientation
Dedicated manager	Resilience
Deserter manager	Rigidity
Developer manager	Situational effectiveness
Divergent style	System alpha
Drift	System beta
Executive manager	System gamma
Experiential learning	Theory of hygiene/
Extension function	motivation
Flexibility	Theory 'X'
Grid (managerial)	Theory 'Y'
Integrated manager	Three 'D' management
Intension function	Vertical thinking

Objectives

Upon completing this chapter you should be able to do the following:

1. Compare and contrast management and learning styles.
2. Outline Theory 'X' and Theory 'Y', the Managerial Grid, and the Contingency Theory of Leadership.
3. Summarize Reddin's approach to managerial effectiveness, commenting on your own management style, in 3 'D' terms.
4. Compare and contrast De Bono's approach to David Kolb's, commenting on your own style of learning and thinking.
5. Outline Reg Revans' contribution to management theory, especially his role in synthesizing manager and management.

Introduction

In this Chapter I want to turn from the 'hardened' notion of management skills to the 'softer' idea of management and learning style.

While skills are impersonal and analytical, management and learning styles are interpersonal and interrelated. Whereas style, like skill, is an object of rational analysis, it is much more subject to individual and situational integration than the principles (skills) of management. Let us see, then, how 'management style', as a subject of theoretical and practical interest, first emerged.

The origins of management style

The development of codifiable management skills, as we saw in the previous chapter, supplanted the instinctive attributes of risk-taking enterprise. Instead of the primal entrepreneur using improvized tactics and imposing his will the rational manager planned and controlled, organized and directed.

However, until the fifties at least, the individual managerial personality – as opposed to the collectively codified managerial functions, operations or principles – remained in a primal state. In other words, personalized management traits, like empathy and integrity, were considered to be 'a good thing', in all situations. These traits were as subjectively based as such entrepreneurial qualities as courage and flair and were seldom tested for predictive validity.

Leadership and management traits

For centuries effective managers have been described and sometimes measured in terms of a list of personal qualities or traits that all effective managers were thought to possess. Traits such as energy and judgment often appeared on such lists. The appeal of this approach is that it is easy to understand, appears sensible, and is widely used.

The weaknesses of the trait approach are that there is no agreement on the best traits that fit all situations, that there is no evidence that one group of traits predicts effectiveness generally and that there are now over a thousand different traits to deal with.

For these reasons the trait approach is becoming less popular with social scientists. It seems likely, however, that as a single sound theory becomes established, sets of traits will become useful but with an important difference.

The traits will not be drawn at will from a list of qualities but will be a set of interrelated ideas associated with a comprehensive theory. It is not the idea of traits that is wrong but rather the absence of a theory to show which traits are important for particular managerial situations.

William Reddin *Managerial Effectiveness*[1] 1970

The origins of learning style in management

Whereas the origins of management style lie in North America, learning style – as a key factor in management – found its home in Britain.

While Edward De Bono, who was orginally Maltese, set managers off in the direction of 'thinking and learning style', and the American David Kolb initially helped them along on their journey of discovery, the key individual behind its development was Reg Revans. His life and work will form the substantive part of this chapter. In fact professor Revans' gift for synthesis, in the fields of management and learning, surpasses that of any of his predecessors or successors.

While management style, in content and form, reached its heyday in the sixties and seventies, learning style has gained popularity in the seventies and eighties. In fact it is learning rather than management style, as we shall discover in Chapter 22, which is the more closely linked to developmental management. Whereas management style merely substitutes interpersonality, or relationships, for impersonality; learning style introduces individuality and, prospectively, development.

Let me start, though, by elaborating upon management style.

Management style

The approaches to analyzing and integrating management style, which essentially evolved in the fifties and sixties, fall in two main groupings. The earlier ones differentiated, primarily, between production-centered task and relationship-centered people, and posed a 'best' style of management. Their orientation was more towards analysis than towards integration.

The later ones not only compared and contrasted a task *versus* a people-orientation, but also introduced situational effectiveness. In other words, these approaches interrelated style and situation in the overall interests of managerial objectives.

Task versus people

Theories 'X' and 'Y'

The first person to systematically compare and contrast a task- versus a people-orientation was Douglas McGregor.[2] In fact management today is still liable to refer to theories 'X' and 'Y', although it is some thirty years since McGregor first introduced these theories to us.

Douglas Mcgregor identified two prevailing 'styles' of management that pervaded America in the fifties. Each was based on opposing sets of assumptions about human behavior – hence 'X' and 'Y'.

Theories 'X' and 'Y'

Theory 'X' assumptions were:

- The average human being has an inherent dislike for work and will avoid it if he can.
- Because of this human characteristic of dislike of work, most people must be coerced, controlled, directed and threatened with punishment to get them to put forth adequate effort toward the achievement of organizational objectives.
- The average human being prefers to be directed, wishes to avoid responsibility, has relatively little ambition, and wants security above all.

Theory 'Y' assumptions, by contrast, were:

- The expenditure of physical and mental effort in work is as natural as play or rest.

- Man will exercise self-direction and self-control in the service of objectives to which he is committed.
- Commitment to objectives is a function of the rewards associated with their achievement.
- The average human being learns, under proper conditions, not only to accept but also to seek responsibility.
- The capacity to exercize a relatively high degree of imagination, ingenuity, and creativity is widely distributed amongst the population.

Douglas McGregor *The Human Side of Enterprise*[3] 1960

To McGregor, how people were treated was largely a self-fulfilling prophecy; if managers assumed that people were lazy, and treated them as such, then they would be lazy. On the other hand, if they assumed that workers sought challenging work, and provided it, the workers would respond positively.

Finally, McGregor did not disguise the fact that he much favored the 'Y' approach over the 'X' one. In fact he saw theory 'Y' as setting the tone for a new approach to the management of human resources.

Motivation/hygiene theory

Following closely behind McGregor was the American management, and motivational consultant, Fred Herzberg. In the mid-fifties he, and his associates, set out to discover what lay at the source of peoples' satisfactions and dissatisfactions at work. What they discovered, having intensively researched some 200 engineers and accountants, was that the 'dissatisfiers', or hygiene factors, were different from the job 'satisfiers', or motivating factors.

Hygiene and motivating factors

Motivating factors – the work content:
- Achievement
- Advancement and growth
- Recognition
- Responsibility
- The work itself

Hygiene factors – the work context:
- Company policy and administration
- Status, salary, security
- Quality of supervision
- Working conditions
- Working relationships

Fred Herzberg, *et al. Work and the Nature of Man*[4] 1959

Whereas the engineers were dissatisfied at work if such 'hygiene' factors as pay and physical working conditions were perceived to be inadequate, these factors in isolation – the work context – could never be a source of satisfaction. Only the 'motivating' factors, inherent within the work itself – the work content – could create satisfaction.

In other words, Herzberg provided substantiating evidence for McGregor's orientation towards theory 'Y'. Two more Americans, Jane Mouton and Robert Blake, then progressed the matter of management style further, in the early sixties. The other major motivational theorist of that era, Abraham Maslow, we shall be considering in depth in Chapter 22.

The managerial grid

The managerial grid, first made public in 1964, has proved the most operationally enduring of all the approaches to analyzing and developing management style. For what Mouton and Blake did was to turn a new theory into an operational technique for developing managers, particularly their managing styles.

The grid, as illustrated in Fig. 21, is based on the simple division between 'People' and 'Production' orientations. In other words, instead of assuming that style 'X' is bad and 'Y' is good, Mouton and Blake implied that there was room for both. What they did, in fact, was to turn 'X' into concern for production, and 'Y' into concern for people. Their stance, therefore, was less value-laden than McGregor's.

'Concern for production', they say, may be reflected in policy decisions, in the number of creative ideas that applied research turns into useful products, in the number of accounts processed, in the quality of thoroughness of support services, as well as in the volume of sales and physical output. Production is therefore not limited to things. It covers whatever it is that the organization or department engages its people to accomplish, whether it be properly accurate records, suitably trained personnel, or adequate levels of productivity.

'Concern for people', in similar vein, can be expressed in a variety of different ways. These include the degree of personal commitment one displays towards a job for which one is responsible; the extent to which one allocates responsibility based on trust rather than obedience; the quality of the working conditions one establishes; and the intimacy of the social relationships one develops.

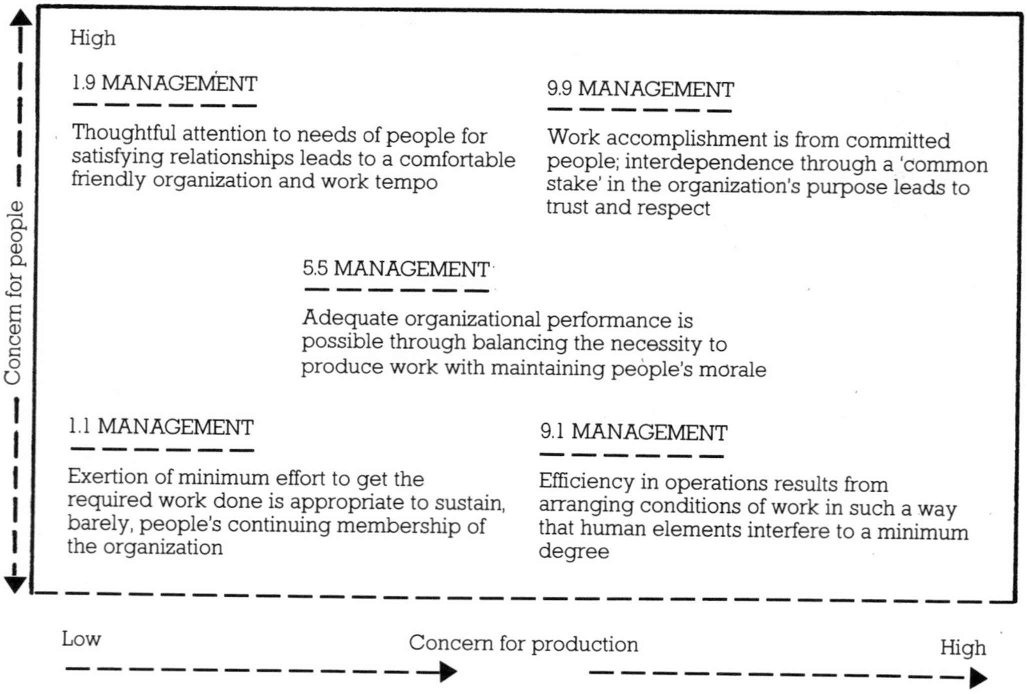

High

1.9 MANAGEMENT

Thoughtful attention to needs of people for satisfying relationships leads to a comfortable friendly organization and work tempo

9.9 MANAGEMENT

Work accomplishment is from committed people; interdependence through a 'common stake' in the organization's purpose leads to trust and respect

5.5 MANAGEMENT

Adequate organizational performance is possible through balancing the necessity to produce work with maintaining people's morale

1.1 MANAGEMENT

Exertion of minimum effort to get the required work done is appropriate to sustain, barely, people's continuing membership of the organization

9.1 MANAGEMENT

Efficiency in operations results from arranging conditions of work in such a way that human elements interfere to a minimum degree

Concern for people

Low   Concern for production   High

Fig. 24 The managerial grid.

Situational effectiveness

A contingency theory of leadership

By the late sixties the differences between leadership and management had become much less visible than in the fifties, when rational management theorists had begun to set their concepts apart from primal leadership traits. The key issue, by this stage, was not leadership versus management, but that of standardized versus situational approaches to leadership or management style.

In other words, the question that the American psychologist Fred Fiedler began to ask was – is there such a thing as a best management style, be it McGregor's 'Y', or Mouton and Blake's 9.9 (see Fig. 24)? His answer was categorically, 'it depends on the situation'.

Fiedler identified three critical factors that impinged on what he termed 'leadership effectiveness'. These were position power, task structure, and the personal relationships between the leader and his followers.

> The Contingency Model ... states that a group's performance will be contingent on the appropriate matching of leadership style and the degree of favorableness of the group situation for the leader, that is, the degree to which the situation provides the leader with influence over his group members. The model suggests that group performance can, therefore, be improved either by modifying the leader's style or by modifying the group-task situation.[5]

The crucial point that Fiedler was making, unlike McGregor or Mouton and Blake, was that – as far as he was concerned – there was no such thing as an optimal management style. Rather he was concerned with matching the leader, in person, with the situation. The situation, in turn, varied according to the leader's power and influence in his organization, the tightness or looseness of the task at hand, and the attitudes and skills of the group of people under his charge.

It is common knowledge today, for example, that a group of professional scientists working in a research laboratory, need to be managed very differently from a group of manual workers on an assembly line. At the same time, and here is the rub, both groups may benefit equally from the sorts of 'shared value' to which Peters and Waterman allude. So Fiedler has a point, but it is not the whole point.

Managerial effectiveness

The person who has done most, though, to advance the cause of situational effectiveness, is not Fiedler, but the Canadian, Bill Reddin:

> Managerial style, with its connotations of effectiveness, simply cannot be defined solely with reference to behavior. It always must be defined with reference to the demands of the situation ... As a simple example, a man who yells, 'Everybody out', in a burning theater would be labelled a 'benevolent autocrat'. Precisely the same comment used to close an office or a restaurant for the night may be labelled an 'autocrat'.[6]

Flexibility and resilience

Reddin, who grew up in Britain, Canada and the United States, has worked out an admirably simple means of relating style to effectiveness. While the effective manager, for Reddin, exercises 'flexibility' and 'resilience' the ineffective one exhibits 'drift' and 'rigidity'.

An effective manager identifies the situation at hand, including the people and events with which he is dealing, and consciously 'switches on' a particular approach (flexibility) or purposefully holds on to a particular style (resilience) for the occasion.

For example – operating flexibly – a natural delegator 'arbitrarily' undertakes a particular task himself because of extreme time pressures; or a manager – displaying resilience – who normally works with his group as a whole, resists the pressure to 'divide and rule' when the going gets tough.

The ineffective manager, by way of contrast, sticks to his same old guns (rigidity) whoever and whatever confronts him, or slips and slides (drift), under pressure, from one approach to another.

For example, he remains an autocrat, when shifted from production to research management; or he slides, willy nilly, from being authoritative to being non-commital, only because he cannot handle a situation.

Tasks and relationships
Although Reddin is concerned ultimately with situational effectiveness rather than with styles, in isolation, he uses the same initial building blocks as Mouton and Blake, that is 'tasks' (concern for production) and 'relationships' (concern for people).

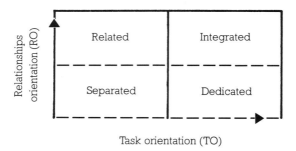

Fig. 25 Task and relationship orientations.

At this initial point (see Fig. 25) Reddin's four styles – separated, related, dedicated and integrated – are neutral. None, isolated as they are from the individual or the situation, is good or bad. They merely reflect different combinations, and also varying degrees, of concern for task or relationships. As a result, then, the 'Separated' – low task/low relationships – manager examines, measures, administers, controls and maintains; the 'Related' – low task/high relationships – manager trusts, listens, accepts, advises and encourages.

The 'Dedicated' manager – high task/low relationships – organizes, initiates, directs, completes, and evaluates; and the 'Integrated' manager – high task/high relationships – participates, interacts, motivates, integrates and innovates.

In each situation, or in each part of the organization, one set of qualities is likely to be at a premium rather than another. For example the 'Separated' style – examining, measuring, administering, controlling and maintaining – may go down very well in an accounts department, and may be disastrous in research. However, effectiveness is not only a function of the situation, but also of the person, that is the manager himself.

Three-dimensional management

Management style for Reddin is three-dimensional (Fig. 26). The four basic styles, as illustrated in Fig. 26, each have their 'effective' and 'ineffective' versions. In the effective version the manager exhibits flexibility and resilience as, say, a successful 'bureaucrat' or 'executive'. In the ineffective version the manager exhibits drift and rigidity as an unsuccessful 'deserter' or 'compromiser'.

The effective manager, who is capable of being flexible and resilient, knows where he stands, and feels sufficiently confident in himself to adapt to people and situations without fear of compromize. The ineffective manager is unsure of where he is coming from and is therefore defensive and inward looking. He is therefore liable to stick to, or drift into, an inappropriate style for the situation at hand.

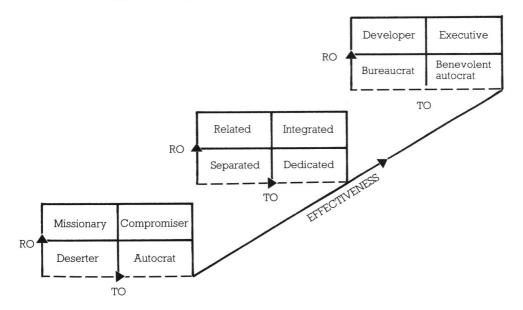

Fig. 26 Three 'D' management.

Each of the four styles, then, has its generic character, combined with its effective and ineffective forms. These are set out below. In each of the four categories – separated, related, dedicated, and integrated – I have cited Reddin's generic indicators first, followed by the ineffective and then the effective equivalents.

1. Separated – deserter – bureaucrat. I start with 'separated', the generic category, followed by the 'deserter' (ineffective) and then the 'bureaucrat' (effective).
   (a) Separated manager: Tends to be cautious, careful, conservative, orderly; prefers paperwork, procedures, facts; looks for established principles; seeks accuracy, precision, correctness, perfection; tends to be steady, deliberate, patient; and is calm, modest, discreet.
   (b) Deserter manager: Works to rule, minimizes output, gives up; avoids involvement, responsibility, or commitment; gives few useful opinions or suggestions; hinders

others from progressing, generally making things difficult for them; resists change, by being generally uncooperative and uncommunicative.

(c) Bureaucratic manager: Follows orders, rules, and procedures; is reliable and dependable; maintains a system and a going concern; watches out for detail and is generally efficient; is rational, logical, and self-controlled; tends to be fair, just and equitable.

2. Dedicated – autocrat – benevolent autocrat. Whereas the separated style is low on concern for both task and relationships, the 'dedicated' one is high on task, but still low on relationships.

(a) Dedicated manager: He is determined, aggressive and confident; tends to be busy, driving and takes the initiative; he sets individual tasks, responsibilities and standards; he is self-reliant, independent and ambitious; he uses tangible rewards and punishments to motivate people; he ensures that the task, rather than people, come first.

(b) Autocratic manager: He is critical and threatening; he makes all the important decisions himself; he demands obedience and supresses conflict; he wants action, and results, immediately; communication is directed downwards only, and he acts without consultation; he is feared and disliked.

(c) Benevolent autocrat: He is decisive, and displays initiatives; he is industrious and energetic; he is committed to tasks and is a finisher; he evaluates performance constantly, taking into account quantity, quality, waste and time; he is cost-, sales-, and profit-conscious; he gets results.

3. Related – missionary – developer. While the dedicated managers are high on task and low on relationships the 'related' ones are the opposite.

(a) Related manager: People come first; he emphasizes personal development; he operates informally, quietly, often unnoticed; he takes time out for protracted dialogue; he is sympathetic, approving, accepting and friendly; he creates a secure atmosphere.

(b) Missionary manager: He avoids conflict; he is pleasant, kind and warm; he seeks acceptance of and for himself; he wants to make things easier for others; he avoids taking initiative, is passive and undirected; he is unconcerned about output standards and controls.

(c) Developer manager: He listens to people, maintaining open channels of communication; he acts as a coach, developing other people's talents; he understands and supports others around him; he easily cooperates with people; he is trusted by others and he trusts them.

4. Integrated – compromiser – executive. While related managers are high on relationships and low on task, the 'integrated' managers, finally, are high on both.

(a) Integrated manager: He derives his authority from the company's aims, ideals, goals and policies; he integrates the individual with the organization; he seeks participation from others; he prefers sharing responsibility to calling the shots himself; he is interested in motivational techniques.

(b) Compromiser manager: He overuses participation; he is yielding and weak; he avoids tough decisions, producing grey, acceptable compromises; he emphasizes tasks, and relationships, each inappropriately; he is an idealist, and not one to be trusted to deliver the goods.

(c) Executive manager: He uses teamwork in decision making; he uses participation appropriately; he invokes commitment to objectives; he encourages heightened performance; he coordinates others at work.

So much then for situational effectiveness, or otherwise, across the task/relationships continuum. What does this all mean, then, for organizational effectiveness?

Individual and organizational effectiveness

For Reddin, the truly effective company, like the effective manager, must be capable of adapting to changing people and circumstances. In other words, it must exhibit flexibility rather than rigidity. It must learn from its experiences.

The effective manager, or organization, is constantly making a diagnosis of the situation he or it faces, using style flexibility or situational management to respond appropriately, and assessing the effectiveness of the resulting actions, with a view to improved intervention in the future. In that sense, management or organizational effectiveness and readiness for both to learn and to adapt are closely intertwined. In fact, as I have already indicated, it is 'learning styles', in the seventies and eighties, which have increasingly gained in managerial popularity and now organizational or 'cultural' styles, in the eighties and nineties.

One of the reasons for this shift in popularity, from management to learning style, is the very complexity of the task Reddin set practising managers. To be able to 'flex' one's style, from one situation to another, is much easier said that done. In order to discover how it might be done it is useful to take a step back from the immediate activities of management, and to analyze and reflect on the way one learns. In the process of doing so we come closer to assessing 'personality style' than Reddin was inclined to do. For despite his emphasis on style, Reddin remained closely identified with the interpersonal, in his case situational, orientation of rational management. The proponents of learning style, on the other hand, were more closely attached to the individual.

Learning styles

Lateral and vertical thinking

Whereas management style has been developed most extensively in North America, learning style has received most attention in Britain. The first person, ostensibly, to bring the subject to management's attention was the redoubtable Edward De Bono.

Edward De Bono has become particularly renowned, though, in management circles, for the development of what he has termed 'lateral thinking'. In fact his differentiation between so called 'vertical' and 'lateral' thinking is about as well known as McGregor's distinction between 'X' and 'Y'. There is indeed some overlap between the two sets of categories. De Bono, like McGregor, has his style preference – in his case for lateral thinking – but he recognizes the complementarity of the two modes of thought.

Lateral and vertical thinking are both required. Lateral thinking is concerned with the first stage of thinking, the stage of patterning, perceptual choice, and approach to the problem. Vertical thinking is concerned with the second stage processing and working out. Lateral thinking is concerned with selecting alternatives, vertical thinking with choosing one and using it. Although the two types of thinking are distinct they are not substitutes; they are complementary.[7]

De Bono provides a wide range of concepts and techniques for effective thinking, in general, and for lateral thinking, in particular. His work is directed at school children and teachers, at politicians and managers, as well as at the lay person. The substance of what he is saying, in comparing lateral with vertical thinking, is set out below:[8]

- Lateral thinking changes. Vertical thinking chooses. Lateral thinking is generative. Its purpose is movement – from one concept to another, from one way of looking at things to another. Vertical thinking is selective. It seeks to judge. It seeks to prove and establish points and relationships. Whereas vertical thinking is looking for answers, lateral thinking is looking for questions.
- Vertical, unlike lateral thinking, uses the yes/no system. The very basis of vertical thinking is that you are not allowed to be wrong at any stage. Vertical thinking is selective and judgemental, thereby relying on the 'yes/no system'. Lateral thinking is not looking for what is right but for what is different. The only 'wrong' for the lateral thinker, is the arrogance or rigidity with which an idea is held.
- Lateral thinking uses information for effect, not for meaning. Vertical thinking is analytical. Lateral thinking is provocative. Vertical thinking is interested in where an idea came from – this is the backward use of information. Lateral thinking is interested in where an idea leads to – this is the forward use of information. Instead of looking at what is wrong with an idea, a lateral thinker will see what can be got out of it.
- In vertical thinking one follows; in lateral thinking one jumps. Vertical thinking seeks to establish continuity. Lateral thinking seeks to introduce discontinuity. In vertical thinking one step follows logically from another. In lateral thinking one makes jumps which only make sense with hindsight – after the jump has led to the opening of a new avenue of thought.
- Vertical thinking is relevant; lateral thinking is exploratory. Vertical thinking chooses only what is considered relevant to the subject at hand. Lateral thinking welcomes chance intrusions, because they can set off new patterns of thought. For the lateral thinker, then, nothing is irrelevant.
- Lateral thinking moves in unlikely directions, not in likely ones. Vertical thinking proceeds along well established patterns of thought. Lateral thinking, on the other hand, seeks to avoid the obvious. This is not because novelty has value in itself, but because the very obviousness of an idea may obscure a better idea which lies beneath.
- Vertical thinking is closed. Lateral thinking is open. Vertical thinking promises a minimal result. Lateral thinking increases the chances of a maximal result but makes no promises – you may come up with a brilliant answer or with nothing at all. It is always an open ended, probabilistic system.

Lateral thinking, then, is both a general outlook and a specific technique. The division between vertical and lateral thinkers also parallels that between 'convergers' and 'divergers', a point brought out by David Kolb, who, in the seventies, was Professor of Organizational Psychology at the Massachusetts Institute of Technology.

Experiential learning

The individual who has done most to popularize 'learning styles' in management circles is not De Bono but David Kolb. Kolb, the one prominent American in this learning context, has become a champion of what is termed 'experiential learning' in management education and development. His approach is, and always has been, to help managers learn from their experiences rather than – primarily at least – from more formalized learning situations.

Kolb, like Revans from whom we shall soon hear much more, cleverly turned traditional scientific method on its head. Rather than using a purely detached (scientific) method of analysis himself, he chose to view management as science in progress. So, as demonstrated in Fig. 27,[9] the manager – in the process of learning and developing – actually lives and works through scientific method. As a result he engages in 'experiential learning'.

The learning cycle

In undergoing the cycle of learning the manager becomes a practising scientist in whatever context he happens to be operating.

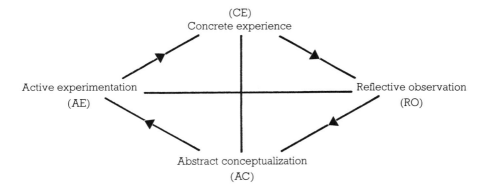

Fig. 27 The learning cycle.

Let us take the example of sales management. A manager tries out (AE) a new promotional campaign, say, replacing costly media advertising with more economical point of sale display. As a result of the change his salesforce experiences (CE) a drop in sales at the lower end of the products' price range, and an increase in turnover at the upper end. He reflects (RO) on this phenomenon, taking particular note of the one item whose sales fell by a full 100 per cent. He concludes (AC) that there is a positive correlation between the value of a product and its susceptibility to in-store promotion. He therefore – beginning again – tries out (AE) a different style of promotion, now blending display and advertizing.

As the example illustrates, the sales manager has – by undergoing the cycle of learning – become a 'scientific' manager with a difference. Instead of exercising scientific and analytic detachment he engages with life, both analyzing and synthesizing his experience. He also becomes, thereby, an 'experiential' learner.

Functions of learning

Having outlined the learning cycle, Kolb goes on, in his more recent book *Experiential Learning*, to elaborate on the functions of learning.

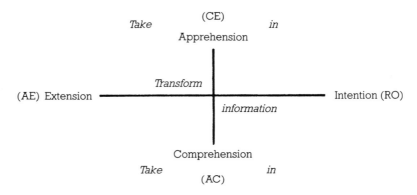

Fig. 28 Learning functions.

We take information in, according to Kolb, through either concrete 'apprehension' or abstract 'comprehension'. (See Fig. 28.) In the first case concrete experience is to the fore; in the second case it is abstract conceptualization.

> Knowing by apprehension is here and now. It exists only in a continuously unfolding present movement of apparently limitless depth, wherein events are often related through apparent synchronicity. Comprehension, on the other hand, is by its very nature a record of the past that seeks to define the future; the concept of linear time is perhaps its most fundamental foundation, underlying the apparently resultant causality.[10]

Apprehension, then, is a personal, subjective process whereas comprehension is an objective social one. The first is only communicable directly to ourselves while the second can be communicated clearly and articulately to others. Having taken information in, we then transform it – through either active 'extension' or reflective 'intention' – in order to learn.

> Learning, the creation of knowledge and meaning, occurs through active extension and grounding of ideas in the external world, and through internal reflection about the attributes of these experiences and ideas in our international world.[11]

Drawing on the Irish poet Yeats, Kolb illustrates how the human being is always moving outward into the external world, and then inward into itself. The greater the contrast between the two the more alive the individual or, to put it another way, the more we genuinely learn, the more we have to alternate between extension and intention. The emphasis, finally, that a manager – learner places on apprehension or comprehension, extension or intention, will determine his learning style.

Styles of learning

Kolb identifies four such 'learning styles' (see Fig. 29), each of which occupies one of the respective quadrants of the circular learning cycle. Interestingly enough two of the styles – converger and diverger – parallel De Bono's vertical and lateral thinking. While the converger comprehends information and learns through outgoing extension, the diverger apprehends information and transforms it into substantive learning, through inner intention. The other two styles, 'Accommodator' and 'Assimilator' are additional to De Bono's more rudimentary classification. Whereas the accommodator apprehends inform-ation, and transforms it through extension into learning, the assimilator comprehends information and learns through intention.

Accommodator

The 'accommodator', therefore, likes dealing with down to earth people and things, and has a generally activist approach to management and to learning. He aptly fits Peters and Austin's description of 'leadership by wandering about', and is liable to possess many primal qualities. He acts more than he reflects, and concretizes rather than theorizes, preferring live activity – in a learning situation – to academic textbooks.

Converger

The converger is active and practical, like the accommodator, but he is guided by abstract rules and principles, rather than by concrete people and situations. He is, in fact, your typically rational manager who manages by objectives and learns methodically, by relating theory to practice. For this reason he is particularly attracted to case studies, through which generalized concepts can be applied to particular situations. He is attracted, moreover, to codified management skills, for just the same reasons.

Diverger

The diverger combines reflective observation with concrete experience. He is, therefore, the person to see a new angle on people, things and on situations. He is De Bono's lateral thinker, looking for lots of variety and stimulation in management and in learning. He is flexible, where the converger might be rigid, and is therefore very much geared towards situational, or contingent responses. He prefers varied and temporary projects to routine, long term ones.

Assimilator

The assimilator, finally, with his preference for abstract conceptualization and reflection, is a typical researcher, staff person or academic. Being opposite in style to the accommodator, he does not like being at the sharp end of either line management or of activity-based learning. He is rational or developmental in his approach, rather than being instinctive, and is, therefore, able to handle complexity more easily than his other three counterparts. He needs time and space in which to operate and does not welcome working under pressure.

The four styles, between them, complete the learning cycle, collectively – within a group, and organizationally – across differently styled departments and functions. The

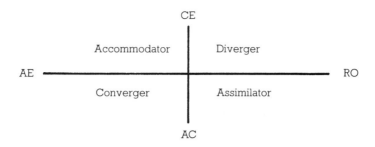

Fig. 29 Learning styles.

implications of this learning-oriented approach, for management and for organizations, became even more wide-ranging for Reg Revans, through 'action learning'.

Action/learning

Action and learning

Reg Revans was a Cambridge physicist and Olympic long jumper in the thirties who subsequently turned his attention to organization and management development in both the public and private sectors. Initiating his scientifically based research in Britain, Revans subsequently has exerted his influence – as both management researcher and educator – in many different parts of the world.

In the forties, Revans began working on the problems of raising productivity and morale in the coal mining industry, spending two years himself down in the mines, and also in Britain's health service. In the fifties he was principally concerned with questions of scale and their implications for communications and learning, in both the mines and in the hospitals. The sixties saw him establish management education programs, most particularly in Belgium, Egypt and in India, while evolving an individualized management science in Great Britain. In the seventies and eighties he devoted himself single mindedly to the dissemination and application of the 'action/learning' approach that he had spent fifty years developing. Finally, spanning the whole of his career has been a religious commitment to action and to learning, that has complemented his scientific research.

> Be ye doers of the word and not hearers only, deceiving your own selves. For if any be a hearer of the word, and not a doer, he is like a man beholding his natural face in the glass. For he beholdeth himself and goeth his way, and straightway forgeteth what manner of man he was.[12]

In the remainder of this chapter I want to trace the development of Revans, and of action learning, and to outline its nature and contribution to management and learning. I shall also illustrate the powers of wide-ranging synthesis, as opposed to narrowly based analysis, that Revans has contributed to manager and management.

The nature and scope of learning

Revans placed at the center of his view of management the capacity for, and opportunity to engage in, learning. On the one hand, he said, 'the underlying structures of successful achievement, of learning, of intelligent counselling, and of what we call the scientific method, are logically identical'.[13] On the other hand, he argued, 'everybody in the organization, from those who frame the policies to those who manipulate the ultimate details of technique, must be endowed to the greatest possible extent with the means of learning ...'[14]

Such learning must demand not only information about the latest shift of policy; it must also demand the power to get the knowledge needed to see one's part in what is going on, and, in particular, to know the effect of one's behavior upon those with whom one works. The organization of learning, then, needs to be built into the structure of an enterprise. The capacity to learn, for Revans, as for Kolb, is intimately connected with the methodology of science.

Science and the manager

In the mid-1960s Revans published his first book on *Science and the Manager*. He had carried his scientific past along with him and had never let it go. But he also ensured that impersonal science was never divorced from personal consciousness.

Management science

There are four forces bearing upon management today that encourage a new approach to its primary task of making decisions. The first is the need for economy of managerial time and effort. The age of science is one of economy, of prudent thought, precise design, exact calculation.

The second is the entry into management of the analytical approach, familiar for over three centuries to the scientist. While intuition, or the unremembered urges of the past, must always be the first weapon of the manager, he must also be able to grasp the underlying structures of the situations that challenge him.

Thirdly, the study of variability through the language of statistics has brought to the manager a language to describe the unexpected, the capricious and the random elements of these tasks.

Fourthly, the social sciences have thrown a little light on the human forces that, in the final analysis, determine whether or not any enterprise will succeed.

Reg Revans *Science and the Manager*[15] 1965

Revans' language flows in and out of subject and object as easily as he moves between thought and action. For Revans, scientific method is merely a model built out of thought just as thoughts themselves are models built from consciousness.

Scientific method and effective management

System beta

In *Developing Effective Managers*, which was published in 1971, Revans turned his general interest in scientific method into a specific methodology for achieving managerial objectives. The resulting model, which he calls 'system beta', involves five distinct elements:

1. Survey, a stage of observation.
2. Hypothesis, a stage of theory, of conjecture.
3. Experiment, in which practical tests are carried out.
4. Audit, during which actual and desired results are compared.
5. Review, relating to the particular result to the whole context.

These stages in fact parallel those of David Kolb's learning cycle, with the addition of a fifth and overall review phase.

'Survey' parallels reflective observation; hypothesis is equivalent to abstract conceptualization; 'experiment' is analagous to active experimentation; and 'audit' approximates concrete experience.

System gamma

Contrasted against system beta is 'system gamma', based on the individual manager's subjective consciousness, or 'predisposing mental set', as this bears upon a particular problem in a particular setting. Thus subject and object are interwoven into the activities of management.

Manager and management system gamma

A real decision, firstly, is always that of a particular person, with his own ends not to be neglected, his own fears to amplify his problems, his own hopes a mirage to magnify his own resources, and with his own prejudices, often called experience, to colour the data with which he works.

A choice of goals, secondly, so much bound up with decision theory, is yet distinct from it, in that the ends for which one strives, deliberately or unconsciously, as an individual or with others, are but partly determined by the calculations of economic strategy: behind them jostle the egocentric drives of the individual as the person he is.

Thirdly, there is the relevance of information, that product of which the raw material is data and the creative process the personal sensitivities of the manager himself.

Fourthly, the theory of systems describes the web in which the world-line of that particular manager is entangled.

The assessment of probability is, fifthly, that farrago of mathematical statistics and simple guesswork, by which we attempt to assess our forgotten experiences, our present wishfulness, and our future hopes.

And, sixthly, the learning process ... integrating everything one has so far become, and one's sole hope for future improvement.

Reg Revans *A Vocabulary of Management Debate*[16] 1972

As we can see, in almost poetic vein, Revans interweaves the managerial subject and the management object of investigation. That leads us on to system alpha.

System alpha

In between the person and the situation is 'system alpha', which forms a bridge between personal values and impersonal circumstances:

- By what values am I guided?
- What is blocking their fulfilment?
- What can I do against such blockage?

In uncovering and negotiating the solutions to these fundamental questions the manager, together with his 'comrades in adversity' seeking their answers too, and helping one another in the process, will be engaging in a process of action learning.

Action learning

The scope of action learning

In the 1950s Revans had stated that the study of industrial behavior was still awaiting its Newton or its Faraday. He confessed the metaphor might oversimplify the problem because, whereas Newton called up one single entity and Faraday no more than three, industrial behavior must take into account scores of independent factors. But this, in itself, he said, should not prevent the discovery of simple laws. Whether or not Revans has discovered even one such, he has certainly evolved a method that is, in one sense, inordinately simple and in another, extraordinarily complex.

In the 1970s the action learning concept was hardened out and applied, for the first time with discipline and design, in British industry. Action learning, at its simplest, is an approach to management education. At its most profound it is a form of personal therapy, a means of social and economic transformation, and even a way of life. Let me try to reconstruct Revans' argument, step by step.

We start with the symbolic amalgamation of 'artisan' and 'scribe'. Knowledge, for Revans, can be only the outcome of action. By wrestling (as artisan) with live problems, and subsequently reflecting (as scribe) upon the results of his achievements, the learner acquires knowledge. The fundamental law of industrial behavior, that Revans was seeking in the 1950s, may well have been discovered by him in the 1970s: '... knowledge is the consequence of action, and to know is the same as to do'.[17]

Self and other

Revans continues with the symbolic intermingling of 'education' and 'industry'. For the knowledge acquired is not so much the facts or techniques imparted by an educator, but, more appropriately, the reinterpretation of the practioner's existing knowledge. This reinterpretation is best achieved through the meeting of 'self' and 'other', that is of 'comrades in adversity'.

This meeting takes place in the context of small groups, coming together at regular intervals, receiving both challenge and support from one another, and directing their efforts at compelling individual projects within their respective organizations. In seeking answers to difficult work-related questions, especially in conditions of risk and confusion, miners, nurses and managers begin to learn who they themselves may be. They come together to learn from one another, through the mediation of a facilitator. To answer their 'work-questions' they must, at the same time, explore their 'self-questions'.

You cannot change the 'system', Revans says, unless you change your 'self'. In other words, external impact and internal development go hand in hand. In giving one another information, support, counsel and challenge, it is not a question of the blind leading the blind, but 'the blindfold shall help the blindfold to strip away the veils and bandages of custom and practice.'[18]

Action learning employs the social processs by which a 'set' of four or five learners, by the apparent incongruity of their exchanges, frequently cause each other to examine afresh both project design and its implementation. Action learning is also a personal activity in that it combines objective analysis ('science') and subjective commitment ('religion'). Its logical foundation is the structural identity of the scientific method, of rational decision making, of the exchange of sound advice and fair criticism, and of the learning of new behavior. Yet, while talking and argument call only for intelligence or quickness of wit, doing and action call for commitment or true belief. For, in taking action, Revans claims, especially after one has clearly exposed one's motives to close and critical colleagues, one is obliged to explore that inner self otherwise so often taken for granted. Action, interaction and learning – in other words – are all inextricably intertwined. Learning is also closely related to change.

Learning/change

In epochs of convulsion, Revans maintains, such as the present, there is nothing more necessary than that we should understand the conditions of our own learning. Moreover, '. . . our ability to adapt to change with such readiness that we are seen to change may be defined as learning.'[19]

Learning, Revans says, for the individual or for society at large, must be greater than the rate of change. What sort of learning are we talking about? When the world does not change, Revans tells us, the son may follow in his father's footsteps, by repeating what is already in the books. But, on the precipice of change, taking the climber into a new world at every rising of the sun, the primary need for learning is no longer current and programmed knowledge, but an ability to pose the questions proper to the microcosm of uncertainty now to be entered.

'P' and 'Q'

Programmed knowledge can be acquired through the published syllabus of the teaching institution, while questioning insight comes only from a recognition within oneself that one's perception of what is going on in the here-and-now falls short of one's responsibility for doing something about it.

Programmed knowledge is the product of technical instruction; questioning insight is to be sought through action learning. If we call the first 'P' and the second 'Q', we might write the general learning equation: L is f(P, Q).

Reg Revans 'Management, productivity and change'[20] 1981

Those able to do tomorrow what there is no need to do today will have learned, just as have those who can do today what was unknown yesterday. Those who brave the unknown frontiers of knowledge, raising awkward questions in conditions of uncertainty, are our latter day hunters. Those who store the accumulated knowledge from the past – upon which present productivity is based – are, similarly, latter day gatherers.

Conclusion

Production and learning

In the early 1970s Revans, having first run the international project for the OECD on *The Emerging Attitudes and Motivation of Workers*,[21] then edited its proceedings. Already at that stage he chose to comment on the Japanese example of good working relations.

He referred particularly to their establishment of small work groups, not only with a high degree of autonomy, but organized in such a way as to endow their members with a continuous opportunity to learn and to develop. The groups were constituted, in other words, not only for effective production, but also for continuous learning. Production and learning, can in fact be related to the American West coast social philosopher, Alan Watts' description, of hunter (masculine) and gatherer (feminine) traits:

> All philosophical dispute can be reduced to an argument between those who are tough-minded, rigorous and precise and like to stress differences and divisions between things [productivity] and those tender-minded romanticists who like wide generalizations and round syntheses, and stress the underlying unities [learning].[22]

Challenge and support

The desirability of harmonizing technological and innovative assertiveness (masculine) with a social and nurturing receptivity (feminine) was stressed by Revans already in the early 1960s. He contrasted the twentieth century with those earlier times, when the master craftsman 'was enjoined by his guild to treat the apprentices as members of his own family ...'[23]. At the same time he lamented how 'we have overlooked the price, in social disintegration, of that final triumph of eighteenth century rationalism, the division of labour'.[24] The social and supportive process engendered by the action learning group, that meeting of 'comrades in adversity' addressing the common foe – an external problem – harks back to a more intimate, primal era of community. The action learner, venturing out to tackle that very same problem, is symbolic of the hunter of old, but stimulated in the 1980s by an intellectual as well as a physical challenge.

Management and learning style

Revans, in synthesizing his own thoughts, feelings and actions has brought a holistic approach to bear upon our organization's social and economic problems. Action learning, in addressing itself to manager and management, to productivity and learning, to stability and change, and to enterprise and community, serves both a multitude and a singleness of purpose.

In fact both De Bono and Kolb, like Revans, have extended their concepts of learning, beyond management, into society at large. Whereas the study of management style has remained limited in its scope, learning styles and processes have wide-ranging applications. Where the one gains, in focus and particularly, the other gains, in its diffuseness and generality. Both sets of concepts, though, have deepened our understanding of management, as an individual and interpersonal, as opposed to an impersonal activity. Revans in particular, in his own unique way, has attempted to synthesize the objectivity of scientific method with the subjectivity of religious conviction. He has also brought together individual and organization, mediated through learning, in a way that is subtly and distinctively European.

At the same time Revans has never gained the visibility and popularity, in management circles, of Mouton and Blake or David Kolb. For the Americans' analytical concepts and techniques are more readily accessible to managers and academics alike than Revans' deeply set synthesis. But all of those cited in this chapter have played their analytical, contingent, and synthesized parts in building up the whole of management theory. I can now move on to organization theory, starting with 'structure'.

References

1. W. Reddin, *Managerial Effectiveness*, McGraw-Hill (1970), p. 20.
2. D. McGregor, *The Human Side of Enterprise*, McGraw-Hill (1960), p. 33–4.
3. D. McGregor, *op. cit.* (1960), p. 47–8.
4. F. Herzberg, Mausner and Snyderman, *Work and the Nature of Man*, Wiley (1959), p. 141.
5. F. Fiedler, *A Theory of Leadership Effectiveness*, McGraw-Hill (1967), p. 21–4.
6. W. Reddin, *op. cit.*, (1970), p. 60.
7. E. De Bono, *Lateral Thinking for Management*, Pelican (1982), p. 221.
8. E. De Bono, *op. cit.*, (1982), pp. 8–12.
9. D. Kolb, *Organizational Psychology*, Prentice Hall (1968), p. 43.
10. D. Kolb, *Experiential Learning*, Prentice Hall (1985), p. 102.
11. D. Kolb, *op. cit.*, (1985), p. 52.
12. St James, *Epistle*, 1:22.
13. R. Revans, 'The nature of action learning', *Omega*, Vol. 9, No. 1 (1981), p. 22.
14. R. Revans, 'Bigness and change', *New Society*, (January, 1964).
15. R. Revans, *Science and the Manager*, MacDonald (1965), pp. 55–6.
16. R. Revans, *A Vocabulary of Management Debate*, unpublished memorandum (1972).
17. R. Revans, *The Psychology of Deliberated Random*, unpublished paper (1981).
18. R. Revans, *op. cit.*, (1981), p. 22.
19. R. Revans, 'Management, productivity and change', *Omega*, Vol. 9, No. 2 (1981).
20. R. Revans, *op. cit.* (1981), p. 137.
21. R. Revans, *The Emerging Attitudes and Motivation of Workers*, OECD, Paris (1972).
22. A. Watts, *Book on the Taboo Against Knowing Who You Are*, Random House (1972).
23. R. Revans, *Industry and Technical Education*, University of Leeds, Institute of Education (1962), p. 1.
24. R. Revans, *op. cit.*, (1962), p. 2.

15 Organization structure

Contents

Key concepts

Once you have fully understood this chapter you should be able to define the following concepts in your own words:

Administrative management	Culture
Autocracy	Decentralized organization
Bureaucracy	Direct democracy
Codetermination	Functional organization
Club structure	Image

Mechanical metaphor	Representative democracy
Organizational culture	Role structure
Organizational politics	Scientific-work design
Power sources	Technocracy
Product-based organization	Visible hand

Objectives

Upon completing this chapter you should be able to do the following:

1. Compare and contrast club and role structures.
2. Outline the impact of the images of power, domination, and culture on the club structure.
3. Trace the development of the modern corporation through American business history.
4. Outline the impact of the image of mechanization on the large-scale organization of today.
5. Describe the workings of functional, territorial, product based, and decentralized organizations in concept and in application.

Introduction

Organizational analysis and integration

In the last two chapters I focussed our attention on management skills, and on management style. In the next two I want to concentrate on organization structure, and on the relationship between the individual, the organization and the environment. In this chapter, therefore, I shall be introducing you to those hardy analysts of 'organization structure' who have influenced managerial thinking in the past, and also to those who are likely to do so in the future. In Chapter 16, I shall turn to those integrators of individual and organization, and of organization and environment.

The approach I shall adopt is a 'building block' one, starting with the structure of the individual enterprise, and building up progressively towards the complexity of modern, large-scale organization. Finally, although organizational analysis and integration is relevant to all forms of public and private institutions, my particular focus will be on the organization of business enterprise. In the course of these two chapters I shall be drawing, in particular, on the work of Charles Handy – *The Gods of Management*,[1] and Gareth Morgan – *Images of Organization*[2]. Professor Handy is the leading organizational theorist in Great Britain and Professor Morgan, a Welshman who is now based at York University in Canada, has applied an unusually wide-ranging set of frameworks to organizational analysis.

The gods of management

Charles Handy was a classical scholar before he joined the ranks of management and subsequently management education. With this classical background he drew on four Ancient Greek gods to inspire both himself and his readers to review alternative organizational structures.

Demystifying organizations

The *Gods of Management* is an inquiry into the state of our organizations and into their likely future ... It is written to encourage more people to think about how organizations actually work and what changes are on the way, because, although 90% of us who study or work still do so in or for an organization, we still take their ways for granted, as if they were nature's laws, to be marvelled at or grumbled about but not by mere man to be altered.

If this book helps to demystify organizations, to make their ways and their assumptions more understandable to ordinary mortals, and causes more people to think about the way they work and the ways in which they might have to work, it will have served its purpose.

Charles Handy *The Gods of Management*[3] 1978

Handy identifies four kinds of organization structure, and corresponding Greek gods, as shown in Table 17. These four are, respectively, 'power-', 'role-', 'task-' and 'person-' centered. I shall be covering the first two of these in this chapter, and the second two in Chapter 16.

Zeus, the head of the gods, famed for his impulses and the power of his presence is one of them. Apollo, fond of rules and order, is another. Athena is the goddess, protectress, as I see her, of problem solvers. Dionysius, for me, is the supreme individualist.[4]

Table 17 The gods of management

Structural focus	Symbolic god	Graphic picture
Club	Zeus	
Role	Apollo	
Task	Athena	
Person	Dionysius	

Images of organization

Gareth Morgan goes further than Charles Handy, and identifies eight distinctively different 'images' or perspectives on organization.

Organizational image and metaphor

The basic premise on which I build is that our theories and explanations of organizational life are based on 'metaphors' or images that lead us to see and understand organizations in distinctive yet partial ways. For the use of metaphor implies a way of thinking and a way of seeing that pervade how we see our world generally ... In highlighting certain interpretations metaphor tends to force others into a background role ...

> Many of our taken-for-granted-ideas about organization are metaphorical, even though we may not recognize them as such. For example, we frequently talk about organizations as if they were machines, designed to operate smoothly and efficiently. By using different metaphors to understand the complex and paradoxical character of organizational life, we are able to manage and design organizations in ways that we may not have thought possible before.
>
> Gareth Morgan *Images of Organization*[5] 1986

I shall be drawing on Morgan's eight 'images', as a complementary basis for structural classification. The first four of his 'images' occupy this chapter, and the second four occupy the next. The eight, altogether (all numbered below), can be seen to parallel Handy's analytical and symbolic structures, in the following way:

Club structure
1. Power and conflict – organizations as political systems.
2. The ugly face – organizations as instruments of domination.
3. Creating social reality – organizations as cultures.

Role structure
4. Mechanization takes command – organizations as machines.

Task structure
5. Nature intervenes – organizations as organisms.
6. Toward self-organization – organizations as brains.

Person structure
7. Exploring Plato's cave – organizations as psychic prisons.
8. Unfolding change – organizations as flux and transformation.

I now want to draw on Handy's and on Morgan's insights, drawing in other organizational theorists as and when appropriate and using the building block approach – constructing the organization from the individual's enterprise, upwards and outwards.

The structure of enterprise

The structure of a free-wheeling, entrepreneurial organization, or primal enterprise, is very different from that of the rationally established organization. Whether it is operating as a small enterprise or as an entrepreneurially run conglomerate, its structural features have more to do with the entrepreneur's mind set, the dynamics of power, the legacy of domination, and the intimacy of a primal culture, than with conventional organization and methods.

In this first section on organizational structure, I shall be considering each of these elements in turn. Inevitably there will be an overlap between those factors affecting the primal and entrepreneurially based company, and those impinging on the rationally based organization. The overall emphasis at this stage, though, will be on the former rather than on the latter.

Before we begin, though, let me remind you of the 'common sense' view of an organization, and its structure, that may well be our mutually understood starting point. If you ask your average man or woman in the street what an organization looks like, he or she will probably present you with a picture of the proverbial 'family tree', or organization chart (see Fig. 30).

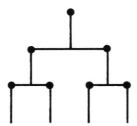

Fig. 30 The 'family tree'.

There will inevitably be someone positioned at the top of the organizational tree and more than one person located at the bottom. In between top and bottom – in the case of a business organization – standard functions – such as manufacturing, sales, purchasing and finance – will usually be identified. Furthermore, lines of vertical command will hold the structure in place. Although this may approximate the structure, seen from a 'mechanistic' perspective, of an established organization, it ignores those structural elements that went into its initial birth and growth.

The entrepreneur's mind set

The structure of the individual entrepreneur's 'psyche', and that of the new enterprise, are very closely interwoven. However, because the former has generally been hidden from public view, the latter has seldom been made explicit.

Enterprising man

Fortunately a team of sociological researchers[6] in America, based at Michigan State University have cast some light (see p. 131) on this previously dimmed matter. They discovered, from their analysis of business entrepreneurs, that:

- The process of business creation does not exist in neatly separated compartments. There is always a flow of events involved, and these events can be conceptually isolated, but the flow is an integral movement.
- Enterprising man, correspondingly, builds his own structure, not functionally and hierarchically, but rather as a system of exchange and transaction, one that he put together by making deals. He does not perceive himself, therefore, as a leader operating within an hierarchically ordered framework, but as a central figure in a transactional system.
- A business enterprise, as a result, is a system of exchange and transaction that has no beginning or end, inside and outside, in any linear or compartmentalized sense. It lies

at the centre of a trading and contact network that is comprised of a never ending circle of unstructured – at least in any formal sense – relationships.

Club structure

The conclusions reached by the Michigan team are not dissimilar to Handy's findings, with respect to his so-called club culture and structure.

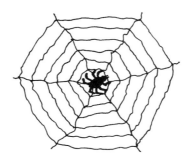

Fig. 31 'Club' or 'power' structure.

The picture (see Fig. 31) is that of a spider's web. Although such a power-centered organization may well have, at least to some extent, the typical functional or product divisions, these are not the structural dimensions that really matter. The crucial lines here are the encircling ones, the lines that surround the spider in the middle. These are the lines of power and influence, reducing in importance as they get more distant from the center. It is the closeness of the relationship with the spider in the middle that matters more in this culture and structure than any formal job title or position.

The dynamics of power

Whereas power-centered structures are typically associated with entrepreneurially styled business enterprises, often at an early stage of their development, 'power politics' is a particular feature of larger organizations. The drive for market territory, and for competitive business influence is turned inward, and reflected in a drive for departmental territory, and even 'empire building'.

The functions of politics

The original function of 'politics' was and is to provide a means of reconciling divergent individual interests, through appropriate systems and procedures of representation, consultation and negotiation. Although organizational politics is most visibly represented by personality clashes, and by countless political intrigues, there is a more mundane and necessary political structure to an organization which is less conspicuous.

The sources of power

Organizational politics arises when people think differently and want to act differently from one another. This diversity creates a tension which must be resolved through political means. Whereas, for the individual entrepreneur, these means are contained within his personally and psychologically based power and influence, in the larger organization the most important sources of power tend to be institutionalized, including:

- The individual's formal authority base.
- His control of scarce resources.
- The use of organizational structure, rules and regulations to resolve differences of interest in one's favor.
- The individual's control of decision processes, including his influence over budgeting and financial control.
- His control over sources and uses of information.
- His knowledge of, and control over, key aspects of technology.
- The individual's informal alliances within and without the organization, and the extent of his influence within them.

Modes of power

Finally, and most importantly from a political and structural perspective. Morgan identifies the forms of 'rule' that organizations, like governments, tend to adopt. Although the six identified are the most commonly found alternatives, institutions often represent a blend of forms of 'rule' rather than a pure form.

Modes of political organization

Autocracy – absolute government where power is held by an individual or small group, supported by their control of critical resources, ownership rights, tradition, charisma, and such claims to personal privilege – typical of the 'classical entrepreneur'.

Bureaucracy – rule exercised through use of the written word, which provides the basis for a rational/legal type of authority, typical of classical and 'formal organization and management'.

Technocracy – rule exercised through use of knowledge, expert power, and the ability to solve expert problems, typical of the modern, technology based enterprise and its management.

Codetermination – opposing parties combine in the joint management of mutual interests, each party drawing on its own power base, pooling their knowledge and influence, as is the practice in Germany, where management and unions in large companies combine together within managing and supervisory boards.

Representative democracy – rule exercised through the election of officials mandated to act on behalf of the electorate and who hold office for a select period of time or so long as they command support from the electorate, as in forms of worker and shareholder control in industry.

Direct democracy – the system where everyone has an equal right to rule and is involved in all decision making, as in organizations such as cooperatives, for example the well known Mondragon in Spain, and Israeli kibbutzim.

Gareth Morgan *Images of Organization*[7] 1986

The politics of organization structure

As we move from personalized power and influence to institutional forms we apparently remove ourselves from the tangible and immediate realities of power in a club culture where Zeus, the god of thunder, holds the reins. However, the basic issue of how power will be manipulated and controlled remains central. In other words, it will be handled:

- Autocratically – 'We'll do it this way.'
- Bureaucratically – 'We're supposed to do it this way.'
- Technocratically – 'It's best to do it this way.'
- Democratically – 'How shall we do it?'

The legacy of domination

The image of business changes – as autocratic, bureaucratic, technocratic, or democratic – depending who you talk to, and the part of the world in which you are based.

Contrasting images of enterprise
As far as the individual entrepreneur is concerned, that is the Zeus character of business, the dichotomy of viewpoint is particularly strong.

Creativity and exploitation

The term entrepreneur evokes various images. In the popular conception the entrepreneur is a risk taker, a man who braves uncertainty, strikes out on his own, and, through native wit, devotion to duty, and singleness of purpose, somehow creates business and industrial activity where none existed before.

At the same time the term engenders certain negative overtones. There is a connotation of manipulation, greed and avarice and grasping acquisitiveness. While it is true that the entrepreneurial hero built railroads, canals ... there is also the implication that in the process he befouled nature, and generally ravished the natural order of things.

Orville Collins *et al. Enterprising Man*[8] 1964

Although the entrepreneur, in particular, has become more popular in the eighties than he was in the sixties, throughout history organizations in general have been associated with processes of social domination, where individuals or groups find ways of imposing their will on others.

Contrasting images of organization
The types of organization which lend themselves to such suspicion are either the entrepreneurial and power-centered ones – characterized as 'autocratic', or else the highly regimented and role-centered ones – tainted as 'bureaucratic', or else some combination of the two.

Construction and destruction

Consider the incredible feat of organization, planning and control required to build the Great Pyramid at Giza. It is estimated that its construction involved work by perhaps ten thousand persons over a period of twenty years.

The pyramid is built from over 2,300,000 blocks of stone, each weighing two and a half tons. These had to be quarried, cut to size, and transported over many miles, usually by water when the Nile was flooded. When we admire this and other pyramids today it is the incredible ingenuity and skill of the early Egyptians that probably strikes us.

From another standpoint, however, the pyramid is a metaphor of exploitation, symbolizing how the lives and hard labor of thousands of people were used to serve and glorify a privileged few ... Organization, in this view, is best understood as a process of domination.

Gareth Morgan *Images of Organization*[9] 1986

What, then, are the structural implications of the image of domination?

Contrasting images of society

A strong case could be made for the idea that organization has always been class based. The first types of formal organization probably arose in hierarchical societies where one social group imposed itself on another, often through conquest. More recently, during the industrial revolution in Europe and America, such domination was less often class based, but it was nevertheless a reality, dividing employer from employed. The emergence of Karl Marx, in particular, and the trade union movement, in general, was in response to both real and apparent physical and social oppression.

The historically determined image of domination lives on particularly strongly in countries, like Great Britain, where political and social institutions – like the Conservative and Labour parties – reinforce the organizational and industrial divide. It also dramatically affects relations, both commercial and political, between industrialized and industrializing countries. Conversely, within the United States itself, where mobility between classes has remained very fluid, and also within Germany and Japan, where internal political differences do not firmly reinforce organizational ones, the image of domination – of one part of the organization over the other – has less of an impact. So the structural separation between management and union in America, in Germany and in Japan, is much less sharp than it is in Britain, in France or in Italy.

The intimacy of culture

The web of culture

Whereas images of organizational politics and of domination both tend to divide, that of 'organizational cultures' has a tendency to unite. In fact, if we return to Handy's picture of the 'club culture' it is as if the spider in the middle divides and rules, while the culture surrounding him represents the web, one strand suitably intermeshing with the other. (See Fig. 32.)

 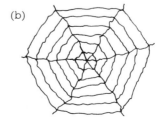

Fig. 32 (a) The spider in the web. (b) The web without the spider.

Culture, in fact, is the 'raw stuff' out of which structure is generated. It parallels, from an organization perspective, the entrepreneur's 'mind set' from a business enterprise perspective. It provides for inner coherence where enterprise provides outward thrust.

A scientific theory of culture

Organizational 'culture' in fact represents much more than even Deal and Kennedy (see Chapter 9) have led us to believe. One of the world's leading anthropologists, Bronislav Malinowski, in his 'scientific theory of culture' has this to say:

> Culture is that integral whole consisting of implements and consumer goods, of constitutional charters, of human ideas and crafts, beliefs and customs, a vast apparatus, partly material, and partly spiritual, by which man is able to cope with the concrete, specific problems that face him.[10]

In other words, for the newly formed enterprise and its primal entrepreneur, organizational culture is not only his reason for being (spiritual purpose), but also his stated intent (organizational charter), and his personal, social and possibly religious values (beliefs and customs). In addition, though, the organization's culture includes its product or service and the technology that underlies each. Such material artifacts are not abstract entities but integral parts of the organizational fabric. For my own entrepreneurial father, for example – who had pulled himself up by his own bootstraps, cloth and clothing were not only extensions of his own skin but also the force that bound many of his employees together.

Culture and structure

Each culture, around the world, brings its own particular influences to bear upon organization structure. This has recently become particularly apparent, of course, with Japan (see Chapters 23 and 24), but it applies with all the other nations, if not also regions, on this globe. Cultural differences will in fact be playing an increasingly important part in business and organization development in the future, as business becomes even more globally oriented. In our primal context here, however, I have focussed more on 'corporate culture', but from a broadened perspective.

> Every culture, from that of a simple, food gathering community like the Eskimos to our own in Britain, has three fundamental aspects: the technological, the sociological, and the ideological ... The technological is concerned with tools, materials, techniques and machines. The sociological aspect involves the relationships into which men enter. The ideological aspect comprises beliefs, rituals, art, ethics, religious practices, and myths.[11]

It is the structure of the entrepreneur's values and beliefs interwoven with the structure of the enterprise's applied technology, in its turn intermeshed with the circle of relationships that prevail, that concern us at this point. If power and intimacy, domination and enterprise shape and influence the club culture or web structure of a primal enterprise, what then impacts upon the role structure of the rationally managed organization? To answer that question we need to investigate the structure and evolution of the bureaucratic enterprise, together with the image of mechanization that is often associated with it.

The structure of bureaucracy

The power-centered organization, with its closely knit club culture, has clearly become part of our business heritage, but one that tends to become eclipsed with age. As the larger corporation begins to dominate the industrial and social scene, so bureaucracy takes over from enterprise.

Small to large

Growth without structural adjustment can lead only to economic inefficiency. Unless new structures are developed to meet new administrative needs which result from an expansion of a firm's activities into new areas, functions or product lines, the technological, financial and personal economies of growth and size cannot be realized.

Whereas in a small firm the same man or group of men buy materials, sell finished goods, and supervise manufacturing as well as coordinate, plan and appraise these different functions, in a large company, administration becomes a specialized, full-time job.

In other words, administration becomes a separately identifiable activity, differing from buying, selling, processing or transporting goods. Moreover, in the large enterprise the concern of executives is more with administration than with the performance of functional work.

Alfred Chandler *Strategy and Structure*[12] 1962

The original concept of bureaucracy

The dominant organizational force in our industrialized societies, and, increasingly in the developing countries too, is the large and bureaucratic institution. It is characterized by a 'role structure' that Charles Handy has christened Apollo, and has been traditionally viewed, in Gareth Morgan's terms, more like a well-oiled machine than as a natural organism. Before we turn to this role-centered structure, and to its mechanized image, I want to trace the path of bureaucracy's historical evolution – towards its currently dominant position. I shall start with Weber's original concept of bureaucracy, and then allow the prominent American business historian, Alfred Chandler, to trace the emergence of the modern corporation. The original formulator of the concept of bureaucracy, one hundred years ago (see p. 80), was the German sociologist, of the late nineteenth century, Max Weber.

The bureaucratic mechanism

The decisive reason for the advance of bureaucratic organization has always been its technical superiority over any other form of organization. The fully developed bureaucratic mechanism compares with other organizations exactly as does the machine with non-mechanical modes of production.

Precision, speed, unambiguity, subordination, reduction of friction and of material and personal costs, are raised to the optimum point in the strictly bureaucratic administration. Its specific nature ... develops the more perfectly the more bureaucracy is dehumanized, the more completely it succeeds in eliminating from official business love and hatred, and all purely personal, irrational and emotional elements which escape calculation.

Max Weber *The Theory of Social and Economic Organization*[13] 1943

The explicit features of Weberian bureaucracy, which set itself so clearly apart from the personality and emotionally of primal management, were:

- A division of labor in which authority and responsibility were clearly defined and officially legitimized.
- An hierarchy of authority resulting in a chain of command.
- Selection through the formal examination, and on the basis of technical, rather than personal qualifications.
- The appointment of administrative officials working as career administrators on fixed salaries.
- The separation of the administrative official, or manager, from the owner of the unit being administered.
- The subjection of the administrator to strict rules, discipline, and controls, impersonally and uniformly applied.

Weber had conceived of his bureaucratic mechanisms as a reaction against the nepotism and corruption perpetrated by the Zeus-like figures of the late nineteenth century. To obtain a full and subsequent picture of the emergence of bureaucratic structures, in twentieth century America, we need to turn to Alfred Chandler.

In fact Chandler might well be seen as the contemporary champion of the formally managed organization. As a business historian at Harvard, Chandler has traced the emergence of the modern corporation, both in terms of individual businesses,[14] and the American economy as a whole.[15] Let me trace, with Chandler, the rise of the American business corporation.

The emergence of the modern corporation

As we retrace business steps, historically, we find ourselves looking back over the evolution of an individual, large-scale organization, even today.

From general merchant to specialized enterprise
In the 1790s the general merchant, the businessman who had dominated the economy of the colonial period, was still the grand entrepreneur. He bought and sold many kinds of products, and carried out all the basic commercial functions. He was an exporter, retailer, shipowner, banker and insurer. By the 1840s, however, such tasks were being carried out by different types of specialized enterprise. Banks, insurance companies and common carriers had appeared. Merchants had begun to specialize in one or two lines of goods. They concentrated more on a single function: retailing, wholesaling, importing and exporting.

In fact, during the first half of the nineteenth century, the specialization of enterprise in commerce, finance and transportation, was a major feature of economic development. Such specialization brought an end to the personal business world of the general merchant of the colonial era and replaced it with the increasingly impersonal world of the commissioning agent.

From personalized business to depersonalized markets
Together with such institutional specialization was an increasing reliance on impersonal

market coordination. Yet such economic expansion and specialization failed, initially, to bring about any institutional innovation. The volume of activity was still not large, and owners had no difficulty in administering their enterprises. In nearly all cases, moreover, business remained a family affair. The two or three people responsible for the destiny of the enterprise handled the economic and the administrative, the operational and the entrepreneurial activities. No managerial hierarchies appeared. Even in the larger enterprises, specialization of function remained distinctly limited. Technological innovation had raced ahead of organization development. Nevertheless, internal specialization was just beginning to emerge.

From enterprise to administration

Within a single textile mill the integration of all the processes of production involved in making cloth stimulated technical innovation in each of the specific processes. Organisational innovation, however, in the 1850s as today, came more slowly.

The merchants who founded the mills and those who came to control them, as well as those who marketed their output, held to traditional ways. Although they incorporated some manufacturing enterprises in order to pool capital, they continued to manage them like partnerships.

The manufacturing firm usually had only one full time officer – normally the treasurer – who was a major shareholder. The day to day operations of the distant mill were left to a salaried agent or superintendent. To the treasurer of the company the mill agent was a mere technician.

The agent's concern was almost wholly with the process of production. He had to manage workers, but his prime task was to maintain a steady flow of materials through the mill.

The treasurer's accounts of that time show clearly that the factories were run by merchants for merchants. Accounting remained merely a recording of past transactions. It was not until after the 1850s, for example, that the owners and managers began using their accounts to determine unit costs.

Selling was undertaken by sales agents, who sold the products through their distribution network. These agents also came to provide the textile companies with the credit they needed as their working capital.

In addition the selling agents paid the insurance and most of the transportation costs for the distribution of the finished cloth. It is hardly surprising, therefore, that they were soon deciding what styles, quantity and quality of cloth the different mills should produce. As a result, in the textile industries long after 1840, the basic functions of marketing, production, finance and purchasing remained under the control of different men in different enterprises. In a word, no central management yet existed.

Alfred Chandler *The Visible Hand*[16] 1977

From individual enterprises to interlocking partnerships

In fact the most powerful businesses of the day were the international, interlocking partnerships. Thus the Brown family, for example, was represented by Brown, Shipley and Company in Liverpool; by Brown Brothers and Company in New York; and by Browns and Bowen in Philadelphia.

Such multiunit enterprises without administrative managers, like Browns', remained little more than federations of autonomous offices. Such federations were formed to control competition between units, or to assure enterprises of sources of raw materials or of outlets for finished goods and services. The owners and managers of the autonomous units agreed on common buying, pricing, production and marketing policies. But such loose federations could not provide the administrative coordination that became a central function of modern business enterprise.

Emergent bureaucracy

The situation began to change quite dramatically in America in the latter part of the nineteenth century. The main and initial instigators of such change were the railroad and telegraph companies. The capital required to construct a railroad was far more than that required to build a textile mill. A single entrepreneur, family, or small group of associates, was therefore rarely able to own and run a railroad entirely themselves. The administrative tasks involved, aside from the capital required, were too numerous, too varied and too complex.

In fact, there is little evidence that the railroad managers merely copied existing military procedures. Instead the evidence suggests that their answers came in response to immediate and pressing operational problems requiring the organization of men and machinery. They responded to these, as engineers, in much the same rational, analytical way as they solved the mechanical problems of building a bridge or laying a railroad.

Administrative supervision on the railroads

1. A proper division of responsibilities.
2. Sufficient power to be conferred to the general superintendent to enable the same to be fully carried out.
3. The means of knowing whether such responsibilities are faithfully carried out.
4. Great promptness in the report of all derelictions of duty, that evils may at once be corrected.
5. Such information to be obtained through a system of daily reports.
7. The adoption of a system, as a whole, which will not only enable the General Superintendent to detect errors immediately, but will also point out the delinquent.

Mr McCallum, General Superintendent, Erie Railroads[17] 1950s

---

The 1850s, then, when McCallum was a railroad superintendent, were a time of building and of learning to manage the railroads in particular, and America's first modern business enterprises in general. The 1860s and 1870s were a period of coordinating and competing for the resulting flows of traffic. Finally the 1890s were the years of system building. After the Civil War and again after the depression of the 1870s, as the market became glutted and prices dropped, companies became more and more willing to combine in order to control or limit competition. Cartels got together to set prices and jointly to schedule production. Occasionally a federation would dissolve into its original parts, but more often it consolidated.

Subsequently then, the transformation of a loose alliance of manufacturing, transportation or distribution firms into a single, consolidated unit with a central headquarters, made possible economies of scale, through standardization and concentration of production and marketing.

From invisible to visible hand

In fact the swift victory of the railroad over the waterway resulted from organizational as well as from technological innovation. Technology made possible fast, all-weather transportation; but safe, regular, reliable movement of goods and passengers, as well as continuing maintenance and repair, required the creation of a sizable administrative organization.

It meant the employment of a set of managers to supervise these functional activities over an extensive geographical area. It meant, too, the formulation of brand new types of internal administrative procedures, including accounting and statistical controls. The overall result was the creation of early forms of modern administration, to cater for the needs of a large-scale organization.

The visible hand

The modern industrial enterprise – the archetype of today's corporation – resulted from the integration of the processes of mass production with those of mass distribution within a single firm. Almost non-existent at the end of the 1870s, these integrated enterprises came to dominate many of America's most vital industries.

The visible hand of managerial direction had replaced the invisible hand of market forces [see p. 15] in coordinating production and distribution.

Gradually, during the course of the twentieth century, the mass marketeers began to replace the merchants as distributors of goods in the American economy, because they internalized a high volume of transactions within a single, large, modern enterprise. They reduced the unit cost of distributing goods by making it possible for a single set of workers, using a single set of facilities, to handle a much greater volume of transactions than the same number could if they were scattered in small facilities.

In production an increase in output for a given input of labor, capital and materials was achieved technologically in three ways: the development of more efficient machinery and equipment, the use of higher quality raw materials, and the intensified application of energy.

Organizationally, output was expanded through improved design of manufacturing or processing plants, and by innovations in managerial practices and procedures required to synchronize plans and supervise the workforce.

By the turn of the century, then, many integrated, multifunctional enterprises had become household names. They had begun to play a significant role in the transformation of the nation from a distended society of island communities into a far more homogeneous and integrated economy and society.

Alfred Chandler *The Visible Hand*[18] 1977

Administrative management

Chandler has crystallized the form and evolution of administrative management, as it emerged in America in the late nineteenth century and which is still so characteristic of large organizations around the world today. Here are his eight propositions, covering the emergence and the scope of administrative management:

1. Modern multiunit business enterprise replaced small traditional enterprise when administrative coordination permitted greater productivity, lower costs and higher profits, than coordination by market mechanisms.
2. The advantages of internalizing the attitudes of many business units within a single

enterprise could not be realized until a managerial hierarchy had been established.

3. Modern business enterprise appeared for the first time in history when the volume of economic activities reached a level that made administrative coordination more efficient and profitable than market coordination.

4. Once a managerial hierarchy had been formed, and had successfully carried out its function of administrative coordination, the hierarchy itself became a source of permanence and power.

5. The careers of the salaried managers who directed these hierarchies became increasingly technical and professional, requiring specialized skills, selection and promotion – based on training, competence and performance.

6. As the multiunit business enterprise grew in size and diversity, and as its managers became more professional, the management of the enterprise became separated from its ownership.

7. In making administrative decisions career managers preferred policies that favored long term stability and growth of their enterprises to those that maximized current profits. For the salaried managers the continued existence of the enterprises was essential to their lifetime careers.

8. As the large enterprises grew and dominated major sectors of the economy, they altered the basic structure of the sectors and of the economy as a whole. As technology became more sophisticated and as markets expanded, administrative coordination replaced market coordination in an increasingly larger portion of the economy.

The thinking that both Weber and Chandler have applied to bureaucracy and administration has been incorporated into Handy's conception of an Apollonian, role culture. I want to turn now to Handy, and thereafter to Gareth Morgan's 'organizations as machines', before concluding this chapter.

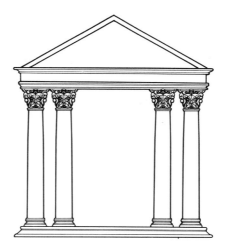

Fig. 33 The role structure.

The role structure

When the average person thinks of an organization it is the role structure that he envisages. The structure is based on roles rather than personalities, projects or tasks. Apollo, for Handy, is its patron god, for he was the god of order and rules. The role structure is built upon the assumption that man is rational and that everything can be organized in logical fashion. The job of organizing can then be divided up box by box until you have a system of prescribed roles held together by rules and procedures. Its picture, as shown in Fig. 33, is that of a Greek temple, for temples draw their strength and their beauty from the pillars. (See also Fig. 34.)

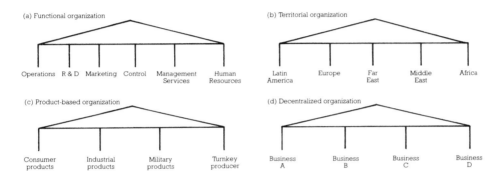

Fig. 34 Departments and divisions.

The pillars represent functions or divisions within an organization. The functions are the standard business ones of purchasing or procurement, engineering or research and development, manufacturing or operations, sales or marketing, finance or control, personnel or human resources and management services or data processing. The divisions may be based on products, geographical markets, or – as in Drucker's federally decentralized organization – on whole businesses.

The functions or divisions are joined only at the top, the pediment, where the heads of department or division join together to form the board, management committee, or president's office. The pillars are also linked by the tension wires, as it were, of policies, rules and procedures. A typical career would involve joining one of the pillars and working up to the top, with perhaps occasional sightseeing visits to other pillars, to broaden one's base.

Apollo

The Apollo style and structure is excellent when it can be assumed that tomorrow will be like yesterday. Yesterday can then be examined, pulled to pieces, and put together again in the form of improved rules and procedures for tomorrow. Stability and predictability are assumed and encouraged.

And thank God for them. That the sun will rise tomorrow can be a most reassuring recollection in some of the bleak moments late at night. Wherever, therefore, the assumptions of stability are still valid, it makes sense to codify the operation so that it follows a set

and predictable pattern.
   Individuals in the role culture are, therefore, part of the machine, the interchangeable human parts of Henry Ford's dream. The role, the set of duties, is fixed. The individual is he or she that is slotted into it.

Charles Handy *The Gods of Management*[19] 1978

Handy's views on the positioning of the role culture and structure are therefore very similar to Revans' views on the relative importance of 'programmed' learning. Furthermore, Handy's thoughts on 'interchangeable human parts' parallel those of Gareth Morgan.

Organizations as machines

Max Weber favorably compared the principles of bureaucracy with the efficient working of machines. Not surprisingly, moreover, it was the mechanical and civil engineers in America who played an important part in establishing the first large-scale organizations in that country.

Scientific management and organization

The best known of these engineers, of course, was Frederick Taylor (see Chapter 11).

Scientific work design

1. Shift all responsibility for the organization of work from the worker to the manager; managers should do all the thinking relating to the planning and design of work, leaving the workers with the task of implementation.
2. Use scientific methods to determine the most efficient way of doing work; design the worker's task accordingly, specifying the precise way in which the work should be done.
3. Select the best person to do the job thus designed.
4. Train the worker to do the job efficiently.
5. Monitor worker performance to ensure that appropriate work procedures are followed and that appropriate results are achieved.

Frederick Taylor *Principles of Scientific Management*[20] 1911

Henry Ford's dream, to which Handy referred, when turned into the reality of the assembly line, involved the building of Taylor's ideas into the technology itself. The technology, in its turn, then captured management's imagination.

The mechanical metaphor

In Gareth Morgan's terms:

> ... organizations that are designed and operated as if they were machines are usually called bureaucracies. But most organizations are bureaucratized in some degree, for the mechanistic mode of thought has shaped our most basic conceptions of what organization is all about.[21]

The strengths and weaknesses of the machine as a metaphor for organization are reflected in the strong and weak points of mechanistic organization in practice.

Strengths
The strengths can be stated very simply. Mechanistic approaches to organization, as Handy has already intimated, work well under conditions where machines work well:

- When there is a straightforward task to perform.
- When the environment is stable enough to ensure that the products or services supplied will be appropriate.
- When one wishes to produce the same thing time and again.
- When precision is at a premium.
- When the human 'machine parts' are compliant.

A well known example of an organization that has operated very successfully on this basis is the Macdonald's hamburger chain. Surgical wards, aircraft maintenance departments, accounting offices, courier firms, selective franchises and other organizations where precision, safety, and clear accountability are at a premium, have often been successful in operating in this way.

Weaknesses
However, in addition to these strengths, mechanistic approaches to organization have severe weaknesses. In particular they:

- Create organizational forms which find difficulty in adapting to change.
- Can result in mindless and unquestioning bureaucracy.
- Can have undesirable consequence as the interests of those working within the organization take precedence over the goals it was designed to achieve.
- Can have dehumanizing effects upon employees, especially those at the lower levels of the organizational hierarchy.

Mechanistic approaches to organization, despite their weaknesses, have proved particularly popular, both in public and private enterprises – beyond a certain size. This is partly because of the demands that large-scale organization places upon management and partly because of the impact that the mechanical image has had on the imagination of the public at large. However, as we shall see in the next chapter, this situation is now changing, not least because technology itself is altering its shape and form.

Conclusion

The power and role-centered structures are the two traditional ones, which still exercise the greatest impact on industrialized, and, increasingly, industrializing societies. The images of Zeus, the God of Thunder, and of Apollo, the God of Rules and Order, lie respectively behind them.

The classical enterprise, created by the entrepreneur who spins a web of deals, is loosely formed, but tightly controlled, through force of personality at the center. It is held together – if successful – not by rules and regulations, but by a coherent culture. Hence the images not only of power and domination, but also of cultural form and formality, pervade. The bureaucratic organization, run by a managerial multitude, who uphold their pillars of function and responsibility, is tightly formed and controlled, but by force of impersonal regulation rather than through personal impact. Hence the mechanical image dominates, though increasingly the organic one – of which we are now to hear more – is making its influence felt.

In the next chapter we shall trace the development of the organic approach to organizational behavior, and identify its key sources and implications.

References

1. C. Handy, *The Gods of Management*, Sovereign (1978).
2. G. Morgan, *Images of Organization*, Sage (1986).
3. C. Handy, *op. cit.*, p. 14.
4. C. Handy, *op. cit.*, p. 17.
5. G. Morgan, *op. cit.*, pp. 12, 13.
6. O. Collins, Moore and Unwalla, *Enterprising Man*, Michigan State University (1964).
7. G. Morgan, *op. cit.*, p. 145.
8. O. Collins, *et al., op. cit.*, pp. 4, 5.
9. G. Morgan, *op. cit.*, p. 274.
10. B. Malinowski, *A Scientific Theory of Culture*, Oxford University Press (1944), p. 1.
11. J. Lewis, *Anthropology Made Simple*, W. H. Allen (1969), p. 42.
12. A. Chandler, *Strategy and Structure*, Doubleday (1962), p. 7.
13. M. Weber, *The Theory of Social and Economic Organization*, Free Press (1943), pp. 215–16.
14. A. Chandler, *op. cit.*
15. A. Chandler, *The Visible Hand*, Belknap Press (1977).
16. A. Chandler, *op. cit.* (1977).
17. D. Wren, *The Evolution of Management Thought*, Wiley (1979), p. 95.
18. A. Chandler, *op. cit.*, (1977), p. 4.
19. C. Handy, *op. cit.*, pp. 20–1.
20. F. Taylor, *Principles of Scientific Management*, Harper & Row (1911), p. 34.

16 Organization theory

Contents

Key concepts

Once you have fully understood the chapter you should be able to define the following concepts in your own terms:

Action learning   Internal elaboration
Adaptive and maintenance   Linking pin
  systems   Managerial subsystem
Contingency organization   Multi-organizations
  theory   Negative entropy
Contrived systems   Mechanistic/organic
Cooperative systems   New psychology
Democratic organization   Organization development
Differentiation and   Open system
  integration   Organizational behavior
Dispersed organization   Organization/environment
Environmental suprasystem   Permeable boundaries
Group development cycle   Psychosocial system
Group effectiveness   Sensitivity training
Group participative system   Social sciences
Group structures   Structural systems
Hierarchy of systems   Systems theory
Human relations   Task achievement/group
Individual/organization   maintenance
  incongruity   Team roles
Integrated organization   Technical subsystem
  system   Values/goals subsystem
Interactive process
  categories

Objectives

Upon completing this chapter you should be able to do the following:

1. Trace the evolution of organization theory from human relations to organization development.
2. Describe the essential elements of human relations theory, comparing and contrasting, in particular, Mayo and Likert.

3. Describe the essential elements of organizational behavior, comparing and contrasting mechanistic and organic approaches and individual and organizational requirements.
4. Describe the essential elements of the systems approaches to organization and environment, comparing and contrasting, in particular, Lawrence and Lorsche with Kast and Rosenzweig.
5. Describe the essential elements of organization development, comparing and contrasting sensitivity training, Revans' action learning, Bennis' changing organizations and Handy's future of work and organization.

Introduction

Management and the social sciences

When we go back to the roots of rational management, as we did in Chapter 11, we find two opposing belief systems. On the one hand, we have 'the old psychology' enshrined within Frederick Taylor's so-called rabble hypothesis – 'men are pulled down instead of being elevated by being herded together'. On the other hand, we have Mary Parker Follett's 'new psychology', which tells a completely different story. 'Group organization', she says, 'will create the new world we are blindly feeling after, for creative force comes from the group'.

The old psychology is associated with the hard analysts, that is with the administrative, bureaucratic, classical or 'scientific' schools of rational management. It sprang out of the early efforts, at the turn of the century, to rationalize, to depersonalize, and to structure the rapidly expanding business organizations in Europe and America. Classical management replaced personal, and idiosyncratic, enterprise. The new psychology is associated with the softer, behavioral or social schools of management. It began to gain credibility after the great depression of the thirties, and once the ills of authoritarian, and even 'dehumanized' approaches to management and organization, became increasingly visible. These 'softer' approaches are no less systematic, at least in the eyes of their proponents, than the 'scientific' management. They merely have a different focus. Specifically, there is a greater emphasis on synthesis (bringing together), than on analysis (taking apart).

Tom Lupton, one of the first of the theorists in the UK to apply the social sciences to management, has compared scientific management with the social sciences.

Administrative and social sciences

'Scientific' management

As engineers concerned with a problem of the organization of manual workers, the scientific managers stressed the significance of physical activities. For them, the industrial worker was a kind of mechanism who would, if he were given the right rewards, produce in predetermined ways, certain defined bits of work.

Taylor and the other scientific managers always stressed the importance of getting the right atmosphere, but the procedures for getting the right atmosphere were never worked out systematically. The theoretical framework of 'scientific management', with its crude psychology and sociology, was inadequate for this task.

Taylor's ideas of human motivation were primitive, and he never understood the significance of groups in organizations. Organizations were seen as disorderly aggregates of individual human beings drilled into formal order and given direction by formal structures and procedures of planning and control, instituted by management.

Social sciences

If I were asked for a brief personal definition of social science I would include all activities which are concerned systematically to investigate and to explain aspects of the relation between the individual and the society of which he is a part.

Economists are chiefly interested in the problems of rational choice between economic alternatives in situations of scarcity, uncertainty and risk. Social psychologists study the problems arising for individuals from their membership of small social groups. Sociologists are concerned chiefly with the structuring and interlocking of social roles at work, in the family, the factory, and in the community. Political scientists are interested in questions of power in society, its origins, and how it is legitimated and administered.

Tom Lupton *Management and the Social Sciences*[1] 1970

Lupton, who has played a major part in bringing the social sciences into management in Britain over the last twenty years, helps us set this softer scene. I should mention, at the outset, that although the 'behavioral' and 'social' sciences are often used interchangeably, the latter is, strictly speaking, the more expansive. Specifically it includes the whole field of economics with which the behavioral sciences (and we in this chapter) are not directly concerned.

The development of the behavioral sciences

Groups and relationships

In this chapter I want to focus on individual, organization and environment, with the group as the mediating force. For the behavioral scientists, of the last fifty years – as opposed to the administrative scientists of the fifty years before them, and 'developmental' theorists of perhaps the next fifty years – the group has been the differentiating and integrating force. On the one hand, the differentiated small group links the individual to the organization; on the other hand, the organization is integrated through an amalgam of such groups.

The behavioral scientists, Abraham Maslow apart (see p. 257), have not been concerned with individuality as such, but rather with the relationship between the individual and the group, or with the organization. Similarly they have not been concerned with the individuality of any organization, but rather with the relationship between the organization and its internal or external environment.

Strands of behavioral thought

There have been, in fact, four major theoretical strands of management thought, for which the behavioral scientists have been responsible. I have excluded from these McGregor, Herzberg, and Maslow, because the first two were included in the chapter on management style (see p. 257), and the third I shall cover in depth in the context of developmental management (see Chapter 22).

Human relations

The first human relations strand, stretching between the 1920s and the 1960s, has connected the individual and the group in the context of the organization. The key figures I have selected therein are, first, the Australian Elton Mayo and, subsequently, the American social psychologist Rensis Likert. Human relations theory has placed particular managerial emphasis on processes of communication within small groups, and has questioned the means rather than the ends of human organization.

Organizational behavior
The second, organizational behavior strand, stretching between the 1940s and the 1960s, has connected individual and organization in the context of the informal organization. The key figures here have been originally the American psychologist, Chris Argyris, and subsequently Burns and Stalker in Britain. Theories of organizational behavior have placed particular managerial emphasis on behavioral processes in organizations, questioning both the means and – to a smaller extent – the ends of human organization.

Organizational and environmental systems
The third strand of organizational and environmental systems, stretching between the forties and the seventies, has connected group, organization and the environment in the context of the individual. The key figures have been originally Chester Barnard, and subsequently the American researchers Lawrence and Lorsche, and the management writers Kast and Rosenzweig. Systems theory has placed its strongest managerial emphasis on processes of differentiation and integration, extending the means and ends of human organization beyond their conventional boundaries.

Organization development
Finally, the fourth and most recent strand of organization development, stretching between the early sixties and today, has been concerned with individual, group, organization and environment. Its key figures have been Mary Parker Follett, and subsequently the American, Warren Bennis and the Englishman, Charles Handy. Organization development theories have placed their greatest emphasis on the management of change, thereby attempting to adapt both the means and the ends of human organization. Let us now consider each strand in turn.

Human relations

Human relations skill in particular is the capacity of a person to communicate his feelings and ideas to others, to receive such communications from others, and to respond to their feelings and ideas in such a fashion as to promote congenial participation in a common task.[2]

The origins of human relations theory

Normlessness and rootlessness
In general terms, the human relations movement can trace its origins to an early group of

sociologists in Europe. Two in particular stand out, that is the Frenchman Emile Durkheim, and the Italian Vilfredo Pareto.

Durkheim, in his first book *The Divison of Labour*, published in 1893, divided society into two primary types, mechanistic and organic. Amongst mechanistic types, he says, Adam Smith's individual self-interest reigns, guided merely by an invisible and impersonal hand. Amongst organic types, the social group overtakes the anonymous individual, as the ultimate source of values. Pareto, then, took a further sociological step, viewing society as a social system, that is as a cluster of interdependent but variable units. For Durkheim and for Pareto, and subsequently for Elton Mayo, individual organizations and whole industrialized societies were in danger of being overrun by 'normlessness and rootlessness'.

Normlessness and rootlessness

In traditional societies people knew their place and their future, and there was social solidarity. The domestic system, built around family and kinship, gave people an identity in their working life as well as in their social life.

The factory system and the process of industrialization destroyed this solidarity through widespread division of labour, increased social and psychological mobility, and the growth of large scale organizations in which the manner of dealing with interpersonal relationships shifted from a personal, friendship basis to one of an impersonal nature.

The result was a normless, rootless life in which individual identities were lost along with the social bonds that provided purpose and continuity to existence. Social invention to keep up with industrial changes had not kept pace with technical inventions.

Elton Mayo *The Human Problems of an Industrial Civilisation*[3] 1933

Interestingly enough Mayo did not advocate going back to the 'gatherer' society of 'the good old days'. Rather he wanted to go forward, into a new kind of cooperative society.

In any primitive society, although the will to work together is active and strong, fear and force nevertheless feature more than in a civilized one. A civilized society is one in which cooperation is based on understanding and the will to work together, rather than on force.[4]

Such a society would be borne out of a conscious process of scientific observation, hypothesis formation, experimentation, and evaluation, that was exemplified by the Hawthorne experiments at Western Electric (see pp. 198–9).

The birth of social scientific method

More specifically, we can trace the beginnings of the human relations movement, back to the Hawthorne experiments to which I referred in Chapter 11. These experiments symbolize the subsequent 'human relations era' in two major ways. Firstly it is scientific in character; secondly it is social, rather than technical in outlook.

The emerging science of human relations

In early research Mayo found that the problems of workers could not be explained by any one factor but had to be dealt with in what he called 'the psychology of the total situation'.

The new man of industry was to be socially as well as economically and technically

> motivated and controlled. Improvements in efficiency and morale were postulated to be due more to improved social or human relations than to material and environmental ones. Management had to be concerned with both the technical and social aspects of work.
>
> The important fact brought to the attention of Mayo's researchers was that the ordinary conception of manager – worker relations, as existing between company officials, on the one hand, and an unspecified number of individuals, on the other, is utterly mistaken. Management, in any continually successful plant, is not related to single workers, but always to working groups.
>
> In any department that continues to operate, the workers have – whether aware of it or not – formed themselves into a group with appropriate customs, duties, routines, even rituals; and management succeeds (or fails) in proportion as it is accepted without reservation by the group as authority and leader.
>
> Daniel Wren *The Evolution of Management Thought*[5] 1979

Mayo himself concluded from his early researches that social study, in organizations, should begin with careful observation of what may be described as communication: 'that is the capacity of an individual to communicate his feelings and ideas to another, the capacity of groups to communicate effectively and intimately with each other. The problem of communication is, beyond all reasonable doubt, the outstanding defect that civilisation is facing today.'[6]

Communication: the individual and the group

The subject of communication, amongst individuals within small groups, and between small groups and the whole organization, was in fact taken over by a generation of human relations theorists, after Elton Mayo. Whereas Mayo was concerned with human relations in organizations, in general, they were concerned with its specific implications, especially with respect to processes of communication.

I shall start by investigating the process of communication within the small group, and then review the process of coordination within the organization as a whole – from a human relations perspective. The first area of investigation has been generally identified with 'group dynamics'; the second area has been identified, at least by Rensis Likert, in *The Human Organization*.

Group dynamics

Task achievement and group maintenance

Theories on group dynamics have been associated with a series of individuals, each applying him- or herself to a part of the small group whole. One of the most prominent of these was the American Robert Bales. I can remember, as a management educator in the sixties, monitoring communications processes amongst hundreds of student managers, using Bales' very helpful form of analysis. Bales developed, in the fifties, a group of twelve 'interaction process categories'[7] (see Table 18) which could be used to differentiate task achievement from group maintenance within groups. Each remark or gesture that an individual makes is registered under one of twelve alternatives. Subsequent to Bales, and over the next twenty years, many variations were developed on his basic theme.

Table 18 Interaction process categories

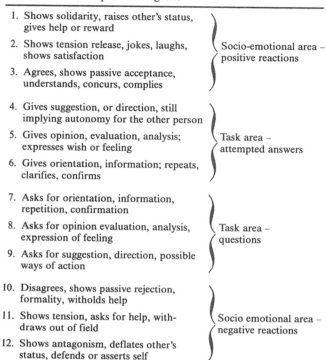

1. Shows solidarity, raises other's status, gives help or reward	
2. Shows tension release, jokes, laughs, shows satisfaction	Socio-emotional area – positive reactions
3. Agrees, shows passive acceptance, understands, concurs, complies	
4. Gives suggestion, or direction, still implying autonomy for the other person	
5. Gives opinion, evaluation, analysis; expresses wish or feeling	Task area – attempted answers
6. Gives orientation, information; repeats, clarifies, confirms	
7. Asks for orientation, information, repetition, confirmation	
8. Asks for opinion evaluation, analysis, expression of feeling	Task area – questions
9. Asks for suggestion, direction, possible ways of action	
10. Disagrees, shows passive rejection, formality, witholds help	
11. Shows tension, asks for help, withdraws out of field	Socio emotional area – negative reactions
12. Shows antagonism, deflates other's status, defends or asserts self	

The overall object of the communications exercize was to balance 'task achievement' and 'group maintenance'. Bales' group process assessment involved an outside analyst observing individuals' interactions within a working group, categorizing them for each individual case, and then – based on his observation and analysis – developing each individual's interpersonal effectiveness. The overall objective, in improving individual and group effectiveness, was to secure a balance between task achievement (the task area) and group maintenance (the positive, as opposed to negative, emotional area).

Group development

Bales also attempted to use his process categories to account for ways in which groups approach problem solving. He divides the process into three sequential phases. The orientation phase, Bales says to begin with, is marked by task categories 7, 8 and 9 (questions); the evaluation phase, second, is characterized by 4, 5 and 6 (attempted answers); and the control phase, finally, is marked by the positive socio-emotional categories 1, 2, 3 and by the negative ones 10, 11, 12.

A more useful approach to categorizing phases of group development, in my opinion, is that proposed by the psychologist, Barry Tuckman. He proposes a four-stage cycle of group problem solving and development. These consist of 'forming, storming, norming, and performing'.

Four-stage cycle of group development

Forming

At this stage the set of individuals has not yet become a group. They are busy sounding each other out. Individuals explore each others' attitudes and background. Members are also keen to establish their individual identities and make a personal impression on others.

Storming

This is a conflict stage in the group's life, and it can easily become uncomfortable. Members bargain with one another as they attempt to sort out what each of them individually, and as a collective group, want out of the situation. It is likely that interpersonal hostility may be generated as differences in individual goals are revealed. The early relationships established in the 'honeymoon', forming stage, may be disrupted.

Norming

The group usually develops a way, though, of achieving its objectives together. The questions of who will do what and how are addressed. Working rules are established in terms of norms of behaviour (e.g. task responsibility will be delegated) and role allocation (e.g. John will be our leader). A framework is therefore created through which each member can relate to the others.

Performing

The final stage is concerned with actually getting the job done. A fully mature group has been created, which can now get on with its prescribed work. Not all groups develop to this stage, of course; many become bogged down at an earlier stage.

Barry Tuckman 'Development Sequences in Small Groups'[8] 1965

Group structure
A great deal has been written about the structure of groups. However, particularly well known is the work of Alex Bavelas in America. In the fifties he conducted laboratory experiments to test out the relative effectiveness of different communication structures for different kinds of task.[9]

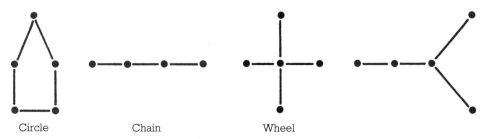

Circle   Chain   Wheel

Fig. 35 Group communication structures.

Communication between individuals was permitted only along the channels prescribed by the patterns shown in Fig. 35, and subjects were insulated from any 'cross talk'. He found that:

- The centrality of position in sending and receiving group messages produces group leaders.
- For organizational efficiency, the wheel is the fastest, followed by the 'Y', the chain and the circle. Thus efficiency reduces as centrality decreases.
- For simple problems which required little interaction the wheel was the fastest; for difficult problems which required a lot of interaction the circle was the fastest.
- Satisfaction was highest in the circle where everyone was involved in the decision making process.

Teamwork
In Chapter 14 we devoted a great deal of attention to management style. At the same time, and in the context of individual and group, work has been done on categorizing the roles of all team members. Particularly well known today are the findings of the British psychologist, Meredith Belbin. Belbin has identified eight roles, based on his extensive observations of management teams, seven of which are needed, he says, for effective communication and teamwork. The 'chairman' and the 'shaper', as we shall see, are mutually exclusive.

Team roles

1. The chairman might also be termed the 'coordinator'. He likes organizing people, mapping their strengths, and using them productively. He engineers consent and develops agreement among different interests. He commands respect and communicates easily, but may come across as unfeeling and impersonal.
2. The shaper is the forceful type who likes to influence group decisions and to make his mark on meetings. He's willing to risk unpopularity to get his ideas across, and tries to ensure that the group's discussions and decisions conform to his own pattern of thought and action. Finally his drive and self-confidence are likely to be balanced by an intolerance towards vague ideas and people.
3. The contacts man often looks further afield than the immediate task and brings in ideas, developments, and phone numbers from outside. He works by personal networks and likes new ideas and techniques. He is curious and willing to see possibilities in anything new. Conversely, he may suffer from over-enthusiasm or a lack of follow up.
4. The ideas man is the innovator, the original, independent, imaginative fellow, who is often frustrated in group work. He is a source of new approaches to old problems who is valued for his independence of outlook as well as for his intelligence and imagination. He may well be impractical at times, and poor at communicating his ideas to others.
5. The critic is the careful, critical member, often slow but right. His judgement wins over his feelings, and he contributes to the group by analyzing problems, evaluating other people's ideas and suggestions. He can poke holes in unsound proposals and make sure all the information is on hand before a decision is made. He is long on critical thinking and objectivity, but probably short on enthusiasm and creativity.
6. The implementer is the practical sort who sticks to it, meeting targets and deadlines. He wants clear objectives and procedures and is sometimes uncomfortable with new ideas. He is the solid, practical member who will make a practical plan to achieve an objective when

the others have finished arguing about it. But he may prove a trifle inflexible and unresponsive to unproven new ideas.

7. The team builder likes people and works easily with them, even when their ideas differ from his own. He'll support the others in their strengths and underpin their weaknesses, while he oils the communication machinery among them. He has humility and listening skills, but they may be offset by a lack of toughness or decisiveness.

8. The inspector's role is to ensure the team is protected from errors of commission or omission, with his fine eye for detail. He also maintains a sense of urgency in the team, acting as its conscience. His strengths include a sense of order and concern. His foibles are likely to include a sense of impatience and intolerance.

Meredith Belbin *Team Building*[10] 1985

So much for the role of the individual within the group. I now want to turn to the role of the group within the organization. In doing so I turn from group dynamics to Rensis Likert's *The Human Organization*.

Coordination: the small group and the large organization

Rensis Likert, to whom we were introduced in Chapter 5 (see p. 83) was extensively involved in the fifties and sixties in applying human relations theory to the problems of management. Unlike the administrative scientists of his time, and before his time, Likert developed a linking pin or 'group pattern of organization'. As an exponent of human relations Likert, like Mayo, believed in the small group, as a vehicle for interaction and influence.

Group effectiveness

The properties and performance of the ideal, highly effective group is as follows:

1. The members are skilled in the various leadership and membership roles required for effective interaction.
2. The group has been in existence sufficiently long to have developed well established, relaxed working relationships.
3. The members of the group are loyal to it and to its leader.
4. The members and leaders have a high degree of confidence and trust in each other.
5. The values and goals of the group are an expression of the values and goals of its members.
6. The members of the group are highly motivated to abide by the major values and achieve the important goals of the group.
7. All the interaction, problem solving and decision making activities of the group take place in a supportive atmosphere.
8. Insofar as group members perform linking functions with other groups, their goals and values are in mutual harmony.

Rensis Likert *New Patterns of Management*[11] 1961

The linking pin

Likert developed his alternative to the formal chain of command, that is a participative organization: 'made up of multiple overlapping groups. The functional line, the product line, and the service line are all parts of a multiple, overlapping group structure'.[12] (See Fig. 36.)

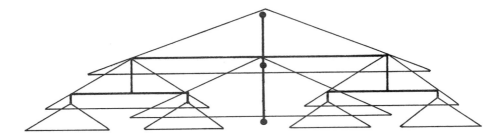

Fig. 36 The linking pin organization.

The linking pin organization was set up to achieve effective coordination between the small group and the large organization.

Achieving effective coordination

To perform the intended coordination well a fundamental requirement must be met. The entire organization must consist of multiple, overlapping group structures, with every work group using group decision making processes skillfully. This requirement applies to the functional, product and service departments.

An organization meeting this requirement will have an effective interaction – influence system through which the relevant communications flow readily, the required influence is exerted laterally, upward, and downward, and the motivational forces needed for coordination are created.

Rensis Likert *The Human Organization*[13] 1967

Alternative management systems

The overlapping group structure worked particularly well in one (group participative) of four different kinds of management system that Likert identified. These four consisted of

Table 19 Alternative management systems

	System			
Trait	1 Exploitative	2 Benevolent	3 Consultative	4 Participative
Motive force	Fear, threat	Reward, punishment	Reward, involvement	Group participation
Flow of information	Downward	Mostly downward	Down and up	Down, up and with peers
Decision making	Bulk made at top	Policies set at top	Broad decisions at top; specific ones lower down	Decisions broadly based in overlapped groups
Control	Highly concentrated	Relatively highly concentrated	Moderate downward delegation	Widespread responsibility set

two authoritative ones – exploitative or benevolent – and two participative ones – consultative or group participative. (See Table 19.)

In Likert's 'human organization', system four was the appropriate form of management, drawing on its linking pin structure and overlapping group processes. Of course, any reasonably progressive organization today would see itself being run more or less along such 'group participative' lines. For a more radical reinterpretation of organizational behavior, in the light of both individual and group requirements, we need to turn from Likert to Argyris, and from human relations to a more fundamental reconstruction of organizational behavior.

Organizational behavior

A new behavioral science 'field' is developing which focusses on understanding human behavior in ongoing organizations. Organizational behavior can stake out a claim as a basic behavioral science because of the documented empirical observation that most of life is organized. There are those who would go as far as to imply that organization is basic to life.[14]

Chris Argyris, in the fifties, first published his contentious findings about the behavior of people within organizations. In the process, he took a step beyond the partial theories of the human relations school by proposing an overall science of organizational behavior. In other words, like the administrative scientists, he focussed on the organization as a whole, but unlike them he saw the individual in organizational life in a fundamentally new way.

For the original administrative scientists, and for Frederick Taylor in particular, the individual was an impersonal entity without any identity of his own. A strong identity was invested in the organizational whole of which the individual was an impassive part. For Elton Mayo, and his fellow human relationists, the small group – rather than the individual or the organization – became the focus of attention. It was human relations between people that counted rather than impersonal structures and systems.

Argyris, then, took a step further than both Taylor and Mayo. He argued that both individual and organization warranted a unique and respectively separate identity. In that case, he concluded, a fundamental conflict was likely to arise between the two. In fact he came out with a series of propositions that bore this out. He emphasized, writing in the fifties, that his propositions were as yet untested, but that together they formed an overall and initial hypothesis.

Individual and organization

Argyris set out eight propositions, pertaining to his perceived incongruency between the healthy individual and the formal organization:

1. *There is a lack of congruency between the needs of healthy individuals and the demands of the formal organization.*

    If one uses the traditional formal principles of organization, including the chain of command and task specialization, to create a social organization; and if one involves people who tend towards a mature state of psychological development, that is they are relatively active, able and independent; then one creates a disturbance because the needs of the healthy individual are incongruent with those of the formal organization, which tends to require its people to work in situations where they are dependent, passive, and use few important abilities.

A manager, therefore, is always faced with an inherent tendency towards continual disturbance.

2. *The result of this disturbance is frustration, failure, short time perspective and conflict.*

If individuals are predisposed towards a mature and healthy psychological state of being, then:

(a) they will experience frustration at the hands of the formal organization, because their drive for self-actualization and for fulfilment will be blocked;

(b) they will tend to experience failure because they will not be able to define their own goals in relation to central needs and the path to these goals;

(c) they will tend to experience short time perspective because they have no control over the clarity and stability of their future;

(d) they will tend to experience conflict because, as healthy agents, they will dislike frustration, failure and short time perspectives.

3. *Under certain conditions the degree of frustration, failure, short time perspective, and conflict will tend to increase.*

The degree of incongruency between the individual and the organization will tend to increase:

(a) as the individual increases in his degree of maturity-exhibiting independence, depth of interest, self-awareness, and a long term perspective; and/or

(b) as one descends down the organizational chain; as directive leadership increases; as management controls are tightened; as jobs become more specialized; and as the degree of structure and formality is raised.

4. *Formal principles of organization cause the subordinate, at any given level, to experience rivalry, inter-subordinate hostility, and to develop a focus towards the parts rather than the whole.*

Because, according to formal principles, the subordinates are directed towards and rewarded for performing their own task well, the subordinates tend to develop an orientation towards their own particular part rather than towards the whole.

The part orientation increases the need for the leader to coordinate the activity among the parts in order to maintain the whole. The need for the leader, in turn, increases the subordinates' degree of dependence and subordination. This creates a circular process whose impact is to maintain and/or increase the degree of dependence and subordination plus the rivalry and competition for the leader's favor.

5. *The employee's adaptive behavior maintains self-integration and impedes integration with the formal organization.*

If the organization is composed of healthy individuals, and if its make up is as already proposed, then individuals will adapt by: either

(a) leaving the organization;

(b) manifesting defense reactions such as aggression, regression, or day dreaming;

(c) becoming apathetic or disinterested towards the organization, its make up and goals. This may be reflected in restrictive practices, industrial sabotage, or absenteeism; or

(d) developing a psychological attitude whereby material aspirations become predominant and non-material ones subordinate.

6. *The adaptive behavior of the employees has a cumulative effect, feeds back into the organization, and reinforces itself.*

All these adaptive reactions reinforce each other so that they have not only their individual impact on the system, but also a cumulative effect. Their total impact is to increase the degree of independence and submissiveness and increase the resulting staff turnover, apathy and disinterest. Thus a feedback process exists whereby the adaptive mechanisms become self-maintaining.

The continual existence of these adaptive mechanisms tends to make them norms or codes which, in turn, act to maintain the adaptive behavior and to make it 'proper' behavior for the system. Employees who may desire to behave differently will tend to feel deviant, and not part of the work community, as, for example, 'rate busters'.

The individual and cumulative impact of the defence mechanisms is to influence the output–input ratio in such a way that a greater input (energy, money, machines) will be required to maintain a constant input.[15]

7. *Certain management reactions tend to increase the antagonisms underlying the adaptive behavior.*

Those managements that base their attitudes and judgements on the logic of the formal organization, will tend to dislike the adaptive employee behavior. They will also tend to diagnose the problem behavior as 'the employee's fault'. The actions they tend to take, as a result, may involve increasing the degree of directive leadership, tightening the management controls, or increasing the number of 'pseudo-human relations programmes'. Whereas the first two reactions tend to compound the problem, the third one 'tends to increase the distance and mistrust between employee and management because it does not jibe with the realities of the system within which the employee works'.[16]

8. *Job enlargement and enrichment, as well as employee-centered leadership, may decrease the incongruency between individual and formal organization, under certain circumstances.*

There are possible means of integrating the individual and the organization, by enlarging or enriching the content and scope of the individual's job – as illustrated by Herzberg (see p. 257) and by Likert. Moreover, people-centered styles of management, as outlined in Chapter 14, may well yield productive results.

However, Argyris makes the point, very strongly, that these forms of employee-centered activity can only work if propositions 1–7 have not become imbedded in the organizational culture, and in the way that individual employees see themselves.

In fact Argyris leads us to believe that nothing short of radical organizational and attitudinal change will decrease the incongruency between individual aspirations and the demands of formal organization. In many ways, Chris Argyris was a man in advance of his times. Unfortunately, in his own subsequent work, he is not particularly adept at showing management how successfully to adapt.

It is the two British researchers, rather, Burns and Stalker, who made the more successful adaptation. In developing the concept of the 'organic' form of organization they provided a viable counterpart to the formal – and 'mechanistic' structure.

Mechanism and organism

It was the sociologist Emile Durkheim who made the original distinction, in the 1890s, between mechanistic and organic types of society. However it was not until the 1960s that this distinction was meaningfully brought into management, in the context of organizational behavior. Two Scottish researchers into the management of innovation made the initial breakthrough. As a result of their investigations into the electronics industry in Scotland, during the mid-fifties, they came to some firm conclusions.

Two types of organizational behavior

There seems to be two divergent systems of management practice. Neither was fully and consistently applied in any firm, although there was a clear division between those managements which adhered generally to the one, and those which followed the other.

One system, to which we gave the name 'mechanistic' appeared to be appropriate to an enterprise operating under relatively stable conditions. The other, 'organic', appeared to be required for conditions of change.

Mechanistic

In mechanistic systems the problems and tasks facing the concern as a whole are broken down into specialisms. Each person pursues his task as something distinct from the real tasks of the concern as a whole. 'Somebody at the top' is responsible for seeing to its relevance. The technical methods, duties and powers attached to each functional role are precisely defined.

Interaction with management tends to be vertical. Operations and working behaviour are governed by instructions and decisions issued by superiors. This command hierarchy is maintained by the implicit assumption that all knowledge about the situation of the firm and its tasks is, or should be, available only to the head of the firm.

Management, often visualized as the complex hierarchy visible in organization charts, operates a simple control system, with information flowing up through a succession of filters, and decisions and instructions flowing downwards through a succession of amplifiers.

Organic

Organic systems are adapted to unstable conditions, when problems and requirements arise which cannot be broken down and distributed among specialist roles within a clearly defined hierarchy. Individuals have to perform their special tasks in the light of their knowledge of the tasks of the firm as a whole.

Jobs lose much of their formal definition in terms of methods, duties and powers, which have to be redefined continually by interaction with others participating in a task. Interaction runs laterally as much as vertically. Omniscience can no longer be imputed to the head of the firm.

Burns and Stalker *The Management of Innovation*[17] 1959

In Table 20 I have represented Burns and Stalker's argument, to reinforce the distinction between the two types of organizational behavior.

By implication, then, the influence of the informal, small group is that much greater in an organically based organization than in a mechanistic one. The organic system also has

Table 20 Mechanistic and organic systems

Attribute	Mechanistic organization	Organic organization
Task division	Specialization of task	Specialized contributions to common tasks
Task context	Specialized tasks are isolated from the whole	Realistic tasks set in the context of the whole
Task integration	Reconciliation of parts to whole perceived by person in authority	Adjustment of parts to whole, through interaction between people
Task responsibility	Precise definition of rights/responsibilities	Responsibility limited and continually shed
Locus of commitment	Rights/responsibilities rest with functions	Commitment spread beyond any functional domain
Organization	Hierarchical structure	Network structure
Locus of final authority	Final authority located exclusively at the top	Ultimate task authority may be located anywhere in the network
Communications flow	Vertical, from superior to subordinate	Lateral, resembling consultation, not command
Content of communications	Instructions and decisions	Information and advice
Locus of prestige	Prestige attached to internal (local) rather than to general (cosmopolitan) knowledge	Prestige attached to affiliations/expertise outside of the firm

softer and more integrative features than the mechanistic one, thereby making itself more attractive to the behavioral scientists than to the administrative ones.

Not only did Burns and Stalker offer a form of organization – the organic – that could circumvent Argyris' incongruencies, but they also made the point that different contexts warranted different forms. This is the particular point that was taken up by the two Americans, Lawrence and Lorsche at the Harvard Business School.

However, before leaving Argyris, I must emphasize once again that he was a man in advance of his times. Even the organic form of organization is unable to cater for the needs of the fully mature individual. For him or her we require, in fact, the more fundamental form of organizational development that we shall encounter in Section D. But before we get to that point we need to reconsider individual, group and organization in the light of environment. This will bring us to systems theory.

Organization and environment

An organization is an open system which exchanges information, energy and materials with its environment.[18]

Mayo, Likert, and Argyris have been concerned with human relations and with organizational behavior, largely in isolation from the surrounding environment. What Burns and Stalker began to do and Lawrence and Lorsche accomplished more purposefully, was to relate the organization to its wider environment. The role of the organizational systems theorists, thereafter, was to develop that form of interdependent thinking in an even more thorough-going way. Kast and Rosenzweig, in America, have played prominent parts in that respect. However, predating the work of all the above-mentioned, was that of the noted Chester Barnard, the American business executive and philosopher.

The cooperative functioning of the executive

Chester Barnard was one of that rare breed, a prominent executive and a thoughtful business philosopher, who wrote *The Functioning of the Executive* during the thirties.

For Barnard the search for a universal organizational theory had been obstructed by the over emphasis on civic and military precursors of business organization. Concepts of military and bureaucratic organization placed too much emphasis on authority structures for Barnard's liking. His particular focus was upon 'that kind of cooperation between men that is conscious, deliberate and purposeful'.[19] Cooperation, for Barnard, was of both social and systemic value.

The spirit of cooperation

The morality that underlies enduring cooperation is multi-dimensional. It comes from, and may expand to, all the world. It is rooted deeply in the past and faces towards the endless future. As it expands it becomes more complex, its conflicts must be numerous and deeper, its call for abilities must be higher, its failures of ideal attainment must perhaps be more tragic...

Among those who cooperate, the things that are seen are moved by things unseen. Out of the void comes the spirit that shapes the ends of man.

Chester Barnard *The Functions of the Executive*[20] 1938

As we shall soon see the visionary executive, Chester Barnard, and the systematic researchers, Lawrence and Lorsche, both came to similar ultimate conclusions. Barnard rejected the view of an organization having finite boundaries, and included investors, customers and suppliers as organizational members.

> The organization's survival depends on the maintenance of the equilibrium of the system. This system is primarily internal, a matter of proportions between the elements, but it is ultimately and basically an equilibrium between the system and the total situation external to it.
>
> This external equilibrium has two terms to it: first, the effectiveness of the organization, which comprises the relevance of its purpose to the environment; and second, its efficiency, which comprises the interchange between the organization and the individuals.[21]

Lawrence and Lorsche, thirty years later, took up where Barnard left off, focussing on both internal and external relationships, but substituting differentiation and integration – as points of emphasis – for efficiency and effectiveness.

Managing differentiation and integration

The organization as a system

Paul Lawrence and Jay Lorsche set out specifically in the mid-sixties to study the functioning of large organizations, consisting of large numbers of individuals and many groups. Like Burns and Stalker they were interested in the way in which the internal functioning of the organization was related to the technical and market conditions of the firm. Unlike their British counterparts they were explicitly interested in the organization's 'systemic' behavior, most particularly in its approach to differentiation and integration.

Systemic differentiation and integration

At the most general level we find it useful to view an organization as an open system in which the behaviors of members are themselves interrelated. The behaviors of members of an organization are also interdependent with the formal organization, the tasks to be accomplished, and the personalities of other individuals ...

As systems become large, they differentiate into parts, and the functioning of these separate parts has to be integrated if the entire system is to be viable.

It is on the states of differentiation and integration in organizational systems that we place major emphasis here. As organizations deal with their external environments, they become segmented into units, each of which has as its major task the problem of dealing with a part of the conditions outside the firm ...

A sales unit faces problems associated with the product, the customers, the competitors. A production unit deals with production equipment sources, raw material sources, and labor markets. Such external conditions as the state of scientific knowledge and opportunities for expanding knowledge and applying it are in the most general sense the purview of the design unit. These parts of the system also have to be linked together toward the accomplishment of the organization's overall purpose. The division of labour among the departments and the need for unified effort lead to a state of differentiation and integration within any organization.

Lawrence and Lorsche *Organization and Environment*[22] 1967

A contingency theory of organizations

The two Harvard researchers methodically assessed the degree of differentiation and integration across three categories of company and environment. (See Table 21.)

Table 21 Comparative differentiation and integration

Industry	Organization	Average differentiation	Average integration
Plastics	High performer	10.7	5.6
	Low performer	9.0	5.1
Foods	High performer	8.0	5.3
	Low performer	6.5	5.0
Containers	High performer	5.7	5.7
	Low performer	5.7	4.8

As a result of these findings the researchers concluded that there is an important relationship between external variables, that is the certainty and diversity of the environment, and internal states of differentiation and integration. More specifically:

We have found that the state of differentiation in the effective organization was consistent with the diversity of the parts of the environment, while the state of integration achieved was consistent with the environmental demand for interdependence.[23]

They also found that the more differentiated the organization the more difficult it is to

achieve integration. Therefore, the more diverse the environment and the more differentiated the organization the more elaborate the integrating devices. Moreover, the more
unpredictable and uncertain the parts of the environment, the lower in the organization is
the locus of decision making. The contingency theory of organizations, then, clearly
indicates that managers can no longer be concerned about the one best way to organize.
Fayol and Weber, Mayo and Argyris – according to Lawrence and Lorsche – are all
guilty of over-generalizing from their own respective standpoints. They themselves, by
way of contrast, emphasize the need for diversity rather than uniformity of organization
structure.

Viable organizations of the future

If our projection of environmental trends proves accurate, the viable organization of the
future will need to establish and integrate the work of organization units that can cope with
even more varied sub-environments. The differentiation of these units will be more extreme.
Concurrently the problems of integration will be more complex. Great ingenuity will be
required to evolve new kinds of integrative methods ...

Global linkages

The viable organizations that we are projecting for the future will have reasonably mastered
the ability to organize work that ranges from basic scientific endeavors to highly standardized and routine production. They will have learned to operate all over the globe and to link
these operations together. They will be able to move repeatedly into new product lines with a
sure-handed grasp of markets and technologies.

They will, in this way, be able to organize effort toward the achievement of human
purposes that are not now even conceived. Such 'multi-organizations' would be able to
undertake and effectively perform tasks in what is currently defined at the public, as well as
the private sector. For the individual, the great diversity of required roles can give meaningful
scope to the potentialities and career aspirations of a wide variety of people.

Culturally based division of labor

We may find a division of labor based more on cultural differences emerging in these
organizations. The different countries have traditionally divided labor partially on the basis
of control of raw materials and, more recently, on technical and organizational capabilities.
These sources of an international division of labor may be supplemented in the future by one
based on differences in values. Basic cultural differences are amongst the slowest-changing
aspects of human life. These values prepare people to play some occupational roles better
than others. Perhaps our multi-organizations will be able to build on these differences, to
design a division of labor around them, and to reduce the present strong trend towards a
universal culture of industrialized man.

Creative leadership

Finally, the multi-organization at its top level will require leadership that can formulate a
general framework of purpose to guide the efforts of the parts. This will require the highest
order of integrative and creative capacity. Perhaps one of the most important functions of

these top managers will be the designing of new forms of complex organization to better achieve the multiple purposes of our evolving civilization.

Lawrence and Lorsche *Organization and Environment*[24] 1967

As we shall see, when we get to Chapter 23, Lawrence and Lorsche were anticipating, twenty years ago, the kinds of multi-organizational forms which are beginning to become prominent today. Kast and Rosenzweig, meanwhile, with their systems approach to organization and management, were setting a trend which has yet to reach its full height.

Organization and management: a systems approach

Definition and scope

In the sixties and seventies so-called 'general systems theory' was gaining popularity. Its founding father, the German biologist Von Bertalanffy, published his seminal work on the subject in 1968.[25] The development of general systems theory has provided a basis for the integration of scientific knowledge across a broad spectrum.

We have defined a system as an organized, unitary whole composed of two or more interdependent parts, components or subsystems, and delineated by identifiable boundaries from its environmental suprasystem. The term system covers a broad spectrum of our physical, biological and social world.[26]

Hierarchy of levels

In considering the various types of system the noted social scientist, Kenneth Boulding, has identified the nine hierarchical levels shown in Table 22.[27] Levels seven to nine are directly relevant to management and organization, while levels four to six are concerned with biological systems, and one to three with physical or mechanical ones.

Table 22 Hierarchy of levels

Level	Description
1.	Static structures or physical frameworks
2.	Simple dynamic systems with predetermined, necessary motions – the level of clockworks
3.	A control mechanism or self-regulating cybernetic system – the level of the thermostat
4.	The 'open system' or self-maintaining structure, where life begins – the level of the cell
5.	The genetic–societal level, typified by the plant
6.	The animal system, characterized by increased mobility
7.	The human level, where symbols and language are in use
8.	The social system through which meanings, human emotions, art and science are developed and conveyed
9.	Transcendent systems of ultimates and absolutes, which I have characterized as metaphysical

Interestingly enough, most of the applications of systems theory within and around the social sciences, have been outside of Boulding's own discipline, which is economics. What, then, are the properties of organizations as systems?

Properties of organizations as systems

Open system. A characteristic of all so-called 'closed systems' is that they have an inherent tendency to run down. An open system, however, is in a dynamic relationship with its environment, receiving inputs in the form of material, energy and information and transforming these into outputs. (See Fig. 37.) These inputs prevent the system from running down. For example the business system imports people, material facilities, money and information, and transforms these into products, profits, and other economic and social satisfactions.

Feedback of information

Fig. 37 The organization as an open system.

Contrived systems. Social organizations are not natural, like mechanical or biological systems, but they are contrived. In other words, they can be established for an infinite variety of reasons and do not follow the same automatic lifecycle of birth, maturity and death of biological systems. They can endure, in fact, for centuries.

Permeable boundaries. Whereas the closed system has rigid, inpenetrable, boundaries the open system has permeable boundaries between itself and a broader suprasystem. Whereas in a physical or biological system the boundaries can be clearly identified, in a social one they are determined by the activities and objectives of the organization. For example, if a company chooses to take part in a programme of urban renewal, it extends its boundaries to include the surrounding man-made infrastructure.

Hierarchy of systems. A system is composed of subsystems of a lower order and is also part of a suprasystem. People are organized into groups; groups are organized into departments; departments are organized into divisions; divisions form part of a company; companies may form part of a consortium or joint venture. Each company is part of a set of surrounding economic, social, political and cultural infrastructures.

Negative entropy. Closed physical systems are subject to the force of entropy, that is a movement towards disorder and ultimately death. Rust in our cars, dry rot in our homes, and general decay in our inner cities are examples of such so-called entropy. Living systems, on the other hand, can avoid an increase in entropy, and can even develop towards states of increased order and organization. For example, a business enterprise can grow in scale and complexity. Such is the force of negative entropy.

Feedback mechanisms. The concept of feedback is important in understanding how a system maintains dynamic equilibrium. Through the process of feedback, the system continually receives from the environment, which enables it to adapt to change.

Adaptive and maintenance mechanisms. Systems must have two mechanisms which are often in conflict with one another. On the one hand, in order to maintain equilibrium, they must have maintenance subsystems to ensure their overall behavior is in accord with their environments. The forces of maintenance are conservative and attempt to prevent the system from changing so rapidly that the various subsystems and overall system become out of balance. On the other hand, adaptive mechanisms are necessary in order to provide a dynamic equilibrium, one which is changing over time.

Growth through internal elaboration. Closed systems tend to run down. In contrast, open systems move towards ever greater levels of differentiation and integration.

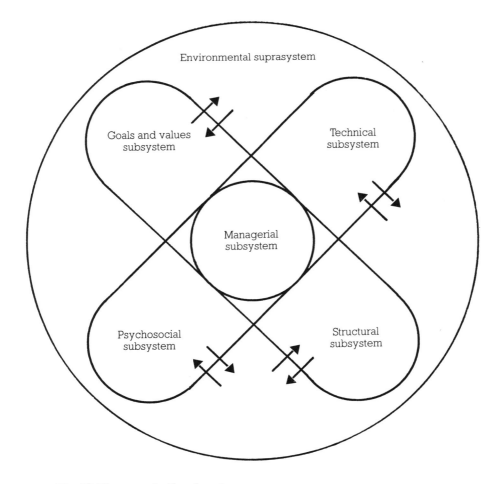

Fig. 38 The organizational system.

Complex social systems are made up of many subsystems, some of which have excess capacity or resources, which creates a continual pressure towards growth. Furthermore, social organizations will often attempt to extend their boundaries of activity and influence in order to reduce uncertainties and ensure survival.

An integrated systems view of organizations

So much for the general properties of social systems. Now let me describe the particular and integrated approach that Professors Kast and Rosenzweig have adopted in America as a way of conceptualizing organization and management.

As illustrated in Fig. 38, the two Americans conceive of the organizational system as a composition of five subsystems, surrounded by an environmental suprasystem. The connecting flows are comprised of materials, energy and information.

The modern view: a systems approach

This figure is an aid to understanding the evolution of organization theory. Traditional management theory emphasized the structural and managerial subsystems and was concerned with developing principles. The human relationists and behavioral scientists emphasized the psychosocial subsystem, and focussed their attention on motivation, group dynamics, and other related factors.

The management science school emphasized the technical subsystem and methods for quantifying decision making and control processes. Thus each approach to organization and management has tended to emphasize particular subsystems, with little recognition of the importance of others. The modern approach views the organization as an open, sociotechnical system and considers all the primary systems and their interactions.

Kast and Rosenzweig *Management and Organization*[28] 1970

In the modern systems view the organization is an open system which exchanges information, energy (human and physical) and materials with its environment. It, therefore, imports people and things from, and exports them to, the surrounding general and task environments.

Environmental suprasystem

The environmental suprasystem is divided into general societal and specific task environments. The general environments span culture, technology, politics, education, law, demographics, physical resources, the economy and society at large. The task environments embrace customers, suppliers, competitors, unions, government departments and collaborators. Generally speaking, and as Lawrence and Lorsche have emphasized, the more heterogeneous and dynamic the environment, the more complex and differentiated the internal structuring of the organization.

Goals and values subsystem

Many of the organizational goals and values are in fact imported from the broader sociocultural environment. A basic premise of the systems approach is that the organization, as a subsystem of society at large, must accomplish certain goals which are determined by the broader system. In other words, the organization performs a function for society, and if it is to be successful in receiving inputs it must fulfil societal expectations.

More specifically, though, goals and values stem from five representative levels, both within and without the organization. These involve individuals, groups, the organization as a whole, the task environments and society at large. Each party brings its own mission, purpose, objectives, targets and deadlines into the organizational system.

Technical subsystem

The technical subsystem, according to Kast and Rosenzweig, relates to the knowledge required for the performance of a particular task. It is therefore prescribed by the task requirements of a particular organization. The technology for manufacturing auto-mobiles is very different from the technology for manufacturing scientific instruments. Similarly, the task requirements and technology in a department store are very different from those in a research laboratory.

The technical subsystem is therefore shaped by the degree of specialization required, the degree of automation that is feasible and desirable and by the amount of routine and non-routine work to be accomplished by people. As a result the technology affects both the organization's structure and its psychosocial subsystem.

Psychosocial subsystem

Every organization has a psychosocial subsystem which is composed of individuals and groups in interaction. It consists of individual behavior and motivation, status and role relationships, group dynamics and influence systems. It is also affected by sentiments, values, attitudes, expectations and aspirations of the people in the organization. Additionally, the psychosocial subsystem is affected by the external environment as well as by the internal tasks, technology and structure. These forces set the 'organizational climate' within which the human participants perform their roles and activities. This climate is likely to differ considerably in different contexts. An assembly line operation in down town Detroit is likely to influence its psychosocial subsystem very differently from a research laboratory on the Californian coast.

Structural subsystem

Structure involves the ways in which the tasks in the organization are divided (different-iated) and coordinated (integrated). In the formal sense structure is delineated by the organization charts, job descriptions and rules and procedures. Structure is also con-cerned with patterns of authority, communication, and workflow. Alongside the planned structure, or formal organization, is the informal organization that arises spontaneously out of the activities and interactions of participants. These informal networks and communication flows are essential to the organization's overall functioning.

Managerial subsystem

The managerial subsystem, finally, spans the entire organization. In the process it relates the organization to its environment, sets goals, develops comprehensive strategic and operational plans, designs the structure, and establishes control processes. Its primary role is that of integrating activities towards the achievement of implicit or explicit goals.

In summary, from an integrated systems perspective, the environmental suprasystem provides the setting within which organizations function. The technology is directly related to structure, both formal and informal. The psychosocial system provides an internal atmosphere for day-to-day operations. The managerial subsystem, finally, is the means of linking the other subsystems together as well as the organization, as a whole, with its environment.

Organization development

A healthy organization is one capable of integrating proactively (purposefully) with its physical, social and biological environment. An effective organization development practitioner is someone who enables an organization to develop the attitudes and processes which will allow it to integrate proactively with its environment.[29]

'OD'

The systems approach to management and organization, that is in its general systems context, has yet to fulfill its potential. Whereas specific and quantifiable applications of systems thinking abound – the new discipline of systems analysis has blossomed in the computing context – general and qualitative applications have been few and far between. In fact hard-hitting analysis has knocked out soft and subtle synthesis in most instances.

As a result, whereas the basic tenets of human relations are second nature to most educated managers, and the dynamics of organizational behavior have become at least somewhat familiar to the rational manager, the general systems view remains, at best, an implicit rather than an explicit part of his organizational understanding.

In fact, during this period in which the systems view was emerging to the academic fore, that is in the sixties and the seventies, another related branch of organization theory was making the more visible running. This newly emerging branch came to be called 'organization development' or, just OD.

Personal growth

Organization development has essentially branched out in two major directions. The first of these, inaugurated in the thirties by Mary Parker Follett, and exemplified in the sixties by 'sensitivity training', is oriented towards individual or 'personal growth'. For the complete flowering of this qualitatively 'growth-centered' approach, encompassing both the individual and the organization, we shall have in effect to turn from rational to developmental management. In fact the boundaries of rational management have turned out to be too limiting to contain OD's full growth potential. For that reason I have delayed our introduction to Abraham Maslow, and his motivational theories, and to John Gardner, and his concept of self- and organizational renewal, until Chapter 22.

The mainstream of growth-centered organization development has been confined, then, to specific techniques of personal growth or self-development, which have actually made little impact on the organizational whole. Well-known examples are the original sensitivity training, which I shall consider here, transactional analysis or TA,[30] and Gestalt therapy.[31]

Within the context of rational management, then, the conflict between the feeling-oriented growth therapies and the thinking-oriented organizational forms has not been resolved. OD has failed to resolve the original incongruency between individual and organization with which Argyris presented us in the fifties.

The planning of change

The branch of OD which has had the more enduring and wide-ranging impact is that concerned with the management or planning of change, which fits more easily within the rational confines of behavioral science.

Planned change

The major foundation of planned change is the application of systematic and appropriate knowledge in human affairs for the purpose of creating intelligent action and change; a conscious, deliberate, and collaborative effort to improve the operations of a human system ... through the utilization of scientific knowledge.

Bennis, Benne and Chin *The Planning of Change*[32] 1968

The initial architect of the changing organization in the sixties was a professor of organizational behavior in America, Warren Bennis. He was one of the few people on either side of the Atlantic who not only took OD seriously, but also saw it carrying business into its next evolutionary step, from bureaucracy to democracy.

The subsequent architect of a new organizational form, incorporating networks as well as hierarchies, freedom as well as order, is Professor Handy. Handy, a leading authority in Great Britain on the future of work and organizations in society, has gone even further than Bennis in prescribing individual freedom within organizational order. However, the person who predated the whole thrust of organization development, both towards individual growth and organizational change, is Mary Parker Follett.

The new psychology

Parker Follett, to whom we were introduced in Chapter 5, was a forerunner of both personal growth and organizational change, in the fullest sense. In her two books *The New State* and *The Creative Experience* she focussed on the full implications of freedom and democracy for the individual, and for the organization, as well as for the community at large.

The new psychology

The importance of the new psychology is that it acknowledges man as the center and the shaper of the universe. In man's nature all institutions are latent and perforce must be adapted. Man not things must be the starting point of the future...

Today the individual is submerged, smothered, choked by the crowd fallacy, the herd theory. Free him from these, release his energies, and he will, with all other freemen, work out quick, flexible, constantly changing froms which shall respond sensitively to every need.

Mary Parker Follett *The New State*[33] 1929

The breadth and depth of Parker Follett's individual and organizational insight, back in the twenties was quite remarkable. Now let us investigate the extent to which her aspirations have since been fulfilled.

Personal growth and self-development

Sensitivity training

The roots of OD reach back to the National Training Laboratories which were established in America in 1947. 'The idea behind the laboratory was that participants, staff and students would learn about themselves and their back-home problems by collaboratively building a laboratory in which participants would become both experimenters and subjects in the study of their own interpersonal and group behavior.'[34]

The seminal influence on the creation of these laboratories was Kurt Lewin,[35] the leading behavioral scientist in the thirties and forties. His followers – Bradford, Gibb and Benne – wrote the leading book on sensitivity training,[36] published after Lewin's death. Sensitivity training, more popularly termed 'T-Groups', became almost synonymous with organization development in the sixties.

Sensitivity training and personal growth

1. In a training group there exists some persistent, incongruent behavior by member A. A is said to be incongruous if others see him as not being fully aware of his own feelings and reactions.
2. To the extent that A's behavior is not considered trivial it is fed back to him by other members.
3. To the extent such reflection causes A to perceive those aspects of his own behavior to be at variance with his own self-concept he experiences some degree of psychological crisis.
4. Should A perceive the group as empathetic his self-concept enlarges to include the reality with which he has been confronted.
5. A's behavior changes in line with his new integration and he therefore tends to be more congruent.

The understanding of self and others increases simultaneously.

James Clark *Authentic Interaction and Personal Growth*[37] 1963

Sensitivity training, with its emphasis on the uninhibited expression of feelings, was never received as well in Europe as in America. The equivalent influence on 'personal growth' within a management context was Revans' action learning.

Self-development through action learning

In Chapter 14 on management style, I introduced Revans and action learning (see pp. 268–74). Whereas sensitivity training is personally oriented, and largely divorced from any specific management context, in an action learning group personal and organizational learning and problem solving go hand in hand.

One cannot change the system of which one is in command, at least in any fundamental sense, unless one is oneself changed in the process. The change in the system we call action, that in the self we call learning . . . and learning consists much more in the reorganization of what was already familiar than it consists in the acquiring of fresh knowledge.[38]

In the process of developing himself, through action and learning, the individual develops his organization. The action learning projects on which he works – and in the context of which a small group of 'comrades in adversity' meet to support and challenge one another intellectually and emotionally – are designed to promote self- and organization development.

> Action learning groups are formed to enable every enterprise to make better use of its existing resources, by trying to engender within it a social process of learning calculated to help it identify its internal strengths and weaknesses, to understand better its inertias and dynamics, and in other ways to make more effective use of its stored experience.[39]

Whereas action learning is broader than sensitivity training in its combined personal and organizational scope neither Revans nor Lewin were explicitly concerned with changing organizational forms, in the same way as Bennis and Handy.

Changing organizations and the future of work

Warren Bennis in fact took on from where Burns and Stalker had left off, by enlarging the implications of the organic organizational form.[40]

Table 23 Mechanistic and organic systems

Mechanistic systems	Organic systems
Focussed on individual skill	Focussed on relationships
Concentrated on authority – obedience relationships	Concentrated on mutual influence and trust
Strict division of labor and hierarchical supervision	Interdependence and shared responsibility
Centralized decision making	Wide sharing of responsibility and control
Conflict resolution through suppression, arbitration, and warfare	Conflict resolution through bargaining or problem solving

The mechanistic and organic approaches (see Table 23)[40] represented, in turn, the old world, that Bennis described as bureaucratic, and the new one that he defined as democratic (see Table 24).[41]

Table 24 Bureaucratic and democratic organizations

Bureaucratic organization	Democratic organization
Division of labor based on functional specialization	Company organized around problems to be solved
A well-defined hierarchy of vertical authority	People organized horizontally according to professional skill
A system of fixed procedures for dealing with work context	Temporary *ad hoc* procedures for dealing with changing situations
Impersonal, formal relations	Personal, informal relationships

There is no doubt as to which approach to management and organization Bennis preferred. He had, in fact, been reacting against his bureaucratic predecessors in the same way as they had reacted against their entrepreneurial ones. Each reaction had come about when the prevailing wisdom had become 'too much of a good thing'.

Bureaucracy and its discontents

The 'bureaucratic model' was developed as a reaction against the personal subjugation, nepotism, cruelty, emotional vicissitudes, and subjective judgement which passed for managerial practices in the early days of the Industrial Revolution. Man's true hope, it was thought, was his ability to rationalize and to calculate... Rationality and predictability were sought for in order to eliminate chaos and unanticipated consequences.

It does not take a great deal of imagination to detect the flaws and problems in the bureaucratic model. We have all experienced them; bosses without technical competence and underlings with it; arbitrary and zany rules; an underworld (or informal) organization which subverts or even replaces the informal apparatus; confusion and conflicts among roles...

Warren Bennis *Changing Organizations*[42] 1966

The way forward for Bennis, then, lies with functional autonomy and learning, rather than with functional specialization and organization. The processes that lead to such individual and organizational autonomy, so necessary in times of uncertainty and change, revolve around individual and organizational learning:

- An ability to learn from experience, to codify, and to store the learning.
- An ability to 'learn how to learn', that is, to develop methodologies for improving the learning process.
- An ability to acquire and use feedback on one's own performance, to develop a 'process orientation', in short, to be self-analytical.
- An ability to direct one's own destiny.

In effect Bennis in the seventies, when compared with Chandler in the fifties, has shifted the emphasis from structure to process, and from organization to individual. What he has not done is to change, even in concept, the basic shape and form of the organization. Such radical change has been left to Bennis' compatriot, Charles Handy.

The future of work and organization

Charles Handy in Britain in the eighties, unlike Bennis in America in the sixties, has been developing organizational concepts at a time when the new communications technology is already upon us. Handy's managerial thinking is therefore influenced as much by modern technology, and by a sense of historical perspective, as it is shaped by the social sciences.

Handy himself is a classical scholar and economist by background, rather than a behavioral scientist. His first important book, *The Gods of Management*[43] bears this out. In it, as we saw in Chapter 15, he relates well-known Greek gods to current organizational structures and functions. Moreover, after a long and distinguished business and academic career, he has emerged as the leading British management theorist. Interestingly enough, Handy has managed to develop some pretty radical views while still retaining good connections with the business and educational establishment.

The dispersed organization

Traditional thinking about organizations has certainly been dominated by the machine. Where the machines were, originally, close to the sources of energy and raw materials, there would the people be. Micro-division of labour became the efficient way to ruin things, breaking work into tiny separate components so that each person could concentrate on one process – a chain of humans looking as much like a machine as possible, and, it was hoped, performing predictably.

The new micro-technologies are changing all that. Mass production is disappearing in factories and offices. Just as significantly, the way in which workers on the floor are organized is changing. Small groups of people with sophisticated tools are being given responsibility for a total operation. The work now comes to them, and they organize how to do it.

We have to build our organizations no longer around the machine, but around people. The new technology makes possible the dispersed organization, which probably means the beginning of the end of the gathered organization, the organizational model of the industrial age, with all its imagery of 'the works' or 'the office', the 'company man' or 'the company team'.

If our contemporary organisations are to survive they must adapt their managerial philosophy to one suited to the needs and attitudes of professionals. This reorganisation calls for not only an adjustment in scale and style, but also for a more profound, qualitative change.

For as the 'organisation man' is pushed into retreat, the apparent organisational imperatives of increased size and greater consistency will tend to be ignored and indeed reversed. Workflows will be broken up, units made smaller and more independent, and employees will be working on contract, but out of sight and out of hearing.

Charles Handy *The Future of Work*[44] 1984

Handy presents us with a much more radical view of our organizational future than does Bennis. The implications for management are dramatic. The shift from a centralized, ordered administration to a decentralized, dispersed professionalism is marked.

Reorganizing work

The principal options are:
- Tools or dials?
- Trains or terminals?
- Wages or fees?

The likely consequences are:
- The contractual organization.
- The federal organization.
- The professional organization.

Charles Handy *The Future of Work*[45] 1984

The actual and potential implications of such professionalism are set out precisely by Handy in the following way:

- Professionals demand a lot of independence and autonomy.
- Their organizations are flat structures.

- A career means advancement in one's profession, not necessarily in the same organization.
- Professionals prefer networks to hierarchies.
- They train the next generation themselves; professional organizations therefore have to be schools as well as workplaces.
- Fixed term contracts will become more common than either casual or indefinite employment.
- Flexible time contracts will be introduced to make part-time work more feasible; many of the professionals will be self-employed for the other part of their time.
- Personal and portable pensions will become more common.

Conclusion

Human relations to organization development

In summary we have come a long way from Mayo to Handy, via Rensis Likert, Burns and Stalker, Lawrence and Lorsche, Kast and Rosenzweig and Warren Bennis. The only person who might have kept up with the successive transformations, from individual and group to group and organization to organization and environment, is the redoubtable Mary Parker Follett. Hers is the only theoretical position that is capable, at least in general terms, of encompassing them all.

As far as the practicing manager is concerned it is fair to say that basic human relations theory has become conventional wisdom, at least in the industrialized nations. In moving on to organizational behavior the practitioner is likely not to have resolved Argyris' incongruencies within the context of the conventionally managed organization. Similarly approaches to organization development, particularly those focussing on personal growth, are likely to have done little more than nibble at the edges of change. It is only once we begin to take Handy's thinking on board, at least in Europe and America, that possibilities of alleviating the incongruencies present themselves.

Resolving organizational dilemmas

Handy is of the opinion that large organizations, in the eighties, face three major dilemmas. These arise, respectively, out of the need to accommodate variety, individuality, and democracy.

Organizational dilemmas

First dilemma: slack, the thermometer of incompetence

The most immediately pressing problem of the organized society is the growing incompetence of many of our organizations. Incompetence results from the wrong management 'cultures'. If you are using the culture you are comfortable with instead of the one that is appropriate to the organization, incompetence is cushioned.

Second dilemma: the rise of individualism

Relieving the pressure problems of obvious incompetence will, however, only uncover a deeper dilemma in the organized society. It is becoming clear that organizations managed for maximum efficiency come into conflict with human needs, the needs of the individual for self-expression and autonomy in everyday life.

Third dilemma: instrument or community?

We would be wise to begin to think of the organization not as an instrument but as a community: a community to which people belong and which belongs to them, whose outputs are measured in units broader than money, whose responsibilities are wider than economic success and whose methods and values mirror those of the wider democratic societies we claim to live in.

Charles Handy *The Gods of Management*[46] 1978

The central thread that runs through Handy's argument links together individuality and variety, reconciling personal freedom with collective order. Even his notion of community, which is so different from the American 'melting pot', is a means of accommodating individuality. Communities, then, which characterize successful organizations, each have their own distinct personality. More importantly, they are not owned by anyone nor do they own anyone. One belongs to a community as a member, and that community can belong to a wider group, in turn, by agreement. Contractual arrangements replace those dictated by authority or even by common identity.

Village communities and the future of work

At present most people are employed by organizations, not withstanding the rising levels of both unemployed and self-employed. In the new organization that Handy forsees, individuals will belong to it rather as one belongs to a village. Villages are small and personal, their people have names and characters and personalities. You cannot be sacked from your village, although life can be made fairly unpleasant for you by your neighbors. But you can leave, or choose not to join. You do not retire from a village. Though you may contribute less and less physically, you may provide more and more, mentally, over time.

Membership organizations such as these are modelled on the village: 'the ancient organic social unit whose flexibility and strength sustained human society through millenia'. Moreover they are based on consent and contract. In other words, fees are paid for work done rather than wages paid for time spent. The organization of contract therefore relies on contractors to provide particular parts or services, which the organization then combines into a whole.

Such organizations of contract and consent also find it hard to insist that all work is done on the premises. There will have to be far more scope, Handy says, for part-time work. Interestingly enough recent statistics indicate that there has been a massive increase in such part-time employment in Great Britain during the eighties.

Establishing organizations of professionals

Individuals, then, will be working for more than one organization simultaneously. Work will be done increasingly from home to be brought in at regular intervals, or communicated electronically to a central point. Electricity allows organizations to be powered from anywhere.

However, we must not lose sight of Lawrence and Lorsche's revelation that different social and economic environments call for different organizational social structures and processes. In the next chapter I want to introduce the two ends of the rational management continuum insofar as actual business organizations are concerned.

References

1. T. Lupton, *Management and the Social Sciences*, Penguin (1970), p 27.
2. F. Rothleisberger, *Training for Human Relations*, Harvard University (1956), p. 156.
3. E. Mayo, *The Human Problems of an Industrial Civilisation*, Macmillan (1933), pp. 128–31.
4. E. Mayo, *op. cit.,* p. 115.
5. D. Wren, *The Evolution of Management Thought*, Wiley (1979), p. 300.
6. E. Mayo, *op. cit.,* pp. 20 and 21.
7. R. F. Bales, *Interaction Process Analysis*, Addison Wesley (1950).
8. B. Tuckman, 'Developmental sequences in small groups', *Psychological Bulletin*, Vol. 63 (1965) pp. 384–99.
9. A. Bavelas, 'Communication patterns in task oriented groups', ex Cartwright, D. and Zander, A. (eds), *Group Dynamics,* Tavistock (1967).
10. M. Belbin, *Team Building*, Gower (1985).
11. R. Likert, *New Patterns of Management*, McGraw-Hill (1961), p. 11.
12. R. Likert, *The Human Organization*, McGraw-Hill (1967), p. 167.
13. R. Likert, *op. cit.,* (1967), p. 165.
14. C. Argyris, *Personality and Organization*, Harper & Row (1957), p. 229.
15. C. Argyris, *op. cit.,* p. 236.
16. C. Argyris, *op. cit.,* p. 236.
17. T. Burns and N. Stalker, *The Management of Innovation*, Tavistock (1959).
18. Kast and Rosenzweig, *Management and Organization*, McGraw-Hill (1970), p. 131.
19. C. Barnard, *The Functions of the Executive*, Harvard University Press (1938), p. 376.
20. C. Barnard, *op. cit.,* p. 283.
21. C. Barnard, *op. cit.,* p. 283.
22. Lawrence and Lorsche, *Organization and Environment*, Harvard University Press (1967), pp. 6–8.
23. Lawrence and Lorsche, *op. cit.,* p. 156.
24. Lawrence and Lorsche, *op. cit.,* pp. 234–5.
25. C. Von Bertalanffy, *General Systems Theory*, Brazillier (1968).
26. Kast and Rosenzweig, *op. cit.,* p. 101.
27. K. Boulding, 'General systems theory', *Management Science* (April, 1956), pp. 197–208.
28. Kast and Rosenzweig, *op. cit.,* p. 112.
29. J. Clark and C. Crone, 'OD in the seventies', ex *Management of Conflict and Change*, Penguin (1971), p. 112.
30. E. Berne, *The Games People Play*, Penguin (1962).
31. F. Perls, *Gestalt Therapy*, Penguin (1976).
32. W. Bennis and T. Benne and C. Chin, *The Planning of Change* Holt, Rinehart & Winston (1968), p. 4.
33. M. Parker Follett, *The New State*, Peter Smith (1929).
34. W. Bennis, T. Benne and C. Chin, *op. cit.,* p. 45.
35. K. Lewin, *Field Theory in Social Science*, Harper & Row (1951).
36. Bradford, Gibb and T. Benne, *T-Group Theory and Laboratory Method*, Wiley (1964).
37. J. V. Clark, 'Authentic interaction and personal growth', ex Bennis, W., Berne, T., and Chin, C., *op. cit.,* p. 397.
38. R. Revans, *Action Learning*, Bland Briggs (1980), p. 67.
39. R. Revans, *op. cit.* p. 122.
40. W. Bennis, *Changing Organizations*, McGraw-Hill (1966).
41. W. Bennis, *op. cit.* (1966), p. 118.

42. W. Bennis, *op. cit.*, (1966), p. 5.
43. C. Handy, *The Gods of Managment*, Pan (1985).
44. C. Handy, *The Future of Work*, Blackwell (1984).
45. C. Handy, *op. cit.* (1985), p. 77.
46. C. Handy, *op. cit.* (1985), p. 185.

17 Business strategy

Contents

Key concepts

Once you have fully understood the chapter you should be able to define the following concepts in your own words:

Commitment	Planning process
Competitive forces	Planning structure
Competitor response profile	Purposes of planning
Competitive strategy	Product development
Confrontative strategies	Product/market evolution
Generic competitive	Rationale for planning
strategies	Sequential planning
Growth share matrix	Strategic appraisal
Growth vector components	Strategic culture
Japanese Inc.	Strategic process
Philosophy of planning	

Objectives

Upon completing this chapter you should be able to do the following:

1. Outline Steiner's basic planning premises and parameters.
2. Describe Ansoff's analytical approach to corporate strategy.
3. Describe Michael Porter's approach to competitive strategy.
4. Analyze the collaborative, competitive and developmental aspects of Kotler's new competition.
5. Compare and contrast the four different approaches to corporate planning and strategy outlined above.

Introduction

Corporate planning and responsibility

The third branch of rational management is corporate planning and its sister discipline, corporate responsibility. Once again Fayol and subsequently Drucker were seminal influences on both. However, in the field of corporate responsibility there is one other early and significant influence, Chester Barnard, the prominent businessman and business philosopher in the 1930s.

In this chapter I shall be focussing on corporate planning, otherwise known as long-range planning, business or corporate strategy. In Chapter 18, I shall move on from toughminded business planning to the more tender end of this strategic orientation: corporate responsibility.

The emergence of strategic planning

Early origins
Strategy and planning, of course, had been part and parcel of military operations for

thousands of years. The great military generals, from Alexander the Great to Napoleon Bonaparte, had been meticulous planners and strategists. However, it was Henri Fayol, writing in the 1920s, who first introduced us to planning in the context of industrial administration.

> The plan of action facilitates the utilization of the firm's resources and the choice of the best methods to use for attaining the objective. It suppresses or reduces hesitancy, false steps, unwarranted changes of course, and helps to improve personnel. It is a precious managerial instrument.[1]

Planning at this point emerged, for the first time in a business context, as an important part of a managerial whole. It was not until the 1950s, however, that 'long-range planning' began to appear as a field in its own right.

From entrepreneurship to planning

For Drucker, one of its early instigators, long range planning was still intimately connected with 'risk taking decision making'. In other words, it was only one small step removed from primal enterprise.

Long-range planning is risk taking

Long range planning is risk taking decision making. As such it is the responsibility of the policy maker, whether we call him entrepreneur or manager. To do the job rationally and systematically does not change this. Long range planning does not substitute facts for judgment; it does not substitute science for the manager.

It does not even lessen the importance and role of managerial ability, courage, experimentation, or even hunch – just as scientific biology and systematic medicine have not lessened the importance of these qualities in the individual physician. On the contrary, the systematic organization of the planning job and the supply of knowledge to it should make more effective individual managerial qualities of personality and vision.

Peter Drucker 'Long range planning means risk taking'[2] 1958

Drucker, of course, had that rare inclination and ability to retain a balance between entrepreneurship and management. He saw the strategic function as a means of mediating between the two. In other words, managerial planning involved a conscious upgrading of entrepreneurial risk taking, to cope with the complexity of large-scale enterprise.

Long-range planning for management

However, Henri Fayol before him, and the corporate planning fraternity afterwards, saw things differently. During the sixties and seventies long range planning became the intellectual discipline of the business day. The first book on long range planning appeared in the late fifties. At the time, as the associate editor of the *Harvard Business Review* said: 'There were no other books devoted exclusively to the subject, the number of articles on planning in business magazines was relatively small, and only a handful of companies had organized formally and systematically for long range planning.'[3]

The planning rationale

All this changed dramatically in the sixties for the seven reasons cited in this first planning text:

1. Long range planning is closely connected with the concept of the corporation as a long-living institution. The more inclined corporate executives are to worry about business prospects five or ten years hence, the more likely they are to engage in some form of long-term planning.
2. Planning symbolizes the purposefulness of modern management. Increasingly, the modern business manager wants to have a hand in moulding, rather than simply reacting to, the future.
3. Planning is connected with the concept of the corporation as an agent of change. Until the seventeenth century, Drucker has pointed out, it was the purpose of all human institutions to prevent change. The business enterprise, on the other hand, was becoming the first human institution with the explicit purpose of bringing about change.
4. Long range planning owes part of its rise to a rapid increase in the level of research and development. As technology became more complex, and the pay off time for the realization of new investments lengthened, so there emerged a strong practical incentive for management to plan far ahead.
5. Planning represents the intellectual movement in management. Ever since administration became a subject of explicit consideration, analysts have emphasized the need to break away from 'managing by the seat of the pants'. As Koontz and O'Donnell – whom we met in Chapter 13 – have said, planning is 'an intellectual process, the conscious determination of courses of action, the basing of decisions on purpose, facts, and considerate estimates'.[4]
6. Long range planning reflects the strategic approach – as opposed to the tactical – to organizational behavior. 'Planning has become a valuable educational tool for managers and managed alike, helping the former to see the folly of exploiting trust and good will for short-term gain, and helping the latter to relate their interests as individuals to the long-term prospects of the organization'.[5]
7. Long range planning is evidence of confidence in the economic and political stability of our society. In an organization where managers cannot afford to take a long-term view, because of political and economic uncertainty, or even warfare, 'long-range thinking must be limited to idealists and visionaries'.

The rise and fall of analytical planning

Interestingly enough the economic uncertainties of the late seventies, in Europe and America, have indeed led to the demise of corporate planning, as a leading business function. In its place have emerged the primal forces of entrepreneurship and shared values, as has been highlighted in Section B, and the combined primal – rational force of 'competitive strategy', as will be highlighted here.

In the eighties, as we shall soon see in this chapter, there has appeared a new mix of primal (competitive) and rational (strategy) ingredients, in the shape of Michael Porter's *Competitive Strategy*, as well as Philip Kotler's *The New Competition*. So, long-range planning has been reformed rather than eclipsed. Before we examine this reformation, though, we need to fully grasp the original strategic formulation. To represent this mainstream I have called upon the two leading figures in the analytical tradition. The one is George Steiner, a Professor at the University of California, who was perhaps the earliest champion of long-range planning, as a function of management. The other is Igor Ansoff, who – over the past twenty years – has moved back and forth between America and Europe. Ansoff has been the true originator of corporate strategy as a discipline in its own right.

Before we hear from George Steiner, it may interest you to notice that all three doyens of rational management – Drucker, Steiner and Ansoff – are Americans of Central European origin. In other words cross-fertilization between European theory and American application has produced this fertile result.

Top management planning

Steiner, in his clear and comprehensive approach, has analyzed the context – background, generic nature, philosophy and purposes, as well as the content – basic characteristics, structure and functions, of planning.

The planning context

Background to planning
Like Ewing before him, Steiner has come up with specific reasons for the emergence of corporate planning in the fifties and sixties. The two sets of reasons are very similar:

1. Business no longer sees itself as standing helplessly before market forces, but rather expects to be able to plan and control its own future.
2. The rate of technological change is ever increasing. Whole new industries are being created, almost overnight, and managers now want to be able to anticipate these changes.
3. The mounting complexity of the job of management has called on a greater degree of analytical planning, in order to cope with its multifaceted demands.
4. The high level of business failures, and the speed up of product obsolescence has accentuated the need for planned development.
5. The increasingly complex environment in which business is operating calls for a more methodical response to competition and to change.

Generic nature of planning
Fundamentally, for Steiner, all planning is concerned with the future. In other words, planning deals with the futurity of present decisions. Planning examines future alternative courses of action which are open to a company. In choosing from among these courses of action an umbrella, a perspective, a frame of reference is established for current decisions.

The philosophy of planning
Planning, for Steiner, is a philosophy, not so much in the literal sense of that word but

more as an attitude to life. Planning necessitates a dedication to acting on the basis of contemplation, a determination to plan constantly and systematically as an integral part of management.

The purposes of planning

Planning also fulfills a particular set of business purposes in that it:

- Simulates the future.
- Reveals and clarifies future opportunities and threats.
- Prevents piecemeal decisions.
- Tests value judgements.
- Establishes a basis for other management functions.
- Acts as a channel for communications.
- Helps to master change.
- Becomes a framework for decision making throughout the company.

So much for the general context in and through which long range planning takes place. Now I want to look, with Steiner, at its detailed content, starting with key characteristics.

The planning content

Characteristics of planning

The key characteristics of planning are those associated with its subject matter, its procedural elements, its time perspective, its features and its organization. These are itemized in Table 25.

Table 25 Characteristics of planning

Subject matter	Procedural elements	Time perspective	Critical features	Structural organization
Research	Rules	Short-term	Qualitative versus	Project
Operations	Procedures	Medium-term	quantitative	Department
Marketing	Budgets	Long-term	Strategic versus	Division
Manpower	Programmes	Perpetual	tactical	Function
Facilities	Strategies		Formal versus	Subsidiary
Finance	Objectives		informal	Company
Acquisitions	Purposes		Flexible versus	
	Creed		inflexible	
	Charter			

The planning process

The planning process may be looked at, alternately, as a strategic or sequential process.

The strategic process

The following sorts of question, for Steiner as for Drucker, underlie the strategic planning process:

- What business am I in?
- What is my place in the industry?
- What customers am I serving? Where is my market?
- What is my company's image?
- What business do I want to be in, in five years time?
- What are my goals for profit improvement?
- What are my plans for product improvement?
- Where is my greatest strength? Am I using it well?
- Where is my greatest problem? How do I solve it?
- What share of the market do I want? Next ...?
- Are my personnel policies acceptable to my employees?
- How can I finance growth?

Sequential planning

At the same time, analytically based planning involves a precise sequence of steps, as follows:

1. Planning the plan.
2. Specifying the objectives of the enterprise:
   (a) forecasting future prospects;
   (b) measuring gaps between aspirations and projections.
3. Developing strategies:
   (a) to fill the major gaps.
4. Developing derivative or detailed plans, in major functional areas, to fit the strategies, covering research and development, operations, marketing, manpower and finance.
5. Carrying out the plans:
   (a) starting out operations;
   (b) introducing necessary controls.
6. Review and recycling.

So much for the planning process, as viewed by Steiner. Now let us investigate its possible structure, within a large-scale enterprise.

Planning structure

Finally, Steiner set out the kinds of major activity in which corporate planning departments were likely to be engaged:

- Environmental analysis incorporating economic, political, industry and competitive scanning and intelligence work.
- Strategic program planning, including the coordination of the entire planning process across the company.
- Venture development involving the analysis and development of new business ventures, as well as the appraisal and implementation of acquisitions.
- Management planning including the conduct of optimization studies, and the provision of analytical problem solving skills to other departments.

Top management planning in perspective

What Steiner did was to set the general parameters within which top management planning should take place. He took Peter Drucker's basic ideas and added both breadth and precision to them. His basic text on *Top Management Planning* therefore takes up some 700 pages of detailed analysis.

Planning as a whole

Since the end of World War II, changes in business planning have been as dramatic as any in the entire history of business. First, there has been the development of comprehensive, structured, corporate plans. Second, there has been a widespread creation of corporate staffs to help top managers operate formal planning programs. The essential characteristics of formal planning are these: plans are prepared on some time scale on the basis of procedures, are well structured, are comprehensive, are developed by many people in a cooperative effort over a lengthy time span and are written.

Third, there has been a development of new and powerful tools to improve the decision making process in corporate planning. Fourth, there has been a systematic effort to look into the future.

George Steiner *Top Management Planning*[6] 1969

What Ansoff did was somewhat different. Although equally analytical in his approach, he attempted, in a much tighter way, to establish a new business discipline, which stood apart from – even though it overlapped with – management. That new discipline, which more fundamentally separated primal from analytical management than Drucker had ever done, he entitled 'corporate strategy'. In its turn it was also closely linked to the managerial skill of 'problem solving and decision making' which became so popular in the sixties and seventies.

Corporate strategy

Strategic decision making

In the fifties, at the same time as David Ewing had been noticing a growing interest in long range planning, Ansoff had been observing an awakening of interest in 'strategy'. Numerous papers had been appearing in the management literature on such topics as product strategy, marketing strategy, diversification strategy, and even business strategy. This interest, as Ansoff saw it, was growing out of a recognition that a firm needs a well defined scope and growth direction. In his opinion objectives alone – as per Drucker – did not meet this need, so that additional 'decision rules' were required if a firm was to have orderly and profitable growth. Such decision rules or guidelines he broadly defined as 'strategy'.

Strategic decision making

From a decision viewpoint the overall problem of the business of the firm is to configure and direct the resource conversion process in such a way as to optimize the attainment of

> objectives. This calls for a great many distinct and different decisions ... called respectively, strategic, administrative and operating, each related to a different aspect of the resource conversion process.
>
> Igor Ansoff *Corporate Strategy*[7] 1964

Strategic decisions, for Ansoff, are primarily those concerned with external, rather than internal, problems of the firm, and specifically with selection of product–market mix which the firm will produce, and the markets to which it will sell. To use an engineering term, the strategic problem is concerned with establishing an 'impedance match' between the firm and its environment, or, in more useful terms, it is the problem of deciding what business the firm is in, and what kinds of businesses it will enter.

> The end product of strategic problems is deceptively simple; a combination of products and markets is selected for the firm. This combination is arrived at by addition of new product markets, divestment from old ones, and expansion of the present position. The change from the previous posture requires a redistribution of the firm's resources – a pattern of investments and divestments.[8]

Conducting a strategic appraisal

The decision as to which strategy to pursue rests upon the results of what Ansoff terms a 'strategic appraisal'. (See Fig. 39.)

Fig. 39 Strategic appraisal.

1. The 'strategic appraisal' begins, firstly, with the specification of objectives and goals, both economic and social. Whereas the economic objectives are likely to exert most influence on management, the social ones are likely to exert a modifying influence.

   The objective is a measure of efficiency of the resource conversion process. It contains three elements: the particular attribute that is chosen as a measure of efficiency (e.g. return on equity); the yardstick or scale (e.g. time scale); and the goal, that is the particular value on the scale that the firm seeks to attain (e.g. 15 per cent).

The central purpose of the firm, according to Ansoff, is to maximise long-term return on resources employed.

2. Following the specification of objectives and goals is the internal and external appraisal. Internally an assessment is made of the strengths and weaknesses of the firm. This involves a construction of a 'competence profile' of the firm, and a comparison between itself and other firms.

Grid of internal competences

Research and development encompasses the entire process of creating a marketable product. Included are pure and applied research, construction of prototypes, industrial design and preparation of manufacturing drawings. Market research is included insofar as it is concerned with determining the price – performance characteristics of the product and the size and structure of the market.

Operating is concerned with the procurement of raw materials, scheduling and controlling production, tooling, manufacturing engineering, quality and inventory control, and manufacturing the product.

Marketing is a broad activity concerned with creating product acceptance, advertising, sales promotion, selling, distributing the product (including transportation and warehousing), contract administration, sales analysis, and servicing.

General management and finance involves:

(a) Determining the overall pattern of relationships between the firm and its environment. This includes the determination of overall strategy and resource allocation, acquisition of new product – market positions for the firm, obtaining necessary financing, and maintaining good public relations.

(b) Providing integrated decision making, guidance and control to the functional (operations/marketing/finance/personnel) areas, particularly in areas of pricing, inventory and production levels, capital expenditures, and individual functional goals.

(c) Providing staff services to functional areas, such as accounting, industrial relations, personnel training, and performing other functions most effectively carried out centrally, such as purchasing.

Igor Ansoff *Corporate Strategy*[9] 1964

Externally an assessment is made of opportunities and threats in the economic, social, technological and political environment.

Both appraisals together have since become known as SWOT – strengths/weaknesses/opportunities/threats – in the business strategy field.

3. Thirdly, and subsequent to the specification of objectives and goals, and to the

Table 26 Growth vector components

PRODUCT MISSION	Present	New
Present	A Market penetration	C Product development
New	B Market development	D Diversification

strategic appraisal, a decision is made as to whether or not to diversify. This involves a selection of 'growth vector components' that have guided strategic decision makers for the past twenty-five years. (See Table 26.)

The firm has a strategic choice as to whether to:

(a) stay with its existing products within existing markets – 'market penetration', or
(b) stay with its existing products, but move into new markets – 'market development'
(c) develop new products, still catering for existing markets – 'product development'
(d) 'diversify' into new products and markets.

This choice will be determined by the results of the strategic appraisal up to this point.

4. Fourthly, detailed strategy components need to be worked out, based on the expansion (market penetration, product development, or market development) or diversification decision. These 'components' cover the operational, marketing, financial and other functional implications of the strategic decision.

5. Fifthly, and finally, decision rules for search and evaluation need to be evolved, to monitor and control the process of strategy formulation and implementation over time.

Corporate strategy in perspective

Since writing *Corporate Strategy* in the mid-sixties, Ansoff has substantially modified his initial position.[10] Specifically, he has placed more emphasis on the organizational and cultural factors influencing strategic decision making.

I personally find his original concepts more valuable than his subsequent modifications. Although *Corporate Strategy* is inevitably several analytical steps removed from 'primal' and – as we shall later see – 'developmental' or 'metaphysical' reality – it is a tightly argued exposition of the purely rational form. As such it is a classic in its own right. Since the 1960s there have been two kinds of reactions to Ansoff's approach. The first reaction – in the seventies – has been to make it more accessible to the practicing manager, while retaining its basically analytical perspective. That is the kind of approach we have seen from Steiner. The second, and more radical response of the eighties, is the one Michael Porter and Philip Kotler have recently adopted. Porter and Kotler have in fact mixed their penetrating analyses with a level of primal aggression that Ansoff and Steiner had never touched.

Competitive strategy

The primal reaction

The ultra-analytical approach to corporate planning was already becoming discredited in the seventies, at least in some business and academic quarters. The Boston Consultancy Group in America, as one of these critics, formulated its own rather crude, and yet very popular framework for strategic analysis.

The Boston Consultancy Group, like many of its clients, found Steiner's and Ansoff's approaches too complex for their liking and substituted their cruder, and more colorful 'growth/share' matrix (see Fig. 40), incorporating:

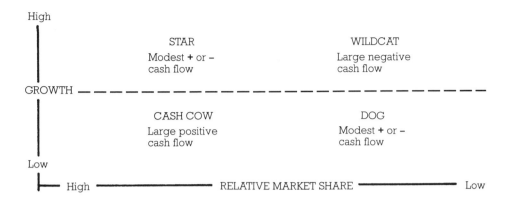

Fig. 40 The Boston growth/share matrix.

Stars – businesses with a large relative share of a high growth market, usually requiring a big injection of cash to sustain their growth, but having a strong market position that yielded high reported profits.

Wildcats – businesses with a small relative share in rapidly growing markets, requiring big injections of cash to finance growth, while being poor profit generators themselves because of their inferior competitive position.

Cash cows – businesses with a high relative share of a low growth market, producing a healthy and sustained, if unspectacular, cash flow, which could be used to sustain other developing businesses.

Dogs – businesses with a low relative share in a low growth market, that would often be suffering a cash crisis. Because of their weak competitive position they were obvious 'cash traps'.

Any large corporation would be likely to have one or more of all four types of business within its portfolio. The idea, however, is to minimize the 'dogs', to maximize on the 'stars' and 'cash cows', and to take a flier on one or two 'wildcats'.

Competitive strategy

Michel Porter, at the Harvard Business School, has taken up the hard nosed flavor of the Boston approach, but has gone much further. In his two books *Competitive Strategy*[11] and *Competitive Advantage*[12] he has developed a fully worked out concept of strategy, like Ansoff's, but one that is rooted in primal hunting grounds. Porter, in the eighties, is living in a very different America from the one that Ansoff inhabited in the sixties. The US is in a much more defensive business position, particularly *vis-à-vis* the Japanese, than it was twenty years ago. Peters, Waterman and Austin have responded by resurrecting a primal form of management, incorporating both hunter and gatherer. Porter, on the other hand, has combined a tough-minded analytical approach with an aggressively primal one, for hunters only!

Competitive strategy

Every firm competing in an industry has a competitive strategy, whether explicit or implicit. This strategy may have been developed explicitly through a planning process or it may have evolved implicitly through the activities of the various functional departments of the firm.

This approach presents a comprehensive framework of analytical techniques to help a firm analyze its industry as a whole and predict the industry's future evolution, to understand its competitors and its own position, and to translate this analysis into a competitive strategy for a particular business ...

The essence of formulating competitive strategy is relating a company to its environment ... The key aspects of the firm's environment is the industry or industries in which it competes ... The goal of competitive strategy ... is to find a position in the industry where the company can best defend itself against these forces or influence them in its favour.

Michael Porter *Competitive Strategy*[13] 1983

In an evolutionary way, Porter adapts the conventional wisdom on corporate strategy formulation to his own competitive orientation. This is demonstrated in Fig. 41.

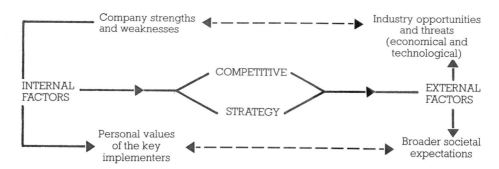

Fig. 41 A framework for competitive analysis.

However, the central thrust of Porter's instincts and analyses lie elsewhere, and that is with the 'competitive factors' in themselves. These he divides into the commitment to compete, the forces driving industrial competition, components of competitor analysis and the generic competitive strategies themselves.

The commitment to compete

Without the basic commitment to compete, as far as Porter is concerned, there is no point whatsoever in entering into a strategic arena. Analysis in itself, for Porter – if not for Steiner or Ansoff – without the instinctive drive to compete to win, is sterile.

There are three major types of commitment, then, each designed to achieve a deterrence of a different type:

● The commitment that the firm is unequivocally sticking with a move that it is making.

- The commitment that the firm will retaliate and continue to retaliate if a competitor makes certain moves.
- The commitment that the firm will take no action or forgo an action.

The concept of commitment

Perhaps the single most important concept in planning and executing offensive or defensive competitive moves is the concept of commitment. Commitment can guarantee the likelihood, speed, and vigor of retaliation to offensive moves, and can be the cornerstone of defensive strategy.

Establishing commitment is essentially a form of communicating the firm's resources and intentions unequivocally.

Michael Porter Competitive Strategy[14] 1983

The forces driving industrial competition

An effective competitive strategy, for Porter, takes offensive or defensive action in order to create a defendable position against five competitive forces. These are laid out in Fig. 42.

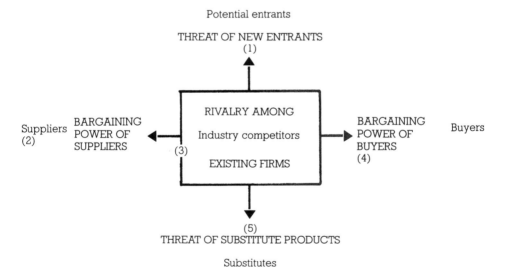

Fig. 42 Competitive forces.

Such a strategy broadly involves three alternative points of emphasis, that is on positioning, influencing, or anticipating:

- Positioning the firm so that its capabilities provide the best defense against the existing array of five competitive forces.
- Influencing the balance of the five forces through strategic moves, thereby improving the firm's relative position.

- Anticipating shifts in the factors underlying the five forces and responding to them, thereby exploiting change by choosing a strategy appropriate to the new competitive balance before the competitors realize it.

Competitive response

Porter's primal instincts are finely tuned to 'competitive response', which therefore makes up a key element of his overall competitive strategy. (See Fig. 43.)

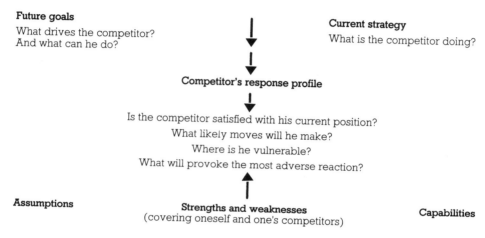

Future goals
What drives the competitor?
And what can he do?

Current strategy
What is the competitor doing?

Competitor's response profile

Is the competitor satisfied with his current position?
What likely moves will he make?
Where is he vulnerable?
What will provoke the most adverse reaction?

Assumptions

Strengths and weaknesses
(covering oneself and one's competitors)

Capabilities

Fig. 43 Components of competitor analysis.

Generic competitive strategies

In the final analysis Porter cites three generic strategies, and only three, for attaining competitive advantage:

1. Overall cost leadership requires the aggressive construction of cost-efficient, usually large-scale facilities; the vigorous pursuit of arising cost reductions; tight cost and overhead control; and cost minimization in areas like research and development, advertizing, after sales service, and so on.
2. Aggressive product or service differentiation, thus providing insulation against competitive rivalry because of the brand loyalty of customers, and a resulting lower sensitivity to price. It also leads to an increase of profit margins, because the customer is willing to pay a price premium. This avoids the necessity of adopting a low cost position. Finally, the resulting customer loyalty, and the need for a competitor to provide uniqueness, creates significant entry barriers.
3. The third and final generic strategy involves focus. This competitive strategy rests on the premise that the firm is thus able to serve its narrow market more effectively or efficiently than competitors who are competing more broadly. This form of strategy has also been termed nichemanship.

Competitive strategy as a whole

As we can see Porter adopts very much the role of the hunter and the hunted, albeit with an overlay of analytical sophistication, in his approach to competitive strategy. He accurately reflects the attitudes and perceptions of most business analysts and practitioners in the eighties, who see the international business arena as a global battlefield.

In fact Porter's compatriot, Philip Kotler, has taken an even more direct step into the military arena, that is by analogy, in *The New Competition*. In seeking to combat the Japanese threat, Kotler – the doyen of analytical marketing[15] – has uncannily merged business analysis with, on the one hand, vehement primal force, and, on the other, a largely subconscious dose of developmental management.

The new competition

The New Competition was the work of three people – Fahey, Jatiesripitak and Kotler. They set out to identify what made Japanese businesses so successful from a strategic point of view. Their most visible conclusions serve to reinforce even further Porter's competitive thesis, albeit within a wider collaborative context. At the same time they do draw our attention, perhaps almost without realizing it, to the developmental aspect of Japanese corporate strategy.

Confrontative strategy within a collaborative context

The collaborative context – Japanese Inc.

Before outlining Kotler's analysis of confrontative Japanese business strategies, let me set out the collaborative context in which they take place. This is the context which is sometimes referred to by the business world as 'Japanese Inc.'. There are, in fact, seven distinct sets of collaborative relationship which are vey much part of a large Japanese company's corporate strategy.

Firstly, one of the key factors underlying the 'Japanese miracle' is the government–business 'partnership'. While in many Western nations government intervention in corporate affairs is unwelcome or distrusted, Japanese companies have generated a more positive view of such relationships. In Japan in fact, the public and private sectors work in concert, thus enabling the Japanese to achieve economic objectives that other cultures have failed to attain.

Secondly, it is important to note that in the post-war period over 60 per cent of the capital that firms required came from the commercial banks' advances; 25 per cent was raised through retained profits and the depreciation of assets, and less than 15 per cent came from stock and bond issues. As a result of the importance of the bank loans, the larger Japanese firms began to group around certain major city banks. Moreover, firms that found themselves in the same banking group also tended to do business with each other wherever possible.

Thirdly, and historically, Japanese businesses have forged strong linkages with *zaibatsu* or huge trading groups. These *zaibatsu* specialize in domestic and international market intelligence, raw material acquisition, distribution, and finance, thereby achieving economies of scale in each.

The trading group does three things for the associated companies: it greatly expands the capabilities/options of the firms, especially the medium-sized ones; it allows Japanese manufacturers to concentrate on their product development; and it reduces the risk of new ventures because of its group support and financing. 'In contrast US firms must develop complete capabilities in finance, marketing, physical distribution, and planning, in pursuing their strategies'.[16]

Fourthly, Japanese manufacturers are aided considerably by trade associations, which can be found in almost every industry. These associations encourage increased communication and information exchange amongst their members. In addition, the associations are often responsible for establishing industry quality standards. Perhaps the most important function, though, is the establishment of priorities, involving output targets, raw material sourcing and supplier related problems and opportunities.

Fifthly, joint ventures serve many of the same purposes for the Japanese as investing in their own manufacturing operations. They gain access to markets, they can adopt products to individual circumstances, they can build in the latest technological developments, they lessen Japan's balance of payments 'problems', and they help with some of the anti-Japanese sentiments.

Sixthly, the Japanese manufacturer is likely to have a particularly close relationship with his suppliers, including very often an equity stake in their businesses. Even if the company does not hold an equity stake, moreover, its senior management team will often sit as directors on the suppliers' board of management. This relatively high degree of influence and control, albeit in an operating context of mutual trust, allows the Japense manufacturers to achieve greater flexibility in the production process than do their Western counterparts.

Seventhly, and perhaps best known to the West, the large company in Japan acts as one big family, with a high degree of mutual trust and support between labor and management. 'Economically, Japan's lack of natural resources has contributed to a sense of insecurity, and therefore encourage greater cooperation at every level. And socially, Japan is a nation where "groupism" predominates ... working is a mode of entry and dedication to a larger social unit.'[17]

Collaborative strategies in business

These seven sets of relationship are characteristic of, but not necessarily exclusive to, Japan. They form a collaborative context within which, as far as Kotler is concerned, the firm can confront the competition in the global market-place that much more effectively.

Confrontative strategies

Kotler and his colleagues went a step further than even Porter in voicing their tough-minded and 'primally' oriented strategic convictions.

Strategic culture

Commitment embodies the 'will to win', the indomitable spirit that separates winners from losers in all spheres of life. Thus the ultimate test of an organization's culture is its capacity in the market-place. This is what determines whether or not it is a 'strategic culture'.

> Stated differently, organizations with strategic cultures are likely to win the lengthy wars that are fought in the competitive battlefield.
>
> Kotler *et al. The New Competition*[18] 1986

The instinctive vehemence of Kotler and colleagues' competitive conviction not only eclipses Ansoff's analytical moderation, but can also be contrasted against Peter's greater balance of hardness and softness. Theirs is indeed a starkly confrontational viewpoint, encompassing Kotler's 'frontal', 'flanking', 'encirclement' and 'bypass' attacks. (See Fig. 44.)

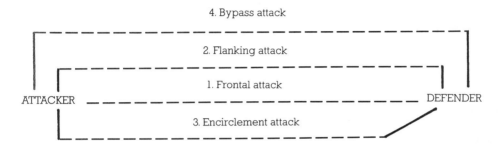

Fig. 44 Confrontation strategies.

As *The New Competition* sees the commercial world – just like the majority of European and American businessmen – 'Japanese firms seem driven by a conception of markets as battlefields'.

Frontal attack
A key ingredient for success in strategic and marketing warfare, Kotler argues, is the establishment of 'competition-centered strategies', and not just customer-centered ones. Here of course he parts company with the less aggressive Drucker.

It is the commitment to competing and winning that shapes and drives the 'warlike' strategic behavior. The most direct form of such is the 'frontal attack' whereby competition is tackled head on through super-aggressive salesmanship, dumping or price wars. 'Going to war over a market and doing whatever it takes to win over the long run motivates the aggressive battle plans so evident in many Japanese strategies since the late sixties'.[19]

In my view the business world at large has tended to exaggerate the 'warlike' aspects of Japanese corporate thrusts because of their relative inability to read the subtle and developmental side of their strategies. In fact Kotler acknowledges that the 'flanking' or 'niching' strategy is the one Japan prefers to the frontal attack.

Flanking attack
Japanese firms first developed a foothold in product-markets where US firms, according to Kotler, were weakest and, in many cases, non-existent. They then 'rolled out' their strategic thrust. This strategic approach is identified as 'flanking'. Its essence is to engage

the competition in areas where they are weak, gradually build up a strong market position on your own, with a view to ultimately launching a major onslaught on the enemy lines.

Patient capitalists

The Japanese are the very model of patient capitalists. Pursuing a flanking strategy over a number of years eventually allows them to adopt the aggressive, combative tactics inherent in frontal attacks.

Many Japanese firms have been willing to incur substantial losses as the price they must pay for later successes. The inclination of many Japanese firms to invest much time and money in bringing their engineers, product designers, and market planners to the United States to learn our customs, tastes and market conditions could only be justified by their plans to enter this market for the long haul.

Kotler *et al. The New Competition*[20] 1986

Encirclement attack

A frontal strategic onslaught will lead the competitor to counterattack. However, if the aggressor encircles the competition – for example, producing many more types, styles and sizes of products – the competitor's possible retaliatory responses are correspondingly reduced. For the enemy aggressor, in terms of *The New Competition* stands ready to block the competitor no matter which way it turns in the given product-market.

At the heart of this so-called Japanese encirclement strategy is technology. Propelled by a technological drive the Japanese are stretching their product-market domain in two ways. On the one hand they are extending and broadening their present market position; on the other hand they are diversifying into new territories. This leads us on to the fourth confrontational strategy.

Bypass attack

Japanese companies seem to understand very well, Kotler argues, that a strong fortified line may bestow a competitive advantage, but that if it remains stationary it invites competitive retaliation. It will ultimately, therefore, result in competitive inferiority.

So, in the main, the Japanese have not relied on a competitive front line. Rather they have employed offensive and defensive strategies to continually move their front, that is their position in the market-place. In other words they have continually adopted 'bypass' strategies.

Strategies of confrontation in perspective

What *The New Competition* has done is to introduce a whole new language to describe business strategy. It draws heavily on primal traditions, involving the hunter and the hunted, the killer and his prey. However, the argument is couched in rational terms, obviously drawing upon contemporary, military terminology. Raw aggression is tempered by a sophisticated rationale that makes for compelling business reading. It undoubtedly reflects an aspect of business strategy that has been underplayed by the purer analysts, such as Drucker, Ansoff and Steiner. What we have to safeguard against, of course, is Kotler's tendency to project, at least in part, a Western viewpoint upon an Eastern phenomenon.

Yet as good analysts Kotler and his colleagues have in fact gone beyond their militaristic analysis, almost without acknowleging it. Because they have not entered consciously into the realms of 'developmental management' their approach to developmental strategy is incidental rather than central. It is nonetheless significant. In fact it represents the subtle and perceptive – as opposed to the raw and instinctive – side of Japanese business.

Developmental strategies

'Niching' strategy

The 'flanking' strategy, so well deployed by the Japanese, is also – in Kotler's terms – a 'niching' strategy. Japanese firms choose particular niches or domains within a broad product-market or industry, and focus their marketing efforts on comparatively narrow 'windows of opportunity'.

> As they achieve success in these initial niches, they improve and upgrade their products, broaden their market focus, extend their distribution channels, and promote their own labels – all the steps necessary to upgrade and extend their product line and penetrate successive segments of the market.[21]

Product and market development

A central tenet of the Japanese strategic mentality, in fact, is that ultimate business success flows from product and market development and not from dealing and trading. In the same 'mental context' they believe that successful organizations develop their people from within rather than 'headhunting' them from without.

Product development

Japanese firms, according to Kotler, pursue three strategies in managing their product lines: product line stretching, product proliferation, and product improvement. Once the Japanese gained an initial foothold in the US market-place, they diligently set about filling out their product line, in order to reach an increasingly broader segment of the total market. That is what Kotler terms product line stretching.

Whereas product line stretching changes product line width, product proliferation introduces a multiplicity of product types or models at each point in the product line. Finally, Kotler and his colleague found, in every case in which the Japanese have been successful, that they have furnished a sequence of product improvements in performance, function, style, features, and quality. A good product, for the Japanese, is crucial but it is only the beginning of what I would term an evolutionary process (see Chapter 20).

Product improvement

Japanese commitment to product improvement is reflected in their commitment to listening and learning about their customers. They will spend long hours in discussion with customers about what limitations and weaknesses exist in their present product offerings, how products might be improved, and how the customers might react to possible product modifications.

> Once collected, these complaints, comments and suggestions are extensively analyzed and critiqued for insight into user needs and potential product development.
>
> Kotler *et al. The New Competition*[22] 1986

Market development

Product developments and improvements make little sense unless targeted at clear customer segments. Furthermore, market segmentation, sequencing and development presume product variation, differentiation, and ongoing improvement. Consequently there is a need to think in terms of product/market evolution rather than in the simpler, but, according to Kotler, 'misleading' product lifecycles.

As the Japanese improve and extend their product lines, they are inherently appealing to an increasingly wider array of market or customer needs, preferences or tastes. As watches, calculators, radios, motorcycles, and so forth, emerge in varying shapes and sizes, styles and functions, 'larger and larger slices of the potential customer base are drawn into the purchasing set'.

Of course, the Japanese do not think in terms of 'slices of custom' but rather in terms of concentric rings of product/market relationships. The linear notion of a product life cycle – with products emerging, proliferating, plateauing and declining – does not fit into their overlapping and evolutionary view of the world. Products are in fact created for, and fitted to, evolutionary technologies and market-place, in terms of both space and time.

Product/market evolution

Many Japanese firms entering the US in the 1950s and 1960s initially concentrated on one geographical region. Once they had achieved some penetration there, they set out to acquire complete coverage of the US in a series of geographical moves.

Toyota and Honda clearly employed this approach. The initial focus for both was California. Once they had established an initial position there, they began to establish their presence in adjoining states and continued in this path until they had attained geographical coverage of the whole of the US. Japanese product/market entries in the 1970s and 1980s tend to be much more upscale and upmarket by comparison with their earlier ones. They have progressed from small, simple and standardized products to complex, innovative and technically oriented versions ...

During the 1950s and 1960s Japanese firms had largely relied on licensing technology from US firms. Increasingly corporation and government-sponsored research and development replaced licensing. During the 1970s and 1980s, however, joint ventures emerged as a major entry strategy. Joint ventures help to overcome technological barriers, lessen distribution problems, and reduce potential competition.

Kotler *et al. The New Competition*[23] 1986

Conclusion

As we can see, 'The New Competition' has come a long way since Drucker, and others even before him, began to address the strategic question from a business perspective. For Fayol, as for Ansoff and Steiner, long range planning was a purely intellectual process, whereby objectives were set for a long term future for businesses, an appraisal was made of its internal strengths and weaknesses and of external opportunities and threats, and appropriate courses of strategic action were selected and implemented.

Whereas Ansoff placed greater emphasis on the analytical process underlying strategy formulation, Steiner addressed himself more specifically to the details of, and parameters surrounding, the organization and implementation of corporate planning. Peter Drucker, in his turn, tried to retain a balance between entrepreneurial risk taking, and strategy formulation, but, as always with Drucker, pursuing a strongly analytical tack.

Michael Porter emerged in the eighties, with, in the one hand, a weighty intellectual pedigree – a Harvard professor – and, on the other, a strong primal instinct. Like Peters and Waterman he was interested in the business of winning in general, and in outgunning the Japanese, in particular. However, unlike his compatriots *In search of Excellence* he has focussed purely on the hard edges of competitive business.

Kotler, Fahey and Jatiesripitak have entered even more aggressively into the primal hunting ground. Their 'combatative strategies', modelled upon their perceptions of Japanese firms today, is based on a framework of analysis that is strongly influenced by military strategy. At the same time, as thorough-going analysts, they have uncovered – almost in passing rather than through conscious intent – the collaborative and developmental aspects of Japanese business.

In the context of strategy I have therefore spilled over into primal and developmental territory. This 'spilling over' not only reflects the natural processes of management's evolution, but also the geographical diversity of our coverage. For, hard as we might try, the Japanese (Eastern) way cannot be fitted into purely American (Western) or European, analytical frameworks. This will become even more apparent when we consider, in Section D, 'developmental management' as a whole. For the time being I want to turn to corporate responsibility, that softer side of business in its environment.

References

1. H. Fayol, *Industrial and General Administration*, Trans. Crobrough, J. M., International Management Institute (1980), p. 64.
2. P. Drucker, 'Long Range Planning Means Risk Taking', ex Ewing, D., *Long Range Planning for Management*, Harper & Row (1958), pp. 7–20.
3. D. Ewing, *op. cit.* (1958), p. ix.
4. H. Koontz and C. O'Donnell, *op. cit.* (1958), p. 21.
5. H. Koontz and C. O'Donnell, *op. cit.* (1958), p. 22.
6. G. Steiner, *Top Management Planning*, Macmillan (1969), p. 14.
7. I. Ansoff, *Corporate Strategy*, McGraw-Hill (1964), p. 11.
8. I. Ansoff, *op. cit.*, p. 12.
9. I. Ansoff, *op. cit.*, p. 126.
10. I. Ansoff, *Implanting Strategic Management*, Prentice Hall (1984).
11. M. Porter, *Competitive Strategy*, Macmillan (1983).
12. M. Porter, *Competitive Advantage*, Macmillan (1985).
13. M. Porter, *op. cit.* (1983), p. 10.
14. M. Porter, *op. cit.* (1983), p. 100.
15. P. Kotler, *Marketing Management: Analysis, Planning and Control*, Prentice Hall (1971).
16. P. Kotler, Fahy and Jatiesripitak, *The New Competition*, Prentice Hall (1986), p. 29.
17. Kotler *et al.*, *op. cit.*, p. 36.
18. Kotler *et al.*, *op. cit.*, p. 254.
19. Kotler *et al.*, *op. cit.*, p. 126.
20. Kotler *et al.*, *op. cit.*, p. 158.

21.   Kotler *et al.*, *op. cit.*, p. 125.
22.   Kotler *et al.*, *op. cit.*, p. 50.
23.   Kotler *et al.*, *op. cit.*, p. 122.

18 Business and its environment

Contents

Key concepts

Once you have fully understood the chapter you should be able
to define the following concepts in your own terms:

Basic responsibility	Open systems
Behavior space	Organizational responsibility
Business roles	Product cycle
Business triad	Social auditing
Change gap	Societal responsibility
Cooperative enterprise	Stakeholder relations
Double entry	Stewardship
Ecological awareness	Synthesis
Field of force	Systemic thinking
Interdependence	Tao
Management by idea	Waste minimization

Objectives

1. To be able to outline, in essence, general systems theory.
2. To be capable of describing Chester Barnard's view of cooperative enterprise.
3. To grasp Albert Low's concept of a company as a set of interacting forces.
4. To understand the three different levels of corporate responsibility and responsiveness.
5. To be able to describe the stakeholder relations, role, and stewardship concepts of business, together with the approach to social auditing that arises.

Introduction

Analysis and synthesis

The corporate strategists, from Steiner and Ansoff to Porter and Kotler, have all been brilliant analysts of the business scene. Porter and Kotler have also added a strong dose of primal aggression to their analytical toughness, demonstrating how businesses can successfully exploit their environments. For a business and environmental synthesis, however, involving more of a coming together than a pulling apart, we need to look elsewhere.

Synthesis

... The action of putting together; a combining of parts or elements so as to form a whole; the juxtaposing of often diverse ideas, forces, or factors into one coherent or consistent complex; the combination of partial truths – of a thesis and its antithesis – into higher truths.
Webster's Third New International Dictionary

Analysis without synthesis only does half the job of rational management. It provides incisiveness and thrust but not integration and coherence. This chapter takes us on, therefore, where the previous one left off, by first introducing systems theory.

Introducing systems theory

General systems approaches, more than any other body of management-related theory, have attempted to bring about business and organizational synthesis. Whereas the analytical strategists have shown management how to control the business environment, the 'systems theorists', have been more interested in identifying ways of interacting with it. In other words, they consider business to be a subordinate part of a 'superordinate' whole.

But there have been two problems. Firstly, systems theory has been used more readily by organizational thinkers than by business consultants or academics. Secondly, many of those who claim to be 'systemic' in their approach are actually nothing of the sort. Unfortunately, the zest present in the work of the genuinely systemic thinkers, like the German biologist, Von Bertallanffy,[1] and the Hungarian systems philosopher, Ervin Lazlo,[2] was lost once brought into the academic and business environments. Wholistic, systemic thinking was turned into computerized business systems, which, for all their undoubted value, had little to do with the business of synthesis.

The business of synthesis

There are valuable exceptions to the rule, and it is with these exceptions that this chapter is concerned. The first of these is Chester Barnard himself, whom we first met in Chapter 10. Drawing on biological sources, Barnard already began synthesizing *The Functions of the Executive*[3] in the thirties. I shall consider his pioneering efforts, within the context of systems theory as a whole, first.

More recently, though, the person who has done most to apply powers of synthesis to business enterprise, is Albert Low. Low was a practising manager in a large Canadian electricity supply company, in the seventies. His exceptional grasp of business, as a system, will form the second part of this chapter. Unfortunately, because Low gave his entirely original book the somewhat esoteric title, *Zen and Creative Management*,[4] it has not acquired the interest and the readership it deserves.

The third and most extensive part of this chapter will be occupied by two men who were in senior public affairs positions within IBM (UK) in the sixties, and who subsequently became independent consultants in the field of corporate responsibility. In the process John Hargreaves and Jan Dauman successfully interrelated business and society,[5] at a time, in the early seventies, when this relationship was preoccupying captains of industry.

Systems theory and the functioning of the executive

Cooperative enterprise

Although Chester Barnard would not have been aware of it at the time, he was the first senior manager to put a 'systemic' approach to business into effect. As we noted in Chapter 10, for him business was essentially a cooperative enterprise. It operated as 'a complex of physical, biological, personal and social components which are in a specific, systemic relationship, by reason of the cooperation of two or more persons for at least one definite end'.[6]

Barnard rejected the traditional, narrowly bounded view of an organization. He included in his concept of a company investors, suppliers, customers and others whose actions contributed to the firm, even though they might not be considered 'members' of the business itself.

> Such a system as the firm is evidently a subordinate unit of a larger system from one point of view, and itself embraces subsidiary systems, from another.[7]

Systems of management

One of the earliest advocates of systemic approaches to business and management, that is after Barnard himself, was a remarkable Englishman, by the name of Geoffrey Vickers. Sir Geoffrey was a High Court Judge in the early part of his career, who later on took a special interest in the ways that industrial societies in general, and public and private institutions in particular, maintained and developed themselves.

In the forties and fifties he began to write about the way institutions worked, and he publicized his findings soon afterwards. This series of publications culminated in a widely read volume, *Human Systems are Different*,[8] that came out in the early eighties. For Vickers, in a nutshell, our institutional and social salvation is dependent upon an ability to regulate our systematically interrelated ecological, technological, economic and political affairs.

Systems and relationships

We are becoming more aware that the individual, around whom the social tissue is woven, is not conveniently to be regarded as an organism continued by its skin, but rather as a system, consisting of two sets of relations, each of which is perhaps indefinitely extensible.

One set comprises the internal relations, psychological as well as physiological, which gives man whatever integrity he personally possesses. The other comprises the external relations which link him to his surroundings, and especially to his fellow men. He extends outward as widely as his interests and his sympathies can carry him, on the wings of communication, especially mutual communication.

The stability of his interior milieu is the condition of his free and independent life. Yet, the life which this stability makes possible is a life of external interdependence.

Sir Geoffrey Vickers *Freedom in a Rocking Boat*[9] 1972

The 'way' of management

The person who really introduced systems theory to me was neither Vickers nor Barnard – who both seemed to skirt around the fundamental systemic issue, and neither Von Bertalanffy nor Lazlo – both of whom were too profoundly philosophical for my managerial liking. It was rather Fritjof Capra who opened my eyes to the managerial potential of a systemic approach.

Capra is an Austrian physicist, now resident in California, who wrote a bestselling book in the seventies in which he described for the lay person the overall significance of the new physics.[10] The symbolism of the 'tao', that is the 'way' of the Ancient Chinese, lay in its qualities of flow and interconnection, within all forms of life.

The tao of physics

In contrast to the mechanistic Cartesian view of the world, the world view emerging from modern physics can be characterized by words like organic, holistic and ecological ... The universe is no longer seen as a machine, made up of a multitude of objects, but has to be pictured as one, indivisible, dynamic whole whose parts are essentially interrelated, and can be understood only as patterns of a cosmic process.

Modern physics pictures matter not at all as passive and inert, but as being in a continuous dancing and vibrating motion whose rhythmic patterns are determined by the molecular, atomic and nuclear configurations.

We have come to realize that there are no static structures in nature. There is stability, but this stability is one of dynamic balance, and the further we penetrate into matter the more we need to understand its dynamic nature to understand its patterns.

Fritjof Capra *Mankind at the Turning point*[11] 1982

Capra's words, in a physical context, echo those of Parker Follett, in a social and organizational one (see Chapter 11). Drawing on one of the founders of the new physics, Walter Heisenberg, Capra affirms, 'the world appears as a complicated tissue of events, in which connections of different kinds alternate or combine or overlap, and thereby determine the texture of the whole'.

If we transfer this kind of thinking into a business context we shall see the world differently from the way Ansoff or Porter have done. Competitive strategies, with finely drawn lines of division between companies and functions, are transformed into interactive ones, with overlapping structures and functions, and flexible patterns of behavior.

> Although the organism as a whole exhibits well defined regularities and behavior patterns, the relationships between its parts are not rigidly determined. Order is achieved by coordinating activities that leave room for variation and flexibility, and it is this flexibility which enables organisms to adapt to circumstances.[12]

Again this is a very different approach to flexible response to the one taken, for example, by Kotler in his assessment of Japanese 'flanking' or 'bypass' strategies. Where Capra alludes to flexibility and variability, as functions of naturally viable physical and social systems, Kotler sees such strategies as a 'warlike' approach to business competition. Where Capra sees emerging life Kotler sees impending death – or at least its avoidance.

Open systems

Living organisms, being open systems, keep themselves alive and functioning through intense transactions with their environment, which itself consists partially of organisms. The activity of systems involves such a transactional process involving a simultaneous and mutually interdependent interaction between multiple components.

The systems view, then, looks at the world in terms of relationships and integration ... Natural systems are wholes whose specific structures arise from the interactions and inter-

> dependence of their parts. Systemic properties are destroyed when the system is dissected. The nature of the whole is always greater than the sum of the parts.
>
> Fritjof Capra *Mankind at the Turningpoint*[13] 1982

Interestingly enough, while Capra – in his *Mankind at the Turningpoint* – refers to economic, social, ecological and political structures, he does not quite get down to business. In other words the new physicists have difficulty in touching base with commercial enterprise, and vice versa. Let us see, then, how much progress Albert Low made in this systemic direction.

Business as a set of interacting forces

Albert Low is a practicing Canadian manager and author of *Zen and Creative Management*. Its central focus is management by and through ideas. Reciprocal order, within a field of interacting forces, constitutes its central theme.

The interactive company

A company, according to Low, is not a personalized enterprise or a depersonalized organization but a 'multidimensional system' capable of growth, expansion and self-regulation. It is therefore not a static thing but a set of interacting forces.

As a set of interacting forces a business consists of independent, but mutually related elements. From a Zen point of view there are no 'things', no enduring entities. Rather the 'thing' or the company is seen to be a field of interacting causes and effects. This view of the world as a 'field' stands in contrast to the more familiar and 'dualistic' view of things. In America and Europe we have tended to view organizations in terms of management and workforce, business and environment, product and market. That is not the Eastern way.

Field theory is the Western counterpart to the Buddhist philosophy of Karma. Under this philosophy not only is the world made up of a multiplicity of interacting causes and effects, but also the resulting field is in a state of dynamic tension. This dynamic is created by the simultaneous opposition, and mutuality, of the component forces. Let me explore, with Low, the business implications.

The business triad as a field

The company's behavior space

The three 'commitments' of the shareholder, market and employee can be looked upon as the forces that make up the field of the company. Out of this field, or behavior space, arises the product (see Fig. 45). It is from this product, or service, that a return can be provided to the shareholder, employee and customer for the commitment each makes.

The notion of a field here is a very important one. It allows for a qualitative understanding of business, based on the notions of fitness, order, harmony, emergence and balance. Let us see, then, where all this leads. The interaction of the three forces gives rise to a system, a set of independent but mutually related entities. The shareholder, the employee, and the customer are each both independent and interdependent. They exist as independent elements of a single, unified corporate will and purpose. A business is therefore a whole, a unity; but it is a composite and multidimensional whole, being the interaction of three forces.

Each of the three forces combines commitment with expectation. The shareholder commits money and expects the highest return for the lowest possible risk. The employee commits his time and capability and expects, in return, a fair rate for the job as well as a continually developing career. The market represents the need that society has for the continued existence of the company. In return customers expect a quality product at a reasonable price. The dynamic tension within the business' force field is created by the simultaneous push and pull. The outward tendency (the push) has its origins in the need that each party has to improve its financial position in opposition to the other. The inward, or centering tendency (the pull), is realized in the product. Each of the three forces collaborates to produce it.

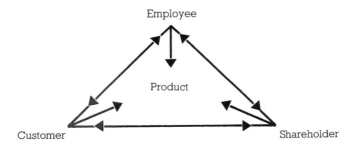

Fig. 45 The business triad.

Furthermore, just as there are three inputs – finance, know how and need, there are three feedbacks – reinvested finance, increased know how and enhanced goodwill. These three feedbacks are all profit in the larger meaning of the words, and it is in that larger context that business and society operates.

The three primary functions
Parallel to the three basic inputs, within the company, are the three primary functions that serve the product: finance, personnel and marketing. The finance function is concerned with realizing the potential that the company has to acquire financial investment, and to make this money available, at the required time and place within the company.

The personnel department has the function of recruiting, maintaining and developing people so that the whole product cycle can be undertaken effectively. The marketing function, finally, is responsible for structuring the needs of the market so that the product cycle can be linked with the willingness and ability of customers to pay. What, then, is this product cycle?

The product: an idea in a form with a demand

The idea as the center of business gravity

A product, according to Low,[14] is an idea in a form with a demand. An idea reveals the connections between people and things. The level of a product, and therefore of a company, is a function of the level of the idea of which that company is an expression. If a company like Sony, for example, merely defined its business as tape recorders or hi-fi its scope would be severely limited. However, it now sees itself 'understanding and exploiting the power of magnetism, to entertain and instruct us by visual and audible means'. That's a much higher level idea.

The business idea is the center of gravity of the field in which it has been perceived. It establishes and holds the connections. Take, for example, a roughly cut, wedge-shaped piece of wood. Is that a product? Most of us would feel that it was not, because nobody would want it. If pressed, however, you may seize on its likely shape and suggest that it could be used as a doorstop. If it happened to be in a place where there was plenty of wind and doors, then it could become a product. Indeed if there was the material and facilities available too, many more such products could be created. So the wedge-shaped piece of wood changes its character from a useless object to a potential product when an idea is introduced.

Through form the idea becomes something

It is through form that the idea becomes 'something'. A person fixes his idea in matter, space and time, and so establishes his idea in concrete terms. This imposes limits on it, separates it from all others, and makes it a thing. So the piece of wood becomes a strong and stylish doorstop, manufactured out of mahogany, colored charcoal and measuring such and such.

The form that a product takes is given by the material, equipment and components of the company. These are provided through the investment that the shareholder makes. The form, then, represents the cost of the product. The form is therefore the commitment of the shareholder in action.

The necessity of demand for an idea to become a product

But there must be a demand for the idea before it can be said to be a product, and this is provided by the customer. By demand we mean need, together with the willingness and ability to pay for it. Through demand the form meshes or fits with other forms. A link or interchange is established between the company-as-product and its environment. The market environment represents a set of potential needs that could be satisfied by the work of the company. These exist amongst an ocean of potential needs. Some of these are already known and clearly defined while others remain vague and unclearly expressed. Others still are unconscious and waiting to surface.

Like water in the ocean, needs are in constant flux, some rising to the surface, others subsiding, some expanding and others contracting. A view of the world which is modeled on field theory is more likely to pick up this floating potential than a more hard-nosed or segmented approach to market research and analysis. Finally, the perception and realization of an idea is the employee dimension in action. A business devoted to the identification of central ideas, and the formulation of strategies for moving swiftly from ideas to operations, will differ in structure and activity from a company purely concerned with the management of money or physical resources. High tech companies today are very much modeled on this premise.

The realization of the idea as the person in action

The recognition of the product as an idea in a form with a demand, and therefore of the idea being the central and dominating value of the company, puts the total human being back into the center of the industrial stage, but in a particular way. For the perception and realization of the idea is seen to be the employee dimension in action. That connects the person intimately with the product itself.

The stereotypical dichotomy between person and product, relationships and task, business and society, therefore disappears out the window. Instead we have the notion of a product cycle that integrates rather than separates people and things.

Integration through the product cycle

In the product development (PD) phase the idea is combined with other ideas; in the product processing phase (PP) it is coalesced with materials to give it form; and in the linking (PL) phase it is combined with need to give it value or meaning. (See Fig. 46.)

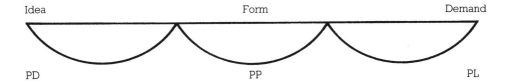

Idea   Form   Demand

PD   PP   PL

Fig. 46 The product cycle.

That, in essence, is the product cycle. It can be applied just as easily to an organizational function as to a physical product.

To the extent that the product cycle, and thereby the management of ideas, becomes the center of the company's field of gravity, so an integrated design function comes into its own. This in fact leads us into developmental management which we have not quite yet reached. For Albert Low stands on the borderline between rational and developmental management. He interweaves a rational, systematic approach with a non-rational Zen Buddhist one. For our purposes here I have stuck closer to the former than to the latter. Nevertheless, Low remains one of the very few management academics or consultants to adopt a truly interactive, systemic approach to business. He is less practical in his approach, however, than the more down to earth Dauman and Hargreaves whom we shall now meet.

Business and society

Business survival and social change

The title of Dauman and Hargreaves' book, *Corporate Survival and Social Change*, immediately sets it in a practical, as well as interdependent context.

> This book is about survival. This, in today's terms, means not just economic but also social and political survival. Because society today is interdependent, business survival depends on its ability to understand the issues facing society as a whole and to adjust to the major political and social forces of our time. In this context, when we talk about social responsibility, we are talking about no more or less than survival itself.[15]

Interestingly enough, then, Dauman and Hargreaves interweave a hard primal (survival), and a soft (systemic) rational orientation. They begin, however, by placing their own integrative orientation in historical perspective.

The protestant ethic and *laissez faire*

At the start of the nineteenth century, they say, the activities of the business community, in the industrializing nations, were generally separated from the rest of society. A *laissez faire* doctrine, often backed by the Protestant ethic of self-help, paid little attention to the needs of the community. Leadership tended to rest, in Europe at least, with the traditional areas of government, the church and the land-owning aristocracy.

A gap in perception existed between the captains of industry and leadership in other fields, which, to this day, in Europe at least, has not entirely disappeared. The drive for profit and growth was unrestrained and the legacy of social inequality marred industrial relations, ruptured human dignity, and ravaged the countryside.

No man is an island

Although the English poet John Donne had written more than a century earlier that 'no man is an Island Intire of Itselfe', there was little evidence of this thinking in our 'dark satanic mills'. The pressures today come from the descendants of those who were exploited. They feel that just recompense is due from the descendants of those who, they claim, established an hierarchy of authority which still exists.

Dauman and Hargreaves *Corporate Survival and Social Change* [16] 1975

The emergence of 'enlightened self-interest'

By the beginning of the twentieth century, many industrialists were of the second and third generation and had the time, power and even the 'necessary quantum of guilt' to act. There was some awakening to human rights and a growing recognition that people and land were assets to be preserved rather than just commodities to be used. There were signs of a more enlightened, even paternalistic attitude, which bore fruit in new amenities at work and for recreation, and in the use of company money for buildings, trusts, foundations and scholarships. On the whole this phase of thinking and doing was centered around the relationship between employer and employee, but it extended also to the immediate community around a factory, and included the patronage of welfare or charitable activities in neighboring districts.

Interdependence and involvement

Today, and emerging particularly strongly in the sixties, another phase of thought and activity has become evident, as a more educated and better-led generation begins to react against the authority and power structure of the past. On both sides of the Atlantic, not to mention the lead taken by Japan, captains of industry are recognizing the interdependence of the system of which they are a part.

For this reason, it is misleading to talk of 'business' and 'society'. Business, for Dauman and Hargreaves, is part of society and a major force within it. In other words, business is an important subsystem of a larger system, that is society. The aims and methods of business cannot be allowed, therefore, to diverge from those of society as a whole.

> Business today has to move side by side with the rest of society. Free enterprise has to add the dimension of social enterprise in which the long term interests of all are also the long term interests of each section. This is the form of the new social contract in which business has to play its leading part.[17]

What sort of society, then, has business today become a part of, and how will underlying technological and social trends affect the part that business plays?

Underlying social trends

Dauman and Hargreaves identified, in the seventies, seven key factors, or social trends, that impinged on business.

Acceleration of change. The graph of material discovery is rising at an almost exponential rate – a rate not matched by institutions designed to manage that change. The problem that needs to be overcome, then, is not change itself but that of reducing the 'change gap' – the gap between material change and institutional (including business) response.

Age of technology. This is an age in which science and technology is making an enormous and continually growing impact on business and society. So it is the job of every manager today to understand the potential of technology, to assess its effect, and to ensure that technology becomes on tap rather than on top.

New forms of control. The structure of both technology and management is changing as the pyramid of authority gives way to new concepts of control. Today the barriers between employer and employee, according to Dauman and Hargreaves, should be disappearing as situations, rather than people, become the dominant factor to which both employer and employee must respond. In this we hear strongly echoed the words of Peter Drucker, in the context of his management by objectives.

Work and leisure. Together with these changes in organizational behavior, Dauman and

Hargreaves see a need to reappraise existing attitudes towards work, leisure, education, and the relationship between income and toil. The Puritan work ethic, through which labor has to be endured and leisure is 'time off', is being challenged. Work and leisure are becoming increasingly blurred as are workplace and home.

Ecological awareness. Our ecological awareness has increased exponentially over the past twenty years. In fact the very science of ecology has only recently been developed. The rapidly emerging interest in health and fitness together with the increased awareness of our fragile and 'finite' planet is something companies can no longer afford to ignore.

Quality of life. Whereas the fifties and sixties were an age of quantity, the seventies and eighties have heralded an era of quality, at least in aspiration. The emergence of design, as a business discipline, and as an individual and social point of focus, reflects this growing, qualitative awareness.

The shrinking world. In any period, man's horizons have been limited by his available means of communication. When communication was restricted to physical transport, he could generally think only in terms of city states, or perhaps nations. With the divorce of communications from its physical limits we can now think and act in new dimensions.

Moreover, it is no longer possible to separate one community from another. The slum at the end of the rich man's garden, as Dauman and Hargreaves puts it, is unacceptable, not only in ethical terms, but also because it visibly jeopardizes his very survival. One community is therefore dependent on another, one nation on another one. The essential unity is not new but its nature is so. Interdependence has become a technological, institution, economic and political reality, even if on a person to person level – as 'civilized' people – we might have become more remote from one another.

The changing role of business in society

The manager or businessman, then, cannot escape the consequences of an interdependent world. What specifically, though, can and must he do about it? Dauman and Hargreaves identify three key activities – environmental analysis, corporate planning, and social auditing. But before we investigate them further, I want to turn to the role and purpose of business, in the light of its developing interdependence within society as a whole.

In the mid-seventies I was involved with Jan Dauman, and with the Battelle Institute in West Germany, in an investigation of the integrated social and economic performance of European-based multinationals. Fifteen companies participated in the programme, and one of the outcomes was a portrayal of the different business roles which these multinationals – in the seventies – could be seen to portray.[18]

The conventional view of the business enterprise, inherited from classical economics, was that of a profit maximizer. Its sole responsibility was to its owner, the entrepreneur. Once joint stock companies were formed, towards the end of the nineteenth century and ownership became diffused, the alleged purpose of business remained the same, but responsibility now shifted to a group of often anonymous shareholders.

Stakeholder relations
The break from this basic pattern of role and responsibility was signalled by Chester Barnard, who broadened the terms of business reference and responsibility, to include employee, customer and supplier. By the sixties and seventies the term 'stakeholders',

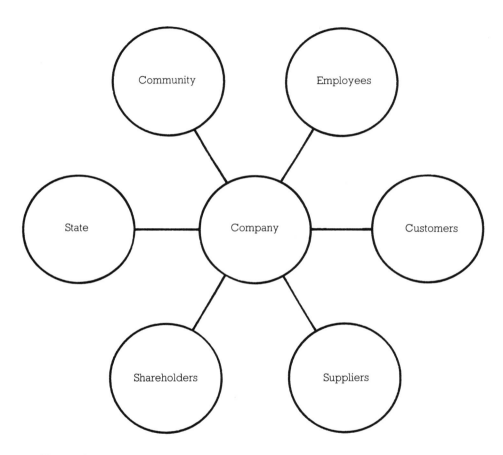

Fig. 47 Stakeholder relations.

representing a range of interested parties as opposed to the single grouping of shareholders, had begun to emerge.

As can be seen in Fig. 47, the stakeholder relations approach to a business and its responsibilities broadens the nature and extent of company transactions.

The roles of business
The virtue of the 'stakeholders' approach is that it spreads the field of responsibility, within which business operates. However, business' basic role remains unchanged, that is to maximize profit, even while its interactions with its diverse stakeholders are made more explicit.

In reconsidering the actual role of business, though, the Battelle project came up with the following and rather novel scheme of classification. The prime functions of business were not divided up according to conventional disciplines, but rather in terms of eight societal functions. For a business, then:

- As a producer of goods and services, its prime function was to fulfil the needs of its customers.
- As employer its function was to create and sustain jobs, thereby offering employment in both quality and quantity.
- As an economic unit its role was to create and distribute wealth.
- As a market partner its function was to participate in the maintenance and development of a healthy economy.
- As a social partner its function was to participate in the maintenance and development of a healthy society.
- As an innovator its role was to create new and better products, processes, and services, for particular customers and for society in general.
- Finally, as organizer, its role was to maintain and develop order, including orderly relationships, amongst people in society.

Stewardship
A third and final view of the function of business in society represented the company as a 'steward' of physical, human and financial resources (see Fig. 48).

Physical, human and financial resources may all be conserved and developed, or alternatively misappropriated and wasted. The stewardship function of a business will be

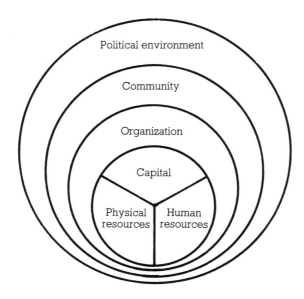

Fig. 48 Business stewardship.

enlarged upon when we come to consider the 'social audit' a little later on. Before that I want to reveal the three levels of corporate responsibility portrayed in *Corporate Survival and Social Change*.

Corporate social responsibility

Dauman and Hargreaves have divided the area of corporate 'social responsibility' into three levels, or concentric circles, as shown in Fig. 49. Basic responsibilities emerge out of a traditional, albeit 'ethical' business perspective. Organizational responsibilities reflect good stakeholder relations.

   Societal responsibilities, on the other hand, imply a more radical shift in the business' view of its role, or of its stewardship function.

Fig. 49 Classification of social responsibility.

Level one: basic responsibilities
The first circle relates to the basic responsibilities of a company, generated by the very fact of its existence. The company has to pay its taxes, obey the letter of the law, observe basic legal standards for employees and satisfy its shareholders. It must also have honorable dealings with its suppliers, customers and creditors. If these responsibilities are not fulfilled then, clearly, it will not take long before the company will be in serious trouble, either from the law or from the disciplines of the market-place.

Level two: organizational responsibilities
Most companies today, though, either through their size or the nature of their business, influence the environment more widely and have to look further in scope and time than is suggested at level one. In terms of the stone-in-the-pond analogy, there is a second ripple or circle. This level relates to the organizational responsibilities of the company to meet the changing needs of all its 'stakeholders', that is its employees, customers, shareholders, suppliers and local community. It is at this second level, according to Dauman and Hargreaves, that most of the thinking on social responsibility is concentrated.

   Pollution from a chemical plant, for example, may well affect a wide range of people in the community, outside the plant, most of whom are in no way associated with the company. If good legislation exists, then the community is protected. But if legislation is inadequate, and it does not stop people being harmed, then, if there is to be a corporate response, it would have to be a 'second level' one.

At this second level, then, the company's organizational responsibilities are principally as follows:

1. To pay heed to the spirit, rather than to just the letter of the law, acting in anticipation of impending legislation.
2. To respond to current attitudes, needs and values of all stakeholders and anticipate and respond to expected changes.

Level three: societal responses

The third and outer circle relates to the societal responsibilities of the company. It represents the stage when the interaction between business and other forces in society are so strong that individual companies are continuously involved in what is happening in society as a whole.

The rationale for this all-encompassing approach is contained within the perception that the health of the community at large, and that of the individual company within it, are as one. In other words, the health of the business subsystem is ultimately dependent upon that of the social system as whole.

The individual company therefore needs to consider the political, social, economic, technological, ecological and cultural foundations upon which the whole society is built, and with which it interacts. Business becomes involved, in essence, in the healthy development of society as a whole. In that capacity it assumes both a wide variety of roles (see p. 366) and also accepts responsibility for stewardship of material and non-material resources.

How, though, does this operationally come about?

Managing the business/society interface

Dauman and Hargreaves, as I mentioned above, identify three major aspects of managing the business/society interface. The second of these, involving planning/organization/control, albeit in a different context, I have already considered in Chapter 13. The first aspect – environmental analysis, and the third – social auditing, I shall consider briefly here.

Environmental analysis and 'issues'

Scanning the business environment is part and parcel of strategic planning as a whole. What is unique to the business/society interface is the elements or issues under consideration. Typical of these issues are:

- Employee relations, including general cultural attributes, the overall industrial relations climate, specific worker participation schemes and government labor regulations in the community or country concerned.
- Individual and organization, incorporating the role of trade unions and pressure groups; civil and minority rights; alienation at work; participation in planning.
- Consumer affairs, including fair trading, customer service, advertizing regulation and control; consumer groups, protection and legislation.
- Environmental pollution, encompassing air, water and noise pollution; resource con-

servations and recycling; land reclamation; environmental legislation and technology.

- Resources, including energy sources and conservation, basic foodstuffs and fresh water, new sources of energy, renewable and non-renewable sources of energy, energy conservation.
- Technological change, incorporating technology assessment, technology transfer, intermediate and alternative technologies, education for a changing world.
- Social trends, including work and leisure, employment and unemployment, growth and no-growth, work and home; attitudes to business, business ethics, business and society; crime and security, international terrorism.
- Urban affairs, incorporating housing, inner city dereliction, transport and communications, social services, participation with the local community and with local government.
- The third world, including the role of private enterprise, the impact of nationalization, population growth and planning, famine and natural disasters, training and education, cross-cultural impacts, the impact of multinationals.
- Government, encompassing general government–industry relations, mergers and monopoly control, political parties and ideologies, internationalization, multinationals and national governments, EEC, the defence industry.
- International affairs, including East–West and North–South relations, GATT, UN and international agencies, expropriation, war and security, South Africa and the Middle East, the role of the multinationals, the international monetary system and national indebtedness, the globalization of business.

As a company moves out of the first circle of basic responsibilities into the third circle of societal responsiveness it becomes more and more actively involved with the wide-ranging, above-mentioned issues. Insofar as it does this the large company's methods of accounting, reporting and control are inevitably affected.

Social auditing

Originators of the social audit

In the late 1960s it appeared as if a new business discipline might be born. It evolved into the late seventies but then seemed to dwindle into insignificance. However, because it was distinctive in itself, and may re-emerge in some new light 'social auditing' is still worthy of consideration here.

Social auditing represented an attempt to account for, and to evaluate, the social as opposed to the economic performance of large companies. The 'auditing' of social performance in general was initiated by the American Clark Abt,[19] and what came to be termed 'human asset accounting', by his countryman Eric Flamholtz.[20] Whereas social auditing involved the evaluation of the whole of corporate social performance, human asset accounting was exclusively concerned with the measurement of 'human worth'.

Where Abt, Flamholtz and most of their colleagues went wrong is that they tried to measure and to quantify human and social attributes, that were essentially qualitative in nature. As a result the validity of their work became increasingly suspect. An excellent summary of the whole range of work carried out in the early seventies is contained in a book entitled *The Corporate Social Audit*.[21]

Accounting for an enterprise's wellbeing

In 1974 I became involved with social accounting and auditing from a strictly qualitative standpoint. I introduced two new elements into the conventional practice of business and social accounting. Firstly, I extended the notion of double entry book keeping and accounts.

> Double entry recognizes the twofold aspect of every transaction ... However, this dual nature is hardly exclusive to business transactions as expressed in monetary values. A bee, for example, interacts with a flower, with pollen being the medium of exchange. In this instance the plant is 'debited' and the insect 'credited' for the receipt incurred.[22]

Similarly, there is no reason why only monetary exchanges should be 'accounted' for within a business. Transactions of a socio-psychological character are just as common as those of a physical and economic nature. It is only that we have not made the same concerted attempt to account for them.

In drawing up the sorts of social and psychological 'balance sheets' and 'trading accounts' indicated in Table 27, I was not proposing – like Abt and Flamholtz – that they be analyzed mainly in quantitative form. My emphasis was on the new way of concept-ualizing business rather than on the new measurements themselves.[23]

Table 27 Psychological balance sheet

Assets/psychological support	Liabilities/psychological demands
Nature and extent of experience: managerial, clerical, skilled manual	Accrued and impending demands for working experience
Nature and extent of knowledge and skill	Accrued and impending demands for utilization of knowledge and skill
Quantity and quality of investment in training	Accrued and impending demands for capacities recently developed

Assets and liabilities, then, represent two sides of a coin. On the 'liability' side a company has some outstanding demand or expectation awaiting satisfaction. On the 'asset' side it has the potential or sufficient support, or facility, to produce that satisfaction. Such demands, and their fulfillment, are 'traded' in not only physical and financial terms, but also in social and psychological ones. In other words, members of the company transact

Table 28 Physics/environmental trading account

Physical revenues	Physical costs
Regeneration of physical life forms	Killing of life forms
Reclamation of land	Desecration of land
Air, water, and noise pollution reduction	Increase in pollution levels
Satisfaction generated amongst conservationists	Dissatisfaction generated amongst conservationists

with themselves and with the outside world, exchanging physical resources, knowledge and skills, goods and services, satisfactions and dissatisfactions. An example of the resulting 'physical' costs and revenues is given in Table 28.

As we can see, the opportunity is there for business to either waste, or to conserve and to develop the physical, economic, social or psychological resources within and adjacent to itself.

Business stewardship and the minimization of waste
Arising out of this conceptual approach, Jan Dauman and myself therefore developed the 'new business ethic' of minimizing waste, within the context of business' stewardship role. This 'ethic' could subsequently be turned into a means of accounting for, and evaluating, total business performance.

The minimization of waste

Our proposal is that the elimination of waste in all aspects of business activities becomes the central ethic according to which business assesses its performance. Not only is the avoidance of waste, at a time of diminishing resources, rapidly being recognized by society as a whole as a prime necessity, it is a term which individuals can easily identify. It is a notion which not only transcends simple egotism but also can be identified with tangible things. Waste can be seen, touched, and smelt. It can be heard and felt.

Waste avoidance, then, interrelates the 'protestant ethic' of thrift with the management scientist's notion of efficiency, with the conservationist's desire for preservation. The more management is able to see physical and human resources as not only scarce but also beautiful creations, that must be nurtured, the more likely it is to succeed in its basic mission.

Dauman and Hargreaves *Corporate Survival and Social Change*[24] 1975

As we can see, especially in the context of social auditing, Dauman and Hargreaves stand at the edge of rational management, pointing one way towards the tangible and primal, and the other way towards the aesthetic and developmental. Nevertheless they remain fundamentally men of reason and method, albeit with a leaning towards business and social synthesis.

Conclusion

The interest in the role of business in society, which gained managerial pre-eminence in the sixties and seventies, extended the boundaries of business enterprise beyond that of the traditional firm. In that sense the movement, from a theoretical standpoint, reinforced the notion of business as a subsystem of a superordinate societal system.

Much debate has ensued, both before and after that particular period, over the role of business in society, from a more philosophical standpoint. On the one hand, the monetary economist Milton Friedman[25] has championed the narrower cause of business, as responsible exclusively to its shareholders, for the generation of profit and wealth. On the other hand, someone like Drucker has championed its wider responsibilities.

The debate will inevitably continue. Today, in the eighties and nineties, we are witnessing a two-way stretch. In one respect business is perceived as ever more competitive and cut-throat, leaving very little room for peripheral responsibilities. In another respect we, as managers and as human beings, are becoming ever more aware of our interdependence, and of business' position as a subsystem of a much wider economic, social and political system. As we enter the domain of developmental management, however, we shall discover that the separation between business and society becomes a contradiction in terms. In Chapter 23 we shall discover how this comes about. But before we do that we need still to analyze and synthesize the abundant fruits of rational management.

References

1. L. Von Bertallanffy, *General Systems Theory*, Brazillier (1973).
2. E. Lazlo, *A Systems View of the Future*, Brazillier (1976).
3. C. Barnard, *The Functions of the Executive*, Harvard University Press (1933).
4. A. Low, *Zen and Creative Management*, Doubleday (1976).
5. J. Dauman and J. Hargreaves, *Corporate Survival and Social Change*, Associated Business Press (1975).
6. C. Barnard, *op. cit.,* (1933), p. 65.
7. C. Barnard, *op. cit.,* (1933), p. 65.
8. G. Vickers, *Human Systems are Different*, Harper & Row (1983).
9. G. Vickers, *Freedom in a Rocking Boat*, Penguin (1972).
10. F. Capra, *The Tao of Physics*, Fontana (1982).
11. F. Capra, *Mankind at the Turningpoint*, Wildwood House (1982), p. 66.
12. F. Capra, *op. cit.,* (1982), p. 289.
13. F. Capra, *op. cit.* (1982), p. 117.
14. A. Low, *op. cit.*
15. J. Dauman and J. Hargreaves, *op. cit.,* p. 1.
16. J. Dauman and J. Hargreaves, *op. cit.,* p. 4.
17. J. Dauman and J. Hargreaves, *op. cit.,* p. 9.
18. D. Van den Berg, *Evaluating Corporate Performance*, unpublished report for Batelle Institute (1976).
19. C. Abt, 'Managing to save money by doing good', *Innovation*, Vol. 27 (1971).
20. E. Flamholtz, *The Theory and Value of an Individual's Value to an Organization*, PhD thesis, University of Michigan (1979).
21. R. Bauer and D. Fenn, *The Corporate Social Audit*, Russell Sage, (1972).
22. R. Lessem, 'Accounting for an Enterprise's Wellbeing', *Omega*, Vol. 2, no. 1, (1974).
23. J. Dauman and J. Hargreaves, *op. cit.,* p. 82.
24. J. Dauman and J. Hargreaves, *op. cit.,* p. 190.
25. M. Friedman, *Free to Choose*, Secker and Warburg (1980).

19 Hierarchies and networks

Contents

Key concepts

Once you have fully understood the chapter you should be able
to define the following concepts in your own terms:

Balanced network	Networker
Continuity mode	Networking organization
Dynamic network	Networker roles
Flexible production systems	Output mode
Full disclosure information systems	Professional management
Hierarchical management	Rational management continuum
Human capital	Vertical disaggregation
Network 'brokers'	

Objectives

Upon completing this chapter you should be able to do the following:

1. Describe the waning of enterprise and the onset of the managerial revolution.
2. Compare and contrast the two ends of the rational management continuum, explaining how they have developed out of the managerial revolution.
3. Describe the development of F International, focussing on the balanced development of formal organization and networking.
4. Compare and contrast the continuity and networking modes within Rank Xerox, relating these to their chairman's beliefs about 'Western man'.
5. Outline, in some detail, the background and structure of the 'dynamic network' that Miles and Snow have conceptualized.

Introduction

The managerial revolution

In the same way as the period from 1770 to 1870 may be termed the Age of Enterprise, at least in Western Europe and in America, that between 1870 and 1970 must rightfully be called the Age of Management. Management, in the context of this book, implies rational management, most particularly the analytical and hierarchical part of it. Indeed the American political philosopher James Burnham, who published his prophetic book *The Managerial Revolution* in the forties, proclaimed that management would rule the roost for approximately fifty years.

The managerial revolution

We are now in a period of social transition ... a period characterized, that is, by an unusually rapid rate of change of the most important economic, social and cultural institutions of society. This transition is from the type of society which we have called capitalist to a type of society which we shall call managerial.

This transition period may be expected to be short compared with the transition from feudal to capitalist society. It may be dated, somewhat arbitrarily, from the First World War, and maybe expected to close, with the consolidation of the new type of society, by approximately fifty years from then ...

James Burnham *The Managerial Revolution*[1] 1941

Robert Reich, a Professor of Business and Public Policy at Harvard University, wrote perhaps the sequel to Burnham's managerial revolution. Calling his book *The Next American Frontier*,[2] Reich traced a path through his acknowledged 'era of management' – 1920 to 1970 – into his 'era of human capital', from 1970 onwards. The respective eras parallel, very roughly, the rise and fall of Burnham's predicted managerial revolution.

The management continuum

In this chapter I want to trace a path, firstly out of the age of enterprise into the era of 'management'. Secondly I want to chart a course out of the management era into that of 'human capital'. Reich's two eras represent, as we shall see, the two ends of the continuum of rational management, one at an early stage, and the other at a late stage of its development. Early stage management (1920s to 1950s), epitomized by Fayol and Weber, emphasized order and organization, often as a reaction against the arbitrariness of enterprise. Later stage management (1960s and onwards), represented by Bennis and Handy, places greater emphasis on freedom and individuality.

Having reviewed the historical development of rational management, then, I shall take a specific look at two organizations in Britain today that are trying to reconcile the two sides of rational management, thereby creating both hierarchies and networks. These two companies are F International, a computer software house and Rank Xerox, the office systems corporation. Let me begin, though, by tracing the emergence of the managed organization out of the business enterprise.

Managerial order and organization

The waning of enterprise

The extraordinary mobility of capital, labour and materials in late nineteenth-century America – as in Britain fifty years before – rapidly transformed inventions into new methods of production and new products. But the organization on which this mobility was founded could not respond to the new demands that industrialization placed on it. The organizational fluidity that had allowed entrepreneurs to summon quickly the nation's resources had become by the first decades of the new century, a fundamental weakness. Once summoned, America's human and capital resources had no coherent structure in which to fit themselves. 'The nation's private enterprises and government institutions were simply too decentralized, piecemeal, idiosyncratic, and unreliable to handle a suddenly complex industrial society'.[3]

The balance between organizational looseness – allowing people and capital to be easily 'unglued', and institutional tightness – facilitating reliability, and economy of production – began to swing from the one way (entrepreneurial) to the other (managerial). In America, this swing to analytical and hierarchical management came through force of business and technological circumstances rather than through national and cultural disposition. Interestingly enough, and as we have seen in the chapters on primal management, there has been a recent reaction and 'regression', in the eighties, back to entrepreneurial ways.

The emergence of hierarchical management

From 1920 to 1970 output per worker in the American economy grew at an average rate of 2.3 per year, faster than in any other industrialized nation. Some of this increase was simply due to more and better machinery. But a larger part of the expansion was due to ways that America organized itself to produce. The first era of American productivity had been a direct extension of Britain's industrial revolution. The United States had merely added huge doses of capital and labor and a large national market, to Britain's basic inventiveness. The recipe had generated enormous increases in production, for a time. However, America could not continue this expansion without an organizational infrastructure to coordinate and monitor the use of its resources.

Its new business enterprises and its newly mobilized society both needed the emerging science of management. 'Management emerged around 1920 as a philosophy, a science and a pervasive metaphor which would dominate the way Americans viewed themselves and their institutions for the next fifty years. Management was America's own creation. No other industrial nation so fully embraced it or experienced its spectacular capacity to generate wealth.'[4]

What happened was that the logic of routine, large-scale manufacturing first shaped its original business environment, and then permeated the larger social environment. American society embraced such scientific or analytical management because it proved to be the very engine of prosperity, and not because the American people took naturally to order and to organization. Hence, again, the backlash in America today. Managers concerned themselves exclusively with the efficient pursuit of productivity, as they were expected to do, and rewarded for doing. The manager's professional code was built upon the ideal of efficiency, and the enterprises they worked in, along with the people they controlled, were cast as agents for achieving that ideal.

The rise of the professional manager

As the practice of management gradually evolved into a fully fledged profession, so the individual and organizational balance began to shift, even if only somewhat.

Specialized schools, journals, societies and management consulting firms, all of which were flourishing by the mid-1920s, buttressed the idea of management as a distinct profession with its own standards, ideals, and frame of reference, transcending any particular business enterprise. They also reinforced the notion that the professional manager could anticipate a career path passing through many different enterprises and managerial situations. His training and credentials made his expertise as marketable as any other professional service. Therefore his primary loyalty was to his profession rather than to any particular organization in which he should find himself.

Whereas the professional manager conceived of a lifetime in management he saw himself progressing through a wide range of companies, from junior to senior positions. In fact the average American manager is likely to have made four career moves before the age of thirty-five. The ascendancy of professional management in America's large companies was nearly complete, according to Reich, by the early 1950s. The professionally managed firm had become the standard form of modern business enterprise, both in America and in Europe. 'By 1962 in none of America's largest non-financial companies did an individual, family, or group hold more than 80% of the stock. In only five did a family or group have majority control. Professional management were clearly in control of 169 out of the 200 companies.'[5]

The character of leadership also changed. The previous generation business leaders had stressed strength of character. For them success in business had been the hallmark of superior personal performance, tangible evidence of the energy and ambition required to mobilize America's resources. Increasingly, however, the business enterprise was too large, and its profitability and growth were dependent on too many factors over too many years for the business manager to be judged solely by demonstrable results.

Personal success came to be weighed by different criteria: the forcefulness of the manager's approach, as evidenced by his ability to shape the organization, and cleverness at juggling numbers, manipulating organizational units, and diagnosing problems. These qualities owed more to the right professional education than they did to strength of character.

The professional manager

The professional manager came to exercise his craft above the industrial din, away from the dirt, noise and irrationality of people and products. He dressed well. His secretary was helpful and alert. His office was as clean, quiet and subdued as that of any other professional.

He organized and controlled large enterprises in a cool, logical and deliberate manner. He surveyed data, calculated profits and losses, and imposed systems for monitoring production, applying a general body of rules to each special circumstance. His professional training was his cachet.

Robert Reich *The Next American Frontier*[6] 1984

The management impasse

The end of an era

The management era – that is the era of what I would term hierarchical management – ended in America, according to Reich, around 1970. Gradually the economic indicators began to turn downward. The proportion of US manufacturing capacity employed in production, which had reached 86 per cent in 1965, fell to less than 70 per cent by 1982.

Measured in constant 1981 dollars, the Dow Jones industrial average declined from 2,624 to 1,000 over the same eighteen-year period. The profit rate of America's non-financial corporations fell steadily from 12.7 per cent in the late 1960s to 10 per cent by 1975. By the 1980s the core industries of this 'management' era – steel, automobiles, petro-chemicals, textiles, consumer electronics, electrical and metal-forming machinery – were in trouble. The problem was being caused, according to Reich, by an obsolete managerial superstructure. This was as applicable, of course, to much of Western Europe as it was to America. Japan, as we shall see in Chapter 23, was in a different position.

Obsolete superstructures

The superstructures of management in America were designed for stability, not adaptability. They were established to cater for high volume, standardized, predictable production. In this way, during the management era, they supported most Americans' prosperity and security.

But America's economic future depends on adjustment to a sharply different world economy. The superstructures of management – organized along industry lines and dominated by the largest and most entrenched producers within each industry – are inappropriate to the new task.

Robert Reich *The Next American Frontier*[7] 1984

A new era begins

What began in the 1960s as a gradual shift became by the late seventies a major structural change in the world economy. Assembly operations were being established in developing countries at an ever-increasing rate, and the manufacturing base of the industrialized world was being steadily eroded. Whereas Third World countries used to provide only primary products to feed the consumers and the industries of Europe and America, the situation was now changing.

A new era has begun in which the more economically advanced, developing countries are becoming the manufacturers of products like fertilizers, steel and heavy engineering goods that used to be made in the developed economies. The industrialized countries are therefore moving into products like precision castings, speciality steel, special chemicals, process control devices, fine ceramics and integrated circuits.

Some of these products or processes require precision engineering, and sophisticated maintenance. Others are custom made to the special needs of individual companies, and of individual market sectors. The remainder are technology driven and rapidly changing.

These three product categories have a great deal in common. They are all skill intensive, and all of them require that the traditionally separate business functions – research, design, engineering, purchasing, manufacturing, distribution, marketing – are merged into a highly flexible and integrated system. Such flexible systems cannot simply be grafted on to business organizations that are highly specialized for producing long runs of standardized goods.

Flexible systems

The premises of high volume, standardized production – the once potent formula of scientific management – are simply inapplicable to the flexible production system.

First, the tasks involved are necessarily complex since any work that can be rendered simple and routine is more efficiently done by low wage labor overseas. Secondly, skill-intensive processes cannot be programed according to a fixed set of rules covering all contingencies. The work requires high level skills precisely because the problems and opportunities cannot be anticipated. Finally, in flexible production systems the quality of the work is more important than quantity. Workers performance cannot be monitored through simple accounting systems ...

In fact, the radical distinction heretofore drawn between those who plan work and those who execute it is no longer appropriate. Not only is advanced planning often impossible, but flexible problem solving also requires close working relationships among people at all stages in the production process. There is no hierarchy to such problem solving. Solutions may come from anyone, anywhere.

In most firms that stake their success on specialized or technology based products, there are few middle managers and only modest differences in the status and income of senior managers and junior employees. The enterprise is typically organized as a set of relatively stable project teams.

Robert Reich *The Next American Frontier*[8] 1984

The net effect of these technologically based changes is to shift the balance of attention from the organization to the individual, both as client and as employee. Custom-made, skill-intensive production requires a perceptive and flexible – as opposed to hierarchical and routinized – approach to management. Reich identifies this approach with an 'era of human capital'.

Managing individuality and freedom

'Human capital'

Unlike high volume production, where most of a firm's value is represented by physical assets, the principal stores of value in flexible enterprises are human assets. Specialized machines and unskilled workers cannot adapt easily to new situations. Flexible machines and teams of skilled workers can.

Financial capital formation is becoming a less important determinant of a nation's wellbeing, according to Reich, than human capital formation. Financial capital crosses international borders with the speed of an electronic impulse. But a nation's store of human capital is relatively immobile internationally, apart from a few high flying scientists and engineers. The skills, knowledge and capacity for teamwork within a nation's labor force will therefore determine that nation's collective standard of living.

The new era of human capital

In the era of human capital, an era that all industrialized nations are entering, high volume, standardized production will to a great extent be replaced by flexible system production, in which integrated teams of workers identify and solve problems. This new organization of work necessarily will be more collaborative, participative, and egalitarian than is high-volume, standardized production, for the simple reason that initiative, responsibility and discretion must be so much more widely exercised without it.

Since its success depends on quickly identifying and responding to opportunities in its rapidly changing environment, the flexible enterprise cannot afford rigidly hierarchical chains of authority. That new organization of work will rest on a new organization of society ... unlike the old management superstructures, new public policies will need to promote adaptability instead of stability, inclusion in the production process rather than exclusion through welfare ... Economic policy will be linked to social policy ... But instead of outright giveaways, the new form of assistance will be tied explicitly to upgrading capital and labour. Businesses will be contractually obliged to restructure themselves, as a condition for receiving the assistance.

Robert Reich *The Next American Frontier*[9] 1984

The next American frontier

In summary, Reich has charted the movement in America, over the last sixty years, from a managerial era – 1920 to 1970 – to an era of human capital – 1970 onwards. Interestingly enough, though, he is not departing from the underlying notion of rational management. Reich is merely shifting from one end of rational management, where the emphasis is on order and organizational worth (financial capital), to the other end, where he focusses on freedom and individual worth (human capital). In emphasizing flexible matrix structures, and project teams, rather than pyramidical structures, and superior – subordinate relationships, he is changing the balance but not the fundamental orientation.

In the *The Next American Frontier* the basic corporate form remains intact, and the depersonalized emphasis – albeit on 'human capital' as opposed to financial capital – remains. What Reich has done, however, is to demonstrate very clearly the differences between the alternately hard, hierarchical, and soft, flexible, outcomes of rational management. He further demonstrates, at least in the industrialized nations of the West and the North, that the former are on the way out, and the latter must be on the way in – if America and Europe are to survive.

The fruits of rational management are therefore changing their shape, if not their ultimate form, from – in Charles Handy's terms – a role-centered to a task-centered one (see pp. 276–7). However, it will take many years still, perhaps another twenty, until the Athenian (task-centered) shape and form becomes predominant in Europe and America. In the meanwhile Apollonian (role-centered) fruit will still be found in relative, though decreasing, abundance.

Finally, we may or may not conclude, as a result of Reich's analysis, that the developing nations should be adopting the hard, Apollonian approach to rational management. I certainly would take issue with such a simple minded conclusion, and – in Chapter 28 – I shall be casting more light on this matter. At this point, though, I want to introduce you to two of the very few organizations that have spanned both ends of the rational management continuum, that is the orderly and the free, the Apollonian and the Athenian. They are F International, a computer software house, and Rank Xerox, both based in the UK. While both are involved in communications systems, the one is dominated by males and the other by females. Rank Xerox is large and powerful; F International is small and efficient; RX is a technological force and F is a social one.

Order within freedom

The origins of F International

Conformity and freedom
F International was started by Steve (Stephanie) Shirley, an emigrant from Nazi Germany into Britain, in the thirties.

Conformity and freedom

My life began in 1933 in Dortmund, West Germany. In 1939, when I was five years old, my family was scattered by the Nazis to the four winds. I was brought over to England by a Quaker family.

I progressed from village to grammar school, via a Roman Catholic convent, and loathed all three. At school, though, I did love maths and literature. I was fascinated by language and European culture.

By the age of eighteen my passions were different from those of other children. I campaigned for homosexual law reform, lobbied for changes in the law on suicide, and campaigned for birth control. I was very extreme. These things were so important to me. I believe in doing as you would be done by, in all walks of life.

Steve Shirley, Founder, F International[10] 1985

Business and society
In her youth Steve pursued freedom initially in a social context rather than in a business one. She was campaigning not for free enterprise but for the freedom of the individual. At the same time she understood the need for a scientific order.

Scientific boldness and order

While I was campaigning for law reform I went to London to look for a job. Ironically I was offered two, and took the one with the Post Office research station because it offered better job security. Whereas some people saw me as a revolutionary, I can see myself, with hindsight, as having been careful and risk-averse. Four years later, with the help of my employer's day release facilities, I obtained my BSc. in maths.

I loved the beauty of maths as I do in classical music. The aesthetics of form are a whole world in itself. But I wasn't clever enough to become an original mathematician.

At evening classes, I came across computers for the first time. They really were primitive in the fifties. I was still working with mechanical calculators, albeit to investigate complex phenomena. There was something very special in the atmosphere where the research station was based. There was an aura of intellectual self-confidence and scientific boldness.

Meanwhile something in me was saying that my future did not lie in being an

> employee. My era of conformity, you might say, was coming to an end.
> Steve Shirley, Founder, F International[11] 1985

Freelance programmers

By that stage in her development Steve was twenty-nine, and she wanted to have children. Matters were brought to a head when, at a staff meeting she made a suggestion and was told, 'That has nothing to do with you, you're technical.' She was furious. 'That's it', she thought to herself, 'I'm off.'

Freelance programmers

I decided to go freelance, thinking I was so good that people would come knocking at my door. Nobody came for three months, until a former colleague – he was then working for a management consultancy – gave me a break. The firm had set up a computer consultancy division, and I was asked to design the management controls for a data processing group.

By the time I finished the job I was eight and a half months pregnant. When I was asked how many people worked for me, I said 'one and a bit'. I called 'our' business Freelance Programmers.

When my son was born I lost interest in work for three months. That was the happiest time of our lives, for my son and I together. I was so pleased we had at least that little time.

He is severely mentally handicapped, and has been hospitalized since he was thirteen years old. It wasn't practicable to have any more of my five anticipated children. Perhaps if I'd had them I would never have developed my other family, F International!

In 1964 I incorporated Freelance Programmers. That was a turning point. It was like laying an official foundation stone. The operation became more credible to my customers and to myself. Business was growing into more of a stream than a trickle. I had earned the status. It was also the time when I began to build up my 'panel' of homeworkers.

They were the real foundation stones, and they enabled the business to extend beyond myself. They have also become the business' reason, my reason, for being. My panel worked from home, or on the client's premises, as three quarters of our thousand, mostly self-employed, mainly female staff, still do today.

Steve Shirley, Founder, F International[12] 1985

A *Guardian* newspaper article, in January 1964, gave the business publicity and context. Entitled 'Computer women', it said:

> Mrs Steve Shirley, a maths graduate who considered herself merely competent at research mathematics, found in computer programming an outlet for her artistic talents – working out patterns. She describes the essential quality required in programming as 'seeing the wood for the trees'. Now 'retired' with a young baby, she has found that computer programming can be done at home, between feeding the baby and washing nappies.[13]

Establishing 'F' for flexible

Soft and hard

If we look at the company policy today, we can see how it emerged out of that need and opportunity:

to utilize, wherever practicable, the services of people with dependants who are unable to work in a conventional environment

As the company's dependants grew, so did its problems, particularly with regard to cash flow. Steve called in a systems analyst who was to become a loyal friend, colleague and ally. He was both alarmed by the company's haphazard approach to cash management and also impressed by what it was doing. So he wrote out a personal cheque of £500 to tide the business over its first cash crisis.

Soft and hard

I remember, soon afterwards, when we got a big job from Castrol and I discovered, after six weeks, that very little had been achieved. I donned my 'troubleshooter' hat, left my husband to look after the baby, and sat on the contract, working sixteen and twenty hours a day. I had to learn Fortran virtually from scratch, but in one week, and two weekends, the job was working. I was exhausted!

In fact during the first ten years, when we were building up our clientele, we struggled quite desperately to keep our heads above water. I vividly recall the time when I needed £1,600 so badly I was compelled to take out a second mortgage on our home. That was a decision my husband and I had to make together. It was clear by then that our son was badly handicapped, and the prospect of moving back to furnished digs was not exactly appealing. But we felt we had to take the risk. The whole of me was at stake.

In the late sixties I realized I needed someone to share the burden of the company with, not just my husband or a friend, but someone with the commitment and commercial acumen to share the load. I found such a person within my panel of freelancers, and we set up a dual management system.

That's when the recession hit. Hardly a month would go by without news of the liquidation of a former client. And plonk in the middle of all this my partner left and took a precious chunk of business from me. That experience scarred me for life, but it's where I got my toughness from.

When I had originally started out in business most people I knew thought I was too soft. But by now I had found out what hard times were like and I realized how much I cared. These two factors together toughened me considerably.

There was much more at stake, after all, than the survival of a smallish company. A completely new way of organizing work would be discredited if we failed. I had tapped a rich vein of national talent (I am a very patriotic person) and nobody was going to stop the flow. In fact after making a loss of almost £4,000 in 1971/1972, by the next year we were back in profit, despite a substantially reduced turnover.

Steve Shirley, Founder, F International[14] 1985

Spreading the word

It was in the early seventies, once the company's survival seemed to be secured, that the idea of going international first came to Steve. The name and structure of Freelance Programmers Limited had already been changed to F, for flexible, International. F had one or two European customers, but it was the company chairman at the time who suggested it establish an overseas operation. The idea was that the company spread its employment philosophy, as well as it computing service, elsewhere. By then F was offering a comprehensive range of data processing services. They included consultancy, hardware and software evaluation, business and systems analysis, software development and computer installation support. The first overseas subsidiary to be opened was in Denmark, soon to be followed by Holland. From a turnover of £50,000 in 1969, the company expanded to £2.5 million in 1979. A loose-knit regional organization was established, all over the UK, run by a small number of entrepreneurial women. F had outgrown Steve's initial pioneering enterprise, but had not yet become a managed organization.

Becoming a managed organization

In 1981 Steve Shirley stepped off center stage and appointed her protegé, Alison Newell, as managing director of the UK company. The first company personnel manager, recruited in 1982, started working on a part-time basis, in the midst of the management transition.

Management transition

When I joined personnel function hardly existed. Alison became managing director in 1981, having evolved into the role from a home to office base and from part to full time employment. She asked me, initially on a part time basis, to help her define the organization structure and jobs.

She wanted a change from the highly competitive, decentralized structure, that existed at the time. It had the best and worst features of an entrepreneurial company, one region competing with the other. Each region had developed its own structures and work procedures, and one hardly communicated with the other.

My aim was to get people talking to one another. I also began to install professional sales and management training.

Jane Wilkinson, Personnel Manager F International[15] 1984

Along with the improved communications, and management training, Alison Newell instituted a formal program and process of strategic planning. Steve Shirley, in the meantime, was busy creating a proper board structure for both UK and overseas operations. By 1984 turnover had risen to £7 millions, 90 per cent of which was still generated from within the UK.

Individual and organization

In 1985 there was also a change at the top, when Hilary Cropper – who had been a senior manager at ICL, took over the managing directorship from Alison Newell. Alison had decided to move on. Hilary immediately shifted the emphasis from structure to strategy, while being particularly anxious, at the same time, to develop the right balance between hierarchical management and freelance networking.

Individual and organization

I've been in F International now for less than a year. The organization is very strong. It's a sure foothold from which to leap to other things. I must preserve the strengths, the culture, the motivation of individuals to express their individual worth and to cooperate with others.

Our 1,000 strong organization has a wide geographic coverage in the UK, so that we can expand rapidly within our markets. We have the right critical mass for a systems house. F also has the managers, the salespeople, and the methods of control it needs to expand. I would say that it is poised for a lift-off.

At the same time F is pretty green from the point of view of understanding the competitive scene. It hasn't assessed its strengths in its existing markets; it's not clear on the company's relative position. It needs to ask itself what business it is in now, and could or should be in, in the future.

This kind of strategic assessment leads to other things, like how we get leverage out of alliances, or takeovers. I've got to percolate that kind of thinking through the organization.

That will mean adding new people to the organization, and installing a 'management culture'. We've got to watch the market trends. We have to outmaneuver our competition! We need to keep our eyes and ears open and to tap our native intelligence. That means each individual contribution and innovation matters even more.

So what I'm doing, at the moment, is firstly creating a forum of debate around the issues. I want to instigate awareness from outside, and graft it on, while preserving our ingrained business culture. It's a very interesting stage.

Hilary Cropper, Managing Director, F International[16] 1986

Combining the technical and social mission

Steve Shirley's primary motive, in setting up her business, was not to make money. However, during the course of its development, the need to create commercially as well as socially viable structures and strategies has emerged. A key requirement has been that of combining technical excellence with social motivation.

Technical and social mission

In the end, of course, it's not money that motivates me. I've been determined to prove a point. I wanted to liberate a few hundred women from some of the constraints of motherhood, and I wanted to control my own destiny. I'm fascinated with the science of computing, and I take pleasure in business, especially entrepreneurial marketing and sales.

You know, people who join our company are very struck by the particular working environment. Apparently we're incredibly honest with one another. The way we say, 'Good God, I didn't know that.' Our meetings are so open. I've developed a credo, a charter to cover the non-quantifiable aspects of our business.

You need to be able to express those absolute qualities that are so important to business and to life. The twinning of technical excellence with a recognition of employees as whole people – writing programs or attending their children's sports days – is essential to our philosophy and structure.

Steve Shirley, Founder, F International[17] 1984

By 1985 the company charter had been formulated, and had gone public to the now 1,000 full- and part-time members of the organization. Within the charter lies the heart of the company, in the same way as Rank Xerox's book on networking speaks its mind.

F's social and economic charter

F International is a group of companies which have sprung from seeing an opportunity in a problem; one woman's inability to work in an office has turned into hundreds of people's opportunity to work in a non-office environment.

Mission

F International's mission is to become a leader in the rapidly growing and highly profitable, knowledge intensive software industry. It aims to achieve this by exploiting, through modern telecommunications, the development of the un-utilized intellectual energy of individuals and groups unable to work in a conventional office environment.

Strategy

F International's strategy is to maximize the value of its asset base by establishing a competitive advantage over conventionally organized firms, and eventually imitators of its approach, through cost and quality competitiveness. This occurs by the development of a methodology which ensures quality and by establishing a company ethos which binds people who work largely independently and often alone.

Values

People are vital to any knowledge intensive industry. The skills and loyalty of our employees are our only asset. Equally important is the knowledge which comes from the exchange of ideas with clients and their personnel. It follows that human and ethical values play a pivotal role in the way in which a company like F International conducts itself.

F International Charter[18] 1985

As we can see, F International clearly reflects Reich's era of human capital within its charter. The same applies to Rank Xerox International, also based in the UK.

Freedom within order

Networks and networking

While F International has adopted networking to a greater extent than any other company in Britain, Rank Xerox has done the most to conceptualize the role of 'networker'. Although only a very small proportion of the company's headquarters staff have been encouraged to take to this new form of employment – today there are 100 incumbent networkers – the concept of networking has now become well developed.

Rank Xerox's management services manager, who has played the major part in the development of 'networking', has an unusual background. As an electronics engineer and personnel executive Phil Judkin's mind is tuned into both physical and personal networks. Phil is also a radar buff so that he is emotionally involved with a lot of the electronic gadgetry with which he is 'playing'. He can happily spend until the small hours of the morning talking about Ethernet, Rank Xerox's distributed networking system, or about the new space-age headquarters that he has masterminded for his company.

At the same time Phil remains spiritually attached to the small Northern community where he still chooses to live. An archaeologist by training, he lives and breathes the traditional community life. In fact, in our conversations he is forever providing analogies drawn from the lifestyles of individual characters from the North of England. Their hardiness and rugged individualism, their wandering spirit and flexible lifestyle, their closeness to nature and practical ingenuity, all appeal strongly to his Northern spirit.

The village-based organization

The village, with its villagers, must replace the Greek temple as the centrepiece of the organization. Villages are small and personal, their people have names and characters and personalities. What more appropriate concept on which to base our institutions of the future than the ancient organic social unit whose flexibility and strength sustained human society through millenia.

Charles Handy *The Gods of Management*[19] 1985

Western (and Northern) man: an individual

Networking was first introduced at Rank Xerox while its chairman was Hamish Orr Ewing. He had the touch of individualism, almost of the English eccentric about him, and not surprisingly Mr Orr Ewing is a great advocate of individual freedom.

In one of the seminal speeches, in which he contrasted Japanese with combined American and European management styles, he summarized his operating premises in the following terms:

- Western man is an individualist.
- It would be therefore foolish to adopt the methods of a social order founded upon the primacy of the group.
- Western (what I have additionally termed Northern) organizational theory has led to rigidity.
- Previously this did not matter as the companies competing one with the other were doing so on the same basis.
- Now the situation is different, and we are facing competition from a source whose philosophy and psychology appears much more adapted, in an evolutionary, even Darwinian sense, to survival; in the present case, to the creation of wealth through the processes of mass manufacture of rapidly changing products.
- If we are to compete, we must do so in a way that builds upon our cultural history and our psychology, but this must be in a way that enables and enhances Western society to cope with change.

Organizations to enhance creativity

The new organizational forms that should emerge in Europe, if not also in America, must according to Orr Ewing:

(a) Be adaptive rather than rigid.
(b) Involve considerably lower overhead costs.
(c) Enhance individual contributions.
(d) Be organic and involve people.
(e) Enhance creativity.
(f) Motivate the production of quality work.

The new forms of organization

What will these forms actually look like? *Ex hypothesi*, they will not be like the huge organizational structures that we now see. On the contrary, the new form will consist of interrelated small structures, each part of which will almost certainly be a separate legal identity, owned and run by its members.

The emphasis will be on output and services rendered rather than on system and service. In that delightfully old-fashioned jargon so beloved by the legal profession, contracts will be for services rather than of service.

The internal hierarchy of the 'parent' organization may still exist but will be much abbreviated and reduced. The use of electronic communications will be common, with as much emphasis upon the use of social communications and on a healthy sense of humour, as upon formal communication.

Hamish Orr Ewing *New Forms of Organisation*[20] 1984

So much for the underlying vision of the networking organization. It has emerged out of an inherently British, you might even say eccentric, consciousness, brought into sharp relief by the comparison with Japan. The vision is also rooted in a fertile combination of traditionally rural and contemporary, sophisticated terrains. Phil Judkins himself strikes me as a mixture of archaeologist and engineer, agronomist and enabler.

Continuity and networking modes

In more pragmatic terms, Rank Xerox management have begun to grapple with the problems of reconciling freedom (networking) and order (continuity), organizationally, personally and technologically.

Redeploying facilities, people and technology

Networking, its originators say in their book *The Rank Xerox Experiment*,[21] has a threefold origin. These fall, conveniently, into the neat and clearcut categories of facilities, people and technology.

First, then, competitive pressures on the company forced it to re-examine its overhead costs, and, by implication, the balance between centralization and decentralization.

As can be seen in Fig. 50,[22] salaries on their own come to as little as 30 per cent of the overall cost of employing a knowledge worker in London. The balance of 70 per cent, for Rank Xerox in 1982, consisted of overheads. Moreover the facilities cost component is not only inflationary, and out of the company's control, but also sterile in that it motivates very few people either within the organization or without to buy its products.

Second, they had observed, over a period of years, the tendency for creative people to be relatively mobile around organizations, seeking the ability to regulate their own work,

Fig. 50 Costing a London-based office.

rather than being controlled in detail. As Rank Xerox depends on many such people, it seemed appropriate to search out ways of retaining their skills without stifling their creativity.

I find it interesting to compare and contrast Rank Xerox and F International at this point. Both have resorted to networking in order to shape work around their people's lives, rather than vice versa. Yet whereas for Rank Xerox mobility was the spur, for F it was the woman's immobility that spurred Steve Shirley on.

The third motivating factor for Rank Xerox was the fact that microcomputing technology, capable of transmitting technology over telephone lines, was becoming widely available at low cost. Networking saves the high, sterile proportion of overhead costs spent on facilities by having certain services provided remotely via microcomputer links.

Two employment modes: continuity and output

So networking is a means of reconciling the need for freedom and order within and betwen people and organizations, man and machine, business and environment. The way that Rank Xerox have gone about this is to distinguish between two modes of employment.

The two employment modes

We began by distinguishing two fundamental modes of employment:
(1) The continuity mode, in which 'being there' (that is, physically being at the point where the work is done) is an essential feature of the job and
(2) The output mode, in which the achievement of defined objectives is prime and where work supporting that achievement is incidental.
                    Judkins and West *The Rank Xerox Experiment*[23] 1986

To illustrate this distinction, take two familiar examples – a front desk receptionist, and a computer programmer. In the first case, to perform the task, the receptionist has to be physically present. The geographical location is at the root of the contract. By contrast, in most cases where computer programmers are employed, organizations are primarily interested in acquiring a program which achieves certain defined objectives. Where the programmer sits is of minor significance.

In practice, jobs usually embrace a mixture of continuity and output modes. The essence of networking is to so define a group of tasks which can be performed almost in the output mode, and then to restructure the surrounding organization to take over the balance of continuity work. Interestingly enough, for Steve Shirley the distinction between the two modes emerged naturally, through the course of her business' development. As a result she has never put the same consciousness as Rank Xerox has done into defining and conceptualizing 'networking'. Now that F International is becoming a large and structured organization such conceptualization is becoming more necessary.

Separating core staff from networkers

Rank Xerox, then, have used their analytical prowess to come up with a pathbreaking form of categorization.

Core staff and networkers

Core staff: the continuity mode workers; a reduced number of full-time salaried employees located on company premises who exist not only to achieve certain objectives but also to maintain day to day management and continuity.

Networkers: the output mode workers; a loosely inter-affiliated group who rarely work on parent company premises.

They are typically oriented towards defined objectives, projects or time defined activities, and make a significant knowledge input to those activities. Nomadic staff also work in this way, since a home base is more relevant to them than an office base which is rarely used.

Judkins and West *The Rank Xerox Experiment*[24] 1986

The communications link between the networker and the core staff is through a micro-computer-based electronic mail system. This employs standard telephone lines to communicate either to another microcomputer, or, in its more developed form, to a Xerox Ethernet local area network system. This system includes workstations allowing messages to be passed on, or work to be composed by the networker and printed out in company offices. Although Rank Xerox has placed much more emphasis on the technological end of networking than F International has done, both companies would agree that the personal and organizational aspects are the more significant. In other words, whether networking will succeed or fail depends much more on people and their attitudes than it does on technology, and its facilities.

The networking roles

Networking is not a single, simple style of work, any more than there is one single, simple type of work under the traditional employment contract. Rank Xerox have differentiated between three kinds of networker:

- The networker who seeks to build his networking skill, as a systems analyst or management trainer, for example, into a business. For me this is the purest type of networker, in the sense that he or she is seeking to express him-/herself in a chosen professional field rather than to build up a significant business enterprise. Once the business grows in scope and significance the networker becomes an entrepreneur.

- The networker-*cum*-entrepreneur will, for example, set up a sports shop while continuing to do technical training for Rank Xerox. In another case a management trainer, in Rank Xerox, has established his own contract research company. These entrepreneurial networkers have placed themselves halfway, as it were, between the North and the West of my business spheres.

- Another kind of networker, probably of an older age group, is the one who wants to spend his time outside of Rank Xerox-based work, enabling other people in business or in the community to make a fresh start in their lives. For such a person, maturity and personal circumstances combine to encourage him to become what I call an enabler. He seeks meaning in life, more than self-expression or individual achievement.

Linking up the networkers: the Xanadu Association

Xanadu was created by and for those people leaving Rank Xerox either to become networkers, or else to set up their own, completely separate businesses.

The association, serving to link up the individual networkers, is Xanadu. Aside from its functional and collective purpose as the Xerox Association for Networkers and Distributed Utilities, the road to Xanadu is paved with imaginative – even perhaps romantic – intentions.

Xanadu

The one person business, in particular, leads to a distinctly solitary working life. We have debated whether it is in fact possible or desirable for the parent company to reduce this feeling of loneliness or of isolation; and, indeed, whether a large business could understand how to do this.

The need for independence is after all one of the reasons why the networkers want to work in the way they do.

Eliminating loneliness or isolation might very well destroy the positive drive and motivation and remove the thrust for independence as the stimulus for success. We decided therefore to reduce, but not to eliminate, the isolation, in two ways:

1. Continuing to identify networkers as associated with the parent company. So networkers are still included in departmental charts, both their company and their name, with a dotted connecting line. They are also invited to departmental briefings, product launches and social functions.
2. Creating a business association, that is Xanadu. Its purpose is threefold: to interchange business leads, services, and information; to coordinate group purchasing of services; to maintain contact with the parent company to the mutual benefit of both parties.

Judkins and West *The Rank Xerox Experiment*[25] 1986

Xanadu Ltd was recently incorporated as a legal entity so that it now trades in its own right. It provides office services to the Mitcheldean Enterprise Workshops, created as a community workspace from part of the company's Gloucestershire plant. Xanadu

Consultants trades as a separate subsidiary. By the middle of 1985, four years after it was established, Xanadu's 200 constituent enterprises had a combined turnover of £13 million.

Organization design: rebalancing freedom and order

What then do Rank Xerox see as the implications of networking for the organization of the future? Interestingly enough they stress that no more than 15 per cent of their headquarters staff are ever likely to be networkers. This excludes the salesforce, although they could well be seen as the 'nomadic networkers'. It also excludes secretarial staff who are seen to be part of the continuity mode.

F International's position is almost exactly the reverse of Rank Xerox's. Some 85 per cent of their staff are presently networkers, including a significant proportion of their salesforce and secretarial staff. I suspect there are two main reasons for this discrepancy. First, F has grown organically as a networking organization and has learnt how to cope with a balance of freedom and order over a period of over twenty years. It is therefore much further along the organizational learning curve, in the networking respect, than Rank Xerox. Secondly, it is my conviction that women are characteristically better at coping with freedom, within constraints, than men. They do not have the same need to control as we menfolk, and are less prone to managerial hierarchies. That having been said, it is Rank Xerox who have after all come out with an 'individual centered organization' design. (See also Fig. 51.)[26]

Individual lifestyle

The word most closely identified with the individual centred organization is lifestyle. Lifestyle reflects the views expressed by our networkers that, against the background of a networker's small business, not only do home and workplace blend, but so also do work and family objectives, work and leisure, paid and unpaid roles. Using our analogy of a small village, it is no new phenomenon, but one which has existed for centuries.

Judkins and West *The Rank Xerox Experiment*[27] 1986

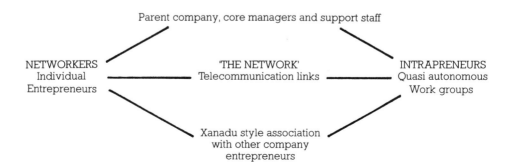

Fig. 51 Freedom within order.

How then does Rank Xerox's concept and F International's application reflect the development of organizational activity in the business world in general? Moreover, where exactly is the era of human capital leading us?

Conclusion

Emerging organizational forms

Companies like F International and Rank Xerox, for all their novel and flexible features, have still maintained the conventional business form. Whereas they have established networking arrangements with individuals outside their respective organizations, they have not yet done so with other corporations. For such forms of collaboration we have generally to turn to 'developmental management' (see Chapter 23).

However, seeds are being sown for a form of interlocking individuality that will overthrow, in time, the conventional and independent business establishment. 'New organizational forms are arising to cope with new environmental conditions. However, no new means of organizing or managing arrives full-blown; usually it results from a

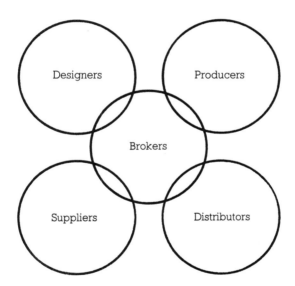

Fig. 52 The network organization.

variety of experimental actions taken by innovative companies ... a few businesses, in the US are on the verge of a breakthrough in organizational form.'[28]

Two American professors of management, Raymond Miles and Charles Snow have labelled this breakthrough organization the dynamic network (see Fig. 52), to suggest that 'its major components can be assembled and reassembled to meet complex and changing competitive conditions'.

The dynamic network

Vertical disaggregation: Business functions such as product design and development, manufacturing, marketing and distribution, typically conducted within a single organization, are performed by independent organizations within a network.

Brokers: Because each function is not necessarily part of a single organization, business groups are assembled by or located through brokers.

Market mechanisms: The major functions are held together in the main by market mechanisms rather than by plans and controls. Contracts and payment by results are used more frequently than progress reports and personal, hierarchically based supervision.

Full disclosure information systems: Broad-access computerized information systems are used as substitutes for lengthy trust building processes, based on experience. Participants in the network agree on a general structure of payment for value added and then hook themselves together in a continuously updated information system so that contributions can be mutually and instantaneously verified.

Miles and Snow 'Network organizations'[29] 1986

From enterprise to network

What we are seeing, then, is a shift in rational orientation that parallels the change in primal orientation of yesteryear. We may recall, from Chapter 1, that the independent enterprise – as it grew and developed – linked up with other such enterprises to form coalitions, cartels, or interlocking partnerships based on personal trust.

However, in time and as the volume of production and distribution grew and grew, these alliances became too brittle, too dependent on personal whim and individual circumstances, to endure. Hence the modern corporation came into being.

> The modern industrial organization – the archetype of today's giant corporation – resulted from the integration of the processes of mass production with those of mass distribution within a single firm ... Almost non-existent at the end of the 1870s, these integrated businesses came to dominate many of America's most vital industries within less than three decades ... The visible and coordinating hand of managerial direction had replaced the invisible and hand of market forces.[30]

The integrated business, according to Miles and Snow, is now disintegrating once again. In its place is no longer a personally based series of alliances but a depersonalized, dynamic network. While it retains the impersonality of rationally based management it overrides the rigidity of the hierarchical organization. While it retains the speed of response of primally based management it overcomes the limitations of personal pride and prejudice.

The balanced network

In order to understand all its ramifications, the dynamic network must be viewed simultaneously from the perspectives both of its individual components and of the network as a whole. For the individual firm (or component), the primary benefit of participation in the network is the opportunity to pursue its particular distinctive competence.

> A properly constructed network can display the technical specialization of the functional structure, and the balanced orientation characteristic of the matrix. Therefore, each matrix component can be seen as complementing rather than competing with the other components.
>
> Miles and Snow 'Network organizations'[31] 1986

Miles and Snow have extended Robert Reich's analysis, then, from the intra-organizational to the inter-organizational. In the process they have shifted the balance between freedom (network) and order (hierarchy) even further towards the former. Individual, as against organization, thus strengthens its hold, though still within the impersonal confines of rational management. The context and form changes once again when we enter the domain of 'developmental management'. While the primal manager attempts, instinctively, to bridge the gap between personality and community, and the rational manager has to sort out, intellectually, the conflict between individual and organization, the developmental manager must use his insight to dissolve the tension between self-development and group harmony.

References

1. J. Burnham, *The Managerial Revolution*, Indiana University Press (1941), p. 7.
2. R. Reich, *The Next American Frontier*, Penguin (1984).
3. R. Reich, *op. cit.*, p. 7.
4. R. Reich, *op. cit.*, p. 14.
5. R. Reich, *op. cit.*, p. 42.
6. R. Reich, *op. cit.*, p. 86.
7. R. Reich, *op. cit.*, p. 118.
8. R. Reich, *op. cit.*, p. 212.
9. R. Reich, *op. cit.*, p. 114.
10. S. Shirley, personal interview (1985).
11. S. Shirley, *op. cit.*
12. S. Shirley, *op. cit.*
13. *Guardian* (January, 1964).
14. S. Shirley, *op. cit.*
15. J. Wilkinson, personal interview (1984).
16. H. Cropper, personal interview (1986).
17. S. Shirley, *op. cit.*
18. *F International Charter,* (1985).
19. C. Handy, *The Gods of Management*, Pan (1985), p. 214.
20. H. Orr Ewing, *New Forms of Organization*, unpublished paper (1984).
21. Judkins and West, *The Rank Xerox Experiment*, Gower (1986), p. 18.
22. Judkins and West, *op. cit.*
23. Judkins and West, *op. cit.*, p. 25.
24. Judkins and West, *op. cit.*, p. 26.
25. Judkins and West, *op. cit.*, p. 49.
26. Judkins and West, *op. cit.*, p. 117.
27. Judkins and West, *op. cit.*, p. 116.
28. Miles and Snow, 'Network organizations', *California Managment Review*, no. 3, (Spring 1986), pp. 62–73.
29. Miles and Snow, *op. cit.*, p. 65.
30. Miles and Snow, *op. cit.*, p. 68.
31. Miles and Snow, *op. cit.*, p. 70.

Section D
Developmental
management

Introduction

The underlying ground

Whereas rational management characterizes the responsible, middle-sized organization, a developmental approach is required when such an organization approaches midlife, and is in need of renewal. This process of business and organizational renewal requires a quality of insight from its managers that is distinctively different from either instinct or intellect.

From a geographical perspective, such 'midlife' behavior is most widespread in the East, most visibly in Japan. At the same time there are elements of such an approach throughout the developed and developing world, most noticeably in design-based enterprises and in community economic development. Developmental management thrives, finally, on a balance of individual and organizational evolution and harmony, both of which are interpersonally, rather than personally or impersonally based. (See Fig. 53.)

The living characters

Whereas primal management is appropriate at the first phase of a business' development, and rational management at the second, developmental management is particularly appropriate at the third stage of an organization's evolution. However, life and business are never that clearcut, and the different stages will inevitably coexist somewhat, at any one point in time. The extent to which this is the case will depend on the personality of the founder, the industry in question, and the cultural origins of the enterprise. The 'soft' side of developmental management is personified by the enabler; the 'hard' side, on the other hand, is personified by the adopter. Whereas the typical enabler encourages individual self-development, the adopter encourages a collective form of association and development that cuts across any ego boundaries. While the 'soft' side is geared more towards self-actualization, the 'hard' is more oriented towards the realization of organizational potential.

Finally, the individual who represents a combination of the 'hard' adopter – characteristically Eastern, and the 'soft' enabler – characteristically Western, is what I have termed the corporate architect.[1] He is personified, in this text, by a plant manager of Sony, in Japan, Shigeru Kobayashi. He embodies developmental management.

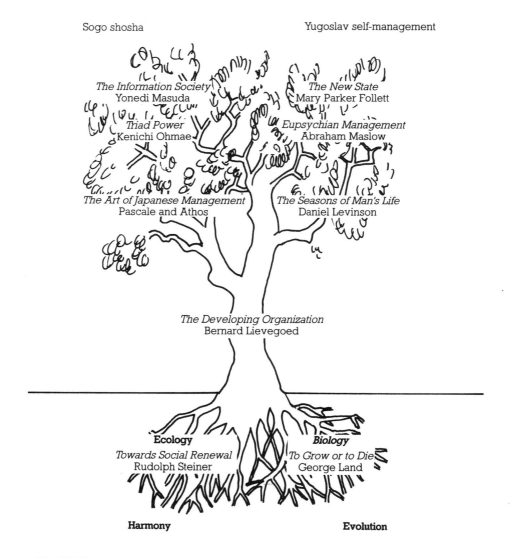

Fig. 53 The developmental tree.

The rational roots

Soft roots

The soft roots of developmental management reach down to 'the other economics' that is the theory of social renewal developed by Rudolph Steiner, an Austrian by birth, at the turn of the century. Steiner was a philosopher and psychologist, economist and agronomist, artist and architect, scientist and educator, who had a very different view of economics[2] from that of Adam Smith.

Steiner, like the classical economists that preceded him, believed in the division of labor, but not in the principle of individual self-interest that underpinned it. For Rudolph Steiner, such a 'division' of economic activity was born out of an underlying connectedness – serving the needs of others – rather than out of separation and self-centeredness.

More specifically he argued that whereas socio-political life was founded upon human rights, or equality and cultural life on human individuality, or freedom, economics was built upon foundations of fraternity. At the heart of economic life, for Steiner, lay principles of interpersonal and interorganizational association rather than of personal self-interest. Steiner's work has been recently updated, in Britain, by the anthropologist, Martin Large,[3] who has used the term 'social ecology' to relate Steiner's economics and organizational theory to contemporary business and social activity.

Hard roots

While the discipline of ecology underpins the harmony and fraternity in which Steiner's economics is rooted, developmental biology is concerned with the processes of evolution in which George Land's work is lodged.

George Ainsworth Land[4] is an American biologist and management consultant whose evocative book, *To Grow or to Die*, charts the developmental principles that underlie personal, organizational and societal evolution. He maintains that all living organisms pass through formative, normative and mutualistic stages of development. Moreover, if they fail to grow, in such qualitative terms, they will die.

Barry McWaters,[5] a humanistic psychologist in America, has added a fourth stage, that of nucleation or centering, to development. Together with his colleague, Barbara Hubbard,[6] he believes that conscious evolution is the unique task of our age, as individuals, organizations and as a planet. Within these grounds of conscious evolution, the soft roots of developmental management are imbedded.

The developmental core

Developmental principles

Bernard Lievegoed[7] is a Dutchman, who started out in life as a clinical psychologist, and has since branched out, as an educator and consultant, into all aspects of organizational life. From the outset he has espoused the developmental principles of Rudolph Steiner, and applied and adapted them to organizations around the globe.

Underlying Lievegoed's work, and those of his fellow, internationally based consultants (working under the umbrella of the National Pedagogical Institute), are such principles as:

- Development occurs in a series of stages.
- Within each stage a particular structure tends to dominate.
- The stages become progressively more complex.
- Development is not reversible (i.e. youth cannot return).

Stages of development

The stages of business development that Lievegoed formulated are pioneering (formative), differentiated (normative) and integrated (mutualistic). Those relate rather closely to the primal, rational and developmental domains within this text. Lievegoed took greatest interest in the third stage, which he thought should be contained within a so-called 'clover leaf organization'. Within each of the four leaves would be specific management activities.

The chairman of such an organization would shift from the top to the center of the enterprise; would harmonize people and things rather than control them; would follow an evolutionary path rather than just manage change; would strive for association and mutual agreement rather than for autonomy of function or authority; and would integrate business, technical and organizational development rather than pursue each separately.

Organizational renewal

Crisis and development

While Lievegoed's work represents the solid core of developmental management, there are two slighter developmental sources, both American, which parallel his own.

Gordon Lippitt, a consultant in organizational renewal, though generally restricting himself to rationally based planning for change, nevertheless came up with a robust developmental model. He maintained that an organization had to resolve a series of issues, or crises, if it was to grow and develop.[8] Lippitt, like Lievegoed, envisaged three phases of organization development. In the 'birth' stage the critical issues were creation and survival; in the 'youth' stage these were 'stability' and 'reputation'; and in the 'maturity' stage the issues to be resolved were 'uniqueness and adaptability' and 'contribution to society'.

Evolution and revolution

The second developmental theory that parallels Lievegoed's is that of Larry Greiner.[9] Greiner maintained that organizations evolve through five stages, interspersed with crises of revolutionary proportions. The young enterprise grows, firstly, through creativity, but has to undergo a 'crisis of leadership' before it can grow, secondly, through articulated direction. The personally directed organization, in its turn, needs to undergo a 'crisis of autonomy' before it can grow, thirdly, through delegation.

Such delegated authority, at a later stage of the organization's development, is subjected to a 'crisis of control' before it can grow, fourthly, through coordination. Finally, and in its more mature stage, an inevitable 'crisis of red tape' precedes any enduring organizational growth, fifthly, through collaboration.

Evolution and harmony

The core of soft developmental theory is lodged, then, in evolutionary phases, interspersed with crises. If the successive crises are anticipated and surmounted the organization grows; if they are ignored or not resolved the organization will eventually die. The hard developmental core, on the other hand, is reflected in the principles of association and integration. These not only enable the organization to evolve, but also, and particularly, characterize the third phase of its evolution. It is for this reason that this phase is identified with conscious evolution.

The developmental branches

Soft branches

The art of Japanese management

The 'soft' branches of developmental management are firmly attached to the core of large-scale Japanese enterprise. As a result most of the management literature, concerned with such harmonious business and organizational integration, is derived from Japan. Probably the best known of these sources is *The Art of Japanese Management*, written by the two Americans, Pascale and Athos.[10] They illustrate not only the strong group identity of the typical Japanese employee but also the strong spiritual bonds that tie the individual to the organization.

Triad power

Whereas Pascale and Athos are Americans, with a particular interest in Japan, Kenichi Ohmae is an American with a particular interest in both Europe and America. Ohmae,[11] in his recent book *Triad Power* (Japan–America–Europe), indicates that collaborative enterprises are taking over from independent business entities as the emerging global norm.

In other words, Ohmae is applying the principle of association, on a global business scale, not as an article of faith, but as the considered judgement of an international business consultant. As he sees it, both the escalating costs of technological investment and the exigencies of running businesses cross culturally, are forcing companies to work together. The result, in his terms, is not the choking of competition, but its emergence in a more dynamic form.

The synergistic economy

Whereas Pascale and Athos refer to principles of harmony and association within the individual firm, and Ohmae alludes to collaboration between them, Yonedi Masuda,[12] a Japanese futurist, forsees the onset of an entirely synergistic economy. Masuda argues that whereas industrial society is characterized by specialization in production, and by a division between producer and consumer, in the forthcoming information society social and economic arrangements will be substantively different. In such a society, he says, information – the axis of social and economic development – will be produced by an information utility. In that context the self-production of information by users will increase, and information will accumulate and expand through synergetic production and shared utilization. The economy, as a result, will change from an exchange economy to a 'synergetic' one.

Organizational, business and economic integration

As we can see, then, the Japanese have a vision of institutional, economic and cultural integration that is foreign to us in Europe and America, and that is largely concealed from the developing nations because of the lack of communication between Japan and, in particular, the South. At the same time, if Europe reaches down to its roots it will find, through Rudolph Steiner, fertile ground for the development of a similarly collaborative outlook. However, there are also distinct differences between the Western and Eastern viewpoints, in the relative importance attached to the individual. This leads us on to the hard branches of developmental management.

Hard branches

Self-realization

The hard branches of developmental management have proliferated not so much in a business and organizational context, but more so in an individual one. Whereas the Japanese have taken the lead in conceiving of approaches to organizational development, through harmony, the Americans and Europeans have led the way in conceiving of approaches to self-development, through stages of personal evolution.

The leading representative here, in the management literature, is the Armenian-American, Abraham Maslow.[13] Already in the fifties, he was introducing managers to the concept of an hierarchy of needs. Maslow maintained that should the individual evolve he or she would satisfy, within him or herself, needs ordered in an 'hierarchy of prepotency'.

In other words, once 'deficiency needs' – initially, physiological and, subsequently, social – were satisfied, only then could 'being needs' – initially, outer directed, and ultimately, inner directed, be satisfied. Not only the deficiency needs, Maslow argued, but also the being ones should be satisfied at work.

Maturation

Whereas Maslow attached some importance to the individual's lifecycle, in the course of his or her self-realization, it was not of major significance to him. In more recent years a number of developmental psychologists have paid particular attention to the process of maturation, in the context of both individual and organizational development. The most articulate of these has probably been the American psychiatrist, Daniel Levinson.[14] In his book *The Seasons of Man's Life* he sets out very clearly his four major phases of personal development, from youth and adulthood through to midlife and maturity. Levinson also pays particular attention to the alternating structure building (life structure) and structure changing (life transition) phases that characterize healthy adult development.

Finally, in a work context, Levinson attaches particular importance to the formation of one's dream, in one's youth (twenties); in the exercise of responsibility, in adulthood (thirties); in the process of self-renewal, in midlife (forties); and in the realization of one's legacy, in maturity (fifties onwards).

Self-development and social synergy

Very few theorists have attempted to combine the soft and hard elements of developmental management. The one major exception has been Mary Parker Follett, who not only had a major influence on rational management, but also has contributed a great deal to the developmental domain.

Parker Follett,[15] in *The New State*, equates personal evolution with interpersonal association, in the context of the small working group. For her individual self-realization is a function of group self-realization, and vice versa. In other words, I become myself through my association with different others, and the same applies to the individual organization as to the individual person. I, or it, can only find my or its part, within the whole.

The developmental fruits

Sogo shosha

In the same way as Mary Parker Follett has been largely ignored by the management establishment of today, so the 'developmental organization', in the terms of this text, has remained almost invisible. In fact Yoshino and Lifson,[16] a Japanese – American duo, who went out in search of the Japanese *sogo shosha*, entitled their book *The Invisible Link*.

The Japanese trading company that they sought out, the *sogo shosha*, has in fact played a major role in the development of that country. It has done so, almost invisibly, at least to those of us outside Japan, by acting as an economic facilitator, intermediary and integrator. The *sogo shosha* links up different companies, different industries and different countries in the course of developing a new technology, a new business, or a new market for its clients. There are no discrete boundaries between itself and its client enterprises, so that it exemplifies the principle and practice of business association.

Yugoslav self-management

While the Japanese have played a unique part in creating cooperative business structures, both within and across organizations, the Yugoslavs – at least in the sixties and seventies – had a related, though different claim to cooperative achievement. The Yugoslavs, unlike the Japanese, have made a genuine attempt to link individual self-development with social cooperation, within the context of their self-managed enterprises. As Ichack Adizes,[17] a close observer of Yugoslavia's industrial development in the sixties, pointed out, the 'self-management ideology emphasizes qualities of self-actualization, self-expression, and social-interdependence'. The organization, as a result, is circular, rather than vertical or horizontal, rippling out from a center based upon the individual economic unit. There is also a community council, in which all the workers are represented, involved in policy making, though not everyday business decisions.

The development circle

What is noticeable within each of the examples I have cited, in the context of developmental management, is that the circle replaces the spider's web, the pyramid or the network as a symbol of the organization's functioning and relationships. Such a circular symbol is one with which Shigeru Kobayashi, of Sony, would certainly feel at home.

The developmental manager

The wholesome, developmental manager, combines individual self-actualization and personal intimacy, with organizational harmony and business interdependence. In doing so he or she becomes what I have termed a corporate architect.

Adaptability and harmony

On the day of the ceremony that marked my assumption of authority, I stood in front of the workers; my mind was refreshingly empty and receptive. Glancing at the girls, I found all of them irresistibly young. They were so cheerful, so smiling and cute – at least they looked that way to me then. So, without thinking, I blurted out something to the following effect: I don't know anything about transistors, but I like human beings very much. Let us do our best together. This was the start of my first encounter with those lovable people.

It was towards the end of 1961, immediately following my taking over the Atsugi plant, that the following incident occurred. In a plant management meeting, the manager of industrial relations reminded us that there had been considerable dishonesty in the handling of time cards. Such cheating, he maintained, could not be tolerated. Watchmen would have to be placed at the time clocks to control the situation.

I had already given some thought to this time clock problem, and hearing this proposal was enough to make up my mind once and for all. Let's abolish the time clocks, I said. All they have done is bring about the war of offense and defense that's now going on between management and labor. Anyway, what in the world is a time clock? It has nothing to do with the existence of this plant. Our plant is one which produces transistors. To put it in a nutshell, we are being used by the time clock.

So I gathered all the employees together and appealed to them. Obviously, I said, we are here to make transistors. Let's decide that beginning tomorrow we will work according to the time schedule without any clocks. Your own reporting of your absences will be sufficient. The company will trust you.

Once we had managed to create an atmosphere of trust all signs of discontent, such as graffiti on the toilet walls, disappeared. However, for some strange reason, a couple of years later someone started scribbling, and others began to follow suit. We naturally had no means of controlling this growing vandalism, since the toilets were private. Then, suddenly, one day, the scribbling stopped. I became curious to find out why. I discovered that the women sweepers, who used to take pride in keeping the walls shining, had been doing their best to erase the scribblings. Finally they got fed up and decided to display posters on the walls. They said: This is our place of work;

please don't stain our walls. The vandalism stopped immediately.

I was tremendously moved when I heard the story. If these women had been undertaking meaningless labor, calling for them only to sweep, they would never have reacted the way they did. You see, in our plant we provide orientation for everybody as a matter of course. Like every other aspect of plant management, clean toilets are a contributing factor in the production of high-quality transistors. So, when we establish our plans for the next six-month period, plans by the sweepers' groups are included.

Every employee, under this kind of system, becomes the master of his job and begins to feel that he is his own president. The only difference between the woman sweeper and the real company president is that the woman sweeps the floors and the president steers the company.

Shigeru Kobayashi *Creative Management*[18] 1971

References

1. R. Lessem *The Global Business*, Prentice Hall (1987).
2. R. Steiner, *Towards Social Renewal*, Steiner Press (1977).
3. M. Large, *Social Ecology*, self-published (1984).
4. G. Land, *To Grow or to Die*, John Wiley (1986).
5. B. McWaters, *Conscious Evolution*, Turnstone (1983).
6. B. Hubbard, *The Evolutionary Way* Turnstone (1983).
7. B. Lievegoed, *The Developing Organization*, Celestial Arts (1983).
8. G. Lippitt, *Organizational Renewal*, Appleton Century Craft (1969).
9. L. Greiner, 'Evolution and revolution as organizations grow,' *Harvard Business Review* (July–August 1972).
10. Pascale and Athos, *The Art of Japanese Management*, Penguin (1982).
11. K. Ohmae, *Triad Powers*, Macmillan (1985).
12. Y. Masuda, *The Information Society*, Institute for the Information Society (1981).
13. A. Maslow, *Motivation and Personality*, Harper & Row (1954).
14. D. Levinson, *The Seasons of Man's Life*, Knopf (1978).
15. M. Parker Follett, *The New State*, Pete Smith (1929).
16. Yoshino and Lifson, *The Invisible Link*, MIT Press (1987).
17. I. Adizes, *Industrial Democracy: Yugoslav Style*, Macmillan (1971).
18. S. Kobayashi, *Creative Management*, American Management Association (1971).

 20 Biology and ecology

Contents

Key concepts

Once you have fully understood this chapter you should be able to define the following concepts in your own words:

Alignment	Developmental stage
Attunement	Developmental thinking
Communal growth	Differentiation/replication
Conscious evolution	Evolutionary driver
Design innovation	Evolutionary spiral

Formation/accretion	Quantum transformation
Integration/mutuality	Recapitulation
Nucleation	Synergy
Personal growth	

Objectives

Upon completing this chapter you should be able to do the following:

1. Compare and contrast developmental management with primal and rational management.
2. Describe the essence of developmental thinking.
3. Describe the three or four stages of development, as described by Large, Land and McWaters.
4. Comprehend the principles of development.
5. Indentify ways in which you personally identify, or otherwise, with developmental management.

Introduction

From rational to developmental management

Developmental management is founded upon the laws of growth and change that under-pin human development. It is rooted particularly in the life sciences, that is in biology and ecology, rather than in the physical or social sciences. It is based neither on purely instinctive behavior nor on wholly rational conduct, but on a process of conscious evolution.

In fact this text so far, while enabling you to manage such growth – through business strategy, action learning or organization development – has not yet introduced you to the laws of growth and evolution, such as they may be. This will be the aim of this chapter.

Biologists, ecologists and some humanistic psychologists, in recent years, have uncovered such laws of growth and evolution, with a view to their being applied to the management of organizations. Unfortunately they have been largely ignored by the OD (organization development) establishment, and have certainly been bypassed by those involved in product, market and systems development. It is my job here to uncover the roots of such developmental management and then to follow up the core concepts, as well as the branch theories and applications, that have become available to us.

Characteristics of evolution

Inclusion
Emergent evolution describes the process of long, slow change alternating with short, rapid change and sudden transformation.

Earlier levels of life are absorbed into later levels.

Emergence

Sudden and sharp discontinuities punctuate the progress of slow change.

These rifts either signal a leap to a new, more complex level of life or they signal a devastating crash to some earlier level.

There is a process of building up as well as a process of tearing down.

Transition

Dominant models reach a certain peak of success when anomalies become numerous and troublesome.

A 'clash of worldiness' between perspectives creates a period of confusion and tension.

The new synthesis invariably incorporates the new apparent partial truths of the older model, provides consistent explanations for the precipitating anomalies, and opens up new territory for exploration.

When evolution gets 'stuck', it may revert to an earlier, more plastic level of order before the leap to a new synthesis.

Acceleration

Galactic change is measured in billions and millions of years, biological change in millions.

Today, change of evolutionary significance is measured in decades and years.

Lipnack and Stamps, *The Networking Book*[1] 1986

In fact I would go so far as to say that it is developmental management, in the eighties and nineties, that holds the key to commercial success and to organizational effectiveness around the globe.

The laws of growth

The laws of qualitative growth, with which this chapter will be concerned, can be divided into three distinctive categories. The first involves patterns of development which seem to follow a somewhat predictable form. The second involves three or four developmental stages – in individuals, organizations and communities. Thirdly, and finally, the interdependent character of developmental management is clearly apparent.

Patterns of development

To grow or to die

One of the greatest contributions to developmental management, whether of individual enterprises or of whole ecosystems, comes from the American biologist and business consultant, George Ainsworth Land.

To grow or to die

History, in every sense, from the biological to the social, demonstrates that what we really have to fear is not so much the perpetuation of our growth failures; much more dangerous is the deliberate attempt to repeat our successes. Today's successes become tomorrow's failures. Life in its very manifestation is growth and change. Not to grow is to die.

Evolution carries with it the message of extinction. If we isolate ourselves from the 'system' of life; if we do not find a balance of trade with our environment, we face a future known in all of its frightening dimensions. The message is abundantly clear: grow or die, evolution or extinction.

George Land *To Grow or To Die*[2] 1985

As an individual or organization evolves to higher levels of being, according to Land, the potential for slipping either backwards or forwards is always present. In other words, if an organism fails to grow with its cultural environment, for example by adopting new technologies or methods of work, then it must of necessity grow against it. People or organizations cannot actually stand still. They choose to move forward or back.

How then, do we evolve and develop?

Developmental thinking

The management consulting group that has done the most to promote developmental management are the NPI (Netherlands Pedagogical Institute) who operate throughout Western Europe. I shall be referring to their work extensively in my next, core chapter. One of their members, the English social anthropologist Martin Large, has represented the 'developmental thinking' very thoroughly in his book *Social Ecology*.[3] He makes the following seven major points:

1. As long as an organism continues to develop and maintain itself then there is life. But as soon as development ceases the organism rigidifies.
2. The concept of development is derived originally from biology and is used to describe the lifecycle of people and things. While growth could be taken to mean a purely quantitative change development involves qualitative or structural changes.
3. Development involves a journey from the past through the heart of the present, into the future. Thus the process of development involves an unfolding of structure over time.
4. An organism grows, unfolding to the point where the original structure cannot be maintained. There is then a crisis, as the architectural forces of development break down the old structure. The process of breaking down is sometimes called involution, which is needed to prepare the way for a more differentiated structure – which can in turn undergo further evolution.
5. Each life crisis involves a progression from involution through chaos to evolution. Each stage of development is initiated by a structural crisis, in which the foundations are laid for a new structure.
6. Such a development is discontinuous, taking place in leaps and bounds, so that sometimes dramatic structural changes can occur, like when a chrysalis turns into a

butterfly. Old structures are then restructured as a higher unity, at a more complex level of organization. This process is irreversible. Development therefore undergoes particular structural crises and evolutionary phases.

7. Development can be pictured as a dynamic balancing process where security needs and the need for challenges predominate in turn.

These seven points can be applied to any living organism, be it an individual, an organization or a whole community. The implications for each of these are significant. For one thing crises are to be welcomed as part and parcel of the growth process, provided they are handled with a conscious awareness of evolutionary forces. For another, organisms develop in stages.

The developmental manager, therefore, should be accustomed not only to viewing crises as opportunities for conscious evolution, but to also working towards progressive, and discontinuous shifts in the degrees of freedom within which his people and organizations will be working. In effect he is designing increasing amounts of complexity into his structures and processes as both he and his enterprises evolve.

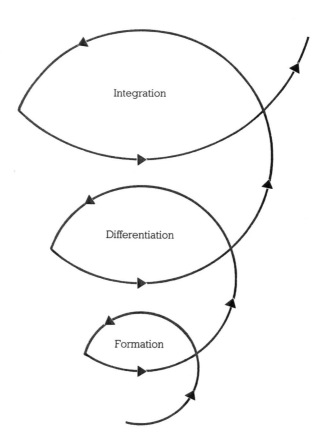

Fig. 54 Evolutionary spiral.

Developmental stages

The developing organism

It is this progressive development, via distinct stages, in the developmental manager's product, market, people or organization that mark him out as an active and even aggressive force. Such staged and conscious evolution is to the developmental manager what business entrepreneurship is to the primal manager and corporate strategy is to the rational manager. This phased development is characteristically divided into either three or four cumulative stages, each representing a degree of complexity exceeding that of the phase that preceded it. For Barbara Hubbard there are three such stages. (See Fig. 54.)[4]

First there is the process of formation or growth of the whole person, product, business or organization, which only begins to split apart as skills, features or functions are separated off and allocated to emergent parts of the whole. Secondly there thus follows a process of differentiation and hierarchization, whereby some capacities, products or divisions become governed by others, after which initial attempts are made to relate one to the other. This leads, thirdly, to a process of integration, involving more technical, economic and social interdependence and greater complexity of structure. Production and risk sharing, consortia and joint ventures become the norm rather than the exception.

From accretion to mutualism

Stages of growth

George Ainsworth Land has written, about the stages of development of individuals, organizations and of whole communities. Drawing on his biological knowledge and subsequently transferring the developmental implications to management, he has also concluded that there are three fundamental stages of development. He has called them 'accretive', 'replicative' and 'mutual'.

Principles and stages of growth

Physical, biological, psychological and social systems are growth motivated; that is their behavior acts in the direction of development of higher levels of, and more widespread, interrelationships. Thus all systems tend to evolve more organized behavior, becoming integrated through the incorporation of diversity.

There are, in fact, three distinctly different forms of growth, each of which merges into the other on a continuum of levels of development. The first of these is purely additive – an extension of the boundaries that already exist. We shall call this form of growth accretive, that is inclusion through sameness.

The second form of growth is replicative; it is growth through influencing other people or things to take on the form of the initiator. As a cell, for example, grows and divides it takes in the environment and transforms it directly into itself. Replicative growth, therefore, is inclusion through similarity

The third form of growth involves reciprocal interaction. Mutual growth incorporates give and take, that is the equilateral sharing or joining process. Such mutualism is inclusive of differentness.

George Land *To Grow or To Die*[5] 1985

Land's stages of development affect the personal and psychological domains as well as in the social and communal ones. I shall consider each, in turn, covering accretive, replicative, and mutualistic forms.

Personal and psychological growth

Drives and complusions for such things as power, possession and dominance – according to Land – are accretive in nature. They involve control of man's internal or external world. Needs for manipulation as well as being manipulated – dependent and counter-dependent modes of behavior – are basically replicative. They involve both modifications of the outside world, to copy the internal, and changes in the inside world, to mimic the external. Mutualistic patterns are found in empathetic and creative behavior, and in the drive for self-fulfillment and self-actualization. They are characterized by recombination and fusion, involving self-extension through sharing. Personal growth is attained through reciprocal exchange with the outside world.

Experiencing the process of creative, mutual (integrated) growth does not preclude us, however, from the manifestations of accretive (formative) and replicative (differentiated) development. Each man, each society, is an ever changing mixture of all forms of growth, working through and with each other.

Societal and communal growth

A cell, person, organization or whole community that has achieved mutualistic growth has done so by building on accretive and replicative behavior. Thus mutualism is founded on lower forms and cannot exist without them. Lower forms of growth provide the self-maintenance necessary for mutualism to be successful. Thus primal and rational management is a prerequisite for the developmental or even metaphysical variety that may follow. The earliest human cultures were fundamentally accretive inasmuch as information and cultural forms were rigidly controlled, and passed to each generation almost unchanged. When written symbols supplemented the organic information storage and retrieval system the shift to replicative societies began. Missionary activity and imperial conquest ensued. Worldwide travel and more sophisticated communications media have provided a broad new base of common information, and have created much higher probabilities of considering new and different ideas and cultures. This forms part of a mutualistic, global village.

Decay and renewal

The demise of the British, French, Portuguese and our own American colonial empires represents only a few examples of how evolution from accretive boundary expansion, absolute ownership and control, to that of replicative influence – 'think, act and value like us' – have both outgrown themselves. We are now being pressured to grow into a new form of mutualistic relationship between ourselves, as the previous colonizers, and themselves, as the previously colonized.

George Land *To Grow or To Die*[6] 1985

A village initially comes into being as people 'accrete' and band together in small groups to form a larger, more defensible, viable organism. The same, you might say, takes place in the early stages of business formation, though usually under the influence of an entrepreneurial individual. Common pursuits, or shared values, unite everyone – farming, milling, mining or in contemporary business terms, being close to the customer. As offspring begin to learn their parents' trades they 'replicate' the original and successful organism. However, when they overproduce their own capacity to use the products that they make (as in the steel and automobile industries today) pressures emerge to develop deeper relations with other communities. 'Mutualism' is developed through the development of specialization, trade and the exchange of information with others.

Finally, as with biological growth, so in social organisms recapitulation of forms of growth occurs with changes in scale and complexity. Companies which renew themselves have not only to collaborate more intensely with their customers, competitors and suppliers, but also to create new business enterprises, both with and without them. The highest form of mutualism begins to transform into a new accretive.

Nucleation

The three stages of growth and development, to which both Land and Large allude, can in fact be stretched to four. In fact the four developmental stages lead to a corresponding number of management domains. In such conditions the creative process underlying the development is included as a fourth evolutionary stage. In the context of this text, that fourth stage represents 'metaphysical' management. Barry McWaters, an American biologist and psychologist, who founded the Institute for the Study of Conscious Evolution, calls this stage 'nucleation'.[7]

> Nucleation describes the emergence of a conscious center that holds responsibility for internal regulation and self-transcendence. In each evolving being a center is formed, a center that has in mind the integrity of the organism itself, the establishment of the right relationship with the environment, and the transcendent evolution of the organism.[8]

The center, or nucleus, embodies in itself the integral pattern of the whole, the DNA, the picture of the organism in its perfect form. The nucleus also embodies the RNA, the messenger unit by which the nucleus will communicate the knowledge of its form to subsequent generations. The nucleus, in other words, is the inspiration behind the organization. It permits differentiation and calls for integration. It fosters communication between the parts, balances their relationship, and controls and transforms processes that are out of synch. 'It is the nucleus which has the capacity for multidimensional communication',[9] at all levels, with diverse cultures, and with multifaceted people. It has the very special role of communicating higher intention, of transmitting vision.

In a continually evolving organism, a nucleus will come forth to assume a central role.

Table 29 Comparative stages of development

Source	Stage			
	1	2	3	4
Large	Formative	Differentiated	Integrated	
Land	Accretive	Replicative	Mutual	
McWaters		Differentiation	Integration	Nucleation

The same applies to society at large as to the single individual or organization. In a business context, genuine nucleation, albeit rarely achieved, is required of the corporate policy making function. In Table 29 I have summarized the three or four stages of evolutionary development, as depicted by Large – the anthropologist, Land – the biologist and McWaters – the psychologist.

I now want to move on from the evolutionary stages of which the development manager needs to be aware, to the interdependent outlook which is characteristic of his operating style.

The interdependent character of developmental management

Principles of interdependence

Progression through the three or four stages represents the developmental manager's aggressive thrust, as he powers the organization through the successively more complex layers of business evolution. At each stage he has to recognize, accommodate and harness progressively more breadth and depth in product, market, individual and organizational functioning. Therein lies the hard edge of development. At the same time, and on the other hand, the process of conscious evolution has a visibly soft edge to it, as McWaters reveals.

Conscious evolution: a definition

1. The emerging potential of human beings to take responsibility, individually and collectively, for a positive future, through sharing in the unfolding of creation.
2. The process by which an individual or organizational entity can transform itself from a state of fear and alienation to one of enlightened cooperation.
3. The capacity of a group to work together synergistically, that is to become a functional entity with capabilities beyond the sum of the individual parts.
4. The potential of individuals and organizations to develop a resonant relationship within the parts of itself, with its environment, and with the world as a whole.

Barry McWaters *Conscious Evolution*[10] 1983

McWaters identifies four so-called 'principles of relationship' which underlie the interdependence that characterizes developmental management. These are synergy, attunement, allignment and quantum transformation.

Synergy

Synergy describes the release of free energy that occurs when a group of entities – be they people or things, individuals or organizations – come together with a common aim. The resultant whole is both quantitatively and qualitatively greater than the sum of the parts.

Synergic release is often experienced at the beginning of group work. A momentary fusion may occur when individuals come together, a 'high' is experienced, and what has been called a 'honeymoon period' ensues for a period of time. The free energy created, that is this 'group high', can be used for productive and collective activity. Synergy can both be created across space, between people or things – as in the case of a really successful merger, and also over time. In effect the principle of synergy describes the evolutionary process we have witnessed, that evolutionary spiral whereby greater and greater levels of integration occur.

> Synergic release from wave/particle formations led to the creation of the atom; atomic combinations resulted in molecules; combinations of molecules resulted in organelles; combinations of organelles produced cells; etc. At each new union an attractive force is realeased that seeks out the next evolutionary stage of union.[11]

It is for that reason that a developing enterprise can never stand still. As entrepreneur links up with customer an attractive force is released that seeks out the next evolutionary stage, the creation of a business organization. As one employee links up with another, another attractive force is released that seeks out the formation of a human organization. As one culture after another becomes involved so yet another attractive force is released that, on this occasion, seeks out the development of a multinational organization. The process is unending.

Attunement

The second of McWater's principles of relationship, or interdependence, is that of attunement. Attunement is an expression of the receptive will of the individual or the organization. Through it a larger context or consciousness is invited and permitted to penetrate more and more deeply into self-consciousness. In this way individual energies are attuned to the wider environment just as a musical instrument is tuned into the dominant key of an orchestral theme.

For example, by way of attunement, a businessman tunes into pervading market trends, a manager of human resources is receptive to the needs of employees, or an interior designer absorbs the surrounding high street atmosphere and incorporates it into his attractive shop front. An individual, an organization or indeed a musical instrument would come across as harsh and cacophonous if one or other was ill-attuned to its surroundings. While each may insist on a way of being that is out of resonance with its environment, such a disharmony must ultimately have serious implications for both the part and the whole. For example, in Great Britain today, any retailing chain which lacks ambiance is likely, over the long term, to lose clientele.

Alignment

Whereas, through attunement, the developmental manager literally tunes into a wider organizational, market or social context, through alignment he or she 'chooses to find meaning and purpose in contributing to the well being or evolution of a higher reality.[12] In a commercial context a developmental marketing manager in a pharmaceuticals company, for example, would be contributing to the physical health and wellbeing of individuals and nations. Such 'physical wellbeing' represents a higher reality than, say, the alleviation of headaches and indigestion. In an operational context a developmental production manager in a steel mill, for example, would be creating a working climate wherein his workforce could fulfill their higher needs, for self-actualization, as well as their immediate needs, for physical health and safety.

Quantum transformation

The principle of quantum transformation offers us hope. All the stubborn parts of oneself, and of one's organization or society, do not have to agree to change and grow all at once. It only takes a clear and definite suggestion from one small part to remind the whole of its inborn preference for evolution and development. An inner ear begins to hear the call, begins to sense the possibility.

Critical mass

In each evolving being, the nucleus works toward turning the attention of a significant percentage of the parts toward evolutionary transformation. When this percentage is reached – critical mass – the idea is transmitted rapidly and directly to all parts of the organism, and a quantum evolutionary leap is experienced.

Barry McWaters *Conscious Evolution*[13] 1983

If a small, yet critical, percentage of the organization or market-place is able to see the light, there will be intonations and ramifications for the whole human enterprise. As a result, evolution in product, market and human development takes place in unpredictable leaps. That seems to have been the case, for example in the United States in the early eighties, when Steve Jobs' Apple Computers began to grow like wildfire. A small, but critical percentage of the computerate market-place had apparently seen the desktop light.

Mutualism in developmental management

Whereas McWaters has developed specific principles of relationship George Land argues that mutualism, in general, lies at the core of human evolution. Although the mutualistic principle manifests itself particularly strongly at his third developmental stage it underpins the whole of his developmental thinking.

Growth and interdependence

If we reach down to the basic nature of the concept of growth we find a single fact. Growth cannot occur independently. It requires interaction and interrelation between the growing thing and its environment. The process requires a joining of things ...

In every natural phenomenon there is the irreversible procession from accretive to replicative to mutual growth, at which point, at a new level of organization, the process repeats itself. Growth, at this stage of our examination, is defined as a process of joining, in which the ratios of interactive effect are continually expressing higher levels of interaction.

George Land *To Grow or to Die*[14] 1985

The process of joining, as an evolutionary development, is particularly apparent in the world of electronics and telecommunications today. The need for computers and companies alike, to talk to one another is becoming an evolutionary requirement. The world of the lone high tech warrior, ploughing his own organizational and technological furrow, has well nigh disappeared.

AT & T, for example, as of August 1985 had developed strategic alliances with no less than eight companies, of various sizes and product lines, including Olivetti, Microsoft, Motorola and Amdahl. These alliances were geared towards joint product, market and systems development within and across national frontiers. They involve a progression from accretion and replication to mutualism.

> By mutualizing our resources we can realize the latent potential of our species. To bring this about, however, will require a rapid and radical integration of the quality of human growth into the processes of planning, forecasting, and creating a future still and always highly unknown. But we can do so with the knowledge that, by and through nature's processes, we can determine the quality and form, if not the content of things to come.[15]

Conclusion

Laws of nature

The roots of conventional, and rational management, lie not in nature but in man-made institutions of antiquity, including the church, the army, and civil administrations. The roots of the currently fashionable, primal management, lie within the hunter–gatherer communities of prehistoric times. The roots of developmental management, however, lie in both physical and human nature, and in the life sciences that underpin them.

From their studies of atomic, molecular, cellular, as well as animal and human beings, life scientists such as George Land, Martin Large, Barbara Hubbard and Barry McWaters have discovered underlying patterns of physical and social development. These are only beginning to enter into the management vocabulary, although Mary Parker Follett had been working along parallel lines some sixty years ago.

The surge of life

The surge of life sweeps through the given similarity, the common ground, and breaks it up into a thousand differences. This tumultuous, irresistible flow of life is our existence: the unity is but for an instant; it flows on to new differings which adjust themselves anew in more varied, richer syntheses ... This is the process of evolution.

Mary Parker Follett *The New State*[16] 1929

Stages of growth

Individual atoms and whole societies alike, evolve by creating ever richer syntheses out of ever-increasing variety. There is also a predictable sequence to the growth process.

The sequence begins formatively. Formation or accretion, in business enterprise, is represented by the primal urge for growth through sameness, thus expanding the entrepreneur's financial base and extending the communally shared values. Replication is reflected in the rational orientation towards expansion through differentiation, of functions, of products, of markets, and of territories, thus replicating business by extending standard procedures into different operations, and by also adapting performance to accommodate such individual differences. Integration is represented by a developmental approach to creating unity out of diversity in people and things, in products and markets, as well as between the stages of their evolution, thereby combining physical and social development with organizational and economic harmony. Finally, at least as far as McWaters is concerned, a fourth stage, which I have identified as metaphysical management, locates the regulative center of the evolving organism, which contains a picture of the enterprise in its perfect form, and enables it to engage in physical, organizational, economic and social transformation.

We shall be considering this metaphysical phenomenon in Section E. Before we do that, however, I want to investigate first the core, and thereafter the branches and fruits of developmental management.

For the core I turn to the NPI in general, and to the Dutchman, Bernard Lievegoed, in particular.

References

1. J. Lipnack and J. Stamps, *The Networking Book*, Routledge & Kegan Paul (1986).
2. G. Land, *To Grow or To Die*, Wiley (1985), pp. 74 and 127.
3. M. Large, *Social Ecology*, published privately (1981), Chapter 2.
4. B. Hubbard, *The Evolutionary Way*, Turnstone Press (1983), p. 26.
5. G. Land, *op. cit.*, p. 197.
6. G. Land, *op. cit.*, p. 196.
7. B. McWaters, *Conscious Evolution*, Turnstone Press (1983).
8. B. McWaters, *op. cit.*, pp. 67–8.
9. B. McWaters, *op. cit.*, p. 73.
10. B. McWaters, *op. cit.*, p. 4.
11. B. McWaters, *op. cit.*, p. 79.
12. B. McWaters, *op. cit.*, p. 78.
13. B. McWaters, *op. cit.*, p. 84.
14. G. Land, *op. cit.*, pp. 11–12.
15. G. Land, *op. cit.*, p. 145.
16. M. Parker Follett, *The New State*, Longman Green (1929), p. 35.

21 The developing organization

Contents

Key concepts

Once you have fully understood this chapter you should be able to define the following concepts in your own words:

Autonomy crisis   Coordination
Clover leaf organization   Crisis of control

Crisis of red tape	Limits to integration
Developmental laws	Limits to pioneering
Developmental picture	Mature responses
Differentiated phase	Mechanization
Enabling company	Pioneer phase
Infant responses	Process management
Information management	Qualitative growth
Integrated phase	Relations management
Inter-organizational	Specialization
collaboration	Standardization
Limits to differentiation	Youthful response

Objectives

Upon completing this chapter you should be able to do the following:

1. Relate the developmental laws to the growth and evolution of organizations.
2. Describe, in some detail, the pioneering, differentiated and integrated phases of business development.
3. Identify the limits to each phase, including the forces which drive the healthy organization onto its next phase of development.
4. Compare and contrast Lievegoed's, Lippitt and Schmidt's, and Greiner's developmental approaches.
5. Outline the key features of the clover leaf organization, including its four major subsystems.

Introduction

The originators of developmental management

The origins of developmental management reach back to the Austrian, Rudolph Steiner, in the 1920s, and link up, via Bernard Lievegoed in Holland, with the modern school of 'organizational renewal' in America. The most important single influence on its formation and impact is Lievegoed.

Lievegoed: the developing organization
Bernard Lievegoed is a venerable Dutchman now in his eighties. He is by far the best known management consultant in that country, and is also a highly respected clinical psychologist. Lievegoed, in turn, has drawn on Rudolph Steiner for his own source of inspiration, with respect to developing organizations.

Steiner: social renewal
Steiner, from whom we shall hear more in Chapter 23, was an Austrian who, at the turn of the century, had developed a reputation as a philosopher, a psychologist, an educator, an agronomist, an economist, a politician, an architect and a medical practitioner. Above

all, he had strong views on the evolution of man, of organizations, and on the processes of social renewal on which Lievegoed subsequently drew.

> Everything that happens to man is an image, having its prototype amid those great events of cosmic evolution with which his existence is bound up.[1]

For Steiner, as for Lievegoed and his fellow management consultants at the Netherlands Pedagogical Institute (NPI) – based in Holland and operating around the globe – human and organizational evolution are intertwined. Each follows a developmental pattern to which we alluded in the previous chapter.

Lippitt, Schmidt and Greiner: organizational renewal

In this core chapter on developmental management I want to unravel the implications of this pattern for organization development. I shall begin with Lievegoed's seminal work, and then enter into the derivative American thinking. The leading Americans in this developmental context are the late Gordon Lippitt, Warren Schmidt and Larry Greiner, all of whom were students of organizational renewal.

Let me start by comparing and contrasting the developmental manager with his primal or rational counterpart.

The characteristics of developmental management

Qualitative growth

Whereas both primal and rational managers are concerned with growth in quantitative terms the developmental manager, as George Land has intimated (see pp. 411–14), focusses on its qualitative attributes. As the British anthropologist, Martin Large, has indicated:

> Whereas objective (rational) consciousness gives rise to mechanistic thinking appropriate to understanding the inorganic world, life-consciousness (developmental) gives rise to holistic thinking appropriate to the understanding of the development of human and social forms in time.[2]

So the questions a developmental manager asks are concerned not with the prediction of physical quantities but rather with the forecast of future socio-technical structures. Such a manager requires special insight into the qualitative development of individual human beings and products, and of collective organizations and industries, over time.

Parallel development

Whereas the primal and rational managers view business and organizational entities as discrete phenomena, the developmental manager views individuals, organizations, products and markets as parallel phenomena, each undergoing similar laws of structural evolution. More specifically, for all living organisms, growth continues within a certain structure until a limit is reached. Beyond this limit the existing structure or model can no longer impose order on the larger mass. The consequence is either disintegration or a step up to a higher level of order.

This phenomenon can be observed in a single living cell or in a complex business organization. A cell does not grow indefinitely but at a certain moment divides into two new cells, which in turn grow only to their limits, and so on. The same can be observed, according to both Land (see Chapter 17) and Lievegoed, in the higher organisms, which pass from one phase of development to the next. This phasing occurs both in individual development and in the evolution of whole species. In other words, as we shall soon see, it affects the development of individual companies, over time, as well as entire product lines, industries or economies.

Developmental laws

In Chapter 17, I introduced laws of development. However, as these are likely to have been somewhat new to you, I shall repeat them here, drawing specifically though on Lievegoed's interpretation and covering developing organizations:

- Development occurs in time, in a series of stages.
- Development is principally discontinuous.
- Within each stage a particular structure tends to dominate.
- The stages become progressively more complex.
- A new structure is not added to the old; rather a shift occurs in the whole new pattern of relationships.
- Development is not reversible.

Let us take a look now at this developmental process as a whole.

A picture of development

Development can be diagrammatically depicted as a flight of steps, as in Fig. 55, or it can well be represented as a process of spreading, whereby the emphasis shifts from old to new centers, as in Fig. 56.

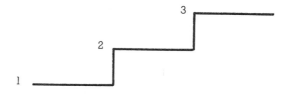

Fig. 55 Flight of steps.

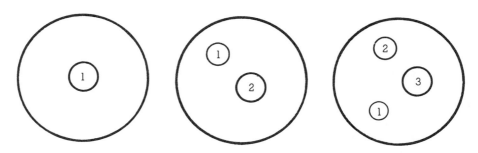

Fig. 56 Spreading process.

A stepwise picture of development represents total transformation from one step to the next, as is the case when a caterpillar becomes a butterfly. This in fact seldom happens in organizational life. Remnants of earlier steps tend to remain in some shape or form.

Thus the ever-spreading picture is more representative of the developing organization. In other words, as an organization evolves we find remnants of earlier structures. For example a rationally managed organization will still have pockets of primal enterprise. Developmental management is full of ambiguity and unpredictability.

Social evolution

The term 'social Darwinism' denotes the survival of the fittest. It befits the primal manager. The term 'social engineering' denotes the construction of logically determined forms of organization. It befits the rational manager. The term 'social evolution' befits the developmental manager. It involves setting in motion organizational changes in the direction of a more advanced stage of development, but of which only the barest outlines are known. The final form and content of the next stage can thus arise out of the actual potentialities of the people involved. Let us now investigate, in outline, these stages. For Lievegoed, as for Land, there are three of them.[3]

The developing organization

Three phases: pioneering/differentiated/integrated

As an enterprise develops, according to Lievegoed, its structure changes from an undifferentiated general beginning to successive stages of ever-increasing complexity. At each successive stage of development a different subsystem is dominant. First comes the so-called pioneer phase. The dominant influence is the pioneer himself. He takes the initiative within the economic subsystem of society. He finds the pioneering answer to a consumer need which he recognizes. This phase reaches its limit when the organization has grown so much that the pioneer no longer knows everyone personally, when the technical equipment needed has become so complicated that specialists are required, and when the market has grown so large that the pioneer finds himself working not for the customer he knows but for an anonymous public.

At this point the pioneer organization either becomes 'overripe' and begins to disintegrate (decrease of profits, increase of customer complaints), or it has to be restructured so that it can start on the next phase of its development.

In this second differentiated phase, the pioneer with his economic achievement is no longer the dominant factor. The requirements of the technical subsystem in the enterprise become pre-eminent. With the help of scientific management techniques, the structure based on personal relationships is transformed into one based on an impersonal and logical division of functions. The man has been replaced by the system. The limit of this second phase is reached when the neglect of the social system in the enterprise begins to make itself felt. The progress achieved through technical improvements is slowed down by a decrease in the motivation of the people involved. Feelings of powerlessness against the 'system' creep in.

The third integrated phase can be established successfully only if the social subsystem is interwoven with the economic and technical ones. This cannot be achieved simply by maintaining the existing structure and adding 'human relations'. What is required is rethinking the whole organization. The dominant factor now is the community of people working together as a combined source of innovation and enthusiasm, towards the common goal.

Comparative phases

Lievegoed's pioneering, differentiated and integrated phases relate to our primal, rational and developmental aspects of management. These three phases have been neatly summarized by Martin Large[4] as shown in Table 30.

Table 30 Lievegoed's development phases

	Phase 1	Phase 2	Phase 3
Approach	Personal	Impersonal	Individual
Leadership	Primal	Rational	Developmental
Goals	Directive	Purposeful	Inspirational
Structure	Simple/flat	Complex/pyramid	Open/hexagon
Response	Improvized	Planned	Evolved
Style	Active	Authoritative	Adaptive
Orientation	Outer oriented	Inward looking	Outer/inner balance
Emphasis	Economic	Technical	Social

I now want to investigate each of Lievegoed's phases in greater detail.

The pioneering phase

Characteristics

The first stage of Lievegoed's developing organization is the pioneering one. At this point an owner–manager is primarily interested in answering a need at a price that his customer is willing to pay. He is economically driven. In its pure form a pioneer enterprise is run by its founder. It comes into being as a result of a creative act by an individual person. This person is an entrepreneur. He has a realistic imagination.

The pioneer runs his firm with an autocratic style of leadership which is based on the prestige he enjoys in the eyes of his people. In other words, he has their trust. If there is trouble he can be relied upon to find a way out. He can typically be relied upon in this way because he knows all his employees and their family circumstances. He engaged them himself and they are 'his' people; he knows all their jobs, having performed all of them at one point or another.

Communication is direct. The pioneer communicates straightforwardly and directly with all his employees. At least in the early years he has worked in very close contact with them. He speaks their language. The organizational form is simple. So there is no need for formal communication channels, for job or task descriptions to regulate employees' rights and responsibilities.

The working style is therefore improvised. All problems are solved by improvisation rather than by planning. This style makes for flexibility. Production or service can be rapidly adapted to demand, and the special requests of individual customers can be met.

The workforce functions as one big family. In many cases, particularly prior to women's emancipation, the wife of the pioneer functioned as a kind of welfare worker for her husband's employees and families. 'We're all one happy family' is a favorite phrase of many a pioneer, until the first company strike gives him an unforgettable shock. The pioneer is not only close to his employees but is also, in the words of Peters and Waterman, close to the customer. He does not know what it is to operate in an anonymous market-place. He works in a limited geographical area and knows each customer personally.

Limits

The healthy pioneering enterprise that Lievegoed has described has highly motivated staff within and loyal customers without. Objectives are simple and clear, and success or failure can be witnessed by all. Such an organization remains healthy as long as the pioneer himself knows all his employees and his customers; the production process or services rendered remain relatively simple; and the accumulation of experience is an asset because technology and the market remain relatively stable.

Close-knit character

The close-knit character of a pioneering enterprise is both its strength and its weakness. As long as influences from outside do not disturb the system, fundamentally, the firm can grow and even be taken over by the next generation without much difficulty.

The advent of change

However, if the 'external' world starts to move, if a new technology becomes available to satisfy needs, if market conditions change and competitors break into the pioneer's field with brand new sales techniques, if the market grows so that personal contacts with customers are no longer possible, if extensive changes take place in the social structure so that a patriarchal style is no longer acceptable, then the pioneering phase has reached its limits.

Loss of confidence

The first thing that happens once the pioneering company has become 'overripe' is that the employees begin to entertain doubts about 'the boss'. His prestige begins to decrease and his autocratic style becomes intolerable. Mistakes then begin to creep in.

Once single mistakes begin to turn into overall failures to adapt, once the negative impact of particular instances becomes so great that the whole ethos and structure of the organization is affected, the pioneer enterprise has reached the threshold of a new development.

Symptoms of decline

The symptoms of such a crisis, heralding a period of transition, are decreasing profits, increasing customer complaints, communication blocks, decreasing maneuverability and decreasing motivation.

In pioneering limbo

In practice the development from a pioneering enterprise into the next stage of a business' development can be forestalled in three major ways.

Cartels

Historically, the formation of cartels, whereby companies clubbed together to forestall competition, and to curb the impact of fundamental changes, has been one way of inhibiting development. However, such arrangements, particularly in today's volatile and highly internationalized business environment, are extremely vulnerable to breakdown.

Conglomerates

Secondly, and more commonly today, conglomerates are formed. The original enterprise is split up into a number of smaller units, each of which is run in the pioneer style. The central holding company becomes a kind of financing body. The pioneering approach, albeit somewhat adapted, can thereby be maintained across a large and diversified scale. However, such conglomerate holdings, because they lack a coherent corporate image, are unduly dependent on one pioneering character – like Lord Hanson of Hanson Trust – for their underlying identity.

Family business

A third and final extension of the pioneering style is that represented by the family business. In such a context a close-knit family-based structure may be retained from one generation to the next. Such features as staff loyalty, goodwill towards the company, integrity of management and social responsibility are more likely to prevail than in a straightforward pioneering enterprise, or in a conventionally managed organization.

In fact, as I indicated in Chapter 2, it is the blend of enterprise and community that characterizes this family business form. Such a blend is more likely to endure, over both time and space, than a more one-sided and 'masculine' enterprising approach. Inevitably, though, if a family business like Marks and Spencer is to grow and develop into a large business, it has to move on to a newly 'differentiated' phase.

The differentiated phase

The historical answer to the problems of the overripe pioneer enterprise came in the form of scientific management. Taylor in America, Fayol in France, and Weber in Germany were the early apostles of such a scientific, administrative and bureaucratic response, each of which was based on rational principles of management and organization.

The main such principles of the second, 'differentiated' phase – according to Lievegoed – are mechanization, standardization, specialization and coordination. Each principle has been formulated to deal with production and distribution on a large scale. For as we move out of the pioneering phase into the differentiated one, single products and markets are replaced by mass production and marketing.

Mechanization

The principle of mechanization implies that technical resources must be used wherever possible, in place of increasingly costly, unpredictable and relatively inefficient human resources. Mechanization or automation, in this context, is not only concerned with labor-saving machinery on the factory floor, but also with enhanced information processing facilities in the office.

Standardization

The principle of standardization is concerned with interchangeability and uniformity. Standardization means that everything, every process, every working method can be whittled down to an exactly described standard. From a number of alternatives one possibility is chosen and is declared to represent the norm for reasons of expediency.

In addition to interchangeable standard parts and quality standards, the differentiated organization has standard job descriptions, performance appraisals, wage and salary scales, and so on. Business and organization therefore becomes, at least to a much larger extent than in the pioneering days, predictable and controllable. Individual departments become more directly concerned with meeting their own budgeted requirements than with the satisfaction of customer needs.

In the early stages of standardization, the production function leaps ahead of sales. The firm, and its scientifically based management, have initially become technically minded and inward looking, rather than economically minded and outward looking. While methods and techniques for controlling and developing the internal organization become increasingly scientific, the sales department continues to function anachronistically in the pioneer style. On the one hand the elaboration of norms and standards has led to a thorough knowledge of production costs and output, but on the other hand much less is known about sales costs and the benefits obtainable from alternative sales techniques. This development leads to an aggressive sales mentality: the firm's products are 'forced' into the market.

As, however, management evolves through its second stage, standardization spreads into mass merchandising and marketing. Marketing plans and strategies are developed to complement production and distribution planning and control. The composite and highly specialized marketing function, inclusive of sales and distribution, then overtakes production and finance at the leading edge of the differentiated organization.

Specialization

Mechanization and standardization lead as a matter of course to specialization. Mechanization requires an ever-increasing perfection of equipment as well as a growing concentration of knowledge and experience of every part and component technology. Standards can be met only if all the causes and effects that could influence the object to be standardized are controlled in minute detail. All of this can be best achieved through specialization.

Three kinds of specialization, according to Lievegoed, appear in the phase of differentiation:

Functional specialization – Similar activities are concentrated in a single department under one specialized department head, who in turn engages further specialists. Purchasing, operations, marketing, finance and human resources become separate departments in place of the all-powerful, all-competent pioneer. These core departments, in their turn, are subdivided so that, for example, marketing is broken down into distribution, sales, advertising, and public relations.

Hierarchical specialization – Managerial authority is established and contained in and by vertical layers. The top is concerned with long-term policy making; in the middle these policies are converted into medium-range strategies and structures, through strategy making; and at the bottom of the hierarchy immediate direction and control is exercised through implementation.

Specialized management processes – the three interrelated management processes – planning, execution and control – are recognized as being distinguishable, and are duly separated, Koontz and O'Donnell, as we saw in Chapter 13, while retaining planning and control, have further subdivided 'execution' into the specialized management processes of organizing, staffing and directing.

Coordination

The principle of coordination serves to counterbalance the forces of differentiation, which tend to pull people and things apart. Such coordination is brought about, directly or indirectly, through:

- Unity of command – to avoid the issuing of contradictory instructions, each person is allocated only one superior.
- Manageable span of control – the number of subordinates that a given superior has to control is limited by the number of people about whom he is able to retain detailed knowledge.
- Reliable communications – clear objectives and direct channels of formal communications are installed to ensure that management remains informed about the activities of its personnel, and that they are informed of the plans of management.
- Systematic training – systematic transmission of knowledge and skills ensures that people will do their work in the way prescribed by the formal plan. Higher levels of management coordinate the training of lower levels in the formal hierarchy.

The phase of differentiation, in sum, is the very antithesis of the pioneer phase. it is rational as opposed to instinctive, impersonal rather than personal, and is based on organizational rather than situational principles of management.

Limits to differentiation

The differentiation that takes place in the second phase is an essential condition for a company if it is to function, over the long term, on some scale. Clearly differentiated functions have to be developed. However, the laws of development are relentless. As growth continues well into the second phase, new crises emerge, and call for a second major re-orientation.

Rigid bureaucracy

Formalization and bureaucratization reduce the flexibility of the organization, so that it fails to respond to market and to social changes. Through specialization divisions and subdivisions are formed which draw further and further apart. They lose their understanding of one another's tasks and can no longer speak the same business language. Small functional kingdoms arise, with their own objectives and standards and communication breaks down.

Excessive control
Problems of communication increase not only across divisional boundaries but also up and down the ever lengthening hierarchy of control. At the top less and less is known about what is happening at the foot of the hierarchy, and vice versa. As the lack of coordination and responsiveness reaches crisis proportions there is a call for strong leadership, which represents a step back into the pioneering phase. Similarly the call for a new style of 'management by walkabout', made in the eighties by Peters and Waterman, arises from the nostalgic desire to return to the days of the pioneer.

Alienation
One of the most serious problems to occur is the steady fall in personal motivation. As the scale and impersonality of the organization increases, so the individual's perceived impotence, vis-à-vis the system, grows relentlessly. People feel that their work has become devoid of meaningful content and therefore experience a kind of qualitative under-employment. They feel reduced to a number, a mere extension of the system. To identify with the objectives of the whole organization becomes well-nigh impossible. Customers, as well as employees, gradually become part of the same alienating process.

  In the early days of differentiation, the move away from personalized customer relations to mass marketing was a necessary and useful development. It was the only way to make goods or services available at affordable prices to a mass market. Automobiles, historically, and personal computers, currently, are good cases in point. However, a highly differentiated company can become so distanced from its market-place that it begins to push products and services at people rather than adapting to their changing needs. Its customers, as Lievegoed vividly portrays, thereby become 'used' rather than being served.

> Advertising and persuasion techniques place the consumer under pressure. He is seen just as much as an instrument as the internal workforce: he must not think or judge or choose for himself; he must just reach for the branded product at the command of his influenced subconscious. A new commandment appears: in the sweat of thy brow thou shalt consume![5]

While the workforce intensify their disruptive practices within the firm consumer organizations are founded to mastermind attacks from without. Industrial and external relations become important, though reactive functions within the company. Tensions and inevitable crises, mount.

Differentiation in limbo

Regression
It is always easier to go back towards the known rather than forwards towards the unknown. Many differentiated companies, in the eighties, have responded to crises of falling profitability, productivity and motivation by regressing. In other words, they have

slimmed down their headquarters, decentralized operations, and installed a tough man at the top, in order to 'turn the company around'. Lee Iaccoca is a legendary example of such a person in the United States, and Michael Edwards – ex Chairman of British Leyland – is a good example in the UK.

All of this represents a return to a pioneering outlook. The advent of 'intrapreneuring', spearheaded by Gifford Pinchot[6] in America, and the trend towards 'privatization', in Thatcher's Britain, also heralds the return of phase one thinking. Moreover, the growth of franchising, of management buyouts, and of subcontracting, have all positioned the differentiated company in a state of limbo, in between phases one and two.

Progression

In addition to this process of regression, however, some of the very same companies – unbeknown to Lievegoed in the seventies – are undergoing a progression in the eighties. In fact they are differentiating their production, marketing and personnel functions more finely, as Robert Reich has illustrated in Chapter 19 (see pp. 375–95). The advent of flexible manufacturing systems, increasingly individualized products and services, and ever-more flexible work patterns, marks a distinct change of emphasis from the mass to the individual.

Alvin Toffler, in his book *The Third Wave*,[7] refers to this phenomenon as 'demassification'. It heralds a development from the personal and communal (phase one), to the functional and organizational (phase two), to the individual and social (phase three).

The integrated phase

Emergence of the social subsystem

For Lievegoed, the third phase of integration is centered on the development of the organization's social system, and its integration with the already-developed economic (phase one) and technical (phase two) subsystems.

> If we start with the entrepreneurial initiative of the pioneer as our thesis, then scientific (differentiated) management is in a certain sense the antithesis, and a third step will have to be the synthesis of the positive elements of the first and second phases with the addition of a new element which makes this synthesis possible – the mature social subsystem.[8]

Lievegoed's third phase is based on the premise that every individual can and wants to develop. Real fulfillment can only be attained at work, therefore, if that individual need for ongoing development is satisfied. A mature social subsystem is therefore required to facilitate this. To accommodate it a new form of organization is required.

The pioneer phase had a shallow, broad form of organization; the phase of differentiation had a deep, pyramid form, with the directing and controlling board of directors at the top. The phase of integration demands a form which Lievegoed has termed a 'clover leaf' organization.

The clover leaf organization

In the clover leaf organization the board no longer stands at the apex of a pyramid. It is now situated at the center of the organization, at the crossing point of all the channels of information and communication.

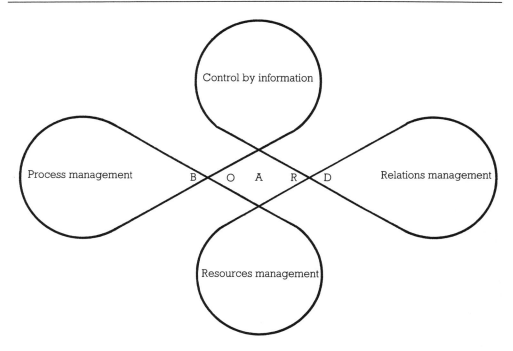

Fig. 57 The clover leaf organization.

The function of the board is to integrate the four subsystems or management activities outlined in Fig. 57. I shall now describe them in turn.

Relations management
The management and cultivation of relations refers to both the internal and external variety. The most important external relations are those involved in marketing. In marketing the true task of the pioneer re-appears: the discovery of a consumer need and the answering of this need by solving problems for others. Everything else is derived from this primary task and is for the exclusive purpose of realizing it.

Other external relations are, historically, with suppliers and distributors, with trade unions and shareholders, and with local and national government. More recently there have been a spate of associated ventures between companies themselves in preproduction research, in joint marketing ventures, and in international consortia. These are becoming an increasingly important part of relations management.

Internal relations form the second part of relations management. This sub-function involves discovering the needs of people working within the company, including their desire for ongoing personal development, and catering for these individually and collectively. These needs are economic, psychological and social. Internal relations, moreover, incorporates the stimulation of innovation as a continual activity of all employees. Such innovation takes place as a process, over time.

Process management

Between the inputs and the outputs of the company there are many activities of a material (production flows) and a non-material nature (information flows), which follow one another over time. Within these flow processes human beings are used, or become superfluous, and therefore process management becomes the crucial test for the genuine integration of the social system.

In the second, differentiated phase, people were organized vertically in a structure that was superior-oriented. In the third phase emphasis is now placed on the organization of people who are work oriented horizontally within the process flow. In these horizontal consultation groups, people are oriented towards those who precede them and influence their work, and towards those who are next in the process flow and whose work is influenced in turn. Within process management there is a close interaction between the technical and the social subsystems. Only through integrating the technical 'hardware' and the social 'software' can a truly functional process flow be guaranteed. Such a flow is also predetermined by the availability and allocation of resources.

Resources management

Resources of different kinds are necessary to make possible the process flow, which is determined in turn by external relations. The procurement, management, and disposal of these resources at the right place, in the right amounts, and also at the right time, comprises the third of the four clover-leaf functions. 'Resources', in this context, includes both material capital and facilities, and non-material people and know-how. In the third phase these non-material resources, inclusive if so-called 'intellectual capital' are more important than the material ones. Thus the board must be primarily concerned with the procurement, allocation, and development of its non-material resources.

Information management

Information processing has grown quantitatively and qualitatively to such a degree, in large-scale enterprise, that it warrants – in the third phase – a completely separate subsystem. It is therefore given a place as one of the leaflets of the clover-leaf organization. Like a nervous system that permeates the whole organism but has its own center, it receives its policy direct from the board. Its task is to send every piece of information to the place where it is required so that those concerned can act intelligently in the interests of the whole company.

Its job is to distribute information in a firm that is useful for everybody as regards content, frequency and intelligibility.

> ... It is the task of the information center to use the assembling, processing and distribution of information to enable people individually and in groups to adjust and control, independently, within the framework of the defined standards. In this way it becomes possible for everyone to act intelligently within the context of the overall objectives.[9]

The information processing center, finally, will have a department concerned with external functions, primarily market research and intelligence, and it will have an internal department serving the administrative, financial and management functions. The section of the internal department serving process management will need to collaborate with engineers. In fact collaboration, mutual consultation, and an attitude of service, are the characteristics of the information processing subsystem.

The board
The board is situated at the center, in the heart of the clover leaf. Instead of being at the top of a pyramid, in splendid isolation, it is now at a point where all the channels of communication cross. Its members, therefore, must have sufficient proficiency and interest in the four main subsystems to ensure that they can make balanced judgements and take corrective action, as well as initiate and innovate. The role of Chairman of the Board, accordingly, changes fundamentally.

Chairman of the center – board

- Instead of seeing himself at the top of a pyramid, he shifts to the center of the organism, at a point where all channels of communication meet. Ideally too the chairman would shift geographically, as well as organizationally, away from a parochial and national centre.
- Instead of making heavy handed decisions and exercising ultimate authority, he selectively guides, encourages, envisages and harmonizes, asking questions, giving support, recognizing potential, and inspiring confidence. He also needs to publically and imaginatively distinguish between these enabling and envisioning functions and the more established ones of entrepreneurship and management.
- Instead of primarily focussing on efficiency and effectiveness progressive corporate chairmen have concentrated on the management of change, on an ongoing basis. What remains to be done is to shift the focus from change – which has no direction or higher purpose to it – to an evolutionary path of interdependent development, serving to link past, present and future.
- Instead of necessarily competing with companies outside, and resolving conflicts amongst people inside, the third stage chairman strives for association with enterprises and institutions and reaches decisions through mutual agreement. What remains is to accentuate this shift of emphasis, particularly externally, away from an autonomous corporation towards an interdependent corporate architecture.
- Instead of pursuing business, technical and organisation development as separate goals, the new chairman strives to integrate all three within a transformed technological, commercial and social vision. What is required is for that transformed vision to percolate its way through the organization, by a process of cultural evolution, stimulated by powerful images and suitably heroic figures.
- Finally, instead of insisting that individual goals and aspirations should be subordinated to those of the organization, the new corporate chairman should adapt the organization to the needs of the individual. What he needs to do is to model the organization on the individual's growth and development from youth to adulthood and maturity, and to identify and accommodate diverse forms of individuality within it.

Ronnie Lessem *The Roots of Excellence*[10] 1986

In the final analysis the primary task of the chairman and his board is to manage innovation and development.

Limits to integration
It is difficult to assess the limits that the integrated, clover-leaf organization might come up against because so few companies have yet become fully integrated, in Lievegoed's terms.

However, as we shall see in Chapter 24, there are problems with 'self-managed' companies, particularly in Yugoslavia, that have attempted to enter into the third, socially oriented phase, without undergoing a proper economic and technical development. In other words many a socially oriented and cooperative enterprise will find itself struggling to survive because it has not built up the economic or technical resilience to compete aggressively and effectively in the market-place.

The developing organization in perspective

Bernard Lievegoed, together with his mentor, Rudolph Steiner, and his fifty or so disciples at the NPI, have attempted singlemindedly to introduce developmental management into organizational life. The concept of the clover leaf organization, transcending functionally based management, is quite unique and, probably for that reason, is somewhat difficult to grasp. It represents a fundamentally new departure in managerial thinking.

The notion of phases of development, however, is a little more commonplace. In Chapter 20, on 'The roots of developmental management', I described its origins in developmental biology. In the chapter that follows I shall be dealing with some of its applications in developmental psychology. However, closer to home, there have been three organizational theorists whose work on phases has paralleled that of Lievegoed.

Gordon Lippitt, Warren Schmidt and Larry Greiner are three Americans who have played prominent roles within the 'organization development' movement (see pages 436–9). Their particular interest has been in the area of what has come to be called organizational renewal.

Organizational renewal

Crisis and development

Interestingly enough in America, Gordon Lippitt and Warren Schmidt – two leading practitioners in organization development – had been coming to similar conclusions to those of Lievegoed. They referred to their phases as 'growth stages', in an organization's development and renewal. Instead of pioneering, differentiated, and integrated phases they have adopted the terms 'birth', 'youth' and 'maturity'.

At a particular stage of its evolution, through birth and infancy, youth or maturity, an organization – like an individual – faces one or two 'issues' that are crucial to that phase of its development. If those issues remain unresolved the organization will enter decline. At each stage, as revealed in Table 31,[11] there are appropriate and inappropriate developmental responses.

Infant responses
With the creation of a new enterprise, then, if it is to survive, the pioneers have to continually decide what to create, in a commercial and organizational sense, and what sacrifice to make in both financial and emotional terms. If the decisions made are inappropriate, the enterprise will be stillborn, or will die in its infancy.

Table 31 Appropriate developmental responses

Critical issue	Correct response	Incorrect response
Creation	New organizational system comes into being	Idea remains abstract. Organization is under-capitalized.
Survival	Organization learns from experience; becomes viable	Organization fails to adjust to realities of its environment, and remains marginal
Stability	Organization develops efficiency and strength, and retains flexibility	Organization over extends itself, returning to survival stage
Pride and reputation	Organization's reputation reinforces efforts to improve quality	Organization places more effort on image-creation than on product quality
Uniqueness and adaptability	Organization changes to take full advantage of its unique capability, and provides growth opportunities for its personnel	Organization fails to discover its uniqueness and spreads its efforts inappropriately, thus inhibiting growth
Contribution	Organization gains public respect for its contribution to society	Organization may be accused of failing to uphold its responsibility to its shareholders

Youthful responses

If the pioneers manage to 'get through the knot hole', and survive into the next youthful phase, they will need to turn into 'scientific managers'. As such they will be seeking after much greater stability, as well as after a solid and enduring reputation. If management fails to plan, organize and control effectively, the company will become overreactive to immediate stimuli, and dominated by short-term crises.

Mature responses

As the differentiated and youthful organization enters its integrated and mature phase its critical concerns duly evolve. It aims now to achieve uniqueness and adaptability, on the one hand, and to contribute to society, on the other. The managers' focus is now long, as opposed to medium- or short-term. The key issues to be resolved are how to change and adapt, and how to share business and management with others. The lack of such a developmental orientation leads to unnecessarily defensive or aggressive attitudes, to a narrowness of approach and to an ultimate failure to adapt. A third and final source of knowledge on development phases, comes from a researcher at the Harvard Business School, in the early seventies, Larry Greiner.

Evolution and revolution

Stability and change

Lippitt and Schmidt's three growth stages, then, encompass creation and survival; stability, pride and reputation; uniqueness and adaptability and contribution to society. They are in fact very similar to Lievegoed's three phases: pioneering, differentiated and integrated.

Greiner,[12] however, maintains that growing organizations move through five distinguishable phases of development, each of which contains a relatively calm period of growth that ends with a management crisis. The calm period of growth he describes as 'evolutionary'; the period of crisis and turmoil Greiner terms 'revolutionary'. The critical task for management in each revolutionary period is to find a new set of organizational practices that will become the basis for managing the next period of evolutionary growth. Interestingly enough, these new practices eventually sow their own seeds of decay and lead to another period of revolution.

Companies therefore find, ironically, that a major solution in one time period becomes a major problem at a future date. The extent and duration of a stage of development, moreover, is not only a function of the age and size of an organization, it is also related to the market environment of its industry. For example, a company in a rapidly expanding market will have to add employees rapidly. Hence the need for structures and systems to accommodate these changes is accelerated. While evolutionary changes tend to be relatively short in fast-growing industries, much longer evolutionary periods occur in mature or slowly growing industries.

Five stages of growth
Greiner, unlike Lievegoed, Lippitt and Schmidt, conceives of five growth periods (see Fig.

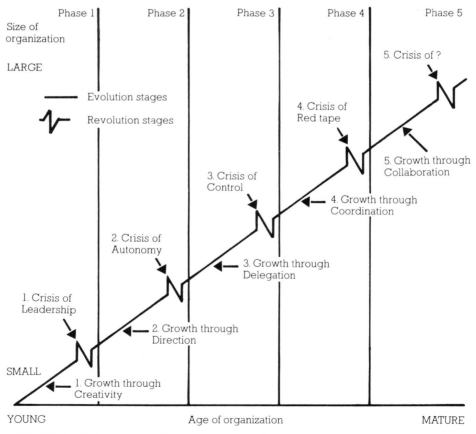

Fig. 58 Evolution and revolution as organizations grow.

58)[13]. Yet, as we shall soon see, three of them merely consist of finer subdivisions of the differentiated phase.

It is important to note that each stage is both an effect of the previous stage and a cause for the next one. When we consider, with Greiner, each stage of development, we find that he is not fundamentally at odds with Lippitt and Schmidt, or with Lievegoed. In fact, Greiner's phases one (creativity) and five (collaboration) correspond with Lippitt's 'birth' and 'maturity' and with Lievegoed's 'pioneering' and 'integration', respectively.

The three intermediate stages represent 'youth', perhaps including adulthood, but involving a more detailed breakdown, (direction, delegation, coordination). Let us now investigate Greiner's evolutions or stages, and revolutions or crises, in more detail.

Pioneering/birth

Phase one: creativity. In the birth stage of an organization the emphasis is on creating a product or service, and a market:

- The company's founders are usually technically or entrepreneurially oriented, and they disdain management activities; their physical and mental energies are absorbed in producing and selling a product or a service.
- Communication amongst employees is frequent and informal.
- Long hours of work are rewarded by modest salaries and the promise of ownership benefits.
- Control of activities comes from immediate market-place feedback; the management acts as customers react.

... Up comes the leadership crisis.

All of this enterprising activity is essential for the company to get off the ground. But therein lies the problem. As the company grows, larger production and distribution runs require the founders to acquire knowledge about operational systems and structures.

Increased numbers of employees cannot be managed exclusively through informal communications; new employees are no longer motivated by an intense dedication to the product or organization. Additional capital must also be secured and new accounting procedures are needed for financial control. Thus the founders find themselves burdened with unwanted management responsibilities. A leadership crisis occurs, which, for its resolution, requires a managerial revolution.

Differentiation/youth

Phase two: direction. Those companies that survive the first phase by installing capable management usually embark on a period of sustained growth under able and directive leadership. This is Greiner's youthful phase, involving the early influence of scientific management.

- A functional organization structure is introduced to separate operations from marketing activities and job assignments become more specialized.
- Incentives, budgets and work standards are introduced.
- Communication becomes more formal and impersonal as an hierarchy of titles and positions builds up.

- The new management take on most of the decision making responsibility.

                                            ... Up comes the autonomy crisis.

While the new management policies and techniques channel employee effort more efficiently and effectively into growth, they eventually become inappropriate. They become ill-fitted for the control of an increasingly complex and diversified operation. Lower level employees find themselves stifled by a cumbersome and centralized hierarchy.

Because, moreover, they have become more in touch with the grass roots than their senior management, they begin to feel torn. Should they take responsive initiative or stick to seemingly outmoded procedures? Thus the second revolution is imminent. There is increasing demand for autonomy at lower levels. However, while the lower levels may be ill-accustomed to making decisions the higher levels may be ill-disposed to surrendering power. The crisis needs to be resolved through appropriate delegation.

Phase three: delegation. The next organizational evolution results in a more decentralized structure:

- Much greater responsibility is given to managers of individual operations and territories.
- Profit centers and bonus systems are used to stimulate motivation.
- Top executives at the center confine themselves to managing by exception, based on periodic reports from the field.
- Senior management may acquire new companies or enter into joint ventures, to supplement the existing, decentralized units.

                                            ... Up comes the crisis of control.

A serious crisis eventually looms as top management begin to sense that they are losing control over a highly diversified operation. Freedom breeds not only autonomy but also parochialism. Revolution gets under way as management seeks to regain overall control. However, an attempt to reassert centralized control is bound to fail, given the emerging complexity of the operation. Those companies that resolve the crisis discover a new form of coordination.

Phase four: coordination. This next evolutionary phase therefore calls for a new and subtle form of coordination. This may involve:

- Previously decentralized units being merged into newly formed product groups.
- Formal planning procedures being installed.
- The hiring of staff personnel at headquarters to initiate company wide technical, commercial and organizational review programs.
- Introducing stock options and companywide profit sharing schemes to encourage individuals and divisions to identify with the company as a whole.

                                            ... Up comes the crisis of red tape.

Gradually, a lack of confidence builds up between line and staff, between headquarters and the divisions. The proliferation of systems and procedures begins to turn into too much of a good thing. Such procedures take precedence over problem solving. A red tape crisis looms. The next revolution is under way. A new form of collaboration is required to resolve it.

Integration/emerging maturity
Phase five: collaboration. The last observable phase, according to Greiner, emphasizes strong interpersonal collaboration to overcome the red tape crisis:

- Focus is now on problem-solving through group interaction.
- Teams are combined across foundations; a matrix structure is often created, linking up temporary projects and permanent functions.
- Headquarters staff are reduced in number, and combined into interdisciplinary teams.
- Experimentation is encouraged throughout the organization.

Greiner is unsure at this point what crisis will emerge next. He hints at the prospect of 'psychological saturation', whereby employees 'burnout'. Perhaps at this stage, he argues, they need more time for reflexion. The fact is that Greiner himself has reached an evolutionary cul de sac. He is unable to fully come to grips with the challenges of, and opportunities for, genuine integration and maturation. His final phase fails to have a real ring of maturity about it, because he is not completely in touch with the emerging technological and social developments of our time, nor with his own emerging maturity.

New patterns of work and organization

Dispersed organizations

While Greiner alludes to a succession of revolutions, characterizing each crisis of transition, only the 'managerial' one assumes genuinely revolutionary proportions. In other words, the step up from a pioneering enterprise to managed organization does appear to be a revolutionary one. The rules of the business game change fundamentally. A science of management replaces the art of entrepreneurship. Thereafter, his 'revolutions' seem to go off half cock.

The problem is that in the 1970s, when Greiner, Lievegoed, and Lippitt and Schmidt were writing, structures of organization and management, of employment and self-employment, were little changed from those that had existed fifty years before. In the 1980s, though, we have a very different situation. With the rapid emergence of the new communications technologies Charles Handy's 'dispersed organization' (see Chapter 16) is becoming a reality, albeit presently on a small scale. Such organizational dispersion reinforces individuality and independence. At the same time collaboration between businesses, as well as within them, is increasing at a very rapid rate.

Interorganizational collaboration
Such interorganizational cooperation enhances commonality and interdependence. It takes the form of consortia, joint venturing, risk sharing, counter trade, piggy backing and several more such collaborative arrangements. (See Table 32[14]).

Table 32 Interorganizational collaboration

Collaborators	Mode	Description
Eurotunnel	Consortium	This Anglo French group is a consortium of major construction and finance companies assembled to build the Channel Tunnel
Barclays/De Zoete	Joint venture	Clearing bank and stockbroker have combined forces to create a whole that is greater than the sum of their individual parts
Rolls-Royce/GE (USA)	Risk sharing	These two major companies, across the Atlantic, have become partners in the development and manufacture of high-powered aircraft engines
Ford/Levi Strauss/Pierre Cardin	Counter trade	Ford trades its cars for Uraguayan sheepskins; Levi Strauss sells a turnkey plant to Hungary, and gets jeans in return; Pierre Cardin gets oriental skills by providing consultancy services to China
Pitney Bowes/small business	Piggy backing	Pitney Bowes markets, through its nationwide marketing and service network, innovative products of small businesses

The enabling company

Whereas the birth phase, in a company's development, is represented by the independent enterprise, and the youthful phase by a holding or parent company, I have argued that the maturer phase is represented by an 'enabling company'.[15] The enabling company is the instrument through which independence and interdependence are combined with dependence.

In other words, the new enterprise and the managed organization have not been eclipsed; rather a rival has appeared in their midst. That rival might be called the enabling company. While the role of 'enabler' has been visible in the training world for years, the enabling company's role is much more wide-ranging. Whereas the enabler develops people's potential, the enabling company harnesses the potential of not only people but also of products, of markets, and of whole businesses.

Moreover, and this is the key, enabling involves not so much holding down but more holding together; not so much employing people and their skills but more deploying individuality and its potential; not so much competing but more cooperating; not so much overpowering people and institutions but more empowering staff, suppliers, customers, associated companies and whole societies. The model of a maturing, developmental organization, is therefore one of hexagonal linkages rather than of hierarchical structures. (See Fig. 59.) It thereby accommodates both independence and interdependence.

Conclusion

Developmental management

In summary, as an organization evolves so its structures and functions are transformed. The transformation from a new enterprise into an established organization is well

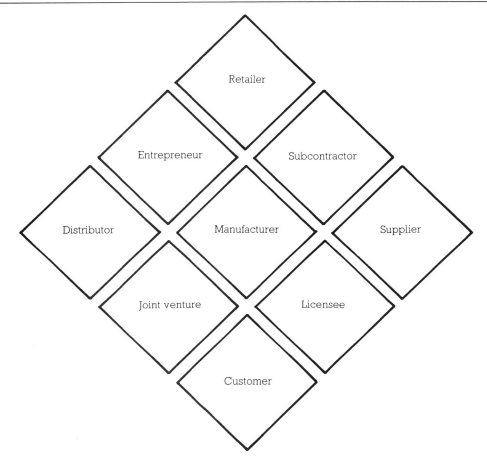

Fig. 59 The enabling company.

substantiated both in theory and practice. We are generally familiar with the conventional business entrepreneur and administrator.

The so-called 'developmental manager' is something of a new breed. His emphasis is social rather than technical or economic. His style is supportive and enabling, rather than dynamic or authoritative. He fosters both independence and interdependence rather than independence on its own, or dependence as the predominating and employed mode of being. For Greiner, for Lippitt and Schmidt, and most other proponents of organization development, that is as far as they go. The form of organization does not fundamentally change, though the style of management does. This new style is less mechanistic and bureaucratic, more organic and democratic.

The new corporate architecture

But for Lievegoed, for Handy, and for the practicing businessman in a dynamic company or industry today, the pattern of work and organization has changed. The boundaries between not only different business functions, for Lievegoed, but also between home and work, for Handy, and between one company and another, for myself, are dissolving. It is as if a new 'corporate architecture' is unfolding within, for example, the chemical industry. I shall be elaborating on this developmental theme, and on the resulting corporate architecture in Chapter 23.

Development and renewal in the chemical industry

The evolutionary perspective in chemistry is rich in deep-seated and significant innovations. The tendency is to break up the industry, to split it up into subsectors which are, increasingly, closely linked to the solution of specific problems, and to rearrange it into new industries, borne from an interdisciplinary perception of the contribution of innovation.

This does not necessarily mean that the major chemical companies will disappear, but in order to evolve they will need to rebuild themselves around specific problems, explicit markets and societal demands. During this process they will be combining with industries which traditionally were buying their products or supplying them with raw materials.

Finally they will no longer be unistrategy companies. They will manifest strong intersectoral synergy.

Umberto Colombo, President of the European Research and Development Committee[16] 1986

Organic development, in that emerging context, overlaps conventional boundaries between home and work, between one company, discipline or department and another, as well as between public and private enterprise. As organizations continue to grow and evolve in the future, therefore, they will undergo evolutions and revolutions of which Greiner has not yet dreamed.

The hard and soft edges of development

Before we unravel such developments, I want to move on to individual lifecycle theories, a subject dear to the developmental manager's heart. These lifecycles, like the organizational evolutions and revolutions, represent the hard edge of development, with their intermittent crises and resolutions. They will constitute Chapter 22. Conversely the subject of individual and organizational, corporate and societal synergy, like the third phase of business integration, represents the soft edge of development. It therefore forms the substance of Chapter 23.

References

1. R. Steiner, *World Economics*, Steiner Press (1979), p. 266.
2. M. Large, *Social Ecology*, published privately (1981), p. 10.
3. B. Lievegoed, *The Developing Organisation*, Celestial Arts (1973), Chapter 5.
4. M. Large, *op. cit.,* Chapter 6.
5. B. Lievegoed, *op. cit.,* p. 75.
6. G. Pinchot *Intrapreneuring*, Harper & Row (1984).
7. A. Toffler, *The Third Wave*, Bantam (1982).
8. B. Lievegoed, *op. cit.,* p. 79.
9. B. Lievegoed, *op. cit.,* p. 86.
10. R. Lessem, The Roots of Excellence, Fontana (1986), p. 209.
11. C. Lippitt, *Organizational Renewal* (2nd edn) Prentice Hall (1982), p. 245.

12. L. Greiner, 'Evolution and resolution as organizations grow', *Harvard Business Review* (July–August 1972), p. 41.
13. L. Greiner, *op. cit.*
14. R. Lessem, 'The Enabling Company', ex *New Problems at Work*, Clutterbuck, D. (ed.) Gower (1986), p. 92.
15. R. Lessem, *op. cit.,* p. 94.
16. U. Colombo, 'Industrial development and renewal in the chemical industry' *Futures*, Vol. 18, no. 2, (April, 1986), pp. 170–191.

22 Personal growth and self-development

Contents

Key concepts

Once you have fully understood this chapter you should be able to define the following concepts in your own words:

Age fifty transition	Lifecycle theory
Age thirty transition	Life phases
'Being' values	Life structure
Deficiency needs	Mentors
The dream	Novice phase
Early adult transition	Occupation
Growth needs	Pathfinding
Hierarchy of needs	Phase of individuation
The 'ladder'	Self-actualization
The 'legacy'	Transition

Objectives

Upon completing this chapter you should be able to do the following:

1. Illustrate the nature and significance of Maslow's contribution to management theory.
2. Describe the 'hierarchy of needs'.
3. Compare the phases of an individual's development, as cited by Levinson, with those of an organization, as cited by Lievegoed.
4. Contrast the stable life structures with the transitional phases, during the course of an individual's development through life, relating both to your own adult development.
5. Compare Sheahy's 'healthy pathfinding' with the unprepared for transition out of employment, cited by Hayes and Nutman.

Introduction

Personal growth and development

In Chapter 16, I mentioned that the organization development (OD) movement in the sixties branched out in two main directions. In one direction its advocates extended rational management, applying the behavioral sciences to the 'planning of change'. In the other direction organization developers produced, over twenty to thirty years, a body of knowledge and an array of specialized techniques, in the general area of humanistic psychology.

What distinguished this 'third force' of humanists from the psychological schools that preceded them, was the extent to which they focussed on the whole person, as opposed to merely concentrating on the individual's basic instincts or behavioral traits. In fact they were oriented towards actualizing (phase three) potential rather than channelling (phase two) or exploiting (phase one) it.

Self-actualization

Orthodox behaviorist theory has assumed that the human species seeks an eqilibrium, needs to reduce tension, and that most behavior can be defined in tension reducing terms. Freud also believed in tension reduction and the pleasure–pain principle, saying that the human species constantly sought pleasure and avoided pain.

All the evidence that we (the 'third force') have indicates that it is reasonable to assume in practically every human being, that there is an active will towards health, an impulse towards the actualization of human potential.

Frank Noble *The Third Force*[1] 1970

Out of this third force, one psychologist stood out, and that was the late Abraham Maslow. Though Maslow is generally linked together with Herzberg and Argyris (see pp. 257 and 307–9), and with motivational theory, his work is of a much more far reaching nature than of his two living compatriots. For that reason he warrants a special attention in this chapter.

Negotiating life's phases

While Maslow focussed on human growth at any stage of an adult's development, Bernard Lievegoed paid particular attention to the course, and phases, of such an individual's evolution. In the same way as he has revealed the stages of a developing organization, so he has uncovered the phases of a maturing person. Drawing on ancient Chinese sources he referred[2] to three phases of life, that in fact parallel the organizational stages of pioneering, differentiation and integration. These he described as times to learn – until twenty, to expand – from twenty to forty, and to grow wise – from forty onwards.

The concept of life phases has been with us for a long time. Shakespeare referred[3] to the seven ages of man. Piaget,[4] the Swiss child psychologist, and Dr Erik Erikson,[5] who is based in America, are particularly well known for their developmental psychology. However, it is only in the last ten years that attention has shifted from child to adult development, and from an academic and psychological to a practical and vocational orientation towards lifecycle theories.

Leading interpreters of the individual's lifecycle, and of its vocational and managerial implications, have ranged from the NPI in Holland, to the two American psychological researchers and consultants, Gail Sheahy and Daniel Levinson. While Sheahy has written the two popular works *Passages*[6] and *Pathfinders*,[7] Levinson completed a major research project on *The Seasons of Man's Life*. I shall begin by focussing on Maslow's work on human growth and development, in the context of 'the third force' in organization psychology, and then move on to Daniel Levinson's research into life phases, in the context of work on 'manager self-development'.

Self-actualization and personal growth

Maslow's hierarchy of needs

In 1954 Maslow published his seminal work on *Motivation and Personality*. In it he first revealed his oft since quoted hierarchy of needs.

Maslow's motivational hierarchy

It is quite true that man lives by bread alone – when there is no bread. But what happens to man's desires when there is plenty of bread and when his belly is chronically filled?

At once other (and higher) needs emerge and these, rather than physiological hunger, dominate the organism. When these in turn are satisfied, again new (and still higher) needs emerge ... Human needs are organized into a hierarchy of prepotency.

Abraham Maslow *Motivation and Personality*[8] 1954

As we can see Maslow's developmental approach is constructed not on the basis of phases of life, but on the basis of 'an hierarchy of need prepotency'. In other words, as one need is satisfied so a next, predictable need rises to the fore.

Deficiency needs

The set of needs that form the starting point for his motivational theory (see Fig. 60) are

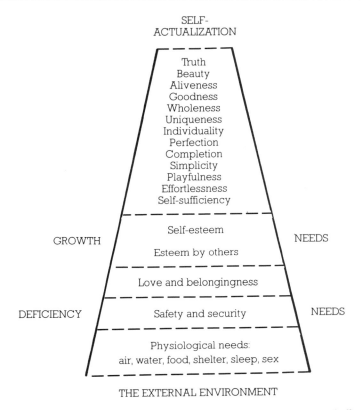

SELF-
ACTUALIZATION

Truth
Beauty
Aliveness
Goodness
Wholeness
Uniqueness
Individuality
Perfection
Completion
Simplicity
Playfulness
Effortlessness
Self-sufficiency

GROWTH   Self-esteem   NEEDS

Esteem by others

Love and belongingness

DEFICIENCY   Safety and security   NEEDS

Physiological needs:
air, water, food, shelter, sleep, sex

THE EXTERNAL ENVIRONMENT

(precondition for need satisfaction, freedom, justice, orderliness, challenge)

Fig. 60 Hierarchy of needs.

physiological ones. Man needs food, water, air, shelter, sleep, sex. Once such physiological needs are relatively well satisfied there emerges a new set of safety needs. Both these 'physiological' and 'safety' drives are, according to Maslow, 'deficiency needs'. In other words, lack of either results in tangible deprivation.

Growth needs

Once both sets of deficiency needs are gratified, then belonging needs take over, that is the drive for love and affection. These are the first of Maslow's growth needs. Next in the hierarchy of prepotency is the need for esteem. Everyone in our society, Maslow says, has need for a stable, firmly based and high evaluation of themselves. This need becomes prepotent once an individual's physiological, safety, and belongingness drives have been satisfied.

Such esteem needs form two subsets. First, there is the desire for achievement, for adequacy, for mastery, for confidence, for independence and for freedom. These are inner directed. Second, there is the desire for status and importance, reputation and prestige. These are outer directed. However, even if all of these physiological, social and psychological needs are satisfied, there is still room for discontent, that is unless a person is doing what he or she is truly fitted for. 'What a man (or woman) can be, he must be ... this need we call self-actualization'.[9] Self-actualization is the ultimate of the growth needs. The full hierarchy of needs, with those attributes comprising self-actualization standing at the top of the pyramid, are shown in Fig. 60.

Towards a psychology of being

The self-actualizing features that stood at the top of Maslow's hierarchy were alternatively identified by him as 'being' (B) as opposed to 'deficiency' (D) values. In fact one of his most fundamental contributions to individual and organizational development was to focus on health rather than pathology, on so called 'peak' rather than mundane levels of experience.

> Man demonstrates in his own nature a pressure towards fuller and fuller being, more and more perfect actualization of his humanness in exactly the same naturalistic, scientific sense that an acorn can be said to be pressing towards being an oak tree.[10]

Maslow in fact coined the phrase 'Eupsychian management' which operates according to such 'being values'.

Eupsychic man

First of all, and most important of all, is the strong belief that man has an essential nature of his own ... Second, there is involved the conception that full health and normal, desirable development consists in actualizing this nature, in fulfilling these potentialities and in developing into maturity along the lines that this dimly seen essential nature dictates, growing from within rather than being shaped from without.

If I had to put it into a single phrase ... we can now see not only what man is but also what he may become. That is to say we can see not only surface, not only the actualities but also the potentialities. We are now able to judge the essential nature of man according to what his highest possible development may be, instead of merely relying on external observations.

Abraham Maslow *Eupsychian Management*[11] 1965

Maslow therefore played a pioneering role in creating a developmental approach to management that took into account the full potential of the human being. Each human being, given a conducive physical and institutional environment in which to live and work, was naturally inclined towards self-actualization, that is once his deficiency needs, and his more basic growth needs were satisfied. Unfortunately Maslow did not go on to relate individual to organizational growth and self-actualization, although you may have already made that obvious connection.

Maslow in perspective

While Maslow's concept of a motivational hierarchy of needs has endured, in management circles, his more prolific ideas on 'being' values and on 'self-actualization' have slipped into the management background.

This has happened for three main reasons. Firstly his need hierarchy has been contested by contingency theorists, like Fiedler (see p. 259), who believe that motivation is situationally determined, rather than abolutely prescribed. In other words, according to the contingency school of motivation and leadership, different people and situations call upon different motivations. They therefore accept no absolutes, no fixed motivational hierarchy or prepotencies.

Secondly, few, if any, organizations have been psychologically mature enough to accommodate Maslow's 'being' values within themselves. Most of our structures and strategies have not yet evolved sufficiently, though there are exceptions such as BCC cited in Chapter 29.

Thirdly, and finally, Maslow restricted his 'being' psychology to human behavior within organizations. He therefore left such business disciplines as marketing and finance largely untouched – a deficiency that, as we saw in Chapter 21, Bernard Lievegoed has been able to overcome. In fact most of the 'growth' psychologists who made an impact on organization development, focussing in different ways on the whole person, restricted themselves to the field of human and organizational behavior. They therefore remained, with Maslow, isolated from the mainstream of business development. Their contribution to developmental management was therefore circumscribed.

Lifecycle theory and self-development

Manager self-development

While the 'human growth' movement in general,[12] and Maslow in particular, were popular in American and British management circles in the sixties and seventies, by the eighties their influence had begun to wane. While the behavioral sciences in the broadest sense have continued to influence management theory and practice, organization development and humanistic psychology have apparently lost their way. In their place has appeared, on the one hand, the subject area of corporate culture, to which I have referred both in Chapters 5 and 22, and, on the other, the field of 'manager self-development'.

Most of the current theory and practice on the subject of manager self-development is very much a watered down version of the originating thrust towards human growth and development. In fact it often boils down to nothing more than self-study methods, or a smattering of self-development techniques, ranging from action learning (see pp. 268–74) and lateral thinking (see pp. 263–73) to speed reading and methods of improving one's memory.

However, in the last ten years, one new and fully developmental area of theory has crept into management, and that is the one concerned with the individual and organizational lifecycle. We have already seen how Lievegoed, Lippitt and Schmidt, and Greiner have introduced such phases of development into organizational thinking. Now I want to introduce you to the current thinking on individual life phases, drawing in particular on Daniel Levinson's work.

Seasons of man's life

The most accessible, and fully articulated of these lifecycle theories, is that developed by the American psychiatrist, Daniel Levinson,[13] and his team of psychological researchers. In fact Levinson is to self-development what Maslow is to personal growth. Although his research has been restricted to men, rather than women, the general findings are not dissimilar to those of Lievegoed and the NPI and Gail Sheahy, both of whom focussed on men and women. Levinson has developed a comprehensive theory of adult development, covering both discrete life phases and the transition periods in between. I first want to reveal the general nature of his developmental theory – life structure – and, thereafter, the particular character of his four transitional periods and life phases.

Life structure

The components of a life structure, for Levinson, are not a random set of events, like pebbles washed upon the shore. Rather, like threads in a tapestry, they are woven into an encompassing design. Recurring themes help to unify the overall pattern of the tapestry. Moreover, lives differ widely in the nature and patterning of the components. His life structure evolves through a relatively orderly sequence during the adult years. It consists of alternating stable, structure building and transitional structure changing periods.

To construct anything, something else must be destructured and restructured. In human reproduction, an ovum and a sperm are joined to create a new being; but many ova and sperm are left to die. The balance of nature is a mixture of destruction and creation. Both are essential to the harmony and evolution of individuals, organizations and societies. In fact, at each phase of development, a new balance has to be created between the forces not only of creativity and destruction, but also of youth and age, of masculinity and femininity, and of separation and attachment.

The primary task of every stable period, then, is to build a life structure that reconciles those four sets of opposing forces in a new and appropriate way. A person must make certain key choices, form a structure around them, and pursue his values and goals within that structure. A transitional period terminates the existing life structure and creates the possibility for a new one. The decision to 'stay put' within a stable period is not always based on reaffirmed commitment. It may stem from resignation, inertia, passive acceptance or controlled despair – a self-restriction in the context of severe external constraints. This kind of surface stability marks the beginning of long-term decline unless new factors intervene (perhaps in the next transitional period) and enable a person to form a more satisfactory life structure.

The primary tasks of every transitional period are to question and to reappraise the existing structure, to explore various possibilities for change in oneself and in one's world, and to move towards commitment to the crucial choices that form the basis for a new life structure in the ensuing stable period. The task of a developmental transition, therefore, is to terminate a time in one's life; to accept the losses that termination entails; to review and evaluate the past; to decide which aspects of the past to keep and which to reject; and to consider one's wishes and possibilities for the future. One is suspended between past and future, struggling to overcome the gap that separates them. Much from the past must be given up, separated from, cut out of one's life; and there is much that can be used as a basis for the future.

In every transitional period, throughout the cycle of life, the internal figures of young and old are modified and placed in a new balance. The end of the preceding period stimulates old thoughts and feelings about being in a rut, rotting, coming to the brink of death. The start of a new period stimulates new thoughts and feelings about being reborn, making a fresh start, discovering fresh possibilities in oneself and new vistas in one's world.

The task in every transition is to create a new young/old integration appropriate to that time of life. With the change of eras there is normally an increase in the old qualities of maturity, judgement, self-awareness, magnanimity, integrated structure, breadth of perspective. But these qualities are of value only if they continue to be vitalized by the young's energy, imagination, capacity for foolishness and fancy.

In summary, the most fundamental tasks of a stable period are to make firm choices, rebuild the life structure and enhance one's life within it. Those of a transitional period are to question and reappraise the existing period, to search for new possibilities in oneself and in the world, and to modify the present structure enough for a new one to be formed. The alternating periods constitute, as Levinson reveals, 'the seasons of man's life'.

Alternating seasons

Spring is not intrinsically a better season than winter, nor is summer better than spring. Each season plays its part in the unfolding of the life cycle, and the sequence follows a prescribed course.

Winter is a fallow, quiet time in which the previous growth comes to an end, and the possibility of new growth is created. It is the ultimate transitional period. Unless the creative work of winter is done and seeds take root, nothing further can grow.

Spring is a time of blossoming, when the fruits of the winter's labour begin to be realized. The blossoms will not appear unless the seeds have been nourished, and the blossoms in turn make way for the blooming, full grown flowers.

Daniel Levinson *The Seasons of Man's Life*[14] 1979

Life phases

Levinson divides the course of a man's life into four transitional periods and four stable life structures, as can be seen in Table 33.

Table 33 Life phases

Age	Transitional period	Stable structure
17–22	Early Adult transition	
22–28		Novice phase
28–33	Age thirty transition	
33–40		Settling down phase
40–45	Midlife transition	
45–52		Phase of individuation
52–57	Age fifty transition	
58–		The legacy phase

Early adult transition (17–22)
The first task, in this early adult transition, is to terminate the adolescent life structure, thereby leaving the pre-adult world behind you. This involves modifying existing relationships with important persons and institutions, as well as the self you formed in adolescence. Separations from family and school friends are required as well as the loss of a certain degree of dependence.

The second task, then, is to make a preliminary step into the adult world: to explore its possibilities, to imagine oneself as a participant in it, to make and test some tentative choices, before entering it.

The first task involves a process of termination, the second a process of initiation. Both are essential in a transitional period. Out of this opening transition emerges the young adult life structure, that is 'the novice phase'.

The novice phase (22–28)
Three major tasks, characterizing Levinson's novice phase, are crucial to the individual's vocational and management development. These comprise the formation of the 'dream', of a suitable mentor relationship, and an appropriate occupation. I shall start with the single most important of these tasks, the uncovering of the dream.

1. Forming a dream and giving it a place in the life structure. The young adult's dream, for Levinson, grows out of 'a primordial sense of self-in-world'. It lends excitement and vitality to the novice's life. It is associated with the 'I am' feeling. The dream may be modest ('I want to be happy') or heroic ('I'm going to change the world'). It is usually vaguely defined and only very occasionally crystal clear; it may be a burning passion or a quiet guiding force, a source of inspiration or of gentle comfort. In dramatic terms, a man's dream is his personal myth, an imagined drama in which he is the central character, a would-be hero engaged in a noble quest.

Forming a dream

The vicissitudes and fate of the dream have fundamental qualities for adult development. In its primordial form, the dream is a vague sense of self-in-adult-world. It has the quality of a vision, an imagined possibility that generates excitement and vitality.

At the start it is usually poorly articulated and only tenuously connected to reality, although it may contain concrete images such as winning the Nobel Prize or making the national football team.

It may take dramatic form as in the myth of the hero: the great artist, business tycoon, athletic or intellectual superstar performing magnificent feats and receiving special honors. It may, alternatively, take the mundane forms that are not yet inspiring and sustaining: the excellent craftsman, the husband–father in a certain kind of family, the highly respected man of one's community.

Daniel Levinson *The Seasons of Man's Life*[15] 1979

Whatever its nature, a young person has the developmental task of giving the dream greater definition and finding ways of living it out. It makes a great difference in his growth whether his novice phase is consonant with, and infused by the dream, or opposed to it. If the dream remains unconnected to his life it may simply die, and with it his sense of aliveness and purpose.

Many young men (and indeed women), in fact, develop a conflict between a life direction expressing the dream and another that is quite different. A young person may be pushed in the latter direction by his parents, by various external constraints, such as lack of money or opportunity, and by various aspects of his personality, such as guilt, passivity, competitiveness and special talents. He may thus succeed in an occupation that holds no interest for him.

Alternatively, for the person who does fulfill his dream he will inevitably find, particularly as he approaches midlife, that the hero of the dream is only one of many figures in the man's life. To the extent that this figure plays a predominant part in the evolution of the novice phase, other parts of the self tend to be neglected. For example, someone who fulfills his dreams by becoming a millionaire may neglect to develop the artistic side of his nature.

Inevitably, therefore, whether or not a person works on and through their dream in early adulthood, it will have to be reworked in later life. Mentor relationships are likely to help in that process. In fact the second task of the novice phase lies therein.

2. Forming mentor relationships. During the novice phase, in particular, a young adult stands to gain, according to Levinson, from an 'apprenticeship' with an appropriately more advanced, expert and authoritative 'mentor'. As the relationship evolves, the novice gains a fuller sense of his own authority and of his capability for autonomous, responsible action.

More specifically the mentor involved may act, firstly, as a teacher, serving to enhance the young adult's skills and intellectual development. Secondly, he may serve as a sponsor, using his influence to facilitate the young person's advancement. Thirdly, he may act as a host and guide, welcoming the initiate into a new occupational role and social world, and acquainting him with its customs, values, resources and cast of characters. Fourthly, the mentor may serve as an exemplar that the protegé can admire and seek to emulate. The mentor has a fifth and final function, and this is developmentally the most crucial one: to support and facilitate the realization of the dream. He fosters the young adult's development by believing in him, sharing the youthful dream and giving it his blessing, helping to define the newly discovered self in its freshly discovered world, and creating space in which the young person can work on a life structure that contains the dream.

3. Forming an occupation. In every period, Levinson says, the developmental tasks are contrasting, even antithetical. Just as the 'early adult transition' requires a young person both to terminate one era and to initiate the next, 'entering the adult world' requires him both to explore freely and to make firm choices.

The exploratory stance requires him to 'hang loose', keeping his options open and avoiding strong commitments. To varying degrees, the outside world provides multiple possibilities. Also his own youthful vitality generates a sense of adventure and wonder, a wish to seek out all the treasures of the new world he is entering. At the same time, in the early to mid-twenties, he must take on adult responsibilities and begin to make something of his life. Externally there are pressures to 'grow up', get married, enter an occupation, and lead a more organized life. Internally there are desires for stability and order, for roots, lasting ties and for the fulfillment of core values.

Certain circumstances are more conducive to what Levinson terms 'forming' an occupation (as opposed to choosing one once and for all) over the course of the novice phase, than others. Supportive conditions, on the one hand, involve the granting of room to maneuver, and the freedom to make mistakes together with the setting of clear limits and expectations. Challenging conditions, on the other hand, involve the setting of appropriate problems and opportunities for the individual to resolve.

No particular set of circumstances, though, is ideal. Forming an occupation, as has been indicated, is inherently paradoxical. Young people who make a strong occupational commitment in their early twenties, without sufficient exploration of external options and inner preferences, often come to regret it later. On the other hand, those who don't make a commitment until their thirties, or who never make one, are deprived of the satisfaction of engaging in enduring work that is suitable for themselves and for society. So there is always a need to redress an occupational imbalance in later life.

Age thirty transition (28–32)

At about twenty-eight, Levinson maintains, the provisional qualities of the twenties begin to end and life becomes more serious, more for real. A voice within the person says: 'If I am to change my life – if there are things in it I want to modify or exclude, or things missing I want to add – I must now make a start, for soon it will be too late.'

The 'age thirty transition', in fact, provides an opportunity to work on the flaws in the life structure formed during the previous period, and to create the basis for a more enduring future. For some people, according to Levinson, the transition proceeds smoothly. A person's life and work thereby becomes modified and enriched. However, for most, the transition takes on a more stressful form, just like the fraught transition from a 'pioneering' to a 'differentiated' organization. The individual often fears that he can neither move forward or back. The integrity of his 'enterprise' is in serious doubt.

As this age thirty transition extends itself, a person moves towards major new choices or recommits himself to existing ones. A great deal hinges on these choices. If they are well made – from the point of view of the individual's dream, values, talents, possibilities – they provide the basis for a relatively satisfactory second, adult life structure. If the preparatory work has been poorly done and the new structure is flawed, life in 'settling down' will become increasingly painful.

The settling down phase (32–40)

In the 'settling down' phase a person has two major tasks. Firstly, he tries to establish a niche in society, to anchor his life and work more firmly, to develop competence in a chosen field, and to become a valued member of a world he in turn values. Secondly, he has the task of striving to 'make it', to advance, to progress according to some inner or outward looking timetable. Establishing a niche involves digging in, forming an occupation and pursuing one's interests within a prescribed pattern. This is the initial step in 'settling down'. A person needs a relatively ordered, stable life, in order to become established in their life and work.

Working at advancement involves striving to succeed, moving onward and upward, progressing according to a pre-ordained schedule. Whereas the first task – establishing a niche – contributes to the stability and order of a defined structure, the second – 'making it' – involves a progression within the structure. The 'settling down' life structure, then, gives certain aspirations, relationships, and aspects of the person a prominent place, while requiring that others be made secondary or put aside altogether. It may, depending on the case in point, permit expression of many or few aspects of oneself.

A relatively integrated structure has a few central elements which serve as focal points for the structure as a whole, while other peripheral elements enrich and expand the structure. For example, a man may become a professionally qualified and commercially successful sales executive (focal points) and have a certain style and love of 'good living' (peripheral elements) to go with it.

Second life structure

The underlying task is to 'settle for' a few key choices, to create a broader structure around them, to invest oneself fully in the various components of the structure – such as work, family, community – and to pursue long range goals and plans within it. An individual has a stronger sense of urgency to 'get serious', to be responsible, to decide what is truly important and to shape his life accordingly.

Daniel Levinson *The Seasons of Man's Life*[16] 1979

To the extent, however, that a person wants order and stability he must be ready to moderate his upward striving which may rock his personal and familial boat. Conversely, an individual who wants desperately to make a mark, to attain great heights of power, virtue or achievement, cannot afford to place great value on stability. The imagery of the ladder, finally, is central to the settling down phase. It reflects the interest in advancement and affirmation so central to this period. By 'ladder', Levinson refers to all dimensions of advancement – increases in social rank, income, power, fame. The ladder has both objective and subjective aspects. It reflects the realities of the external world, but it is also defined by the person in terms of his own meanings and strivings – be they economically, technically, socially or psychologically circumscribed.

The midlife transition (40–45)

At around forty, when a person reaches the top rung of his early adult ladder, he has to reappraise the ladder itself. It is not just a matter of evaluating how well he has done within the current definitions of success and failure. He has to question the basic meanings of success and failure, including the value of the ladder. In reworking the dream, then, he needs to modify the meaning of the ladder, to evaluate his success or failure in more complex terms, and to give more emphasis to the quality of experience, to the intrinsic value of his work and productivity, and their meaning to himself and to others. Interestingly enough a similar shift in emphasis marks the transition from 'differentiated' to the 'integrated' organization.

For the great majority of men, according to Levinson's research into people from all walks of life, the mid-life transition spans a period of great struggle. The individuals he investigated began to question nearly every aspect of their lives, feeling they could not continue as before. Past and future coexist in the present, but the individual suffers from corrosive doubt as to whether they can be joined. During the period from forty to forty-five, then, a man needs to reduce his heavy investment in the external world. To do the work of reappraisal he must turn inward. He has to discover, Levinson says, what his turmoil is about, and where it hurts. Having been overly engaged with worldly struggles, he needs to be more engaged with himself. Hence the recent wave of interest, particularly amongst the maturer business enterprises, in 'corporate culture', that inner manifestation of a corporation's outer being.

Inner mapping

The 'geographical study' is a mapping expedition in a territory often experienced as a desert, with long stretches of sand enlivened by occasional oases. The traveller discovers that some of the perceived water holes are mirages, others real, and that the territory contains far more resources than he has been able to see. Slowly he learns how to look below the surface and to make use of the treasures he finds there ...

Beyond the concern for personal survival, there is a concern for meaning. It is bad enough to feel that my life will soon be over. It is worse to feel that my life has not had – and never will have – sufficient value for myself and for the world.

The wish for immortality plays a powerful part in a man's reappraisal of his life at 40. He often feels that his life until now has been wasted. He has not fulfilled himelf sufficiently and has not contributed enough to the world. What he has been, and what he has produced, are of little consequence. In the remaining years he wants to do more, to be more, to give his life a meaning that will live after his death.

Daniel Levinson *The Seasons of Man's Life*[17] 1979

In this transitional period in mid-life the individual begins, for the first time, to come to grips with his real self. 'It becomes a more active internal figure, someone that the conscious ego must learn to talk with, and listen to'. Man needs to separate himself from his 'striving ego' and the external pressures it brings with it, so that he can better hear 'the voices from within'.

The midlife phase of individuation (45–52)

Every developmental transition presents the opportunity and necessity of moving towards an integration of each of the four sets of polarities – young/old; destruction/creation; masculine/feminine (see Chapter 4); attachment/separateness.

At midlife, however, the demand for integration is particularly strong. The energy and vigor of youthful aspiration needs to be tempered by the durability and perspective of seasoned wisdom. The destructive features of primal cut and thrust need to be counter-balanced by the creative features of organizational development and renewal. The power of 'masculine' analysis and competitiveness needs to be tempered by 'feminine' intuition and cooperation. Attachment to self-centered, material goals needs to be rebalanced, through a growing separation from tangible aspirations, towards a more spiritually oriented search for self-actualization (see p. 447).

Every life structure, Levinson maintains, gives high priority to certain aspects of the self and neglects others. In midlife these neglected aspects seek particularly urgent expression. Internal voices that have been silent for years now clamor to be heard. At times they are heard as a vague whispering, the content unclear, but the tone indicating grief, outrage or guilt. At other times they come through as a thunderous raw, the content all too clear. A person hears the voice of an identity prematurely rejected, of a goal lost sight of or not pursued, of a valued connection given up in acquiescence to authority, of an internal figure who wants to be an academic or an entrepreneur. He must learn to listen to these voices and decide consciously what part he will give them in his life.

In fact, the great developmental task of this era – for an organization, perhaps, as well as for an individual – is not to retire early from wordly responsibilities but to seek a new balance between power and love. It is critically important, Levinson says, both to society and to the individual in middle adulthood, that he accepts the burdens and the pleasure of responsibility, that he learns to exercise authority with more wisdom and compassion, and that he tolerates the guilt and pain that are the price of the self-conscious use of power.

Society in midlife

The rapidly lengthening lifespan in modern society has stimulated widespread concern with the era of late adulthood. We are beginning to seek ways of improving the quality of life for the elderly, and of managing the economic burdens involved. Much less attention has been given to a problem of equal and greater significance: what about the rapidly growing percentage of the population in middle adulthood?

Unless the quality of life in this generation is improved, the middle aged will be under strain and society will continue to be short of creative leadership. We need more people who can contribute as leaders, managers, mentors, sources of traditional wisdom as well as vision and imagination. Modern society requires a vital, developing contingent in middle age.

Daniel Levinson *The Seasons of Man's Life*[18] 1979

In midlife, then, the individual should consciously set out to rebalance the needs of self and society. He can develop greater wisdom if he is less focussed on the acquisition of specific skills, knowledge and rewards, and more focussed on the intrinsic pleasure of work and of having more individualized, loving relationships. While he still enjoys the power and tangible rewards of leadership, in some shape or form, he gains even greater satisfaction from empowering others.

Age fifty transition into maturity – and the legacy phase (52–   )
Daniel Levinson undertook his research into the season of man's life while in his forties. Having not yet entered his own mature years he founded it difficult to enter fully into the evening of man's life. The transition into maturity, from the age of fifty-two to fifty-seven, and what he terms 'the legacy phase', from the age of fifty-eight, are therefore merged together. The imagery of the 'legacy', he maintains, begins to emerge in the mid-life transition. A man's legacy, according to Levinson, is what he passes on to future generations. It includes material possessions, creative products, business enterprises, influences on others. Men, he says, differ enormously in their views about what constitutes a legacy. Although the real value of any such legacy is impossible to measure, in his mind it defines, to a large degree, the ultimate value of his life. In every era, in fact,

a man has the need and the capability to generate a legacy. But it is in the final phase of his life that the task of building one acquires its greatest developmental significance. It can also become his ultimate vision, or source of profound creativity.

> Knowing that his own death is not far off, he is eager to affirm life for himself, and for the generations to come. He wants to be more creative. The creative impulse is not merely to make something. It is to bring something into being, to give birth, to generate life.[19]

Life's seasons in perspective

Levinson's research was exclusive to men rather than women, and to individuals rather than to organizations. Yet, as we shall soon see, the passages in women's lives have a lot in common with man's 'seasons'. Moreover, if we cast our minds back to Chapter 21, we shall find that the developing organization that Lievegoed, Lippitt and Schmidt as well as Greiner described, is in many ways analogous to the developing individual. Birth, youth and maturity (Lippitt and Schmidt) have a lot in common with the novice phase, the settling down phase, and the phase of midlife individuation, respectively. Similar comparisons can be made between pioneering, differentiation and integration (Lievegoed) and the three phases of the individual's lifecycle.

Moreover, with just a touch of imagination, the transitional periods in the individual's life can be applied to similar such transitions in an organization's life. In other words, the transition from adolescence to young adulthood can be readily compared with the act of creating a business. The transition from the novice phase into settling down, with all its accompanying dangers, is very similar to the crossing from entrepreneurism to professional management. Finally, the inward journey heralded by the midlife transition has much in common with the transition from rational management towards a new form of integrated organization.

So organizations, like individuals, need to continually balance and rebalance the four polarities of young/old; destruction/creation; masculine/feminine and attachment/ separation. To the extent that they fail, at each phase of their 'life structure', like individuals, they will form 'inner contradictions that will be reflected in the flaws of the next life (organizational) phase or structure'.[20]

Phases, passages, and pathfinders

Daniel Levinson has been by no means the only researcher into life's phases over the past decade. Probably the best known investigator of life's 'passages'[21] in popular circles has been the American researcher and writer, Gail Sheahy. The Dutch based NPI, to whom I have already referred in Chapter 21, have done similar, individually oriented developmental work, more specifically related to Lievegoed's research into developing organizations.

I shall begin, then, by comparing and contrasting the life phases espoused by Levinson, Sheahy and the NPI. I then want to draw on specific insights that Gail Sheahy has developed into the process of negotiating life's passages, that might be of particular interest to you.

Table 34 Seasons, passages and phases

Age	Levinson's seasons	Sheahy's passages	NPI's phases
		AGE OF EXPLORATION	
18–22	Adolescent/young adult transition	'Pulling up roots': we begin to separate our own individuality from our parents'	'Opening up': freeing ourselves from adult authority, to learn through personal insight
22–28	Novice phase	'Trying twenties': trying on life's uniforms to establish provisional identity	'Seeking out' a variety of challenges to put ourselves on map
		AGE OF CONSOLIDATION	
28–32	Young adult/transition	'Catch thirty': reappraising ourselves with a view to extending our capacities	'Self image': designing and fitting the roles we create for us
32–40	Settling down phase		
		AGE OF RENEWAL	
40–45	Midlife transition	'Midlife crisis': potentially leading to strengthened self and and sense of purpose	'Birth of new self': potentially leads to coming to terms with what we are
45–52	Phase of individuation	'Comeback period': men become more interested in people and environment; women become more assertive	'Age of meaning': a sense of meaning becomes central, together with a desire to share
		AGE OF TRANSFORMATION	
52–58	Midlife/maturity transition	'Freestyle fifties': giving ourselves permission to do what we wish	'Age of compassion': developing a broader sense of vision and compassion
58–65	Legacy phase	'The selective sixties': separating out what is truly important in life from what can fall by the wayside	'Age of review': decide what remains to be done, and what is still worth doing

Comparative phases

In Table 34 I have set out, in brief, Sheahy's and the NPI's lifecycle, grouped according to Levinson's basic schema. As you can see, there is a broad correspondence between each of the approaches.

As we can see, all three sets of researchers come to very similar conclusions. Roughly speaking we can group all their cycles into four main phases, which I have termed 'ages' of exploration, consolidation; renewal and transformation. Interestingly these correspond, roughly speaking, to our four categories of management: primal, rational, developmental and metaphysical.

One can also argue, as indeed Maslow has done, that the mature years are potentially those in which we are best equipped for self-actualization, and that life, up till then, involves a progressive build up through the hierarchy of needs. The one major variance between our respective schema does occur, according to Sheahy, at midlife, when men become more receptive and women more assertive. Each seemingly needs to balance out, but starting from opposite vantage points. It is, in fact, Gail Sheahy who has given most thought to ways in which we might successfully negotiate life's phases.

Negotiating life's phases

Sheahy approaches the subject of actively managing one's self development in two ways. Firstly she identifies a series of attributes which characterize the successful 'pathfinder'. Secondly she compares the process of successfully managing life's transitions to creative activity.

Pathfinding

There are five attributes, according to Sheahy,[22] that the successful pathfinder possesses. These are:

- Capacity for insight.
- Possession of foresight.
- Tolerance of uncertainty.
- Willingness to risk.
- Courage to change.

Pathfinders, firstly, have sufficient insight into themselves, at a particular stage of their lives, to realize that they are undergoing a phase of development. This kind of insight requires a certain sensitivity to needs emerging from within. It also often means discarding roles and behaviors expected from without.

Secondly, pathfinders successfully engaged in their own self-development, have sufficient foresight to avoid going down blind alleys. They can somehow tell which path of development offers the greatest potential for personal growth.

Thirdly, pathfinders are able to tolerate uncertainty in that they allow their lives to move in fits and starts. Development, as we have already seen, is not a smooth and continuous process. Thrusts of energy are often followed by periods of uncertainty and retrenchment. Progress is usually slow, and seldom steady. Pathfinders know and can accept this, even though it makes their lives uncomfortable.

Pathfinders, fourthly, are willing to take 'psychological' risks whereby they are willing to give up personally restrictive practices. In other words, for example, they are willing to change jobs – whereby they temporarily enter a vocational backwater – because of the developmental prospects that arise. A secondment to a new venture, or to a community project, is a typical case in point.

Fifthly, pathfinders engaged in self-development, have the courage to change their closely held beliefs, in the light of new information and experience, and also dare to include others, in their pathfinding, whose values are fundamentally different from their own. Finally, they have the inclination to set out on their own, despite personal or family misgivings, in order to pursue their dream.

Creative self-development

If these are the general attributes of successful pathfinders, what are the particular, and creative steps that they have to take in negotiating a life transition? Sheahy identifies, as shown in Table 35, four such steps, each of which parallel a phase of the creative process.[23]

Anticipation, firstly then, like the gathering of impressions and images, involves preparing to meet a prospective transition rather than becoming lost in everyday detail,

Table 35 Managing personal transition

The creative process	The process of transition
PREPARATION Gathering impressions and images	ANTICIPATION Imagining oneself into the next phase of one's life and work
INCUBATION Letting go of certainties	INCUBATION/SEPARATION Letting go of an outlived identity
ILLUMINATION Leaping into the unknown	EXPANSION Being swept along in a fast current
REVISION Conscious restructuring, and editing of creative material	INCORPORATION Reflection on, and integration of, new aspects of one's life and work

or in vague procrastination. People who are particularly well prepared have:

- Collected the skills they are likely to require.
- Developed a picture, an image of how things will be.
- Couched the picture in positive terms and enthusiastically pursued it.

In the separation and incubation period, secondly, as they painfully let go of old certainties, people give up increasingly destructive aspects of their old selves to form space for newly creative aspects. So an expanded identity replaces the previous and restricted one. Outgrown social roles and 'shoulds', along with old fears and handicapping defences, are re-examined in the light of new possibilities for integrating their personalities in the stage to come.

Thirdly, as they leap into the physical, economic, or psychological unknown, a pathfinder plunges into new territory of one kind or another, often experiencing heightened sensations through this process of expansions. Their senses are thereby enlivened, their insights quicken, and their focus often becomes selective. However, having dared to get their feet wet in a new stream, they may well be swept along in such a fast current of events that they become temporarily out of control.

Finally, after the hurly burly of expansion, there is a dormant period in which they are able to consciously restructure themselves and their world. Through this process of incorporation they reflect on what has changed, and integrate the meaning of these changes into their philosophy of life and work. It is important to allow time for the whole of themselves to absorb and clear, and to allow for their batteries to be recharged.

Transition from employment

In fact it is interesting to compare and contrast this positive and successful approach to life transition with an unmanaged process that two academic observers of people becoming unemployed, in Great Britain, have codified.

In a study undertaken in 1981 Hayes and Nutman[24] observed six discrete phases in the transition out of employment. Unlike Sheahy's pathfinders, their subjects were not prepared for transition in anything like the full sense. The resultant transition path is shown in Fig. 61.

The first phase, in this unanticipated transition, is that of immobilization. The person is

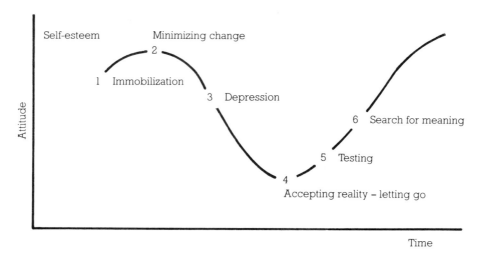

Fig. 61 Transition out of employment.

overwhelmed by his change in status and is unable to reason, plan or understand what is happening. He has no positive image of the future. He is in a state of shock, experienced as a state of numbness, as a detachment from reality.

In the second phase, the individual attempts to minimize change. This is in direct contrast to the pathfinder's willingness to let go of certainties. The unemployed (or demoted or deserted) person attempts to maintain reality as if the offending event had not occurred.

But eventually most people realize that some changes in their way of life will have to be made. At this stage they become depressed. While beginning to face the prospect of change, they neither wish to face it, nor do they know how to deal with it. After an extended period of time, though, the person realizes that he has to accept the changed reality. He begins to let go of his old identity, attitudes and assumptions. Only then does he actively begin to test out his new position in life. He starts to develop a new way of dealing with the present reality, perhaps through voluntary work, or through setting up a little business based at home. At this stage, however, he may still be governed by stereotypes. Some things – like full-time employment – are good, and others – like self employment – are bad. Some things are worth considering, for the long term, and others are definitely not. There is a lack of fluidity.

If the individual is to break through this stereotyping he must be willing to fully let go (separation) of his old identity and to get caught up with the new stream of events (expansion), even risking loss of control. It he does so new possibilities will emerge. The individual may then begin a successful search for new meaning (incorporation) out of which a positive future may prospectively arise, should he engage in the necessary exploration (anticipation).

Conclusion

Personal growth, and individual self-development, each follows a series of somewhat predictable steps, that is if the individual is to grow and develop. Of course for all sorts of reasons, both extenal and internal, he or she may choose not to. The outer environment may be too cushy or too harsh, or the individual's inner constitution may be too weak or too brash.

The growth steps, for Maslow, consisted of a progression, or hierarchy, of prepotent needs to be cumulatively actualized. Once the deficiency needs, at the base of the hierarchy, were fulfilled, then the individual was ready to move on, and to fulfill a succession of growth needs. At the top of the hierarchy lies self-actualization. Maslow's motivational theory has been criticized by 'contingency theorists' who maintain that needs vary according to the person and the situation. Advocates of the lifecycle approach, though, claim that the critical variable is neither personality nor situation but age and developmental stage.

For Levinson, who undertook particularly extensive research into adult life phases, there are a series of four life structures – structure forming, and four life transitions – structure changing, that underpin self-development. Thus for Levinson the dynamics of the human lifecycle are more important than Maslow's hierarchy of need prepotency. In each of his phases, duly interspersed with transitions, the polarities of creation and destruction, youth and age, masculinity and femininity, separation and attachment, need to be newly and appropriately balanced. If the individual is to develop, in his life and work, he will pass through four 'ages' – of exploration, consolidation, individuation, and transformation – each of which needs to contain different resolutions of the above-mentioned polarities.

In order to successfully negotiate these phases, passages, or ages – according to Gail Sheahy – the individual needs to do four things. At each phase such a 'pathfinder' needs to anticipate the future, separate from the past, expand outwards without overdue self-control, and incorporate his or her self into the evolving situation.

Sheahy's 'pathfinder' can be compared with the individual who is unprepared for self-development, in the same way as the 'pathfinding' organization can be compared with the one that has lost its way. The healthily growing organization, like its individual counterpart, needs to anticipate the future, to separate from the past, expand its horizons into the somewhat unknown, and incorporate its developing self into its evolving environment.

Thus the developing process – in individuals, in organizations, as well as in whole societies – has common themes running through it. Each 'grows' or it dies, as George Land (see pp. 408–9) tells us. If we do grow we mature. If we mature we become self-actualized. Maslow, Levinson and Land, like Steiner who we are about to meet again, therefore share common developmental ground. Within that common ground development integrates over time, that is through our lifecycle (Maslow found that most of his self-actualized people had entered their sixties), and across space. It is that process of integration across space, sometimes referred to as 'synergy' to which we now turn. In fact our starting point will be Steiner's economics which are of a much more developmental nature than Adam Smith's.

References

1. F. Noble *The Third Force*, Grossman (1970).
2. B. Lievegoed *Phases*, Steiner Press (1979).
3. W. Shakespeare, *As You Like It*, Oxford University Press (1957).
4. E. Piaget, *The Child and Reality*, Penguin (1976).
5. E. Erikson, *Identity, Youth and Crisis*, W. W. Morton (1968).
6. G. Sheahy, *Passages*, E. P. Sutton (1976).
7. G. Sheahy, *Pathfinders*, Sidgwick & Jackson (1979).
8. A. Maslow, *Motivation and Personality*, Harper & Row (1954), p. 83.
9. A. Maslow, *op. cit.*, p. 91.
10. A. Maslow, *Toward a Psychology of Being*, Van Nostrand (1962), p. 57.
11. A. Maslow, *Eupsychian Management*, Irwin & Dorsey (1965).
12. E. Berne, *The Games People Play*, Grove Press, (1965).
13. D. Levinson, *The Seasons of Man's Life*, Knopf (1979).
14. D. Levinson, *op. cit.*, pp. 319–20.
15. D. Levinson, *op. cit.*, p. 91.
16. D. Levinson, *op. cit.*, p. 139.
17. D. Levinson, *op. cit.*, pp. 216, 251.
18. D. Levinson, *op. cit.*, p. 329.
19. D. Levinson, *op. cit.*, p. 222.
20. D. Levinson, *op. cit.*, p. 197.
21. G. Sheahy, *op. cit.*, (1976).
22. G. Sheahy, *op. cit.*, (1979).
23. G. Wallas, *Creative Techniques in Management*, American Association of Bloodbanks (1985).
24. Hayes and Nutman, *Understanding the Unemployed*, Tavistock (1981).

23 Synergy in business and organization

Contents

Key concepts

Once you have fully understood this chapter you should be able to define the following concepts in your own mind:

Buddhist economics	Heterogeneity
Co-creation	Information society
Craftsmanship	Information utility
Design management	Japanese 'form'
Division of labor	Joint development
Economic association	Joint marketing
Field of forces	Joint ventures
Harmony	Logical incrementalism

Meta-enterprise	Reciprocal order
Organismic society	Self-determining economy
Production sharing	Synergistic economy
Quality	Synergy
Quaternary group	Threefold commonwealth
Reciprocal economics	*Wa*

OEM deal — *Sangyo kyoryko*

Objectives

Upon completing this chapter you should be able to do the following:

1. Compare and contrast the Japanese philosophy of '*wa*' with Mary Parker Follett's 'new psychology'.
2. Ascertain the significance of Rudolph Steiner's associative economics for developmental business strategy.
3. Reveal, in its essence, the art of Japanese management, and relate it to generic design philosophy and application.
4. Outline the major developmental approaches to business strategy.
5. Describe in what way, and to what extent, you are personally able to relate to the different aspects of 'soft' developmental theory.

Introduction

The role of synergy in organization

Individual and social synergy

In Chapter 20, on the roots of development, I introduced you to the term 'synergy'. Such synergy, that is the release of free energy caused by a combining of people or things, can arise over time, or across space. In Chapter 22 we saw how synergy could arise, over time, through a process of evolutionary development. 'At each new union an attractive force is released that seeks out the next evolutionary stage of union' (see p. 414).

In this chapter we shall investigate the incidence of synergy across business and organizational space. In other words, we shall discover the role of cooperation, collaboration, harmony and interdependence in business strategy and organizational behavior. In the process we shall gain more familiarity with the Japanese approach to business and organization. Abraham Maslow, whom we referred to extensively in the last chapter, commented on the close correlation between self-actualized people and synergistic societies. He cited the work of the famous American anthropologist, Ruth Benedict, in which she investigated individual and social synergy.

> Societies where non-aggression is conspicuous have social orders in which the individual, by the same act and at the same time, serves his own advantage and that of the group ... Non-aggression occurs, not because people are unselfish and put social obligations above personal desires, but when social arrangements make these two identical ... Their institutions insure mutual advantage from their undertakings.

Versus:

> In societies which have low social synergy the advantage of one individual becomes a victory over another, and the majority who are not victorious must shift as they can.[1]

Flexible rigidities

Interestingly enough Ronald Dore, a British researcher into Japanese business and organizational practice, comes to a parallel set of conclusions, when comparing classical economics with Japanese economic tradition.

Market morality and social morality

'It is not,' said Adam Smith, 'from the benevolence of the butcher, the brewer, or the baker, that we expect our dinner, but from their regard to their own self-interest.'

The trouble with the Japanese is that they have never really caught up with Adam Smith. They do not believe in the invisible hand. They believe that you cannot get a decent, moral society, not even an efficient society, simply by the mechanisms of the market powered by the motivational fuel of self-interest, however clever, or even divinely inspired, these mechanisms may be.

The morality has got to come from the hearts, the wills, and motives of the individuals in it. The butcher and the brewer have got to be benevolent. They need to have a conscience about the quality of the meat and the beer they supply. They need to care.

Ronald Dore *Flexible Rigidities*[2] 1987

The concept of *wa*

It was only in the 1970s, in fact, that Japanese businessmen and business analysts accepted the idea that there was something unique in their culture which gave them a significant edge over Western nations. It was not until the early 1980s, moreover, that they began to feel at ease in attributing their accomplishments to such traditional concepts as *wa*.

Then, suddenly, *wa* was on the lips of almost every executive who got up before any kind of audience, including his own employees. Here was a concept, sanctified by age, with which he could really get to grips. Boye De Mente, an American who has spent most of his life in Japan, analyzing the Japanese, describes the situation, and the concept, concisely.

Wa

It has been endlessly pointed out since the early eighties that *wa*, the ancient word for peace and harmony, literally means 'circle' and that the secret of Japan's economic success was based on employees and managers functioning in human-oriented circles – instead of the series of horizontal layers favored by Western management. As manager after manager explains, *wa* incorporates mutual trust and unselfish cooperation between management and labor, harmonious relations among employees at all levels and mutual responsibility for results.

Boye De Mente *Japanese Etiquette and Ethics in Business*[3] 1987

As we can see, then, the Japanese in the East have played a significant role in introducing the soft edge of developmental management into organizational life. What part has America, that experimental management laboratory in the West, played, if any?

Harmony in diversity

Whereas the Japanese have tended to focus on social synergy and cultural integration, and the Americans and Europeans on individual energy and self-actualization, the unique Mary Parker Follett – a cross Atlantic character – (see Chapter 5) has managed to combine the two. In fact, for her, self-development and social renewal go hand in hand. As you may recall (see p. 417) this early and innovative management theorist developed a 'new psychology', through which she was 'feeling out for a new conception of modes of association'. For her, both the individual and the organization, are respectively enriched by collaboration. 'Man lives on several planes, and his development depends on uniting them.'

The several planes of existence – primal, rational, developmental and metaphysical – are indeed united in the course of individual, organizational and social evolution.

The surge of life

The surge of life sweeps through the given similarity, the common ground, and breaks it up into a thousand differences. This tumultuous, irresistible flow of life is our existence. The unity, the common, is but for an instant, it flows on to new offerings which adjust themselves anew in more varied, richer syntheses.

That is the process of evolution. Social progress involves coadapting, but coadapting means that the fresh unity becomes the pole of a fresh difference leading again to new unities which lead to broader and broader fields of activity.

Mary Parker Follett *The New State*[4] 1929

As we witness (see pp. 282–3), for example, an OEM deal becoming a joint development, and then a fully fledged joint venture between Honda and Austin Rover, we shall see that evolutionary and synergistic process at work.

Parker Follett, then, is a great synthesizer, who manages to link together the 'hard', evolutionary, and the 'soft', synergistic sides of developmental management. For her, unlike the largely communal ethos of the East, and the largely individual ethos of the West, it is 'the unifying of difference' that represents the highest act of social and commercial co-creation. Heterogeneity, not homogeneity, she says, makes for genuine unity. Through the interpenetration of one person or organization and another, differences are conserved, accentuated and reconciled, in the greater life that is the issue. Out of this activity of interpersonal or institutional 'co-creation' true democracy results.

The business world, she was already arguing in the twenties, will never again be directed by individual intelligences, but by intelligences interacting and ceaselessly influencing one another. There is of course, she says, competition between large firms, but the 'cooperation between them is coming to occupy a larger and larger place, relatively'. For Parker Follett, then, our personal, organizational and business lives consist of manifold relatings. The power of our corporations, she maintained, depended upon their ability to interknit themselves into such 'genuine relations' that a new personality is therefore evolved. That new and composite personality is synergy in Parker Follett guise. The fallacy of self-and-other fades away, and there is only self-in-and-through-others.

Unity, not uniformity, she says, must be our individual and organizational aim. We attain this unity only through variety. Differences must be integrated, not annihilated, nor absorbed. Every difference that is swept up in a bigger commercial or organizational conception feeds and enriches society; every difference which is ignored feeds on society, and eventually corrupts it. Europe 1992, beware!

Fraternity in business

Interestingly enough Parker Follett was not the only social scientist presenting these kinds of synergistic views in the twenties. Another redoubtable exponent of individual and economic association was the Austrian economic philosopher, Rudolph Steiner.

The threefold commonwealth

Steiner, who was also an educator, agronomist, and social reformer, developed the concept of the 'threefold commonwealth'. These three and respectively economic, socio-political and cultural parts of a national whole were not to be united and centralized in some abstract body. Each of the three was to be centralized within itself, and then, through their mutual cooperation, the unity of the overall society could come about.

> It will then be evident that human cooperation in economic life must be based on fraternity which is inherent in associations; in the civil rights system it is necessary to strive for the realization of equality; and in the relatively independent cultural sector of the social organism is is necessary to strive for the realization of the idea of freedom.[5]

Thus Steiner related the guiding principles of the French revolution – fraternité, égalité, liberté – to the social organism. The basis of economic life is, he said, fraternal, which sounds less like Adam Smith and more like *wa*. However, economic fraternity needs to be interwoven with political equality and, unlike the Japanese, blended with individual freedom, in order to maintain a healthy social organism.

Liberty: equality: fraternity

If he is to contribute his share to the wellbeing of the social order in modern society, if he is to add to the welfare of his community by cooperation in the production of values, he must first of all possess individual capacity, talent, ability. In the second place, he must be able to live at peace with his fellow man and to work harmoniously with him

Thirdly, he must find his proper place, from which he can further the interests of the community by his work, by his activity, by his achievements.

Rudolph Steiner *The Threefold Commonwealth*[6] 1945

The economics of association

Interestingly enough, Steiner was a great advocate of the division of labor, but for reasons that were somewhat different from Adam Smith's classical economics, or, for that matter, from Frederick Taylor's scientific management. For Steiner, then, the specialized division of labor meant that it became impossible to work for oneself. All one can do is to work for others and to set others to work for one.

In other words, the division of labor makes for a social organism in which the individual shall live in accordance with the conditions of the whole of the body of the community. 'One can no more work for oneself than one can eat onself!' To that extent the onset of the division of labor represents a progressive step in business and economic evolution. However, economic judgements are best made in association, not in water-tight, hierarchical compartments. 'Economic judgements cannot be built on theory; they must be built on living association where the sensitive judgements of people are real and effective'. Specialization, then, is a means to an associative end and not a separatist end in itself.

Within the economic circuit of goods and services, then, whose flow has been speeded up by the division of labor, associations must be formed to create the flow itself. Specifically, Steiner argues, representatives of different occupations should meet, consumers and producers should come together. The resultant contracts should then be entered into by – and in the spirit of – association, and not purely through legal dictate.

In the economic world, Steiner maintains, everything should rest on contracts, everything should depend on mutual service rendered. Corporations should carry on business with other corporations. An association of efficiency – I shall have to be productive in my own branch of work in order to enter into contracts with other branches – will be formed by means of contract. In the final analysis Rudolph Steiner emerges as an advocate of an economic system which is neither American nor Japanese, neither conventionally capitalist nor socialist, but a unique amalgam.

Economic life

Economic life is striving to structure itself according to its own nature, independent of political institutionalization and mentality. It can only do this if associations, comprised of consumers, distributors and producers, are established according to purely economic criteria. External planning sacrifices the free, creative initiative of the individual, thereby depriving the economy of what such initiative alone can give. At the same time the individuals who labor in industry are caught in a routine, and the formative economic forces are invisible to them.

In the associations each individual would learn what he should through contact with another. Through the participants' insight and experience in relation to their respective activities, and their resulting ability to exercize collective judgement, knowledge of what is economically possible would arise.

Rudolph Steiner *Social Renewal* 1977

Steiner's 'associational economics' sounds less and less like Adam Smith and more and more like whomever Smith's counterpart in Japan might be. In fact there was such a person, a sixteenth century Zen priest by the name of Shosan Suzuki. But before we hear from him (see p. 472), I want to introduce a disciple of Steiner's, a modern German economist by the name of Folkert Wilken.

A self-determining economy

Folkert Wilken, a German economist who died very recently, wrote his seminal work *The Liberation of Capital*. In this book he advocates the formation of a 'need-oriented economy', which he locates at a 'higher level', compared with the two dominant and rival private and state systems. In the private sector, he says, demand is met according to the business logic of each individual company in isolation. This means that a decline in profit and turnover causes redundancies, in both physical and social terms. The state-controlled economies try, in the name of socialism or communism, to overcome these difficulties by nationalizing the entire economy. This imposes on the state the task of determing the amount of production and consumption. Neither of these two examples represents a true 'self-determining economy'.

Such an economy, Wilken argues, does not replace individualism, but it makes it more socially effective. People would still work for personal motives but they would have to collaborate with one another and maintain a common understanding about economic trends. The economy would then be formed on the basis of organic cooperation, in which every individual part reflects, and is in harmony with the whole. The whole exists only to the extent that the individual parts continue to associate with one another, giving to the whole and taking from it; whereas an individual and hierarchical organization is lifeless, like a tree without leaves.

Reciprocal economics

It is reciprocal understanding which forms the guiding social principle for the development of an economic plan and implementing it. The process of reaching this understanding must be continuous, since the economy is in constant movement, with new impetuses continuously taking place in both production and consumption, and old ones dying away. Each achievement of social harmonization represents a point of departure from a new social process.

This dynamic aspect of the economy can only be handled effectively by means of associations. The whole issue is dependent on a particular form of consciousness, and that at a level unattainable by the individual, and reachable only by joint effort. Whereas the social forms of ancient times were religious and impersonal, and based on consanguinity, society can now develop on the basis of wills of individuals who are conscious of their mutual responsibilities, and so form communities based on the spirit of brotherhood.

Folkert Wilken *The Liberation of Capital*[8] 1984

Wilken, like Steiner, saw economic life as essentially fraternal, and capital as a means of freeing human capacities, albeit within an egalitarian social context. Their view of a need-oriented and associatively based economics, was similar to that of the originators of Japanese capitalism. Yet ironically, despite the Japanese economic miracle, the views of Adam Smith, if not those of Karl Marx, continue to eclipse those of Rudolph Steiner and Folkert Wilken in Western Europe and in America

Buddhist economics

It was E. F. Schumacher who first popularized the motion of a 'Buddhist Economics' in the West.[9] Long before Schumacher, though, a Japanese writer, publisher and biblical scholar, by the name of Shichihei Yamamoto, had credited a sixteenth century priest and a seventeenth century clerk-turned-economic philosopher for the development of a Buddhist based capitalism in Japan. The Zen priest was Shoshan Suzuki and the redoubtable clerk was a certain Baigan Ishida.

In his book *The Spirit of Japanese Capitalism*[10] Yamamoto says that Suzuki, whose ideas were further developed by Ishida, preached that businessmen should become like 'living Buddhas'. In other words, they must travel round the country distributing goods as if they were on a pilgrimage. Any businessman who pursues his trade purely to make a profit will inevitably fail. It is only by keeping the needs of the consumers and the nation in the forefront of all thinking, planning and working, that one can succeed.

Ishida's economic philosophy, in fact, drew on Suzuki's ethical base but extended his ideas in a practical and pragmatic vein. Ishida held that social order and progress could be brought into conformity and harmony with the cosmos if people followed the precepts of honesty, self-restraint and order. Ishida taught that the inner heart (the true heart of man) and the natural order (the cosmos) were one and the same.

In summary, and drawing on the social and economic theories of Ruth Benedict, Ronald Dore and Mary Parker Follett, on the one hand, and of Rudolph Steiner, Folkert Wilken and Shoshan Suzuki, on the other, we have a whole underpinning to developmental management that is absent from conventional business and management theory. So developmental managers can combine together notions of synergy, harmony, reciprocity and association to create a new orthodoxy that Japanese business enterprises, rather than European or American ones, have consciously and practically espoused.

I now want to enter into this synergistic and developmental approach in more detail drawing first on organizational and second on business, theory and practice.

Harmonic management and organization

Quality East and West

Quality circles have become the rage in America and in Europe, over the past decade. In most instances, though, companies have failed to capture the quality consciousness that pervades most Japanese business enterprises.

The reason for this failure is patently obvious. We have adopted a Western approach to an Eastern phenomenon. While statistically based quality control was invented in America, and had been successfully adapted by the Japanese, quality consciousness on a large scale, at least in business, was invented in Japan, and needs to be adapted by the rest of us around the world.

The key to such successful application is a broader appreciation of the concept of design than the one which we have hitherto adopted in most European and American companies. Such a concept would need to embrace both physical and social aspects of design, within an integrated organizational context. Ultimately we should then be able to link up with notions of 'strategic design' via the same kind of developmental thoughts, feelings and actions.

The management of design

The design dimension
In 1986, Chris Lorenz, management editor of the UK's *Financial Times*, published *The Design Dimension*. At the time design was re-emerging as a force to be reckoned with in business, in Britain.

The power of design

In the arcane, but descriptive, language of behavioural science, industrial designers who are given pivotal rôles display a combination of several skills which are generally considered necessary to the success of any management team. At one and the same time they seem to be acting, alone or in conjunction with the official project leader, not only as an invaluable source of ideas, but as facilitator, coordinator, evaluator and completer.

This is a far cry from the stereotype of the 'designer as stylist', and much closer to the all round role of coordination and integration which, in many countries, an architect plays in the building process.

Underpinning the ability of many designers to play a full part in the development team, and the potential of some to become even the team's coordinator, is a set of unusual personal attributes and skills. Some are inborn, others are learned. They include imagination; the ability to visualize shapes and the relationship between objects in three dimensions; creativity, a natural unwillingness to accept conventional solutions; the ability to communicate in words as well as sketches and, finally, the ability to synthesize all sorts of multidisciplinary factors and influences into a coherent whole.

Chris Lorenz *The Design Dimension*[11] 1986

Design management
The design dimension to which Lorenz alludes is being increasingly incorporated into what is called 'design management'. Unfortunately, however, the developmental aspects of design, including the capacity to synthesize and to harmonize, are all too often left to the designer, while the design manager continues to work along conventional rational lines. To the extent that there is to be any 'cultural cross-fertilization' between design and management, then we should see the kind of outlook developing that is described in Watts and Hayes' *Corporate Revolution*. These two British design managers have a particular interest in corporate image.

Corporate image and design management

Few companies have a truly sophisticated design management system in which each product and brand relates to the other and the whole projects a coherent idea of the corporation.

Despite what stockbrokers and bankers would have us believe, success cannot be measured in terms of quantifiable phenomena, such as bottom line alone, but in terms of management philosophy, style and context. Qualitative data are as important as quantitative. Dealing solely in money is distorting.

We cannot stress enough, therefore, the importance of developing an overall corporate identity as an umbrella for programmes directed at specific audiences. That provides the philosophical theme running through all the promotional programmes anywhere in the company.

Reginald Watts *Corporate Revolution*[12] 1986

Hayes and Watts go some of the way towards integrating industrial and organizational design under a developmental umbrella. However, they do not go far enough. Design management in Europe and America, with the possible exception of Italy, is still a fringe activity in most firms. In Japan, because of the more widely spread appreciation for harmony, it can be different.

The Japanese appreciation of form

Lorenz's and Watts' and Hayes' European approach can be compared and contrasted with that of two Japanese authorities on the same subject.

Ken Takaoka, director of Japan's prestigious Modern Human Science Institute, describes the Japanese approach to business as a matrix of nature, culture and modern technology. A systems and aeronautical engineer, Takaoka says that a deeply spiritual orientation, combined with a highly refined sense of form, has conditioned the Japanese to approach their work with care and precision.

Kenji Ekuan, president of the GK Industrial Design Research Institute, has been quoted as saying that centuries of practicing the arts of swordsmanship, calligraphy, judo, flower arranging, and the tea ceremony, led the Japanese to develop a keen 'sense of how things ought to be, of proper processes and conclusions . . . to judge proportion with a trained intuition, to reach beyond the arrangement of particulars to a holistic order'.[12]

As can be seen, this attachment to form, to taste, and to style characterizes the design of Japanese social and organizational arrangements as much as that of their physical artifacts. The Japanese, seemingly, can move more fluidly between the two than the Europeans. However, there is another way of reaching that design sensitivity within ourselves, outside of Japan, at least in the eyes of Robert Pirsig.

The pursuit of craftsmanship

A longstanding tradition of craftsmanship exists in all countries, around the world, both developed and developing. An American social philosopher, Pirsig, wrote an amazing book in the mid-seventies entitled *Zen and the Art of Motorcycle Maintenance*. The book in fact became a bestseller with Pirsig skillfully blending philosophy and narrative.

The central theme of Pirsig's book is, in effect, quality. Tangible and externalized achievement, he says, represents quality discovered in the outer direction only. Such a 'mountain of achievement' becomes relatively meaningless, as well as often unobtainable, unless taken together with 'the ocean trenches of self-awareness'.

This self-awareness arises from peace of mind, which is in its turn the key to quality's inner direction. Notice again how the emphasis shifts from the restless pursuit of gain to the restful attainment of quality. Pirsig then describes this quality in the work of the craftsman, which might be likened to that of the successful Japanese 'manager'.

Quality craftsmanship

Craftsmen have patience, care, and attentiveness to what they are doing. But more than this, there's an inner peace of mind which isn't contrived but results from a kind of harmony with the work, in which there is no leader and follower. The material and the craftsman's thoughts change together in a progression of smooth, even changes, until his mind is at rest at the

exact instant that the material is right.
Robert Pirsig *Zen and the Art of Motorcycle Maintenance*[13] 1976

Quality, or its absence, does not reside in either the subject, that is the person, or in the object, that is the product. It lies in the relationship between the two. When there is genuine caring by the producer for the product, quality results. Such caring is born out of the kind of immersion that not only the craftsman has in his artifact but also the developmental manager can have in his or her activity.

There is no such thing, for example, as ugly technology or an ugly product per se. The real ugliness lies in the relationship between the people who produce and the things they produce. The ugliness similarly lies in the relationship between the people who use the technology or product, and the thing that they use. The Japanese pursuit of perfection and the quality of the products they are now manufacturing need to be understood in that light.

The design of organizational meaning

Linking person and product

There is a direct analogy between the caring relationship that exists, between ourselves and our artifacts, and the context and role that organizations play in our lives. This is a key point that Pascale and Athos made in their splendid book on *The Art of Japanese Management*.

Making meaning

By an accident of history, we in the West have evolved a culture that separates man's spiritual life from his institutional life. Our companies freely lay claim to mind and muscle but they are culturally discouraged from intruding on our personal lives and deeper beliefs.

Splitting man into separate 'personal' and 'productive' beings makes somewhat artificial parts of what is the whole of his character. When we do so, our cultural heritage not only too strictly enforces this artificial dichotomy, but deprives us of two rather important ingredients for employee commitment.

First, companies are denied access to higher order human values, which are among the best known mechanisms for reconciling one's inner life with one's working life. Second, the firm itself is denied a meaning-making role in society, and thus puts excessive attention on instrumental values such as profit, market share, and technological innovation.
Pascale and Athos *The Art of Japanese Management*[14] 1981

Of course it is no accident of history that spiritual and material values have been split apart in the West. Indeed it has served to advance the cause of individualism. It is only that now we are beginning to realize the costs. Secularly based individualism detracts from the making of shared meaning.

Pirsig particularly laments the way that technology has become removed from matters of the spirit and heart. The solution that Pascale and Athos propose is 'a non-deified, non-religious spirituality that enables a firm's superordinate goals to respond truly to the inner meanings that many people seek in their work'.

Interestingly enough that kind of solution is exactly opposite to the Zen belief in the holiness of the simplest of tasks. There is no need for the individual to respond to superordinate goals when he is engaged in the quality of relationship and craftsmanship that Pirsig describes. In fact, the great American automobile designer in the forties, Walter Teague, makes a similar point from a purely design perspective.

Garage or temple?

The function of a thing may be trivial or magnificent; it may serve a very humble or a very exalted end. The potentialities of beauty in a thing are in direct proportion to the importance or the wonder, or the worthiness of the end it serves.

But we are influenced by the degree of success with which a function is performed. Complete adaptation to a humble station in life, perfect fulfillment of a modest destiny, may be far more admirable than meretricious performance in a more exalted role.

Walter Teague 'In good shape'[15] 1979

In the same way as a designer such as Teague has captured the shape and meaning of good design, Pascale and Athos have succeeded in capturing the nuance and subtlety, that is the art or style, of Japanese developmental 'management'. However, the so-called soft s's (see p. 113 above) that they came up with – staff, skills, style and shared values – fail to do justice to the intricate patterns of thought, feeling and behavior that the two Americans so astutely observed. For me the most important such stylistic feature is that of pattern formation.

Pattern formation

Human nature may be universal but the lens through which we view and experience things is not. The Japanese perceive the drawing of lines between 'self' and 'other' as arbitrary. While the American and European cultures emphasize individuality and separateness their culture emphasizes group interaction and togetherness.

Classically, a Japanese does not see his world in terms of separate categories, but as concentric rings of relationship from the most intimate to the most remote. Those within the innermost circle are free to lay claim to the individual's or to the corporation's energies and psychic resources. Those without are not.

Japanese businessmen, therefore, pursue self-interest in the name and spirit of the collective interest. In doing so it is harmony rather than conformity which is the guiding principle. Division and subdivision of tasks, and the spelling out of organizational principles and practices will never accomplish the job that experiencing, watching, feeling, sensing and intuiting will. It is the form and harmony amongst people and things that counts, or, if you like, the aesthetic fit.

Being in tune

In management, as in music, there is a bass clef as well as treble. The treble generally carries the melody in music, and the melody's equivalent in Japan is the manager's style.

A Manager's style – the way he focusses his attention, and interacts with people – sets the 'tune' for subordinates, and communicates at the operational level what his expectations are and how he wants business conducted. Beneath these messages is a deeper rhythm that communicates more fundamentally. In Japanese organizations a great deal of attention is devoted to ensuring the continuity of these bass clef messages.

Pascale and Athos *The Art of Japanese Management*[16] 1981

A business is only in tune if both the manager's style and the organization's purpose are in harmony. As in music, harmony does not call for imitation but for syncopation. Such concepts as harmony and syncopation, as you may gather, are more familiar to the musician or architect in Europe or America, than to the manager.

Design in developmental perspective

The pursuit of quality is universal, but has received particularly strong emphasis, of late, in business and management circles. The success of the Japanese quality circle programs has undoubtedly spurred the Americans and Europeans on. However, all too many primal and rational managers have missed the developmental boat. For primal managers the apparent answer lies in a tangible closeness to the customer, and in a physical involvement with product quality. For rational management quality control is a matter of human participation and statistical quality control. Both miss out on the brand of craftsmanship, to which Pirsig alludes, and on the sensitivity towards both form and substance, that the Japanese designer, Kenji Ekuan declares to be part of a long-standing cultural tradition.

For quality goes together with subtlety and harmony, peace of mind and interdependence of spirit. These are not the kind of qualities that come easily to your average Western business manager, though the emerging design professional has easier access to such attributes. The challenge such designers now face is to round out, thereby becoming adept at social and commercial as well as physical pattern formation.

It is to such commercial 'pattern formation' that we now turn, linking the designer's aesthetic sensitivities to the developmental requirements of strategy formation. In the process we shall also be drawing on Rudolph Steiner's associative economics and Albert Low's notion (see p. 359), of a company as a 'field'.

Synergistic business strategy

Albert Low is the practicing Canadian manager who wrote that very fine, if somewhat obtuse book, *Zen and Creative Management*,[17] to which we referred in Chapter 0. As you may recall, Low is unique, in the business and management literature, to the extent that he focusses on a company as a set of interacting forces. I want to remind you of his basic theory, at this point, because of its synergistic relevance to business.

The company as a field

A set of interacting forces

A company, according to Low, is not a personalized enterprise or a depersonalized organization but a multidimensional system capable of growth, expansion and self-regulation. As a system it is a set of interacting forces. As a set of interacting forces a business consists of independent, but mutually related elements. From a Zen point of view there are no 'things', no enduring entities. Rather the thing or the company is seen to be a field of interacting causes and effects.

This view of the world as a field stands in contrast to the more familiar and dualistic view of things. In America and Europe we have tended to view organizations in terms of management and workforce, business and environment, product and market. That is not the Eastern way.

Field theory is the Western counterpart to the Buddhist philosophy of Karma. Under this philosophy not only is the world made up of a multiplicity of interacting causes and effects, but also the resulting field is in a state of dynamic tension. This dynamic is created by the simultaneous opposition and mutuality of the component forces. Let me explore, with Low, the business implications of reciprocal relationships.

Reciprocal order

The three 'commitments' of the shareholder, market, and employee can be looked upon as the forces that make up the field of the company (see Fig. 62). Out of this field, or behavior space, arises the product. It is from this product, or service, that a return can be provided to the shareholder, employee and customer for the commitment each makes.

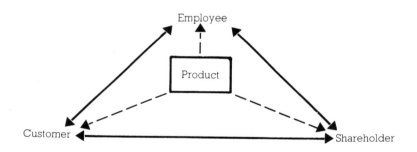

Fig. 62 The company as a 'field'.

The notion of a field here is a very important one. It allows for a qualitative understanding of business, based on the notions of fitness, order, harmony, emergence and balance. Let us see, then, where all this leads.

The interaction of the three forces gives rise to a system, a set of independent but mutually related entities. The shareholder, the employee, and the customer are each both and independent and interdependent. They exist as independent elements of a single, unified corporate will and purpose. A business is therefore a whole, a unity; but it is a composite and multidimensional whole, being the interaction of three forces. The dynamic tension within the business' force field is created by the simultaneous push and pull. The outward tendency (the push) has its origins in the need that each party has to improve its financial position in opposition to the other. The inward, or centering tendency (the pull), is realized in the product. Each of the three forces collaborates to produce it.

Beyond the basic triad

Albert Low stops short at the basic triad of customer–employee–shareholder, incorporating their reciprocal interactions. Perhaps because he was writing in the seventies he had not yet become aware of the extension of this triad, beyond the bounds of an individual business enterprise. Ironically enough it has been another business analyst, who has been able to cross the East–West conceptual divide, who has taken the next, synergistic step.

What Kaimichi Ohmae has done in his book *Triad Power* is to extend the boundaries of the individual business across the global 'businessphere'. His triad is not the three business stakeholders, but the three-quarters of the globe – North (Europe), West (America), and East (Japan and the Pacific rim). Ohmae's field of interacting business forces thus extends far wider than Low's. Let me now review the synergistic approaches to business strategy, ultimately resulting in Ohmae's global reach!

Developmental strategy

Logical incrementalism

Harmony, interdependence and reciprocal order are unfamiliar terms within conventional business strategy. Neither Ansoff nor Steiner, the strategic gurus of yesteryear; and neither Porter nor Kotler, the strategic gurus of today (see Chapter 17), would be particularly familiar with them. After all, for them, it is 'competitive' rather than collaborative strategy that characterizes business enterprise.

Interestingly enough, though, and before we focus on strategic collaboration externally, in particular, it is worth noting James Quinn's views on 'strategies for change'. For Professor Quinn is one of the most prominent of a new wave of strategic thinkers in America, who focus on what is termed 'logical incrementalism'. Such incrementalism, falling half-way between rational and developmental management, focusses on interdependent strategy formulation, internally.

Fermentative strategy

The total strategic process is anything but linear. Integrating all the subsystem strategies is a groping, cyclical process that often circles back on itself, encountering interruptions and delays, and rarely arrives at clear-cut decisions at any one time.

The strategy's ultimate development involves a series of nested, partial decisions (in each subsystem) interacting with other partial decisions, like fermentation in biochemistry, rather than an industrial assembly line ...

A somewhat common series of management processes seems required for most major strategic changes. Most important amongst these are sensing needs, amplifying understanding, building awareness, creating credibility, legitimizing viewpoints, generating partial solutions, broadening support, structuring needed flexibilities, putting forward trial concepts, creating pockets of commitment, crystallizing focus, managing coalitions and, finally, agreed upon commitments.

James Quinn *Strategies for Change: Logical Incrementation*[18] 1980

Quinn's observations of strategy formulation in major American and European companies, at least from an internal perspective, yields more in the way of concentric rings rather than linear thrusts. In Japan, however – according to Ronald Dore – this non-linear approach characterizes both external and internal business and social relationships.

Flexible rigidities

Ronald Dore, the British analyst of Japanese business alludes to their complex, and interlinked pattern of business organization as 'meta-enterprise'. He also considers Japanese business strategies to be 'flexibly rigid'.

Enterprises combine strategically together, Dore maintains, in three ways. There are, first, groups of firms, made up of a major firm and its satellites. These are possibly tied by capital ownership and by the strategic 'posting' of the major firm's staff to the satellite 'colonies', but at least by long standing relationships – contacts for the purchase of parts or intermediaries, exclusive dealerships, and so on. All the major firms like Hitachi, Toyota, Kubota, have such *keiretsu* – such satellite clusters.

Secondly, there are the groups of firms of relatively equal status, usually including a major bank as an important component, who maintain continuous liaison over such matters as corporate strategy, and give each other marginal preferences in interfirm transactions.

The third form of linkage is the industrial associations. These play an important part in joint R & D projects. The effectiveness of the associations results from a strong sense, evidently shared by the top managers of the membership, in the 'industry', as a community, within a larger community, that is Japanese industry as a whole. Here we have echoes of Rudolph Steiner.

Industrial association

The general propensity to prefer cooperation to competition, when it can be clearly shown to be in one's long term interest, often gives industrial associations considerable power to constrain individual firms in the interests of the industry as a whole. This makes them ideal interlocuters for MITI [Ministry in Trade and Industry] officials' attempt to impose direction on particular industries ...

When MITI established a new biotechnology section in 1982, its first task was to be midwife to a new association. The relevant technical expertise was scattered – firms in the food industry, pharmaceuticals, fibre making, petrochemicals, brewing, all had their own 'home' industry. No forum had until then existed to bring them all together.

Ronald Dore *Flexible Rigidities*[19] 1987

Whereas Dore likens collaboration, in Japanese business, to 'flexible rigidity' and James Quinn associates 'logical incrementalism' with such a straight approach, Louis Turner has a yet another view.

Industrial collaboration

Turner, of the Royal Institute of Affairs in the UK, led an extensive international investigation into collaboration between Japanese and non-Japanese firms in the 1980s. His overall conclusion was that an industrial policy cannot work nowadays unless it creates companies capable of competing globally. This will almost certainly involve, he says, creating links with companies from all over the world, 'the exact pattern of linkages depending on the precise combination of technological, marketing and geographical strengths that each company can bring to the collaboration'.

With a view to such collaboration, Turner maintains that not only do the Japanese have a broader concept of association than we do in the North and West, but also they distinguish their particular and collaborative approach to multinational enterprise from the more old-fashioned and competitive, European and American one.

Sangyo kyoryoku

The Japanese use the words *sangyo kyoryoku* which have a much wider meaning than what the Westerners understand by collaboration. The Japanese words convey the ideas of common action and collaboration, but also a sense of 'cooperation' whereby economic activities in two countries are linked together. In this latter sense, the Japanese do not just envisage intergovernmental agreements, but also 100 percent foreign controlled direct investment.

Westerners would not tend to count such investment as true collaboration, because it lacks the symmetry of partnership which is inherent in the Western world. On the other hand, the Japanese believe that direct investment involves elements from the two economies working together and thus counts as a form of collaboration. In particular, the Japanese see collaboration as an integral part of international industrial adjustment. In the words of a recent statement from a high level study group on Japanese direct foreign investment:

'Industrial cooperation through direct foreign investment contributes to increased employment, production and exports, to the vitalization of regional economies, and to the efficient use of resources. It is hoped that a horizontal international division of labor between Japan and other developed countries will develop from industrial cooperation, benefiting both partners'.

Louis Turner *Industrial Collaboration with Japan*[20] 1987

There is a range of collaborative strategies between firms, then, some of which are wider in scope than others. I shall start with the more modest associations before moving on to the more ambitious ones.

Technical assistance and licensing.
A company with a distinctive product gives another one the right to produce it for a fee. These licensing arrangements have existed for a long time. Joint marketing, however, is a more recent phenomenon.

Joint marketing
There can be agreements between companies to sell jointly in specific markets where, for some reason, neither company feels strong enough to go it alone. AT & T, in America, has in recent years entered into several agreements with Olivetti in Italy, involving cross marketing of their respective, electronically based products in Europe and America. Joint marketing, in its turn, is generally less wide-ranging in collaborative scope than production sharing.

Production sharing

It was Drucker who first referred to 'production sharing', in the late seventies, as a vehicle for transnational integration. 'In production sharing', he says, 'the resources of the developing countries – their abundant labor for traditional jobs – are brought together with the resources of the developed countries – their management, their technology, their educated people, their markets and purchasing power'. He then cites several examples of this. The electronic calculator is one.

Production sharing

The hand held electronic calculator may carry the nameplate of a Japanese company, but that may be the only part of it that is 'made in Japan'. The electronic chips probably come from Texas or from Silicon Valley. They may have been assembled in Singapore, in Indonesia, or perhaps in Nigeria. The casing may be the product of an Indian steel mill and of course the final product will be sold all over the world. The design, the quality control and the marketing will have been done in a highly developed country, Japan, and the labour intensive work in developing countries. Whereas the former has expertise readily on tap the latter have surplus labour on hand.

There is more to production sharing than comparative costs alone yet there is no acknowledged theory to explain this new pattern of international trading: 'We are about to enter the stage of integrated trade, for this is what production sharing means. Yet economists, theoreticians, and policy makers are totally unprepared for the challenge'.

Peter Drucker *Management in Turbulent Times*[21] 1979

Drucker claims that the multinational of tomorrow will need to be organized quite differently from its predecessor. It will be organized around two focal points, technology (or design) and marketing. Instead of being a multinational corporation, he says, it will have to become a transnational confederation. The local subsidiary 'will not be a business as it has traditionally been, one that produces and markets the full range of the company's products, but only in its own country. The products it makes will be sold all over the world'.

Tomorrow, Drucker says, the developing countries will matter to the multinationals as they have not mattered before. They will provide the manufacturing work. The parent company should thus become increasingly dependent on them. Top management will lead an orchestra rather than an army.

Production sharing, Drucker tells us, makes high demands on design, quality control and marketing, and even higher ones on the management skills of planning, organizing, integrating and coordinating. So production sharing lies half-way between rational and developmental management. There is evidence of interdependence and a need for mutual trust, but conventional management skills are still most strongly emphasized. OEM deals, joint developments, and, above all, joint ventures and consortia involve thorough going, synergistic strategies. A good example of such, as we shall see, is the strategic association between Honda and Austin-Rover.

Original equipment manufacturing (OEM) deals

Further along the collaborative spectrum is the OEM phenomenon, whereby a company manufactures a product, based (possibly including a minor variation), by specific agreement, on another company's original equipment.

Joint development

A fairly passive OEM deal will usually evolve imperceptibly into a more active relationship whereby companies work together to develop some part of a new product. A good example is that between Honda and Austin-Rover.

A joint automobile development

Austin-Rover's involvement with Honda resulted from an approach by the UK company. Austin-Rover, at the time, needed to turn its fortunes round rapidly. Its overstretched management could not develop the complete range of models which the company badly needed, without outside help. Collaboration was called for.

The initial deal was an 'OEM' one. The Austin-Rover Group licensed a Honda model, the Ballade, for assembly as the Acclaim in the United Kingdom on a knockdown basis (i.e. the bulk of the components were imported from Japan). Honda earned a license fee, and also earned income from the provision of major components, such as engines and gearboxes.

The limited collaboration between the two companies grew with the joint development of the 'XX' luxury car range, which was eventually known as the Legend range by Honda, and as the Rover 800 by Austin Rover. This 2,000cc and 2,500cc range was developed by the engineers of both companies, and the work was shared as equally as possible to draw on the respective strengths of the two design teams. The Honda designers were considered to be stronger in electronics and engines, while the UK team was judged to be good at interior and chassis design, and at suspension systems.

The two companies are committed to further cooperation in the form of the 'YY' project ...

Louis Turner *Industrial Collaboration with Japan*[22] 1987

Whereas a joint development is product specific, joint ventures, and consortia, are more wide-ranging in scope.

Joint venture and consortia

In his recent book *Triad Power*,[23] Ohmae makes two key points, one spurred on by competitive advantage, and the other by the need for cooperation. His first point is that major companies in America, Europe and Japan (the triad) have all now to plan and implement their strategies globally. Nothing else will do. This is the new economic imperative for any large company that wants to remain competitive. Ironically, in order to compete, companies need to cooperate. Ohmae's reasoning is not founded, like Drucker's, on the comparative availability of labor on the one hand and on comparative management and design expertise on the other, but is centered upon today's technology.

As the development and commercialization of new technological breakthroughs become increasingly costly, he argues, there is a threefold movement towards integration and cross-fertilization.

The need for integration arises first downstream, to control interfaces with the customer; second, upstream, to acquire new technologies; and third horizontally, to share complementary technologies prior to market exploitation.

Ohmae then cites the example of the IBM personal computer. The interface with the customer is controlled not directly by IBM but through a group of third-party companies, such as the consumer retail experts of Sears Roebuck. IBM moved upstream, to acquire new technologies, by adopting Intel processors that originate from Hitachi; finally, by linking up with an Epson printer IBM shared the exploitation of the small business market with a competitor. How odd it is, Ohmae goes on to say, that the general public holds on to the perception of Detroit fighting against Japan. For never before have the respective national car makers been so close to one another.

GM, as the biggest of the Detroit three, in 1985 boosted its equity in Isuzu of Japan to 34 per cent. It also has a 5 per cent share in Suzuki motors, from which it is gleaning minicar technology and for which it serves as a marketing arm in the States. That is the way companies now cooperate and mutually benefit as a result. 'The current consortia and joint ventures encourage dynamic competition; mergers tend to choke it'.

Economic integration

Industrial collaboration is by no means confined to America and Japan. In Western Europe, over the past five years, a transformation in economic relationships has been taking place. Both commerce and technology have become too complex for single companies and homogeneous cultures to handle. While Silicon Valley is populated by Europeans, Chinese, Indians and Americans, Europe is populated by Latins, Anglo Saxons, Teutonics among others. As one of the leading influences behind the European Eureka project, Yves Stourdze, has said: 'Europe's technological renaissance requires the coming together of different intellectual backgrounds, nationalities and cultures'.

Developmental business strategy in perspective

Whereas primal strategies, like Porter's and Kotler's focus on competitive thrust, and rational ones, like Steiner's and Ansoff's, are oriented towards the fulfillment of objectives, developmental strategies are geared towards harmony, reciprocity, and mutual benefit. That is not to say that aggressive thrust and thoughtful analysis are precluded. It is rather the case that they become secondary, while synergistic collaboration becomes primary. Harmony in diversity takes over from directness of thrust, or from unity of objective.

At the same time, and as a direct result, developmental strategies are seldom restricted to single departments or even companies. In pursuit of natural association they inevitably spill over individual divisions, businesses, and countries, while – in the best cases – retaining the individual diversity within the newly formed whole. In due time, perhaps, the demise of the sovereign company will follow the demise of the nation state, as multicompany enterprises take over from the unitary, multinational business.

While such an eventually might appear far-fetched, for the time being, the need for collaboration, association and interdependence within the business organization is becoming more evident. Again it is the Japanese, and their followers, who have played a dominant part in shifting our orientation in this developmental direction. On an even broader, societal level, Yonedi Masuda, the Japanese futurist, has again taken a lead.

Towards the synergistic economy

Industrial versus post-industrial society

In 1981 Yonedi Masuda, on behalf of Japan's Computer Usage Development Institute, published a 'Plan for the Information Society – a national goal towards the year 2000'. The plan was entitled *The Information Society as Post-industrial Society*. In it he compared and contrasted industrial- and information-based societies in the most intriguing ways.

Comparative goals

Masuda begins by comparing and contrasting the goals of the two forms of society: if the goal of industrial society, he says, is represented by volume consumption of durable goods, or by the realization of heavy mass consumption centering around motorization, the information society will be centered upon highly intellectual creativity where people may draw future designs on an invisible canvas and pursue and realize individual lives worth living.

Comparative symbols

Masuda arrived at his futuristic conclusion on the basis of both technological and historical insight. He is particularly adept at combining his technological rationality with a developmental outlook, comparing and contrasting industrial symbols past and future: In industrial society, the modern factory, consisting of machines and equipment, became the societal symbol, and was the production center for goods. In the information society the information utility (a computer-based public infrastructure) consisting of information networks and data banks, will replace the factory as the societal symbol and become the production and distribution center for information and goods.

Comparative industries

Masuda goes on to investigate the 'quaternary' industries which he considers to be replacing the primary (extractive), secondary (manufacturing) and even tertiary (non-information-based services) industries: In industrial societies, the leading industries in economic development are machinery and chemicals, and the total economic structure comprises primary, secondary and tertiary industries. In the information society the leading industries will be intellectually based, the core of which will be the knowledge industries. Information-related industries will be newly added as the quaternary group to the industrial structure of primary, secondary and tertiary.

Quaternary industries

Quaternary industries can be divided broadly into four main industrial groups.

The first information industries will produce, process and service cognitive information, or produce and sell related equipment. The second knowledge industries will be of two types, that is to say education industries and research and development. The third, arts industries, are particularly important in that in an information society individual and creative activity will flourish.

The fourth and final group of ethical industries will become growth industries in that human life will be elevated through the renewed belief in the existence and strength of humanity. In the information society, on the one hand, each person will attach more importance to scientific thought, and, on the other, will be humble before an absolute existence that transcends human abilities.

Yonedi Masuda *The Information Society, as Post Industrial Society*[24] 1981

These quaternary industries are analyzed by Masuda, in more detail in Table 36.

Table 36 Industries of the future

Group	Industries	Industrial participants
Information	Privately operated information industries	Investigators, forecasters, freelance writers, public opinion surveyors
	Printing and publishing industries	Printing plate making, book-binding, publishing, photocopying
	News and advertising industries	Papers, magazines, advertising, new agencies
	Information processing and service industries	Computer centers, data banks, software houses, timeshare services
	Information machinery industries	Printing presses, computers, terminal equipment, typewriters, photocopiers
Knowledge	Privately operated knowledge industries	Lawyers, accountants, consultants, surveyors, designers
	Research and development industries	Think tanks, research institutes, engineering and development companies
	Education industries	Schools, colleges, universities, distance learning, conferences, training courses, libraries
	Knowledge equipment industries	Electronic calculators, personal computers, computer aided instruction and teaching materials
Arts	Privately operated 'affective' information industries	Novelists, composers, singers, painters, photographers, agents, promoters
	'Affective' information service industries	Theatre groups, orchestras, film producers, TV companies, recording companies, cinemas, arts complexes
	'Affective' information equipment industries	Photographic equipment, musical instruments, filming and recording equipment, television and video
Ethics	Privately operated ethics 'industries'	Philosophers, religious leaders, prophets
	Religious 'industries'	Religious groups, churches, shrines, mosques, synagogues
	Spiritual training 'industries'	Spiritual training centers, volunteer service groups, fencing, calligraphy, astrology, Zen

Although we might quarrel with the use of the term 'industries' in the artistic and ethical context Masuda's overall quaternary thrust is nevertheless a revealingly synergistic and developmental one.

Comparative structures

Masuda goes on to deal with two aspects which are of particular relevance to developmental management, that is, synergistic structure and global spirit. He starts with structure: the economic structure of industrial society is characterized by a sales-oriented, commodity economy; specialization of production, utilizing divisions of labor; and by a complete division of production and consumption between enterprise and household.

In the information society, information, the axis of socio-economic development, will be produced by the information utility; self-production of information by users will increase; information will accumulate and expand through synergetic production and shared utilization; and the economy will change structurally from an exchange economy to a synergistic one.

Masuda's last two points, relating to synergistic production and utilization, on the one hand, and to a wholly synergistic economy, on the other, are particularly significant for us. In other words, intimate and interdependently based sharing, cross-fertilization, collaboration and association will replace arms-length and independently based business negotiations, commercial trading or watertight divisions of economic labor. A good example of this synergistic movement is provided by the semiconductor industry in America, in the latter part of the eighties.

Independence–interdependence

Until four or five years ago, hardly anyone would have questioned the organization of the American semiconductor industry. The independent silicon chip manufacturers were regarded as one of the marvels of the electronic age, exemplifying all that was best in the buccaneering American entrepreneurial tradition.

Changes in technology, however, have begun to prompt increasing doubts about the viability of the independently-based producer.

Product lifecycles have shortened radically. In their relationships with their customers, the producers are therefore having to form much closer ties. 'If we are going to develop a piece of technology of the complexity we are now dealing with, we have to understand exactly what our customers want', says Pat Brockett, Managing Director of National Semiconductor's European semiconductor division.

Such partnerships, or strategic alliances with customers, Brockett goes on to emphasize, should help companies to develop products faster; they ought also to enable customers to secure greater reliability and quality; most of all they will allow chip designers to get closer to systems designers.

Terry Dodsworth 'Why the speed of technology is chipping away at the independents'[25] 1987

Comparative spirit

Finally, then, Masuda compares and contrasts the 'spirit' that pervades an industrialized as compared with an information-based society (see Fig. 63)[26]. The spirit of the industrial society is drawn from the Renaissance spirit of human liberation, which involves, ethically speaking, respect for fundamental human rights and emphasis on the dignity of the individual. In other words, the spirit that infused 'the age of reason', and gave birth, simultaneously, to scientific inquiry and to freedom of personal thought and action, underpinned the industrial revolution in Great Britain.

HIGH MASS CONSUMPTION SOCIETY/HIGH WELFARE SOCIETY

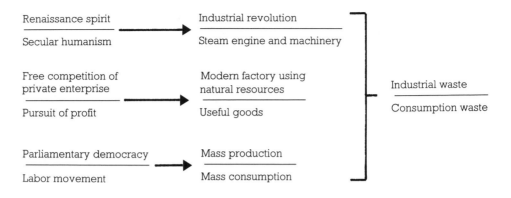

Fig. 63 Industrial society.

The spirit of the information society (see Fig. 64)[27], Masuda argues, will be one of globalism, a symbiosis in which man and nature can live together in harmony, consisting ethically of self-discipline and social contribution. Within this emerging spirit the image of fraternity, drawing, on the one hand, on George Land's developmental biology, and, on the other, on Rudolph Steiner's associative economics, rises to the fore. The hypothesis can be formulated, Masuda concludes, that the future information society will be a highly organismic one, a multi-centered complex society in which many systems are interlinked by information networks. In fact Masuda has much in common with the great French biologist, Catholic priest and social philosopher, Teillard De Chardin, with whose developmental view of the world we shall conclude this section.

HIGH MASS CREATION SOCIETY

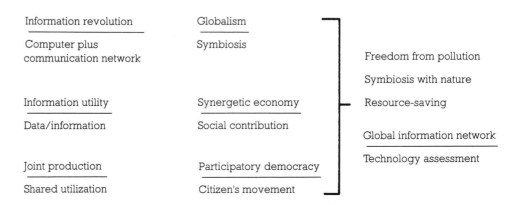

Fig. 64 Information society.

Conclusion

Developmental management

In conclusion, I have argued that developmental management combines an evolutionary thrust with an interdependent form. It is not personality or funtionality but the emergence of individuality, in people, in products, and in businesses, that should pre-occupy developmental managers. Moreover, as Mary Parker Follett so eloquently argued, genuine individuality cannot be realized without profound interdependence. Synergy in time and space are thereby interlinked.

De Chardin, in his book *The Future of Man*, first written in the fifties, sees the universe spreading like a fan, as it progressively evolves. 'If there is any characteristic clearly observable in the progress of nature, it is that such progress is achieved by increasing differentiation, causing ever stronger individualities to emerge'.[28] This process of evolving individuality is not achieved, moreover, by individuals, or by organizations, working in isolation. In fact it is quite the opposite.

The super-evolution of man

The first stage in mankind's evolution was the elaboration of lower organisms, up to and including man, by the use of combinations of elementary sources of energy, received or released by the planet.

The second stage is the super-evolution of man, individually and collectively, by the use of refined forms of energy scientifically harnessed and applied, thanks to the coordinated efforts of all men working reflectively and unanimously upon themselves.

Teillard De Chardin *The Future of Man*[29] 1977

As man and civilization matures, then, reflection takes over from action, as the dominant evolutionary principle. More specifically, De Chardin describes the development of what he calls a 'noosphere' – not unlike Masuda's 'quaternary' industries – within a post-industrial society.

Towards a post-industrial society

The enormous surplus of free energy released by the unfolding of the noosphere is destined, De Chardin maintains – by a natural and evolutionary process – to flow into the construction and functioning of what he calls its 'brain'. In other words, he says, humanity is in the process of 'cerebralizing' itself.

Our proper biological course, according to De Chardin, in making use of what we call 'our leisure', is to devote it to a new kind of work on a higher plane. Hence, in Masuda's terms, such work leads to the growth and development of the arts and ethics 'industries'.

The noosphere

Traditions of every kind, hoarded and manifested in gesture and language, schools, libraries, museums, bodies of law and religion, philosophy and science – everything that accumulates, arranges itself, recurs and adds to itself, becoming the collective history of the human race –

heredity, hitherto primarily chromosomic becomes primarily noospheric – transmitted, that is to say, by the surrounding environment.

Teillard De Chardin *The Future of Man*[30] 1977

In the post-industrial society not only does man, then, become increasingly reflective and interdependent, but so do machines. To an increasing extent, De Chardin argues, every machine comes into being as a function of another machine. Ultimately, 'a single, gigantic network is formed, girdling the earth'. And the basis, the inventive core of this vast apparatus is the noosphere.

Amazingly enough De Chardin was writing in the forties and fifties, before distributed networks, cellular or satellite communications had even been dreamed of, never mind actualized. Yet we can now see a noospheric or quaternary pattern to our individual, organizational, and societal evolution.

In the final analysis, the noosphere, De Chardin says, or the quaternary industries, Masuda might say, can function only by releasing more and more 'spiritual energy'. As a direct result, according to De Chardin, research, which until now was a luxury pursuit, is in the process of becoming the principal function of humanity. Doubtless such mature corporations as IBM, ICI, Olivetti, Hoechst, 3M, or Mitsubishi would agree, at least in part, with our developmental philosopher. In Chapter 25, that is in Section E, I want to explore these issues in more depth, starting with an investigation of modern physics, and of the roots of 'metaphysical management'.

References

1. R. Benedict, 'Synergy in the society and in the individual' *Journal of Individual Psychology*, Vol. 20 (1964).
2. R. Dore, *Flexible Rigidities*, Athlone Press (1987), p. 7.
3. B. De Mente, *Japanese Etiquette and Ethics in Business*, Passport Books 5th edn (1987), p. 3.
4. M. Parker Follett, *The New State*, Peter Smith (1929), p. 35.
5. R. Steiner, *Social Renewal*, Steiner Press (1977), p. 81.
6. R. Steiner, *The Threefold Commonwealth*, Steiner Press (1945), p. 14.
7. R. Steiner, *op. cit.* (1977), pp. 19 and 20.
8. F. Wilken, *The Liberation of Capital*, Allen & Unwin (1984), p. 193.
9. E. F. Schumacher, *Small is Beautiful*, Abacus (1973).
10. S. Yamamoto, 'The spirit of Japanese capitalism', ex De Mente, B. *op. cit.*
11. C. Lorenz, *The Design Dimension*, Blackwell (1986).
12. R. Watts, *Corporate Revolution*, Heinemann (1986), p. 27.
13. R. Pirsig, *Zen and the Art of Motor Cycle Maintenance*, Harper & Row (1976), p. 168.
14. Pascale and Athos, *The Art of Japanese Management*, Penguin (1981), p. 23.
15. W. Teague, 'In good shape', ex Design Council, Products 1900–1960 (1979), pp. 45, 46.
16. Pascale & Athos, *op. cit.*, p. 214.
17. A. Low, *Zen and Creative Management*, Doubleday (1976).
18. J. Quinn, *Strategies for Change: Logical Incrementation*, Irwin (1980), p. 9.
19. R. Dore, *Flexible Rigidities*, Athlone Press (1987), p. 7.
20. L. Turner, *Industrial Collaboration with Japan*, Routledge & Kegan Paul (1987), p. 14.
21. P. Drucker, *Management in Turbulent Times*, Heinemann (1979), p. 87.
22. L. Turner, *op. cit.*, pp. 54, 55.
23. K. Ohmae, *op. cit.*, p. 124.
24. Y. Masuda, *The Information Society, as Post-Industrial Society*, Institute for the Information Society (1981), p. 88.
25. T. Dodsworth, 'Why the speed of technology is chipping away at the independents', *Financial Times* (27 May 1987), p. 24.
26. Y. Masuda, *op. cit.*, p. 34.

27. Y. Masuda, *op. cit.,* p. 35.
28. T. De Chardin, *The Future of Man*, Fontana (1977), p. 48.
29. T. De Chardin, *op. cit.,* p. 183.
30. T. De Chardin, *op. cit.,* p. 168.

24 Organizational harmony and self-development

Contents

Key concepts

Once you have fully understood this chapter you should be able to define the following concepts in your own terms:

Catalyst of common effort   *On* and *giri*
Cellular organization   Product system
Circular organizational form   Ripple effect
Concentric organization   Self-management
Industrial faciliator   *Sogo shosha*
The New Man

Objectives

Upon completing this chapter you should be able to do the following:

1. Describe the workings of the *sogo shosha*, most specifically their implications for developmental management.
2. Relate the interdependent aspects of developmental theory to Japan's 'invisible link'.
3. Assess the developmental origins and impact of Yugoslav self-management.
4. Compare and contrast the Japanese, communal approach to developmental management to the Yugoslav one, which is both individually and communally centered.
5. Assess the desirability of working in one or other of the organizations considered in this chapter, from a personal point of view.

Introduction

Developmental management

The fruits of developmental management are much less visible today, than primal or rational ones. It would seem that they are still at an early stage of their evolution. British and American management theory and practice still seems to be dominated by primal – particularly entrepreneurial – and by rational – both administrative and behavioral – features.

However, both primal and rational approaches are in a state of flux, and some fruits of developmental management have become to appear. They have emerged, albeit partially formed, from two main directions. The one direction is Eastern, specifically Japanese; the other is Northern, and specifically central European. Developmental management, as we have already seen, recognizes and harnesses potential, in people and in things, by combining previously isolated parts into newly formed wholes. This developmental process takes place over time – evolutionary – and across space – synergy. Moreover, it can be oriented towards a whole corporation within a society (business development), or towards a whole self within an organization (self-development).

Japanese managers have made particular headway in the first respects, both within individual businesses and in whole industries, and Yugoslav managers have made significant progress in the second, via 'self-management'.

The Japanese communal way

The Japanese have been able, in their unique way, to upgrade the primal gatherer from her instinctive and communal base into a developmental organizational form. They have succeeded in doing this because their business organizations represent an evolved form of the Japanese household (see p. 149).

In other words, the Japanese have taken attributes of mutuality, trust, and harmony from their traditional and family origins, and developed them into distinctive forms of economic and social exchange, in a modern organizational context. As a result they have evolved trading companies (*sogo shosha*) that cross business boundaries in the same way as a son-in-law, for example, becomes an accepted part of his newly acquired household. The Japanese have also evolved companies, like Sony, which have adapted the 'pair system' of husband/wife, to their own organizational arrangements.

In this way, Japanese enterprises have evolved from closely knit households (primal) into both hierarchical organizations (rational) and also interdependent communities (developmental), in a relatively short period of time. What the Japanese have not done is to upgrade the hunter or warrior, out of a primal heritage, into an individual in his or her own right. Moreover, in many instances, they are experiencing difficulties in transplanting their interdependent business communities from Japan into foreign soils.

The Yugoslav approach to self-management

In fact, and in time, we might find that the full flowering of developmental management – whereby individual self-development and organizational interdependence become mutually reinforcing – takes place in Eastern Europe rather than in Japan.

It is well known that whereas the East has traditionally emphasized the collective or universal, the West and North – at least since the days of the Ancient Greeks – has focussed on the individual. In fact Eastern Europe lies geographically between the two. Once it manages to rid itself of the more dogmatic aspects of 'Scientific Socialism' we are likely to see some very intriguing developments.

Indeed already in the sixties and seventies some very interesting experiments in self-management took place in Yugoslavia. These will be reviewed in this chapter. In the eighties and nineties, moreover, and with the advent of Gorbachov's *perestroika* we might see something similar, and even more far-reaching, emerging in the Soviet Union.

In this chapter I shall start, then, with the Japanese approach to developmental management, with its communal orientation towards economic and social interchange. I shall then move over to the Yugoslav one, with is focus on self-development and human evolution, within the context of business enterprise.

The invisible link: the sogo shosha

The first of the barely visible fruits of developmental management is the uniquely Japanese trading company, the *sogo shosha*.

According to the American business magazine, *Forbes*, by 1984 six of the *sogo shosha* had become the largest companies in the world, outside of the United States. Yet, as the president of the biggest of these, Mitsubishi Corporation, said in 1981: 'we are like the air, invisible but pervasive, providing essential things to sustain life'.[1]

A third institutional form

A *sogo shosha* is like no other company. It is not defined by the product it handles or even by the particular service it performs, for it offers a broad and changing array of products and functions. Its business goals are equally elusive, for maximization of profits from each transaction is clearly not the major one, at either the operating or philosophical level.

Although it sometimes owns a partial or controlling interest in the corporations actually performing the activities of production or distribution, the primary role of the *sogo shosha* lies in the coordination or linkage of them.

Between and beyond Adam Smith's 'invisible hand' of the market, and Alfred Chandler's 'visible hand' of the vertically integrated firm, the *sogo shosha* stands out as a third institutional form. It provides a system of governance, channelling money, information, ideas, raw materials, products, services and other economic goods into a coherent system of activity.

While it is a coordinator, the *sogo shosha* is not a dictator or boss. It does not exercise the same degree of power over its clients as does an integrated corporation. The clients remain, in most cases, independent firms, with the freedom to act on their own, in the market-place, rather than participate via the mechanism of a *sogo shosha*.

In fact the subtle and ever changing dynamics of power between a *sogo shosha* and its client firms, and the utility to both of the coordinating function it performs, challenge us to rethink many assumptions of the nature and boundaries of the firm and to look at the basic organization of economic activity with fresh eyes.

The challenge of managing complex interdependency, rapid change, and fierce external competition, has been met by the evolution of a distinctive organization system. In a *sogo shosha* organization it is not so much the conventional bureaucratic structures and processes, as the systematic use of informal interpersonal exchange processes, that serves to govern the most important aspects of the organization's activity. These informal processes form an invisible link.

In the sum the *sogo shosha*, according to Yoshino and Lifson, is an example of a third type of institutional form, with some characteristics of both vertically integrated firms and the market.

The *sogo shosha's* context and impact

The *sogo shosha*, unique among the world's corporations, is active from the very earliest or upstream activities of raw material extraction, through multiple stages of production, fabrication, and distribution, downstream to the end user, in most of the basic categories of economic commodities: food, fuel, fiber, metals, chemicals, and the end-products for which they are used.

The six largest *sogo shosha*, including the well known Mitsubishi and Sumitomo Corporations, affect the lives of most participants in the world economy. Collectively they are the largest purchaser of US exports in the world.

Yoshino and Lifson *The Invisible Link*[2] 1986

An industrial facilitator

The evolution of the *sogo shosha* began as an ingenious Japanese response to the overwhelming needs for large-scale trading organizations and led to a broader role as facilitator and even leader in the industrialization process. Its character and functions were much shaped by the distinct needs of the period. Not only did the *sogo shosha* become a window to the world for a nation long isolated, it came to occupy a crucial role in the Japanese economy.

Inside Japan the *sogo shosha* promoted the division of labor in burgeoning industries saddled with a scarcity of resources. The *sogo shosha* gave important advantages to their fledgling industrial ventures. It enabled them to enjoy economies of scale in procuring raw materials and made it possible for them to concentrate on manufacturing, by providing them with ready access to export markets.

Particularly important in this regard was the role the *sogo shosha* played in providing export opportunities for the myriad of small Japanese firms in cottage industries. The *sogo shosha* fed them market information, helped them design products, extended credit, and, most important, developed foreign outlets for their products. Their contribution to the nation's economic development transcended the narrow definition of foreign trade. They have played a vital role as catalyst of new industrial activities.

In post-war Japan, after the *sogo shosha* had been unformed and reformed, it began once more to assume a dominant role in Japan's economic development. In the period 1960 to 1977, for instance Mitsubishi's sales increased from 644 billion to 9,609 billion yen. By 1977, moreover, the six largest *sogo shosha* held stocks in nearly 6,000 companies.

Coordinator–developer–intermediary

The *sogo shosha* has three distinctive attributes. It coordinates a wide-ranging and integrated product system; it simultaneously develops new business opportunities for itself and its clients; and it acts as an intermediary within a complex business system. I shall start, then, by elaborating upon its role as coordinator.

Coordinating product systems

The primary function of the *sogo shosha* is trading, that is matching buyers and sellers of diverse products. In that respect it is by no means unique. Traders and middlemen have existed, all over the world, for many thousands of years. What is unique about the *sogo shosha* is its capacity to provide essential links between stages in a product system for a client firm.

The *sogo shosha*, in fact, coordinates product systems that can be larger and more complex than the operations of a large and integrated firm. For example, in steel production, a *sogo shosha* may be concerned with many more operations than even a typically integrated manufacturer.

Sogo shosha organize large-scale coal and iron mines, arrange shipping, often sell or lease ships to the shipping lines, provide insurance and arrange delivery to the iron and steel producers, and manage inventories all along the way. They are also involved in a wide number of downstream fabrication and sales operations.

To further coordination they have organized groups of small and medium-sized firms into quasi-captive networks for which they provide the materials to be fabricated, market the fabricated products, and, of course, extend financing for working and capital investment.

In fact it is not uncommon, for example, for steel mills and the *sogo shosha* to own fabricators jointly. The *sogo shosha* often sell steel to the very shipyards building bulk carriers to transport iron ore and coal, which will be sold and leased by the same *sogo shosha*.

Finally, through its diverse dealings, the *sogo shosha* tends to enjoy superior access to information about a market, a customer, or a country. Thus it enables its clients to assess the magnitude of its risks more accurately and efficiently than would otherwise be possible.

A business constellation

A *sogo shosha* product system is best understood not as a rigid body whose constituents are mechanically linked into a tightly balanced system but as a constellation of firms, active at various stages of a complex production process, whose links with each other are shaped by the *sogo shosha's* influence.

The *sogo shosha*, with its system perspective, induces members of the system to act in ways that maximize what it perceives as the system welfare, in which all members want to share in the long run. For every client there is a constant tension between maximizing its own welfare and maximizing the welfare of the system. The *sogo shosha* acts as interpreter of system welfare and also attempts to act as enforcer of system discipline.

Yoshino and Lifson *The Invisible Link*[3] 1986

Developing new business opportunities

A product system does not necessarily exist, ready made from the outset. Often the different components, as outlined in Fig. 65 in the case of a steel system, evolve throgh incremental modification of industrial and commercial practices.

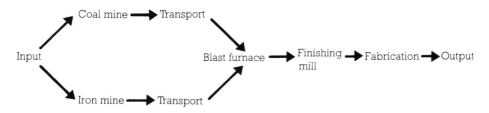

Fig. 65 A product system.

However, a *sogo shosha* can often spot new opportunities that require the coordination of several firms to create a distinctively new set of financial, information, and product flows amongst them.

The process of pulling together these actors, negotiating common understandings and arrangements to govern the product system, and establishing the initial flows may be considered, according to Yoshino and Lifson, the system development stage of the *sogo shosha's* lifecycle.

System development

In Japan, as in a number of other countries, the traditional method of producing and marketing chickens had been small scale, part time endeavours by farm families. The *sogo shosha* identified the potential to replace this antiquated system with a modern and efficient one, and imported the technology and breeding stock necessary to undertake mass production.

Advancing the capital necessary for construction of huge poultry houses and processing plants, arranging for the import of grains, mixing feeds, growing and processing birds, setting up supply routes for distribution of chicken meat, eggs, and by products, and arranging delivery are only the most basic activities of the *sogo shosha* in this product system.

The actors include some units wholly owned by the *sogo shosha*, some partly owned, and some independently owned. The *sogo shosha*, earn commissions based on the volume of goods and services and are also able to realize ownership profits at certain stages.

One of the *sogo shosha*, Mitsubishi, has even extended its involvement in broiler chickens to include becoming the Japanese franchisee of Kentucky Fried Chicken, via a joint venture.

Yoshino and Lifson *The Invisible Link*[4] 1986

When a *sogo shosha* links previously unrelated actors in a new system, it can charge relatively high fees for its services, because of its catalytic role and function. Once the system stabilizes the individual actors may question the continuing need for the *sogo shosha's* services

In practice this means that the *sogo shosha* must always be developing new business opportunities to add to its existing array of services to clients. It also means that the *sogo shosha* must constantly strive to identify the emerging points of greatest leverage over a particular product system, and then undertake activities, such as research or investment, that give them influence or control over these points.

Acting as intermediary

The *sogo shosha* often acts as an intermediary, bringing corporations together to alter traditional flows or to create new sources of production. In the early sixties, for example, the *sogo shosha* C. Itoh began actively to diversify out of textiles into other areas, namely heavy industries. At the same time the company became interested in establishing ties with major corporations in the United States and Europe.

The Japanese automobile industry offered an another excellent opportunity to accomplish both these goals of product and geographical diversification.

Sogo shosha as intermediary

Through the 1960s the Japanese automobile industry was fragmented and by the end of the decade it became increasingly apparent that shakeouts were imminent. Isuzu was one of the marginal producers whose future was very uncertain. Its management, however, did not want to be acquired by another company.

C. Itoh's management, seeing an opportunity to strengthen its ties with the manufacturer, concluded that the only way that Isuzu could survive was to enter into some sort of working relationship with an American firm. After an abortive effort with Ford, it approached General Motors.

Isuzu, although an old and respected company in Japan, lacked skills of negotiation on the international scene, and C. Itoh undertook much of this activity on Isuzu's behalf. After almost a year of confidential and complicated negotiations agreement was reached. General

Motors became a minority shareholder of Isuzu.

As part of the agreement Isuzu gained immediate access to General Motors' worldwide sales network for certain of its automobile models, resulting in a dramatic increase in the company's exports. C. Itoh became Isuzu's sole agent for such exports as well as one of its primary suppliers of steel. General Motors was not only to establish a foothold in Japan, it also gained several new product lines ... the arrangement proved to be satisfactory to all parties concerned.

Yoshino and Lifson *The Invisible Link*[5] 1986

The organization of the sogo shosha

The strategy of a *sogo shosha* requires it to manage exceedingly complex systems governing the flow of goods and services from raw materials to ultimate consumers. To carry out such a strategy the *sogo shosha* has adopted a distinctive form of organization.

Business and organization development

In essence the *sogo shosha* performs a linkage function, connecting buyers and sellers into multistage systems. Unlike markets, though, the *sogo shosha* must be able to continually seek out new linkages for its clients. Without this latter activity its ability to maintain fees, and therefore its existence, would soon diminish.

The creation of new linkages is possible because the range of its activities exposes its managers to a wide variety of opportunities to imagine new combinations of institutions and resources. This gives them the impetus to create or modify systems. 'We can label this creation of new activity development, for the ability of the *sogo shosha* to grow, or even maintain its present strength in existing terms, depends on it'.[6]

Initiative must usually be taken at comparatively low levels of the organization by managers scattered throughout the world, often also separated by 'product distance'. The most common type of opportunity, a chance to make a deal on especially favorable terms, requires that a group of traders coordinate a complex and varying mix of services within the firm – financing, shipping, insurance, storage, delivery, and other customer services.

Most *sogo shosha* trading is done not for the firm's account but rather for the accounts of clients. Therefore close liaison with the client's organization must take place, if the *sogo shosha* is to keep in touch with its needs, and is to keep the client informed. Moreover, when the *sogo shosha* is working within a product system in which its client ties are extensive, a single transaction often involves buying from one client and simultaneously selling to another, further complicating the coordination that must take place.

The network of subsidiaries and affiliates

Besides trading activities a *sogo shosha* is involved, *via* a network of separately incorporated entities, in a number of other business lines. Most of the companies involved were founded or purchased as the outgrowth of the trading business, though some have been taken over after defaulting on credit lines owned to the *sogo shosha*.

About half of these businesses, overall, are likely to be in Japan and the other half in other countries, all over the world. In the number of employees they dwarf the *sogo shosha*. There may be as may as 100,000 people working for an affiliated company, in which the *sogo shosha* holds a part of the equity.

There are basically five types of subsidiary or affiliate:

- Resource development affiliates in such fields as mining, paper and pulp and agricultural products.
- Sales organizations that handle specialized products such as certain types of machinery or textiles.
- Support service organizations such as warehousing and forwarding agents.
- Manufacturing firms whose raw materials and output may be handled by the *sogo shosha*.
- Financing organizations that are set up to deal in specialized services and financial markets.

Subsidiaries and affiliates are usually established at key points in the product systems that the *sogo shosha* manages. Finally, whereas subsidiaries and affiliates are more closely integrated into the trading network than clients are, they are less integrated than the sub-units of the *soga shosha* itself. How exactly, then, are the *soga shosha* able to weave these complex organizational fabrics?

Interunit coordination

On and giri

We have seen that the *sogo shosha*'s distinctive activity is the building and managing of product systems. This involves coordinating the numerous clients and institutions that are in contact with the different subunits of the *sogo shosha*. Vast amounts of information must be gathered and channelled. Complex tradeoffs must be made under uncertain conditions. All of this means that the *sogo shosha* must develop the ability to integrate itself to a high degree.

According to Yoshino and Lifson such coordination and cooperation is not achieved, in the main, through formal mechanisms. Rather, they say, it is 'the emergent system', that is the sum total of informal interactions created by the social system of the firm, that is the source of interunit coordination. Fundamental to this social system are the communication networks that have been established, over an extended period of time, and during which 'shared meanings' have been exchanged via a culturally based system of mutual obligation.

Two concepts, *on* and *giri*, are essential to understanding the very large role a strongly internalized sense of obligation plays in determining mutual obligation in Japan. *On* can be thought of as part of the cement that holds together important vertical relations. It binds superior and subordinate together in a web of emotionally-tinged obligations.

Giri is a much more mundane and measurable category of obligation. It is subject, in other words, to precise calculation and repayment. What makes it distinctively Japanese, however, is the widely held agreement about the necessity of repayment, and the common understanding about what degree of obligation is produced by a particular act.

As a result, all sides – be they one unit and another, parent and subsidiary company, or *sogo shosha* and trading partner – have a fairly precise sense of the implications of favors given and received. Since group life is so important to the Japanese, few individuals are

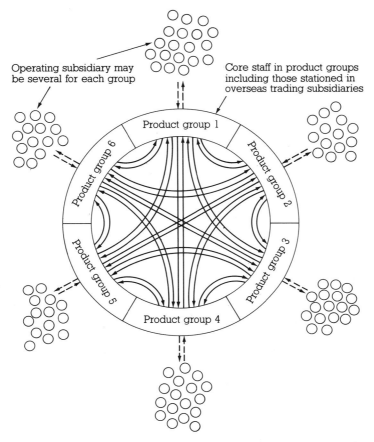

Operating subsidiary may
be several for each group

Core staff in product groups
including those stationed in
overseas trading subsidiaries

Product group 1

Product group 6

Product group 2

Product group 5

Product group 3

Product group 4

Fig. 66 Schematic of product group, subsidiary and affiliate patterns of coordination
at a *sogo shosha*.

willing to violate the commonly held sense of propriety by failing to discharge an
obligation. In the business context that means that even informal bargains or tradeoffs
can occur with regularity and with certainty of repayment.

Sogo shosha–client relations

Figure 66,[7] drawn up by Yoshino and Lifson, represents a schematic of the predominant
relationships under the informal system. Subsidiaries and affiliates are linked to a specific
product group as the group's staff members are 'loaned out' to them. These staff members
enable the subsidiaries and affiliates to be integrated with the parent company.

The 'loanee' is also in an excellent position to pick up various kinds of information that
may be useful to the overall trading network. In this way he can at least partially repay
the obligations he incurs when calling on members of his network to help the subsidiary.
Moreover, the more wide-ranging the units – both within and without the parent
company – to which he is loaned, the larger his network becomes.

Finally, both *sogo shosha* and client are interested in seeing their relations run smoothly. There is an enormous investment of time and energy in building numerous network connections between them at all levels of the two firms. So, a trader who abused a client confidence to produce a large short-term profit would find himself heavily censored within his own firm.

Interestingly enough such interunit coordination is also very much a feature of Yugoslav self-management, except here, as we shall find, the emphasis is somewhat different. Finally, and as we saw through the eyes of our corporate architect from Sony, Shigeru Kobayashi (p. 404), in Japan interdependence without is matched by harmony within.

Developing the 'New Man': Yugoslav self-management

Whereas the cooperative enterprises described in Chapter 10, especially those established in mainland China, were created out of a communistic impulse, those developed in Yugoslavia in the fifties were the result of a unique blend of individualistic and socialistic orientations. Moreover, unlike the Japanese case, they have drawn less consciously on Slav traditions in particular than on European ones in general – both Eastern and Western.

Having concentrated, up until now, on the social and interdependent features of developmental management, I want to focus on those elements that help to foster the integration of the individual person. In other words, having focussed on the whole community, I now want to shift our attention to the whole individual. The two combined make up developmental management.

Between East and West

Since the 1950s Yugoslavia, positioned between Western and Eastern Europe, has been attempting to develop a 'New Man' in the context of a self-managed enterprise. Within one generation, in fact, the country has moved at an accelerated pace from a pre-industrial era into an industrial one, and is now fostering the values of a post-industrial society.

Unfortunately, however, because Yugoslavia has fallen behind in the primal and rational stages of its economic evolution, its developmental achievements have been inhibited. In other words, the relative absence of primal enterprise and rational organization has held back the progress of self-management. Too much has been attempted, perhaps, in too short a period. Moreover, Unlike Japan, Yugoslavia is not a homogenous society.

The economic and political context

Before the Second World War, Yugoslavia's economy was based on its agrarian and largely illiterate population. In 1921, 78% of the population was agrarian, enterprises were on a small scale, and the level of international trade was low. By 1960 the ratio of agricultural to non-agricultural population had fallen to only 50%.

In addition to this process of industrialization Yugoslavia experienced extreme political

> and social turbulence during and after the Second World War. The country in fact went from a centrally-planned economy immediately after the war to a market-socialist one in the fifties and sixties.
>
> In 1945 all economic resources and means of production were nationalized. Obligatory plans, indicating what and how much production should be carried out, were made on the federal, regional and district levels. By 1950, the Yugoslavs had replaced the centrally planned system with an approach whereby the workers in the plants were granted considerable collective autonomy. Workers Councils replaced central government at the helm.
>
> Continuing decentralization took place during the period 1950 to 1970, including the gradual deregulation of pricing, a steady increase of the share of the revenue that remained within each company, and a gradual thawing of political authority over decision making.
>
> Ichak Adizes *Industrial Democracy: Yugoslav Style*[8] 1971

Nevertheless, the Yugoslav attempt to create 'self-managed' enterprises has been a genuine and unique developmental exercise with which – as whole managers – we should become familiar. For what the Yugoslavs have done is to try and bring Maslovian ideas on individual development, and progressive self-actualization, into the center of organizational life. That is something neither the Japanese nor the Americans or Western Europeans have attempted to do.

The ideology of self-management

Not only, then, are the Yugoslavs undergoing industrialization and economic decentralization, but they are seriously attempting to develop a society with post-industrial values.

The basic concept of self-management, according to the leading American authority on Yugoslav business enterprise, Ichak Adizes, involves four key elements:

- A transition period, in which a 'new man' will be educated and trained to operate in a stateless society and in which he will be guided by his conscience.
- A new form of organization, in which the individual member has the right to manage himself through having the power to govern, if not the power to administer. In other words, while the general membership governs (policy making) the nominated or elected administrators administer (strategy making and implementation).
- Pure authority by acceptance in that the sources of influence in self-management are not supposed to be based on vested hierarchical positions but on professional authority.
- Social ownership Yugoslav style, which is a very different proposition when compared with, say, the style of ownership in Soviet Russia. 'As the ownership is by society, an abstract legal identity, and as all the members of the organization have rented the means of production, there is legal equality amongst the members to manage on equal terms those resources. In self-management there is no elite group which manages others; all members of the organization manage themselves. There is a group of coordinators and administrators, but not managers'.[9]

Self-management versus free enterprise

It is apparent from the self-management ideology that it emphasizes qualities of self actualization, self expression and interdependence, in addition to encouraging collaborative relations, linked objectives and social ownership of resources.

These values are different from those of the industrializing society, which emphasize achievement rather than self-actualization, self-control rather than self-expression, independence rather than interdependence, competitive rather than collaborative relations, separate rather than linked objectives, and a state in which resources are regarded as owned absolutely rather than belonging to society as well.

Ichak Adizes *Industrial Democracy: Yugoslav Style*[10] 1971

The self-managed organization

Concentric organization

The organization of Yugoslav self-management, at the level of the individual plant, is built up and around the basic economic unit. Each such unit of production or distribution has a key task to accomplish. No one can tell from the organization chart (see Fig. 67)[11] who is in charge of whom. It represents the wholeness and equality of the Yugoslav system.

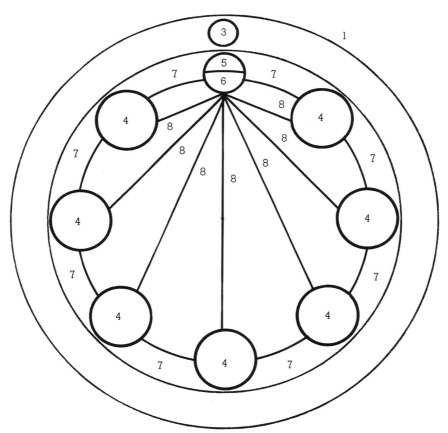

Fig. 67 The whole organization of an economic unit.

Each economic unit, then, has the following eight organizational attributes:

1. A boundary line separating one unit from another.
2. A governing body of members, that is an assembly of all the workers, known as the Zbor.
3. A governing board of the unit, usually the senior administrators, known as the Collegium.
4. Working places, either different jobs or different groups of workers each performing a certain technological process.
5. The group coordinating the economic unit.
6. The foreman, organizing the work of the unit.
7. The technological and economic interrelationships between the working places or work groups.
8. The links between the foreman the coordinating group and the working places or work groups.

As we can see the relationships are circular and interactive rather than vertical and insular. Moreover, whereas policymaking responsibility is shared by the whole work-force, some line responsibility does exist for the implementation of particular tasks. However, even responsibility for the implementation of decisions is not strictly linear in nature.

The ripple effect
The flow of authority and influence, as well as the process of decision making, is circular

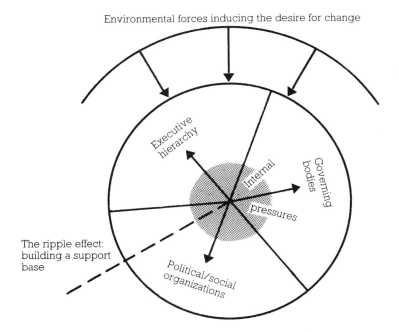

Fig. 68 Making major decisions.

rather than linear, especially if the decision is being made is non-routine in nature. This is illustrated in Figs. 68[12] and 69[13].

The ripple effect

An originator of a proposal must be strongly motivated to propel his suggestion through the various phases of decision making, because his suggestion will have to pass through a series of 'filters'. If personal interest is his only motivation, this fact will be detected early in the process and his suggestions will be defeated.

In order for a proposal, for example to invest in new machinery, to gain initial credibility, a support base from a nucleus of people is necessary. Such a nucleus is neither appointed nor elected, but is comprised of volunteers. This volunteer group, in turn, needs to gain an even wider support base.

First an exchange of opinions is conducted within the economic units from which the core members come, and influential people need to become involved. Several alternatives are then discussed, new alternatives are formulated, and new nuclei formed.

Because an extremely strong core is needed in order to propel a major decision, the proposal does not have a chance of ultimate acceptance until such time as the various nuclei are integrated, thus creating a joint front. In the final analysis, then, on a policy matter or significant strategic issue, the general membership will have to be won over.

Ichak Adizes *Industrial Democracy Yugoslav Style*[14] 1971

The evolution of self-management

Whereas the specific approach to decision making is not dissimilar to the Japanese *ringi*

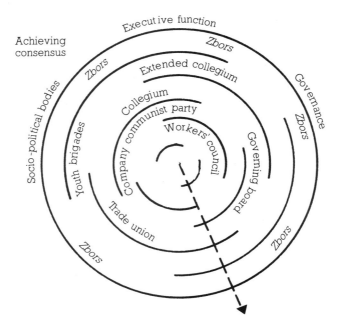

Fig. 69 The ripple effect in making major decisions

system, the democratic nature of the organization, and the concept of the 'New Man' is certainly dramatically different. In fact, the Yugoslavs have taken Maslow's ideas on self-actualization and conceived of an organizational form to support them.

Inevitably expectation has run ahead of achievement. For not only is the Yugoslavian economy still much less developed than that of the United States, Japan or Western Europe, but the country has had to cope with a somewhat fraught political situation. Given such trying circumstances the progress made through self-management has been significant, both in economic and socio-political terms.

For unlike other Eastern European countries, Yugoslav socialism accommodates a considerable degree of individual autonomy, both at the personal and at the enterprise level. Moreover, unlike Western European nations, Yugoslavia has attempted to introduce democracy into the workplace.

Conclusion

The fruits of developmental management, especially insofar as the development of the self is concerned, are much more scantily spread, around the world, than those of primal or rational management. In a sense, business and economic development has not caught up with the kind of humanistic psychology that Abraham Maslow and Bernard Lievegoed have introduced.

Interestingly enough, as far as business and organization development is concerned, the American and European contribution has lagged behind the Japanese one, not only in commercial terms but also in humanistic ones. On the one hand, the Japanese have succeeded in successively upgrading their communal and Eastern traditions from a primal (communal household) to a rational (hierarchical organization) and subsequently to a developmental (interdependent economy and society) level of management.

On the other hand, Europe and America have only succeeded in upgrading their individualistic and Western traditions from a primal (nuclear family) to a rational (network organization) level. The subsequent evolution of a developmental (self-managed) form – symbolized by a circle rather than a pyramid or net – has been restricted to isolated examples, although the Yugoslavs have made determined efforts in this respect. The trouble is, of course, that the same Yugoslavs have probably not evolved primal and rational structures and processes sufficiently.

Interestingly enough the Soviet Union, under Gorbachov, is now making a determined attempt to stimulate individual and cooperative enterprise (primal) as well as efficiency and effectiveness (rational), but under the possible overall umbrella of self-development and mutual interdependence (developmental).

Mikhail Gorbachov has a clear understanding of the need for individual self-determin-ation and global interdependence on the world's political stage. Whether he can trans-plant that developmental outlook into the economic sphere, within the broad context of a progressive brand of socialism, will probably depend on the amount of cooperation he receives both from within and without the Soviet Union. As progressive managers, then, we should not only take note, in the nineties, of developments both in Russia and in mainland China, but also cooperate with those nations in order to gain mutual advantage.

If such cooperation is to take place it will more than likely be influenced by metaphysical management, to which we now turn.

References

1. Yoshino and Lifson, *The Invisible Link*, MIT Press (1986).
2. Yoshino and Lifson, *op. cit.,* p. 14.
3. Yoshino and Lifson, *op. cit.,* p. 28.
4. Yoshino and Lifson, *op. cit.,* p. 64.
5. Yoshino and Lifson, *op. cit.,* p. 58.
6. Yoshino and Lifson, *op. cit.,* p. 112.
7. Yoshino and Lifson, *op. cit.,* p. 156.
8. I. Adizes, *Industrial Democracy: Yugoslav Style*, Macmillan (1971), pp. 11–28.
9. I. Adizes, *op. cit.,* pp. 29–32.
10. I. Adizes, *op. cit.,* p. 84.
11. I. Adizes, *op. cit.,* p. 276.
12. I. Adizes, *op. cit.,* p. 86.
13. I. Adizes, *op. cit.,* p. 88.
14. I. Adizes, *op. cit.,* p. 87.

Section E
Metaphysical management

Introduction

This is the one section in the book which I introduce with an apology to you readers. The word 'metaphysical' will be off putting to some of you at least. It certainly is not conventionally associated with management. Though I feel it conveys the right meaning for our purposes here, it does require a bit of a stretch of the imagination.

I was tempted by such alternative labels as creative, innovative and even transcendental, but they have all become rather hackneyed because of their prolific usage, in very varied contexts, of late. So please do stay with us, and if you continue to have problems with the word, select one of the others – like innovative – instead.

The underlying ground

Whereas, then, developmental management characterizes the consciously evolving, and interdependent organization in midlife, a metaphysical approach is best suited to the mature, large-scale enterprise, in the process of transformation. Such transformation of energy, and of spirit, requires a quality of inspiration from managers that is distinctive from not only instinct and intellect but also insight.

From a geographical perspective such 'mature' behavior is difficult to pinpoint, but is more likely to be found in the South than in the North, and in developing countries rather than in developed ones. However, not only are there the inevitable exceptions, but because the developing countries have yet to grow their own large-scale business enterprises, we are very much open to speculation in this metaphysical domain.

Metaphysical management does thrive, though, on a balance of energy and vision, both of which are 'transpersonally' – rather than personally, impersonally or interpersonally – based. In other words, we are entering the realms of nature and of spirit. (See Fig. 70.)

The living characters

Whereas primal management is particularly appropriate at the first stage of a business' development and rational and developmental management at the second and third stages, metaphysical management comes into its own at the fourth stage of an organization's evolution. However, it is likely that the metaphysical domain, albeit in a barely visible sense, will be present, embryonically, from the outset of the business' development.

In fact there is often an uncanny linkage between the primal and metaphysical management domains. This is evidenced by Peters' and Waterman's[1] strong interest in 'corporate culture', which contains both primal and metaphysical elements. It is as if the cycle of development is a spiral, continually returning to its origins, rather than being linear in its form.

The 'soft' side of metaphysical management is personified by the adventurer; the 'hard' side, on the other hand, is personified by the innovator. Whereas the typical adventurer is both bounding with physical energy and also closely bound up with nature, the business innovator is both bounding with imagination and also closely bound up with his dream, which he wants to turn into a reality.

Finally, the individual who represents a combination of 'hard' innovator and 'soft' adventurer is the visionary. He is personified, in this text, by John Hillbery, a cofounder of the Bank of Credit and Commerce. Though somewhat tarnished by alleged 'drug money laundering' in 1988, the company is, in its essence, metaphorically based.

The metaphysical roots

Hard roots

The implicate order

The hard roots of metaphysical management have only been very recently tapped. With the emergence of the new physics, particularly in the last decade, a new view of the universe is making itself apparent. Time and space, having once already been transformed this century, by Albert Einstein, is being transformed yet again by a veritable collection of physical scientists.[2]

The implications for management have barely become apparent, but are nevertheless there to be tapped. Most importantly, if we draw on the American David Bohm's[3] pathbreaking work on the 'implicate order', we discover that matter and consciousness are inextricably linked. In other words, what is invisible, implicate and 'metaphysical' is closely interwoven with what is visible, 'explicate' and 'physical'. According to Bohm we only respond more readily to the explicate, or, in terms of this text, to the 'primal', if and when we are culturally attuned to doing so.

The self-organizing universe

Re-ligio

Erich Jantsch,[4] a Swiss born physicist, who also became an internationally renowned management consultant, sees mankind as poised to enter a great new synthesis. Such a synthesis of intensity, autonomy and meaning, as he sees it, is beginning to emerge out of all forms of life and organization.

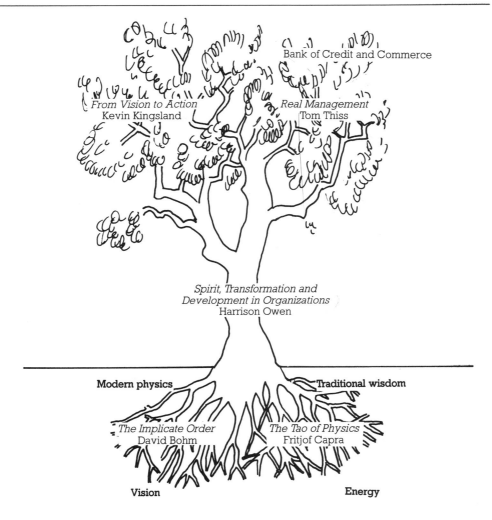

Fig. 70 The metaphysical tree.

In the course of this unfolding process of universal self-organization, Jantsch viewed the linking back to our origins, re-ligio, as both our main spiritual concern and also the core of creative action.

Coevolution
The Belgian physicist and Nobel prize winner, Ilya Prigogine,[5] has since introduced us to the term 'coevolution', whereby living organisms are transformed not in the course of selective adaptation to specific environments, but as a result of the flux and flow of all surrounding phenomena. In other words, the world in general, and organizations in particular, are imbedded in a holographic universe.

In every part, be it individual, departmental or divisional, is contained the whole – as is well known to the Bank of Credit and Commerce – and vice versa. Not only that, but, in the course of its coevolution, every product or market is interpenetrated by the whole of the universe.

Soft roots

Whereas the hard roots of metaphysical management are closely attached to the experimental findings of sub-atomic physics, the soft, and much deeper roots, reach down to the philosophers of antiquity. The Austrian Fritjof Capra,[6] himself a physicist, has drawn, in particular, on the Ancient Chinese taoist philosophies, to draw out the broader implications of his scientific researches. Capra pictures the subatomic universe as 'a dance of energy', and nature as in a state of 'dynamic equilibrium'. These resulting energy patterns are in a constant state of movement, interaction and transformation.

In the Ancient Chinese view of the world, according to Capra, the harmonious cooperation of all beings arose, not through any external dictate, but through the internal dictates of their own nature, identifying themselves with the ultimate reality. That ultimate reality was represented in the highest level of consciousness known to man. In fact, common to many of the different philosophies or religions of antiquity, be they Judeo-Christian, Buddhist or Taoist, was the notion of four levels of being. Capra has identified them as personal (primal), social (rational), existential (developmental) and transpersonal (metaphysical).

The developmental core

Corporate culture

Operating at such a transpersonal level, the American lay preacher and management consultant, Owen Harrison, has played a unique part in turning 'corporate culture' into an essentially metaphysical – rather than primal – field of management activity. For Owen, the essence of corporate culture is neither visibly shared values (primal), nor researchable attitudes and beliefs (rational). It is not even the climate (developmental) or atmosphere that pervades the organization, albeit barely visibly. Rather it is the mythos, that is the combination of myth and ritual, that lives beneath the organization's surface.

Such corporate mythology, in particular, can be uncovered through an understanding of the seminal stories that characterize an organization, including those of its origins, and potential re-creation. The transformation of a corporate culture is only possible if the mythos is first grasped, and second, re-created through a process of collective story telling.

Organizational transformation

Real transformation can only take place, then, if the essence of the story is uncovered, revealed and transcended. In fact, for Owen, the difference between organizational development (OD), and organization transformation (OT), is that the one deals with the emotional resources of the organization and the other with its spiritual ones.

In fact, he argues, the organization's spirit is its most essential resource. Drawing on

David Bohms' ideas on implicate and explicate order, we can infer, on Owen's behalf, that the implicate controls the explicate, so that 'spirit' is of a higher order than matter – money, people or things. (See Fig. 71.)

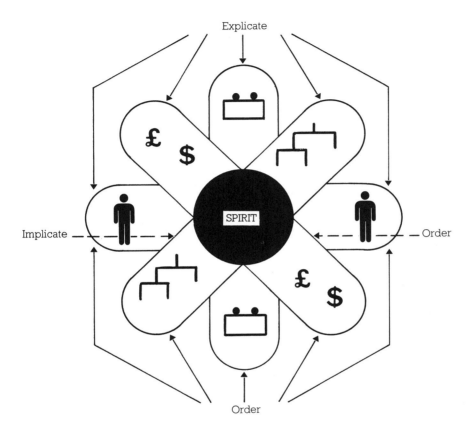

Fig. 71 Spirit.

In order, to 'turn around' a mature company, at least as far as Owen is concerned, you will get much further by transforming its spirit, prior to, or at least in the course of, transforming its material base.

The metaphysical branches

Hard branches

From vision to action
If you are to transform the spirit of an organization you need to be able to follow, or lead it, along its journey from out of the depths of the unconscious into the physically

conscious. The British psychologist and philosopher, Kevin Kingsland,[7] has traced such a journey in the course of his physical and metaphysical travels between East (India) and West (America).

Kevin Kingsland, relating modern psychology to ancient wisdom, concluded, after working for some fifteen years with thousands of students in small groups, that there are basically eight personality types. I have adapted these, in turn, to the cast of managerial characters that appear in this text. Within each person, in fact, although one attribute predominates and predetermines his or her 'type', the full set of other attributes are contained to varying degrees.

These 'horizontal' personality attributes – physical, social, perceptive, emotional, analytical, aesthetic, imaginative and spiritual – can be 'vertically' related to the processes of learning and innovation. As you learn you journey upwards, from immediately physical activity through to the acquisition of knowledge about the divine mysteries of the universe! As you innovate you journey downwards:

- From out of the mysterious depths of the origins of all things.
- To the extraction of an imaginative vision of the future.
- To recognition of the aesthetic fit between product and market.
- To an organized structure capable of channelling your vision.
- To willful commitment to acquiring the resources you need.
- To a mental perception to adapt to changes along the way.
- To social aptitude in involving people in your enterprise.
- To the physical energy to make things happen.

Soft branches

Real management

Whereas the hard metaphysical branches support individual innovation, the soft branches merge into the surrounding environment. They are an integral part of nature's network, that is of the entire ecosystem. The theory and practice of 'real management'[8] has been worked out interactively, at the Bank of Credit and Commerce (BCC). BCC was originated in Pakistan less than twenty years ago, has more branches in Africa than any other commercial bank, and now operates in over seventy countries around the world. Real management has been developed by its Pakistani president, Agha Hasan Abedi, its English marketing executive, John Hillbery, and its American organization developer, Tom Thiss.

Four fundamental laws of nature underpin it. These are the laws of totality – all is one and one is all; of integrity – the material is subordinate to the moral; of flow – all is flux and change; and of latency – possibilities are infinite. As a result the interconnectedness (totality), the levels of being (integrity), the dynamic interplay (flow) and the infinite potential (latency) of energy forces support the organization in its transcendent purpose. In BCC's case this purpose is the attainment of world peace, through enabling the developing countries to overcome the crippling burdens of poverty.

The metaphysical fruits

BCC, not surprisingly, as a metaphysically oriented company has been cited in this text. Not only is the submission to God an explicit part of the Bank's purpose, but it also has a transcendent economic and ecological mission to attain. More importantly, however, through the theory and practice of real management, BCC has not only originated but also implemented an approach to business that is rooted in thousands of years of natural, social and economic history. For not only does it heed the laws of nature, but it closely observes, and responds to, the shifting patterns of trade and of immigration, as they have evolved through the centuries.

Finally, BCC is ultimately concerned with the transformation of physical, economic and human resources by virtue of its banking operations. That is not to say that every one of its employees are in touch with its metaphysically based purpose. Because the bank is less than twenty years old it straddles all four of the primal, rational, developmental and metaphysical domains. Its employees, in their turn, and as we have recently seen (see p. 510), reflect this disparity. However, its visionary leaders, as we shall soon see, are metaphysical managers.

The metaphysical manager

The wholesome, metaphysical manager, combines a love of adventure and involvement with mother nature, with a capacity to innovate and a mastery of him or herself. In bringing the two together he or she becomes a visionary, as is the case for John Hillbery. John sees himself as Agha Hasan Abedi's *alter ego*, and as 'the guardian of the spirit of BCC'. He is responsible for the key communications function, in conjunction with his 'invisible' supporters. Although he was born in Britain he sees himself as truly cosmopolitan, with the spirit of Portugal lodged firmly within him. Once you have read John Hillbery's story you may choose to look at your own life, so far, in a similar vein! You will be getting further help, in that respect, in Chapter 27 on 'Vision'.

Visionary
John Hillbery   Director, BCC International
Adventurer

The movement of goods
It's important for me to divorce my own life from BCC. I'm forty-four years of age now. I left school at fifteen, and came to work in the City of London. I became a clerk in a shipping company. In fact, between the ages of fifteen and eighteen I was given a very responsible administrative job. I costed the cargo, made up accounts and bills of lading. Unknowingly I became involved with the very paperwork which makes up banking. It was and is all to do with the movement of goods.

Miracles do happen
At the age of fifteen I still didn't know my alphabet properly. I had missed two years of schooling because of a disease of the hip I had contracted as a young child. The doctors were poised to cut off my right leg, and then a miracle happened. My leg was saved.

Outward bound

When I returned to school I was sent on the first outward bound course ever put on. I came back with honours. I wanted to learn. I had a passion to know. My father came from German stock. He ran away from a wealthy family. He never had a proper job in his life. He was a park keeper, verger, grave digger, life saver ... He had over fifty jobs in his time, including five years as a desert rat, when he became Bedouin!

Father left us for the desert when I was six months old. When he returned, five years later, it was as a Bedou. He was a whimsical and mystical man. It took me fifteen years to get to know him. My mother was a tigress. If Hitler had known of her existence he wouldn't have dared to attack this country!

Educating myself

On leaving school I decided to educate myself. I remember, when I was taught history, telling the teachers that I wanted to study it from different national perspectives. I wanted to learn the relationships between everything. The totality. I've met some outstanding people in my life. I absorb them. I remember a lawyer from Cambridge who joined the shipping company, and taught me about language. I've always had a fascination for music. I feel that I know Mozart, Beethoven, and Mahler, individually.

There are many great people that I haven't physically met, but I've reached them through their work. Tolstoy and Dostoevsky played a very important part in my life. My own children have taught me a great deal, and my wife, who is Portuguese. She's been ill most of her life, but she has an amazing spirit. Immersing myself in Portugal has taught me a great deal. I love nature too, and have had some strange experiences out in the wilds.

My odyssey

At nineteen, when I left the shipping company, I went to sea. I was the only English speaker on a foreign ship. I worked as a deckhand, and we were almost shipwrecked off the coast of Portugal. I feel that my voyage at sea was my epic, my odyssey, so to speak. When I came back to England, I got a job as an assistant to a stockbroker. I gradually felt, though, that I was living a lie. The market was more of a gambling centre than a stock exchange. So I took a job selling advertising space with the Thompson organization. I met people by the score and was promoted to the *Sunday Times*, as Deputy Financial Advertising Manager. We were still poor, my wife and I. But it didn't matter to us. We always had been.

Innovator

The spirit of a corporate body

I did very well as a salesman. In 1965 I first saw the 'spirit' of a corporation. AB Foods. I got through to Charles Forte. I could see his future. While others saw him as a trumped-up ice cream salesman, I could see – in a vision, in advertising terms – where his future lay. I knew how to capture the true, underlying reflection of a company. I knew the secret.

I had discovered, you see, that Forte owned a few hotels, Terry's Chocolates, and some property. His shares were standing at 21 shillings. People hadn't realized what a bloody good buy his stock was. So I phoned him up and told him I knew how to double his share price. We ended up carrying a full page advert, which his corporate affairs director and myself designed, in the *Financial Times*. We had it published the day his shareholders were meeting, showing photographs of all his assets. In ten days his shares went up 40 per cent. Six days after that there was a reverse takeover, and Trust House became Trust House Forte.

I then travelled to Brazil. I knew how to attract investors to a market. I sold the Brazilians space in the *Financial Times*. The bankers followed. I portrayed vividly the true seeds of Brazil's greatness, surpassing the underlying weaknesses, the lack of purpose and direction in the country. The huge foreign debts, today, reflect the discrepancy between those seeds and the actual fruit ... Then I went off to Japan and sold them a twenty-page *Financial Times* survey. The Japanese wanted to be seen as international. The survey captured the spirit of that nation and its times. I did this sort of thing all over the place. It yielded a bumper crop of advertising for the *FT*.

It's all about patterns and relationships

But I've left out something important. In 1960, after my sea voyage, I took off on the road, and arrived first in Paris. I had £20 to take me round the world. When I got there I was told about some very cheap accommodation at 24 Rue de Tuileries. A huge iron gate was opened by a little Indian girl. At the end of the garden there was a chicken run, divided into cells. I stayed in one of them, and it turned out I was living with Sufis. One of them was a gentleman named Vilaid Khan.

The girl told me, after a little while, to run away from those Sufis. 'They all,' she said, 'considered life to be an illusion.' Many years later, when I'd already joined BCC, a colleague brought in Mohammed Ali to the bank. 'Does anyone know Hasrod Khan,' the boxer asked. 'I know his son, Vilaid,' I said. 'That's the man,' Ali said. 'I want to find him.' So when I was next in Paris, now of course in my Mercedes, I went to look for Vilaid Khan. But the chicken run had been burned down. I was told, would you believe, that Vilaid was on his way to Los Angeles, to seek out Mohammed Ali. Yet neither knew the one was looking for the other.

It's all about patterns, relationships. When I was at sea I soaked up bits of Iran and Algiers, Naples and Barcelona. They each came to form part of my pattern of internal relationships, part of me. You know, T. S. Eliot, in *The Wasteland*, helped me understand the spirit of the word, and the pattern of relationships that each one sets up. We have words, even in the financial sphere, like 'pro-vision' and 'goodwill', and we lose sight of their deep and invisible meaning.

The search for re-unification

The journey we make in life is a search for re-unification. People give up their identity to a club in Pall Mall, or to the 'working class'. I've never been lured by any such constraining identity. I've learned to use shibboleth, and myth to set off catalytic reactions, rather than being submerged by dead ritual. After my stint at the *Financial Times* I joined the Bank of America. The Bank wanted me to write the president's speeches, handle investor relations, take on PR, the house magazine, and also prepare their high fliers for senior positions. I became, in fact, the first English vice president of the company. But soon I began to realize that I was operating as merely a part of the whole. The American approach to multinational business, at the time, didn't allow other parts of the world to develop and evolve independently. When senior American management went overseas they failed to discover how other people really lived and felt. Yet to make a good credit investment you need to know the soul of a people, 'the credit for the nation'.

Turning a dream into a reality

Then one day I got a call from Mr Naqvi, who is now our Chief Executive. The Bank of

America had, at one stage, a 30 per cent investment in BCC. That's why Naqvi and I had got to know each other. BCC was struggling to gain recognition in the developed countries. I had a vision. I knew that the mission of the third world was contained in BCCs spirit. I wanted to help turn that dream into reality. Now, some twelve years later, that dream has indeed become a living and growing reality. I see myself as the public face of BCC. Mr Abedi calls me the guardian of the spirit of the company. I'm his alter ego. The president and I have joined our purposes to achieve unity, to fight arrogance and prejudice, to realize the spirit of the South.

London, England 1986

Conclusion

You will now be introduced more fully to metaphysical management, that is its roots – in modern physics and traditional wisdom (Chapter 25), its core – spirit, transformation and development (Chapter 26), its branches – from vision to action and 'real' management (Chapter 28), and its fruits – BCC. All together they represent the fourth and mature management domain. We shall explore its metaphysical characteristics in the chapters that follow. Thereafter we shall investigate, more fully, the full cast of managerial characters.

References

1. T. Peters and B. Waterman, *In Search of Excellence*, Harper & Row (1982).
2. Briggs and Peat, *Looking Glass Universe: The Emerging Science of Wholeness*, Fontana (1985).
3. D. Bohm, *The Implicate Order*, Fontana (1984).
4. E. Jantsch, *Design for Evolution*, Brazillier (1974).
5. I. Prigogine and Y. Stengers, *Order and Chaos*, Fontana (1981).
6. F. Capra, *The Tao of Physics*, Fontana (1983).
7. R. Lessem, *The Global Business*, Prentice Hall (1987).
8. T. Thiss, ex Adams, J. (ed.), *Real Management Transforming Leadership*, Miles River Press, (1986).

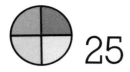

25 Contemporary physics and traditional wisdom

Contents

Key concepts

Once you have fully understood this chapter you should be able to define the following concepts in your own terms:

Aristotle's causes	Cosmic dance
The 'atomists'	Dissipative structures
Coevolution	The dynamic universe

Energy	Order through fluctuation
Explicate order	Outer way
The flow of time	Re-ligio
Holomovement	Self-organization
Implicate order	Self-renewal
Levels of consciousness	Self-transcendence
Levels of interaction	Systemic interconnectedness
Meaning	

Objectives

Upon completing this chapter you should be able to do the following:

1. Portray, in brief, the origins and development of physical science.
2. Appreciate the influence of the new physics on a new and metaphysical approach to business and to management.
3. Understand the concept of levels of consciousness, and be able to relate it to levels of management.
4. Compare and contrast dynamic principles of self-organization with holistic notions of implicate order annd systemic interconnectedness.
5. Appreciate the influence of so-called 'invisible' forces on visible science and management.

Introduction

Two-way stretch

Having covered the primal, rational and developmental ground, we can now proceed to the realms of the metaphysical. In so doing we shall enter territory that has only been probed in depth by a select group of managers. These managers in fact range from Henry Ford, the first person to mass produce automobiles, in America in the 1920s, to Anita Roddick, 1987 Businesswoman of the Year, in Great Britain.

This chapter is the most philosophical one in this text. If you are particularly averse to abstract thought, and therefore find the chapter a struggle, try and stay with it. For it is vital to the text as a whole. For the metaphysical roots stretch all the way from ancient wisdom, reaching down thousands of years, to modern physics in the 1980s.

From traditional wisdom to modern science

The developmentally oriented corporations of modern Japan are a unique amalgam of ancient wisdom and new technology. Somehow the traditional and the modern appear, when joined together, to produce a powerful combination. The same would seem to apply to the roots, or foundations, of management as a whole. The primal manager, firstly, draws on traditional anthropology and on contemporary economics. The rational manager, secondly, draws on traditional administrative theory and on modern behavioral science. The developmental manager, thirdly, draws on traditional ecologically based wisdom and on modern biological science.

The metaphysical manager, finally, draws on traditional mystical beliefs about the functioning of the universe, and on the most contemporary thinking in modern physics. It is with these developments in contemporary physics, set in the context of traditional belief systems, that this chapter is concerned. A bridge between these ancient and modern approaches is formed by what Dennis Milner, a modern philosopher of science, has termed consciousness.[1] Having explored the inner path of consciousness and the outer path of analytical science, I shall investigate the different levels of being that characterize the metaphysical approach, before returning to the origins of the physical sciences.

Explorations in consciousness: science and metaphysics

The outer way and the inner way

There are essentially two ways in which a person, and a manager in particular, can seek an understanding of his role and function. The first is the 'outer' way, and the second is the 'inner' way. The outer way is based on the sense experience of the material world. This way has been espoused by both primal and rational managers. It is also the approach taken in classical and analytically based science. By contrast, through the 'inner' way a person, or a manager, seeks to raise his or her level of consciousness. His aim is to gain direct perception of whatever forces and activities lie behind existence. This is more the approach of the developmental or, even more particularly, the metaphysical manager.

To understand phenomena, including those contained within and without organizations, we need both outer and inner viewpoints. Rational science provides a detailed knowledge of substances, that is of the bricks and mortar of the world, while metaphysics provides knowledge of the planning and organization behind the construction. To become a true organization builder you have to begin by learning how to deal immediately (primal) and prospectively (rational) with people and things. Once this has been mastered you need to learn how to become an architect, and design (developmental) buildings or organizations. Finally, you have to learn how to perceive and actualize worthwhile purposes for which buildings or organizations are required (metaphysical).

Analysis and integration

When you apply the analytical, scientific method to the phenomena of your organizational experience you find that the totality of your existence is far too great for you to grasp. You therefore divide and subdivide management into fragments small enough for you to comprehend. You then investigate these fragments in detail so that you can get a clear understanding of what they involve. Any knowledge you thereby gain is effective, detailed, working knowledge. But in the process of dividing and subdividing it into fragments you lose sight of the wholeness of management.

The metaphysical approach deals only cursorily with the detailed behavior of people and things. Instead the metaphysical manager conceives and acts upon forces and activities that lie behind and beyond the material world. He or she is able to do this because of an 'expanded state of consciousness', or highly evolved state of managerial or moral being.

Levels of consciousness

The metaphysical view, in fact, means that we have to see every single thing in the universe in terms of being at different levels of consciousness.

Aristotle's causes

The most common basis for such a division of levels is a fourfold one. Aristotle,[2] for example, the Ancient Greek philosopher, described four levels of causal influence:

1. A formal cause, e.g. the blueprint or concept of a table, affecting its shape and proportion. This formal cause corresponds with 'the objective general', with body and substance.
2. An efficient cause e.g. the work of the carpenter in making the table. This efficient cause corresponds with the 'objective particular'. His work produced this particular table. He is concerned with ends and means.
3. A material cause, e.g. the wood or other raw substance of which a table is made. This material cause corresponds with the 'projective general'. Wood is general because it can make many things besides tables. It is full of potential.
4. A final cause, e.g. the function of the table. This final cause corresponds with the 'projective particular', that is with the table's particular function and purpose of holding things.

Two thousand years later an American physicist was still drawing on Aristotle's original thinking.

The geometry of meaning

The American physicist, Arthur Young, from whom I discovered Aristotle's 'causes', also describes four levels of being, or of consciousness.

Four levels of elements

Hydrogen is the first and most basic element, like the light that started it all.

The second row – carbon, oxygen, hydrogen – are the elements that make up the carbohydrates, fats and the proteins, that is the bulk of the body. These molecules are the building material and the fuel. They have no fixed character, no identity.

The third row of elements contrast sharply with this. They are elements which make molecules which have a special purpose and retain their identity.

The fourth row of elements also have special functions, but it would appear that the combining motif is emphasized.

Arthur Young *The Geometry of Meaning*[3] 1976

For Young atoms or molecules are not separate things but expressions of an evolving entity. At each state of its evolution the entity, be it a living cell or a human organization, acquires a new power. Since the powers are cumulative, an atom cannot achieve cell-ness, say, without previously having mastered molecular combinations. Furthermore, it cannot deal with genuine combination, as a molecule, unless it has previously learned personification, as an atom. The same of course, we would argue, goes for a business enterprise, that is its powers are cumulative.

In summary, for Young, as for the metaphysical manager, the geometry of meaning unfolds thus:

- The universe is a process, put in motion by purpose.
- The development of process occurs in stages.
- Each stage develops a new power.
- Powers are cumulative; each one retains the powers developed in the previous stages.
- Powers are evolved sequentially in what are called 'kingdoms'.

Levels of being

This notion of different 'kingdoms', or levels of being, has in fact been developed by E. F. Schumacher, the well known German economic philosopher and author of *Small is Beautiful*. Schumacher describes four levels of being – matter, life, consciousness and self-awareness – each of which is 'in their fundamental nature, different, incomparable, incommensurable and discontinuous'.[4]

While Schumacher was a Christian economist and philosopher, a contemporary of his, Adin Steinsaltz, has come to similar conclusions, from a Jewish metaphysical standpoint. The world of action (matter), Steinsaltz says, is only one of a general system of four fundamentally different dimensions of being. He calls these dimensions, 'action', 'formation', 'creation', and 'emanation'.

A system of worlds

The physical world in which we live, the objectively observed world around us, is only a part of a vast system of worlds. Three of these are of a different order from the immediately known world – which does not necessarily mean that they exist somewhere else, but rather that they exist in different dimensions of being.

What is more the various worlds interpenetrate and interact in such a way that they can be considered counterparts of one another, each reflecting itself on the one below or above it, with all the modifications, changes, and even distortions that are the result of such interaction.

It is the sum of this infinitely complex exchange of influence back and forth among the four different domains that comprises the specific world of reality that we experience in everyday life.

Adin Steinsaltz *The Thirteen Petalled Flower*[5] 1980

The domains of experience to which Steinsaltz refers, are probably analogous to the four underlying our own evolving management principles.

Each domain or 'world' is distinguished from the other by the way that time and space is manifested in it. Moreover, for the reasons Steinsaltz gives, the interaction between the worlds often makes it difficult to distinguish say, primal from metaphysical, or rational from developmental management. The spatial division between one world and another is as nonlinear as the flow of time.

The flow of time

In our domain of experience, time is measured by the movement of physical objects in space. Upon ascending the order of the worlds, this time system becomes increasingly asbtract and less and less representative of anything we know as time in the physical world. It becomes no more than the purest essence of change, or even the possibility of potential change.

The concept of time moreover, in the Jewish way of thinking, is not one of linear flow. Time is a process in which past, present and future are bound to each other, not only by cause and effect but also as a harmonization of two motions: progress forward and a countermotion backward, encircling and returning.

It is more like a spiral, or a helix, rising up from creation. There is always a certain return to the past, and the past is never a condition that has gone by and is no more, but rather one that continually returns, and begins again at some significant point, whose significance changes according to changing circumstances. There is therefore a constant reversion to basic patterns of the past, although it is impossible to have a precise counterpart at any moment of time.

Adin Steinsaltz *The Essence of Jewish Belief*[6] 1980

Spiral flow of time

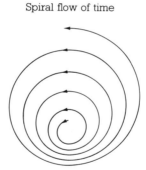

Fig. 72 Spiral flow of time.

Having explored the metaphysical world of inner consciousness and levels of being, I now want to relate these concepts to the origins and development of physical science.

The origins and development of science

Science and metaphysics

To what extent, then, is physical science, today, in a position to embrace these metaphysical viewpoints? Is there a place for Aristotle, for Young, for Schumacher and for Steinsaltz in the scientific worldview? Similarly, what foundations might such metaphysicians be building for a more mature management?

There is no doubt that science is evolving in a direction which is able to accommodate such underlying metaphysical foundations. In fact, the contemporary physicists who will be represented in this chapter – the American David Bohm, the Swiss Erich Jantsch, the Austrian Fritjof Capra, and the Belgian Ilya Prigogine – are not only noted scientists in their own right and trailblazers of the new physics, but also popular philosophers. Before we hear from these illustrious people, however, let us briefly trace the history of physical science, drawing on the insights of the Nobel prize winner, the Belgian Ilya Prigogine, and his French associate Isabelle Stengers.

From the Greek atomists to quantum physics

The Greek atomists' main aim, according to Prigogine and Stengers,[7] was to describe a godless, lawless world in which man is free, and can expect to receive neither punishment nor reward from any divine or natural order. By way of contrast, classical science was a science of engineers and astronomers, of action and prediction. Nature becomes law abiding, docile and predictable instead of being chaotic and unruly. In the twentieth century, ironically enough, we are again, through quantum physics, witnessing the clash between lawfulness and random events. In place of actuality and certainty the quantum physicists recognize only potential and probability. In a sense, therefore, we can draw parallels between the atomists, the classicists and the quantum physicists, and the primal, rational and developmental or metaphysical approaches to management.

A transition in epochs

Each epoch and each society is rooted in some fundamental beliefs and assumptions, which are acted upon as if they were true. They justify all other things that follow from them, while they themselves are accepted as faith.

A change in philosophy is a change in the accepted canons of faith, whether that faith is of a religious or a secular character. And conversely, when a given people, society or civilization is shaken or shattered, this calls for fresh thinking, a new philosophical basis.

We shall need to create new myths to make transition in our society possible. Two myths in the making are: the myth of the unity of the family of man within the context of universal sympathy for all; and the myth maintaining that the cosmos is pervaded with spirituality, which leads to the reality that we are part of a sacred tapestry.

Henri Skolimowski *Eco-Philosophy*[8] 1981

I now turn to the new beliefs and assumptions that underpin the new physics, and that also underlie, in my view, so called metaphysical management. The first person to publically cross the bridge between modern physics and ancient wisdom has been the Austrian scientist, now working in California, Fritjof Capra. He has called his construction the 'Tao of Physics'. The 'tao', for the ancient Chinese, was the way of all things.

The way of all things

The ultimate reality

Fritjof Capra is a young physicist who took the scientific world by storm, in the early eighties, when he compared the concepts of contemporary Western physics with the tenets of traditional Eastern mysticism.

The cosmic dance

In contrast to the mechanistic Cartesian view of the world, the world view emerging from modern physics can be characterized by words like organic, holistic, and ecological. The universe is no longer seen as a machine, made up of a multitude of objects, but has to be pictured as one indivisible, dynamic whole whose parts are essentially interrelated and can be understood only as patterns of a cosmic process ...

Living organisms, being open systems, keep themselves alive and functioning through intense transactions with their environment, which itself consists partially of organisms. Thus the whole biosphere – our planetary ecosystem – is a dynamic and highly integrated web of living and nonliving forms.

Most organisms are not only embedded in ecosystems but are complex ecosystems themselves, containing a host of small organisms that have considerable autonomy and yet integrate themselves harmoniously into the functioning of the whole.

Fritjof Capra *Mankind at the Turningpoint*[9] 1982

In the Ancient Chinese worldview, Capra tells us, the harmonious cooperation of all beings arose, not from the orders of a superior authority external to themselves, but from the fact that they were all parts in a hierarchy of wholes forming a cosmic pattern, and what they obeyed were the internal dictates of their own nature.

Although the various schools of Eastern mysticism differ in many details, they all emphasize the basic unity of the universe. The highest aim of their followers – whether they are Hindus, Buddhists, or Taoists – is to become aware of the unity and mutual interrelation of all things, to transcend the notion of an isolated individual self and to identify themselves with the ultimate reality.

Self-renewal and self-transcendence

Capra, accordingly, has a view of consciousness, also based on four levels, that evolves from the personal 'ego' to the collective and 'transpersonal'. Firstly, at the ego level, specifically, one does not identify with the total organism, but only with a personal representation of it, known as the self-image. Hence, for us, the relevance of autonomy and entrepreneurship at this level.

The second major level of consciousness he calls the 'bisocial' because it represents an aspect of a person's social environment, including family relationships, cultural traditions and beliefs that profoundly affect the person's perceptions and behavior. Hence, for us at this level, the importance of the behavioral sciences in management.

The third existential level is the level of the total organism, characterized by the integrated individual who is exploring his or her full potential. At this third level of 'self-renewal' developmental management, for us, is of obvious relevance.

The final transpersonal level is the level of the collective unconscious. The individual now feels connected to the cosmos as a whole, and so may be identified with the traditional concept of the human spirit. In the final analysis, for Capra, it is the processes of self-renewal and of self-transcendence (levels three and four) which are of greatest interest. These together take him into the realms of self-organization with which Erich Jantsch and Ilya Prigogine have been intimately concerned.

Self-organization

The internal plasticity and flexibility of living organisms, whose functioning is controlled by dynamic relations rather than rigid mechanical structures, gives rise to the principal of self-organization.

The two principle dynamic phenomena of self-organization are self-renewal – the ability of living organisms continuously to renew and recycle their components while maintaining the integrity of their overall-structure – and self transcendence – the ability to reach out creatively beyond physical and mental boundaries in the processes of learning, development and evolution.

Fritjof Capra Mankind at the Turningpoint[10] 1982

Now let us turn to Erich Jantsch and to his self-organizing universe.

The self-organizing universe

'Re-ligio'

Erich Jantsch initially established a reputation for himself, in industry, as a technological forecaster in the fifties and sixties. As he matured he broadened his perspective and in the seventies wrote his seminal work, *Design for Evolution*.[11] The book was addressed not only at corporate planners but also at executives and statesmen. He wrote as a physical scientist who had become increasingly interested in processes of social, as well as physical, evolution.

We may experience evolution, according to Jantsch, in terms of roots branching in the direction of historical time, and accessible by means of 're-ligio', which literally means a linking back to the origin. Re-ligio opens up the unformed with its wealth of open possibilities, and new evolutionary lines of development, thereby giving us a kind of dynamic security.

In a civilization or an organization with a true history, therefore, the concept of irreversible time undergoes a significant modification. Not only does re-ligio, the linking backward to the origin, become the main spiritual concern, it also becomes the core of creative action.

Levels of interaction

A close scientific colleague of Erich Jantsch's was Ilya Prigogine. Prigogine is a Russian-born Belgian physicist who has gained such a reputation in the United States that he has been given his own research laboratory at the University of Austin, Texas. He thus spends his time commuting between Europe and America, and furthering his research into 'dissipative structures'. In order to gain a meaningful perspective on Prigogine's work we need to go back to the original principles of thermodynamics.

Dissipative structures

Nineteenth century thermodynamics had portrayed a universe in which entropy (the running down of structure) increases. In other words, structure inevitably breaks down unless it is 'fed' with information or order. Prigogine, however, through his research, discovered a twentieth-century thermodynamics that is fundamentally different. He found that in far-from-equilibrium situations structures will inevitably form. Prigogine called these forms 'dissipative structures'. Furthermore, he called the dynamics of such structures 'order through fluctuation'.

If such a dissipative structure, then, is subjected to intense perturbation, and is unable to damp these jolts and jars, it may, in Prigogine's words, 'escape to a higher order'. But there is another possibility. The system may generate inside itself, on a lower level, a dissipative structure which compensates for the change. There are two major implications of Prigogine's findings. First, he argues, there is no hierarchy of levels as such. Instead there are different levels, each dependent on the other in complex ways. 'Lower' levels depend on higher ones for their existence as much as higher ones depend on lower. One level does not come before or after another. Similarly the universe cannot be disassembled into simpler and simpler parts.

The management inferences we are led to make are indeed significant. Primal management, Prigogine would argue, is not a lower order phenomenon subordinate to, say, developmental management. There are different levels of management rather than an hierarchy of them. One managerial domain depends on the other each to an equal extent, as indicated in Fig. 73.

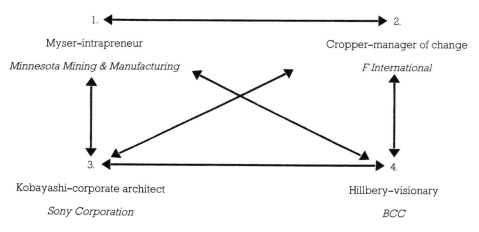

Fig. 73 Domains as levels of interaction.

John Myser needs John Hillbery as much as John Hillbery needs John Myser. Shigeru Kobayashi needs Hilary Cropper as much as Hilary Cropper needs Shigeru Kobayashi.

Coevolution
The second implication of Prigogine's research findings is even more radical. For it cuts across the Darwinian theory of evolution.

Prigogine's concept of coevolution

According to neo-Darwinism, over the course of history, new biological forms appear as the result of the struggle of individual species for survival. Darwinian evolutionary theory emphasizes adaptation to competition. As creatures contend with one another those that are the fittest will survive. Coevolution overthrows neo-Darwinism and asserts that life forms are not created piece by piece in small changes: they're dissipative structures arising spontaneously and holistically out of the flux and flow of macro and micro processes.

Coevolution explains the delicacy of the tropical fish, the gay markings of the butterfly, and the curiosity of the human mind not as simply responses to the demands for survival, but as the creative play and cooperative necessity of an entire evolving universe.

Briggs and Peat *Looking Glass Universe: The Emerging Science of Wholeness*[12] 1985

The picture that emerges from both Erich Jantsch's design for evolution and Prigogine's dissipative structure is wholly different from either the primal or rational worlds with which traditional managers are familiar. Competitive strategies and hierarchical structures are increasingly called into question by the metaphysical foundations laid by the new physics. The development of business enterprise today is part of the coevolution of business and society, on the one hand, and of East, West, North and South, on the other. No one sector of activity and no one quarter of the globe can be disconnected, one from the other. All are coevolving. David Bohm, through his concept of an 'implicate order', takes the metaphysical argument a step further.

The implicate order

The matter–mind continuum

David Bohm is an American physicist, now in his seventies, who has divided his working time between Britain and America, and between scientific research and philosophical breakthroughs. Perhaps more than any of his contemporary physicists he has contributed to the current evolution in scientific thinking.

As Einstein brought us the space–time continuum, seeing space and time as one inextricably linked process, Bohm brings us the matter–mind continuum, seeing matter and consciousness as inextricably linked. Matter, Bohm calls explicate order, and consciousness is closer to what he terms 'implicate order'. According to Bohm, ordinary consciousness responds to the explicate because it had been trained, through acculturation, to screen out and suppress vast dimensions of its implicate nature. One of the explicate forms of order that the explicate adopts is a sense of personal identity. 'Bohm believes that there is a grave fallacy lurking in individual consciousness. For him individual consciousness is an abstraction'.[13]

Letting go of the *ego*

When the binding power of the physical atom is released in an accelerator the resulting energy – staggeringly huge – becomes freed. Analogously, huge amounts of binding energy are needed to sustain the ego and the illusion that it is an independent, ultimate entity. That energy is tied up and thus unavailable for 'the high energy state'.

Energy thus preempted cannot flow into other grooves. The sage who has seen through this principle and understood it no longer exhausts himself trying to hold his bonded energy together, but lets go of the ego and releases its energy, opening a channel to the limitless, universal energy.

Rene Weber *The Search for Unity*[14] 1987

The holomovement

In classical physics the observer was separated from the observed. They were separate parts of the universe. With quantum physics some theorists proposed that the observer actually affects what is observed. Both these views subtly retain the idea that the observer is separate, though in the second case he and what he observes are 'interfacing'. For Bohm both observer and observed appear from the same underlying, indivisible process and flow in and out of each other like a stream through vortices. They are both, in a sense, causing each other, and being caused, by the same movement. Bohm calls this the 'holomovement'.

Enfolded order

The implicate order provides the ground for the explicate order that ranges from particles to planets. A radio wave can carry 'enfolded' in its movement various orders that can be unfolded by the electronic circuitry of a TV into a two-dimensional image. With the hologram, the movement of interference patterns of coherent (laser) light enfolds a much subtler range of structures and orders.

When these are recorded on a plate and retrieved by a laser beam, the readers sees three-dimensional scenes from many points of view. In a similar, but unthinkably vaster way, the whole movement or holomovement of the universe carries the implicate order and allows us to see and experience our four dimensional space–time world.

Briggs and Peat *Looking Glass Universe*[15] 1985

In the implicate order, then, what is going to be visible is only a very small part of the enfolded order, and therefore Bohm introduces the distinction between what is manifest and what is non-manifest. 'It may fold up and become non-manifest or unfold into the manifest order and then refold again. The fundamental movement is folding and unfolding'.[16] In other word there is much more to management than what meets the primal or rational manager's eye. One reality, or domain, is enfolded within the other. Moreover, whereas the primal and rational domains are more 'explicate' or manifest, the developmental and metaphysical ones are more 'implicate' and nonmanifest. Whereas, then, the visionary and the corporate architect are primarily guided by the implicit, invisible order, the manager of change and the intrapreneur are guided by the explicit and visible.

Conclusion

Matter and consciousness, implicate and explicate order, self-determination and self-transcendence, levels of interaction and coevolution, are all familiar concepts to the manager grounded in the new physics. His operating universe is therefore, quite paradoxically, metaphysical; his invisible faculties, of imagination and intuition, are more focussed than his visible tendencies to manage by objectives or by 'walkabout'. At the same time, he carries within him both yang and yin, both hard and soft edges to his management style. His hardness is reflected not so much in autonomy and enterprise but more in the creation of order through fluctuation, in far-from-equilibrium situations. Through his awareness of the implicate order, in which his enterprise is lodged, he is able to tap hidden sources of spirit and energy, thereby transforming them into successful business outcomes.

His softness, on the other hand, is reflected in an openness, a humility, and a willingness to be absorbed by the cosmic dance of physical, economic and cultural activities. He not only understands the fundamental laws of nature, in their totality – latency – flow – integrity (see pp. 91 and 576–7) but is able to enter into their innermost existence. As a result, and as we shall see in Chapter 29, he is able to create an enterprise such as the Bank of Credit and Commerce, which is not only highly successful – commercially – but is also engaged in transforming this very planet, economically and commercially.

In the chapters that follow, then, we shall first be exposed to the core of metaphysical management as conceived by the American business thinker and consultant, Harrison Owen. Second we shall investigate the process of generic innovation, whereby vision, contained in the implicate order, is converted into action, manifested in the explicate order. Third, we shall uncover the theory and practice of 'real' management whereby systemic interconnectedness and unified consciousness in management and organization is clearly revealed. Finally, I shall exemplify the process of metaphysical management in prominent business instances.

References

1. D. Milner (ed.), *Explorations in Consciousness*, Neville Spearman (1978).
2. Aristotle, ex Young, A. *The Geometry of Meaning*, Delacorte Press (1976).
3. A. Young, *op. cit.* (1976), p. 63.
4. E. F. Schumacher, *A Guide for the Perplexed*, Jonathan Cape (1977), p. 32.
5. A. Steinsaltz, *The Thirteen Petalled Flower*, Basic Books (1980), p. 3.
6. A. Steinsaltz, *op. cit.*, p. 124.
7. Y. Prigogine and I. Stengers, *Order and Chaos*, Fontana (1985), p. 37.
8. H. Skolimowski, *Eco-Philosophy*, Marion Boyars (1981), p. 114.
9. F. Capra, *Mankind at the Turningpoint*, Wildwood House (1982), p. 66 and 297.
10. F. Capra, *op. cit.*, p. 290.
11. E. Jantsch, *Design for Evolution*, Brazillier (1974).
12. J. Briggs and D. Peat, *Looking Glass Universe: The Emerging Science of Wholeness*, Fontana (1985).
13. D. Bohm, 'The implicate and the explicate order', ex Weber, R., *op. cit.* (1987), p. 27.
14. R. Weber, *The Search for Unity*, Routledge & Kegan Paul (1987).
15. J. Briggs and D. Peat, *op. cit.*, p. 122.
16. D. Bohm, *op. cit.*

26 Spirit and transformation

Contents

Key concepts

Once you have fully understood this chapter you should be able to define the following concepts in your own terms:

Collective story telling
Covenant
Cultural review
Functions of myth
Historical scan
Information

Inspired
Interactive
Journey of the spirit
Kairos
Language
Liturgy

Meta-operations	Proactive
Meta-policy	Reactive
Metaphysical management	Responsive
Meta-strategy	Ritual
Myth	Spirit
Mythograph	Transformation
Mythos	Understanding
Out of the depths	Vision

Objectives

Upon completing this chapter you should be able to:

1. Compare and contrast organization development and transformation.
2. Outline the core language of metaphysical management, relating it to Sony Corporation as and when appropriate.
3. Describe the 'journey of the spirit', with due reference to KMC – as a live example.
4. Understand the facilitating process of a cultural review, including the nature and significance of a 'mythograph'.
5. Determine the actual and potential applicability of metaphysical management to yourself, both now and in the future.

Introduction

The metaphysical spirit

The emergence of 'corporate culture' – in the eighties – as a new business discipline, has had two major influences on management. On the one hand, as we discovered in Chapter 9, it has served to reinstate the role and function of the 'gatherer', on the soft side of primal management. On the other hand, and this is our concern here, it has lifted management into a newly 'metaphysical' realm.

The individual who has done most to lift corporate culture out of a primal, visible immediacy into a metaphysical, invisible 'spirituality', is Harrison Owen. While for Peters and Waterman 'shared values' can be seen, touched and felt, for Harrison Owen they are intangible, invisible 'spirit'.

'The point,' Owen says, 'is not that organizations become more spiritual, but rather that we might recognize that organizations, in their essence, are spirit, and then get on with the important business of caring intelligently and intentionally for this most crucial and essential element.'[1]

Metaphysical management, then, is concerned with the identification, generation and support of 'spirit' with a view to its transformation into material energy. Metaphysical management is equally concerned with the way physical matter and energy, whether in the form of technology, products or material aspirations, can be transformed into individual, team, or company spirit. As Pierre Curie, who with his wife Marie created radiography, said, 'It is necessary to make life a dream, and of that dream a reality.'[2]

Organizational transformation

Innovation and transformation

The use of the term 'transformation', as opposed to development, is quite deliberate. For, as first suggested in Chapter 5, while 'development' is evolutionary 'transformation' is 'revolutionary'. Whereas the developmental manager recognizes and enhances potential in people or things, the metaphysical manager creates potential, where seemingly none existed before. Two such managers from the past were Ludwig Mond and Alfred Nobel, the forerunners of Britain's Imperial Chemical Industries (ICI).

Transformation and innovation

Ludwig Mond's unique sense of predestination enabled him to visualize the result of an experiment long before it could be established – as one sees the light at the end of a tunnel, although the tunnel itself is dark.

Jane Goodman *The Mond Legacy*[3] 1984

I left in early youth
A home for distant lands beyond the sea
But strange to say, even when the ocean spread
Its grandeur round, it struck me not as new,
My mind has pictured oceans far more wide.

Alfred Nobel[4] 1980

This creative activity is well known to the great artist or inventor – as exemplified by Alfred Nobel and Ludwig Mond – though less commonly associated with the innovative manager.

Development and transformation

Harrison Owen uses the compelling analogy, in comparing and contrasting development and transformation, of the creation of a butterfly, as against a frog. Whereas a tadpole develops bit by bit into a frog, first losing its tail, then growing its legs, a caterpillar becomes a butterfly in a very different way. The essence of transformation, as the word suggests, is a movement across and through forms. Transformation takes place in the 'odyssey or passage of the human spirit as it moves from one formal manifestation to another'. How this actually happens is indicated by the caterpillar transformation.

Butterflies start out as caterpillars, just as great organizations, symphonies, or technological breakthroughs start out as much simpler material forms. These initial forms may range from a basic commodity, in the case of the organization, to a simple melody, in the case of the symphony, to a basic compound, in the case of the innovation. Then, when the time is right, the caterpillar spins a cocoon about itself, and, after a period, emerges with beautiful colors and wings to fly. That might have been a 'development', but it is not. For once the caterpillar is inside it literally dissolves, as a small business enterprise or simple melody might dissolve rather than evolve. The caterpillar has gone to its essence, which Owen terms 'spirit', and is then transformed into a butterfly – assuming that being a butterfly is a better way to be.

The only way to get to that butterfly state is to allow the old form to dissolve, thus freeing the spirit of the thing to achieve a new form. This may seem, at first glance, to be like 'asset stripping'. The asset stripper, however, is dealing with material assets, at least that is the way he sees them, rather than with 'spiritual essence'. To achieve transformation in a commercial context the businessman must be able to identify, release and reform 'spirit' rather than physical, economic or human matter. How, then, does he go about this?

Metaphysical management

There are three specific parts to becoming a 'metaphysical manager'. They cover, in a manner of speaking, metaphysical policymaking, strategy formulation and operations management.

Meta-policy
The first policy making requirement is for the would-be metaphysical manager to learn a new language. The primal manager expresses himself, for example, in terms of winning, of intrapreneuring, of sharing values, and of managing by wandering about. The rational manager uses the language of planning, organizing, directing and control. The developmental manager focusses, amongst other things, on attunement, alignment, enhancement and on interfusion. The metaphysical manager expresses himself – both verbally and non-verbally – through myth and ritual, through liturgy and covenant, through spirit and culture.

Meta-strategy
The second strategic requirement of metaphysical management, whether in a manufacturing, marketing, financial or personnel context, is not to have a passion for excellence, to compete efficiently and effectively, or to recognize and develop synergy, but to transform spirit into matter or energy or vice versa. In order to do either such a manager needs to be capable of undergoing what Owen terms 'the journey of the spirit', or, what I have called 'vision to action' (see Chapter 26).

Meta-operations
Finally, and in operational terms, the metaphysical manager must be able – not to make things happen, to perform to standard, or to fulfill potential, but – to uncover, translate, act out and reveal both original and derivative stories that convey the spirit/energy of the organization. Should he not be entirely successful in this operationally metaphysical respect it is possible to intervene, indirectly, and facilitate effective transformation. This is achieved through a process of 'collective story telling'. For it is these stories, in their right form in their right time in their right place, that imaginatively and materially transform energy into spirit and back again. I shall now deal, via Harrison Owen, with each of these elements in their policy making, strategy and operational turn.

Meta-policy

In the course of describing the policy making language that enters into metaphysical management I shall be citing examples from Sony Corporation. I have selected Sony not because its chairman, Akio Morita, is a particularly 'metaphysical manager', but because he is one of the company's founders and has chosen to reveal its formative myths to the public at large.[5]

Mythos

Mythos is the collective term for organizational myth and ritual. These two elements in combination make up the fundamental building blocks of the metaphysical manager. In fact, they represent, to him, what for example capital and labor represent, to the primal manager.

> Myths are the stories of a group's culture which describe its beginning, continuance, and ultimate goals. These stories are so much part of the institutional fabric as to define it. To know the myth is to know the institution in a way that balance sheets and organization charts can never tell.
>
> Ritual, then, is the dramatic re-enactment of the myth. In a ritual the group acts out its central stories in such a way that the members experience really being there and participating in the original event.[6]

The nature of mythos

A myth, then, may be defined as a likely (but not necessarily true) story, arising from the life experience of a group, through which it comes to experience their past, present, and potential. The story does not reveal systematically the workings of the group or organization, but rather re-presents it in an immediate and gripping way.

> A myth is a good story that grips you, creates a world, and, to some significant degree, transforms it. Working with or in a given myth is like living in a good novel. The difference is that you cannot put the myth down. A myth not only reflects life. It becomes life.[7]

We can see this in Sony's early days, and in its co-founder Morita's early and formative experiences in the company.

To live is to learn

Finding good magnetic material to coat our tape with after the war was almost impossible in that time of shortages. It seems incredible to me now, but Ibuka, Kihara (a brilliant young engineer) and I made those first tapes by hand. We would cut enough tape for a small reel and then we would lay out the long strip on the floor of our laboratory.

The first tapes were terrible of course, but we were proud of them. In those early days the tape was the key to the future of our business ... and I was absolutely convinced that after all this work we were finally on the road to success ... We were in for a rude awakening. A tape recorder was not something, in the early fifties, that people in Japan felt they wanted ...

I was going to have to be the merchandizer of our small business.

Akio Morita *Made in Japan*[8] 1987

Whereas a rational manager views his organization's systems and procedures as the natural channel for his activities, the metaphysical manager sees myth and ritual performing that channelling function. Where the image of efficiency for the 'organization man' is reflected in return on investment, for the metaphysical manager the image of transformation is reflected in dreams turned into reality. In just a few words Morita has presented us with an image of his company, capturing its spirit of activity and learning, interspersed with creativity and humility.

The function of mythos

The true function of mythos, according to Owen, is to say the unsayable, to express the ineffable, but most importantly, to bring the participant employee, customer, or business associate into an immediate, self-validating relationship with the spirit of the organization. With a few lines and some color a whole world is created. To be sure there are details, but just enough to set the stage and invite your imagination inside.

Hunger for development

In 1948 Ibuka, the company's co-founder, and I, had both read about the work of William Shockley and others at Bell Labs, and we had been curious about their discoveries ever since. On Ibuka's trip to America in 1952 he first learnt that a license for this marvellous, solid-state transistor might soon be available.

I must say, though, that the transistor being made at the time was not something we could license and produce off the shelf. This marvellous device was a breakthrough in electronic technology, but it could only handle audio frequencies.

In fact when I signed the license agreement with the people at Western Electric a year later they told me that the hearing aid was the only consumer product we could expect to make with it.

We wanted to make something that could be used by everybody.

Akio Morita *Made in Japan*[9] (1987)

How Sony proceeded to create and market the world's first transistor radio might be public history, but the imagination of the employee or customer listening to Morita's brief story of creation is still free to roam.

There are so many technical, personal and social details to be filled in. It is just like looking at one of Picasso's abstract paintings. The net result of any active observation is one of co-creation. You and Morita or Picasso, subsequently, create the reality that results.

These results are more than Morita could originally have imagined, for it includes what you have contributed. This means, of course, that the function of mythos in corporate policy making is not a static one. It continues to grow, over time, as succeeding generations add their imagination – their spirit – to the original act and its re-creation.

In the process of such re-creation, spanning both the imagination and also reality, those involved imbibe fascination, meaning, morality and even awe into their lives.

Functions of myth

- The first function is to awaken us to the fascinating mystery of life.
- The second function is to interpret that mystery in order to give meaning to life.
- The third function is that of sustaining the moral order by shaping the individual to the requirements of his geographically or historically conditioned social group.

> • The fourth function is the most vital one of fostering the unfolding of the individual, in accord with himself, his culture and the universe, as well as that awesome ultimate mystery which is both beyond and within himself and all things.
>
> Joseph Campbell *The Hero with a Thousand Faces*[10] 1969

The life cycle

Unfolding

Myth and ritual, just like the organization as a whole, goes through a lifecycle. In the early days of a business' formation stories are being acted out, and told, in real time. They are part of everyday reality rather than carriers of meaning.

It is only later on, once the stories have become increasingly familiar to an ever growing number of people, that their presence begins to offer comfort and security as well as excitement and drama. Eventually it becomes important that the stories are told in the right way, if they are to continue to be meaningful.

In their more flexible form, organizational stories provide an outlet for creativity and innovation. At the point where stories have become fixed in people's minds they need to be broken in order to give them a fresh and updated touch.

In fact, to the extent that mythos is alive and well in an organization, those who participate in it will experience the moment of breaking as one of release. Yet they will also experience such release as fearful.

Mythos completes its lifecycle with renewal, whereby the individual or organization is infused with new meaning and purpose. This new spirit is generated during the time of 'breaking', and is created under conditions of what Owen terms 'open space'.

Here is an example from Akio Morita's family circumstances, in which open space was created by Akio's father in the presence of Sony's co-founder, Ibuka.

Break with tradition

In Japan it was considered a serious thing to take a son, especially a first son as I was, out of his home and family environment and bring him permanently into a new atmosphere in the world of business, outside of his own family firm. Our own brewing company had been passed on from one generation to another for hundreds of years.

... Ibuka told my father about our new venture and what they hoped to accomplish, and said I was absolutely needed in the new business. When he had finished we all waited tensely for a response. With very little hesitation he said that he expected me to succeed him as head of the family and had also expected me to take over the family business.

Then he turned to Ibuka and said, 'But if my son wants to do something else to develop himself or utilize his capacities, he should do it'. He looked at me and smiled. 'You are going to do what you like best', he said ...

My younger brother volunteered to take over as the sake brewer of the Morita family when the time came for my father to retire. There were smiles all round. Everyone was relieved and happy.

Akio Morita *Made in Japan*[11] 1987

As the individuals participate in the story, and specifically its breaking, they discover that the spirit has been freed to explore new possibilities. In this way Akio was freed from the traditional role of first son, following in his father's footsteps. The old mythos was broken, and yet the family business could still go on.

Role

The role of myth and ritual, in fact, changes as it reaches different points in its lifecycle. At first it serves as a mere record of transformation. Such a transformation may involve the initial conversion of a speculative idea into a fully established business, the handover of a business from one generation to the other, or a diversification into a new product line. The intent of mythos at this point is not just to talk about what transpired, but rather to create the conditions under which that prior journey of the spirit (adventurous, enterprising, innovative, or whatever) may be experienced. In other words the younger generation of Morita's will have vividly experienced the transformation of the family business, through successive generations, in advance of themselves taking over.

The second role of myth and ritual is to become an agent of transformation. By virtue of the fact that mythos, within a dynamic regime, is being constantly broken, it exists within the corporate psyche as an uneasy bedfellow. Just as everybody has become accustomed to the tale it shifts, and exposes some new area of meaning.[12] For Akio, the meaning of 'brewed by Morita in Japan' became transformed into the more wide-ranging 'Made in Japan'. In moving out of sake and into electronics, Akio Morita moved the spirit of innovation and enterprise into the twentieth century, his father having created the 'open space' for him to do so.

This ongoing shifting continually creates new open spaces which invite the group spirit to consider new forms of expression. For example, a previously conceived act of bold diversification may be subsequently viewed as a deliberate attempt to catch the competition offguard. This in turn leads to a new subtlety in corporate strategy and to a fresh sense of humor in its interpretation. A strategy of deliberate 'fun making' takes over from jungle fighting tactics.

Thirdly, and finally, mythos may be itself transformative. Clock time (Greek *chronos*) is replaced by *kairos*, that is meaning – filled time, which in turn defines time for the group or organization. In other words, eras – for example, pre- and post-merger – replace months or years as focal points in an organization's historical progression.[13]

Similarly, the advent of Sony signified a meaningful shift in the Morita family's role in Japanese business and society. It even heralded a transformation in Japan's role in the world. Sony's development spearheaded, and reflected back, that of Japan, from a resourceful but conservative to a resourceful and adaptive nation, technologically and commercially. Through this the country's spirit of self-sufficiency was both retained and upgraded.

Re-membering and upgrading self-sufficiency

Japan

One of the most significant value concepts that we Japanese have cherished from ancient times is *mottainai*. It is an expression that suggests that everything in the world is a gift from the Creator, and that we should be grateful for it and never waste anything.

Yoishi

Yoishi Yokoi had gone into hiding when the US forces took Guam in 1944 and he had eluded capture for 28 years. Yoishi had bathed in, and had taken his drinking water from, a small stream near his cave. He had dug the cave eight feet below ground level, using a spent artillery shell as a shovel. He shored up his roof with bamboo, and he fashioned drains and a latrine for survival.

For his clothing he stripped the pliable bark from pago trees and made thread of it, which he wove into a cloth on a makeshift loom. Then he cut the cloth with the tailoring scissors he had saved – Yokoi had been a tailor before being drafted – and sewed trousers, shirts, and jackets. He had made needles by pounding and shaping pieces of brass cartridges. He also learnt to make fire by rubbing sticks together. He trapped freshwater fish and managed to grow some vegetables. He came home, in 1982, to a hero's welcome ...

Akio

I had to teach myself because the subjects I was really interested in were not taught in my school in those days [1930s]. But I managed to build a crude electric phonograph and a radio receiver of my own.

Sony

We Japanese have always been eager to develop our own technology, absorb aspects of technology from aboard, and blend them to make suitable objects or systems. Today, at Sony, we are developing new materials for uses in machines that are not off the drawing board, but that we know will be needed along the developmental time line.

Akio Morita *Made in Japan*[14] 1987

Liturgy

Liturgy, of which the raw material is myth and ritual and the manufactured process is form and structure, provides the peculiar sense of time, space and propriety indigenous to a particular people and culture. Liturgy is formed from two Greek words – *iaos*, meaning people, and *ergos*, meaning work. In literal translation it means the people's work, or what people do. In fact it is the sum of what the people do and say as an expression of their deepest being. When myth and ritual is deeply and continuously integrated into the life of an organization, that is liturgy. 'Liturgy at its best is the conscious production and orchestration of myth and ritual such that spirit is focussed and directed in a particular, intended way.[14] This is clearly in evidence within Sony.

Spirit and image

Traditionally, it has been the role of the priest to care for the story of the people, and to provide the means whereby that story can be continually re-membered. In contemporary business organizations we now find the public relations function sometimes taking on the role as guardian or protector of the spirit, or of the image, of the corporation. Akio Morita had adopted this role in Sony, from early on.

Trademark

I had decided during my first trip abroad in 1953 that our full name – Tokyo Tsushin Kogyo Kabushiki – was not a good name to put on a product. Ibuka and I then came across the Latin word *sonus*, meaning sound ... Sony carried the connotations of lightness and sound that we wanted ...

In June 1957 we put up our first billboard carrying the Sony name. One day we learnt that somebody was selling Sony chocolate. Seeing this stuff on sale made me sick. We took these imposters to court and brought famous people in, such as entertainers and newspapermen, to confirm the damage that was being done to us.

We won the case ... I have always believed that a trademark is the life of an enterprise and it must be protected boldly.

Akio Morita *Made in Japan*[15] 1987

Form and structure

While the raw material of liturgy is myth and ritual the processes for 'liturgy making' are form and structure. Form is the way we do things, as in the phrase 'good form'. Structure is the delineated field of operation within which things get done. To be effective in metaphysical terms, both form and structure should accord with, and be expressive of, the image and channel of the spirit of the organization.

Family form

The most important mission for a Japanese manager is to develop a healthy relationship with his employees, to create a family feeling within the corporation, a feeling that managers and employees share the same fate ...

On the 25th anniversary of Sony America, Yoshiko (my wife) and I flew to the US where we had a picnic or a meal with all the employees in Alabama, San Diego, Chicago and New York. It was not just part of my job; I like these people. They are family.

Akio Morita *Made in Japan*[16] 1987

Covenant

At some point in the life of an organization this special sense of time and space, form and structure, will be given formal verbal expression. Initially this expression will be very sparse, limited to some general agreement of 'the way things ought to be done around here'. Over time the expression will become more detailed, eventually constituting some kind of 'rule book'. This is what Owen terms the organizational 'covenant'.

Ibuka's dream (1940s)

If it were possible to establish conditions where persons could become united with a firm spirit of teamwork, and exercise to their heart's desire their technological capacity, then such an organization could bring untold pleasure and untold benefits.

Ibuka's management philosophy (1950s)

1. We shall eliminate any untoward profit seeking, and shall constantly emphasize the real substance of our products, not seeking expansion in size just for the sake of it.
2. Rather, we shall seek a compact size of operation through which the path of technology and business activities can advance in areas that large companies, because of their size, cannot.
3. We shall focus on highly sophisticated technical products that have great usefulness in society, regardless of the quantity involved.
4. Utilizing to the utmost the unique features of our firm, we shall open up through mutual cooperation our production and sales channels.
5. We shall guide and foster subcontracting factories in directions which will help them become independently operable, and shall strive to expand the pattern of mutual help with them.

Mick Lyons *The Sony Vision*[17] 1976

The extent to which the organizational covenant reflects the real behavior of the people within the enterprise varies enormously. It will all depend on the extent to which the spirit of the organization, reflected in and through myth and ritual, has inspired the people within it. How then might this, or might this not, come about?

Meta-strategy

The journey of the spirit

The journey of the spirit may be described as a series of stages which constitute, in Owen's terms, the course of organizational transformation. Each stage indicates some different quality or mode of that spirit, as it becomes progressively and strategically transformed into matter (See Fig. 74). In illustrating the point I shall now move from Sony in the East to an embryonic mining enterprise in the South.

The Zimbabwean company involved is Karanga Mining Company (KMC), which has recently been started by a spirited indigenous technologist, Trivanu Karanga. The journey begins with diffuse spirit. However, the emerging potential is gradually being transformed into increasingly concrete and specific, actual energy.

The creation of potential

Out of the depths
At the beginning of any organization's creation there is a moment when some individual, or some small group, has what amounts to an 'Aha' experience. Something might be done, something of particular moment. We saw it with Ibuka of Sony, with the founders of 3M, with Steve Shirley of F International, and now with Karanga of KMC.

This is the creative moment when something emerges out of nothing. It appears, as it were, from out of the depths. One might think of Edwin Land, when the mere possibility of an 'instant camera' popped into view or a thousand other emergent moments when the pot began to boil. At the instant, the originator may not know precisely what to do, and where it all might lead. But the thing is definitely there – hot, powerful, and moving.[18]

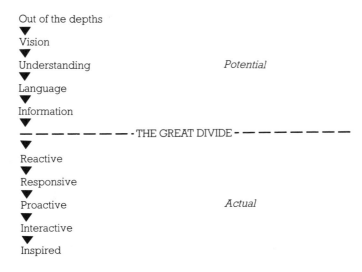

Fig. 74 The journey of the spirit.

Void gives shape to substance

Three years ago I decided to quit – temporarily – regular employment as a mining engineer to investigate business prospects for myself in Zimbabwe. Zimbabwe, and indeed most African countries at the time, were in a chronic state of hunger, poverty and political uncertainty.

In the early eighties the country was riddled with drought. I observed that some of the worst hit areas were mining regions, but it never dawned on me that I might become a prospector for minerals. My background was far too comfortable for a risky venture like that.

So despite my concern, and love for the peasantry, my intentions to create a new enterprise brought neither them nor myself any financial reward. I couldn't get a job, let alone a bank loan that could fund any one of the thousand plus investment projects that I had identified in the rural areas. Then, one day, I heard that my aged grandfather was dying of cancer in the communal lands. The whole of my family and clan decided to spend a weekend with him before he died, as a gesture of love. During the evening the 'spirit' (*mudzimu*) of my great grandfather spoke to us through the spirit medium (*svikiro*).

'The time has come to give wealth to our children, and they must then choose how to spread it amongst their children'. However, we had to perform certain culturally based rituals before getting such support from the spiritual world.

A month later my family conducted such rituals, and I was directed to go back into regular employment. A job was going to be secured for me in less than two weeks. A week later I was offered employment by three different organizations, none of which I had applied for. This was my first tangible experience of direct spiritual intervention in my life. My *mudzimu* also stressed that my future fortunes lay in the mining industry.

Trivanu Karanga, KMC[19] 1986

Vision
As substance is created out of the void, so a vision may begin to form, that is literally a

picture or image of where the future lies.

> In colour, shape and form, the idea is embedded in some descriptive way. But the vision is not only clothed in garments of the world; the vision also reaches out to shape, form, and change that world. The nascent organization expands its power base as sympathetic individuals are brought within the expanding energy field. What the vision may lack in concreteness, it more than makes up for in raw power.[20]

Tradition and modernity

Despite the risks associated, mining has proved itself to be the breadbasket of Rhodesia and now Zimbabwe. An interesting feature of particularly goldmining today is that the vast majority of major mines are on 'primitive' sites, on which iron ore has been mined for centuries.

The nineteenth century settlers dispossessed the indigenous owners of their customary rights. Karanga Mining Company, on the other hand, has adopted the local Shona culture as part and parcel of its enterprise. The workers, the communal chief, and the *mhondoro* or ancestral chief are all important members of the family. Our culture revolves around *ukama*, that is the real support gained from the cooperation between living and deceased members of the family.

With this combination of traditional cultural forces and modern production techniques we in KMC feel we can surpass all previous production records in mining iron ore. History is set to both repeat and outreach itself, as gold mining is renewed to reach even beyond its former glory.

Trivanu Karanga, KMC[21] 1986

Understanding

With 'understanding' the vision assumes clarity of form. Shape is measured, force is calibrated, products and goals are specified. Planning must be applied so that what emerged' out of the depths' can move from vision to the real world. Trivanu Karanga has thus related the journey of the spirit to a planned development, engineered by 'architects on the board'.

Architects on the board

It is my belief that the liberation struggle that resulted in the transformation of Rhodesia into Zimbabwe was engineered by our ancestors, especially our past chiefs, or *mhondoro*. They were the architects in a grand strategy to repossess the land. My own ancestors are a dynasty of successful merchants who traded in gold and ivory before the first Portuguese settlers entered East Africa in the seventeenth century.

It is in that context that I envisaged the birth and development of KMC. Since independence in 1981, egalitarian reforms introduced by the new government brought about a rapid improvement in the economy. This was so because of the vital cultural linkage between the land, the people, and the *mhondoro* [past chiefs of the so-called spirit provinces]. The government has planned for a 67% increase in minerals production over the next five years. This remarkable feat can only be accomplished by forging the same traditional and cultural linkages. Modern practices in the mining industry are inadequate to meet this requirement.

Our ancestors are the custodians of our natural resources. Land based enterprises thrive on the goodwill of these 'owners' of the land. In fact the early Portuguese settlers, in the eighteenth century, participated in the indigenous culture and rituals, and reaped their rewards in gold and ivory.

My own experience in 1985 lends support to this view. We had been prospecting for base minerals for four months without success. Despite all indications of failure we persisted in the search, basing our hope on the legends and folk stories of the wealth within the area. Eventually, though, we were on the point of packing our bags.

But a local labourer urged us to pay a visit to the area's spirit medium. He, in turn, advised us to perform certain rituals. More than sixty people danced, drank, ate and sang for three days. In the course of these rituals I was singled out by the local medium and questioned as to my motives and plans. I explained my mission and was subsequently given assurances of support. After that we had no more trouble in locating mineral deposits in the area.

I attributed our success to the harmony of interest between myself, my own ancestors, and the *mhondoro* of that particular area. I could see then that I was fulfilling a plan that had been designed by architects within a higher world.

KMC had therefore passed the first stage of business development, including the necessary financial and psychological investment, a stage that directly involved the world of 'spirit'. Now, as was the case in the past, our ancestors had asserted their authority over the land, and were actively keeping pace with, and leading the way for, the cultural and economic transformation of our country.

Trivanu Karanga, KMC[22] 1986

Language

Something arising out of the depths, represented in a vision, and located in a context that can be readily understood, must then be named. The possibility of expression comes through language. When something is named it is literally called into existence, as a conscious element in the life of the organization. In this way TTK came to be called Sony, and KMC was named – after the dynasty into which Trivanu was born. 'It is fitting', he says, 'to name an enterprise engineered by my ancestors after them'.

Until you know the name, the products and the functions of an organization, you cannot know it in a unique sense. In that sense IBM or Sony are more familiar to us than 3M or F International because – in the first two cases as opposed to the second two – the company names reflect the products and functions of the enterprises.

Information and data

Harrison Owen does not separate out 'information and data', as impersonal abstractions devoid of spirit. In viewing them as means whereby progress is measured and plans are measured and changed, he sees still a continuity of flow. In other words such data are a record of the movement of spirit, along its journey from out of the depths onwards.

There is a continuity of flow. The same spirit moves on through a sequence of manifestations. There is also a discontinuity of effect. Each appearance of spirit must end before the next emerges. That is the story of the butterfly, the story of transformation.[23]

Appropriate adaptation has led to the progressive transformation of KMC from just about a one-man band – mining in one area – into an early stage-managed organization, with a series of gold mines. However, these are still very early days. Hope and potential still far exceed actual production. In other words, potential has been recognized, and to some degree realized, but is only beginning to be actualized.

From potential to actuality

Crossing the great divide separating 'might be' from 'is' brings the organizational spirit from the level of good idea to that of being there. In this process of 'actualization' the spirit brings about reaction, response, proactivity, interaction and finally, inspiration.

Reaction

On the first days of business, Owen points out, things are more than a little confusing. Events and demands pile on top of one another. The style of management may be described as 'reactive'. You just keep things moving.

A punch drunk boxer

KMC, as of 1985, was myself – Trivanu Karanga – as sole proprietor. I had no capital nor prospects for getting capital. I was neither an experienced miner nor geologist. Yet somehow I had faith that my ancestors would see to the capital need as we went along.

At many a stage I could not even see my way through the next two days. Somehow I persisted despite the hardships incurred in trying to raise capital, the threats from creditors, pilfering management, dishonest workers, stringent labor regulations, and family obligations. I went through a living nightmare. The blows were getting heavier and heavier and I still came on for more, like a punch drunk boxer.

What kept me going was my instinct, faith, and the spirit of my ancestors. Eventually I gained a kind of immunity to hardship and soldiered on. Whenever I was at the bottom of the barrel something would happen that would enable me to carry on.

As one *mhondoro* put it to me, 'Where there is honey there are fierce stinging bees.'

Trivanu Karanga, KMC[24] 1986

Responsive

Once things begin to move ahead without constant disruption you will have learnt to distinguish what works from what does not. In other words you will have learnt to respond appropriately. As Owen says: 'It becomes clearer who you are and what your business is, so that your organization may be responsive to your own needs, and to those of the outside world.'[25]

Productivity and adaptivity

When we started mining most employees were on fixed hourly rates. We found later that this practice was inadequate because most local people had an alternative job going at home or in the communal fields. Attendance and productivity therefore left a lot to be desired.

We then decided to introduce an hourly rate coupled with a productivity bonus scheme. Productivity was the key and there was no better way of emphasizing the point.

Trivanu Karanga, KMC[26] 1986

Proactive and interactive

Proactive organizations are at the opposite pole from reactive ones. They not only respond appropriately but they exhibit a strong sense of purpose.

Interactive enterprises approach particular problems, albeit purposefully, as they individually arise, whereas interactive ones have a more wholistic and integrated approach. They merge with their environment, seeking progressively more interactive ways of expressing themselves.

The distinction between 'in here' and 'out there' becomes increasingly more blurred, as boundaries and constraints are turned into linkages and opportunities. This has indeed been the case for KMC. 'Already opportunities are opening up for integrating vertically in processing mineral ores for manufacturing industries'.

Inspired organization

The journey of the spirit is completed when the matter it has infused becomes fully transformed. In other words, the organization through its people – as a whole – now becomes totally inspired.

Although the quality of inspiration is similar to that of the individual's original vision, it is now diffused throughout the organization. The whole enterprise has become 'spiritualized'. All forms of energy are vibrating with spirit!

Spirit–energy–spirit

The potential for the inspired organization is given by the out of depths experience with which the organization began. The experience was powerful in the sense that something dramatic and new appeared from nowhere. What it was and what it would become were all unknowns.

Over the course of the succeeding stages of the odyssey, that primordial spirit, having emerged from out of the depths, became more focussed and particular. The spirit appeared in successive modes of being, each one of which allowed for a fuller expression of its potential. Yet even at the interactive level, form and structure were important and constraining considerations. The Inspired level brings the possibility of going beyond these constraints.

Harrison Owen *Development and Transformation*[27] 1987

KMC, as a youthful enterprise, has a long way to go before it might become an inspired organization. Yet a lot of potential has already been created. Trivanu Karanga has certainly emerged out of the depths. The vision he now holds powerfully motivates him to link Zimbabwe's spiritual and cultural heritage with its material resources.

Through his enriched understanding of indigenous business and society, moreover, he has fused together ancient Zimbabwean culture and modern European technology. He has even created a new business language through *mhondoro* (spirit) and *ukama* (cooperation) into his mining operation. That operation will be monitored, via this special language, and through 'purpose built' information.

Furthermore Karanga has crossed the great divide between potential and actual. In doing so he at first reacted instinctively to adversity, carrying on relentlessly and fuelled by the support of his family and ancestry. He is now beginning to tackle responsively technical, social and economic problems as they arise, and has been proactive enough to draw on traditional practices to reinforce current productivity.

He has not yet reached a stage in which his interactive activity is as commercially evident and viable as it is, communally. For at this point he has not yet won over a sceptical business establishment, for reasons that will soon become apparent. So KMC is still being called upon to react to adverse financial circumstances.

Finally, when and if Karanga creates a wholly inspired organization, and so actualizes his vision, he is likely to be ten or twenty years down the road. 'We must not fail and cannot fail because the stakes are too high for not only KMC but also for Zimbabwe and Mozambique to whom we are spiritually bonded.'[28]

Facilitating the journey

Policy and strategy

The journey of the spirit is an odyssey that a metaphysical manager, like Trivanu, undergoes over a long period of time. At one stage he will have emerged from out of the depths to gradually formulate his vision. He will have established his metaphysical policy. Over time the vision will have been placed in context, and converted into a business language that those around him could understand. In his own mind he will also have planned a series of steps for its accomplishment.

In fact this process, whereby potential is created, will often recur during the metaphysical manager's lifetime. If KMC is to continue to develop Trivanu will have to descend into the depths on many more occasions. In subsequently turning actualizing potential he will continually and successively react, respond, become proactive and then interactive, and then infuse his whole organization with inspiration. That is, if you like, his ongoing metaphysical strategy.

This strategy or journey takes place, however, in the wider context of an organization, as I revealed in the first part of this chapter. As Fig. 75 indicates, spirit is inevitably and necessarily moulded by corporate culture. The 'family culture' pervading Sony and the *ukama* culture pervading KMC are ever present.

This culture is in its turn re-presented through myth and ritual (*mythos*), with which both Akio Morita and Trivanu Karanga have imbued their organizations. Japanese and Zimbabwean mythology, whether pertaining to self-sufficiency or honey and stinging bees, have become part of the organizations' fabric. The heroic exploits of their current and ancestral originators live on through stories acted out, ritualized and re-presented.

Mythos creates liturgy, that is the everyday activities of people in the organization, which is more or less infused with myth and ritual. Every time Sony makes a technological breakthrough the spirit of *mottainai* is relived. Every time a new mine is discovered the chiefs of the spirit provinces are remembered.

Liturgy is codified, at a later stage of the organization's development, as the organizational covenant (see Ibuka's management philosophy on p. 542) which serves, in its turn, to produce a coherent spirit. In the business' early stages, as for KMC, the covenant and the vision are as one.

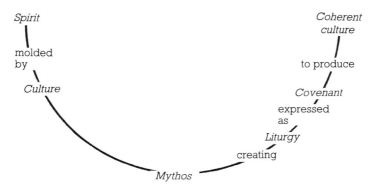

Fig. 75 Spirit and culture.

Operations

Whereas the metaphysical manager undergoes the journey of the spirit, the developmental manager can, at least to some extent, facilitate it within the organization as a whole. This is a useful developmental role because organizational members seldom perceive their institution as spirit, represented by *mythos*. Moreover, even for those who are so inclined, really seeing your own culture, your own stories, and your own spirit, is difficult because they are so much part of your life.

Harrison Owen's approach to facilitating the journey of spirit involves four distinct steps. In step one a general understanding of the organization is developed through a consideration of its history. In step two the facilitator focusses on the leader, and on his personal vision and understanding. Finally, in steps three and four, the organizational culture is studied, described, and reflected back to its members, through a variety of methods.

Particular and novel use is made of what Owen calls a mythograph.

Historical scan

The process begins with a historian's approach to the organization, unravelling at the outset objective facts and figures – when did the organization all start, where and under what conditions? Who are, or were, the major figures, founders, associates and adversaries, and what have been their major characteristics and contributions? What is the structure and shape of the organization, including its external affiliations? What are the major locations and product lines?

Having found this all out the facilitator then must uncover what significant events have occupied the organization's past. He is therefore interested in the development of brand new products and services, market breakthroughs, mergers and takeovers, reorganizations, struggles for succession, and so on. His aim is to uncover, at this initial stage, not only facts and figures but also the key words and names – particular to the organization – which recur.

Owen calls these heavy words, because of their depth of historically based meaning and significance. Sony itself, from the Latin *sonus*, meaning sound, is a good case in point.

After completing this historical scan, and having identified several 'heavy words', the facilitator interviews the leader of the organization.

Uncovering the leader's vision

During this interview – step two – the essential question that the facilitator asks is 'Where does the organization think that it is going, or would like to go?' The question is asked of the current leader, and is aimed at uncovering his vision and understanding of the organization. The discussion starts with facts and figures – production targets, plans for relocation, and recitation of major problems and opportunities – but should proceed to the uncovering of the leader's personal and qualitative vision of the long-term future. The question of 'What would it look and feel like if success were achieved?' addresses the quality of spirit desired.

Cultural analysis

Exploration

Step three begins at the conclusion of the interview with the leader, at which time he or she is asked to identify a dozen important people in the organization. 'Importance' may be defined in any way the leader chooses, though he would inevitably include several members of his or her senior staff. In interviewing these important people one cannot begin by asking 'What are the key myths and rituals around here?'. Rather one centers upon three questions: 'Who are you and how did you get here? What is this place? What should it be?'

Who are you? The first question is designed to set the stage and allow the person to talk about himself. It serves to place him or her in the context of the organization, and its historical evolution.

What is this place?/What should it be? The second two questions go to the heart of the matter, but they get there indirectly. Inevitably the person interviewed will initially respond with facts and figures, but will be likely to turn to stories and incidents that emerge out of, or exemplify, these. Their words might go something like: 'You really don't understand this place ... it's like ... well last week', and out comes the tale.

In listening to the interview responses, it is important to remember what, in particular, you are investigating. The factual information is of interest, but only from the point of view that it establishes the context. The real concern is for the 'little stories' that are told. Sometimes the telling of a tale will be an extended performance; other times it may involve just a few key words, for example 'John is a mysterious character'.

Although only a select few stories will be told by those twelve people, in Owen's experience the seminal ones will recur. The actual number of major myths (stories 'pregnant' with meaning), in his opinion, is unlikely to succeed half a dozen, even within a major corporation.

Preliminary assessment

The role of the focus group. Once the initial interviews are complete, they must be analyzed in terms of the stories present. Of particular importance is the way in which these stories function together to represent the spirit of the organization. Areas of similarity and difference between the leader's vision and that of his 'followers' should be identified.

Step three of the process comes to an end when the findings are presented to a preselected focus group of the organization's leader and his key associates. The function of this group is twofold – firstly, to validate the stories, and secondly, to assess the proposed interpretation and corrective actions.

The role of the full group. In step four, stories are sought from all levels and sectors of the organization. Specifically this means interviewing a representative sample from the executive, middle management, and working levels of all major departments and divisions. This may involve a total of, say, one hundred people in an organization of ten thousand. The facilitator simply proceeds until stories begin to repeat themselves, continually, at any one level or in any one sector.

Observing ritual. In addition to uncovering these stories through interviews, it is important to observe closely the rituals that characterize different parts of the organization. These may range from board and departmental meetings, to sales drives, to 'rites of passage' for new recruits, to company prize givings, to golden handshakes. One needs to identify their precise range and character.

Constructing the mythograph

Classification. Once the tales and ritual acts have been gathered, the problem is to make sense out of this collection by arranging the material in such a way that the quality and direction of the spirit emerges. Furthermore, one needs to identify how strongly focussed or weakly diffused the spirit may be and apply any corrective actions that may be appropriate. The means whereby this analysis is accomplished is Owen's mythograph.

Table 37 The mythograph of KMC

Levels	Sectors		
	Operations	Banking	Community
Executive	11. Dynasty of merchants	12. The guy's crackers	13. Nehanda at the gallows
Supervisory	21. The Wedza *bira*	22. The Zimbabwe ruins	23. The dying grandfather
Workers	31. Where there's honey there are stinging bees	32. His father went under	33. Ukama

The mythograph is a formalized representation of the organization onto which may be plotted the elements of myth and ritual. By way of an example, and applying more than a little of my own imagination (in absence of the complete facts) I have used KMC to illustrate the mythographic points (See Table 37).

Assessment. In assessing the mythograph (see Table 38), the key thing to remember is that each element (myth) re-presents, and in a sense contains, the spirit of the place. Furthermore, it provides indications of the quality, force and direction of the spirit.

Table 38 An mythographic analysis of KMC

11.	'Dynasty of merchants'	Trivanu's ancestors, stretching back hundreds of years, were all gold and ivory traders
21.	'The Wedza *bira*'	In the Wedza area, after Karanga had unsuccessfully prospected for four months, he held a *bira*, that is a traditionally communal festival, and iron ore was subsequently found
31.	'Honey/stinging'	There is a traditional story, told within the local Shona culture that tells of the bees that sting (hardships incurred) by those gallant folk seeking honey for all
12.	'The guy's crackers'	The European bankers in Zimbabwe are skeptical of 'spiritual' forces, especially in business. Most regard Trivanu, the self-styled visionary, as not only a poor investment, but also 'crackers'
22.	'Zimbabwe ruins'	The indigenous banking supervisors, more receptive to Karanga, tell the story of the ancient Zimbabwe ruins, in which gold was mined 500 years ago – Trivanu is seen to be following in those footsteps
32.	'His father went under'	The low level staff within the banks, easily influenced by the big bosses, tell jokes about the family of bankrupt Karanga, Trivanu's father having himself gone in
13.	'Nehanda at the gallows'	The spiritual leader Nehanda, vowed, as she was taken to the gallows in 1890, that her bones would rise to liberate her country
23.	'The dying uncle'	As Karanga was beginning to despair over his self-determined future, the spirit of his dying grandfather intervened, and pointed towards Trivanu's future in mining
33.	'Ukama'	Many a story has been told within the traditional culture of how, through a spirit of cooperation, great things have been achieved

Under ideal circumstances, when the metaphysical management of the organization is functioning effectively, all cells would show the same seminal story, with minor and due variations, according to level and sector. That sort of coherent picture would represent a 'one pointed' spirit, creating the potential for an unimpeded, powerful flow of physical and human energy. In this situation not only is the culture coherent, but the spirit remains free and flexible – free to develop and transform.

As we can see from the mythograph characterizing KMC the company and the indigenous community are in harmony. One story, whether current or historic, KMC or Zimbabwe, related, reinforces the other. The company–community spirit is coherent at all levels. In contrast the banking establishment is out of step. Its spirit lies some place else. 'The guy's crackers'.

Applying corrective metaphysical action

The futility of direct intervention

Corrective metaphysical action will smooth out the flow – avoid side eddies and bottlenecks – toward the achievement of the business' vision. Such action must recognize the present situation in which the spirit flow is disconnected in one particular respect and mutually reinforcing in all others.

Simply telling someone – the banking establishment in this case – to adopt a different *mythos* can never work. Such statements, as for example 'don't shut yourself off from the spirit of Karanga's ancestors', literally fall outside of the frame of reference of the listener. Consequently it is 'nonsense' to him. In fact a direct challenge to the European's own *mythos* that 'mining empires are created by heroic personalities with material resources at their command', will merely strengthen his original position. As Owen says: 'Since *mythos* represents the field of meaning, denial of *mythos* will subject the holder to meaninglessness, which is obviously not a condition that anyone will willingly enter into.'

Leadership by indirection

The alternative route that Owen proposes is 'leadership by indirection'. The object is to create a new and composite story out of the existing elements contained within the mythograph. By using the existing *mythos* the basic, conservative nature of culture is acknowledged. However, the very power of the newly shaped story, overrides the existing negativity. Let me illustrate. In constructing the new tale a place must be found for the heroes and rebels of the past, as a basis and connecting point for the future. In KMC's case, then, a linkage needs to be established between such characters as Rhodes and Jameson – the heroes of the European establishment, and Nehanda, the heroine of the indigenous Zimbabweans.

Furthermore, in the process of reconstruction the spirit of Zimbabwe's ancestors needs to be interlinked with that of Rhodes himself, who indeed lives on through the European's historical connection with 'Rhodesia'.

Collective story telling

The new *mythos* cannot be created impersonally, but has to be installed through a process of collective story telling.

Collective story telling

Weaving the new tale is the essence of leadership and lies at the heart of the process of transformation. In constructing it, it is necessary to consciously link back to the organizational potential, created through its depths, vision, and language, and also the ways in which its potential may have become actualised in everyday business life.

Whatever this new tale may be it cannot simply jettison all that went before ...

The leader may start with a 'story line', but that is just the framework around which need to be orchestrated all of the other elements. In fact it should be possible to touch, smell, and move with a story that is well told. Each part should be able to contribute in its own way, and none should be allowed to dominate.

But most of all, the story should be constructed with sufficient open space to allow members of the organization to partake in its creation, through their own imagination. The story must become their story, 'our story' . . . Telling a four-dimensional story is a real art. Indeed it may be the highest form of art.

Harrison Owen *Development of Transformation*[28] 1987

Conclusion: the creation of liturgy

A story once told will be quickly eroded unless it is retold and embedded within the organization. It must become real, and an ongoing part of organizational life. In other words it must become liturgy – or what the people do. No longer is it the leader's prime function to direct the organization. Rather it is his responsibility to orchestrate the new story in all its forms. The structure of the institution, its physical fabric, the cycle of organizational activities – all need to reinforce it.

Suitable 'rites of passage' for new recruits to the enterprise need to be developed. Celebrations, at regular intervals, must reflect the *ethos*, the *mythos* and the appropriate heroes. In the KMC case Trivanu, as leader of his enterprise, would assume a position central to not only his workforce and the indigenous community but also to the commercial and political establishment in Zimbabwe. Akio Morita has already assumed such a position in Japan.

The rounded structure of his organization would reflect the spirit of *ukama* (cooperation) indigenous to the country, and pictures of Cecil Rhodes (colonizer) and Mbuya Nehanda (liberator) would be located alongside one another. Sony has achieved this harmonization of opposing forces by Westernizing its Japanese operation, in one sense, and Easternizing its American one, in another.

New recruits to KMC would be able to share the story of its birth and growth, alongside stories of the founding of both Rhodesia and Zimbabwe. The *bira* festival, which had such a formative influence on the KMC's development, would be regularly celebrated. In Sony Akio Motita makes a point of addressing all new recruits in Japan, once a year, and revealing to them the journey of Sony's spirit.

In time, the spirit of the organization, moulded by the Sony or by the KMC culture – through the prevailing myths and rituals – needs to create an enduring liturgy, expressed in the form of a written covenant, serving to produce a coherent spirit. Should this process not happen naturally it is possible to intervene, albeit indirectly, and help the transformation of energy and spirit along. It is that spirit, for Harrison Owen and for all metaphysically inclined cultures, which is the most precious and powerful of all organizational resources. In Chapter 27 we shall take a further look at the metaphysical process of transformation – of energy into spirit and back again – this time via Joseph Campbell's *Hero of a Thousand Faces*.[29]

References

1. H. Owen, *Transformation and Development in Organistions*, published privately (1987), p. 3.
2. P. Curie, ex J. Goodfield, *The Imagined World*, Penguin (1982).
3. J. Goodman, *The Mond Legacy*, Weidenfeld & Nicolson (1984), p. 42.
4. A. Nobel, ex N. Hale, *Nobel*, Robert Hode (1980), p. 21.
5. A. Morita, *Made in Japan*, Collins (1987).

6. H. Owen, 'Myth, Transformation and Change', ex J. Adams, *The Transformation of Work*, Miles River Press (1984), p. 216.
7. H. Owen, *op.cit.*, p. 217.
8. A. Morita, *op.cit.*, pp. 52–60.
9. A. Morita, *op.cit.*, p. 64.
10. J. Campbell, *The Hero with a Thousand Faces*, Princeton University (1969), p. 37.
11. A. Morita, *op.cit.*, p. 48.
12. H. Owen, *op.cit.*, p. 35.
13. J. Brady, *Keeper of the Corporate Image*, unpublished paper (1987).
14. A. Morita, *op.cit.*, pp. 18, 227 and 237.
15. A. Morita, *op.cit.*, p. 66.
16. A. Morita, *op.cit.*, p. 87.
17. M. Lyons, *The Sony Vision* Crowell (1976).
18. H. Owen, *op.cit.*, p. 39.
19. T. Karanga, unpublished paper, Zimbabwe (1986).
20. H. Owen, *op.cit.*, p. 40.
21. T. Karanga, *op.cit.*, p. 4.
22. T. Karanga, *op.cit.*, p. 6.
23. H. Owen, *op.cit.*, p. 42.
24. T. Karanga, *op.cit.*, p. 9.
25. H. Owen, *op.cit.*, p. 45.
26. T. Karanga, *op.cit.*, p. 7.
27. H. Owen, *op.cit.*, p. 48.
28. H. Owen, *op.cit.*, p. 140.
29. J. Campbell, *op.cit.*, p. 116.

27 From vision to action

Contents

Key concepts

Once you have fully understood this chapter you should be able to define the following concepts in your own terms:

Asserting yourself	Mystical union
Adapting to change	Natural inclinations*
Blocks to vision	Protector
Born hero	Recognizing needs
Call to adventure	Risking yourself
Compass hero	Road of trials
Corporate vision to action	Role of myth
Criteria for vision	Roots*
evaluation	Source
Developing vision	Structuring a business
Enhancing yourself*	Taking action
Inhibitions to vision	Unravelling vision*
Innovation	Vision to life*
Involving people	Visionary attributes
Learning	

Objectives

Upon completing this chapter you should be able to do the following:

1. Outline the significance of myth and of heroism, in metaphysical management.
2. Describe the course taken in a heroic journey of the kind described by Joseph Campbell.
3. Outline the resultant approach to learning, and to innovation.
4. Undertake at least two, and up to five, of the personal vision building exercises.
5. Apply the 'vision to action' process to both yourself, and also to an organization, in, at minimum, a sketchy and illustrative fashion.

Introduction

The functions of myth

It has always been a central function of mythology to supply the symbols that carry the human spirit forward, in counteraction to those other images that constantly hold us back. As Joseph Campbell says in *The Hero with a Thousand Faces*, 'We remain fixated to the unexorcized images of our infancy, and hence disinclined to the necessary passages of adulthood'.[1] This disinclination can apply just as much to organizations as to individuals.

It is with these individual and organizational passages that this chapter is concerned. However, unlike the developmental manager, who is concerned with processes of personal and collective evolution, the metaphysical manager, or hero, is geared towards creative action. In other words he is an agent of transformation, as opposed to development, a revolutionary as opposed to an evolutionary. As such he is engaged in a

* Exercises.

journey of truly heroic proportions, equal in dramatic impact to the mythological journey of antiquity.

As we saw in the previous chapter, Joseph Campbell describes the four primary functions of the myth – accompanying such heroic journies – as follows:

- First, to awaken consciousness to the fascinating mystery of the existing universe.
- Second, to interpret that mystery in order to give meaning to life.
- Third, to sustain the moral order.
- Fourth, to foster the centering and unfolding of the individual.

The role of the hero

The leading character in the great myths, throughout the centuries and across the globe, are the heroes and heroines, engaged in their triumphant or tragic journies.

Peters and Waterman,[2] as we indicated in Chapter 2, point out that heroes abound in excellent companies. Deal and Kennedy, in their *Corporate Cultures* (see Chapter 9), differentiate between the 'born hero', the mainstay of the business, and the 'compass hero', an important but lesser mortal.

Organizational heroes

If values are the soul of the culture, then heroes personify values and epitomize the strength of the organization. They create the role models for employees to follow. The hero is the great motivator, the magician, the person everyone will count on when things get tough. They have unshakeable character and style. Heroes are symbolic figures whose deeds are out of the ordinary but not too far out. They show, often dramatically, that the ideal of success lies within human capacity.

The success of the born hero lies in not only having built an organization, but also in having established an institution that survived them and added their personal sense of values to the world. Their visions changed the way we do business and their influence is still pervasive.

A second type of 'made' hero is the compass hero. If a company is in a situation where things have to change and there are no role models for it, it is good management practice to find role models, plant them inside the company, and make them heroes. By doing so, management communicates that, in the future, business will be done either more 'aggressively' or more 'courteously'; in any case, less as it was done and more as the new hero style conveys.

Deal and Kennedy *Corporate Cultures*[3] 1982

Our concern here is with the born hero, although, as budding metaphysical managers, we all have a chance of becoming such heroes in the course of our maturation. It does necessarily involve, as I have indicated, a truly heroic journey.

The journey of the spirit

Harrison Owen, engages, via his 'journey of the spirit' in metaphysical depth. Like Joseph Campbell he is both interested in entering into the great mysteries of the universe and also in the centering and unfolding of the individual.

As we saw in Chapter 21, Owen[4] traced the hero's journey:

through potential

- From out of the depths of the hero's subconscious motivation.
- Into his vision of individual and organizational potential.
- Via understanding of the context in which he was operating.
- Through a special language that enabled him to communicate.
- The information to accomplish his prospective task.

By this point our hero has equipped himself with the motivation, imagination, understanding, language and information to accomplish his historic mission. But he still has to cross that great divide between knowledge and action, between potential and its actualization. As he journeyed on:

towards the actual

- He reacted first to the onset of circumstances.
- Before becoming more deliberately responsive to situations.
- Therefore growing truly purposeful or proactive.
- Becoming, at a later stage, genuinely interactive as well as.
- Ultimately, and wholly, inspired.

Joseph Campbell, via his *Hero with a Thousand Faces*,[5] presents us with a heroic journey which is more visual and dramatic. I want to become involved, with you, in Campbell's metaphysical and heroic journey before converting it into more accessibly analytical language. In the process, and we shall see, I shall journey with you from action towards vision – that is the way of learning, and from vision back to action – that is the way of innovation.

The heroic journey

Campbell's hero, and the passages he undergoes, reflect something of the flavour that John Hillbery conveyed (see pp. 516–18), in his journey through life. The image of the eventful journey rather than that of the successful destination is the one that sticks in our minds. It begins with a call to adventure (action) and ends with the discovery of power (vision). The result of a successful journey is the unlocking and release of a flow of life into the body of the world.

Responding to the call

The call to adventure is the first stage of the mythological journey. John Hillbery's sojourn as merchant seaman corresponds with this phase. Destiny summons the hero and transfers his center of gravity from within the pole of society to a zone unknown. In other words, our hero disregards social convention, and instead of going to university or landing a good job, he sets out towards an unfamiliar destination.

Often in actual life, and not infrequently in the myths and popular tales, we encounter cases of the call being unanswered. In business parlance opportunities go unrecognized. Refusal to follow the call results in boredom, or disintegration of the individual or enterprise. All the person can do is create problems for himself and await the gradual approach of his demise: 'His flowering world becomes a wasteland of dry stones and his life seems meaningless'.

The myths and folk tales of the whole world make clear that the refusal is essentially the rejection of one's own individual self-interest or social purpose or 'dream'. So John Hillbery might have remained a journalist rather than becoming 'the guardian of the spirit of BCC'. In choosing to follow his call he is effectively crossing the threshold.

Opening yourself to a protector

For those who have not refused the call, the first encounter on the heroic journey is with a protective figure. In Hillbery's case the linguist he met at the shipping company shielded him from boredom and mundanity. Such a person also provides the adventurer 'with amulets against the dragon forces he is about to pass'.

Having responded to his own call, and continuing courageously as both positive and negative consequences unfold, the hero finds the powerful forces of the unconscious on his side. In so far as the hero's actions coincide with that for which his society is ready, he seems to stride along the great rhythm of the historic process. Hence BCC was able to grow at such an enormous rate during the seventies.

Entering the road of trials

Having responded to the call, then, the hero crosses the threshold of the known into the world of the unknown. Armed with a protector, he moves into a dream landscape of curiously fluid, ambiguous forms, where he must survive a road of trials. These are well known, of course, to the risk taking entrepreneur, to the proverbial adventurer and to the business visionary.

Risking loss or gain

World mythology has produced a vast literature of miraculous tests and ordeals. The hero, however, is aided by the advice, resources and even 'secret agents' of the magical helper whom he met before entering into the unknown. But he still has to stand the ultimate test alone. Is he able to put his old self to death? Is he willing to put his own security, both physical and psychological, aside? 'For many headed is the surrounding Hydra; one head cut off, two more appear.' Dragons have now to be slain and surprising barriers to be passed, again and again. There will meanwhile be a multitude of preliminary victories and momentary glimpses of the promised land.

Engaging in a mystical union

The ultimate adventure, when all the barriers and ogres have been overcome, is commonly represented by a mystical marriage of the triumphant hero-soul with the queen goddess of the world. When John Hillbery left the Bank of America to join BCC that mystical union occurred. He helped the Bank's founder, Agha Hasan Abedi, create an organization capable of receiving their visionary impulse. The 'corporation', a term whose origin lies in the word 'cup', should be seen as the great receptacle for the heroic spirit.

The 'mystical union', to which we refer, also involves a marriage of yang and yin, of active heroism and receptive appreciation, of power and love, of product and market.

Penetrating to the source

Subsequent to the mystical union, and further heroic accomplishments, the hero quest is accomplished only when and if he succeeds in penetrating to the source. Within the source lies the true vision to be realized. In order to reach that vision our hero has to acquire supreme power.

In order to gain such power the hero must proceed to the threshold of adventure. There he encounters the shadow presence of the guards of the ultimate passage. If he overcomes them he enters into another new and unfamiliar world of strange and yet intimate forces, some of which challenge him and others of which give him magical aid.

Acquiring the power of vision

When he arrives at the nadir of his mythological round, he undergoes a supreme ordeal. If he survives he gains his reward, the power of vision.

The full round of departure and return requires that the hero now begins the labor of bringing the golden fleece, as it were, back into the kingdom of humanity. In other words the vision has to be converted into action, whereby the individual, the corporation, the community or planet can realize itself. This is a task in which the Bank of Credit and Commerce is actively and currently engaged, but still has a long way to go. Agha Hasan Abedi and John Hillbery have acquired the power of vision, but have only just begun their 'return' journey, that is the journey through which vision is turned into enduring action.

From vision to action

Learning: the departure

The hero with a thousand faces, with all his mythological overtones, may appear as somewhat fanciful to the hardened realists amongst you. For some twenty years now a British philosopher and psychologist, with strong Indian connections, Kevin Kingsland, has been developing an approach to business and to life which turns the mythologies of antiquity into everyday realities. While Kevin has worked with thousands of students in Britain, in India, and in America, running programs on personal communication, I have been applying this 'vision to action' approach to businesses small and large in America, in the UK and in Zimbabwe.[6]

The call to adventure: the first physical step

Kingsland's vision to action approach,[7] like Jacob's Ladder linking heaven with earth, spans the complete spectrum of human endeavor. We learn in business and in life by ascending, as it were, Jacobbs Ladder step by step, thus following the path of the hero. That, if you like, is the heroic departure. The 'call to adventure' represents the first and physical step. Without activity there is no learning. The newborn babe learns about life through physical challenge and response. When learning ceases to be an adventure it loses its primordial aspect.

The role of protector: making a social connection

The role of the protector symbolizes the supportive part to be played by a mother figure, a caring teacher or by 'comrades in adversity'. Without a social context into which learning can be placed it becomes depersonalized and sterile. If we fail to open ourselves to the supportive influence of coaches and of mentors, who inevitably cross our heroic path, our journey will be in vain. We shall remain insular and insulated.

The road of trials: learning from experience

The 'road of trials' quite obviously represents the processes of trial and error, action and reflection, that the individual or enterprise undergoes in order to learn from experience. This is the period of mental alertness, and of youthful discovery, that is such an important part of growing up. This is Levinson's youthful phase, built into the learning process, before we settle down in an adult way. Any task we tackle, then, should involve some degree of exploration and experimentation before we commit ourselves to a particular line of thought or action.

Taking a risk: committing yourself

'Risking the loss of your old self' is the inward equivalent of the outward risk taking that accompanies business and personal enterprise. Professor Revans, in Chapter 14, has argued that there is no real learning without risk.

Whatever ideas you pick up intellectually you have to develop the emotional commitment to put both them and yourself to the test. In the process you may become a different person, disassembled and reassembled, as a result of the emotional wrangles you have undergone. You may remember how Steve Shirley of F International was 'toughened' by the experience of losing her partner (see pp. 381-6).

The marriage of interest: defining your role

As your new self fully emerges or a new business comes into its own, a further learning step is required if there is to be continued development. A 'marriage of interest' between the thrusting force of the newly formed ego (the hero soul) and the receptive force of an existing organization (the mother goddess) is needed for both individual and enterprise to outgrow narrowly based self-interest. The combined result is a rounded business concept, an individual with role integrity, or an organization with a coherent philosophy.

Penetrating to the source: developing insight

A person may have role integrity or a business may have a clearly defined mission, but neither will ensure that the individual or organization has 'penetrated to its source'. That degree of understanding of the source and destination of one's personal or organizational being requires a particular brand of personal and social insight. Such insight is developed through a capacity to listen, a power to observe, a willingness to be overawed, and an ability and inclination to link like with unlike, actual and potential, visible energy and invisible spirit, whether in the person or in the business.

The power of vision: engaging in creative action

The 'acquisition of visionary power', finally, only comes when the insight developed through penetrating the source of the individual's or company's being, is tested out in practice.

You only learn about the power of vision when you engage in the kind of creative action that serves to bring it about. There is much of the chicken and the egg about it, and it is always difficult to tell which came first. But when you have acquired the power of vision, nothing will hold you back.

Attributes of vision

When you have found your vision you do not ask yourself whether you have one. You inform the world about it. If you're wondering whether you have a vision, then you haven't got one.

When you've discovered your vision you abound with inspiration. Your eyes sparkle. You can see it in the atmosphere. It is pulsing with life.

When you have a vision everything you plan and do stems from it. Its all-consuming nature makes all previous attitudes and ideas seem like a training ground for the ultimate vision.

When you feel part of an overall vision you don't think of rest and reward. Total absorption removes all sense of personal effort. You cannot help but pursue the vision.

When you have a vision that is all you want to talk about. Everything people say or do is a readout of that vision. The world becomes a theater for your visionary script.

When the vision is present in you everyone around gets included or ignored, depending on whether or not they feel associated with it. In other words, people become actors in your production, or else they remain off stage.

When you find your vision nothing will be permitted to stand in its way. Obstacles must be overcome or else life won't be worth living for you.

Kevin Kingsland *The Whole Personality*[8] 1985

Innovation: the return

Learning reflects the mythological hero's outward journey, from the call to adventure on to the acquisition of power. Innovation represents his return. In other words, having ascended Jacob's Ladder, rising from action up to vision, he now descends the ladder, this time turning vision into action. This descent constitutes the process and substance of innovation. The highest point on the ladder, the one most filled with spiritual substance, emerging from out of the subconscious depths, is personal imagination and corporate vision.

Developing your vision
- What is your personal mission?
- How is it going to change the world around you?

- How will its fulfillment change your life, work and vocation?
- What universal problem will your unique idea solve?
- Where does your imagination lead you?

Vision will be stillborn unless it is united with insight and understanding, and thereby with social need.

Recognizing market need

- Does your idea have market potential?
- How is technology and society evolving and where does your vision fit in with such developments?
- What particular market trends pertain to your idea?
- What underlying need will you serve?
- What business partnerships and alliances will arise?

If vision is father to the innovation, and need is mother, the resultant offspring is the business concept and organization, expressed in a unique language, and both yielding and drawn from particular information.

Structuring a business and organization

- What product or service is being designed for what market?
- How is the product created, developed, produced and sold?
- How do the different business functions interact with one another and with the outside world?
- How is a balance maintained between freedom and order?
- How are physical and human resources procured and channelled?

The product and organization, once designed as a 'mystical marriage' of vision and need, are brought to life through the commitment of inner will and outer resources, resulting in a defensive/aggressive reaction to adverse circumstances.

Asserting your will/acquiring resources

- What is in it for you personally and financially?
- What is your competitive advantage?
- Who will champion your product's cause?
- What financial resources need to be committed?
- What is the risk and what is the likely return?
- How do you sell yourself?

Once the commitment is made, and business is under way, progress needs to be planned and monitored, so both individual and organization can purposefully respond to change.

Adapting to change

- How are targets and programs established and monitored?
- How are tasks planned and implemented, step by step?
- What systems have been installed to process information?
- What experimental forms enable individual and organization to adapt to change?

- How does the organization provide scope for free expression?

Envisioning (acquiring creative power), unravelling (penetrating to the source), integrating (entering the mystical union), committing (risking yourself) and learning (engaging in the road of trials), take the innovator almost all the way along his chosen path. The interactive and inspired steps still remaining lead him closer to the social and physical end points of his journey.

Involving people

Step six involves people, that is symbolically the protector and magic helpers, and literally all those employees, customers, suppliers, shareholders and other allies that comprise the human body of the organization.

- How do you effect shared values, so that people feel they belong?
- What myths and rituals bind people together?
- How do you bring about a family atmosphere, and a sense of community?
- How do you maintain closeness to the customer?
- How do you achieve productivity through people?

Finally, and ultimately, the complex and ethereal vision needs to be embodied in simple tangible form, to inspire effort.

Taking action

- How do you keep the energy level up?
- What is physically produced, at the end of the day?
- How do you ensure that the product remains constantly and physically visible both inside and outside the business?
- How do you impose a sense of urgency?
- How do you maintain a bias for action?

Having responded to all these questions, the heroic innovator, or innovative organization, will have completed both departure and return. Of the steps along the journey's way it is the extraction of vision which is probably the most difficult for us to perceive, largely because the unconscious spirit has been well concealed from us, like the night is from the day.

I now want to investigate, with you, how personal and corporate vision can be both inhibited and acquired.

Acquiring the power of vision

What inhibits vision?

The first question we have to ask ourselves is what stops us embarking on, and returning from the heroic journey, the combination of which ultimately results in the extraction of vision? Why do we fail to grow up? Why do our organizations fail to mature? Why do our visions fail to come out?

Personal transformation

All the life potentalities that we never managed to bring to adult realization, those other portions of oneself are there; for such golden seeds do not die. If only a portion of that lost totality could be dredged up into the light of day we should experience a marvellous expansion of our powers, a vivid renewal of life.

Moreover, if we could dredge up something forgotten not only by ourselves but also by our whole generation or our entire civilization we should become the heroes of the day.

Joseph Campbell *The Hero with a Thousand Faces*[9] 1949

What specifically, then, blocks our vision, what are the consequences of such inhibition, and how do we become unblocked? Let me deal with each of these questions in turn.

Blocks to vision

To begin with, the first way we block our vision is by seeing ourselves as down to earth and feet on the ground. We get stuck therefore on the first rung of the ladder of learning. A desire to work hard and 'go for it' overwhelms any desire for reflexion. The call to adventure leads us nowhere rather than somewhere. We are too busy getting on with life to take time out to contemplate the future. Companies are too busy 'getting the stuff out the door' to plan ahead. There is too much 'real work' to be done for us to bother about 'fancy stuff dreamed up by people with their heads in the stars'.

The second stumbling block on the ladder arises when we see ourselves as 'just one of the boys or girls'. It is comfortable and comforting to allow ourselves to have undemanding expectations. Our protectors then shield us from experience rather than guiding us through it. Being like everyone else is much easier going than becoming distinctive. Being just another cornerstore is much simpler than becoming a department store.

We get stuck on the third rung of the ladder when we flit from one activity and experience to another just for the fun of it. The road of trials then becomes a distraction rather than an intention. How better to distract ourselves from our real vision and purpose than by the fascination of novelty. How quickly time goes by when we are busy doing one thing, or project, after another. There are so many things to be done that we, individually or in our organizations, seem to have to run merely to keep still.

The fourth step along the way becomes a stumbling block rather than a stepping stone because we take a risk 'just for the hell of it'. So we manage to command everyone's attention except that of the people who really count. We surround our lives with drama but become a tragic hero rather than a triumphant one. We lose our old selves and never find a new one, as an individual or organization. Shaking everything up is an excellent way to avoid making real headway.

Fifthly, we cling to established principles to avoid having to deal with uncertainty, ambiguity or conflict. Instead of effecting a union amongst opposites we divide and rule. Anything that fails to fit in with preset personal or institutional attitudes we dismiss as diversionary, divisive, improper or unnecessary.

The sixth block occurs when open-mindedness leads not to empathy and sensitivity but to confusion and indecision. Everything becomes a kind of haze. Different issues, problems or opportunities are all lumped together into the same pot of insubstance. Floating along in a haze or getting lost in the fog is a way of cushioning ourselves from the real world.

We slip and fall at the seventh and last rung when we feel we already have all the answers. Nobody can tell us anything that can improve on what already is. Other options are inevitably suspect rather than enriching, dangerous rather than enticing. Such total suppression of total possibility is a perfect way to sustain ignorance rather than empower both ourselves and other people.

The consequences of inhibited vision

To the extent that vision is blocked, in the individual or in the organization, there are the inevitable adverse consequences. The development of vision is then inhibited through:

- Lack of purpose. Without purpose there is a lack of direction in life. We lack spiritual substance. Our activity lacks lustre or intrinsic worth. Life is hollow. There is no ultimate vision of the future. The sole purpose of it all is survival.
- Lack of meaning. Our activity lacks a meaningful context. There is no penetrating source of demand for what we are doing. We are lacking in foundations. Other people's work is not respected because we fail to respect our own. The atmosphere becomes soured. The physical environment deteriorates. Depression sets in. Who cares anyway!
- Lack of planning. To what ends can any plans be directed? There seems little point in planning for the ephemeral. Why plan when disorder will nevertheless follow? How can we build on the past when there is no forseeable future? Nothing makes sense.
- Motivation is lacking. Drive is reduced. Going around in circles is unrewarding. Energy may be filled digging holes and filling them up again. Effort does not seem to get us anywhere.
- Lack of priorities. There is nothing to distinguish one task from another. How can priorities be set when so many things demand attention? How can time be found for anything when there is no energy?
- Lack of pride. Why bother to put up a front when we feel down and out? Keeping up appearances or maintaining good relationships seem futile when there are no priorities set.
- Lack of activity. Procrastination is natural when we have nothing special to do. Tomorrow will probably be like today, so what is the hurry? When we feel we have nothing to offer we may as well sit back and see what others have to offer us.

Jacob's Ladder then – from vision to action and vice versa – can function as a negative or positive cascade. It becomes positive when the higher step nourishes the lower one. You are active, rung number one, to be attractive, rung number two. You take pride in what you do, rung number two, because you know or have been told what is worth doing, rung number three.

You have bothered to sort out your priorities, rung number three, because either you are self-motivated or else someone is motivating you, rung number four. You are committed to taking risks, rung number four, because there is an overall structure, rung number five – like a formal religion, scientific order or bureaucracy – which provides overriding stability.

It is worth planning ahead, rung number five, because there is a wider context, rung number six, for which to plan. Finally, there is meaning to life and work, rung number six, because there is an ulterior purpose, rung number seven, that surpasses the mere fulfilment of personal or customer need. That ultimate purpose, which is true vision, is something other than shared values. It requires the full extent of the heroic departure and return to acquire it.

Extracting a personal vision

There are specific methods, in fact, of overcoming both personal and corporate blocks to vision, removing the inhibitors in the process. These methods are not simple, once and for all techniques, but more like ongoing and iterative processes. I shall begin with the personal approaches, drawing on Kevin Kingsland's methodologies,[10] and then move on to my own corporate applications.[11]

Recognizing a vision
Before we embark on our vision building exercises, though, let me reveal to you an example of one, drawing on the experience of Mary Quant, the British designer.

Black and white image

As a child I didn't like stiffness or artificiality. I didn't want to grow up. I wanted people around me to move, run, dance. The image came to me first when I was eight. A tap dancer with a bullet haircut, wearing black tights, black shirt, black patent leather shoes, and white socks. This black and white image branded my mind. It has stuck with me forever.

Mary Quant 'Enterprise development'[12] 1986

A vision, then, arises out of the imagination, and infuses the rest of our lives with purpose. Naturally the original image will be less focussed than the ultimate manifestation, should we realize our dreams. Mary Quant has since built up an international business in cosmetics, fabrics, soft furnishing and stationery products, all drawing on that original image, and manifested today in bold colors and designs.

Developing a vision
The practical necessity for developing a vision arises for people like Mary Quant when the already described symptoms of lack of vision reach an intolerable stage. The tolerance level of different people, varies enormously. Generally speaking, the more sensitive you are, the more intolerant you will be of lack of vision. Quant was appalled by the dowdy fashions in the fifties. Conran was deeply offended by the ugly furniture he saw in the high street. Both were sufficiently incensed to pursue their emergent visions.[13]

Discovering your natural inclinations
By the time you feel the urge to seek after your vision it is probably close at hand. It is perhaps working its way through your awareness, but has not yet actually been perceived.

So how can you extract it from the realms of semi-darkness?!

Start by looking at your life, and see what is actually going on. Look, particularly, at what you are doing at your own discretion. Most of your obligatory work may be taken up with activities that are a relic of your past. The momentum remains but you may be beginning to question their value. So note down what you do. Now think about what you like doing. Distinguish between those things that are done only because they have to be, and those things which you enjoy doing. Treat those things which you get no satisfaction out of as red herrings.

Then begin to enliven, enlarge, and invigorate those realms of activity which you naturally want to do. In sum, they will comprise your vision.

Discerning what enhances you

A variation on the above theme is to ask yourself, for a start, what really enhances you. What do you love doing? What captivates your imagination in the context of what you do? Now write down, as a list, the most enjoyable, fulfilling and creative aspects of your existence. It would be nice to think that you could now take all those things and make them your life's work. But, in practice, that is too simplistic an approach. Negativity gets in the way.

So write down a list of all the things that go on in your life, which are incompatible with the first list. Form two lists, on the left-hand side those things that enhance you, and on the right-hand side those which cancel out each of the items on the left. Reflect on this list from time to time and resolve to remove the items on the right-hand side.

Both of the above approaches to developing a vision require relatively modest effort. Now we come to three approaches that require more thought.

Unravelling your vision

In order to unravel your vision you need to project yourself into your desired future:

- What will you physically look like? What energy level will you be operating at? How will you be physically occupied? What kind of sporting activity will you be undertaking and when?
- What will be your social standing? Will you have a reputation to be proud of, and of what sort? What kinds of organization will you be closely associated with, and how will they affect your self-image? What social groupings will be represented in your work and life and how will you meet them?
- How educated and informed will you be? What degree of knowledge and skill will you require and how, specifically, will it be different from now? What kind of communications will you have with others? What kind of training will you be undergoing? How will you keep in touch with artistic and technological developments? How will you develop your ability to learn?
- What will your economic standing be? What sorts and value of assets will you have acquired? How will your assets be apportioned as fixtures and fittings, land and buildings, and investments? Will your assets all be owned outright or rented or leased? How secure will those assets be? How much control will you have over your future? How acquisitive will you be in your approach, and in what way? What return on your investment will you be seeking?

- How much authority will you have? To what extent will your opinion matter and to whom? What titles, awards and accreditations will you acquire? What role will you be playing in your local, national and international communities? How will you structure your activities to achieve efficiency and effectiveness?
- How will you develop yourself and others? Will you become more sensitive and caring, and in what way? How will you have improved the quality of your physical and social environment? How will peoples' minds and hearts have become elevated?
- What will be your original and longlasting creation? Will you be able to look at your life and regard it as your greatest work of art? What will you have contributed uniquely to the world that will give you a deep sense of fulfillment? At what will you be able to point, and say, 'That is the reason for my being.'

Bringing your vision to life
The previous exercise was future-oriented whereas this one begins with the past and the present. You are invited to consider, first of all, where you are most alive.

- Physically, do you relish your strength, endurance and versatility? In what way? Do you love being physically close to other people, playing contact sport, undertaking exercise, working hard and playing hard?
- Socially, do you really enjoy being with others? Do you happily rely on one another? Is there a strong family feeling? Are you pleased when someone drops unexpectedly into the house or office? Do you go to lots of parties and outings, just for the fun of it?
- Intellectually, do you have insatiable curiosity? Do you eagerly anticipate the next book or computer program that you come across? Do you eagerly scan the television and radio pages for programs that will expand your mind? Are ideas common currency in your conversations? Do you make sure that you are up to date with the latest concepts and techniques in your field?
- Entrepreneurially, do you thrill in anticipation of challenge? Do you love a good fight for justice, good service or market share? Are you irrepressible in spirit? Do you champion your pet product or favored cause? Do you ever give up championing something you believe in? Can you be beaten off? Are you a risk taker?
- Organizationally, are you fanatical about order, including filing, record keeping, budgeting, systems? Are things habitually straightened out, systematized and organized? Do you derive pleasure out of creating systems and devising procedures? Do you find putting order into chaos deeply satisfying?
- Aesthetically, do you look in awe upon beautiful settings, elegant buildings, and well-designed products. Are quiet moments of contemplation greatly valued? Does the sense of fulfilled potential excite you? Conversely, does unfulfilled potential cause you despair.
- Creatively, do you suffer greatly when you go a day without making something beautiful, making a breakthrough, or transforming some aspect of your life? Do you ascend to seventh heaven as brilliant ideas enter your mind, and flow out verbally, pictorially, physically, or organizationally. Is the world your stage, canvas, or magic garden?

Now determine those areas which you could identify with. Did you find yourself alive to all realms, to some of them, or to none? Write down one new area of emphasis for each of the weeks that follow. You may find yourself dismissing some areas as inapplicable. These may be areas where you are blocked; in other words they lie underdeveloped. By getting to grips with those neglected areas you will be removing the shroud that covers your vision up. As you allow yourself to enjoy your total being, then the intensity of your vision will be raised. In fact it will become brilliant and unmistakable.

Going back to your roots
So much for vision, plucked out of the ground, as it were. For a more throughgoing and enduring attempt to extract vision we have to go back to your roots. To start with, then:

- List on the left-hand side of a page the key events in your life history.
- Then identify, alongside, your emotional reactions to these events, as and when they happened.
- Now list, alongside these, actions that you took, or you think should have been taken, as a result.

You will now have three columns containing histories of activities and events in your life, emotional reactions and resulting behavior.

The combined result of your uncovering of the past and of the roots of your identity, should provide you with the raw material for your vision. You now need to summarize and condense your personal history. That will take a little time and effort. You should be in a position, after paying particular attention to the experiences and actions uncovered on your historical journey, to do the following:

- Create a name for your vision.
- Create a logo that represents it.
- Create a suitable motto.
- Compose a new statement of your personal mission, one that will capture the imaginations of all that matter around you.

Criteria for visionary evaluation

In the final analysis, then, how can you tell whether you have tapped the real depths of your personal vision? The sorts of criterion for evaluation are laid out below.

Vision criteria

Consciousness

You need to become obsessed by your vision. If this does not happen there is no way in which it can become all-pervading.

Internal consistency

Various elements of the vision may be incompatible. It may be manifested differently in one part of you as compared with another. It may be reflected in your outer image but not in the inner behavior. This will detract from your vision.

Clarity

Your vision may be confused. It may not yet have penetrated the minds of people. The message may still not have got across. Such lack of clarity will get in the visionary way.

Intensity

Visions need to be brilliant to show up against the background of images and attitudes that get in the way. They need to be impactful, colorful, captivating and energizing.

Confidence

Acceptance of your vision can be delayed by your concentrating too much on its alternatives, and too little on itself; too much on the negative and too little on the positive.

Recognition

Without the outside world to encourage you, your vision will be devalued. You need people around you who can recognize your creative potential.

Faith

To manifest a vision, you must increasingly act as if it were a reality. Without the conviction to do this the vision remains a fantasy.

Kevin Kingsland *Extracting a Vision*[14] 1986

The same criteria can be applied to the assessment of the power of a corporate vision, as to the evaluation of the strength of a personal one.

In fact, all five of the methods I have revealed for extracting a personal vision are equally applicable to the extraction of a corporate one. In each case you will be substituting either part or the whole of an organization, collectively, for yourself, individually. Obviously that increases the layers of complexity, but it can nevertheless be done. For example, you can just as well assess the 'aliveness' of a corporation – physically, socially or intellectually – as an individual. Equally, you can just as well assess the most fullfilling and creative aspects of your organization's being, as your own. A vision, however, once extracted, has still to be actualized. This is indeed what the heroic journey is ultimately about, converting vision into action. In the concluding part of this chapter I shall illustrate how a corporate visionary may go about it.

Conclusion

From corporate vision to action

So now we come to the extraction of vision from the depths of the organizational (similar principles apply to the individual) subconscious, and to its subsequent and cumulative conversion into action.

- Uncover the historically based vision of the company, as reflected in:
  - The origins of its national culture and economy.
  - The historical roots of the product and technology.
  - The founder's underlying motives and psychology.

What powerful and captivating vision has emerged out of your company's unique cultural, economic, technological and personal heritage? How can it be stated and visually represented in the word and picture language of uplift and idealism? How might it serve as a 'meta-vision' to embrace each of your people's own personal visions?

- Relate the acquired vision to an underlying context, thereby discovering its meaning or significance:

What unique cultural and economic context, in the pattern of geographical space and historical time, marks your evolving enterprise?

- Structure and conceptualize the union between vision and context, thereby defining the product and organization in practical terms:

What particularly appropriate principles and structures of management and organization have you developed in your company?

- Harness the will and motivation of your people to drive the company forward, committed to profitable growth, so that the resources can be acquired to put its principles into practice, to fulfil the needs of its people, and to serve its mission:

How have you tapped the egotistical drives of your people while providing means of channelling these self-centered motives into the common cause, organizationally, contextually and spiritually?

- Adapt to change, so that the forces of single-minded persistence, clearly principled management, sensitivity to the customer, and submission to a higher purpose, do not cause rigidity and inflexibility:

How do you keep your organization and resource-base fluid so that strength of commitment can be linked with flexibility of response?

- Establish a family atmosphere whereby values are shared and people feel they belong together, even though individual flexibility and enterprise is encouraged, and individuals can dream their own dreams within the context of the whole:

How do you cultivate a family atmosphere in your company with a common identity and culture, reinforced by social ties and binding myths and rituals?

- Ensure that vision is continuously manifested in action, through which the dream ultimately becomes a reality; the true power of vision is realized, and the resources of the earth are transformed:

How are you deploying energy to transform energy so that, in turn, your vision can be refuelled, reformed and renewed?

Vision and adventure

Unlike the purely technological inventor or the artistic creator, the visionary, immersed in his heroic journey, is both innovator and adventurer. Be he an Alfred Nobel or Henry Ford from the nineteenth century, or Agha Hasan Abedi or John Hillbery from the twentieth, he harnesses spirit and transforms energy on his heroic journey.

Adventurers, however, can only become visionaries if they combine their toughest venturesomeness with their tendermost purpose. The explicit order (see David Bohm, pp. 529–30) of their thrust has to be received by the implicit order of the universe. This is where 'real management', basing itself on the laws of nature, plays its harmonizing part.

In Chapter 27 we shall become acquainted with such 'real management' and, in Chapter 28, with the company, BCC, that has created it. By that stage we shall have completed our global, and managerial journey. All that will then be required is for us to link the primal, rational, developmental, and metaphysical strands together. For in that undertaking lies both our internal and managerial vision and our external and global adventure.

References

1. J. Campbell, *The Hero with a Thousand Faces*, Princeton University Press (1949), p. 43.
2. T. Peters and B. Waterman, *In Search of Excellence*, Harper & Row (1982), p. 11.
3. T. Deal and A. Kennedy, *Corporate Cultures*, Addison & Wesley (1982), p. 43.
4. H. Owen, *Spirit, Transformation and Development*, Abbott Publishing (1987) p. 62.
5. J. Campbell, *op.cit.*, p. 64.
6. R. Lessem, 'Linking ancient wisdom and modern business practice', *Journal of Enterprise Management* (Autumn, 1980).
7. K. Kingsland, *The Whole Personality*, unpublished manuscript (1985).
8. K. Kingsland, *op.cit.*
9. J. Campbell, *op.cit.*, p. 17.
10. K. Kingsland, *Extracting A Vision*, unpublished manuscript (1986).
11. R. Lessem, *The Global Business*, Prentice Hall (1987), pp. 216–19.
12. M. Quant, ex R. Lessem, *Intrapreneurship*, Wildwood House (1987), p. 84.
13. R. Lessem, *op.cit.*, p. 102.
14. K. Kingsland, *op.cit.*, (1986), p. 8.

28 'Real' management

Contents

Key concepts

Once you have fully understood this chapter you should be able to define the following concepts in your own terms:

Autonomy   Integrity principle
Beings in progress   Interfusion
Dynamic planning   Joint personality
Flow principle   Latency principle
Humility   Marketing as totality

Real management	Totality principle
Seven Ps	Unitive consciousness
Timing	Vision

Objectives

Upon completing this chapter you should be able to do the following:

1. Outline the fundamental laws of nature, as they relate to metaphysical management.
2. Analyze the key features of real management.
3. Identify the similarities and differences between the soft sides of developmental and of metaphysical, management theory.
4. Compare and contrast real and traditional management in both theory and practice.
5. Assess the extent to which you are receptive to the real management approach, and identify those aspects of yourself which might get in the way of your receptivity.

Introduction

In Chapter 25 we focussed on the individual business innovator, or hero, who turns an imaginative idea, emerging out of his spirit into an ongoing activity, containing material energy. In this chapter we investigate the laws of nature that underpin this creative process, drawing on the formidable Bank of Credit and Commerce (BCC) for both the theory and the practice. BCC has grown, in fifteen short years, from virtual scratch to seventeen billion dollars in assets (see Chapter 27), because its founders have understood the laws of nature, and have deliberately applied them to the development of an international business.

As its president and cofounder, Agha Hasan Abedi, has said: 'All creeds, all nationalities, all people are governed by the laws of nature. Nature transcends ethnic differences and national boundaries. The laws of nature are universal. They are part of the vast unconscious world which governs the more limited conscious world of our perception and reason.'

There are four principles, or natural laws, which have governed the bank's thoughts, feelings and actions from the outset. They have been described by BCC's cofounders, John Hillbery and Agha Hasan Abedi, along with the resulting processes of 'Real Management', in a dozen or so of the bank's internal publications. I shall begin by outlining the fundamental, natural laws and then move on to the derivative real management processes.

The totality principle

By aligning an organization with the organization of the cosmos, Abedi and Hillbery argue, you gain the support of the laws of nature. 'We live enfolded within the laws of nature, and we hope to be worthy of their support'.

Nature operates as an integrated system in its dynamic state. All parts of the system are interrelated and interdependent. They interfuse in and through the phenomenon of change, and assume their dynamic shape in the form of evolution. The realization of this relationship, and of the energy that is generated in the process of fusion and fission, is generic to the natural order.

The balance – in nature, in man, and in organization – between parts and totality, is a delicate one. No organization can remain only as a collection of parts, nor can it function purely as a totality. There is a natural bond between the two.

The global village

Modern technology has shrunk our world to make it easier for us to grasp the totality. We are no longer like our forefathers confined by the limits of our particular village, unfamiliar with the strange ways of the foreigner in the next valley and deeply suspicious of their intentions. Today the world is a global village.

It is sometimes said by psychologists and other cartographers of the human psyche that a healthy personality unites and integrates diverse and disparate elements of experience and character. Perhaps world wisdom has some of the same characteristics as personal wisdom: the coming together of diverse cultures, religions, races, and politics, within a recognition and respect for the totality and continuity of the planet earth and the human beings who live there.

Agha Hasan Abedi *Survival in the Nuclear Age*[1] 1985

The flow principle

The dynamics of existence are in a state of constant flux. The process of change flows on and on. We live in and through change. We live within the fold of change. Nature is process; nature is change. The Bank of Credit and Commerce, for example, exists because people, throughout the world, and through the centuries, have changed their status and place of residence. One wave of immigration and of emigration has followed another. In the wake of these movements follow transfers of capital and commodities and BCC has made it its business to ease that flow, through the supply of credit.

Through humility we open ourselves to change. If we tried to protect our egos with rigid boundaries, we could never be in tune with evolution. Every change creates a vacuum and an opportunity. Through humility we have the flexibility to move into that vacuum and take full advantage of whatever situations occur.

The latency principle

No-existence, which is infinite, is the container of existence, which is finite. With due humility and lack of preconception, man and businessman can remain open to the infinite realm of opportunity. Nature has the capacity to be the state of existence and the state of no-existence at the same time. From this relationship emanates the process of change. In fact, change began when the state of existence emerged from the state of no-existence. In that sense, BCC was in a state of no-existence, or latency, before its time. It came into existence because its founders combined a vision of total possibility with the humility of pure receptiveness.

The role of humility

There can be no purposeful growth without awareness. Yet with awareness comes our habits and beliefs. The problem for us then becomes: how to be aware of our essence without all this clutter that comes with it?

This is the role of humility. It brings the essence to the surface of our awareness. Humility distils off the surface overlays, leaving behind only the distillate, the pure concentrate of our being. Sensing this essence in others, whether as fellow members of the organization or as customers, is a more intense experience than routine communication. It is like breathing pure oxygen. It has the power to vitalize.

Tom Thiss *Bridging the BCC World*[2] 1986

The vision of BCC is born out of humility 'In the not too distant future,' Abedi claims, 'BCC will be one of the largest profit earning financial institutions in the world. We will then be able to meet the ultimate challenge contained in our major purpose. The intention is to give hope to people who have nothing.'

To realize that vision BCC needed the humility, born out of a spirit of no-existence, to be open to change, that is the process of life itself. The ebb and flow of international trade and finance across the globe has presented BCC with just that. 'We were there,' John Hillbery has said, 'when the flux of petro-dollars changed the financial structure of the world. During the first ten years of our existence we were one of the major beneficiaries of this change.'

The integrity principle

The moral, which is equivalent to the laws and principles of nature, governs all that is material. Hence, both must be acknowledged, treated and felt as inseparable. No company can assume its ultimate identity and its pure quality without becoming one with its moral substance.

The spirit of the organization

Just as each of us has a spirit, so does each organization. Attending to the spiritual needs of the organization is the job of management. Much has been written in recent years about work values and corporate culture. The culture determines how things get done in business. Managing this culture is the principal task of the chief executive officer.

The culture, in turn, then manages the people. We call this culture the ethos, the energy psyche, or the spirit. It is the vitality of the organization. Its collective energies determine the quality and the quantity of our company's performance. As custodians or keepers of the spirit, we are the ones who nurture its growth through leadership and vision.

Without this vision the energies will wane and collapse in the misdirected efforts and random activities. But with this vision, management has the energy to transform a company. Collectively, it has the power to transform a nation.

John Hillbery *Real Management*[3] 1984

We need, therefore to account for our human and spiritual gains as well as for our financial ones. We need to expand our concept of profit to include, with the material, a moral dimension, a new 'bottom line' that accounts for both: 'If we can say we have given more of ourselves than we have taken from others,' Hillbery says, 'we have made a spiritual profit. If we cannot say that then we have a deficit, and no company can grow in the long run by operating spiritually in the red.'

'Real' management

The philosophy of management that Abedi, Hillbery and their core group have developed is unique. Not only is it born out of direct experience but it also brings fundamental laws of nature into management. For those two reasons it has been termed 'real'. Its starting point is energy.

Process, change and the role of energy

What makes human energy different from all other sources of energy is its qualitative dimension. If only quantitative aspects were to be considered then human beings could be placed in the same category as barrels of oil or tons of coal. Qualitative energy resembles the lines of force in a magnetic field. They are invisible but the stronger the lines of force, the stronger the magnetic pull. Conventional management tends to be concerned with visible manifestations of energy, such as output and productivity, rather than with intangible forces behind tangible effect. Organization is visualized as a static structure, composed in an hierarchy of levels. People belong when they have a place in the hierarchy within the structure.

Real management is visualized as a process through which physical, emotional and spiritual energy flows. To and from this vast stream of energy, everyone contributes and draws. The manager concentrates therefore on the quality, vitality, velocity, quantity and direction of this energy. In order to do this well, the real manager needs to be familiar with the laws of nature, in one context or another. Such a manager sees the organization as a dynamic, fluid and ever-changing process. He views organizational changes as continuous and evolutionary, rather than as desultory and episodic. The major and discontinuous restructuring, which is characteristic of conventional management, is therefore alien to him.

For the 'real' manager, moreover, planning is a dynamic process and not a static perception. Planning is energized by the planners through their feelings. Planning is the reflection of the release, flow and interfusion of the streams of psychic energy, and of the feelings of the entire management when it has become synthesized with the corporate objectives and purpose. Planning and strategy is life flowing in tune with totality.

People, accordingly, are viewed as 'beings in progress', as self-directed sources of energy. They have no fixed position on the organizational tree. Formal reporting chains are non-existent. People belong, not by virtue of having a place in the formal structure, but by relating to the process of flow. The first thing that strikes you as you walk into the fourth floor of the bank's City of London office is the open plan. There are no private offices. The whole floor has an atmosphere of what one visitor called 'dynamic serenity'.

Initiative, persistence and the role of enterprise

Dynamism and personal initiative go hand in hand with the spirit of enterprise. But the real management flavor is somewhat different. Perception and awareness of what needs to be done determines the scope of individual responsibility. There is less emphasis on personal conviction and more stress on timely perception. There is also much less emphasis upon prescribed responsibility than in the traditional organization, and more inclination to respond appropriately to need.

The conventional manager tries to control time, and the proverbial entrepreneur often tries to force time and space into a pattern of his own will. The real manager, on the other hand, knows that one cannot control time. One can only control the timing of one's own interventions. He therefore pursues a course of action with determination and persistence, but exercises patience in waiting for the right moment. He acts, after sensing the momentum for an opportunity, that is the critical momentum for change.

By a process of intuition he perceives others' needs for support, direction and inspiration, and he intervenes accordingly. Although he might be greatly tempted to take a personal initiative, he never forgets that he is part of a greater whole. Every manager, in the final analysis, must have a clear perception, a strong vision, and a clean instinct for a balanced relationship and interaction between seven Ps – purpose, people, planning, priorities, possibilities, products and profits. (See Fig. 76.)

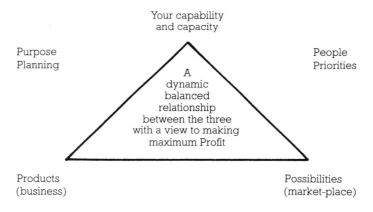

Fig. 76 The seven Ps.

Totality, wholeness and the role of development

Real managers deal with the whole person, and with the whole management process that bears upon their realm of activity. Everyone in the bank is expected to take an interest in the marketing of its services: 'In BCC we are gardeners. Our crop is people. Our harvest is success.' Marketing is seen as the high road to business success, as well as providing the opportunity for suppliers and customers to get together. Thus, through marketing, people increase their sense of belonging. Marketing is the external application of the real management process.

Marketing as totality

Our personalities are growing through marketing. It charms and fascinates us. It is so enriching. Through marketing we meet all sorts of people. Marketing brings us the chance to win the most precious thing in life – the hearts of the people we meet.

We can win their good feelings and their love. We can exchange with them our feelings about the value of life. Each time this delicate process happens it adds to our personality. The fullness of life comes through marketing.

John Hillbery *The Dynamics of Marketing*[4] 1984

Conventional management, on the other hand, breaks marketing down into separate functions and principles. Conventional marketeers either sell, distribute, promote, or cost/price their product or service. They plan, organize, direct or control. The fullness of marketing and of life is broken down into segregated pieces. Employees are categorized as manual or clerical, skilled or unskilled workers.

Wholeness, however demands the inclusion of opposites. So managers need to be active physically and mentally, producing and marketing, as do employees. In fact everyone is both manager and employee.

Unitive consciousness

The common purpose, faith, humility, and the spirit of giving are leading to the emergence of unitive consciousness, i.e., the ability to perceive two dimensions simultaneously. In effect what is being seen is at the same time universal and particular; something that both exists here and now but whose ends also extend to eternity.

This is making it possible for us to perceive the is and the ought, the immediate and what might be, the end value that not only could come to pass but is there now existing before our eyes. The polarity, the dichotomy, the assumption that more of one means less of the other is fading away.

Ali Rashid 'Corporate magic'[5] 1986

The ability to perceive the undivided and cooperative whole, where others see divided and competitive parts, is dependent upon an individual's or an organization's state of evolution. Some people and some institutions, at a given time, are more evolved than others. 'People and organizations evolve as they interfuse with one another.'

Feeling, autonomy and the role of interfusion

The conventional management tradition grew up as a direct reaction against the emotional, intuitive and irrational modes of entrepreneurism. The belief in thought, logic and analysis subsequently reigned supreme. Corporate planning, management by objectives and managerial problem solving were all outcomes of this rational spirit.

Along with this conventional viewpoint has come the bureaucratic organization, the belief in 'pyramid power', and a formal hierarchy of authority and responsibility. In recent times, spurred on by the American spirit of enterprise, there has been a resurgence of entrepreneurism, but now also within a corporate context. The quest for autonomy is shared by real management. Where BCC parts company with entrepreneurial management is in the degree of attention it places on independence, as opposed to interdependence. In fact it focusses, particularly, on the merger of energies resulting in what it calls 'joint personality'. In other words, each person is simultaneously autonomous and interdependent, both independent of mind and also interfused within a network of relationships.

The role of interfusion

Traditional banking practices are being reshaped in the light of the evolution of our culture. Interfusion is taking the place of ordinary communication. The support of an officer in one department gives an officer in another involves the interfusion of psychic energies. As this interfusion takes place within the whole of BCC we are starting to merge with the totality of the energy that is available.

Although we remain parts or individuals, we are blessed with the ability to interfuse with the cosmic totality. The corporate psyche of BCC is nothing less than this. We have a natural desire to merge with the whole of creation. We would like to be completely identified with everything that exists, with all power and all energy, and to live in the interfusion of this power.

To the extent that we become so interfused we will feel at home in all situations and with whatever changes take place in us or in our environment.

John Hillbery *The Dynamics of Marketing*[6] 1984

In such an interfused context, success is important but winning is a non event. People do not talk about it. Here BCC strongly parts company with the American tradition. Even win-win situations are not part of its business reality. For within the cooperative pursuit of purpose one's only competitor is oneself.

Success then is geared to the evolution of the person; therefore what real managers often talk about is the evolution of one's self. Some people are actually referred to as being 'very evolved'. To be less so, though, does not carry a stigma. The bud is no less valuable than the flower; it is just at a different stage in the process of evolution.

People, management and the role of work

Conventional management is defined as the process of getting work done through people. In real management the relationship is reversed. Management is defined as the process of getting people 'done', or rather developed, through work. The task provides the opportunity to interfuse – the creative process of change – and to relate to a purpose larger than oneself.

So management becomes the process of developing people through work. Instead of merely focussing on the individual's business and technical skills, the real manager focusses on his life process. The first requirement is to be a whole person of quality. Then, it is believed, the quality of performance will follow.

Communication

We should give 10 per cent of our time to plans, policies and problems. We should give the rest of our time to human beings. Building up human resources takes time and attention and also communication.

> Communication involves establishing clarity of vision, precision in articulation, lucidity in expression, quality and volume as well as flow and fusion of feeling.
>
> John Hillbery *The Dynamics of Marketing*[7] 1984

The means of achieving all this is not, primarily, through management training and development. Rather, managers need to develop other managers to be better than themselves. The key to all this lies in humility. 'The quality and rise of our organization is determined by the quality and stature of the individuals within it. If the boundaries to individual psyches are removed there will be no boundaries to the growth and quality of our organization.'[8]

Morality, purpose and the role of vision

Conventional management is beset by goal setting, strategy formulation, and by tangible measures of success. These have an important part to play in real management, but a subordinate one.

Serving humanity

Our relationship with the company is not just the contractual relationship whereby we sell our energy and expertise. It is much deeper than that. It is a relationship that encompasses the totality of our lives. It is a relationship of life itself.

We give our total lives to BCC and BCC gives total life to us. BCC is a bridge between us as individuals and the totality of the phenomenon of existence. Through the company we bcome part of all that is and all that happens.

Even if you work in a small branch and the objectives seem limited, if you work with love and inspiration, you are serving humanity and fulfilling the call of history.

BCC, Paris Regional Conference[9] 1984

The real manager sets his objectives in the context of a wider moral dimension. The guiding principle is to give more than one takes, and to serve the needs of people and societies. In BCC's case the 'service' happens to be banking, and those served – primarily – the Third World.

BCC, in 1985, instigated a policy whereby everyone in the bank was provided with an extra 2½ per cent of his salary to be given, by the individual at his own discretion, to his chosen good causes. There are, in fact, no controls on what the individual chooses to do with the money. It is based entirely on trust.

Charitable donations, however, are a small part of the moral whole. The greater part is contained in the overall mission, or vision of the company. A real manager is one who sees his contribution to be one part of a much larger socioeconomic and geopolitical force, in the unfolding stage of history. (See Fig. 77.)[10]

Vision

Vision is not only the perception or comprehension of your environment. Vision is the ability to comprehend and capture all that is and that happens in its dynamic state. Vision is experiencing life and existence in the flux of its totality.

> Vision is the synthesis of the individual psyche with the psyche of the environment and the purpose. Vision in its finality is the fusion of the individual with the psyche of the totality of existence and the purpose of life.
>
> Every individual member of management should have a vision of the identity, the dynamics and the dimensions of the corporation, and of the corporate environment as well as the purpose in which he lives.
>
> Agha Hasan Abedi *Real Management*[11] 1984

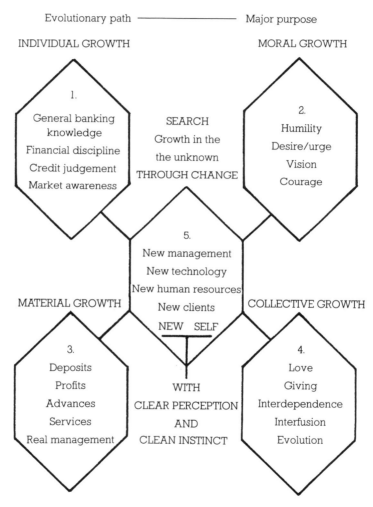

Evolutionary path ——————— Major purpose

INDIVIDUAL GROWTH   MORAL GROWTH

1.
General banking knowledge
Financial discipline
Credit judgement
Market awareness

SEARCH
Growth in the
the unknown
THROUGH CHANGE

2.
Humility
Desire/urge
Vision
Courage

5.
New management
New technology
New human resources
New clients
NEW   SELF

MATERIAL GROWTH   COLLECTIVE GROWTH

3.
Deposits
Profits
Advances
Services
Real management

WITH
CLEAR PERCEPTION
AND
CLEAN INSTINCT

4.
Love
Giving
Interdependence
Interfusion
Evolution

Fig. 77 The evolutionary path.

Conclusion: real versus traditional management

To conclude this chapter, on the 'soft' side of metaphysical management, I want to compare and contrast real management with the traditional variety – that is, in our terms, rational. In each case I shall be using the rational (traditional) perspective to highlight the comparative significance of the metaphysical, (real) alternative.

The management truth: visible or invisible?

Specific or cosmic?

The traditional manager accepts the rationally focussed principles of management and organization, as defined by such founding management fathers as Fayol and Taylor, Mayo and Likert, and Drucker and Mintzberg. These sets of principles can each be precisely defined and analyzed, as separately delineated parts. The best known of these conventional management processes are those of planning, organizing, staffing, directing and control.

Real managers, on the other hand, search for a management truth that lies beyond conventional wisdom, both administrative and behavioral. Their 'truth' even surpasses the emerging primal and developmental wisdoms that, in themselves, bypass the rational management logic.

Real truth often lies in the unseen world behind everyday perceptions. Real managers seek a greater understanding of this truth in themselves, in others and in nature itself. This process of inner and outer discovery is forever unfolding. It also reflects the larger and cosmic truth in which the smaller and conventional managerial wisdom is contained.

Strategic or visionary?

The traditional manager commits his thoughts and actions to a strategic plan. Such a plan determines the long-term direction of a particular company within a competitive environment, and the allocation of its component – physical, human and financial – resources. Tactical plans, particular to the company, are then set to implement this competitive strategy over the short to medium term. The 'real' manager commits his thoughts, feelings and actions to a business vision. Such a vision arises out of a purposeful view of the organization within a larger, and ultimately cosmic environment. It is unbounded, individually or geographically, and unconstrained by resources or competition. It involves an integrative process that unites rather than divides the microscopic and the macroscopic. For example, a John Hillbery who sees BCC (see Chapter 29) in the context of larger socioeconomic forces, playing a 'bit part' on the wider, and largely invisible, stage of history.

Material or moral?

The traditional manager sets goals for material growth, in profitability and productivity. These may or may not be related to a larger, and qualitative objective, such as 'serving the community'. He believes that objectives must be measurable, and emphasis is on numbers, and on the 'bottom line'.

The real manager sets his objectives in the context of a larger purpose that has a moral dimension. This gives meaning and perspective to day to day operations, and prevents the person from becoming a mere instrument in a corporate goal setting process. In that sense the larger Japanese business enterprises are infused with metaphysical purpose.

The manager's world: divisible or indivisible?

Tangible or intangible?
The traditional manager lives in the conscious world of tangible perceptions – men, money, machines and materials – and of objective reality. The real world is one which can be seen and heard, and – for the primal managers – also touched and felt. The real manager, on the other hand, lives simultaneously both in the tangible and intangible worlds. He or she recognizes the invisible forces, or psychic energies, governing our visible actions, or visible manifestations of energy. The 'real' world is the interaction of the seen and the unseen – an indivisible, living system that does not separate the material effects from the moral, or natural causes.

Part or whole?
The traditional manager sees the management process in parts, in principles, in separate processes or activities. He plans and controls, motivates and communicates. Individuals and groups are seen as separate entities, as are managers and workers, skilled and unskilled.

The real manager perceives of the management process as a whole. He believes that the managerial essence is lost in pursuit of the parts. He sees himself managing the whole process and the whole person. He integrates individual and organization, business and environment, people and things into a management ecosystem.

Division or unity?
The traditional manager sees opposing parts as competitive, and hence formulates competitive strategies within a 'hostile' business environment. Such competition may be healthy, as in retailing, or unhealthy, as in the semiconductor industry, but it is inevitably seen to exist.

The real manager sees opposing parts as elements of his interdependent whole – an all-encompassing commonality. Wholeness in fact demands the inclusion of opposites, so that actual competitors become potential collaborators. He realizes that wholesome and purposeful interaction, between opposites, produces evolutionary changes for each. When General Motors and Isuzu, for example, joined forces, each had the potential to evolve, commercially and technologically.

Management and organization: structure or flow?

Mass or energy?
The traditional manager visualizes the organization as a structure. He concentrates on organizational form and managerial content. His institution is structured, via a series of pyramidical levels, which are periodically reformed. People belong when they have a place in the amassed structure.

The real manager visualizes the organization as a process, a vast stream of energy to which all contribute and from which all draw. He concentrates on the energy of flow and merger, its quality, velocity, vitality, quantity and direction. Organizational changes are viewed as continuous and evolutionary, rather than as episodic. Finally, he views each person as a being in progress, a self-directing source of energy rather than as an inert mass. People belong to the organization when they are able to relate to its energy flow.

Dependence or interdependence?

The traditional manager, especially in the tradition of Fayol and Taylor, believes in 'pyramid power', that is in an hierarchy of super-subordinate relationships. Control is exercised vertically and authority and responsibility are clearly defined up and down the organization. The real manager, conversely, believes in interfusion power and in the resultant merger of energies known as 'joint personality'. He sees each individual as autonomous, but within an interdependent network of relationships, within which he is 'free to interfuse'. Responsibilities are, therefore, less clearly defined. The real manager is both managing and managed, autonomous and enmeshed.

Thought or feeling?

The rational manager inevitably maintains that thinking is primary, and, as a result, that scientific management is the ultimate management force. Feelings have their place, but they tend to cloud the scientific process. Intuition is suspect because it cannot be scientifically verified. The real manager believes that thinking is important but that feelings are primary. In fact feelings energize and humanize thought. Without feelings thoughts are lifeless, they lack movement and flow. Intellect and reason have their limitations. Thoughts can develop and communicate ideas but they cannot originate them, on their own. Intuition, rather, is the source of creativity.

People and management: which comes first?

Work or people?

The traditional manager defines management as the process of getting work done through people. People are therefore the means through which work is accomplished. This can sometimes lead to the manipulation of people, as 'hands' or as units of labor, rather than as human beings.

The real manager defines management as the process of getting people done (or developed) through work. In other words, work is the means through which people are developed. The work task provides the opportunity for people to interfuse – the creative process of evolution – and to relate to a process greater than themselves. Such a manager therefore has the capacity to empower others.

Work skills or life skills?

The traditional manager focusses on the person's business and technical skills with a view to improving performance. His first requirement is to ensure that both he and the people he manages perform a task at a satisfactory level. Such performance can be enhanced through training and development.

The real manager focusses on life skills for the whole person, inclusive of his technical and commercial abilities. He therefore concerns himself with the individual's physical, mental and spiritual wellbeing. His first requirement is to be a whole person of quality. The quality of performance will then follow. Furthermore, he believes that managers must develop fellow managers to be better than themselves.

Control or humility?

The traditional American or European manager sees control as a strength and humility as a weakness. For submission involves loss of control. As a result he tends to produce firmness or fixity, hardened positions or positions of conflict. He therefore visualizes central headquarters as a control centre (CHQ).

The real manager sees humility as a strength. In effect, real control occurs by taking the risk of relaxing control, by releasing one's ego attachment to a position. To let go of one's need to control is to let interfusion happen. This permits change to occur through a merger of thoughts and feelings. Thus through humility one may gain access to greater resources by becoming a relatively smaller part of a greater whole. The real manager therefore visualizes the central headquarteres as a support centre (CSO).

The winning streak: reality or fiction?

Self-assertiveness or self-improvement?

The traditional 'jungle fighter' of a manager believes in the survival of the fittest. The world, for him, consists of winners and losers. There is nothing in between. The more contemporary 'gamesman' (see Chapter 8) believes in win/win situations. Nevertheless he retains the language of winning and losing.

For the 'real' manager winning is a nonevent, irrelevant in the cooperative pursuit of purpose, competition is only with oneself and this takes the form of self-improvement. The real manager commits himself, therefore, to unique success in pursuit of extraordinary vision and purpose. 'Extraordinariness', for him, rather than 'winning', is the norm.

Responsibility or responsiveness?

The traditional manager takes action if it is within the scope of his responsibility, as defined into his role. The real manager takes initiative when it seems to be the appropriate thing to do. Perception and what needs to be done determine the scope of his responsibility.

Time or timing?

The traditional manager tries to control time. He imposes his time schedule on others. This forcing of events may accelerate or delay achievement. While recognizing the importance of timing, this may be subordinated to the need for power or task achievement.

The real manager knows that one cannot control time but only the timing of one's interventions. He pursues a course of action with persistence and perseverence, exercising patience and waiting for the right moment. He acts after sensing an inner readiness and an outer momentum (critical mass for change) of an opportunity. He intuitively perceives others' need for direction, support and inspiration, and intervenes accordingly.

Real and metaphysical management

In the final analysis, real management is an amalgam of developmental and metaphysical approaches. It retains the evolutionary and interdependent perspectives of the former, and the spiritual and energetic foundations of the latter.

Above all, though, it is founded upon laws of nature that have been absorbed, in their turn, into the fabric of an ongoing business. In that sense Agha Hasan Abedi, as President of BCC, John Hillbery as 'guardian of the spirit of the organization', and Tom Thiss, as organization developer, have played a unique and combined role in the evolution of management theory. Let me now investigate the fruits of this metaphysical approach to management.

References

1. A. Abedi, *Survival in the Nuclear age*, BCC (1985).
2. T. Thiss, *Bridging the BCC World*, BCC (March 1986), p. 14.
3. J. Hillbery, *Real Management*, BCC (1984), p. 10.
4. J. Hillbery, *The Dynamics of Marketing*, BCC, (1984), p. 13.
5. A. Rashid, 'Corporate magic', ex Thiss, T., *op.cit.*
6. J. Hillbery, *The Dynamics of Marketing* (*op.cit.*), p. 21.
7. J. Hillbery, *The Dynamics of Marketing* (*op.cit.*), p. 21.
8. A. Abedi, *Quality and Consolidation*, BCC (June, 1985), p. 10.
9. BCC, ex Hillbery, J., (*op.cit.*).
10. Hillbery, J. *Real Management* (*op.cit.*), p. 12.
11. A. Abedi, ex Hillbery, J., *Real Management* (*op.cit.*), p. 8.

29 Vision and energy

Contents

Key concepts

Once you have fully understood this chapter you should be able to define the following concepts in your own terms:

Culture	Joint personality
Interfusion	Re-ligio

Objectives

Upon completing this chapter you should be able to do the following:

1. Reveal the 'originative' impact of the developing countries on management and business.
2. Uncover the origins and development of the Bank of Credit and Commerce.
3. Locate BCC within the cultural foundations of the South and the East.
4. Compare and contrast the structure and dynamics of BCC and 3M.
5. Relate the structure and dynamics to the roots of metaphysical management.

Introduction: North and South

The Bank of Credit and Commerce, as has been revealed in Chapter 28, has transformed the very nature of business through the real management concepts that it has developed. In fact, BCC have founded their principles of management on the originative laws of nature. Most of the current business and management debate centers on the similarities and differences between West, centered upon free enterprise, and East, centered previously on state socialism and, more recently, on 'the art of Japanese management'. In this text we have compared and contrasted the enterprise and shared values of America with the adaptability and harmony of Japan.

However, there is another polarity which, in business and managerial terms, has received much less attention, and that is between North and South. In fact business and economic analysts who have focussed their attention on the North–South divide have displayed sympathy or cynicism rather than comparative managerial insight. Whereas the North, that is particularly Europe, prides itself on its rationality and explicate order (to use Bohm's terminology), the South, as we saw in Chapter 4, is closer to the metaphysical, and to Bohm's implicate order. In effect it is closer to nature, and to the origins of things. Not surprisingly, therefore, BCC, while having a strong base in the developed world, is intimately connected with the developing ones.

The Bank of Credit and Commerce

Birth of a vision: pioneering years

The roots of the Bank of Credit and Commerce are to be found in the early career of Agha Hasan Abedi, in Pakistan, during the fifties. There is a story about him, when he was still a young banking officer in the Habib Bank. The senior management at the time were engaging in a little exercise. Each was asked to write down on a piece of paper where they saw themselves in ten years. 'Abedi, you too,' they said to their junior clerk. He resisted, but they obliged him to speak. 'I shall be in charge of you all,' he wrote. Of course he turned out to be right. Abedi became head of what was then called the United Bank of Pakistan. The story of the early days emerges from the current general manager of the UK region, of BCC, who was there from almost the beginning.

He caused a banking revolution

I shall never forget when Agha Hasan Abedi, who subsequently opened the United Bank in 1959, came into our bank one day. 'Here comes the lunatic', they said. 'This man wants to open a bank of his own, and provide his people with their own new cars, villas, and foreign holidays.' Our president, then, was only in his early thirties. I knew there and then where my future lay. I joined on January 1st, 1960. In three years Mr Abedi had translated his words into deeds. He had caused a banking revolution.

I can remember vividly, in those early days sitting around, and the president telling us young upstarts, 'You are my future senior management.' I couldn't visualize it. The picture I had in my head of a senior manager was someone bald, fat and gray. We were still in our twenties and thirties. Yet, sure enough, that too materialized ...

He would notice the slightest thing. 'Cut your nails short, Mr So and So.' We had to set professional and social standards. I remember someone recognizing me in Pakistan and saying. 'I'm sure you must work for the United Bank. You officers put your suits on first, and then have them ironed around you!' Mr Abedi started the practice of bankers, in Pakistan,

> wearing suits. He really brought true professionalism into banking in the subcontinent. But there was much more to it than that.
>
> V. H. Abidi, Regional Manager, UK[1] 1987

Initially Abedi built up United Bank in Pakistan. Then, when that was being nationalized, he resolved to develop a bank that would be free to pursue its own destiny. At the time, during the sixties, he was in touch with the spirit of the Middle East. He anticipated what was going to happen there, and at the same time befriended the oil sheikhs. That was all prior to the Yom Kippur War and the great rise in oil prices. Then the world changed, and Abedi changed with it.

Combined vision

In 1972 a group of people with a joint vision came together. They had a vision of a multinational, multilingual, truly international bank with a philosophy that would accommodate all nationalities, all races, all creeds. A universal institution that belonged to all nations but no nation: one that would link the individuality of the North with the energy of the South, the intuition of the East with the enterprise of the West, in a global network of trade and transactions.

Tom Thiss, Consultant to BCC[2], 1987

Abedi started up BCC with $2½ million and forty of his own bankers in Abu Dabi. That was in 1972. They gradually built up a branch network in the Gulf. He himself stayed on with United until 1976, in order to honor his commitments. His early followers could not quite grasp his mission, but they had faith in him.

Taking advantage of change: expansion

During those formative years, in the sixties and seventies, the pioneers had engaged in lots of intensive discussions. That is how Abedi gradually passed on his philosophy of management.

Raising your sights

I remember his telling me about mental telepathy and 'joint personality'. The foundations kept on growing. What he impressed upon us was to look at the big things in life rather than squabble about the little ones. He always told us to raise our sights: 'Small people get involved in small things,' he said, 'and big people in big ones.' That is how the hazy dream of my future was beginning to be transformed into a clearer one. I was getting to know the vision. We were being introduced to the management of human energy.

V. H. Abidi, General Manager, UK[3] 1987

The physical energy situation on the Gulf, together with the financial ramifications, had meanwhile altered dramatically. The changes brought about by the rising oil prices changed the economic climate globally. BCC was in the Gulf when the flux of petrodollars transformed the financial structure of the world, and a major part of this flux flowed into the banking system. It heralded, for BCC, a period of extraordinary growth and expansion. In the ten years, 1974–83, the bank's assets had grown from a quarter of a million to US$1 billion!

In 1977, BCC came to the UK. They opened branches in Paris and Hamburg without knowing what they would do in either. They tried to act as bankers without having any banking to do. In the mid-seventies, the Middle East began to burgeon. In came the capital. The newly oil-rich began to buy land in America and property in Germany and Britain. That's where BCC came in. The Kenyan Asians and emigrés from Iran also made use of the bank's facilities.

BCC got in before the other banks. They spoke the people's languages, gave them first-class treatment and helped their trade and investments grow. The bank also took advantage of the developing countries' need to assert their independence from their former colonial masters. So slowly, as people moved out and created a worldwide diaspora, the customer base expanded. In independent Africa BCC became partners with the indigenous people. They formed a relationship. As people moved physically and psychologically BCC positioned itself accordingly.

Interfusion

A young and promising international officer posted in Africa saw an opportunity to open an agency office in a neighboring country. Sensing it was the right thing to do and the right time to do it, he took initiative and moved quickly. Regional management was informed after it was done. He was commended for his entrepreneurial efforts. Flushed with his success he pushed on to contract with the government for full banking status and the legal right to open a branch. As before, he informed management after the fact. This time they were not pleased.

The young officer had gone too far too fast. Neither the bank nor the government was ready. He had forced the process of change with a premature initiative. He had not 'interfused' beforehand. Had he done so, he would have known the timing was not right.

In BCC, if you know what's best, you are expected to take the initiative. If you have any doubt you are expected to interfuse. This process, done openly and caringly, will suggest the appropriate direction.

Tom Thiss, Consultant to BCC[4], 1987

BCC was conceived in change and continues to change, responding to it and creating it, simultaneously and continuously. During 1983 the company sensed it was time for another development.

Coping with complexity: developing

BCC in 1984, with over 300 branches operating in over seventy countries, had so grown and developed in size and stature that a new strategy was warranted. This perception coincided with a turbulent and uncertain climate in the banking world that called for consolidation and greater quality. The new impetus for change was not a regional phenomenon as it was in the Gulf in 1972 but rather a global phenomenon of complex and ever-changing proportions. International banking was becoming a highly intricate operation.

So, by 1984, the financial results were already reflecting the shift in emphasis from quantity to quality. The capital asset ratio was improved from 6½ per cent to 7 per cent, and liquidity from 50 per cent to 53 per cent. But quality is not reflected in financial terms alone. There has been an overall shift in orientation from quantitative expansion to qualitative development. A new International Development Unit was in fact established in 1984 to coordinate the development of people, of services, of marketing and of overall business on a worldwide basis.

The unit is part of the Central Support Organisation (CSO) based in London. There is no central headquarters as BCC does not believe in centralized control. The function of the CSO is to support various regions and not to control them. The same is true for the regions in relation to their branches. BCC is a bridge, linking people, cultures and nations through its banking services.

By 1986 the company's asset base had grown to no less than $17 billion, a massive expansion in fifteen years. Yet its 'implicate order' has little to do with material advancement in and of itself, but is lodged in a natural order. In a speech delivered to a peace symposium in New York in 1985, Agha Hasan Abedi extolled the sort of ecological awareness that underpinned BCC's operations.

Ecological awareness

I am impressed that a connection has begun to be made by individuals who have developed an awareness of the world as a whole, between disarmament, development and security ... This connection sees the world as one fragile, yet potentially bounteous ecology.

We are dealing with what our engineers would call a total system. Yet our politics, and the values that underlie and shape them, are still locked in the divisions of an earlier age.

We must move on – and it is my contention that it is the cruel necessity of the nuclear age that could be the spur to political evolution and its real progress, that the horror of nuclear suicide faced squarely by masses and their leaders alike could bring the dawning of a new world awareness. We must live together or die together on a spaceship Earth.

Agha Hasan Abedi 'Survival in a nuclear age'[5] 1985

In 1986 BCC had begun applying its philosophy of global interdependence to a new marketing thrust: correspondent banking. Correspondent banking involves the handling of other banks' business related to international trade transactions, such as the advising and negotiating of letters of credit, collections and remittances, the issue of guarantees and the maintenance of their accounts.

A Dynamics Committee was formed, worldwide, under the International Division of the bank, to realize the possibilities inherent in this major departure. 'This Dynamics Committee would create a power base and an environment of possibilities which will be the nucleus of the action. The energy system of the International Division would be channelled into the creation of Correspondent Banking Desks in important places to encash on relationships with other banks and actualize the possibilities.'[6]

In 1987, the bank was poised, ready to interfuse with a selected group of major national and commercial partners, thereby spreading its collaborative philosophy and transcending psychological, cultural and national boundaries in the process.

Conclusion

Tradition and modernity

The Bank of Credit and Commerce, while hurtling on towards the year 2000, at the same time constantly returns to its origins, or 'links back' (re-ligio) with its past. Time, for BCC, 'is a process in which past, present and future are bound to each other . . . it is like a spiral or a helix, rising from creation' (see p. 524).

As Erich Jantsch, the physicist, has said: 'Not only does re-ligio, the linking back to the origin, become the main spiritual concern, it also becomes the core of creative action' (see Chapter 25). In metaphysical conclusion, natural laws of interfused banking, not only lie at the core of creative action, but also become the main spiritual concern of the company. Its physical and economic 'explicate' performance, to use David Bohms's terminology, draws off a more profound and 'implicate', natural or moral order. Ultimately, for BCC, the 'tao of business', to catch a phrase from Capra, unites yin and yang, the cosmic dance and the self-organizing universe, in a new synthesis as Jantsch would have it, of 'universal, unfolding energy'.

Manager self-development

So much for matters metaphysical, which may or may not be close to your way of thinking, feeling and doing, as a manager.

In the final section of this text I want to present to you the full array of managers, that is eight of them in all, reflecting the alternately hard and soft sides of primal, rational, developmental and metaphysical management. You yourself are likely to have a particular affinity with one, if not two of them. At the same time one or more are likely to be inaccessible at this stage of your development.

References

1. R. Lessem, *The Global Business*, Prentice Hall (1987), p. 145.
2. R. Lessem, *op.cit.* (1987), p. 147.
3. R. Lessem, *op.cit.* (1987), p. 146.
4. R. Lessem, *op.cit.* (1987), p. 147.
5. A. Abedi, 'Survival in a nuclear age', *BCCI* (April 1985).
6. J. Hillbery, 'Correspondent banking', *BCCI* (March 1986).

Section F
Manager
self-development

Introduction

Now that you have covered each of the four management domains, you should be in a position to decide which one suits you the best. In making your choice you will inevitably be influenced by the national or ethnic culture of your origin and residence; by your age and phase of development; and by the particular organization in which you may be working. Most important though, in this section of the text, will be your particular individuality.

In helping you develop yourself, as an individual manager at this point, I am not implying that you should discard any flexibility you might have, in being able to manage across domains. Rather, I want to help you find your natural, and developing managerial self, while still cultivating your ability to respond flexibly. In the appendix to Chapter 1, there is a 'spectral inventory' to help you uncover your managerial self if it has not already become apparent to you.

Becoming a primal manager

In becoming a primal manager, that is either a tough-headed entrepreneur, a tender-hearted animateur, or some combination of the two, you undergo a series of stages and transitions, before you realize your full managerial potential. The entrepreneur and animateur, between them, or within one person, make up the pioneering enterprise.
As an entrepreneur, you may:

- Start out in your youth as a salesman or merchandizer.
- Become, in adulthood, a fully fledged intrapreneur.
- Turn, in midlife, into a business developer.
- Become, in your maturity, the very spirit of enterprise.

As such an entrepreneur, you may well be marginal to the managerial establishment;

your work and life will be full of drama; you will naturally gravitate towards buying and selling; you will be rewarded by tangible and financial returns for your commercial achievements, and you will develop naturally and circuitously if given far-reaching business challenges and family-like emotional support.

As an animateur, that is the soft counterpart to the hard entrepreneur, you may:

- Start out in your twenties as a craftsperson.
- Become, in adulthood, a skilled operator, with people or things.
- Grow, in midlife, into an animateur, enthusing all those around.
- Become, in your fifties, the very spirit of community.

As such an animateur, you are liable to be a gregarious person, seeking to belong to a close circle of people; your progress at work will be with and through other people and things, and you will be rewarded by being able to improve their lot; you will develop naturally and roundedly if able to exercize and advance your social or technical skills to an ever-increasing extent, especially in operations, personnel or sales.

Becoming a rational manager

In becoming a rational manager you will develop as either a tough and judgemental executive, as a tender and flexible change agent, or as some combination of the two. The executive and the change agent between them support the established organization.
As an executive you may:

- Start out in your twenties as a trainee manager.
- Become, in adulthood, a functional manager.
- Grow, in your forties, into a business executive.
- Represent, in your maturity, the very spirit of leadership.

As such an executive you are likely to be an authoritative person, who advances through conventional promotion within the structured organization, being rewarded by the status and esteem that goes with it, and being developed through a succession of progressively more senior management postings.

The counterpart to the force of order, within the established organization, is the change agent, that is the force of freedom. As such a manager you may:

- Start out in your youth as professional troubleshooter.
- Gravitate, in your thirties, into becoming an agent of change.
- Develop, in midlife, into a more wide-ranging manager of change.
- Evolve, in maturity, into the very spirit of freedom.

As such a change agent, and free spirit, you like variety and mental stimulation, being rewarded by interesting and varied work in a flexible project setting; you develop laterally within a professional network, and want to keep continually, and mentally, on the move, often within R&D, management services, management training or advertising and public relations.

Becoming a developmental manager

The primal and rational managers are the better known ones, at least to those of us in the West and North. However, there are still four more managers to come. The first two are the adopter and the enabler. In becoming a developmental manager you will evolve either as a faithful adopter, that is committed to your company or creed, as an insightful enabler, sensitive to potential, or as some combination of the two. Between you, you stimulate corporate renewal.

As an adopter, you may:

- Submit yourself, in your youth, as an apprentice to a master.
- Develop, in your thirties, as a journeyman along your way.
- Practice multi-leadership, in midlife, by 'interfusing'.
- Acquire mastery, in your fifties, of your management craft.

As such an adopter you are characterized by your humility and willingness to imitate those people and things that you respect; you are rewarded by being allowed to serve your faith, thereby acquiring meaning in your life; you develop by following respected people, and by becoming progressively more absorbed in your work, as a manager and follower.

The counterpart to the agent of harmony, the adopter, is the agent of evolution, the enabler. As such an enabler of physical or human development you may:

- Start out in your twenties as an artist or scientist.
- Become, in adulthood, a technically or socially based designer.
- Turn, in your forties, into an enabler of development,
- Become, in your maturity, the spirit of development.

As such an enabler, you are able to recognize potential in people, in products or in markets that others cannot see; you feel rewarded if given the opportunity to develop that potential alongside your own, often by making diagonal movements within or without your organization; you grow or evolve your role rather than relying on conventional promotion, particularly in the fields of organization development or industrial design.

Becoming a metaphysical manager

In becoming a metaphysical manager you will develop as a charismatic innovator, as a romantic adventurer, or as some combination of the two. Between you, you are capable of organizational transformation.

As an innovator you may:

- Start out as an inventor in your twenties.
- Grow into a fully-fledged innovator in your adulthood.
- Become a visionary in your forties.
- Develop, in maturity, into the very spirit of creativity.

As such an innovator you will be recognized, from the outset, for your powers of imagination, and will be particularly sought after in research and development; you will seek to promote your ideas rather than be promoted within the formal hierarchy; your reward will be the realization of your creativity, in tangible form.

Finally, as an adventurer you may:

- Start out in your youth as an action man or woman.
- Become an adventurer in your thirties.
- Start activating others in your midlife.
- Become the very spirit of adventure in your fifties.

As such an adventurer you will be recognized for your incredible energy, particularly in sales or operations, and be rewarded by surmounting physical challenges that are put your way; between your energy and the innovator's creativity a vision is materialized.

Conclusion

Starting out in managerial life as a sales or craftsperson, as a management trainee or professional troubleshooter, as an apprentice or artist, or as an action man or inventor, you have the potential to round out, over the course of your development.

In fact, if and as you develop, say as a primal manager, you absorb aspects of rational management in adulthood, developmental management in midlife, and metaphysical management in maturity. As a proverbial 'Westerner', you will need to imbibe elements of the 'North', the 'East' and the 'South', in turn. In this penultimate section of our text, therefore, you will have the opportunity of recognizing and developing your managerial self, in some detail. In the final section of this text, then, we can focus on the implications for global business and organization, as well as for the domains of management.

 **30** Becoming a primal manager

Contents

Key concepts

Once you have fully understood this chapter you should be able to define the following concepts in your own terms:

Animateur   Entrepreneur

Objectives

Upon completing this chapter you should be able to do the following:

1. Compare and contrast the entrepreneur, or intrapreneur, and the animateur.
2. Analyze how the primal manager develops over the course of his or her work and life.
3. Describe how the intrapreneur can be recognized, recruited, rewarded and developed.
4. Describe how the animateur can be recognized, recruited, rewarded and developed.
5. Assess the nature and extent of your own entrepreneurial, and your animateurial attributes.

Introduction

Factors impinging on the individual manager

In the penultimate section of this global management text I want to help you identify and develop your individual, managerial potential, over the course of your lifespan. In the process I shall be exposing you to eight real-life managers from all around the globe who have developed their respective and managerial individualities.

At the same time, in focussing on you, as an individual manager, I am exhibiting cultural bias towards the North and West. I therefore owe some of you in the South and East an apology, though the fact that this book is written in English already makes such bias inevitable. Before I embark on this individual orientation, however, let me emphasize that a manager's operating domain will be influenced by three major factors, other than his or her individuality. See Fig. 78.

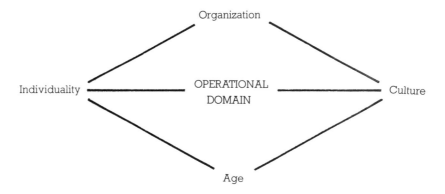

Fig. 78 Factors impinging on you as an individual.

In other words, the national and ethnic culture of your birth and residence; the particular organization and industry in which you are working; and the age you have reached, will each have an important bearing on the domain in which you are operating. However, in this section of this text, I shall be placing special emphasis on the development of your individuality over the course of your lifecycle. As a result I shall be focussing on your maturation, as it unfolds through your youth, adulthood, midlife and maturity.

The process of individuation

Although you each have a different career path to forge, or to follow, each one of your paths will be crossed by somewhat predictable demands (see Chapter 22) at particular stages of your life. In other words, if you choose to open yourself to life, and to personal growth, you will progressively round out your managerial personality, but still operating from a unique, and individual base. There is a natural cycle of development, then, that applies to all individual managers, at least in an approximate way. In fact, if you are to 'mature' as an adult, in the best sense of the word, you need to develop through Levinson's four major phases.

Exploration phase

In your youth, from your late teens to late twenties, you need to explore, to experiment and to take risks – just like the pioneering enterprise.

Consolidation phase

In your young adulthood you need to settle down into more of a routine, to establish yourself and to specialize. Thus in the period between your late twenties and thirties you can model yourself on the conventionally managed organization.

Phase of renewal

Then as you enter midlife, in your forties, you have to change direction – that is to broaden your horizons. More often than not you need to help yourself by helping others in one capacity or another. You become involved in the conscious development of yourself, of other people, or of products or markets in the broadest sense.

Individuation phase

Finally, as you mature, you tap the true center of your being and become, for the first time, your true self. In the process you realize your youthful dream.

Domains of individuality

As has been indicated throughout this text, management theory and practice occupy distinct, though necessarily overlapping, operational domains. Each can be divided into softer and harder realms of thought, feeling and action. Thus we have a total of eight subdomains. For each I have identified a managerial character. Finally, each one is prospectively, though seldom actually 'actualized', to use Maslow's term (see pp. 446–7), over the course of an individual lifetime.

For example, as a rational manager you may become a 'hard' business executive or a 'soft' agent of change. Moreover, you actualize yourself, as an executive, by progressing from a trainee, in your youth, to a functional manager, in adulthood; and from an executive, in midlife, to a leader, in your maturity.

Of course these are tendencies rather than inevitabilities. The factors that inhibit so-called individuation in management, are:

- Lack of self knowledge.
- Poor management recruitment.
- Inappropriate reward systems.
- Inadequate training and development.

as well as the overall personal, organizational and cultural inhibitions that foster these inadequacies. In the next four chapters I want to help you – as an individual, as a company or as a country – overcome these limitations, in both theory and practice.

A model of individuation in management

A hero and heroine in each domain

For each of the four management domains, there is both a soft and a hard individual domain. This is summarized in Table 39. Furthermore, in the Appendix to Chapter 1 I have provided a rough and ready means of your checking which of these subdomains seems to befit you most at this point of time.

Remember that, as an individual, you are capable of inhabiting more than one such subdomain at any one time. In fact, the more versatile you become, the more able you will be to switch between one domain and the other. Interestingly enough, as and if you grow and develop, within any one domain, you will inevitably broaden, as well as deepen, your abilities. The point does remain, however, that you are likely to remain most at home within one of the four domains, be it primal, rational developmental or metaphysical.

Table 39 Domains and subdomains

Domain	Subdomain		Personal Quality	Managerial Attribute
	'Hard'	'Soft'		
Primal	Entrepreneur		Dynamic	Enterprise
		Animateur	Enthusiastic	Shared values
Rational	Executive		Flexibile	Adaptability
		Change agent	Analytical	Structure/strategy
Developmental	Enabler		Magnetic	Potential
		Adopter	Humble	Spirit
Meta Physical	Visionary		Charismatic	Vision
		Adventurer	Active	Energy

I shall now investigate each of these domains, and individual subdomains, in turn. In each case I shall invite you, for yourself or on behalf of your colleagues or employees, to discover:

● What kind of individual manager you are.
● How to recruit people like yourself.
● What rewards you seek.
● How you develop your managerial individuality, over time.

In each case I shall also be providing a role model from different corners of the globe. I begin, in this chapter, with the two primal individuals, the entrepreneur and the animateur. Inevitably, of course, some of you may be some combination of the two.

The individual: primal domain

The entrepreneur or intrapreneur

Are you an entrepreneur, or intrapreneur?
As such a primal manager:

- You are a marginal operator, establishing an edge.
  - You are, by birth or by choice, marginal to the establishment.
  - You seek to find your niche rather than to fill a role.

- You are a risk taker, taking chances.
  - You believe that the future will turn out in your favor.
  - You enjoy taking calculated risks.

- You are an opportunist, spotting chances.
  - You see the creation of customers as fundamental to you.
  - You expand outwards, like an amoeba, and then fill the spaces.

- You are a wheeler dealer, making chances.
  - By negotiating you create a system of exchange and transaction.
  - By scheming you create profitable combinations – out of people.

- You are an achiever, securing results.
  - You bring your desired future into being.
  - You are competitive, determined and persistent.

- You are a gamesman, who enjoys winning.
  - You respond to work and life as to a game.
  - You maintain control by making the first moves.

- You are powerful, influencing people.
  - You seek, defend and increase your power base.
  - You get into a position where you can dictate the moves.

- You are a champion, committing yourself.
  - You personally identify with an idea and vigorously promote it.
  - You combine self-interest with commitment to your organization.

The qualities of the corporate entrepreneur, or 'intrapreneur', are to a large extent instinctive and therefore difficult to cultivate. However, through appropriate challenges and support, mentorship and coaching, you can develop entrepreneurially, within an organization, if you have the innate tendencies in the first place. Those of you who scored highly on category (e), on the spectral inventory, are likely candidates!

Do companies recruit you as an intrapreneur?

As an entrepreneur, or intrapreneur, you are therefore marginal to the establishment, a risk taker – taking chances, an opportunist – spotting chances, a wheeler dealer – making chances, an achiever – securing results, a gamesman – who enjoys winning, a powerful person – influencing people and a product champion – committing your all.

Most people believe that no self-respecting entrepreneur will join a large organization. That is only a half truth. After all it may take a prospective entrepreneur like you, many years before you are ready to take the plunge. Moreover, there are many shades of entrepreneurship.

Some of you entrepreneurs may find that the balance of risk and security offered by an autonomously structured organization is more acceptable to you than a business of your own. Within a go-ahead company there will inevitably be a number of opportunities for entrepreneurs who can recognize a main chance, and also make and take one. The areas in which entrepreneurship is particularly encouraged are in merchandizing, in sales and in customer services, in new ventures, and in the general management of rapidly changing products in highly competitive markets.

How do you reward your entrepreneurs?

Entrepreneurs are not motivated to climb up the corporate ladder in the conventional sort of way. In fact the naturally entrepreneurial path is circuitous rather than direct. As part of your wheeling and dealing, as an entrepreneur or intrapreneur, you need to be able to step sideways, or move in a zigzag path, rather than stick to the straight and narrow. As such a primal manager, you love to overcome obstacles and to take calculated and emotionally thrilling risks. Your life and workstyle is full of ups and downs, and of mistakes from which you are able to learn. Each new territory lost or gained is a landmark in your dramatic journey.

As an entrepreneur you need to be given the rope either to hang yourself or to climb commercial mountains. You need capital both as a form of outward recognition and as a means to acquire personal freedom. You want to achieve the targets that you have set yourself and to be rewarded directly and financially for your accomplishments. The entrepreneurial sector of the business you need to work for will not only offer you scope for financial gain, but it will also encourage new ventures within which you can take an equity stake. Such new, or joint ventures are the lifeblood of Analog Devices in Norwood, Massachusetts, where Ray Stata has developed as an entrepreneur over the past twenty years.

The developing entrepreneur

Ray Stata   President, Analog Devices

Background

I come from farm country. My father was a self-employed contractor. I got to observe his form of livelihood. Eventually it became my own. By the time I left high school I was clear in my mind that I wanted to run my own company.

A budding entrepreneur

Preparing the entrepreneurial ground

I got my masters in electrical engineering from MIT and then left. I first joined Hewlett Packard and worked in a sales function. Not long afterwards an old and casual acquaintance of mine became a room mate. We started plotting together with a view to forming our own business. We had some knowledge of testing gyroscopes, and in 1969 there was a strong military market for the product. So we started Solid State Instruments. In retrospect, it was a failure in every respect, except one, namely we were able to sell out in good time, and raised a bit of capital. At that stage we had very limited knowledge and experience, and very little capital, but the urge to create our own business was still very strong.

We stayed on for a couple of years with the company who bought us out and picked up more knowledge. Toward the end of our agreed term with them we began to think again. The idea of a new company began to form in our minds. Analog Devices grew directly out of our experiences in our former company. We often had to decide whether to make or buy particular components for our manufacturing operation. Inevitably it was more economical to buy in. Yet the small companies from which we were buying were very poorly run. They had developed good ideas which were poorly executed.

Outdoing the competition

So we left our old company and went into competition with our vendors. Within two or three years we had managed to capture a major share of the market. That provided our genesis and our roots. We outdid our competition, in the execution of our business, in every respect.

When we started out our vision didn't extend beyond outdoing the competition. But, having achieved our initial goals we had to decide how to continue to be successful. The clues lay in the nature of our business. Our customer base was extremely fragmented. While our sales had reached only five or six million dollars, we had acquired literally thousands of customers. That established the foundations for our subsequent marketing techniques. We had to find a way of staying in touch with them all.

So we converted a problem into an opportunity. We came out with an appropriate survey instrument, and got an enormous response back. Amongst other things we asked our customers which components they preferred to buy, and which to make. This took us back, again, to our genesis. Overall, we got such an enormous response back from our survey that it established a product agenda, virtually to the present day. We restricted ourselves, though, to products with a coherent, linear technology base.

There was another key event close to the inception of our company. When we began the company our manufacturing techniques were very primitive. Then, in 1967 and 1968, integrated circuits began to show their face. It was clear to us, at the time, that this manufacturing technology was going to become predominant in the industry. As a young company we envisioned the need that was going to arise, which we could potentially be in a position to fulfill.

Leveraging success

In order to put ourselves in such a position we formed our first joint venture. We set this company up, while installing our rights to acquire it if we so wished. In fact, we bet our company on the venture. We had to leverage our success, totally, The venture established the roots for our semi conductor technology.

There was another key event in our historical development. The first minicomputers were beginning to appear on the horizon in the early seventies. They needed devices to convert from analog signals to digital. We saw this as a major opportunity. We had some of the knowledge to do the conversion, but not all. We cast around for a small company that was expert in conversion techniques, and acquired it. Those strands, brought together, became the roots of our products, as they stand today. This also set up another pattern. We're able to identify an emerging market opportunity early in the game, and fulfill it by supplementing our skills by merging with others.

Becoming an entrepreneurial manager

Setting targets

As we began to grow larger, we decentralized into small work units with a self-contained set of resources and information. In the early stages cf Analog, of course, this was all done instinctively. It was only from 1972 onwards that we began to formalize in order to perpetuate a way of life. So we now have documents that set forth our assumptions, our value system, our vision. If people don't buy into our vision they're better off going someplace else. We try to get people of a like mind. You're bound to be more successful if you get people who are on the same wavelength as you are. We formalized our first set of corporate objectives in 1974, after we'd been working on them for a couple of years.

Resolving the crisis of adulthood

In fact, in 1970 we had faced a real crisis. At that stage our turnover was ten or twelve million dollars. The country was going through a recession. The company was in a shambles. We had just gone public and brought in a professional as president. I chose to remain more of a strategist. I saw the presidency in terms of administration, an upgraded clerk. I wasn't prepared for it. I hadn't realized the distinction between administration and leadership. I was in my early to mid-thirties at the time.

That particular arrangement fell apart. I remained the principal stockholder and yet I was reporting to this other guy, who was running the show. He didn't have the power base to enforce his vision and I lacked the nominal authority to enforce mine. I decided that I had to take on the job. I had to learn to be president. So I established a program for myself. I did some reading and also decided to go on a management course for presidents who shared a concern about developing themselves as professionals. There I met a person I was very taken with. I invited him to become a director of my company, and he became a kind of tutor for me. He taught me basic principles of supervision and leadership. They applied to both our domestic and foreign operations.

International enterprise

Back in 1967 I took a trip to Europe and saw that half our market was out there. So we set up wholly owned sales and marketing operations first in England, and then in all the important markets round the world. Subsequently we have established manufacturing units in Ireland, Japan and the Phillipines. Forty per cent of our sales and the greater proportion of our profits now come from overseas, and that's on an overall, current turnover of some $400 million now.

Business development

Developing a broader outlook

We've developed a joint venturing capability out of our experience of nurturing one company after another. In four out of eleven cases we have since acquired the companies. Joint venturing, all along the way, has enhanced our ability to exploit our customer base. A major recent development, amongst our customers, involves a movement from buying in components to buying in systems. Our customers have been coming to us to help them convert not only components but also, increasingly, systems. The time has now come for us to be more proactive in this respect.

Increasingly, as we move into VLSI technology, the division between components and systems manufacture will become blurred. To continue to look at the world through a component manufacturer's eyes is to become obsolete. We have to develop a systems outlook. Companies will want to buy more complete building blocks, that is subsystems and systems products. The thrust for the future is to be able to supply the complete set of building blocks.

Coping with commercial complexity

So our marketplace and our organization are both becoming more complex. As things become more complicated there's a tendency to grow more inward looking. I have to try ever harder to get our general managers and our marketing managers out into the field.

Now I need to re-establish the critical importance of being close to the customer. As a young company you have no problem. You have nothing on your desk, so you have to go out and acquire something. Nowadays my people's desks are full, which gives them every excuse for remaining deskbound. Admittedly a lot of technology development is internal, but the coupling of technical seeds to market need is the real trick.

Embodying the spirit of enterprise

Keeper of our culture

I feel now, like seventeen years ago, that we're going through another watershed. And my role is changing, at least in emphasis. If I look at my priorities, I see myself now as, first and foremost, the keeper of our culture. I have to make sure that we slowly evolve it rather than allow it to disintegrate, or totally depart from its roots. That's the key. But I have to play that role in a participative manner.

Becoming a mentor

When we were smaller we relied on pirating professional people with technical and commercial know how and experience. Now we cannot afford to bring in huge numbers of people with their own agendas. It's too risky. So we have to provide an environment in which young people can grow. So we've got to get people committed to being mentors. Bottom line results are no longer enough. People have to see mentoring as part of their responsibility.

Actualizing myself

A second major area of priority revolves around vision. We have to be able to articulate a long-term direction that makes sense. We have to establish a direction that is both reinforcing and synergistic. I have to grow, from a professional manager and incipient leader, into a fully fledged one. If I can nurture the spirit of enterprise, the management functions can always be added on.

A critical part of the whole thing is the alignment between personal and corporate goals. The corporation, in fact, is an instrument for the realization of my personal goals, and so it should be for the employee. The interplay of these two things is essential.

Norwood, Massachusetts 1986

How do you develop as an intrapreneur?

As an entrepreneur or intrapreneur like Ray Stata, you do not develop, managerially, by going on formal training courses. You need to set or be set, rather, challenging personal and business targets to which to respond. You also need to be provided with coaches and mentors who can not only live up to your entrepreneurial expectations, but also supersede them.

Your dream is to be rich and powerful!

In your youth you are likely to find the most opportunities in marketing, or else in championing a particular product or service in any one of the other functions. Travel to far-flung places and rewards directly related to your achievements are likely to enhance your performance, as an itinerant salesman, market trader and budding entrepreneur. In your adulthood you should have the opportunity of managing a profit center of semiautonomous function in your own particular way. Challenge needs now to be accompanied, as it was for Ray Stata by growing territory and responsibility, as an entrepreneurial manager.

In midlife – in your forties – the entrepreneurs among you, like Ray Stata, should be broadening your terms of reference. Instead of being preoccupied only by money and markets you should also be widening your field of concern to encompass, to a much greater extent, the development of people and the business as a whole. This is a natural time for you to enter a development function therefore, without losing your marketing or financial touch. Such a role would also and naturally serve to broaden the base of a personnel or R&D department, with you as a business developer.

Finally, as you fully mature, in your fifties and sixties, you might become involved in overall business renewal, through which the transformation of the company, its culture, and its overall direction may be achieved. This is a role that Ray Stata is now playing at Analog Devices, as he becomes his ultimate and primal managerial self, thereby embodying the spirit of enterprise.

So much then for the entrepreneur, in his own company, or for the intrapreneur, within someone else's organization. He represents the 'hard' side of primal management. However, if he is to be successful over the long term, like Stata, he needs to open up to other management domains – rational in adulthood, developmental in midlife and metaphysical in maturity. While you retain your fundamental and, in this case, primal identity, you therefore progressively round out, as you grow and develop. This will only happen in this instance, however, if you are open to the soft, as well as to the hard, attributes of primal management.

That leads us on to the 'animateur'.

The animateur

The entrepreneur and animateur, like the hunter and gatherer of old, are the formative primal couple. As one rounded person, or as a management duo, they spearhead the youthful phase of a business' development. More often than not it is the entrepreneur who takes the hunting lead, and the animateur – in the background – who provides the nurturing support. This may occur both within the business and also at home.

However, in recent years, as more and more women have set up in business, we find instances where the animateur in fact takes the nurturing lead, and the hunter – entrepreneur plays the supportive role. An example of this, in the UK, is the interpreting and translation company, Interlingua, which has recently merged with TTI to become the largest such company in the world. The role of the 'animateur', a term I have borrowed from the French (see p. 157), has also been brought in to recent focus as a result of the growing interest in corporate culture. Let me now investigate, with you, who the animateur is, and how she is recruited, rewarded and developed.

As an animateur:

- You operate informally, making personal contacts.
  - You establish a strongly cohesive, informal organization.
  - You create ways and means of keeping in constant touch.

- You establish rituals and ceremonies, uniting people.
  - You hold 'revivalist' meetings, especially for sales people.
  - You establish rituals to protect staff from fear of the unknown.

- You establish a 'family feeling', in which everyone partakes.
  - You ensure that needs of individuals serve those of the whole.
  - You become like a mother to your business children.

- You are an animateur, activating people's social lives.
  - You provide access to an active and creative group life.
  - You widen people's horizons and enlarge their social circle.

- You create a corporate culture, thereby sharing values.
  - You create heroes who pass on your primary corporate values.
  - You make sure that formative corporate legends live on.

- You embody the spirit of the community.
  - You become a 'mother earth' figure.
  - Your business becomes identified with the community.

You may be such an animateur, then, if you scored highly on category (g) in the spectral inventory.

As an animateur you are not a cartoonist, but, in the original context, a person who animates individuals and groups within a particular locality. You accomplish this not only through your own charm and enthusiasm but also by drawing on your organizational and cultural heritage.

Do organizations recruit animateurs?

As an animateur, then, you operate informally – making personal contact, you establish rituals and ceremonies – thereby uniting people, you create a family feeling – in which everyone partakes, you activate people's social lives – as an animateur, you create a corporate culture – through which values are shared, and you come to embody community spirit. Animateurs are more likely to be found in America or in Italy than in the UK or Japan, and generally more amongst women than men. However, there will be many exceptions to these very generalized rules, and you may well be one of them.

In functional terms, animateurs are most likely to be found amongst the salesforce, amongst the secretarial staff, or amidst those individuals in personnel or in operations who are seen to be natural and gregarious 'people people'. In fact, in Britain at the present time, with the growing emphasis on 'customer care', animateurs are in ever-increasing demand. British Rail, British Airways and Barclays Bank are just three examples of companies which have rapidly developed their emphasis on service.

Moreover, in the world at large, as the importance of the 'services sector' increases, so the role of animateurs will become ever more significant, that is if they are allowed to develop themselves through their supportive functions.

How do you reward your animateurs?

As an animateur you seek out a social circle to which to belong, whether or not it is entirely of your own making. The last thing you want is to be promoted into a position of isolation from your familiar friends, colleagues and workmates, and from the product or service which matters to you. However, if you are ambitious and are encouraged to grow, you will need progressively to broaden your circle of contacts. As an animateur you will be intent on bringing your practical and social skills to bear on situations, and you will be frustrated if prevented from doing so. You therefore need to be recognized for your skill, whether as a skilled craftsman, or for your innate social skills.

You are rewarded, though, not so much by individual recognition, but by recognition of your group of skilled workers, whether as joiners or linguists, in which you may have become a leading influence. In fact, the reason that cooperative enterprises are more widespread in Italy or Spain than in Britain or Scandinavia is because of the gregarious, Mediterranean influence. Cooperative activity, in its inherent nature if not necessarily in its legally constituted form, comes naturally to the animateur. Rewards for cooperative achievement are therefore welcomed.

Nelli Eichner of Interlingua is a good case in point. Although she and her husband sadly died in 1986, her memory lives on within the newly amalgamated company.

Becoming an animateur

Nelli Eichner   Co-founder, Interlingua

Background

The story of my life
I am now the director of a translation company called Interlingua.
  In this short story I shall tell you how we started, grew and prospered. 'We' means my husband, our five children and now, with the help of a few grandchildren ...

Acquiring the craft of translation

Lonely in a strange land
I, Nelli Eichner, née Nelinka Kleinova, was born on the family farm in what is now called Czechoslovakia. We spoke Czech and German at home. Some war prisoners who were left behind and who were working on our farm in the Austro-Hungarian

Empire were Italians, and some of them were Russians. These men were lonely in a strange land. They found it hard to learn Czech. I could not really blame them. It is a language with sentences such as STRC!

These lonely men were only too glad to tell the stories of their homelands to little Nelinka, who loved sitting on a cosy lap and listening to stories. Gradually I started to understand the legends of old mother Russia, full of werewolves and the Italian stories about the singing mermaids of Venice. In the evening, in bed, I repeated these stories in Czech to my little sister.

Becoming a translator, without knowing it

Without knowing it, I became a translator. When our dairymaid found out that I had learned to communicate with her Russian lover, which she could not do, at least not verbally, I was frequently sent to the pub to fetch him. The mill foreman asked me to tell the Italians that they had not filled the sacks of grain right up to the top. Thus I became an interpreter at the ripe old age of four years.

My parents tried to make me into a young lady (unsuccessfully, as you will note) – that's why I was sent to school in Vienna, Austria where I learned my lessons in German, while still speaking Czech at home. French and English grammar were painfully drummed into me when I was eleven years old, but I am glad to say that I actually learned to speak these languages later, at an international scout camp.

I was not a particularly brilliant scholar, but my languages were soon just a little better than my schoolteachers'. That's how I managed to pass exams – somehow.

I spent several holidays abroad, usually hitch-hiking, which brought me into contact with local people. I learned to communicate, at a superficial level, in other languages. Later I was able to improve on these by reading books, papers and learning local folk songs.

Developing into a skilled operator

Interpreting for a living

Hitler made it impossible for me to stay at home and continue my studies. I accepted a job in Rome for one year, then moved to France, then England. When war broke out, I was working in the Czech Embassy in Paris. When the Germans occupied Paris, I fled again. This time with the Czech Army. I interpreted for them and for the English officers in England who were suddenly swamped with a Czech Army, a Polish Army and the Free French Army, most of whom could not say a word in English.

I was then twenty-five years old and doing well interpreting for a living. That's when I met my husband. This was the greatest stroke of luck in a very lucky life. His name is Fred. He is a chemist, a good linguist and, to me, the most wonderful man in the world.

Involving the family in the business

We were married in a registry office in London during the blitz. I soon became pregnant. Our first child, Jona, was born under a shower of bombs. I had to stay at home to look after my baby, which meant living on only one salary. We were very short of money. We had to think of some way to supplement our income. My languages came in useful. They provided me with pocket money. It helped a bit. Fred was writing a text book for an Oxford publisher. I translated the stuff. It helped a bit more.

Then our second child, our son Mike, fell ill with polio. We thought that the world had come to an end. But – somehow – he lived. He survived the illness, but his lungs had collapsed. There was but one way to save him. Take him out of London, into the fresh country air – immediately!

Becoming an animateur

Cultivation

When we moved to Ashurst Wood in rural Sussex, my husband could not continue travelling to north London. He stayed on with his firm as consultant chemist. At home he spent his time fixing the roof, the plumbing, the drains and cutting the overgrown hedges. One of our florist friends told him that the cypress hedge clippings were in demand by florists. That's how we started supplying Covent Garden flower market greenery.

Since my husband could no longer rely on his salary, money had to be found from somewhere – in Ashurst Wood. We raised and bred chickens, ducks and geese. Meat was in short supply during the period of food rationing after the war. Our poultry prospered but – at Christmas time we had to pluck 110 hens, plus ducks and geese, draw out their innards and truss them. Another farming venture produced seventeen goats.

Languages and family life

Meanwhile the translation side of our money-making efforts had increased and prospered in a small way. We found several locally available, university-trained women who were equally tied down by their families. Together we tackled languages which I could not cope with on my own. There was enough money, at long last, for the down-payment on our first, second-hand electric typewriter, and one of the other mums did the typing work, which gave me more time to get on with translations.

Working as a husband and wife team

My husband, Fred, having a scientific turn of mind, insisted that every single translation was checked before being sent out. In this way we started to provide good, technical translations which made sense. The word got around in Crawley New Town where many new, export-minded companies had set up shop. More technical translations were sent to us – more helpers were needed, more typwriters, more dictionaries. In a small way we were in business – but still broke.

Then we received our first order for a translation of a big, fat, technical manual. We all worked like the devil, for weeks. The last few pages had to be done at night, to get the job finished and sent out, and get paid for it. The next day was a Saturday, the circus had come to East Grinstead.

The children pitch in

Our children had looked forward to going – but … After a night's work I was so exhausted, I fell ill. I could not take the children to the fair and to the famous circus. The children were terribly disappointed! A family council was convened over supper. The children agreed that Mummy and Daddy are working too hard and, 'We shall have to help.' And help they did, from that day on.

They delivered and collected jobs, folded leaflets, learned to answer the 'phone intelligently. They painted foreign accents on finished work, and they were prepared to do the eternal fetching and carrying to and from the translators, typists, printers. The experience of the circus set our family into a new pattern of life. 'We' became one family, one group of people who pulled together for the common good.

Creating the Interlingua family

We became a very happy group, keen and proud of our ever-growing and expanding translation company. Translation jobs included flight simulators, aeroplanes, potato peeling machines, harvesters and diving gear. The office expanded into a second room and then a third. Clients must have been satisfied with our work.

That's when the construction of Concorde was being planned. The first Concorde was going to be an Anglo-French combined effort. One of our clients 'phoned: 'How would you like to translate all the specifications for us from and into French, so that designers and engineers on both sides of the Channel could understand each other, because them frogs don't speak no English!' Would we? Oh, boy! What a lovely job this was going to be. We were all delighted, but ...

This was a Government job and we could not really supply Government departments, the British aircraft industry and sundry boffins in Parliament with invoices in triplicate under the name of 'Fred and Nelli Eichner'. The contract was to be signed on the next day. So, we all sat down to tea in the evening after work and we cooked up a respectable sounding name, suitable for a company with Government contracts.

The name Interlingua was born, and Fred had to rush to London to register it, first thing in the morning, before we actually signed the contract. Fred and I were now a properly constituted and registered partnership. Our little Interlingua had grown to be a reputed, but still only local company. Our children were as proud of Interlingua as we were, and they were overheard bragging to their friends about 'our company'. Yes, they felt a part of it, having worked with us since they were babies – well almost babies.

A telex machine joins the family

In our pride and boundless enthusiasm we were always working, thinking and forward planning. That's when Fred had a brainwave. Instead of fetching, carrying and delivering our translations on bicycles, why don't we install a telex machine. The idea was new. Telexes were still regarded as a rare and costly installation which was used only by large, well-heeled industrial companies. It was a gamble. Would it ever pay? The new machine, a huge noisy monster, was installed in our lounge! Yes, no other location would have been elegant enough. It stood on one side of the fireplace in front of the piano – and a new carpet was purchased in order to set it off to best advantage. Then we all, yes all, including the children, learned how to use the telex machine. When we were almost sure what we were doing, I started to send out short messages to other telex subscribers, informing them that: 'Interlingua provide instant translations by telex.'

Our very first telex translation job came from a paper mill in the Midlands. It was just a few lines, an urgent message about a pulp shipment. I translated it and typed it and sent it back to the client within minutes. He was surprised. No, he was amazed! No, he did not believe it was possible, it could not be done! He sent another translation by telex, just to see if we could really do it again. We did! He told all his friends in the club about Interlingua. They all tried out the new services. Yes, it really worked!

Within a couple of weeks, one of the newspapers had heard about this incredible 'Interlingua Instant Translation Service'. Yes, one could send a message in Rumanian to Sussex, via telex, and have the translation back in Scotland with the hour! The story made headlines in forty-two newspapers.

The world links up with Interlingua

Visitors came to see us from America, from Japan, from all over Europe. They brought work and 'could Interlingua please accept them as subscribers'.

It was the turning point. Within months Interlingua expanded from a local company to an international company. Our house was full of offices. Our children became expert telex typists, checkers, proof-readers. We were all so proud – and oh so enthusiastic. The large companies who were then the only telex users became our clients. The workload increased and became more and more varied and interesting. One day the BBC asked us to translate a film script. It was the first of many more. We were asked to translate books, film scripts, secret documents, urgent communications between heads of state.

Cultivating the spirit of community

There are, of course, many more episodes, in many languages about Interlingua. A woman's and a translator's work is never done. I am a happy grannie now. The company is in my children's capable hands. Our conference interpreters are travelling all over the world. A solid bank of computers helps to process translation faster and better. New ideas were added to those, now old fashioned, which made Interlingua grow and expand into an international company with offices in many countries.

The company became one big, happy family.

During one of his inspired moments, Fred bought twenty acres of beautiful Sussex countryside surrounding an elegant mansion. This is now the Interlingua head office. On the same plot of land each of our five children has built their own house ...

Our grandchildren play in the pool. The older children come into the office to help, and leave when the job is done. These children are my greatest blessing. They fill my heart with joy and pride. Interlingua is our family business. There is no happiness like shared happiness.

Ashurst Wood, England 1986

How do you develop as an animateur?

In your youth you will welcome the opportunity of meeting lots of warmhearted people, and of working with people and things which you really care about. Like Nelli Eichner you are more of a craftsman than a technologist or professional. You learn best from people with whom you feel a natural rapport. Because Nelli did not have that rapport with her teachers at school she learnt virtually nothing from them. Any training programs you go on therefore have to be fun and friendly if these courses are to achieve the desired effect.

Your dream is to be happy

As you enter adulthood, in your thirties, you need to substantiate the base of your activities and relationships, thereby becoming a skilled operator in commercial and social, as well as technical terms. The role of a supportive coach, and an admired mentor, are particularly important for you at this stage. Nelli Eichner in fact drew on her own family in those respects. In midlife you need to broaden out even further, beyond the relatively limited circle of sales, production or personnel activity in which you might have been working. A natural development is from production or sales to regional, divisional or company animateur. You will need to become more involved with consciously creating a corporate culture, rather than with just instinctively generating a family feeling.

Though your enthusiasm and charm, rather than your dynamism or authority, will still remain to the fore, more of these latter qualities will begin to come out. Moreover, you will begin to acquire a reflective capacity that was not in evidence before. Finally, as you approach maturity, you develop the potential to create a new and powerful culture in your organization. That is what Nelli never quite achieved and has therefore left to her successors. Such a corporate culture may be more in tune with the times than the one you inherited. You, in your turn, as you mellow, and become more philosophical, will come to embody the spirit of community.

Conclusion

Entrepreneur and animateur

So we can see the way in which, between the two of you as entrepreneur and animateur, you build up the base of your business. Enterprising cells and a cohesive culture are now in place. Autonomy and entrepreneurship, combined with shared values, are your joint creation. The net result is a profitable and growing business – in itself or within an existing organization – as well as contented customers and employees. In a functional context it is sales, rather than marketing, the product or service rather than operations, people rather than human resources, and money rather than finance, which are the primal preoccupations.

Developing yourself as a primal manager

However, as you develop towards maturity, the scope, if not the essential nature, of your managerial role changes. It becomes more broadly based and more deeply founded. In other words you absorb, if you open yourself to growth and development, some of the rational, developmental and metaphysical attributes that characterize others around you. In other words, while product is paramount, more rationally based notions of product standards, and more developmental notions of quality do begin to have their place.

Although sales remain primary, design and marketing assume important secondary, rational and developmental functions. Similarly, while it is basically people that count, rationally based human resource management and even the metaphysically oriented corporate culture have their supportive roles to play. Finally, while profit is all-important, profitability and productivity have their rational part to play, and excellence its developmental one, in the evolving, primal whole.

In sum, the primal essence is retained, but its shape and form is broadened and deepened over time. As a result Peters and Waterman go out 'in search of excellence' rather than in pursuit of fame and fortune.

Primal and rational management

All the same, a developing business needs more than its primal and instinctive duo. The bigger and more complex the business the greater the need for the executive and for the change agent, whether within manufacturing or marketing, finance or human resources, management services or general management. While it is viable and sufficient for you as an individual manager, or for a nationally based company, to round out primally, if you and it develop internationally, you both have to acquire 'new cultural spots'. Moreover, and in any case, in order to grow into the other three domains, you have to understand their inner nature. So we now turn, in Chapter 31, to the two inhabitants of the rational management domain. In Chapters 32 and 33 we shall turn to the respective couples in the developmental and metaphysical domains.

 **31** Becoming a rational
manager

Contents

Key concepts

Once you have fully understood this chapter you should be able to define the following concepts in your own terms:

Change agent   Executive

Objectives

Upon completing this chapter you should be able to do the following:

1. Compare and contrast the executive and the change agent.
2. Analyze how the rational manager develops over the course of his or her working life.
3. Describe how the executive can be recognized, recruited, rewarded and developed.
4. Describe how the change agent can be recognized, recruited, rewarded and developed.
5. Assess the nature and extent of your own executive, and change agent attributes.

Introduction

Business enterprise and the management of change

As a business evolves from a pioneering enterprise to a managed organization so it requires a new, or transformed cast of leading managerial characters. No longer do entrepreneurs and animateurs dominate the show. The world has grown too complex for those two alone. Hence Western Germany or Japan supersede the United States as models of industrial efficiency and effectiveness.

The personal age of enterprise – entrepreneur, and community – animateur, gets left behind or is pushed into the background, while the functional age of order – executive, and freedom – change agent, takes over.

The era between the fifties and the seventies was dominated, in the industrialized nations at least, by the managed economy and by the managed organization. The more recent era has been characterized by more adaptive economies and organizations, with more flexible structures and systems. Hence so-called managers of change have gained ground over their more establishment counterparts.

The executive and the change agent

The hard edge of the managed organization is provided by the executive who establishes competitive strategy and clear structure. The softer edge of the adaptive organism is provided by the change agent who instils flexibility of response and learning at a rate that exceeds the rate of change. While the executive establishes order the change agent instils freedom; between the two of them they achieve the right rational balance.

To recap, then, the entrepreneur and animateur have an important part to play in the managed organization, but not the primary one. They occupy the wings rather than the center field, creating and nurturing new business ventures. The center field is now occupied by executives, differentiated by function and integrated by means of an hierarchy of fixed command; and by change agents, differentiated by project and integrated via networks of temporary relationships. Let me begin, then, with the executive, and then move on to the agent of change.

The individual: rational domain

The executive

Are you an executive?
As such an executive manager:

- Your direction is clearcut.
  - · Clear objectives have been set at all levels.
  - · They are internally consistent and collectively exhaustive.

- You have a competitive strategy.
  - · Your mission is clearly and fully articulated.
  - · You have filled a gap in the market.

- Your management activities are clearly differentiated.
  - You plan, organize, direct and control operations efficiently.
  - You link up with other business functions effectively.

- Your communications are effective.
  - Authority and responsibility is purposefully delegated.
  - Horizontal and vertical communications operate effectively.

- You run a well-structured organization.
  - Your organization functions smoothly as an integrated whole.
  - Line and staff functions are effectively linked.

- You serve society.
  - You serve your customers efficiently and with integrity.
  - You make a recognized contribution to the community at large.

As an executive, then, you have a particular, and rational management orientation. As such you are more of a planner, a coordinator and a controller rather than a schemer, a networker or a self-starter. You are likely to have scored highest, therefore, on category (d) in the spectral inventory.

As a bureaucrat, in the best sense of the word, it is the qualities of impartiality, fairness, and justice which should mark you out rather than those of, say, regimentation and impersonality. As a prospective leader, like John Harvey Jones, you are a conciliator or referee, a person of integrity who rises above the competitive fray.

Do companies recruit potential executives?

The systematic recruitment of managers has been going on for the past two decades, both from the business schools and from within the managed organizations themselves. If anything too many prospective executives have been sought because of the recruiter's narrowly based – in our terms 'hard' and rational frame of managerial reference. There is one other problem, though, to be addressed.

Prospective executives have been traditionally recruited from the ranks of men rather than women. Although this is rapidly changing in Europe and America, particularly in the retailing sector and in the personnel function, there is still a long way to go before equality of opportunity becomes a reality. In particular, women in clerical and secreterial positions, who may well have latent executive potential, are not brought out into the limelight. The functional areas which place a premium on this kind of practical and organized mind are management accounting and control, production engineering, the analytical side of marketing, and human resource management.

The executive, then, who is being sought in such a context, has a clear direction within his function or unit; can structure such a unit efficiently and effectively; has a well defined concept of business in his mind; communicates clearly at all levels; understands succinctly his management discipline or function; and is both able and willing to serve the organization and the wider community.

How do you reward potential executives?

Sophisticated schemes have already been developed for rewarding executives. For it is the potential executives amongst you who particularly appreciate the increasing authority and responsibility, as well as the enhanced remuneration and status that goes with conventional job promotion.

Moreover once it is recognized that it is only executive types who seek that particular form of remuneration there will be less pressure, within the organization, for a single line of promotion. The organizational ladder – whether functionally, sectorally or territorially based – should serve only the hierarchically inclined amongst you. At the moment our one-dimensional orientation leads to unnecessary overcrowding.

Executive

John Harvey Jones   Ex Chairman, ICI

Background

I survived with difficulty

I was born in London but spent my early years in India. My father was a professional prime minister! He was hired by an Indian state to run its affairs, and I was brought up with the Maharaja almost as an elder brother.

When still very young I was brought over to this country and dumped in a British prep school in Kent. It was notable for its building, and I hated it. I was basically unequipped to cope. Other boys had homes to go to, and I was on my own. I vividly remember a friend going home for his fifth birthday, and there was I ... I survived with difficulty.

The school was, basically, a middle-class crammer, and one thing it did do was to teach you how to concentrate and work. I've never believed in all this inspirational stuff. It's the 90 percent perspiration that really counts. So I did reasonably well at school, through effort. I wasn't an academic. After school, I decided to go into the navy. Law was my first choice, but my parents couldn't afford it.

I loved the discipline

Anyway, I went on to Dartmouth Naval College. The discipline was draconian. I loved it. It was a totally institutionalized set-up. They didn't educate you. You were trained. They barely attempted, for example, to teach you economic history as a discipline in its own right. You merely learnt about Nelson's battles of the Nile. What they were trying to do was to set a high standard for failed officers.

A trainee officer-manager

Working in a close-knit team

When I finished at college, I went to sea. It was during the war, and I was under seventeen. We were sunk a couple of times before I was eighteen. I became a sub-lieutenant specializing in the submarine service. After the war was over, the submarine I joined was in a mess, in fact so much so that the first eight months of peace were more dangerous than ever. My submarine experience did a lot of things for me. There was rigorous discipline. We all worked in close proximity. There was a high degree of mutual respect. After all, we were all capable of sinking the sub. So it was friendly and uninstitutionalized. The discipline was real, but we mucked in together, officers and men. It was a team thing.

Meeting the top brass

I then went on to do some jobs with naval intelligence. For the first time I came into contact with the workings of government, and with the really top brass like Montgomery. I always envisaged the top brass doing these really big jobs, but I was quickly disillusioned. After one or two weeks in the Cabinet office I was asked to draw up the British strategy for a matter of great importance. I knew virtually nothing about it, and just used my common sense.

Globetrotting

Then I was sent off to occupied Germany. I did a series of intelligence assignments. I was naval officer in charge of Hamburg, and at Kiel, on the Baltic. Although German discipline can be draconian, I made sure that we ran the thing as a team.

Establishing mutual respect amongst officers and men

We then went off to the Antarctic. That was a fascinating experience. When I came back from the Antarctic, I was put into the Admiralty, to do another intelligence job.

I was there a year when my daughter got polio. A year later it became apparent that she wouldn't recover the use of her legs. She has been in leg irons since, and in continual pain. It's been a bloody hard life for her. I concluded I couldn't go on globetrotting. It was too disruptive of family life. I was twenty-six at the time.

Undergoing management training

I selected ICI for my new job. I felt the need to get into something basic. I had a need to perform a service. Something socially responsible. I'm not driven by money, and never have been. I know what I think a 'man' ought to do. I have this inner compulsion. I have to perform, and ensure that I make things happen. I joined the works study department as the lowest example of a manager. I spent the first years trying to find out what a manager was. I was very naive about industry, and very poorly paid. In the navy I had been getting £1,700 per annum, and at ICI I started on £800.

Becoming a functional manager

Managing a section

I then became a section manager. Being a section manager, for me at that time, was a marvellous job. I had a lot of junior staff and a discreet job to do. I became deputy supplies officer, and had a tremendous time. I still get letters from men and women who worked for me then. It was all about achieving high productivity through people. Every damn year we reduced our numbers. But we did it nicely, through natural wastage. Then our plant at Wilton was taken over. It was traumatic. It taught me a great deal about how not to do things. All of our top brass was shunted off or fired. It was unprecedented for ICI. Wilton was taken over by the Heavy Organic Chemicals Division. I was the only Wilton man given promotion. It wasn't a deliberate choice. I was your token someone! I became supply manager, in any case, for both Wilton and Heavy Organics. It was one of the least important jobs around, given to some erk!

Managing a function

I had 150 people in my department. Heavy Organics had 12. We combined together under my overall direction. The supply role in fact proved extremely important. In petrochemicals, 30 per cent of the costs go into feedstock. I figured that it could be bought in cheaper. I was sent round the world, on a fact-finding mission, and I concluded that we were paying far too much. I recommended that we build our own refinery. I was sent out to find a contractor, and we got the refinery built. That broke the naphtha price, at least for a while. We then created two selling organisations, and I was put in charge of one, hydrocarbons.

Becoming an executive

Personnel director

They subsequently put me on the board, as Wilton's personnel director. Within a year the deputy chairman's role became vacant. I was the only guy around at the time, so I got the job. I managed to manage, but I was moved on too quickly. I took over from the old guard and when I left it was handed over to them. There was no continuity.

Division Chairman

I was amazed to be appointed Division chairman. I was given a clear-up job. The business base wasn't sound enough when I took over. In my first year in the job we only avoided making a loss by selling off our waste heat. In three years there, though, I doubled the profits in every one of them.

Main board director

Then I was put on the main ICI board. Initially, I was put in charge of organization. I made three attempts to change the way the board did its business. The first one got me a bloody nose. The other two achieved a bit. In fact, the way the board operated hadn't changed for yonks. It had grown up its collectivist approach, as a reaction against the power mongering of two previous chairmen.

Company chairman

Then in 1981, against all the expectations, I was appointed chairman of ICI.

I'm a strong believer in group leadership but not in compromise and consensus. My job is to manage the board, and to make sure it makes decisions. I have to polarize things. Argument there must be, but good humoured stuff. I'll listen and change if I can't carry people. If anyone is bypassed, then they still must be heard. They must have a kick at the ball. And if things turn out wrong for me, I shall always say, 'Well Alan and Charles did say this might happen'.

Creating a leadership spirit

The board's job is unique

What I had to create was an adaptive company that had some of the values you need to survive in tomorrow's world. I believe passionately that you should not have any organizational layers, unless they visibly add to the party.

The board's job, meanwhile, should be unique. It is concerned more with the what than the how. When you mix the two you get into trouble. The art of jacking up any business is to continuously set people targets, a bit beyond their perceived capacity and then to ensure that they achieve them.

We need to become the chemical problem solvers of the world, by the year 2000.

Whenever you have a chemistry problem, you ring up ICI, and, of course, we get paid for it. We're not doing good for love. But our customers must profit from working with us.

I'm a total believer in people

I'm a total believer in people. It's like a lot of things in life. You get what you expect, and you get back what you give. The job of leader is to get extraordinary performances out of ordinary people. There's no achievement in taking over a company, firing everybody and bringing in seven whizz kids, that's not my style. I like to build the leaders I've got to be leaders.

London, England 1986

How do you develop towards executive leadership?

The formal, credential-based training programs which are run by business and management schools are geared towards the typically rational manager, eager to establish his authority. Each business discipline has a body of knowledge that underlies such hard worn authority. However where the greatest difficulty is still found is in schooling individuals for a more generalist role. For it is in fact the school of working life which offers the best form of training for such general abilities. In your youth you are likely to either undertake formal business studies, or else enter the practical business school as a trainee manager. Harvey Jones took the second route rather than the first, first in the Navy and then in ICI. Your dream, in fact, is to become a responsible leader in society.

It may well be, in adulthood, that progressively more challenging job assignments, coupled with an action learning approach, provide the best of both theory and practice. For within such action learning groups, and live projects, scope is provided for design and implementation, as well as for objective knowledge and subjective insight. In your thirties, though, your major managerial activities are likely to be within a functional management role. To develop in midlife from a section or functional manager, as Harvey Jones did, into a business executive on the Board, requires, as John found, exposure to a wide range of business disciplines, situations, problems and opportunities. It also requires, amongst ordinary management mortals, the kind of wisdom, empathy and perspective that comes with age and experience.

As you enter midlife and then maturity, in your fifties, you may be able to provide that extra amount of authority and conviction that comes with depth as well as breadth of perspective. Your determination to make a fundamental contribution to society will be embodied in the spirit of leadership that you have now built up. Together with your flexible counterparts, the agents of change, you will be in a position to adapt your organization to its fast moving environment, as was very much the case for ICI, under Harvey Jones' leadership. For, as is well known in the UK and in America, the company, infused with his dynamic and authoritative spirit of leadership, was effectively transformed in five years from an ailing one, to a company that is now supremely fit and healthy. Let us now turn to the role and functioning of that softer manifestation of rational management, the agent of change.

The change agent

Are you a change agent?

As a prospective agent of change:

- You are a professional.
  - With in-depth knowledge and experience in your particular field.
  - Often with greater loyalty to your profession than to your firm.

- You learn from change.
  - By observing, conceptualizing, experimenting and validating.
  - By accommodating variety through flexible communications.

- You troubleshoot.
  - Rapidly identifying opportunities for change.
  - Coming up with alternative courses of action to exploit them.

- You adapt to change.
  - By mapping out the internal and external environment.
  - By creating systems and procedures for dealing with change.

- You experiment with change.
  - Continually forming temporary project groupings.
  - Solving ongoing problems in interdisciplinary teams.

- You plan for change.
  - You construct long-term plans with contingencies built in.
  - You monitor changes and adapt your plans accordingly.

- You embody the spirit of change.
  - You are respected as a free thinker.
  - You embody the organization's cause.

The scope for the change agent is rapidly growing in today's managed organizations. In fact Harvey Jones at ICI called for such heroic individuals to take the company into the future.

Typically you can be found in technical research and development, in computer programming and management services, in management training, in market research and public relations, and in the emerging, and flexible end of financial services. Steve Shirley, as you will see, is a good case in point. If you scored highest, on the spectral inventory, in category (f), you may well be one yourself.

Who recruits change agents?

There is a potentially rich crop of change agents to be picked from amongst the rapidly growing knowledge workers. However, because you change agents are characteristically freedom loving souls, like Steve Shirley, you are often put off the large and established organizations. You either choose to remain independent freelancers or else join the more flexible design groups, advertising agencies, computer software houses or management consultancy groups. Should you choose to join a large corporation, you are often kept well away from the corridors of power so as not to disrupt things, unless an enlightened boss or mentor recognizes your potential. This conventional behavior turns into self-fulfilling prophesy in that prospective change agents might not become sufficiently mature or politically streetwise to develop and implement desirable changes. Typically you will be involved in project, rather than in line management.

However, in recent years there has been a welcome rise to power of designers and electronic buffs, many of whom are beginning to act in such a change making capacity. They are adding weight and strength to the opportunities for change being opened up every day by changes in lifestyles and by the emerging communications technologies.

How should companies reward you change agents?

You agents of change, by definition, want to be free to make the sorts of change you consider appropriate. Such adaptations in products and processes, systems and procedures often cut across conventional functions. As a result you want to be able to move across functional boundaries freely and constantly. As a change agent you seek continual mental stimulus. If you do not feel you are learning and developing yourself you will seek a change. Bureaucratic, unadaptive organizations can be particularly stifling for you in that respect. Your primary motivation is neither financial reward nor formal promotion but variety of experience and opportunity for self-expression, as has been the case for Steve Shirley.

Becoming a change agent

Steve Shirley   Group Director, F International

Background to liberation

My life began in 1933 in Dortmund, West Germany. In 1939, when I was five years old, my family was scattered by the Nazis to the four winds. I was brought over to England by a Quaker family. I progressed from village to grammar school, via a Roman Catholic Convent, and loathed all three. I would have liked to go to university, but the family could not afford it. At school I loved maths and literature. I was fascinated by language and European culture.

A young troubleshooter

Rebel with a cause

My passions at eighteen were different from those of other children my age. I campaigned for homosexual law reform, lobbied for changes in the law on suicide, and campaigned for birth control. I was very extreme. These things were so important to me.

Seeking intellectual stimulus

While I was campaigning I went to London, at eighteen, to look for a job and took one with the Post Office research station. There was something very special in the atmosphere at Dollis Hill where the research station was based. There was an aura of scientific self-confidence and scientific boldness. I had three bosses in eight years; the

---

last, T. H. Flowers, had been at Bletchley Park, scene of the dramatic cracking of Germany's Enigma code during World War II.

Four years later, with the help of its day release facilities, I obtained my BSc in maths. At evening classes, I came across computers for the first time. They really were primitive in the fifties. I was still working with mechanical calculators, albeit to investigate complex phenomena.

Change agent

New breed of engineer

Then I joined a new company called Computer Developments Ltd, jointly owned by GEC and ICL's predecessor, ICT. During my years there I helped design one of the early computers, the 1301, and I also became one of the first of a new breed of software engineers. The job was highly skilled, and well paid for those days. But my career as an employee was coming to an end. For one thing, something in me was saying that my future did not lie in being an employee. My era of conformity, you might say, was coming to an end. For another thing, I was twenty already, and wanted to have children, preferably five. Matters were brought to a head, when, at a staff meeting I made a suggestion and was told 'that has nothing to do with you, you're technical'. I was furious. 'That's it, I thought to myself, I'm off'.

Going freelance

I decided to go freelance, thinking I was so good that people would come knocking at my door. Nobody came for three months, until a former colleague – he was then working for a large management consultancy – gave me a break. The firm had set up a computer consultancy division, and I was asked to design the management controls for a data processing group. By the time I finished the job I was eight and a half months pregnant. When I was asked how many people worked for me, I said 'one and a bit'. I called 'our' business freelance programmers.

When my son was born I lost interest in work for three months. That was the happiest time of our lives, for my son and I together. I was so pleased we had at least that little time. He is severely mentally handicapped, and has been hospitalized since he was 13 years old. It wasn't practicable to have any more of my five anticipated children. Perhaps if I'd had them I would never have developed my other family, F International.

In 1964 I incorporated Freelance Programmers. That was a turning point. It was like laying an official foundation stone. The operation became more credible to my customers and to myself. Business was growing into more of a stream than a trickle. I had earned the status. It was also the time when I began to build up my panel of homeworkers. They were the real foundation stones, and they enabled the business to extend beyond myself. They have also become the business' reason, my reason, for being.

A *Guardian* article, in January 1964, gave our business publicity and context. Entitled 'Computer women', it said: 'One of the fanatics is Mrs Steve Shirley. A maths graduate who considered herself merely competent at research mathematics, found in computer programming an outlet for her artistic talents – working out patterns. She describes the essential quality required in programming as "seeing the wood for the trees". Now "retired", with a young baby, she has found that computer programming can be done at home, between feeding the baby and washing nappies.'

Freeing other women from dependence
If we look at the company policy today, we can see how it emerged out of the need and opportunity to utilize, wherever practicable, the services of people with dependents who are unable to work in a conventional work environment.

Managing change

Toughening myself up
As our dependents grew, so did our problems, particularly with regard to cash flow.

In the late sixties I realized I needed someone to share the burden of the company with, not just my husband or a friend, but someone with the commitment and commercial acumen to share the load. I found such a person within my panel, and we set up a dual management system. That's when the recession hit. Hardly a month would go by without news of the liquidation of a former client.

And in the middle of all this my partner left and took a precious chunk of business from me. That experience scarred me for life, but it's where I got my toughness from. When I had originally started out in business most people I knew thought I was too soft. But, by now, I had found out what hard times were like and I realized how much I cared. These two factors together toughened me considerably.

F (for flexible) International
It was also in the early seventies that the idea of going international first came to us. I had already altered the structure of Freelance Programmers, to accommodate one of my colleagues, and renamed it F (for flexible) International.

We had one or two European customers, but it was our chairman at the time who suggested we establish an overseas operation. The idea was that the company spread its employment philosophy, as well as its computing services, elsewhere. By then we were offering a comprehensive range of data processing services. They included consulting, hardware and software evaluation, business and systems analysis, software development and computer installation support.

The basic demand for our service is there in most countries. But cultural and legislative differences can make it hard to winkle out a formula for implementing our unique employment policies. They are exportable, but not in their pure, original form.

Embodying the spirit of freedom

Spreading the word
We now have operations in Holland and in France, as well as in Denmark. Now, in my early fifties, I am no longer involved with day to day operations. I see my main responsibility in spreading out our operations overseas, and in holding the ethos of the company together. Our present turnover is 90 percent UK-based. I would like this reduced to 50 percent over time, as we become truly international.

You know, I used to see my literary interests as a side track. Now I can see how my involvement with different cultures has become so important for our work.

We have also set up regional headquarters in the UK, and have delegated project management responsibilities accordingly. Our turnover has gone up, from a few thousand in the sixties, to over £10 million in 1987, and we have more than a thousand women involved with us, most of who work from home.

Becoming a public figure

In the meantime, I have been seduced into becoming more of a public figure. Between 1979 and 1982 I was a Vice-President of the British Computer Society. During the International Year for Disabled People I developed several IT based projects. I am also preoccupied with the damaging effect that computers can have on the human spirit.

In the end, of course, it's not money that motivates me. I've been determined to prove a point; I wanted to liberate a few hundred women from the constraints of motherhood, and I want to control my own destiny.

Our credo

I'm fascinated with the science of computing, and I take pleasure in business, especially entrepreneurial marketing and sales. Our meetings are so open. I've developed a credo, a charter to cover the non-quantifiable aspects of our business. You need to be able to express those absolute qualities that are so important to business and to life.

The twinning of technical excellence with the recognition of employees as whole people – writing programmes or attending their children's sports days – is essential to our philosophy and structure.

I hate the way life and people get divided up. As for the future, it's like the past and the present. I started the business as an outsider, with a whole new approach to employment. Now, twenty-five years and a thousand people later, we're putting across a new, even revolutionary message to the world.

Berkshire, England 1987

How do you develop yourself as an agent of change?

Characteristically you start out in organizational life as a professionally qualified designer, computer programmer like Steve Shirley, training officer, or technologist.

In your youth you may be called in as a troubleshooter, to investigate problems and opportunities of a technical, commercial and human nature. You will typically be involved in a variety of time bound tasks and projects.

Your dream is to be free to be yourself

As you develop through adulthood, in your thirties, you are likely to have attended specific and often short courses, travelled around the company, and visited different locations. You thus become a more knowledgeable agent of change, able to take on more significant assignments. You will be called in not only to solve particular problems but to apply more generalizable solutions.

In midlife, as you consolidate your position within a function, or in your own organization as Steve Shirley did, you will be in a position to enter the ranks of functional management as a manager of change. Your need for variety and mental stimulus will be tempered by a willingness to focus on longer-term problems and opportunities. Your own need for self-expression will be matched by your desire to help others express themselves within your functional area, be it in operations or in R&D, marketing, or management services, or else – through organization development – in the organization as a whole.

Finally, as you mature your role will become more symbolic than practical, as is the case now with Steve Shirley in F International. You then come to embody the spirit of freedom rather than continuing to rush mentally and physically from one project or product to another. In other words you will come to represent and even lead a particular cause, like 'shaping work around the individual' or 'giving people the freedom to pursue wild ideas', rather than solely managing a particular and adaptable function or project.

Conclusion

Stability and change

On your own, however, even with the support of entrepreneurs and animateurs, you may be unable to steer your company in the right direction. For all the intellectual and adaptive leadership that you are able to provide, you may lack the necessary stability, staying power, and sense of continuity to provide rounded leadership. That is where your counterpart comes in, the business executive. On the other hand, if you round out into a fully fledged manager of change then you may come to represent all the qualities of rational management in yourself.

Developing your rational individuality

Both the hardened, more organized executive and the softer, more flexible agent of change, need each other in order to mature. If you are to remain open, over the course of your working life, then your rational qualities will be tempered, at first primally, and subsequently developmentally and metaphysically. In other words, and for example, while the management of human resources may be of paramount importance for you, in your youth you may be open to people as people; in midlife you may become involved in organization development; and in maturity you may become engaged in the transformation of your corporate culture. While all these activities, for you, will fall within the management of human resources, this function will take on broader and deeper connotations than would have been the case had you not matured.

Similarly, for you, while management services may be your source of primary identity, in your youth you may open yourself to risk-laden projects undertaken in new disciplines and in foreign lands; in midlife you may broaden your base from technology to people, and from project control to management control; finally, in maturity, you may progress from ongoing individual and group learning to the creation of a companywide learning community.

While all this evolving activity would still be contained within management services, the nature and extent of this rationally based function would be significantly rounded out. In fact, as we saw in Rank Xerox (see pp. 387–95), that is exactly the way in which Phil Judkins, their management services manager, has been developing – his individuality and his function, as a change agent.

In the process of maturing, then, whether as an executive or change agent, you maintain your fundamental rationality, but gradually round out, thereby imbibing qualities from the other three domains. This is not a smooth and continuous process, as we recall from Chapter 20, but one interspersed with transitions, during which your evolving identity becomes confused. If you are able to withstand these periods of doubt and uncertainty, suitably reassured by your image of change and development, you should be able to realize your rational potential, and in the process interweave qualities both soft and hard. This was achieved by both Harvey Jones and by Steve Shirley, starting from their differing management perspectives. What then about the developmental duo, the adopter and the enabler?

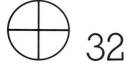 32 Becoming a
developmental manager

Contents

Key concepts

Once you have fully understood this chapter you should be able to define the following concepts in your own terms:

Adopter   Enabler

Objectives

Upon completing this chapter you should be able to do the following:

1. Compare and contrast the adopter and the enabler.
2. Analyze how the developmental manager evolves over the course of his or her working life.
3. Describe how the adopter can be recognized, recruited, rewarded and developed.
4. Describe how the enabler can be recognized, recruited, rewarded and developed.
5. Assess the nature and extent of your own adopter and enabler attributes.

Introduction

From rational to developmental management

The dominance of rational management
The change agent and executive, between the two of them, have established many a conventionally managed organization. While the one designs and implements adaptive systems and procedures the other devises and maintains an overall business strategy and organization structure.

However, it is only a certain proportion of you who are suited to developing along this path of rational management. Too often you are led to believe that, should you not be an entrepreneur, then functional or general management are the only paths open to you. For most managers, at least in America and Western Europe feel reasonably familiar with such business individuals as the entrepreneur, change agent and executive, even if the animateur remains a little remote from our everyday awareness. The flexible change agent and authoritative executive in fact take us to the limits of conventional wisdom within a managed organization in the West and North.

Our blindness to developmental management
So we resist real understanding of, as a major example, the Japanese in the East, because their particular brand of adaptability and harmony falls beyond our common business consciousness. We find it relatively easy to identify with their primal aggression and sense of community, as well as with their rational organization and market flexibility. We find it very difficult to acknowledge the Japanese's cooperative and developmental orientation.

In addition, we are yet to see what brand of management emerges from China and from the Soviet Union, now that these two Eastern countries are just beginning to evolve their own approaches, independent of the ideologies of Karl Marx or Adam Smith – both of whom originated from Western Europe. For unlike America, Europe and Japan, these very important nations have not yet evolved a form of business and of management that emerges from their sophisticated, indigenous cultures.

Moreover, we have not yet begun to understand the generic styles of management in the South, outside of my own very limited assessments and projections.[1,2]

However, as 'Japan Inc.' takes the business world ever more by storm, we shall eventually be obliged to wake up to the more Eastern and developmental approach.

Enabler and adopter

Thanks to two major sources of information and insight, an Eastern view of management is now emerging from both Japan and from the Indian subcontinent. The Japanese approach, untainted by significant Western bias, is best conveyed in Pascale and Athos' *The Art of Japanese Management*[3] and in Boye De Mente's *Japanese Etiquette and Ethics in Business*[4]. Both highlight the interdependent view of the world reflected in the Japanese psyche (see Chapter 23).

The role of enabler

It is this kind of interdependent view that characterizes the enabler's sensitive, managerial behavior. However, the enabler does not limit herself to the recognition of such interdependent potential in the external organization or market-place. She is also sensitive to her own potential, and to that of other people and environments. In that capacity it is the organization developers and designers in Europe and America who have taken the lead. One of these, John Sculley, is represented as an enabling role model in this chapter.

The role of enabler has been very much underplayed in American and European organizations, and in fact relegated to a fringe position – within the training and development function. The trouble is that this conventionally soft character, at least in Europe and America, has lacked a hard edge. Fortunately in the eighties, the design function – at least in Great Britain – has risen to prominence, as a potentially 'hard' developmental candidate. Unfortunately most designers have more of an affinity for physical environments than for social and commercial ones. Yet, as a fully functioning enabler, your appreciation for harmony and interdependence across both time and space, needs to involve both people and things.

The role of adopter

The 'soft' edge of developmental management has in fact emerged, uniquely from the East, in the form of what I have termed an adopter. Such an individual manager is both similar to and different from an adaptive, or flexible manager.

The key to his personality lies in such Japanese concepts (see Chapter 23) as *amae* – total dependence on a mother figure – and *mu* – total openness to the world around you. As an adopter, therefore, you have no inhibitions about adopting a belief, a technology, or a mentor, as long as you have total faith in them. Interestingly enough, the Japanese have had such total faith in Western technology, but not in Europe's or America's people or methods of organization. For these they have trusted their own indigenous culture.

The Japanese are by no means the only Eastern culture to deny the self or the ego, thereby to submit themselves to the purposes of the organization. It is only that they have been particularly successful at it. Through the Bank of Credit and Commerce we have been able to gain another perspective on such humility, which has originated from the Indian subcontinent. Unfortunately, we in the North and West have been all to quick to dismiss such adoptive behavior as paternalistic, or robot like. We all too easily forget our own behavior within the context of the church, where humility and devotion has its proper place. In addition John Hillbery of BCC, in the context of real management, has illustrated the broader implications of humility in organizational and business life, as has David Bohm (see p. 510) in the context of the new physics. I shall start, then, by introducing you to the adoptive, subdomain of developmental management before moving on to its enabling counterpart.

The individual: developmental domain

The adopter

Are you an adopter?
As such an adopter:

- You are submissive.
  · You dedicate yourself to the purposes of your organization.
  · You submit to the will of your superior or mentor.

- You are trusting.
  · You place complete trust in people you know well.
  · As you develop trust, you merge into others' activities.

- You are open.
  · Your mind is empty and receptive, unbound by preconception.
  · Your ears and eyes are constantly on the alert for opportunity.

- You are humble.
  · You have no ego, no self to defend.
  · You give more than you receive.

- You have peace of mind.
  · You are totally absorbed in and by your work.
  · You and what you do are as one.

- You have faith.
  · Your activities are attached to a higher spiritual purpose.
  · You see yourself as following a path of destiny.

As an adopter, then, you are prepared to immerse yourself in the world around you, at least that part of it in which you have faith and trust. You draw such religious conviction from that trusted authority, literally or figuratively, that you are prepared to give your all. If you scored highest on the spectral inventory, in category (h), you may well be an adopter yourself.

Do companies recruit potential adopters?
The individual adopter, as a manager, is much better known in the East, and perhaps in the South, than he is in the West and North. However, any company with a strong culture, like IBM in America or Marks & Spencer in Great Britain, may be looking out for individuals who are prepared to submit themselves to such all-pervasive cultures.

Of course the practice of lifetime employment, whether in Japan as a whole or in a company like IBM in particular, lends itself to the adopter mentality. After all the individual is being recruited for life! The manager being sought, then, in this adoptive context, has a weak individual ego – in that he is prepared to be absorbed by others; he is willing to place complete trust in the recruiting organization; he has evident humility – displayed through his obvious courtesy, respect, and lack of self-centeredness; he has faith in the purposes of the organization and wants to attach himself to its higher purpose; he is open to influence – both in an organizational and market context; and is willing to immerse himself in his work, through which he acquires ultimate peace of mind.

How do you reward adopters?

The way in which you are rewarded, as an adopter, follows from your personality characteristics. The offer of lifetime employment, to begin with, enables you to place complete trust in your employer, which is a reward in itself. Moreover, should the organization espouse such higher purposes as service to God or to the nation, then you will be provided with the meaning in life that you seek. Moreover, because your ego boundaries are very weak you need the protection of an intimate group of trusted colleagues with whom to work. Similarly you will seek out the prospect of identifying such intimate associates, as suppliers, as distributors, and as commercial partners, in order to reinforce both your sense of security and also of opportunity. You will require a very close relationship with your superior, from whom you will both seek and gain trust. Finally, because there is no tight ego boundary surrounding yourself or your company, you will be rewarded by having the opportunity to work with government, and with other like-minded companies, to attain the higher purposes to which you are attached.

Becoming an adopter

V. H. Abidi   Bank of Credit and Commerce

Background

My dream of youth

Whatever I am is related to BCC. Knowledge and memory of the past is vitally important for the present and the future. I am a cosmopolitan. Born in India, I lived in Pakistan and in Bangladesh while I was still very young. I got my first full-time job when I was fifteen. I come from a family of middle-class landlords. My father lived until his eighties, my grandfather into his nineties. Neither had to work a day in their life for a living. That was the environment I was brought up in. I never liked it. Even when I was twelve I wanted to get out. It was much too slow moving. A rusting environment. I had this hazy dream in adolescence. I wanted to achieve something of substance, to give new life to things. I needed to create a platform for my family to be.

Submission to a master: the apprenticeship

Here comes the lunatic

So at the age of fifteen I left home and joined the National Bank of Pakistan. At the time, and for many years to come, banking in the subcontinent was a totally backward profession. As a young banker you drove a second-hand car and lived in very poor conditions. I shall never forget when Agha Hasan Abedi, who subsequently opened the United Bank in 1959, came into our bank one day. 'Here comes the lunatic', they said. 'This man wants to open a bank of his own, and provide his people with their own new cars, villas, and foreign holidays'. Our President, then, was only in his early thirties'. I knew there and then where my future lay. I joined on January 1st, 1960. In three years Mr Abedi had translated his words into deeds. He had caused a banking revolution.

You are my future

I can remember vividly in those early days sitting around and the president telling us young upstairs, 'you are my future senior management'. I couldn't visualize it. The picture I had in my head of a senior manager was someone bald, fat and gray. We were still in our twenties and thirties. Yet, sure enough, that too materialized ...

He would notice the slightest thing. 'Cut your nails short, Mr So and So.' We had to set professional and social standards. I remember someone recognizing me in Pakistan and saying. 'I'm sure you must work for the United Bank. You officers put your suits on first, and then have them ironed around you!' Mr. Abedi started the practice of bankers, in Pakistan, wearing suits. He really brought true professionalism into banking in the subcontinent. But there was much more to it than that.

Becoming a journeyman: raising your sights

I remember Abedi telling me about mental telepathy and joint personality. The foundations kept on growing. What he impressed upon us was to look at the big things in life rather than squabble about the little ones. He always told us to raise our sights: 'Small people get involved in small things', he said, 'and big people in big ones.'

That is how the hazy dream of my future was beginning to be transformed into a clearer one. I was getting to know the vision. We were being introduced to the management of human energy.

Developing mastery: coordinating the flow of energy

Practicing humility

We practice humility. That allows energy to flow into you. We always recognize the qualities of others. I have never moved an inch without drawing on a colleague who will be superior to me, at least in one particular respect. We practice multi-leadership here. I'm merely the coordinator of other people's energies. When I'm negotiating with a client I bring in people better than me, and the client appreciates the combined service we offer. My ability, on my own, is very limited.

Originally, then, my vision was projected in terms of specific designations and personal power. I was trying to move, and fast. Mr Abedi kept telling me I had to change. How? What? I wondered. After all, I was bringing in the results.

Now I know what what was missing. Five years ago the block was removed. Position and power gets in the way. Dismantling both gave me clarity.

Now I am as ambitious to grow as before, but to grow in myself, and through others. This is no longer my ambition. It is my life.

Acquiring mastery: becoming attached to a higher purpose

More than money

I've had offers time and again, at twice or three times my salary here. Money is important, but here I'm getting something else. My own personal growth and my love for this organization is what really matters.

Five years ago the realization came to me of what's really important in life. You have to be able to connect the material substance with the visionary spirit. What we call interfusion amongst people, and service to humanity is what really counts. You can keep going for one, two or three years – in a conventional organization – and then you get tired.

People can't continuously give of their best. It's not possible unless you're attached to a higher purpose. Bonuses, profit sharing, that's not high enough. When I was brought over to the UK we had forty-five branches. In five years we've grown 7½ times. And qualitatively we've grown even more.

The importance of faith

The most important thing of all, of course, is faith. Faith is blind. We all had faith in Mr Abedi from the start. We were trying to explore in every way. Each of us went out on our own, and, at the same time, we pooled resources. Growth is part of our soul. One person would bring in a new location, another a new executive. Peoples' potential was released in the most unlikely ways. Our head of computing, for example, has become our marketing director. We are structured, but it's dynamic.

In today's world, you need a culture or a society which will bring the moral aspects back into the material world. Voluntary work may take up a few hours in one's week. What we have created is a worldwide, full-time organization to bring the dimensions of ethics and morality back into people's lives. We want to create the largest possible organization performing a service to humanity.

London, England 1986

How do you develop as an adopter?

The first stage, as a prospective adoptive manager in your youth, is to submit yourself as an apprentice to a master–manager in the same way as Mr Abidi submitted himself to the principles and practices of Agha Hasan Abedi. In fact, the process is not unlike that of the apprentice who submits himself to a master craftsman. In the course of such submission you are obliged to let go of your personal attitudes and beliefs, pride and prejudice, and absorb everything the master has to offer. That places a great developmental responsibility on the master's shoulders. You will be imbibing not only knowledge and skill, but also attitudes and beliefs from him.

In your adulthood, to continue the apprenticeship analogy, you become a journeyman, making your way through the organization, acquiring different disciplines and rubbing shoulders with different cultures. You engage in a journey with a purpose, that is to build up managerial mastery, and to serve your chosen organization. Thus your journey takes place within a specific business and organizational context, and is not easily transferrable.

In midlife, having acquired a wide range of knowledge of skills, you begin to develop mastery by applying them across a broad front. In other words, you graduate from specific applications to more general ones, and consciously interfuse with other managers in the process. In fact, you practice multi-leadership rather than becoming a leader in your own, individual right. Like V. H. Abidi at BCC, you are a coordinator of other people's energies rather than an energizer yourself.

In maturity, if you have journeyed along your predestined path, you will finally acquire the power of mastery. In so doing you will enter into direct communion with powers higher than yourself, on whose behalf your mastery is being exercised. As Abidi begins to enter that phase himself he is able to make the direct link between material and spiritual well being, with the latter firmly guiding the former.

In his case, he becomes fully aligned with BCC's higher purpose, that of creating the largest possible organization performing a service to humanity. He is at one with the totality.

Now let me turn to the adopter's softer counterpart, the enabler.

The enabler

Are you a prospective enabler?

As such an enabler:

- You are a harmonizer.
  - · You have a talent for invoking consensus.
  - · You focus on areas of mutual benefit.

- You recognize potential for development.
  - · You release potential by opening up hidden, connected pathways.
  - · You help people and enterprises to fulfill their potential.

- You are a link person.
  - · You are moored by many interlocking lines of connection.
  - · You build up alliances, as well as networks of mutual support.

- You recognize the flow of energy.
  - · You focus on energy's quality, velocity, vitality and direction.
  - · You view changes in energy flows as evolutionary, not spasmadic.

- You harness the power of interfusion.
  - · You focus on mergers of individual or corporate entities.
  - · You view all entities as both autonomous and interdependent.

- You are in touch with evolution.
  - · You can recognize the individual's level of evolution.
  - · You embody the spirit of development within your company.

As an enabler, then, you are at home within an organization in midlife, whose prime focus is on development.

You have an acute appreciation of subtlety and balance, amongst products and markets as well as people and organizations. Your approach is individually and collaboratively oriented rather than personality-based and competitive. This applies in person to person, business to business, supplier to customer or corporate to government dealings. You therefore enable people and organizations, or products and markets – as John Sculley is doing – to realize their unique identity and potential. You achieve this by recognizing and harnessing opportunities for synergy across space and time. You recognize that true individuality is acquired through genuine interdependence, and vice versa.

Who recruits enablers?

The role of the enabler has only become widely recognized in the areas of management and organization development. As someone who can recognize and develop human potential you will often have a background in social psychology or in industrial design. So you can indeed be recruited via conventional graduate channels. Personality-wise, you naturally seek our harmony in people or things; you recognize potential for development in one or the other; you are characteristically a link person within an organization; you have the distinctive capacity to recognize the qualitative flow of energy; and you are uncannily in touch with the level of evolution of an individual or organization, product or market.

I have deliberately broadened usage of the term enabler to include industrial designers who are adept at recognizing and developing the potential of new products, materials and technologies – in fulfilling market needs. As design and technology becomes an integral part of business development so the scope for recruiting the design based enabler increases. Finally, fertile ground for enabling recruits lies with the functional specialist or manager who has reached midlife, and who needs to broaden out rather than deepen his or her involvement with management. To the extent that such individuals could be redirected at mid-career, so the infamous plateauing of management could be stemmed.

Particularly if you scored highest in category (c), in the spectral inventory – whether you are a technologist, a designer or a functional manager – you should be positioning yourself within a broadly based development role.

How can you be rewarded as an enabler?
As an enabler you feel rewarded when you can see development – of people, of products, of businesses or of landscapes – arising before you. You hate to see physical or human potential go to waste.

You need to combine with other people, as Apple's Sculley has done, often outside of your own organization, so as to enable change and evolution to take place. As a result you find opportunities to step outside of the confines of your particular department or company most rewarding, particularly if you can create some joint venture that is of mutual benefit. Conventional salaries, derived from a single source, run counter to your interest in building up a combination of linked economic, personal and social benefits. You would rather, over time, build up a composite reward package, made up of a number of corporate constituents, than be limited to a single source. This has in fact been the case for Apple Computers.

Becoming an enabler

John Sculley   Chief Executive, Apple Computers

Childhood and youth – fantasy versus reality

I grew up in a formal tradition-bound world, on the upper east side of New York. As a child I suffered from a speech impediment up until my middle teens. There was so much I wanted to talk about, and yet I couldn't even walk into a candy store and ask for a pack of Lifesavers without stumbling over the words. It drove me into a world of my own where I would fantasize about building my own car or conducting my own scientific experiments – inspired by early morning sessions reading the books of knowledge, I'd express my thoughts on paper because I couldn't get them out of my mouth.

Young adulthood – ascending the ladder

At the age of twenty-one, a year before graduating, I got married to the step daughter of Don Kendall, the president of Pepsico. He became a close friend and a distant mentor to me. I had planned to study architecture and to become an industrial designer. However, my mentor convinced me that my future lay not with architecture but as a marketeer. That led me to do an MBA.

I joined Pepsi Cola, the soft drinks part of Pepsico, in 1967 as a new oddity, their first MBA. My training completed, I was assigned to Pepsi Cola's market research department. It was an inauspicious start. I was given neither an assignment nor an office. What became clear was that I was in an essentially meaningless department.

Later, as a director of market development, I began to learn the marketing ropes and also proved myself very successful at it. Yet successful marketing, I found, could not be reduced to a set of quantitative skills or measurements. Market builders, like myself, attempt to get mentally inside their products. My ideas about marketing leant towards the creative and intuitive – not the rigidly analytical.

By the age of thirty, it seemed my approach to marketing had proved successful. For I was promoted to marketing vice president, the company's youngest ever. From then on I never looked back. By the age of forty-three, that is in 1982, I had become president of the entire Pepsi Cola company.

Midlife – redefining the meaning of the ladder

One day, as I was getting ready to leave the office for the upcoming Thanksgiving Day holiday, I received a 'phone call from an acquaintance – the only headhunter, in fact, that I was even prepared to listen to. Apple Computers, in California, were looking for a chief executive.

Steve Jobs revealed to me that if he weren't working with computers he could envision himself as a poet in Paris. I confessed that if I weren't in business I'd probably be an artist. But I still couldn't see myself leaving Pepsico. Then Steve delivered the real body blow. 'Do you want to spend the rest of your life selling sugared water or do you want to change the world?'

It was as if someone had reached up and delivered a stiff blow to my stomach. Steve was telling me that my whole life was at a crossroads. The question was a monstrous one.

On 4 April 1982, two days before my forty-fourth birthday, I went up to Kendall's magnificent office to tell him of my decision to leave. It was the most difficult thing I had ever had to do in my life.

I couldn't understand what was going on when I first arrived at Apple's small Cupertino headquarters. It was almost as if there were magnetic fields, some spiritual force, mesmerizing people. Their eyes were just dazed. Excitement showed on everyone's faces. It was nearly a cult environment.

When I arrived to take over the chief executiveship of the company, the Mackintosh team, headed by Steve, was in full swing. A group of young, disparate individuals, they were going all out to accomplish the creation of a product that they believed would change the world. To get each artist to exceed his abilities Steve would go to any length.

The Mac buildings were named after Picasso, Matisse, Rembrandt and other great luminaries. Steve transformed a building into a creative incubator because all these differences became symbols that Apple was dramatically different from your normal company. In fact Steve Jobs was less a manager than an impresario.

Steve and I were convinced that we had the secret formula – a combination of his revolutionary technology and my creative marketing – to fulfil his vision for the personal computer. The 'bicycle for the mind', the computer would be an intellectual tool to enhance the individual's work, mind, life.

In late 1984 we thought we held the future in our hands. We developed an intoxicating overconfidence. In October Steve and I were on the cover of *Business Week*, dubbed the 'Dynamic Duo'. Our revenues had jumped 54 per cent to more than $1.5 billion. Already we were beginning to think of hitting $5 billion in the near future.

Racing to grow fast was fine – as long as things were growing. But if they ever stopped, the price you were going to pay was astronomical. I was hired to be a consumer-marketing person. Yet Apple didn't warrant a consumer-marketing perspective.

Then Steve turned on me, completely without warning. At an extraordinary board meeting he declared, 'I think you're bad for Apple and you're the wrong person to run this company,' in a tense but controlled voice. 'You should really leave the company. I'm more worried about Apple than I have ever been. I'm afraid of you. You don't know how to operate and never have. You've taught me nothing.'

As the market downturn had hit us I had begun to realize I was failing. Steve's outburst, coming from someone I had loved, made it all the worse. For the first time in my life my power, prestige, and self-assurance were in jeopardy. I had never lost my self-confidence. I had never known failure before. But now I wondered whether I was capable of leading the company through its crisis. If it was not for the unanimous support I received from the board, and from my wife Leezy, I probably would never have pulled through.

In the event, Steve was asked by the executive to let go of his operational responsibilities. I then resigned myself to the task of bringing Apple back.

Turning the company around wasn't the difficult part. Cutting expenses isn't much of a mystery. Closing down an unprofitable plant or operation, while one of the toughest decisions a manager might make, isn't all that difficult either. The hard part is knowing what to turn the company into. A tremendous amount of advice poured in from all quarters during the crisis. We would have destroyed the company if we had followed most of it. Instead, we held close to our dream and vision.

The new organization that I built up turned out to be a combination of vastly different nonconformists, an organization in which almost everyone wasn't quite prepared for what they would have to do to turn the company around. We were a team of individuals – as paradoxical as that may sound. But, as such, we could make dramatic changes while holding the company together at the same time. Yet, we hadn't ever worked as a team before, because Steve and I had previously called all the shots.

Unlike a Jobs or a Bill Gates, I hadn't grown up in the personal computer industry. I hadn't founded my own company. I was brought in and had to adopt someone else's vision and beliefs about where the industry was going. I had now reached the point where I had to develop beliefs of my own. To go back and reach deep inside myself to discover what John Sculley believed in. And I had to do it when the entire industry's future seemed in doubt.

I made it my business to meet with all the Valley's pioneering inventors. I devoured books – *The Universal Machine, Literary Machines* and *The Mechanical Bride* – whose authors dreamed of the possibilities of what computers could be. I had to go on a search to track the dream back to its source. Jack, my son, gave me Douglas Hofstadter's *The Mind's I*, to broaden my perspective.

In a major change of Apple's philosophy, I publicly announced that we would begin to introduce devices that would allow Apple users to plug into IBM and Digital Equipment Corporation communications networks.

It was not easy. I felt the blacklash of what I could only call religious crusades in Cupertino. Even faced with Apple's possible ruin, people still resisted reaching out to business markets, connectivity, and coexistence with IBM – their old enemy, the symbol of evil. At a time when morale was low, the repositioning triggered greater anxiety. Yet we had to build products to connect to other computers – 'systems' products – something we had never done before.

My legacy: combining fantasy with reality

We are developing our own new business paradigm at Apple by creating a federation of spinouts. The mothership manages the federation through the bonds of interdependency. This is not cell division but cell association. We are creating not just a company here or a company there but a greater cell around which all its parts are interconnected.

The lifeblood of the network is the free flow of information and mutual support. Any single entity is only as strong as the parts that make it. Within the living organism lie not only entities partially owned by Apple but independent ones whose survival is dependent on the mothership.

The odyssey ahead is to assure that we create the ancestor of a tool that may well be crucial to us in the next century. This is the context in which our dream to change the world with personal computers like Apple II and the Mackintosh is so compelling. It's why we see our role as artists and impresarios.

John Sculley *Odyssey*[5] 1987

How can you develop as an enabler?

Enablers, inclusive of designers, particularly amongst the older members of a company's staff, are the largest, to my mind, the most unexploited management resource. Your potential, albeit often latent rather than actual, generally goes to waste because there are so few recognized channels for your deployment. The best recognized of the currently available channels in a large company are in R&D, and in people and organization development. Emerging channels today include industrial design and community economic development.

You are likely to enter one or the other of these channels as a natural or social scientist, or as a fine artist, in your youth. Your dream is to enhance potential. However, until the enabling path becomes recognized right across the functional board, it will remain – conventional designers perhaps excepted – largely stillborn. As an enabler, who is recognized in adulthood, you can only consolidate your position if you are given opportunities to work in product, market, business, organization or community design. Only in that way can you exercise and develop, your distinctive competences in young adulthood.

It is also important to recognize that you are likely to follow a path that is neither linear nor bounded. It will tend to be diagonal and associative, like John Sculley's, picking up threads of involvement within and without the organization. To that extent the recent spate of joint ventures – whether technologically, commercially or community based – are right up your street, if you are allowed to round out your position as a broadly based enabler, in midlife. In your forties and fifties you may develop the breadth of interest, and the depth of conviction, to coordinate a major shift in the design and orientation of a business operation – based upon changing tastes and technologies. In order to achieve this you may have to bring together engineers, psychologists and marketeers within the company, and design and technology consultants from without. You become, at one and the same time, your actualized self and the embodiment of the developmental spirit within your company.

Conclusion

Adopter and enabler

Whereas the adopter, firmly aligned to the organizations' higher purpose, acts as a channel for the visionary thrust, the enabler ensures that such a thrust is received by the organization and its environment. In the pioneering context the entrepreneur exploits potential and the animateur ensures that his aggresive exploits are warmly received both within and without.

In the conventionally managed organization the executive channels potential and the change agent ensures that such potential is adapted for the range of applications required within and without. In a development context, though, potential is not only exploited and channelled but also firmly aligned, thanks to the adopter, to an all-powerful vision. It is then the enabler's responsibility to ensure that human, product or market potential, thus aligned with the powers above, is suitably attuned to the people and things alongside and below.

Evolving as a developmental individual

The adopter and the enabler need one another in order to mature. For the one has fixity of purpose and the other has sensitivity of response. If both are to remain open, however, during the course of their working lives their developmental orientation will be tempered. For example, in relation to the marketing function, the developmental manager in his youth will open him or herself to aggressive salesmanship and to closeness to the customer, albeit in connection with a broader and deeper purpose.

In adulthood such a manager will espouse analytically based marketing, though again as a means to an evolutionary end. The longer-term end may be the development of the market as a whole, whereas the shorter term means may be an effective marketing mix.

References

1. R. Lessem, *The Global Business*, Prentice Hall (1987).
2. R. Lessem, *Heroic Management*, Mercury Press (1987).
3. Pascale and Athos, *The Art of Japanese Management*, Penguin (1982).
4. B. De Mente, *Japanese Etiquette and Ethics in Business*, Passport Books (1987).
5. J. Sculley, *Odyssey: From Pepsi to Apple*, Collins (1987).

33 Becoming a metaphysical manager

Contents

Key concepts

Once you have fully understood this chapter you should be able to define the following concepts in your own terms:

Adventurer   Innovator

Objectives

Upon completing this chapter you should be able to do the following:

1. Compare and contrast the innovator and the adventurer.
2. Analyze how the metaphysical manager evolves over the course of his or her working life.
3. Describe how the innovator can be recognized, recruited, rewarded and developed.
4. Describe how the adventurer can be recognized, recruited, rewarded and developed.
5. Assess the nature and extent of your own innovator, and adventurer attributes.

Introduction

From developmental to metaphysical management

A developmental manager, like V. H. Abidi or John Sculley, may participate in a fundamental transformation of spirit, and of energy, but will lack the power to complete the revolution in which each has played an important part. For that reason Anita Roddick has superseded Mary Quant as a source of transformation in the UK today, and V. H. Abidi subordinates himself to the vision of Agha Hasan Abedi.

For while adopter and enabler merge with, and harness, potential, innovator and adventurer – between them – actually create it. While Henry Ford created an entire automobile industry, Anita Roddick is creating a new industry founded upon naturally based cosmetics. Both have combined innovation and adventure in their far-reaching activities. While Ford ventured out on the open seas, engaging in his somewhat bizarre peace missions, Roddick travels about the world, discovering and transforming traditional methods of skin and hair care. Both have missions that transcend the material world, and yet partake fundamentally of it.

While entrepreneur and animateur infuse an organization with enterprising activity and shared values; while executive and change agent provide stable organization and adaptive systems; while adopter and enabler align the organization to its ultimate vision and attune it to technological, social and economic evolution; the innovator provides the creative nucleus of the organism, and the adventurer infuses it with energy.

Adventurer and innovator

The most basic element of business life is not money, nor is it people, but it is energy. It is the adventurer who releases raw energy, in its purest form, and it is the genuine innovator who is able to create new energy forms. The most highly evolved corporations, like the Bank of Credit and Commerce, will take particular note of these two metaphysical managers. There is a strange bond between the adventurer, compelled to risk life and limb, and the innovator, compelled to devote his whole life and livelihood to the realization of his dream.

While the one enters into the physical unknown, the other enters a technical, social or artistic void. Both, like Joyce Choto and Terence Conran (see below), are obsessive in their managerial pursuits.

The individual: developmental domain

The innovator

Are you a prospective innovator?
As such an innovator:

- You have the courage to dream.
  - · You have the courage to tap powerful, subconscious images.
  - · You remain close to nature and to the spirit of your nation.

- You can envisage the future.
  - · You are connected with the distant past and the full present.
  - · A little corner of the infinite has been revealed to you.

- You impart fundamental values.
  - · You express your vision in a language of uplift and idealism.
  - · You raise your organization's emotional and spiritual plane.

- You are impassioned.
  - · You experience pain and ecstacy through your work.
  - · You love what you do, as an all embracing obsession.

- You are a master.
  - · You have conquered yourself.
  - · You are, like the conductor of an orchestra, leading – in unison – the many parts of your personality.

- You are an originator.
  - · You are in touch with the roots of your company's being.
  - · You are newly connecting those roots with contemporary soils.

- You transform people and things.
  - · You are consciously transforming the world's physical resources.
  - · You are fitting all the corporate pieces into a new whole.

Broadly based innovators, as opposed to the purely technical variety, are few and far between in our society, and they are more visible in politics – Disraeli, Ghandi, Luther King – than in business. Yet this was not always the case. Brunel in the railways, Nobel in the chemical industry, and the first Henry Ford in the automobile industry – just to mention three – were powerful innovators of yesteryear. If you see yourself as such a person, and you are honest with yourself, you will have genuinely topped the spectral inventory with category (b).

So fully fledged innovators, like one or two of you, are around and about. It is just that it will take a lifetime for you to realize your dream. At a young age you can usually only identify the seeds of your vision, rather than the ripening fruit.

Who recruits innovators?

Such innovators as described above are like golddust. Unfortunately the popular business press brackets innovators and entrepreneurs together as if they were the same breed. This is not strictly true. You innovators are to be found amongst the ranks of highly imaginative artists or scientists. If corporations can succeed in attracting such creative technologists and designers they will do both you and themselves a great service. In order to attract you, as a budding innovator, a company will have to project its image in brilliantly imaginative terms. Companies, rather than being mere patrons of the arts, would need to create and project their own art forms, as the more innovative high tech businesses are now doing. Innovation becomes central rather than peripheral to your company's existence – something towards which ICI, for example, is now aspiring.

As such a creative artist or scientist, then, you have the courage to dream; you are impassioned by your technological or social vision; you are in a position to transform the earth's resources; you impart fundamental values through your activities; you are both a master of yourself and an originator of a new technology of society, drawing from artistic, scientific or cultural roots.

How do you reward your innovators?
You innovators gain your ultimate satisfaction from seeing your dreams turned into reality. In other words the far-reaching potential of your technical, artistic or social imaginations needs to be recognized, converted into a product or service, furnished with adequate resources, adapted to changing conditions and circumstances, and warmly accepted by people inside and outside the organisation. To the extent, then, that your far-reaching idea was turned into reality you would feel duly rewarded. You might then see your creative idea spiral upwards and outwards like nuclear fission, just like what is happening to Sir Terence Conran today. Landmarks along the road to transformation would be scientific or design breakthroughs, together with the flashes of inspiration that served to achieve them.

Ultimately you have no direct interest in progression along a career ladder. A progressive spiral, technologically or socially based, which serves to elevate you from the bottom to a top which – in association with many others – is of your own making. In business terms you can but create your own products and markets. This has certainly been the case for Terence Conran in the UK.

Innovator

Sir Terence Conran   Chairman, Storehouse (UK)

Background

My early mentor
I was born into a typical middle-class family, where my father just managed to make ends meet. He spent more money sending us to good schools than on anything else. Fortunately my school was different. There was a very strong creative bias. I had an inspired man to teach me craft subjects. With him I worked in metal, wood and clay.

Young dreamer
That gave me a great desire to make artifacts. I set myself up with a workshop at home, and built my own pottery kiln. I also did a lot of welding. But to make the activity viable I had to sell my wares. I was thirteen at the time.

One memory that stands out in my childhood is that of a typical English pottery. It made terracotta flower and chimney pots. It was a completely self-contained unit. They dug the clay themselves, made the pots, and then sold them on the spot. I used to cycle seventeen miles there and seventeen miles back, just to be part of it. I remember working at a foot-pedal wheel, making little flower pots. Funnily enough I enjoyed doing one, repetitively, after the other.

I loved the whole circular process, from digging at one end to selling at the other. It was a wonderful example of self-sufficiency. I used to dream of potteries like this one all over the country.

Inventive designer

Imagining new relationships

At school I completed my higher certificate in organic chemistry, engineering and art. I seemed particularly good at imagining new relationships in molecular structures, in plants, and in artifacts. So I took a course at the Central School of Arts and Crafts, in London, in textile design.

After about eighteen months at Central School I began to get itchy feet. I had become friendly with the sculptor, Eduardo Palozzi. We started a workshop together. He taught me form and I taught him practical skills. At that stage I was beginning to get interested in making furniture. There was nothing on the market that I liked. So I started to make things for myself and my friends. I had a very particular style.

The new world was slowly coming

Then I got offered a job with a design centre. It was 1949. Britain was just starting to pull itself together after the war. We did a lot of work for the Festival Exhibition that year. There was terrific enthusiasm. The designers thought that the new world had come. But industry failed to seize the opportunity.

So I got only a few more orders for my furniture designs. I had to start thinking more seriously about selling. I was terribly inept on the business side. Things were always hand to mouth. There had to be more to life, I thought, than this! I felt very deeply that well designed artifacts should be made available to people at a mass level. So I asked myself, how can I get out of this backwater, and touch the real world? I needed capital.

Accumulating capital

The way I accumulated capital, in the early fifties, was to renovate the buildings we worked in, and then sell them off at a profit. I needed capital to buy machinery. Nevertheless, I was always desperately short of money. A psychiatrist friend of mine was also going broke at the time. Together we hit on the idea of a cafe-cum-soup kitchen. We eventually established four of them. When I sold my share I made a bit of money.

I bought machinery. By 1956, aside from my two small workshops, I had created a design group. We designed and made up furniture and textiles. By 1962 we had made a quantum leap into purpose-built factory premises. We decided, for the first time, to make a whole range of domestic furniture. It had a somewhat similar look to the furniture you see in our Habitat stores today.

Business innovator

Creating a prototype

We sold our range to about eighty different retailers in the country. Then we went off to see how they looked. We were appalled. The quality of presentation was awful. But what could we do?

We had no alternative. We had to open a prototype shop ourselves, embodying various principles. Most furniture shops were great stagnant pools filled with brown lumps of scum. Above all, ours had to look busy.

So we developed our prototype, with 50 per cent furniture, and 50 per cent household goods – like kitchen utensils, lighting and floor coverings. Because we expected our customers to be young we also incorporated a toy department. We filled our store with stock, using a supermarket approach, that is making the goods available on the shelves. This was an innovation at the time. The stocky, warehouse feel was very attractive to customers. We provided an exciting environment for them.

In 1964, then, the first Habitat was opened in London. The new clothes shop were just opening. There were lots of Italian restaurants. We sensed the signs of the times, educating our customers in the process. The shop opened with lots of publicity, though we had no experience of retailing. We made every mistake under the sun, but we had enough energy to ride over the problems.

Commercializing the product

After that early period of getting to know the ropes, and experiencing the frustrations of learning from our own mistakes, we began to realize that we enjoyed retailing, and making ourselves visible on the High Street. So the idea of a retail chain came to us. That meant we would really have to teach ourselves retail management, including distribution, stock control, and so forth.

We also decided that our future lay in creating something unique. Habitat merchandise was to be designed by us. That was our approach from the outset. In order to source that uniqueness we had to expand fast, to give the manufacturers large enough throughput to make things economical. In the process we discovered that if you could design talent with efficient and flexible manufacturing capability, you have a formula for success.

Singleminded expansion

We went for success singlemindedly. Fifteen stores were opened in the UK between 1964 and 1973. Then we thought to ourselves, if we could do it in London and Manchester, why not New York and Paris? By 1980 we had forty-seven stores, spread over Britain, in particular, but also over parts of Europe and America. I was in my late thirties and early forties during this very expansive period.

Designing the future

Habitat-Mothercare

In the early eighties a banker friend, who had helped us finance our development abroad, seeded the idea that we should be applying our design and retailing philosophy to companies other than ourselves. It was purely coincidental that Mothercare, who had always been generous to us with their computer facilities, and whom we greatly admired, were reviewing their future direction at the time.

Selim Zilkha had built up a fine business which had many parallels with Habitat. Both companies were specialist retailers who did a high percentage of their business through mail order, and both addressed themselves to the same target customer. But Mothercare had slipped downmarket in recent years. Zilkha, an extremely astute man, knew, when his profits began to fall, that his merchandise had become lacklustre. He recognized that the cure lay in the design-led Habitat concept.

The alliance has proved a great success. Both companies have since learnt a lot from one another. We now have the best retail systems in the world, alongside our unique retailing philosophy.

Storehouse

I then realized there must be many other similar opportunities. We took over Richard Shops, who are in women's clothing, and Heals, in upmarket furnishing, and have injected our design philosophy into them. In the meantime we have invested in a large design team, to ensure exclusivity, well-designed merchandise and strong graphic style. Moreover, we have never been satisfied with existing standards.

In 1986 we took the opportunity to merge with British Home Stores. Overnight our turnover more than doubled, from £600 million to well over a billion. But much more importantly we were now able to reach out, as designers with our own unique style, to a much wider group of people. Time will tell to what extent we shall succeed with our deisgner-led revolution.

Design, essentially, is a matter of function, taste and style. It involves a feeling for a mood. A good designer can express a mood before the population has realized what is happening to it. Through observing what people are doing, thinking or feeling, he or she sensitively captures something in the air and reveals it in, say, clothes or furnishing. The result excites people's imagination. That's something, incidentally, the Japanese are particularly good at.

We, on the other hand, have created a style. Through Habitat well designed furniture is now accessible to people of modest means, whereby twenty-five years ago they were the prerogative of the well off. The Habitat look has gathered an increasing number of converts as their eye becomes educated to appreciate fresh, simple and imaginative furnishing.

So now, not only in furnishing but also in clothing, we are making good design accessible to everyone. Moreover, as retailers we are coming to understand that we can exercise our power to create merchandise that is unique to us. Also, there is a new breed of buyer in the retail world who is a creative person rather than a number cruncher.

What I enjoy now is the feeling that we can make any product we require, thanks to our designers' abilities. We've created and stand by our own case in the high streets.

London, England 1988

How do you develop as an innovator?

The point about you, as an innovator, is that you reach your prime in maturity, that is from your late forties onwards. Unfortunately many an innovator never realizes his or her ultimate vision because he is not encouraged to follow a natural line of development.

In your youth you need to explore, to experiment, to risk your personal resources or identity in a new technological or social invention. Travel into the physically, economically, or psychologically unknown is therefore a natural feature of healthy, youthful development. This is certainly reflected in Terence Conran's youth.

In adulthood, authority and responsibility now come naturally to the developing innovator. Thus the free wheeling inventor needs to come to grips with the problems of managing innovation – from idea generation to commercialization. Whereas the twenties are therefore a time for enterprise, the thirties are prime time for structured organization, as was the case for Habitat.

Midlife is the time to listen to your heart first, and to your head, second. As a technological innovator you need to broaden your social awareness, thereby becoming a true visionary. In fact it was in only in the seventies that Terence Conran, now in his forties, was beginning to be seen as such, a designer visionary offering well-designed merchandise at prices people could afford.

Finally, if you have successfully undergone life's transitions, as a mature individual you are ready to tap the very core of your own being, your spirit of creativity. In so doing you also connect yourself with the roots of your company's being. The relationship between the one and the other is a particularly powerful one, resulting in a fully developed vision.

Let me now turn from Terence Conran to Joyce Choto, and from Britain to Zimbabwe, to our adventurous manager.

The adventurer

Are you a prospective adventurer?

As such an adventurer:

- You're always on the go.
  - You work long hours and travel to far flung places.
  - You have lots of staying power.

- You work hard and play hard.
  - You balance physical, emotional and intellectual activity.
  - You take time off to unwind.

- You are fit and healthy.
  - You exercise regularly, in your work or in your leisure.
  - You are full of energy.

- You move people.
  - You make a physical impact on others.
  - You galvanize people around you into activity.

- You're an explorer.
  - You risk life and limb in your ventures.
  - You travel into the physically unknown.

- You embody the spirit of adventure.
  - You are recognized as a wandering spirit.
  - You imbue your organization with the spirit of adventure.

Adventurers have been part of our recorded heritage for centuries. Marco Polo, Vasco Da Gama, Christopher Columbus, Francis Drake and Lawrence of Arabia are all good examples from the past. Today, in the business world, we have, for example, Armand Hammer, the itinerant oil magnate from the USA, and Richard Branson of Virgin Atlantic, in the UK.

With the advent of an increasingly leisure-oriented society, in which health and recreation has an increasing part to play, the role of adventurer is creeping ever more strongly into business. If you scored highest in category (a), on the spectral inventory, you may be one yourself.

Do companies recruit adventurers?

As companies spread their international wings, particularly towards the remoter parts of our globe, and even our planet, so the call for the adventurer is increasingly heard. As research take us up into outer space and down into the depths of the oceans, this demand for adventurers is likely to grow. The mercenary or merchant adventurer of old is being replaced by a more-educated business adventurer of the eighties and nineties.

At the same time, as the pressures of competitive business mount, the demand for adventure training, for adventure holidays, and the like, increases. Work hard, play hard becomes both a desire and a psychological necessity. The particular parts of a business organization that are likely to be most interested in you, as an adventurer, are export sales, publicity and promotions, research and exploration, and the more physically hazardous operations, especially in mining and agriculture. Finally, as an adventurer you are always physically on the go; you continually intersperse hard work with hard play; you are an explorer, venturing into the physically unknown; and you may come to embody the spirit of adventure within your company.

How are you rewarded, as an adventurer?

Adventurers, like Anita Roddick, Richard Branson, and Armand Hammer, need to keep constantly and physically, on the move. If they are not physically on the go they feel no sense of achievement. So as an adventurer you have physical challenges to surmount like Branson's attempt to cross the Atlantic in a hot air balloon, and Roddick's desire to keep picking up skin and hair-care recipes from all over the world.

Equally, you may seek physical comfort in good food and wine, in exercise and massage, in sunny beaches on the Caribbean, or in pleasurable sporting holidays. Joyce Choto, in Zimbabwe, sees food and nutrition as an indispensable part of her self-image.

Adventurer

Joyce Choto   University of Zimbabwe

Background

Disowned

We were eight girls in the family. My father didn't believe in the female sex. In fact he virtually disowned us.

We were hungry for love, you might say, but not for food. Our plot of land at home was very fertile. Because our plot was fertile we could afford to pay for help from those who lived around us. We needed the labour. They needed the food.

Food for thought

My mother always told us girls that all difficult things to accomplish would turn out well, as long as we never stopped working for them. I got through high school because I worked hard, and knew exactly what I wanted to do, as my vocation. Nutrition.

We had this home economics teacher at high school. She was terribly smart. I admired her for her intelligence. She seemed to know about everything. I often sat down and thought, I wish I knew all those things.

Adventure and return

Action woman

At the local university there was no course in nutrition. So when I heard, one day, of a trade unionist who was giving students scholarships to study overseas, I looked him up immediately. He agreed to give me a scholarship, but said I had to go Malawi first, in order to become eligible. So I went straight to the passport office. I had to bribe the official to get him to produce a passport for me in time. It cost me all of $2.

On 6 April 1970, I can remember to this day, I set out for Malawi. I had all of $79 in my pocket. The trade union official met me at the airport. He took me back to his house and locked up my passport.

'Any cash on you?' he asked, 'I have to keep your passport in a safe.' Naively, I gave him everything I had. Afterwards he left the house, and his wife stayed on with me. 'You should never have come,' is all she said.

After three days the man eventually returned, with some official looking colleagues. 'Come to a movie with us,' he said. His wife looked at me, almost in tears by now. But I thought nothing of it.

The protectors

So I went to the movies. When I got there I was seated next to another man. He was introduced to me as 'Doris' father'. I had never heard of Doris. Halfway through the film the man who had originally taken my passport left, never to return.

When the movie ended Doris' father said to me, 'Didn't you know you were staying with me. I'll take you home and explain.' I thought he was joking.

Anyway, I went home with him. He sat on the sofa opposite, looking at me. 'Read this,' he said, passing a letter over. The letter was from Zambia. It was from a friend, telling the man sitting opposite me how his daughter had been made pregnant.

'If I hadn't received this letter,' he said, 'I may have done the same thing to you. But now I just can't. I'm going to help you instead. But you'll have to play the game with me and pretend you don't know anything.'

He went to the trade union people and asked for my papers. He told them that he'd be marrying me after I got back. He then told me that he had arranged with a friend, Bernard, who was working for the UN in Nairobi at the time, to fly me over to Kenya.

So I got my passport back but not my money. My ticket was waiting for me at the airport. I think the fellow who helped me was called Alphonso. I never saw Alphonso again, but I owe him my life.

I got to Nairobi, then, and found Bernard waiting for me. He was helping a fellow Zimbabwean. I had come through a traumatic experience. As it happened, the university had already started in Nairobi, and I was too late to enrol for a course in nutrition. So I went to a commercial college.

While I was at college a group tried to kidnap me. They abducted me and took me to their rooms in Nairobi. Luckily enough, on the day when it happened, a Zimbabwean who knew me happened to be walking in the street nearby. He heard us talking in Shona, our indigenous Zimbabwean language, from the street. The window happened to be wide open.

The man rushed over to Bernard and the two of them immediately dashed over. They bundled me out and Bernard saved my skin once more.

Test of courage

Eventually I got into university, in Nairobi, and studied nutrition for two years. By this time I was terribly homesick, and returned to Rhodesia. When I got there with my British passport it was immediately confiscated by the Rhodesian police force. This was in the 1970s during the liberation war.

The police asked me for my home address, and I gave them a false location in a remote area on the Mozambique border. Eventually they hunted me down in Salisbury. From that moment on I was always followed. I couldn't cope with that, together with the whole apartheid situation, so I decided to return to Kenya. But I had no passport!

I had to think of a way. Then I heard of a guy in Bulawayo who helped people cross over into neighbouring Botswana. I went to Bulawayo and looked all over for him. When I eventually caught up with the boy – he turned out to be no more than sixteen –he was ready to leave immediately. 'You have to put on completely different clothes,' he said, 'or you may be recognized.'

So I went along to this aunt of mine and asked her for some old clothes. I also picked up some baby's nappies and tennis shoes. Looked like a real old lady. I folded my mini skirt around me, attached it to a diaper, and wrapped both around my middle. Then we set out for the border.

As we got to the roadside a white guy, travelling in an open van, stopped for us. It was as if he had been sent by God. He even happened to be going to the same place as us. 'Get in the back', he said. It rained all the way.

We had to walk for miles from where he had dropped us to get to the border. We walked and walked. At about five in the evening we got to the Tokwe river. But, being the rainy season, it was too full to cross. We had to spend the night in the bush and wait for the river to go down in the morning.

Next morning we started to cross. We had almost got into Botswana, on the other side, when I heard this sharp whistle from behind. I froze. We looked back and saw a whole bunch of soldiers on the Rhodesian side. I was convinced they were going to kill me. 'Walk on,' my companion said. He was my source of strength. Though only sixteen he had ceased to be scared. 'You go in front of me,' he said. 'If they shoot they'll shoot me first'.

We eventually got to the other side and starting running, spurred on by fear. After a while my guide told me to change back into my mini dress. He had been listening to the nearby road and had heard a sound. A car was coming.

Another person sent by God. The car stopped and took us to the railway station. As soon as I had got on the train my sixteen year old guide asked the guard to look after me and departed. I had paid him $24. I was on my own.

When I got to the Botswana capital, Gaberone, I went straight to the British Embassy to get a new passport. 'Where is your old one,' the official immediately asked. He dismissed me immediately. So I was stuck.

Then I remembered a fellow I had met, studying with me in Kenya, who came from Botswana. Those of us who had come from a similar part of the world had stuck together. I'd almost forgotten his name, but I did remember it was something like 'Lebang'. So I stopped people in the street and asked them if they knew Lebang.

Eventually somebody said: 'Of course I know him. He's a big security adviser of the President'. Good, I said, where is he? 'Just over there', the man pointed, 'in that building right opposite. But you can't go and see him just like that!'

Well, I walked right over and asked the guard standing there for Lebang. 'We don't let strangers in to see him,' he said. 'Just take my name to him,' I responded. 'He will remember me.' So the guard went into him saying 'this women is here. This is her name.' 'My goodness,' said Lebang, and came right down to see me.

'What are you doing here in Botswana,' he asked me. 'I can't get a passport,' I told him. 'You have to help me.' We went over to the passport office and in ten minutes I had a new one. I had held on to my old passport number. So they called Malawi and had it verified.

Now for me to get back into Zimbabwe, in the Smith era, I had to leave a Rhodesian airport with a British passport. As I hadn't done so I decided to return, and get my passport stamped. I had to take the risk if I wanted to return home.

Thinking on my feet

So I took the train from Gaberone back to Bulawayo. At the border between the two countries the customs officials began checking passports. When the officer looked at mine he insisted it was invalid, that is unless it had a special piece of paper from the Rhodesian government, accompanying it. He said he'd have to confiscate it.

Oh my God, I thought to myself, not again. I had to think fast. I could see that the customs official was pretty drunk, so – while he had slipped off to check on something – I took off my long African gown, put on my miniskirt and some bright red lipstick. When he returned he stared at me. 'There was a woman sitting where you are. Where has she gone?'

'It's me,' I said. 'Come and sit down, and have a beer. And what about this paper you mentioned? You'll have to give one to me.' At that point he turned around suddenly, noting that the train he was supposed to join, going in the other direction, was about to pull off.

He pointed at the official paper that I needed, which he placed in front of me, and insisted that he would not be able to give me one. At that precise moment the train going in the other direction whistled, and he dashed off, mistakenly leaving the piece of paper behind him. It was all signed and sealed. All I had to do was fill in my name.

I arrived at Harari station in the evening, and dashed to the airport to catch the flight to Kenya. I had no ticket and was wait-listed. Someone failed to turn up and I got on.

New horizons

Out of Africa

I returned to Kenya to finish my degree but before completing it I went on a sponsored holiday tour to Denmark. It was my first time out of Africa.

The culture shock was unbelievable. Our hosts insisted on taking us to live sex shows. People were doing all sorts of things in the park and swimming naked in the sea. I had been educated in a mission school and had been led to believe that Europeans up North were whiter than white, the purest of the pure. I hated the missionaries at that particular point for their pretence. The shock was too much for me and I was eager to go back to Nairobi.

After I graduated I returned to Rhodesia, and, of course, the authorities took my passport again. But by now I knew what to do. I crossed the border into Botswana again and went to see Lebang. This time I went on to Johannesburg and took a South African Airways flight to Nairobi from there.

The American dream

By this point I knew I had to go to America. The teachers at my university in Nairobi were American, and told me that the best nutrition schools were there. So I called on Bernard again and asked him to get me addresses of those universities to which he thought I should apply.

I applied to Cornell, Harvard, Princeton and Columbia. Cornell came back to me first and offered my a place, plus tuition fees and plane fare. I couldn't believe it. I had been sitting for eight months in Mombasa, on the Kenyan coastline, gazing forever watchfully at the waves carrying myself off, in my imagination, across the sea.

Now my dream became a reality. Within eight weeks I was over there. I flew on to Cornell where I met my foster parent. She was one of the Sears family. She welcomed me to America, and told me that I had a furnished flat and a car, at my free disposal. Not only that, but we used to go to the library together, and read till two a.m. She was committed to my education. I learned to work very hard.

Feeding the hungry

Research and development

I completed my Masters in Nutrition at Cornell, and returned to Kenya to do research on vitamin A deficiency, and its relationship to malnutrition. I also got involved in a project to feed the starving refugees in Northern Kenya coming from Ethiopia.

By the time I had completed my research I had become determined to become involved in something that involved feeding people. I didn't want to be a pure academic.

Administering to others

In the meantime, back in America, I got married to Bob, who had been expelled from Rhodesia eighteen years ago, and was now practicing in the United States as a doctor. We went on to UCLA and I did more courses in biochemistry, physiology and food services administration. I got registered in diatetics and went on to work in a hospital. I discovered that I hated feeding hospital patients!

I had to work with food but not with sick people. So Bob suggested that I go to the University of Nevada and study food service administration. I did my practicals at one of the Hilton hotels. Thereafter I became Director of Food Services at the University of Southern California, where I was responsible for providing food for 20,000 students.

Renewal

Director of Food Services

In 1980 Zimbabwe became independent. Bob was quite at home in America, but I told him I had to go back. He didn't want to, and it was only when he had to face the prospect of his wife and baby living thousands of miles away that he changed his mind. Maybe he'd be of some use to the new country, he thought.

I knew what I wanted when I got back, and that was to be director of Food Services at the local university. After working for a short while in a hospital I got the job, which is where I still am now. But that's not where I'll ultimately be.

My vocation

When we came to the country there was no school of nutrition. In the past few years Bob and our vice chancellor have been raising money for one. We've now virtually got enough to set up the school. Hopefully, not too long from now, Bob and I will be teaching there together.

I want Zimbabweans to use their local foods in a way that gives them a balanced diet. I've seen the effects of malnutrition, in Kenya, in this country, and even in America. Often it is this result of a dietary imbalance.

I love my work. I'm thirty-eight now. I feel I am able to achieve whatever I want, as long as I'm dealing with nutrition. Mind you, nutrition and agriculture can hardly be separated. I like to see people eat.

It could only be God's wish that I am where I am now.

Harari, Zimbabwe 1987

How do you develop as an adventurer?

In your youth you may come across as an action man or woman. Like Armand Hammer, for example, you may have sold to more countries than anyone else in your company, by footslogging around the world. Like Joyce Choto, you may have undergone physical risk or hardship.

In young adulthood, you become more visible in the company as a whole, as an adventurer. Like Richard Branson you are physically 'on show' so as to publicize your product and your business, or, like Joyce Choto, you may have engaged in innumerable chancy escapades.

In midlife, as Joyce Choto is doing, you become less involved in your own physical accomplishments, and more so in activating others, in sales or on exploration, through coaching or through 'mentorship'.

Finally, in your fifties, sixties and onwards, as has been the case with Hammer, as you actualize your true self, you come to embody the spirit of adventure, by broadening the base of your physical accomplishments. Instead of leading from the front you inspire from up above, by, for example, transforming a physical environment rather than keeping yourself physically on the go.

As you develop towards maturity, then, you come close to the role of innovator, your counterpart. Between the two – energy and imagination, a vision is materialized.

Conclusion

Vision and energy

The metaphysical paths of adventurer and innovator are somewhat more identifiable than those of enabler and adaptor, but as yet only barely accommodated within conventional organizations. Technological innovators and rugged adventurers are generally relegated to the mature business periphery, even though it is acknowledged that their role has been indispensable.

Without Alfred Nobel there would have been no ICI; without George Eastman there would have been no Kodak; without Masaru Ibuka there would have been no Sony. Yet our commercial memories are short. All too quickly we lose sight of our real energy source, both in its conception in its continued activation. Therein lies the creative nucleus, the 'soul' of the business, and its physical outcome.

For the metaphysical manager, in fact, be he or she an innovator or an adventurer, it is the dream rather than the reality which is the launching point for his or her managerial activity. Although this does become more evident as the person matures, it is always there in the background.

So feeding the hungry, for Choto, or furnishing your home, for Conran, may be material necessities, but they are a means to an imagined end. As the metaphysical manager grows and develops so his or her dreams become tempered by the necessity to survive, the need to be productive, and the requirements of people around him or her.

So primal, rational, and developmental management has its evolving place in the metaphysical manager's self-realization. But that place remains subordinate to his or her ultimate dreams.

In the final analysis, though the adventurer begins with action, and the innovator with imagination, both realize that the ultimate possibility and constraint is neither money nor organization, but the laws of nature, reflected in human energy.

Becoming your managerial self

In conclusion, there are eight managerial subdomains, or paths, each of which has been made visible to us in these last four chapters. Each path makes its way through four stages of development, interspersed with transitional phases (see Table 40).

In realizing your managerial individuality, you will probably be best suited to forge, or to follow, one or other of these. In the process you will explore in your youth, consolidate in adulthood, renew yourself in midlife, and become your ultimate, and managerial self in maturity.

Table 40 Becoming your managerial self

Exploration (youth)	Consolidation (adulthood)	Renewal (midlife)	Individuation (maturity)
Action Man	**Adventurer**	Activator	Spirit of Adventure
Craftsman	Skilled operator	**Animateur**	Community spirit
Troubleshooter	**Change agent**	Manager of change	Free spirit
Budding entrepreneur	Entrepreneurial manager	Business developer	Enterprise spirit
Trainee manager	Functional manager	Business **executive**	Spirit of leadership
Artist/Scientist	Designer	**Enabler**	Spirit of Development
Inventor	**Innovator**	Visionary	Creative spirit

In the final section I shall attempt to pull all the threads together, tentatively relating the domains of management to the functions of business.

Section G
Conclusion

34 Functional domains

Introduction

In this chapter we shall explore the implications of the global management principles, encompassing the four domains, for the basic functions of business. Such functions, in this context, are not planning, organizing, directing and control, but financial, marketing, operational and human resource management.

At this stage of the development of management theory and practice we can do no more than explore the four domains in each functional case. For, explicitly if not implicitly, functional theorists have not yet made visible the evolution of their disciplines, at least beyond the rational stage. Moreover, it is important to mention that each business function may not necessarily evolve, in linear fashion, from a primal to a metaphysical state. In fact, to take what will be our last example of 'human resource management', although it is theoretically probably the furthest advanced, the primal domain has taken a very long time in coming.

In this chapter, then, we shall be investigating the four domains – both hard and soft – of finance, marketing, operations and human resource management, in turn. We start with money and 'finance', because many see it as the essence of business, and conclude with 'human resources' because the function is, theoretically, the most developed.

Finance

Money and business have never been very far apart. In fact, particularly for those who have not been involved in business themselves, the two may appear to be inextricably connected.

Finance: the primal domain

Money, though is actually an abstraction. People who are instinctively adept at making money start off from some other place, deep within their own subconscious. In fact, there is a whole range of 'inspirational' American business literature, which helps managers tap those subconscious motives, that is should they wish to grow rich.

Secrets of success

By far the best known of these books is by Napoleon Hill, written in the twenties and entitled *Think and Grow Rich*.[1] Still a best seller today, the book declares on its front cover: 'This could be worth a million dollars to you.' Hill in fact spent some twenty years with such business geniuses as Andrew Carnegie, Henry Ford and Nelson Rockefeller, uncovering their secrets of success.

The starting point for all great men of business, Hill concluded, was desire. The means whereby such a desire for riches can be satisfied, he says, involves six practical steps:

1. Fix in your mind the exact amount of money you desire.
2. Determine exactly what you want to give in return – there is no such reality as 'something for nothing'.
3. Establish a definite date by which time you want to possess the money you desire.
4. Create a definite plan for carrying out your desire, and begin at once to put your plan into action.
5. Imprint on your heart and mind the amount of money you intend to acquire, the time limit for its acquisition, and what you intend to give in return for the money.
6. Remind yourself twice daily of your intentions, once before you go to sleep, and once when you wake up in the morning. As you remind yourself, see and feel yourself already in possession of the money.

As you can see the primal approach to finance starts with the person, and his or her concrete desires, rather than with money, which is abstract. Although Napoleon Hill's work is the best known, of this kind, there are at least a hundred other such books, albeit not as well researched.

Moneylove

Hill's primal approach, and a hundred other similarly tough-minded ones, focus on the desire to succeed, and hence to make a fortune. Jerry Gillies' tenderhearted approach, and several other American ones like it, are oriented towards 'moneylove'.

> One of the major premises of moneylove is that one of the best things you can do for your own prosperity consciousness is to lift someone else's. Every dollar you help someone else to earn will come back to you multiplied, along with large helpings of love.[2]

The theme of moneylove is echoed by Mary Kay, whom we met in Chapter 7. Money is not only a means to a personal end, that is self-love, but it is also multiplied by the love of others.

> I suppose I'm like a mother who wants to give her children – my salesladies – the things they didn't have. The first thing they need is to hear is 'you can do it!' Sometimes nobody has ever told them that in their life. But we also make sure they learn the necessary skills, as beauty consultants. And when they do that they begin to improve in other ways too. Their confidence builds.[3]

As we can see, then, a primal approach to finance, whether hard or soft, builds on personal desires not only for success and achievement but also for love and self-worth. Whereas the literature in this primal area is largely American, other such tough-minded primal sources exist, in Japan for example, in descriptions of the art of oriental warfare.[4]

Finance: the rational domain

Whereas the proverbial entrepreneur or animateur, like Andrew Carnegie or Mary Kay, sees personal psychology and business finance as intimately linked, for the rational manager they are worlds apart. This is the case, particularly, within the rigid field of management accounting. As we shall see, it is less strictly the case in the looser realms of business finance.

Management accounting

In fact the entire discipline of accounting has grown up – double-entry book-keeping having originated in seventeenth-century Italy – as an abstract and impersonal tool of business.

> Book-keeping is the systematic recording of business transactions in a manner which enables the financial relationship of business with other persons to be clearly disclosed, and the cumulative effect of the transactions on the financial position of the business itself to be ascertained. Business transactions comprise the exchange of value, either in the form of money, or of goods and services which are measured and expressed in terms of money.[5]

Double-entry accounting, then, enables a businessman or financial controller to gauge at any time his company's financial position, and its 'financial relationship with other persons'. Thus an abstract relationship takes over from a personal one. Precise, rationally derived measurements overtake emotionally laden bonds of trust, or mistrust. Stable financial accounts, and corresponding managerial accountability, supplant 'back of the envelope' records of transactions. Similarly, an accountant may overtake a craftsman, technician or salesman at the head of the company.

Subsequent developments of the financial function, often mathematically based, have extended its rationality, and impersonality. Discounted cash flow, capital budgeting, portfolio analysis, and financial model building and simulation, have added further degrees of intellectual sophistication to an already analytically refined discipline. In that analytical context its primal origins are all too often lost. However, in the last few years, a combination of primal instinct and intellectual wizardry has produced a financial revolution.

The financial revolution

In the words of Walter Wriston, head of Citicorp – the world's largest bank – between 1970 and 1984:

> The information standard has replaced the gold standard as the basis for international finance. Communications now enable and ensure that money moves anywhere around the globe, in answer to the latest information or misinformation. There now exists a new order, a global marketplace for ideas, money, goods and services that knows no national boundaries.[6]

In the financial heartlands of London, New York, Hong Kong and now Tokyo, the primal nature of money making, however, has retained its underlying identity. Brokers, jobbers and floor traders have continued to draw on their primal instincts, particularly those of the tougher variety. The drive for personal gain has maintained its influence on every deal. However, with the onset of computerization, and with the internationalization of the world's stock markets, there has been a new twist to the financial tail.

An intellectual superstructure has been built directly upon a primal substructure, resulting in great fluidity and instability. Fixed and archaic primal instincts have become intertwined with a flexible intellect, contained in both people and technology.

'Soft' markets

For generations (centuries in the case of many of the great financial capitals of the world) the principles guiding the financial markets have been specialization and control. The Chicago commodity markets concentrated on futures in pork bellies, the Baltic Exchange in London developed the markets for freight rates by sea. Markets for short, medium and long term funds were separated and the whole structure buttressed by central authorities that controlled interest rates and currency movements.

In the nineteen eighties, however, technology has made it possible to trade huge volumes on screens and on the exchange floors. What is more, it has made it possible to develop increasingly sophisticated and complicated products such as options (when the investor takes out an option to buy or sell a share, bond or commodity at a future date), swaps (when the borrower can swap, for example, his fixed rate debt, raised in one country with the floating rate debt raised by a company elsewhere).

In summary, as both investors and borrowers grow more sophisticated, so new products are developed that enable companies to swap their obligations, investors to convert their bonds into equity shares or different currencies, and banks to take advantage of their spread of customers to organize flexible instruments that could be made short term or long term, moved into one currency or another, and switched from floating to fixed interest rate at will.

Adrian Hamilton *The Financial Revolution*[7] 1986

The shift from gold – through coin, paper money, and credit – to information as a unit of exchange, progressively removes finance from its primal origins.

Finance: the developmental domain

As finance evolves from its position, as a vehicle and outlet for personal ambition or social generosity, to a channel for organizational effectiveness or commercial flexibility, to a medium for personal, organizational, industrial, and economic development, so its role and perspective changes.

Finance for development

Ever since the formation of joint stock companies, in the nineteenth century, finance for business development has been acknowledged. More recently, as international economic awareness has increased and finance for national development has also become recognized. However, such recognition has been at best, partial, in that a genuinely developmental outlook has seldom been adopted. Such an outlook has been the one adopted, albeit perhaps in a more philosophical than practical vein, by Rudolph Steiner (see Chapter 23) at the turn of the century. Disciples of his, that is the economists Folkert Wilken in Germany and Christopher Budd in Britain, have since adopted the term 'capital economy' to underline his developmental approach.

Capital economy

A 'capital economy' is distinguished from other forms of economy by the emancipation of capital within it. It is a mode of economy in which the economic process has more or less freed itself from inclusion within the cultural and political spheres. It has, as a concomitant, the emancipated consciousness of the individual. A capital economy only finds its true setting in the social order when capital finds its way to the individual, solely on the basis of his capacities.

The social order appropriate to capital will never be discovered unless men realize that it is the evolutionary task of capital to call forth from man a new social order, based on self-knowledge and self-initiation, not high authority.

Without capital, in fact, self-expression and individual development are impossible. Capital, in this sense, may be a paint brush or a machine; it can be the stock for a shop or the right to mine a vein of ore. What turns nature into capital is the fact that it is used to unfold the capacities of man.

Christopher Budd *Prelude in Economics*[8] 1979

For Budd, then, capital is a financial means to a psychological end, the unfolding of the capacities of man. The same developmental outlook applies, for economists like Folkert Wilken, in relation to the unfolding of the capacities of a whole nation.

Financial and economic reciprocity

As the capacities of a nation unfold, so they become ever more closely intertwined with other nations. Mary Parker Follett's[9] pairing of individuality and interdependence, then, works on both an individual and on a national plane. For that reason we see, for example with Kenichi Ohmae's *Triad Power*,[10] the advance of economic interdependence across a worldwide stage.

In fact interdependence, together with reciprocity, is built into the underlying nature of double entry. For basic book-keeping recognizes the twofold aspect of every transaction, namely, the receipt of something of monetary value by one person and the parting of it by another. In essence, assets and liabilities represent two sides of the same coin. On the one side we have some outstanding demand or expectation awaiting satisfaction and, on the other, we have the potential or sufficient support to produce such satisfaction.

Table 41 Psychological balance sheet

Assets/psychological supports	Liabilities/psychological demands

Total years experience:
  managerial
  clerical
  skilled manual
	Accrued demands for work experience

Accumulation of knowledge	Accrued demands for utilization of knowledge
Investment in training:	Accrued demands for utilization of capacities developed

skill based
  knowledge based
  self-development based	

Recognizing this fact, in the mid-seventies, I developed[11] a double-entry system, covering not only financial transactions, but also physical, social and psychological ones within a business enterprise. This system was used to audit the 'social performance'[12] of companies. One such 'account' is illustrated in Table 41.

The developmental aspects of financial management are often verbalized, particularly in an international context, even if they are seldom approached in the purist vein indicated by Steiner and his economic disciples. The metaphysical aspects, though, require even deeper probing.

Finance: the metaphysical domain

Business inspiration

Interestingly enough, there is a strong element of the metaphysical in Napoleon Hills' work, to which we referred at the beginning of this financial section. In fact much of the so-called inspirational business literature draws explicitly and, to my mind, unsatisfactorily, on religion. The approach tends to be crude and exaggerated. Hill, on the other hand, is more subtle and sophisticated.

Such phrases as 'infinite intelligence' and the creative imagination, 'autosuggestion' and 'the power of the subconscious mind', sixth sense and 'the stream of life', as well as 'the magnetic force of faith', fall naturally into *Think and Grow Rich*.

Magnetic force

Every man who has accumulated a great personal fortune has recognized the existence of the stream of life. It consists of one's thinking process. Thoughts that are mixed with any of the feelings constitute a magnetic force which attracts other similar or related thoughts. The human mind is constantly attracting vibrations which harmonize with that which dominates the mind.

All thought impulses intended for transmutation into their physical equivalent, voluntarily planted in the subconscious mind, must pass through the imagination and be mixed with faith. The subconscious mind is the 'sending station' of the brain, through which vibrations of thought are broadcast. The creative imagination is the 'receiving set', through which the energies of thought are picked up.

Napoleon Hill *Think and Grow Rich*[13] 1960

Acquiring a fortune, according to Hill, requires metaphysical as well as physical activity. Invisible intelligence is as important as visible energy. Christopher Budd, although very different in his overall approach, ends up with some similar conclusions.

Nature–man–spirit

Economics has two tasks, Budd says, to derive from nature the things necessary to human material life and to derive from spirit the capacities necessary to individual development. Hill would equate riches with material life and thought with spirit. In fact the connection between Rudolph Steiner's metaphysical approach and Napoleon Hills' becomes even more apparent when we hear from Steiner himself.

So long as a mode of organization due to the Spirit is narrowly bound to a certain kind of labor, Nature will still shine through. But the moment we emancipate ourselves, thinking only of how to make fruitful what we gain by the application of the spirit, the more we do this, the more we shall observe the labor becoming indistinct within the total mass of Capital. In its peculiar and specific character, it vanishes.[14]

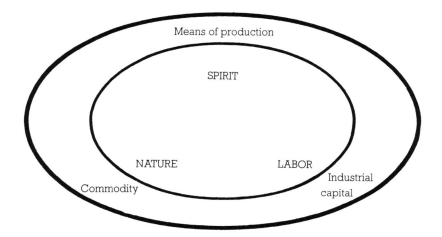

Fig. 79 Metaphysical economics.

(See Fig. 79.)[15] In other words, in Hill's terms, labor becomes invisible intelligence, mere spirit. Thereby, for Hill, the entrepreneur makes his fortune and, for Steiner, the economy flourishes. In both cases, moreover, finance has evolved from a physical and personal to a metaphysical and transpersonal phenomenon. The same kind of perspective can be applied to marketing.

Marketing

While business is generally identified with money and finance, its origins lie closer to marketing. As Peter Drucker has emphasized, in a modern business context: 'The purpose of a business is not to make a profit . . . Rather a business exists for its economic contribution. Its purpose is to create a customer.'[16]

Marketing: the primal domain

Barter and trade

If we look for the primal origins of marketing we shall find them in the market-places of antiquity. For wherever there is buying and selling, marketing of the most basic kind is going on. In fact trade, by way of bartar, preceded economic exchange, mediated by money, by thousands of years.

When, on my last trip to the Victoria Falls in Zimbabwe, the affable sculptor by the roadside offered me a wooden elephant, that he had carved in exchange for a tee-shirt, or 'something like that', he was continuing a tradition that stretches back thousands of years. Having sensed that my need for his carving was not all that great, and that British-made tee-shirts were easy for me to come by (but difficult for Zimbabweans to acquire), he made his proposition. In the event my little boy accepted, on our behalf!

Young children acquire experience of 'primal marketing' long before they learn how to handle money. When my ten year old boy 'sells' his friend Jim the idea of playing monopoly, having previously ascertained that Jim is bored and needs stimulus, he is already marketing – in a primal way. Indeed, a Canadian management consultant, Jean Marc Chaput, has written a book called *Living is Selling*,[17] in which he elaborates on this primal theme.

Salesmanship

Primal marketing, in a contemporary business context, is best represented by salesmanship. Hundreds of books and courses on the subject remind us that such marketing is as much to do with 'touch and feel' as it is to do with 'intelligent perception'.

A veteran salesman himself, Harry Turner, in his book *The Gentle Art of Salesmanship* indicates that good salesman has two particularly dominant personality traits, ego drive and empathy. These, incidentally, correspond very nicely with the hard (ego drive) and soft (empathy) traits that a feature of all our management and functional domains.

> Ego drive is the urge to succeed. If it is not balanced by empathy it can be a destructive force. Empathy is about sensitivity to the reactions and feelings of others. Very few people have both these qualities in equal proportions. Strong empathy and reduced drive means less cutting edge, which will make the closing of sales difficult. Too much ego drive and too little empathy produces the killer instinct.[18]

Another authority on salesmanship in Britain, Heinz Goldman, has taken on from where Turner left off, introducing us to 'AIDA', well known in salesman's circles!

The AIDA rule

means that the successful salesman needs to arouse the attention of the customer, make him personally interested in the offer, and increase his desire to buy the product, in order to stimulate him to the action of buying

Heinz Goldman *How To Win Customers*[19] 1971

Marketing: the rational domain

From sales to marketing

The transition from primal salesmanship to rationally based marketing has been described, in picturesque fashion, by Harry Turner. Years ago, he says, larger than life characters like 'King Gillette' created products which they virtually willed into existence. Such men followed hunches, took breathtaking chances and finally conquered the world with their determination to succeed. They had charisma, and buccaneering style. Their business talents were as much instinctive as academic.

Modern marketing man

Modern marketing man is different. Charisma? He thinks charisma is an Indian restaurant in suburbia. Buccaneering? Thats in old black and white movies on TV. Modern marketing man is often dull, studious, careful, safe. He does everything by the book. But although this type doesn't get my adrenaline flowing, I won't condemn him out of hand.

Big business is now exceedingly complex; there is a compelling need for high volume sales, and the degree of competition is so keen that only the most economical methods of design and production or distribution, will maintain profitability.

It is therefore blindingly obvious that marketing – as it is now understood – embraces a whole lot more than simply selling the product. It must identify what product should be made, how, when and where it should be sold, how much it should be sold for, and to whom?

Harry Turner *The Gentle Art of Salesmanship*[20] 1985

But the high priest of modern marketing is not the British salesman Harry Turner, but the American academic, Philip Kotler.

Analytical marketing

Marketing is the analyzing, organizing, planning and controlling of the firm's customer – impinging resources, policies, and activities with a view to satisfying the needs and wants of chosen customer groups at a profit.[21]

As we can see the abstract world of resources and customer groups replaces the concrete world of people and things. The new science of analytical marketing was diagramatically represented, in the sixties,[22] in the way indicated in Fig. 80.

Fig. 80 The marketing manager's framework.

Rationally based management had come a long way from its primal origins, substituting analytical cut and thrust for the emotionally based ego drive. In fact by the 1970s marketing had become the most intellectually demanding of the business disciplines.

Relationships marketing

Kotler's approach to analytical marketing has remained undisputed, at least within the mainstream of corporate life, until well into the eighties. Just recently, however, a new marketing orthodoxy – equally rational but more flexible in its approach – has begun to emerge. Its advocates are, not surprisingly, more Scandinavian than American or British.

In fact it was the Hollander, Bernard Lievegoed who, already in the early seventies, came up with the notion of 'relations management' (see p. 431).[23] Supplanting marketing and personnel management, this function, as the organization moved out of the 'differentiated' phase, combined both internal and external relations, that is relating to both employees and customers.

The 'Nordic School of Services', based in Finland and Sweden, has gone a step further, replacing the old concept of analytical marketing with a new 'interactive' one.

Developing long-term interactive relationships

Marketing can be seen as relationship management: creating, developing, and maintaining a network in which the firm thrives. Such a network is interactive, that is involving bilateral and multilateral supplier–customer relationships, to produce goods and services. These relationships, finally, are long term, stressing that relationships need time to be built and to be maintained.

Evert Gummersson 'The new marketing'[24] 1987

The interactive approach to marketing, then, stresses the building of relationships rather than the promotion of products or the satisfaction of individual customer needs. Moreover, these relationships extend beyond customers to suppliers, distributors and investors. 'A company can be viewed as a node in an ever-widening pattern of interactions, in some of which it is a direct participant, some of which effect it indirectly and some of which occur independently of it.'[25]

The cut and thrust of tightly bound analytical marketing is being supplanted – though not replaced – by the fluidity and interactivity of loosely bound 'relationships marketing'. This development parallels the shift from fixed hierarchies to changeable organizational networks, and from rigidly based financial systems of yesterday to the more flexibly based financial instruments of today. The interactive approach to marketing requires as much intellectual acumen as the analytical approach, even though there is a shift from conceptual sharpness and rigor (hard, vertical thinking) to fluidity and flexibility of perception (soft, lateral thinking). It is in the context of the deepening relationships, however, to which the Nordic School refers, that a fundamentally new management domain is called into being.

Marketing: the developmental domain

The primal salesman both warms up, and warms to, his customer, responding to his visible wants. It is a personal involvement. The rational marketing manager both provides for, and interacts with, the market-place, generating intangible customer benefits. It is an impersonal involvement. The developmentally minded marketeer becomes intensively involved with his institutional customers, in an interdependent and evolving relationship, responding to their invisible inner needs.

Synergistic marketing

As relationships marketing turns into its synergistic equivalent so the boundaries between supplier and customer are dissolved. The customer, in fact, becomes a coproducer. In Fig. 81, adapted from Evert Gummersson, we can see a range of interactive and synergistic connections between seller and buyers. In some instances, involving joint ventures, the division between the two parties dissolves and in its place there is fusion.

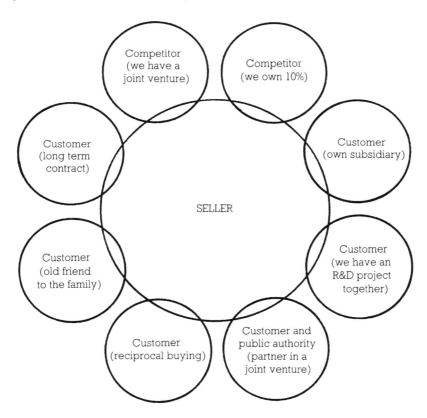

Fig. 81 Interactive and synergistic marketing.

Within these intensive relationships there is both the time and the scope to uncover and fulfill potential needs which were previously invisible, as actual wants. In Mary Parker Follett's terms the meeting of individualities, within an interdependent context, leads to creative opportunities for mutual development. This has, for example, obviously been the case in the intense relationship between Marks & Spencer and Psion Computers (see below) in the UK. New hardware and software, hitherto undeveloped, has been created, out of mutual need.

Evolutionary marketing

The harmonious and interdependent relationship that characterizes synergistic marketing is not an isolated phenomenon. It emerges out of an evolutionary perspective. For, in the same way as a developing individual matures, or, in Maslow's terms, moves towards self-actualization, so a marketing relationship holds such potential. For example, David Potter of Psion started out by packaging games software, on a one-off basis, distributing each product as widely as possible. His primary, and primal concern, was to sell a lot of product, and to generate quick profits. However, once Psion had the time and space to think, it turned its rational attention to matching the knowledge and skills of his growing software house to the evolving needs of the marketplace. Psion's attention turned to more intellectually demanding products.

The process, in fact, is reminiscent of the 'product stretching and proliferation' that Philip Kotler and his colleagues have introduced us to, in *The New Competition*, describing one of the Japanese strategic competencies.[26] No sooner, then, had this

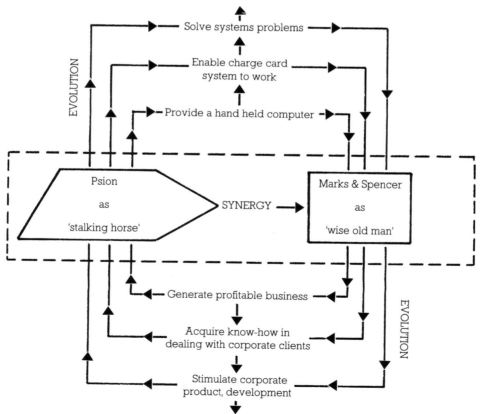

Fig. 82 Evolutionary and synergistic marketing.

intellectual upgrading taken place, than Psion began to become involved in an ongoing relationship with Sinclair Research. They provided the software for Sinclair's hardware. The relationship was interactive, without being synergistic. In other words, it was not a joint venture, involving a genuine fusion of people and ideas. In the Marks & Spencer case, however, such interfusion has taken place (see Fig. 82). Psion has enabled M & S to solve problems, in the course of the retailer's systems development, that neither had previously anticipated.

In the process, as David Potter has said, Psion has acted as a 'stalking horse' for Marks, while Marks has helped Psion become a more professionally run organization. As their interdependence intensifies, moreover, mutual benefits will arise of an increasingly invisible, extensive and long term nature.

Marketing: the metaphysical domain

Tapping the spirit of a nation

Ultimately marketing, at least for Agha Hsan Abedi at BCC, involves bringing together the visible and the invisible. This was the theme of a speech he gave at a recent conference, in China, to a distinguished gathering of marketing and advertising directors from multinational companies, around the world. In the national context Abedi was attempting to harmonize China's current economic pragmatism with the essential nature of its cultural heritage. That, for him, involved tapping the spirit of the world's most populous nation – potentially the largest market-place on this globe.

Marketing is about the glory and grace of mankind

To my mind the practical spirit is, in the deepest sense the only right spirit. To harmonize business life with spiritual life; business practice with spiritual practice; business ideas with spiritual ideas is not merely some cloudy aspiration. It makes hard pragmatic sense.

In my understanding of it, moral complementarity is at the centre of Chinese thought and practice. In the life of business and trade, in the world of marketing and market places, the encounter of man with man, facing each other with mutual respect and regard, and sharing a common pursuit of mutually beneficial regard, and sharing a common pursuit of mutually beneficial exchange – we see a mutuality of feeling and a commonality of satisfied need that forms a small, perfected complimentarity.

Agha Hasan Abedi *Bejing Speech*[27] 1987

For Abedi, and for John Hillbery, BCC's Marketing and Communications Director, there can be no more potent marketing activity than that of tapping the very spirit of a nation. This is what the bank has been attempting to do in China. This is metaphysical marketing.

Exchange and marketing

When you look for a job at a labor exchange, or exchange one piece of computer software for another, you are unlikely to be entering the realms of the metaphysical. However, for Christopher Budd 'exchange', so closely linked with both economics and also marketing, does indeed have far-reaching implications.

The metaphysics of exchange

The great expanses and distant horizons of economic life focus and meet in exchange. Exchange is the absolute distllation of economics and takes place at the moment when man resolves the dichotomy he has created between spirit and nature. Exchange is where production meets consumption ...

Exchange is the human element of economics in the sense that, while production is done for others and consumption for oneself, exchange belongs to neither pole alone. It is neither selfless nor selfish. It is a resolution of the two ...

The stuff of exchange is perception. Regulating the economic life, countering the discrepancy between production and consumption, and thereby allowing the value process to fulfil itself, is a task of perception. The more accurate the perception, the greater its economic value.

Christopher Budd *Prelude in Economics*[28] 1979

As marketing management shifts from the primal to the metaphysical so the degree of abstraction is increased from buying and selling, at the level of the market stall, to the regulation of production and consumption, at the level of a whole industry or economy. Moreover, such regulation is achieved through heightened perception rather than through rational calculation.

The 'hard' attributes of metaphysical marketing, then, involve firstly tapping the spirit of a nation, thereby uncovering a proliferation of need, and secondly creating an awareness of that need amongst the population at large. The 'soft' ones, on the other hand, involve such heightened perception of exchange values that buying and selling activities – across a wide range of products and services – are accelerated due to inspired positioning, promoting and pricing. The product itself (or service), and the production thereof, is what we now have to consider.

Operations

Production and operations management, in America and Great Britain, though not in Japan and West Germany, is the poor relation of the business functions. For on the one hand it is considered too close to engineering to be a business discipline in its own right. On the other hand, it has become too mathematical to be accessible to the average manager or business student. However, the emergence of communications technology, in the past ten years, has given operations management, together with management services (computers and data processing) a new lease of life.

Operations management: the primal domain

Homo faber

Man is a technological animal – hence he is sometimes called *homo faber*, man the maker. Other animals have technologies (beavers construct dams and birds build nests), but only for man are tools a central factor in his existence. In other words, only man has evolved culturally to the point where 'he consciously can alter radically his physical environment and his own biological make up'.[29]

As we saw in Chapter 3, one of the reasons that Britain was the first country to undergo an industrial revolution was its innate (primal) affinity with technology. Such a primal drive, to tinker with physical things and physically to fashion your environment, is more of an innate than an acquired skill. However, skills of craftmanship, with wood or metal, textiles or plastic, can indeed be acquired. Conventionally, however, they lie outside of a business or management curriculum.

Product quality

Craftsmanship
West Germany has a particular strong reputation, today, for craftsmanship, which is reinforced by its solidly based apprenticeship schemes. Production and engineering skill is acquired on the job, backed up by personal example. It is the immediate and tangible experience, at this primal level, reinforced by personal supervision, that counts. Zen Buddhist traditions, in Japan, have had a similar affect on its working population, inculcating a desire for perfection that has been largely absent in America and Britain in recent years.

People-technology

Quality, or its absence, doesn't reside in either the subject or the object. The real ugliness lies in the relationship between the people who produce the technology and the things they produce, which results in a similar relationship between the people who use the technology and the things they use.

Robert Pirsig *Zen and the Art of Motorcycle Maintenance*[30] 1976

Quality circles
The major vehicle, in Japan, for maintaining quality production has been the quality circle. Interestingly enough rationally based techniques for quality control were imported from America after the war, which, combined with primarily Japanese features, were woven into unique form. Kagu Ishikawa, a Japanese production engineer who has written a book on the subject, defines the quality circle as 'a small group, performing quality control activities, voluntarily within the same workshop, carrying on continuously as part of a company-wide program, focussing on mutual development, with all members participating'.[31]
The basic ideas behind quality control, Ishikawa says, involve:

- Contributing to the improvement of the enterprise.
- Building up a worth-living-in, happy and bright workshop.
- Exercising human capacities fully.

Quality management
Ishikawa[32] has an interesting way of looking at management as a whole, which in many ways offers a primal approach to operations management. It contains three aspects:

People. The first concern of management is the happiness of the people who are connected with it. If the people – employees, subcontractors, consumers – do not feel happy, and cannot be made happy, the company does not deserve to exist.

Quality. Secondly, defective products will not only inconvenience consumers but will also hinder sales. If a company makes too many products that cannot be sold, it will waste raw materials and energy. This waste will be a loss for society. A company must always supply products with the qualities the consumer demands.

Price, cost and profit. Thirdly, the consumer's main demand is for a just quality at a just price. No matter how inexpensive a product, if its quality is poor no one will buy it.

Operations management: the rational domain

Operating systems

Although Ishikawa has partially begun to move into the rational domain, once we wholly get there, the tone changes completely. As probably the best known professor of operations management in the UK, Ray Wild, puts it: 'an operating system is a configuration of resources combined for the provision of goods or services.'[33]

The nature of operating systems

Bus and taxi services, motels and dentists, tailors and mines, fire services and refuse removers, retail organizations, hospitals and building contractors are all operating systems. They all, in effect, convert inputs in order to provide outputs that are required by a customer.

Physical inputs will normally predominate, hence: operating systems convert, using physical resources, to create outputs, the function of which is to satisfy consumer wants, that is to provide some utility for the customer.

Ray Wild *Essentials of Production and Operations Management*[34] 1980

The bulk of any operations management text will contain mathematical and statistical techniques for such functions as facilities location and material handling, work study and measurement, activity and project scheduling, and inventory control. However, there is a rationally based and qualitative logic that underlies it all. This can be divided between overall function and structure.

Function of operating systems
Four principal functions can be identified:

- Manufacture, whereby something is physically created. Process or mass production involves the continuous manufacture of a commodity in bulk. Batch production occurs where the number of discrete items to be manufactured is insufficient to enable mass production to be used. Finally jobbing manufacture is intermittent.
- Transport, through which the location of someone or something is physically moved, within or without the organization.
- Supply, through which the ownership or possession of an item is physically changed.
- Service, whereby – as in a dentist, launderette, or welfare department – something or someone is treated or accommodated.

Structure of operating systems

The nature of the operations manager's job will to some extent depend on the nature of the system he is managing, albeit in a rational context. All such systems may be seen to comprise inputs, processes and outputs.

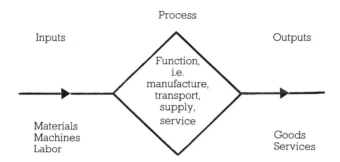

Fig. 83 A simple operations system.

This basic analytical model (see Fig. 83) underlies the 'hard' and rational approach to operations management. In the last five years, in the wake of what the late Bill Abernathy at Harvard called an 'Industrial Renaissance', in America, a softer approach has emerged.

The technology of learning

Abernathy, and his production-minded colleagues at the Harvard Business School, have called for the kind of renaissance in manufacturing technology that effectively 'de-matures' such large and mature companies as General Motors and General Electric. With a different view of maturity from the one adopted in this text, Abernathy calls for technology based revitalization of large-scale manufacturing enterprise. In the process he exposes the limitations of the conventionally analytic approach to operations management.

The possibilities of de-maturity

Our task today is to incorporate particular new technologies and heightened product variety into high volume manufacturing systems and to do so without the luxury of long lead times.

What is therefore needed is a view of production as an enterprise of unlimited potential, an enterprise in which current arrangements (as those set out above by Wild) are but the starting point for continuous organizational learning. No omniscient engineer ever handed down a design for product or production that could not stand improvement.

We do not mean, of course, that learning should proceed while schedules and shipping deadlines get ignored; competent management requires simultaneous attention to both current tasks and future possibilities. What gets lost in the shuffle, however, is the intimate connection between the two.

Only when grafted on to a production system dedicated to ongoing learning and communication, only when used in tandem with a skilled and responsible workforce, can new technologies realize their potential as competitive weapons. Only when such a workforce is truly engaged in the enterprise and encouraged to learn and excel, can a company hope to introduce competitively successful new products in a timely fashion.

Abernathy, Clark and Kantrow *Industrial Renaissance*[35] 1983

The 'Industrial Renaissance' takes America, if not other nations, a long way from the world of machines, materials and labor towards one where it is 'human capital',[36] mediated through information technology, that will make the difference between success and failure. In fact Koji Kobayashi, Chairman of the Japanese semiconductor company, NEC, makes a similar point.[37]

In order to respond to the shift from mass orientation toward product diversity and individuality, and to meet a wider variety of customer needs, he says, very large amounts of information will need to be generated. The transfer and processing of the information, moreover, will be done at the plant. And if sudden changes in the market occur, it will be necessary to rapidly adjust the design and manufacture of products accordingly. Computer and communications technology has already begun to be the basis of such manufacturing, and as it evolves the sophistication of manufacturing will grow.

Economies of scope

A new vocabulary has emerged. Programmable automation permits an automated machine to perform a range of tasks. This permits a single range of equipment to produce a variety of components or to assemble a variety of products, creating flexibility. Economies of scope stand alongside economies of scale.

Cohen and Zysman *Manufacturing Matters*[38] 1987

The argument is taken a step further, into the developmental domain, by two technologists from Berkeley, California.

Operations management: the developmental domain

Evolutionary operations

In a recent and illuminating book Cohen and Zysman argue *'manufacturing matters'* in a way that simplistic arguments about post-industrial societies fail to reveal. For them, services are not a substitute, or successor, for manufacturing. One needs the other. The process of development is not one of sectoral succession but instead it is one of increased sectoral interdependence, driven by an ever more extended and complex division of labor. Manufacturing, in days gone by, was conducted by individual craftsmen, or by small groups of workers, engaged in cottage industries. This was the era of primal production. For the last hundred years, though, in industrialized countries, mass production has taken over as the rationally dominant mode. It is only recently, with the advent of flexible manufacturing systems facilitated by the microprocessor revolution, that this stable model is being overturned.

Interdependent operations

As manufacturing enters the developmental domain so the acknowledged interdependence between manufacturing and services, as well as between one manufacturing sector and another, becomes commonplace. In fact technological innovation depends on a series of subtle and complex interconnections. Knowledge of auto manufacturing, for example, or of airplane manufacturing, promotes innovation in machine tools. The French, in the early eighties, used the word *filiere* to refer to the fact that there are critical interrelations in pieces of the economy.

The more advanced or modern the production process, the longer and more complicated the chains of linkages. 'A primitive farmer has his wife scratch the ground with a stick. He also has a very low productivity. A modern American farmer is really the pivot man in a long, elaborate chain of specialists. Everything is linked to everything else, in a way that is similar to – but surely different from – the Hare Krishna view that everything is one.'[39]

Operations management: the metaphysical domain

The noosphere

It was the French biologist, Catholic theologian and worldly philosopher, Teillard De Chardin (see p. 489) who came up with the term 'noosphere'. Like the atmosphere or my businessphere, the noosphere encompasses the entire globe, but, in its turn, represents the totality of cultural expression, both artistic and technological, known to man. For De Chardin, then, our evolving technological base is becoming ever more metaphysical.

Spiritualized technology

We may be reassured. The vast industrial and social system in which we are enveloped does not threaten to crush us, neither does it seek to rob us of our soul. The energy emanating from it is free not only in the sense that it represents forces that can be used; it is moreover free because, in the whole no less than in the least of its elements, it arises in a state that is ever more spiritualised.

Teillard de Chardin *The Future of Man*[40] 1977

De Chardin's view is not an isolated one. Folkert Wilken, the German economist, comes to similar conclusions. If you look at the working activity of a given individual, he says, you find that it is made up of three elements, each of which can be – and increasingly is – substituted by technology:

- Every job develops out of a mental perception and conceptualisation of the purpose that it is to achieve. This is arrived at by planning. Such purely intellectual work can largely be handled by microprocessors and computers.
- The working process itself consists of the forming or shaping of all sorts of material. This activity is directly assisted by tools.
- Every job is helped by auxiliary energy that is harnessed and channelled through technology.

This seemingly inevitable process of technological substitution is not only economically driven, but also spiritually. 'We should understand that people confined in the material world have to find fulfillment in the inner yearning to raise themselves above it.'[41]

Providing evidence from the Old Testament, Wilken indicates that, after Cain, Jabal–Cain invented house building and cattle raising; Thubal–Cain established the craft of metal work; and Jubal–Cain converted inert matter into a means of artistic creation, with his invention of the violin and flute. All of this moved in the direction of transcending the purely physical content of the work.

A philosophy of industry

Strangely enough this kind of industrial and technological perspective was one shared, at least in part, by the first Henry Ford. The fact that Ford's reputation as a technological innovator was marred by his despotic, and sometimes even bigoted, character, should not deter us from appreciating his unique philosophy of industry.

At least part of the man – for Henry Ford was a hugely paradoxical character – was steeped in a metaphysical world that underpinned his technological breakthroughs. 'The function of the machine is to liberate man from brute burdens, and release his energies to the building of his intellectual and spiritual powers for conquests in the field of thought and higher action. The machine is the symbol of man's mastery of his environment.[42] For Henry Ford, then, who created the automobile industry as we know it today, industrial advancement was not some depersonalized, technocratic process, but the realization of an individual's vision.

Technological vision

Every advancement begins in a small way and with the individual. The mass can be no better than the sum of the individuals. Advancement begins with the man himself, when he advances from half interest to strength of purpose; when he advances from hesitancy to decisive directness; when he advances from an immaturity to a maturity of judgement; when he advances from apprenticeship to mastery; when he advances from a mere dilettante at labor to a worker who finds a genuine joy in work, why then the world advances.

As far as individual, personal advantage is concerned, vast accumulations of money mean nothing. But if one has visions of service, if one has vast plans which no ordinary resources would possibly realize, if one has a life ambition to make the industrial desert bloom like the rose, and the work-a-day life suddenly blossoms into fresh and enthusiastic motives of higher character and efficiency, then one sees in large sums of money what the farmer sees in his seed corn – the beginning of new and richer harvests whose benefits can no more be contained than the sun's rays.

Henry Ford *My Life and Work*[43] 1924

As operations management, like the financial and marketing functions, evolve then, they become less concerned with the immediate and primal, and more with the remote and metaphysical. The same applies, finally, to human resources.

Human resources

Elements of the human resource function first began to appear in Europe and America, at the turn of the century, in reaction to the harsh behavior of autocratic businessman like Henry Ford! It was not until the forties and fifties, though, like most of the business disciplines, that it began to acquire fuller shape and form. In fact, due to its peculiar origins – a reaction against unscrupulous entrepreneurial behavior – 'Personnel' missed out on its primal origins. It has been suffering ever since, relative to the other major functions, from a lack of power and influence. It is only in the 1980s, swept along by the powerfully primal wave, that a more instinctive (less intellectual) approach to managing people has been widely documented and disseminated.

Human resources: the primal domain

In 1964, Collins and his fellow sociologists at the University of Michigan,[44] concluded that entrepreneurship involves, most essentially, 'the bringing together of people into new and profitable combinations'. Although the book, *Enterprising Man*, that they wrote was a classic, in its time, it completely by passed the human resource establishment.

It was not until the redoubtable Peters and Waterman[45] appeared on the primal scene, almost twenty years later, that the penny began to drop. 'Business is people', either in the shape of employees or as customers and suppliers. That was the primal conclusion. There was both a tough and a tender approach to this argument.

Winning friends and influencing people

The tough and 'macho' approach to influencing people was in fact introduced to us many years ago by the American doyen of public speaking, Dale Carnegie. Although his book *Winning Friends and Influencing People*,[46] is not normally incorporated into a management curriculum, it is a classic in its own right. More recently, though, the prolific sports promoter, Mark McCormack, has written the definitive, primal antidote to the rationally based management of human resources. As we noted in Chapter 8, its appropriate title is *What they Don't Teach You at Harvard Business School*. For McCormack, in truly primal vein, the management of people, as insiders or as outsiders, involves the same basic approach.

> Whether I'm selling or buying; whether I'm hiring or being hired; whether I'm negotiating a contract or responding to someone else's demands, I want to know where the other person is coming from. I want to know the other person's real self.[47]

Of course McCormack is merely putting into words what thousands of entrepreneurs around the globe may have been thinking for centuries. However, not only has he taken the trouble to articulate his thoughts so that they now become codified knowledge, but his focus on the self gives it a particular Western and Northern flavor. It is also important to point out that the tough and primally oriented McCormack is naturally self-interested. He is neither philanthropic nor is he paternalistic. He is a businessman who knows that business is people. He is also a man.

P&L is for profit and love

It is interesting to note that business entrepreneurs have traditionally been viewed as men, and thus in some cases paternalistic. Yet Mary Kay in America has developed a $300 million cosmetics company in thoroughly maternal fashion (see Chapter 9). We also know that Nigerian market women exercise a great levelling influence on economic life (see p. 147).

Profit and love

No matter how much profit a company makes if it doesn't enrich the lives of its people it will have failed.

To me P&L doesn't only mean profit and loss – it also means people and love.

When all our people come to understand one another, a familylike atmosphere remains intact and the customer is better served.

The most important justification for being in business is to fulfill a need.

Mary Kay *On Managing People*[48] 1985

For Mary Kay, who had no need of a personnel manager, idealism and realism go hand in hand. For the genuine animateur the source and destination of business is people – both within the company and out in the market-place. For her it is the tender side of people management that takes hold.

Ironically many human resource managers are not innately 'people people'. The reason is that they are cut off from their primal selves. Having acknowledged that heritage, via such influential practitioners as Mark McCormack and Mary Kay, they are in a more powerful position in moving on to the rational domain.

Human resources: the rational domain

As businesses grew in size and scope, during the early part of the twentieth century, entrepreneurs or even animateurs were no longer able to cope on their own. While some fell by the wayside others were astute enough to take on 'scientific' advice. The evolution of a rationally based, personnel function can be traced historically. It develops similarly with the growth and evolution of an individual firm.

Again, the development of a rational approach to human resource management can be divided into harder and softer orientations: respectively analytical and behavioural. The first we term 'human resource management' and the second the 'management of change'. I shall now describe the onset of each.

Human resource management

Bureaucracy

In the early days of management's evolution, attempts to rationalize production and organization were tentative and *ad hoc*. However in the first decades of the twentieth century, businessman did come under the influence of engineers. Such 'social engineers' sought to substitute rational, 'scientific management' for the highly personalized, idiosyncratic style of the owner manager.

Some of the earliest efforts at substituting rational procedures for intuition and family traditions simply involved better record keeping, for which purpose many personnel departments were first established. Personnel records indicated such information as when the employee was hired, educational background, succession of jobs, and provided a record of time and production for payrolls. These were relatively routine clerical tasks.

This concern with methods was one precursor of personnel's concern today with training. It also represented an irrevocable and powerful drive towards increasing specialization.

Industrial psychology

In the last years of the 1920s rationalization and efficiency were the watchwords. The need to rationalize production arose from the new kinds of problems created by competition and demand, and from inventions in machinery and techniques.

Many jobs were broken down. In order to rationalize manufacture combines were formed and amalgamations took place. Planning and efficiency in all aspects of a business became essential. Rationalization brought complexity with it. Selection assumed increasing importance during the 1920s because of the requirements of efficiency and the demands of complexity.

As a result of government experience of classifying recruits during the First World War, psychologists were brought into industry to help pick out the most able workers. They developed testing techniques for assessing individual differences, and personnel began concentrating on selection methods.

Industrial relations

The influence of personnel expanded during the 1930s and 1940s. With their title changed to Industrial Relations many personnel departments began to take charge of hiring, firing, wage determination, handling union grievances and deciding who should be transferred and promoted.

The personnel department suddenly gained so much power, partly because of management's widespread recognition of the importance of the human element, but chiefly because of the threat of unionism. Personnel managers were now called upon to be negotiators, drawing on tough primal qualities of stamina and risk taking. Unfortunately, though, the industrial relations manager's foe was not the external competition but the internal labor force.

Professionalization

By the end of the Second World War the functions of a personnel department could be clearly differentiated between employment, wages, joint consultation, health and safety, and education and training. By 1939 the perception of the range of personnel activities was fairly clear to the boards of larger, more highly organized companies, but the specialist sectors of the work were not always well coordinated.

However, all this resulted in a much fuller functioning of human resource management. Within a few years half a dozen of its component parts were distinguished, each with its own theory forming behind it and its own skills being defined. Recruitment, training, performance appraisal, industrial relations and personnel administration each became subdisciplines in their own right. As a profession 'human resource management' was coming of age.

The management of change

Human relatons

Human resource management, by the fifties and sixties, was seen to be relevant to the whole work situation, to the interrelationship between the work to be done, the individuals and the groups carrying it out, and the environment in which the whole activity took place.

A new phase of professionalism began in the middle 1950s, with specialists developing in depth certain elements of personnel management, and identifying new approaches with the help of the social sciences. Of course, the application of sociology, as well as psychology, to the management of organizations, had been initiated by Mary Parker Follett,[49] by Elton Mayo[50] and by Chester Barnard[51] – all in America – in the twenties and thirties.

Towards organization development: the planning of change
The origins of what came to be called 'organization development' lie in the 1950s, when the then director of the UK Institute of Personnel Management was beginning to identify two distinct aspects of the personnel function.

> 'On the one hand', he said at a European Personnel Conference in 1956, 'there are the processes of analyzing the existing conditions and resources in the light of the requirements of the enterprise, of diagnosing and defining its problems, of prescribing and executing the appropriate action to bring about change. This may be regarded as a predominantly creative and dynamic aspect.
> 'On the other hand there are the routine administrative duties involved in the execution of established policy, the solution of minor problems as they occur, the maintenance of healthy relationships, and the provision of personnel services'.

As Warren Bennis said, in the sixties: 'Bureaucracy was a monumental discovery for harnessing muscle power via guilt and instinctual renunciation. In today's world it is a prosthetic device, no longer useful. For we now require organic/adaptive systems, as structures of freedom, to permit the expression of play and imagination and to exploit the new pleasure of work.'[52]

Some large companies, like Texas Instruments in the United States, and ICI in Britain, tried to introduce Bennis' ideas in the sixties and seventies. However, those early attempts were often only half-hearted, partly because organization development had not yet come of age.

In the meanwhile, and during the seventies, there was some very interesting developmental work going on in Holland, led by the social psychologist Bernard Lievegoed. His book *The Developing Organization*[53] has influenced many people since that time including myself. For Lievegoed has a much more thorough understanding of development than his better-known American counterparts.

Human resources: the developmental domain

We glibly talk about personal, organization or business development and yet few of us are familiar with the intrinsic nature of it. Development is qualitative, discontinuous, irreversible, interspersed with evolutionary crises and dynamically balanced. As a good human resource manager, and organization developer, you need to be able consciously to work within such an evolutionary framework. Such an approach leads in two directions, one vertically toward manager self-development, and the other, horizontally towards organizational harmony.

Manager self-development

Particularly in Britain, today, the subject of manager self-development has become very popular in personnel circles. In most cases, however, no more than lip service is paid to development. The idea that a manager should take responsibility for his own learning is built in, but no conscious path of development is established. On the other hand, an evolutionary perspective was built into Abraham Maslow's work, some twenty years ago, when he traced a personal and managerial path towards self-actualization,[54] through an hierarchy of needs. More recently Daniel Levinson, in *The Seasons of Man's Life*,[55] has indicated that we evolve through alternating structure-building and structure-changing phases, during our life span.

In my own work *Intrapreneurship*[56] I have related seven kinds of individuality to the four structure-building phases – youth, adulthood, midlife and maturity. Each intrapreneur or individual manager, in the terms of this text, develops in a unique way, but passes through similar phases and transitions.

Organizational harmony

A developing organization, then, not only consciously enables the individuals within it to evolve, but also evolves, in itself, and as a whole. Vertical development, whereby one stage is interwoven with the other, over time, is accompanied by horizontal development, whereby one part of the organization is interwoven with the other, across space. In fact, during such integration the protective membranes, isolating one function or business from the other, are broken down and reformed into open filters. An exchange of energy between personnel and marketing, or between human resources and information technology, thus becomes possible. Each becomes a part of a continually re-emerging whole. This horizontal, developmental perspective has been made to work most successfully in Japan. Japan's ability to interweave individual and group, group and organization, and public and private enterprise, as well as interrelate large companies and small ones, banks and manufacturers, and finally industrial and trading companies, is all part of the same harmonious phenomenon.

Japanese harmony

One's sense of self is enhanced by being selected to join a group, and the standing of that group is enhanced by its ability to attract individuals of quality and achievement.

Once taken in, however, powerful sanctions – of which the threat of ostracism is only the most severe – are brought to bear on the individual, who is expected to pursue personal interests only to the extent that the other members of the group agree that such a course does not contravene principles of harmony and effectiveness.

Robert Smith *Japanese Society*[57] 1983

The management of human resources, outside of Japan, has yet to reach a point where it truly harmonizes with the other disciplines. To that extent the rational domain, recently counterbalanced by the primal one, eclipses the developmental domain, notwithstanding claims that might indicate otherwise. In fact, despite the fact that organization development has never really had its day, 'organizational transformation' has now arrived on the American scene.

Human resources: the metaphysical

In America a whole new school of thought has developed, around corporate culture, focussing on organizational transformation (OT) as opposed to organization development (OD). The focus of this new thinking is not on individuals and groups but on myths and rituals, emerging out of the historical depths of an organization's being. The emergence of corporate culture,[58] as a new field of management concern, and of 'spirit' as an area with which to be concerned, is a reflection of this metaphysical aspect of personnel management.

Organizational transformation

Myths are the stories of a group's culture which describe its beginning, continuance and ultimate goals. These stories are so much part of that fabric as to define that fabric and institution. To know the myth is to know the institution in a way that balance sheets and organization charts can never report.

I view ritual as the dramatic re-enactment of a myth. In a ritual, the groups acts out the central stories in such a way that the members experience really being there and participating in the original event.

The role of myths and rituals in organization transformation is critical, for they shape and form the culture, which in turn provides the power, purpose and values of the organization.

The focus of development in the high performing frame of reference is on continuing transformation and renewal.

Harrison Owen *Spirit, Transformation and Development in Organizations*[59] 1987

Corporate culture

As a topical subject, within business circles in Europe and America, corporate culture has displaced management style and organizational behavior, as the prevailing soft side of concern to human resource managers. The language of myth and ritual, of beliefs and values, and of stories and heroism, has taken over from the more rationally based 'interpersonal' or 'socio-technical processes'. The focus on symbolic management, and on the spirit of the organization, has provided the metaphysical overtones.

Organization transformation

The process of transformation, then, supersedes that of enterprise, strategy of development, as the source of cut and thrust at this metaphysical stage. Such a process is of epic, and heroic proportions, as indicated in Chapter 27. It is the stuff of which visions are created, and realized. It carries with it emotional, as well as intellectual and behavioral overtones.

The human resource manager, then, as an agent of social and psychological transformation, joins forces with those marketing, financial and operations managers engaged in technological and commercial transformation. While he or she enables the spirit of the place to be transformed, they revolutionize the material base of the operation.

Conclusion

Functional evolution

Financial, marketing, operations and human resource management each occupy all four of the management domains, potentially if not actually. To the extent that the potential has not yet been actualized so, as in the case of management in general, each quarter of the globe has not yet fully asserted itself commercially, organizationally and most specifically here, functionally.

As a result the developmental and metaphysical domains, in particular, need to evolve. Theory is in fact falling behind practice. Moreover, where a function like 'human resource management' has evolved in isolation – from primal McCormack to metaphysical Owen – it remains relatively inhibited. Organizational transformation, for example, has little hope of accomplishing its purposes apart from the transformation of operations, marketing, and finance. In other words, Harrison Owen (human resources), Henry Ford (operations), Christopher Budd (marketing), and Napoleon Hill (finance) need to draw off one another. Whereas the rational, and more recently primal functions have generally evolved in parallel, the same cannot be said for the other two domains.

Moreover, at every point, the 'hard' approach has superseded the 'soft'. Interestingly enough, it is the soft approach which facilitates structure changing, in Levinson's terms, whereas the hard one facilitates structure building.

Business policy and strategy

The same applies to the whole area of business policy and strategy, as can be inferred from Chapter 17. The hard and rational approaches of Igor Ansoff[60] and George Steiner,[61] recently infused with tough primal dosages from Michael Porter,[62] have continued to reign supreme. Developmental and metaphysical inroads, at least as far as strategic theory is concerned, are yet to be made.

The result is that whereas functional integration has recently been attempted, by Peters and Waterman, at the primal level, and – over the last twenty years – by the business strategists at a rational level, there is no further integration of the functions. No wonder so many business and organizational departments remain segregated from one another.

Functional reconstruction

However, as we have seen from this concluding chapter, the building blocks are there for a thorough reconstruction of the business functions. Such a reconstruction can only come through processes of personal and cultural, as well as business and managerial reorientation. We need to rediscover and recombine soft and hard within ourselves, youthful and mature within our businesses, as well as East and West, North and South within our cultures. I can only hope that, through the global management principles developed in this text, a start has been made for the business functions in general, and for the management of organizations in particular.

References

1. N. Hill, *Think and Grow Rich*, Fawcett (1960)*.
2. T. Gillies, *Moneylove*, Warner Books (1978), p. 23.
3. M. Kay, *Mary Kay*, Harper & Row (1987)*, p. 8.
4. P. Kotler, Fahy and Jatiesripitak, *The New Competition*, Prentice Hall (1986).
5. W. Bigg, H. Wilson, and A. Langton, *Bookkeeping and Accounts*, HFC, London (1963), p. 19.
6. W. Wriston, quoted in Hamilton, *op.cit.* (below), p. 31.
7. A. Hamilton, *The Financial Revolution*, Viking (1986)*, pp. 15–54.
8. C. Budd, *Prelude in Economics*, privately published (1979)*.
9. M. Parker Follett, *The New State*, Peter Smith (1929).
10. K. Ohmae, *Triad Power*, Macmillan (1985).
11. R. Lessem, 'Accounting for an enterprises' wellbeing', *Omega*, Vol. 2, No. 1 (1974).
12. J. Dauman, and J. Hargreaves, *Business Survival and Social Change*, Associated Business Programmes (1975), prt 4.
13. N. Hill, *op.cit.*, p. 238.
14. R. Steiner, *The World Economy*, Rudolph Steiner Press (1936), p. 51.
15. R. Steiner, *op.cit.*, p. 93.
16. P. Drucker, *Management*, Pan (1979)*, p. 67.
17. J. Chaput, *Living is Selling*, Habitex Books (1975).
18. H. Turner, *The Gentle Art of Salesmanship,* Fontana (1985), p. 137.
19. H. Goldman, *How to Win Customers*, Pan (1971)*, p. 173.
20. H. Turner, *op.cit.*, p. 140.
21. P. Kotler, *Marketing Management: Analysis, Planning and Control*, Prentice Hall (1968).
22. J. McCarthy, *Basic Marketing: a Managerial Approach*, Irwin (1968), p. 22.
23. B. Lievegoed, *The Developing Organization*, Celestial Arts (1980), p. 12.
24. E. Gummerson, 'The new marketing', *Long Range Planning,* * Vol. 20, no. 4 (1987), p. 11.
25. D. Ford, H. Wakannan, and D. Johnson, 'How do companies interact?' *Industrial Marketing and Purchasing*, Vol. 1, no. 1 (1986).
26. P. Kotler, *et al.*, *The New Competition*, Prentice Hall (1985).
27. A. Abedi, 'Marketing is about the glory and grace of mankind', *BCCI Magazine*, 38 (July 1987).
28. C. Budd, *op.cit.*, p. 55.
29. V. Ferkis, *Technological Man*, Heinemann (1969), p. 27.
30. R. Pirsig, *Zen and the Art of Motorcycle Maintenance*, Corgi (1976), p. 284.
31. K. Ishikawa, *What is Total Quality Control?*, Prentice Hall (1985), p. 139–40.
32. K. Ishikawa, *op.cit.*, pp. 99–100.
33. R. Wild, *Essentials of Production and Operations Management*, Holt Business Texts (1980), p. 3.
34. R. Wild, *op.cit.*, p. 3.
35. W. Abernathy, K. Clark, and A. Kantrow, *Industrial Renaissance*, Basic Books (1983), p. 125.
36. R. Reich, *The Next American Frontier*, Penguin (1984)*.
37. Quoted in S. Cohen, and J. Zysman, *op.cit.*, (below), p. 179.
38. S. Cohen and J. Zysman, *Manufacturing Matters*, Basic Books (1987), p. 156.
39. S. Cohen and J. Zysman, *op.cit.*, p. 14.
40. T. De Chardin, *The Future of Man*, Fontana (1977), p. 190.
41. F. Wilken, *op.cit.*, p. 7.
42. H. Ford, *My Philosophy of Industry*, Harrap (1929), p. 167.
43. H. Ford, *My Life and Work*, Heinemann (1924), pp. 277–79.
44. Collins, Moore and Umwalla, *Enterprising Man*, University of Michigan (1964)*.
45. Peters and Waterman, *In Search of Excellence*, Harper & Row (1982)*.
46. D. Carnegie, *Winning Friends and Influencing People*, 2nd edn, Heinemann (1986).
47. M. McCormack, *What They Don't Teach You at Harvard Business School*, Collins (1984), p. 15.
48. M. Kay, *On Managing People*, Pan (1985).
49. M. Parker Follett, *The New State*, Peter Smith (1929).
50. E. Mayo, *The Human Problems of an Industrial Civilisation*, Macmillan (1953).
51. C. Barnard, *The Functions of the Executive*, Harvard University Press (1938).
52. W. Bennis, *Changing Organizations*, McGraw Hill (1966).
53. B. Lievegoed, *op.cit.*
54. A. Maslow, *Motivation and Personality*, Harper & Row (1964)*.
55. D. Levinson, *The Seasons of Man's Life*, Knopf (1978).
56. R. Lessem, *Intrapreneurship*, Wildwood House (1988).
57. R. Smith, *Japanese Society*, Cambridge University Press (1983), p. 90.
58. T. Deal and A. Kennedy, *Corporate Cultures* Addison Wesley (1983)*.

59. H. Owen, *Spirit, Transformation and Development in Organizations*, Abbott Publishing (1987).
60. I. Ansoff, *Corporate Strategy*, McGraw Hill (1964)*.
61. G. Steiner, *Top Management Planning*, Macmillan (1969).
62. M. Porter, *Competitive Strategy*, Macmillan (1982)*.

* Important references

35 Managing difference

Introduction

Differentiation

This has been a book about variety rather than uniformity in management. It has been based on the spatial differentiation between national cultures, and between individual personalities, and on the temporal differences between life phases, and between organizational stages.

These variations in personal and cultural space, and in individual and organizational time, serve to differentiate the four management domains. The implication, therefore, is that the domain of management you will inhabit at a particular point of time depends on your personality and culture, on the one hand, and on the phase of your individual organizational development, on the other.

Integration

The question that remains is how, once the domains have been divided up from one another, can they be reintegrated within a dynamically evolving whole? For living reality, both spatially and temporarily, is ultimately whole rather than in parts. The key to such integration lies within that alternating current between the soft and hard edges of management.

Planning and love

Where planning, the masculine element, aims at stabilization which in turn makes it possible to act out power or focussed energy, love, the feminine element, introduces the instabilities which elevate the plane of human action to ever new dynamic regimes, thereby ensuring the continuously renewed conditions for human creativity, and for the life of human systems.

Erich Jantsch *Design for Evolution*[1] 1975

Whereas hardness provides the underlying structure that stabilizes a particular domain, softness provides the ongoing flow, that connects one domain with another, in both space and time. In Daniel Levinson's terms (see Chapter 22), hardness provides the structure building materials, and softness the structure changing ones. Moreover, if this alternating current breaks down, development will be inhibited.

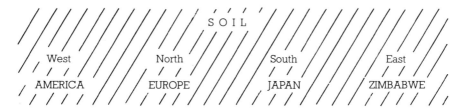

Fig. 84 The global management soil.

In this concluding chapter, therefore, I shall relate these processes of differentiation and integration to the underlying soil, to the roots, to the core, to the branches and to the foliage and fruits of globally based management.

The global management soil

Differentiation

Spatial and regional
The theory and practice of business management has emerged, particularly over the past one hundred years, from Europe, in the North, and from the United States, in the West. In the last twenty years new management concepts and applications have emerged from the East, specifically from Japan. What is still missing is any explicit management theory developed in the South. (See Fig. 84.) Furthermore, major economic zones in the North and East, like Russia, India and China, have not yet come up with their indigenously based and differentiable concepts.

Temporal and historial
The earliest form of management was that carried out by prehistoric hunter–gatherer communities. In fact, the term economics was derived from the Ancient Greek word *oikos*, which means household. Such household or communal management survives to this day in the home, and in the rural areas within the developing countries.

However, in scale and visibility, it was overtaken by the military, civil and religious bureaucracies of Egypt, China and Rome – in antiquity – and of feudal Europe and Japan – in the Middle Ages. The hunting instinct was upgraded and transformed, in modern times, into the spirit of free enterprise, and the feudal bureaucracies were similarly converted into large-scale business organizations, managed efficiently and effectively.

In the 1980s the differentiation between enterprise and bureaucracy, on the one hand, and between intrapreneurial and harmonious organizations, on the other, has emerged as a new point of focus, stimulated particularly by the rivalry between America and Japan.

Integration

Spatial and regional
Each part of the globe is likely to have to reconcile its own managerial dilemma, between

alternately hard and soft forces, if it is to unlock its indigenous economic potential. For the West this involves reconciling enterprise, the personal frontier spirit, and community, the family melting pot. For the North this means reconciling order, the collective rule of law, and freedom, individual self-expression.

For the East this entails reconciling adaptation, or selective imitation, with harmony, general cohesion. For the South finally, and rather speculatively, this may mean reconciling vision, the capacity to dream, with reality, the closeness to nature. Each part of the globe, then, has to establish its own particular alternating current of hard and soft forces. These forces need to be drawn from indigenous soils. Unfortunately, and particularly in developing countries, this approach has not been sufficiently adopted.

To the extent, moreover, that any one region fails to contribute to the economic whole, the global economy suffers. This is becoming particularly apparent in the eighties, as international economic interdependence – between East and West, and between North and South – become ever more apparent. Trade imbalances, debt crises, and breakdowns in cultural understanding all inhibit global business and management development.

Temporal and historical

I have already indicated that the management heritage reaches back to hunter–gatherer communities. In fact, while the hunting instinct was subsequently built into entrepreneurship, the gatherer got left behind. The hard aggressive instinct eclipsed the soft and nurturing one, in business in the North and West, for hundreds of years. It was left to the Japanese, in the sixties and seventies, to demonstrate how soft communal soils could enrich business enterprise. Subsequently the Americans, in search of excellence, rediscovered their shared business and cultural values.

The Europeans, in recent years, have failed to draw sufficiently on their alternate cultural heritage. In other words they have secured a reputation for order, to the point of stodginess in business, without fully developing their capacity for individual self-expression. They have been weighed down by their bureaucratic heritage, insufficiently lightened, in business, by their democratic traditions.

The developing countries, in their turn, have not yet been able to grow into themselves,

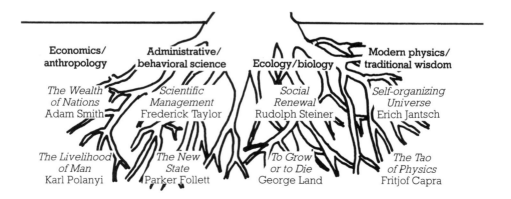

Fig. 85 Global management roots.

through themselves. In effect, they have managed, inadequately, to absorb new structures into their old traditions. Instead smatterings of modernity have overturned their richness of heritage, so that they have often ended up with the worst of both worlds.

In all these cases, and in different contexts, nations and economies have emerged in an imbalanced way. The result is that none have been able to tap the full richness of their indigenous soils, while also soaking in the nutriments from the, as it were, global biosphere. To the extent that they have succeeded, most notably in the case of Japan today, so they have been able to exercise their historical role in the world's economic evolution.

Global management roots

Differentiation

Spatial and disciplinary

Anthropology and economics
The disciplines in which management is rooted are widespread. (See Fig. 85.) Its true academic origins, for me, lie not in concepts of administration, but in anthropology and in economics. For the hunting band was the first managed group, and the village community was the first, elaborated organization. Barter and trade, at the same time, is as old as the hills, but it was only in the seventeenth century that it first began to be conceptualized into a body of economic theory. At that point a theory of enterprise, both relevant to the individual firm and to the economy at large, was spelt out.

Administrative and behavioral science
If the most deeply set roots of management are imbedded in anthropology – soft and pervasive, and economics – hard and penetrating, the most commonly acknowledged ones are represented by the administrative and behavioral sciences. The tradition of scientific management, reflected in the work of Taylor in America, Fayol in France and Weber in Germany, in fact reaches back to the bureaucracies of antiquity. The behavioral tradition, which emerged in the twenties as a reaction against the hardness, and impersonality of administration, was developed by such concerned Anglo Americans as Elton Mayo and Mary Parker Follett.

Biology and ecology
These primal (anthropology and political economy) and rational roots (administrative and behavioral science) underpin popular (primal) and conventional (rational) management wisdom in Europe and America. However previously hidden roots are emerging, ones which are not yet firmly set, but which are likely to become the source of organizational renewal. These draw generally from biology and ecology, and specifically from the American biologist George Land and from the Austrian social ecologist, Rudolph Steiner.

These roots contain within them the blueprint, as it were, for growth and development in association with surrounding business organisms.

Modern physics and ancient wisdom

Finally, and most tenuously, there are roots that are more latent than manifest, lodged in the unlikely realms of modern physics and traditional wisdom. In a management context these have been uniquely tapped by the late Erich Jantsch, the contemporary Swiss physicist, philosopher and corporate planner, who took a particular interest in what he called 'the self-organizing universe'. The new physicists, amazingly enough in tune with ancient philosophers across the globe, are discovering a continuum linking mind and matter that has significant, 'metaphysical' implications for global management.

Temporal and historical

Anthropology and economics

In terms of our stages of historical development, the academic disciplines in which management is widely rooted are at disparate points. Anthropology is still in its youth. It is only with the advent of 'corporate culture' in the eighties that managers, and management academics, are taking it at all seriously.

Economics, in its turn, has entered late adulthood and stopped. It has retained and substantiated its conventional wisdom, but in the process has lost much of its youthful, and primal vigor, and has not yet entered midlife or maturity. Ironically, it was Rudolph Steiner, in the twenties, who developed economic theory into midlife and towards maturity, but he has been totally ignored by the economic establishment. As a result microeconomics (the economics of the firm) has largely lost its relevance to both pioneering and developing enterprise today.

Administrative and behavioral science

Administrative science, having entered its youthful phase with Max Weber and with the American railroad engineers, has emerged into late adulthood within the business and academic establishment. It has been finely differentiated and integrated.

Moreover, in the last twenty years, what with the emergence of Charles Handy's thinking on task-based, and dispersed organizations in Britain, administrative science has entered midlife, and, through the German Schumacher's work on the metaphysical base of management and organization, potential maturity. However, still in the late eighties, the emergent view is eclipsed by the established one.

Behavioral science, having entered its youthful phase with Elton Mayo, is hovering between youth and maturity. Whereas political concepts of management and organization are still largely in a youthful phase, psychological and sociological thinking has advanced, through adulthood and midlife, and is beginning to touch maturity.

The problem is, however, that the evolution of the discipline and its managerial application remain far apart. Whereas academics like the extraordinary Mary Parker Follett and the exceptional Abraham Maslow approach behavioral maturity, the mainstream of theory and practice remains left behind, locked into adulthood.

Biology and ecology

Biology, as an underlying discipline in management, is somewhere between infancy and youth. Although Chester Barnard, the philosophical President of General Electric, introduced developmental biology into management in the thirties, it has never taken substantial root. Whereas Darwin's evolutionary theory, incorporating the survival of the fittest, has had significant implicit influence on management, evolutionary theories – George Land apart – have rarely been explicitly applied.

Ecology, though a subject of increasing environmental concern to managers, is still in its childhood as far as generic influence is concerned. In other words, management academics, in the main, still do not think ecologically, in the sense that Rudolph Steiner did. The images of quantitative growth and of competition still dominate, while concepts of qualitative growth and of symbiosis, synergy or symmetry remain on the fringe. Much developmental ground remains to be covered.

Modern physics and ancient wisdom

Modern physics, though enormously influential as far as the development of new technologies is concerned, is still in its early infancy with respect to management development. While Erich Jantsch, in corporate planning, and Fritjof Capra, in organizational development, have made slender inroads, the bulk of management theory and practice remains untouched by the revolutionary findings of such Nobel prizewinners as David Bohm and Ilya Prigogine. Yet their respective work on the 'implicate order', and on 'dissipative structures' has enormous implications for the development and maturation of organizations.

Ancient wisdom from the East, including Chinese Taoism and Japanese Zen Buddhism certainly has had an impact on the fringes of business life, especially with the economic emergence of Japan. However, in terms of its overall impact on the mainstream of management its influence remains marginal, and in a youthful stage of development. As we can see, then, most of the academic underpinnings, or roots of management, remain historically underdeveloped, or selectively 'overdeveloped', as in the case of 'adultlike' approaches to economics and to administrative theory. Why then is this the case?

Integration

Spatial and interdisciplinary

In the first instance, the interweaving of disciplines has been restricted at all levels. Economics and anthropology, firstly, have largely pursued paths of separate development. In that sense economics has lost touch with its origins, and anthropology has not been developed and renewed. Economics has been deprived of a soft touch, and anthropology has lacked cut and thrust. Administrative and behavioral science have kept closer in touch with one another, in theory, but in practice the administrative and hierarchical view has dominated over the behavioral, networked approach. In my view, this is largely due to the imbalance created at the primal stage between soft and hard. Specifically, the communal (anthropological) network and the trading (economic) have not been integrated.

Biology and ecology have emerged strongly, as disciplines in recent years, but outside of the context of management. They are yet to be integrated within the mainstream of its development. Finally, while physics has undergone a series of revolutions – through Newton, Einstein, and the quantum physicists, much of management remains rooted in a Newtonian world. While some managers are beginning to grapple with Einsteinian relativity, the quantum world remains far apart from their conscious awareness, that is to all except the most enlightened.

Temporal and historical

In historical terms, what we can see is the accumulated repression of the soft side of management theory and practice, especially at the earlier phases of its development. Hence I have seen the need, in this text, to recast both in more balanced terms. For, more often than not, the roots of management are traced back to the bureaucracies of Ancient Egypt or Rome, rather than to the prehistoric communities of Africa or Asia. Within business enterprise itself, moreover, the entrepreneur rather than the animateur is seen to hold sway.

Thereafter, at the second stage of an organization's development, the image of the hierarchical organization dominates that of the communal household. The entry of women into management, in recent years, is beginning to right that imbalance, albeit very slowly.

Finally, the third and fourth stages of development, in which the softness of ecological interdependence, and of 'the cosmic dance of energy', becomes more apparent to us, are still largely in their infant form. The mature roots are still emerging. Yet it is from these particular roots that our large-scale enterprises, in the future, will especially need to draw.

How, then, does this all affect the actual core of management?

The management core

Differentiation

Spatial domains

Because, in this text, we have drawn on the full combination of management roots, including those still at an early stage of their development, and because we have drawn on the composite richness of culturally diverse soils, we have had four, distinctive management domains to investigate. (See Fig. 86.)

Each of the primal, rational, developmental and metaphysical domains has a different

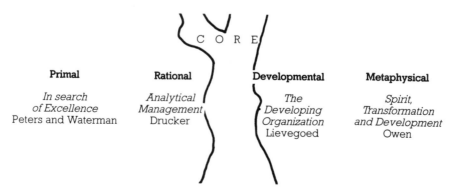

Fig. 86 The management core.

set of roots, both soft and hard attributes and a different cultural heritage, on which to draw. The result is a set of global management principles.

Primal management

The core of primal management, ironically, only recently came to light. Strangely enough, for all its youthful and primal characteristics, America had no eloquently primal spokesmen until the 1980s.

In fact it is because Tom Peters, for all his protestations against rational management, had at least the necessary analytical capability to develop a set of principles, that a new form of 'primal' management was born. Its hard attributes are centrally featured in autonomy and enterprise in the economic market-place, and its soft ones in shared values in the business' community. Both are instinctive, innate and subconscious.

Rational management

Before Tom Peters exposed, so vigorously, the limitations of rational management, it monopolized the academic and business establishment. All management concepts were mere variations on a basic theme, composed, so astutely, by Peter Drucker. The titles of his seminal works on management the effective executive, managing for results, and management: tasks, responsibilities and practices represent that essential theme.

The variations, either administratively or behaviorally rooted, veer respectively towards organizational order or individual freedom. Moreover, drawing off Drucker's integrated lead, they lean more or less towards management, organizational, or business functions (hard) or behavior (soft). All are intelligent, explicit and conscious.

Developmental management

Whereas the core of primal management is rooted firmly in American soils, and rational management is strongly based in Europe and parts of America, developmental management has a dual cultural heritage. Most visibly, amongst practitioners, it draws off Japanese soils, and is reflected in *The Art of Japanese Management*. However, in an academic context, its heritage is European, reaching back to Rudolph Steiner, and represented in Bernard Lievegoed's the developing organization.

The phases of individual, organizational and societal evolution are reflected in Livegoed's work, embodying the hard side of the developmental core. The soft side is represented most strongly in the approach to business and organizational harmony, evident in the East, and reflected in the manager's total faith in the organization's purposes. The core of developmental management, finally, being still split between East and North, is still only barely visible. Moreover, the attributes involved are intuitive, relying on revealed insight rather than rational analysis.

Metapysical management

Metaphysical management, almost by definition, is even less visible still. If it had not been for one major business enterprise, the Bank of Credit and Commerce, and one bold academic, Harrison Owen, it would still remain totally invisible, within the recesses of a hitherto dormant South.

Harrison Owen has successfully rescued the emerging area of corporate culture from a purely primal level of consideration into a metaphysical one, where spirit becomes the primary management resource. The Bank of Credit and Commerce, at the same time, have turned their so called laws of nature – totality, integrity, flow, no-existence – into their basis for real and metaphysical management. Such metaphysical management is essentially imaginative, originative and inspirational.

How do these domains apply to business, then, as it develops?

Temporal domains

Pioneering enterprise

The instinctive, primal domain functions at its peak at the pioneering stage of an organization's development. It is similarly in evidence in youthful and immigrant societies, and the individual, in his twenties, is primally receptive.

As the organization grows and develops the primal need becomes secondary rather than primary, relegated to new ventures, or rendered part of a more adult, managerial whole. In organizational midlife it should receive separate recognition, but again be subservient to a fundamentally developmental purpose. Finally, in maturity, the narrowly economic, primal instinct, should serve the more broadly based mission of economic, social and cultural transformation.

Established organization

The established organization, at the second stage of a business' development, should be run along intelligent, intelligible, rational lines. This is the adult phase of the individual, organization or society.

As the organization grows and develops into midlife rational principles of management should become secondary rather than primary. Functional management should serve the developmental needs of product, market, business and organization development. Finally, in maturity, such management rationality needs to become even less visible, serving now not only developmental requirements but also the company's inspiring vision.

Transnational enterprise

The transnational, transfunctional, transdivisional enterprise, at the third stage of a business' development, should be run along intuitive, insightful, developmental lines. Now the individual, organization or society is entering a period of renewal, in midlife.

As the organization grows and develops into maturity so the developmental functions become secondary, and the transforming one becomes primary. Moreover, in the first two stages of evolution, the developmental function is subservient to, first, primal enterprise, and, second, rational organization and management.

Global corporation

The truly global corporation is the one that has fully matured, thereby exercising its originative imagination in transforming the world's physical, economic, and human resources. In its maturity, the individual, organization or society is capable of accommodating, within it, all phases of development, and therefore each of the core management domains. However, the guiding spirit of the corporation, which the other three domains serve, will operate in the metaphysical domain.

How, then, has the whole subject area of management developed over time?

Integration

Spatial domains

The core of management – as it has developed over the last 100 years – has been historically restricted to the rational domain. By implication it has befitted, particularly well, only the second stage of an organization's development.

As I have indicated, it is only in the eighties, that the rational stronghold has been fundamentally and primally contested. Previous developmental thrusts, from Parker Follett or Maslow, have been swept aside by the prevailing rational tide.

Inside the rational domain the harder, functional approach has led the way, and the softer, behavioral approach has followed. The main reason is that, in Europe and America at least, the operational and financial functions have remained bereft of soft touches, and the soft sides of marketing and human resource management have been dominated by the hard. This has not been the case, of course, in Japan, where – for example – quality circles have made major inroads on the shop floor.

The onset of the developmental and metaphysical domains has been held back for three sets of reasons, each of which has inhibited integration and evolution. Firstly, there has been a lack of partnership between men and women, operating on an equal level, within management. Secondly, there has been limited association between cultures, each bringing with them a part of the managerial whole. Thirdly, because the soft edge of management has lagged behind at both the primal and rational stages, integration at the higher levels has been inhibited.

How, finally, has this affected practicing managers?

Temporal domains

Whereas, in most parts of the world, pioneering enterprises are in evidence, and established organizations are very much part of our indutrialized scene, further developments are thin on the ground. There are four good reasons for this.

The entrepreneur, reinforced by the economics of free enterprise, and by the bravado of the proverbial macho man, has ruled the pioneering roost, generally to the exclusion of his softer primal counterpart (sharing values), the animateur. Moreover, in the developing countries where the communal tradition is still close to hand, it has tended to become economically eclipsed by a form of socialism – created by Karl Marx in England – which has little to do with their own communal heritage.

We shall have to await interesting developments in China and Russia to see how an indigenously upgraded communal tradition might come to light. The established organization is, therefore, built on unduly rough ground, in Europe and America, and on foreign soils, in the developing countries. In its turn, Europe, the originator of political democracy, has failed to install an adequate balance between freedom and order within its economic institutions. Mary Parker Follett's seminal attempts to achieve just that were essentially ignored by a more narrowly based academic establishment.

Thirdly, as established organizations are beset by their own bureaucratic limitations, they fall back on their enterprising past, exclusively, rather than leaning forward into their developmental future. They thus fail to enter fully into their organizational midlife, and, in the process, fail to tap the emerging enabling and adoptive qualities of their management – in their forties and fifties. Again, in this respect, the Japanese are more adept than the Americans and Europeans.

Finally, our lack of real contact with the south, with our own subconscious, and with the inner meaning of our outer business lives, precludes us from applying our spiritually based inspirations to the fourth stage of our organizations' development.

Now we come to the branches of management.

Management branches

Differentiation

Spatial differentiation

Primal branches

The primal core, resurrected by Peters and Waterman in America, and drawing off economic and anthropological roots, has quickly sprung new primal branches. (See Fig. 87.) In fact, in the mid-eighties, a whole new wave of management literature has sprung up, moving on from where Peters left off. The most significant result has been the

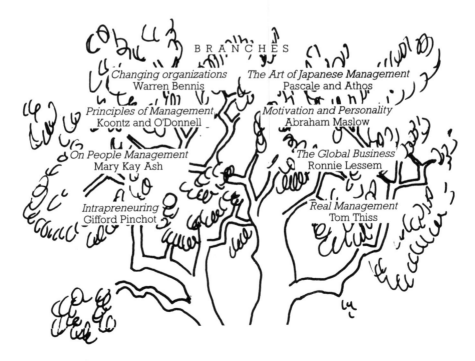

Fig. 87 Management branches.

development of the intrapreneuring concept, on the one hand, and of the concept of people management, on the other.

In promoting intrapreneurship, Gifford Pinchot has attempted to stimulate the same free-market environment within the firm as without. In other words, he has introduced the notions of intracapital and intraprise, as organizational equivalents of capital and enterprise in the market-place.

At first glance, there might appear to be nothing new in the concept of people management. But what Mary Kay has done is to replace the rational concept of personnel or human resource management with a much more down to earth notion. For her business is as much about people and love (P&L) as it is to do with profit and loss.

Rational branches

Whereas Pinchot and Kay represent hard and soft branches of primal management, Koontz and O'Donnell, on the one hand, and Warren Bennis, on the other, may be seen to be the rational equivalent.

Koontz and O'Donnell, following in the administrative tradition of Fayol, Taylor and Weber, have elaborated upon the functions of management – planning, organizing, directing, staffing and control – in supremely analytical vein. Within their organized view of managerial life, functions of management and layers of authority are neatly ordered within a clearly hierarchical organization.

Equally rational, but much more flexible in his approach is Warren Bennis. He was one of the first organizational theorists to compare and contrast fixed and autocratic organizations with changing and democratic organizations. Bennis was in favor of temporary, participative, project-based structures instead of fixed, mechanistic, functionally based ones. He has also been one of the leading figures in the 'organization development' movement, which has focussed on the achievement of planned change.

Developmental branches

Developmental management has branched out, albeit much more thinly than the rational domain, in two major directions. The first one, initiated by Abraham Maslow, leads to the personal growth and development of the individual, reflected in the progressive satisfaction of increasingly higher order needs. At the peak of such development lies self-actualization. Further developments of Maslow's work, not necessarily within management, have led in the direction of the human lifecycle, drawing on concepts of developmental biology and psychology.

The second major developmental thrust has been towards business and organizational synergy and harmony, as complementary to individual self-actualization. Such harmony is a reflexion of an Eastern, and ecological view of the world. The relevant concepts, here, have generally emerged out of the study of Japanese organizations, most particularly through Pascale and Athos' work on *The Art of Japanese Management*.

Metaphysical branches

The metaphysical branches of management are the most poorly developed of all. In one direction, from vision to action, Kevin Kingsland has illustrated how spirit, or imagination is turned into matter, or energy, in a business setting. In my own work I have compared this process to the journey undertaken by heroic figures in the great myths.

Whereas vision to action both draws on ancient wisdom and also on my personal familiarity with the South, the Bank of Credit and Commerce's philosophy of real management can be linked with modern physics. BCC's concepts of energy, of interfusion, and of totality, are close to Capra's cosmic dance, to Jantsch's 'design for evolution', and to Bohm's 'implicate order'. They also draw heavily on the notions of corporate culture introduced by Harrison Owen.

What stage of development, then, have the branches reached?

Temporal differentiation

Primal

'Intrapreneuring' and 'people management', as concepts, are still very much in their youth, and it is open to question as to how much further they can be developed before they become fundamentally transformed. As they do become so, it is likely that individuality will supplant intrapreneuring, and corporate culture will overtake people management.

Rational

Managerial functions are well into adulthood, and awaiting renewal in midlife. It will need more cross-fertilization with concepts of managerial work, managerial decision making, and manager self-development before this happens. In fact what is happening instead is that we are going back to leadership traits, rather than forward to an evolved form of management.

The management of change, though is in a more fluid and fertile state than the management functions. For it is both drawing back on traditionally behavioral concepts, and also leaning forwards towards new ideas brought on by changing communications technology. In this transition between adulthood and midlife there is plenty of scope for future development into individual and organizational networking.

Development

The work on manager self-development, potentially drawing on evolutionary, lifecycle concepts, tends to get stuck in more static, rationally based notions of flexibility and change. Such developmental concepts are being inhibited from developing from youth to midlife and maturity, by an inappropriately prolonged period of adulthood. Conversely, the work on organizational harmony, thanks largely to Japanese practice and some American theory, is proceeding healthily from semi-articulate youth into articulated adulthood. All too often, though, a Western or Northern bias creeps into the analysis of an Eastern, developmental phenomenon. We must await more management theory from the East itself before that can be rectified.

Metaphysical branches

The metaphysical branches are undoubtedly in their infancy. Whether we are referring to corporate culture, to organizational transformation, to business vision, or to 'real' management, each is at a very early and formative stage. The great danger, of course, is that the enthusiastic and sometimes overbearing primal youth might bury the metaphysical concepts in his concrete, everyday reality.

There are three ways to stop this. First, we need to enable our managers to mature, and in the process to encourage them to uncover the spirit of their organization. Second, we need to touch base much more with the spirit of the South, that is in the developing world. Third, we need to bring our new physicists into the mainstream of management.

How, then, have the different branches been integrated?

Integration

Spatial integration

Tom Peters has done a marvellous job in integrating the hard (enterprise) and soft (people) sides of primal management. However, subsequent primal branches run the recurrent danger of over-emphasizing the hard – success and aggression, to the exclusion of the soft – love and belonging. A balanced part needs to be played by men and women, and by different cultures, in the development of management theory and practice, if this is to be avoided.

Peter Drucker, like Peters, has attempted to adopt a balanced rational approach. The problem, though, is that he has not moved as far towards individual freedom as some of the European theorists, like Charles Handy, are willing to go. On the other hand, someone like Handy lacks the respectability in the management establishment of a Drucker, or even of a Warren Bennis. So we are caught on the horns of a dilemma. The issue can only be resolved if the Charles Handy's of this world take themselves, and are taken, as seriously as Drucker or Bennis.

Developmental management has particular difficulty in integrating itself, given the cultural and subject diversity on which it draws. For although biology and ecology form its disciplinary core, it has some roots in psychology and even in economics. Yet because of that very diversity it has tremendous potential.

As a domain, it has also suffered in the past from the very half-hearted and misshapen attempts – albeit well meaning ones – made by the organization developers to evolve their established organizations. If this domain is to enhance itself, then it needs to integrate its developmental approach across the business functions of research, marketing, finance and human resources, as well as of management services. Finally, metaphysical management, like modern physics, must make a concerted attempt to link contemporary management science with the wisdom of the ages. Through modern communications technology, and through Teillard De Chardin's concept of the noosphere (see p. 489) it has the chance to do just that.

Furthermore, metaphysically inclined managers need to make a sincere effort to disentangle themselves from the commonplace notions of culture and vision, which have played their part in opening metaphysical doors, but now need to be abandoned in favor of more subtle concepts.

Temporal integration

Like 'vision' and 'culture', intrapreneuring has emerged as a reaction against rational management. In many ways it is a regression rather than a progression, except in so far as it maintains a better balance between the primal and rational domains than more purely analytical approaches. People management, on the other hand, represents a more spontaneous emergence of a hitherto unrecognized and unexpressed soft approach to primal management.

This soft, primal approach had been unavailable to planners of change, like Warren Bennis, when they developed their more democratic alternatives to hierarchical organizations. As a result, organization development has lacked instinctive ground upon which to build its intelligent theories. This has remained a fundamental weakness, which is only now being addressed by Tom Peters, Mary Kay, and primal others. Similarly, the hard intrapreneurial approach had been unavailable to those constructing the functions, or skills of management. The result has been an overly rational approach to the development of management principles. The transition from rational to developmental branches of management, supposedly facilitated by the 'organization development' movement, has generally fallen short because of the predominance of analysis over intuition. Where intuition has held sway, it has been in marginal contexts, like in 'sensitivity training'.

The problem has been that, unlike in Japan, where intuitive approaches have a solid cultural underpinning – as Pascale and Athos have aptly pointed out – in Europe and America such aesthetic sensitivity is limited to the arts. It has been left to the design function, alone, to redress this imbalance, sadly in isolation from organization development. In effect, outside of Japan, no strong base for developmental management has been established. Neither industrial designers nor organization developers have had the necessary cut and thrust, or – more importantly *vis à vis* the East – the essentially hard-earned faith and commitment.

The transition from developmental to metaphysical management, on the other hand, has been inhibited in America and, particularly, in Europe, by the overly rigid divide – as again Pascale and Athos have pointed out – between purposeful religious life and

FRUIT AND FOLIAGE

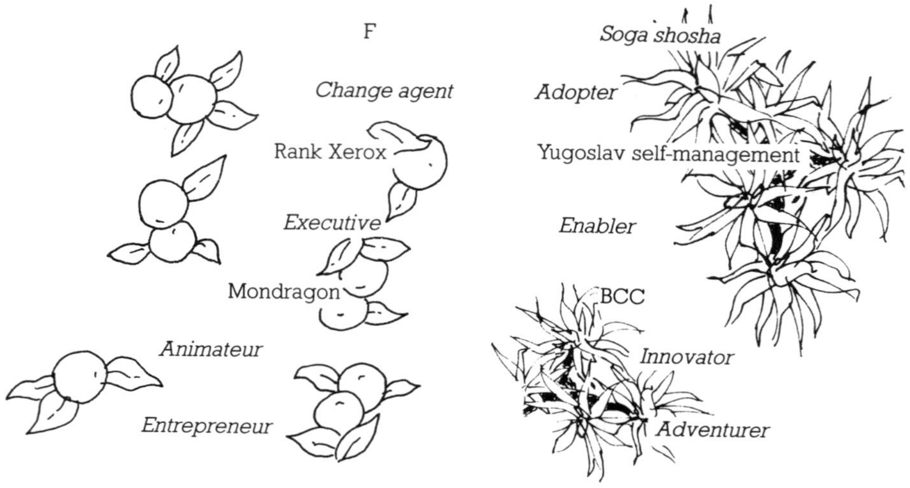

Fig. 88 The fruits of management.

subsequently meaningful business activity. In fact when the two are linked it is in the much too limited context of so-called business ethics.

The essence of metaphysical management lies in the crossing of the boundaries between the secular and the sacred so that, in my own terms, the heart and 'soul' of business become as relevant a managerial concern as its body and mind. BCC go even further in seeing the submission to God, and to the laws of nature, as fundamental to their business mission.

The fruits of management

Differentiation

Spatial and institutional
A fundamental – perhaps the most revolutionary – implication of this text is that there are four significantly different institutional forms, coresponding with each respective management domain. (See Fig. 88 for examples of these.)

Independent enterprise
The first form is that of the well-known independent enterprise, either personally or collectively run. It is owned by an individual or group. 3M in America, particular through its new business ventures, and the Mondragon cooperatives in Spain, typify this small scale enterprise. Within the large organization new ventures, spurred on by individual enterprise and collective enthusiasm, reflect this primal form.

This primal enterprise, finally, is either power or people centered, or both (see Fig. 89). Its function is to create and maintain a profitable business.

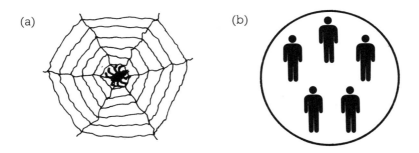

Fig. 89 Independent enterprise. (a) Power-centered enterprise.
(b) People-centered enterprise.

Public company
The second, also well known form, is that of the public company, accountable to its stakeholders. Such an established organization has either an hierarchical or network form, or a combination of these two. It is owned by the public at large, strongly represented by institutional shareholders.

Rank Xerox, in the UK, is an example of a predominantly hierarchical organization. F International, also based in Britain, is more of a network. The hierarchy, because of the 'hard' orientation of most established organizations, is much more common than the network. However, increasingly, progressive organizations in the West and North are combining the two structures. The established organization, then, is either role (function) or task (project) based, or both (see Fig. 90). Its function is to deploy the public resources under its sway efficiently and effectively.

1. Role-based structure   *2. Task-based structure*

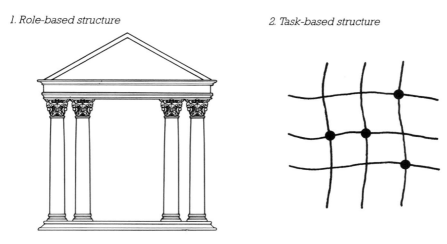

Fig. 90 Public company.

Enabling company

The third institutional form, the enabling company, is just beginning to emerge into public awareness around the globe. It is owned by an association. This might either be commercially and nationally based, like a Japanese Trading Company, or communally and spiritually based, like Yugoslav self-management. In its pure form the enabling company is rounded in its structure, built up of overlapping circles of associated parties. Its function is to enable its people and organizations, its product and markets, its businesses and communities, to develop. Characteristically, its associated organizations either consists of public–private partnerships or, increasingly, of joint ventures, which have yet to form themselves into truly enabling companies. (See Fig. 19).

Nuclear company

The fourth institutional form, which I have termed a nuclear company, has its creative nucleus at the center, and is owned by this originative or spiritual force. The one clear example of this is BCC, although the Bodyshop International, to the extent that its naturally based source of energy forms its center, could be seen as another 'nuclear' case in point.

Its function, as a nuclear company, is to transform itself and the world around it, from lower forms of physical and human energy into higher ones.

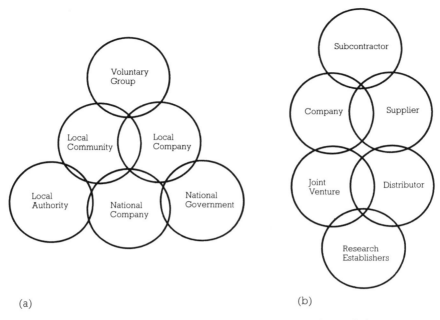

(a)   (b)

Fig. 91 Enabling company. (a) Public–private partnership. (b) Joint venture.

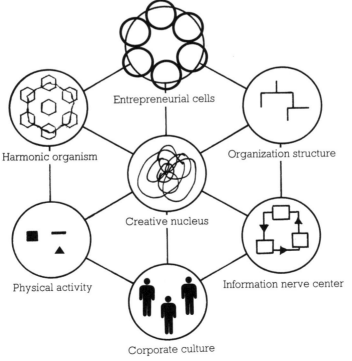

Fig. 92 Nuclear company.

Now I want to move on from the institutional and organizational outcomes to the corresponding personal and managerial ones. We start with the entrepreneur and animateur.

Spatial and personal

Entrepreneur and animateur – enterprising and people managers
The independent enterprise is managed by its dynamic 'hero' and enthusiastic 'heroine'. Both have finely honed instincts. The hero is the entrepreneur, with dynamism and flair. The entrepreneur spots chances, turns them into opportunities, and persistently drives his or her way through one challenge after another. The heroine is the animateur, with charm and enthusiasm. The animateur involves people, shares values, and creates a family feeling within her or his enterprise.

Both are more 'earthy' characters than the two that follow.

Executive and change agent – analytical and adaptive managers
The public company is managed by an authoritative 'hero', and a perceptive heroine. Both are intellectually capable. The functional or business executive is firm and authoritative. This executive is reliable, methodical and well coordinated in approach. He or she formulates effective strategies and efficient structures in the organization. The change agent is flexible and knowledgeable. This agent of change is adaptable, flexible and varied in his or her approach, developing changeable systems and procedures in the company. Both are more 'heady' characters than the two that follow.

Enabler and adopter – developmental managers
The enabling company is managed by its particular, faithful heroine, and its farsighted hero, both intuitively attuned to their environment. The adopter is committed to his calling and humbled by the greater powers of the universe. Such an adopter is faithful, responsive and submissive to influences, both within the organization and without, greater than him or herself. The enabler is sensitive and insightful. Such a manager is naturally cooperative and inherently developmental in his or her approach. He or she recognizes and harnesses physical, human or economic potential as it emerges. Both are more responsive characters than the two that follow.

Innovator and adventurer – innovative and action managers
Finally, the nuclear company is managed by its charismatic innovator, and effervescent adventurer, both bounding with energy.

The business innovator is imaginative, original, impassioned and creative, while the adventurer – active, carefree, risk-prone and energetic.

How, then, do all these organizations and managers function over time?

Institutions in time
Businesses, if they are to grow and develop, undergo alternate structure-building and structure-changing phases. While the hard edge of management plays the dominant, stabilizing role, the soft edge plays the major transitional one.

The pioneering–independent company
Having survived its birth crisis, a pioneering business becomes stabilized for a time, in a

stage of dynamic and youthful independence. At this particular and youthful stage hard work, natural enthusiasm, native wit, emotional resilience, a capacity for improvisation, a gut feel for the market-place and imagination enough to see round corners keeps the business going and growing. Then, as complexity and variety advances, the crisis of control ensues.

The established–public company

Having survived the crisis of delegation and control, a pioneering business turns into an established one, in a stage of adultlike dependence on outside stakeholders. Should it fail to recognize and negotiate its crisis of adulthood the company will return to excesssively exuberant youth, or be acquired, or die. At this particular and adult stage high productivity, effective teamwork, integrated management control, a competitive strategy, a formal organization, analytically based marketing, and systematic innovation, keeps the business going and growing. Then, as complexity and variety advances, the crisis of bureaucracy ensues.

The self-renewing–enabling company

Having survived the crisis of bureaucracy and alienation, an established organization turns into a self-renewing one, in a stage of midlife interdependence between itself and its associates. Should it fail to recognize and negotiate its midlife crisis the company will return to overgrown adulthood, or to excessively exuberant youth, or be taken over, or die. At this particular and midlife stage intense interactivity, interdependent quality circles, manager self development, a cooperative strategy, a new corporate architecture, a planned evolution, and a programme of continuing corporate renewal, keeps the company going and growing. Then, as complexity and variety advances, a crisis of meaning and purpose ensues.

The global corporation–the nuclear company

Having survived the crisis of meaning and purpose, a self-renewing company turns into a transformed one, in a stage of mature transcendence over its material self and environment. Should it fail to recognize and surmount its crisis of maturity the company will return to prolonged midlife, to overgrown adulthood, to excessively exuberant youth, or be acquired, or become extinct.

At this particular and mature stage a high rate of energy flow, a cohesive corporate culture, a focus on process and change, concerted and strategic interfusion, an involvement with natural management, the recognition of unlimited possibility and a spiritually based vision keeps the company going and growing. Thereafter, it returns to the first and youthful point in the cycle, while retaining all the other stages within it. Meanwhile individual managers, like the institutions they run, undergo similar stages of development.

Managers in time

As an individual manager, you have different development paths open to you. Whereas you are individually unique your development path has a particular pattern to it. The developmental phases and the ascribed ages, though, will vary in their particular duration. For example, you may enter managerial 'adulthood' in your mid-thirties rather than at the end of your twenties. However, if you only become an 'adult' manager in your fifties, you will have problems. In the final analysis, for you or for your organization, it is never too late to develop, but it becomes progressively more difficult, the more ground that you leave uncovered.

Youth – twenties

Having developed in a particular way – physically, mentally and emotionally – through childhood and adolescence, you may consciously choose or be chosen by others in your youth, to enter management. Alternatively, you may develop into a manager through an unsuspecting route. In either case, you will need to resolve a crisis of independence, as you depart from your nearest and dearest in late adolescence – at least to some extent. In your twenties, then, you create a provisional identity for yourself, which has prospective managerial significance.

In fact, you may see yourself as a salesperson or as a craftsperson; as a trainee manager or as a professional; as a management apprentice or as an artist or scientist; as an inventor or as a doer. Only a few of these roles could be readily, and initially, ascribed to management. Then, in between youth and adulthood, as you become more conscious of your personal responsibilities, a formative growth crisis ensues.

Adulthood – thirties

Having recognized and surmounted your growth crisis, that is your crisis of dependence, you develop from youth into adulthood. Should you fail to resolve it you become, at least to some extent, managerially irresponsible. As a developing adult manager you may become an entrepreneur or an animateur; a functional manager or an agent of change; a managerial journeyman or a designer (technical or social); an innovator or an adventurer.

Then, between youth and adulthood, as you feel the urge to round out as a person and as a manager, a formative growth crisis again emerges.

Midlife – forties

Having recognized and surmounted your growth crisis, that is a crisis of interdependence, you move from adulthood into managerial midlife. Should you fail to resolve the crisis you will remain over-controlling, or youthfully reckless. As a manager in midlife you may become an intrapreneur; a manager of change; a corporate architect; or a visionary. The soft and hard edges of management, in your developing midlife, merge. Then, between midlife and maturity, as you feel the need to center yourself, as a person and as a manager, the formative crisis of maturity ensues.

Maturity – fifties and onwards

Having recognized and surmounted your growth crisis, that is a crisis of transcendence, you move from midlife into managerial maturity. Should you fail to resolve the crisis you will be held back by managerial indecisiveness, rigidity, or irresponsibility. As a mature manager you come to embody enterprise or community; you personify leadership or freedom; you embody development or mastery; or you become the spirit of creativity or adventure.

You therefore make your fundamental impact, at this mature stage, on the 'top line', that is upon the spirit, rather than on the bottom line, that is upon the body of the organization. In actual fact, of course, life and business is never as clear cut as this section of my concluding chapter might have led you to believe. Individuals and institutions ultimately function as wholes rather than in neatly differentiated compartments. So what are the implications for management and for managers, both in space and time?

Integration

Spatial domains

Firstly, in the same way as a power-centered culture and a people-centered one need to be combined, in a successful intraprise, so do the entrepreneur and animateur need to combine into a successful intrapreneur. Both 3M and Mondragon, therefore, represent such combinations.

However, it also needs to be stressed that the image of the entrepreneur, at least in Western Europe and America, is considerably stronger than that of the animateur. This creates an inevitable imbalance, and prevents many a pioneering enterprise from moving on. In developing countries with a strong communal tradition, of course, the reverse may well apply.

Secondly, in the same way as role and task-centered cultures need to be combined within an effective matrix organization, so do the executive and change agent need to combine into an effective manager of change. Both Rank Xerox and F International, therefore, represent such combinations. However, it also needs to be emphasized that, in traditionally based organizations, executives may hold undue sway over change agents, and in more fringe organizations the reverse may well apply. Both are thereby inhibited in their growth and stabilization, respectively.

Thirdly, in the same way as harmonious and evolutionary cultures need to be combined, within a fully developed enabling company, so do the adopter and enabler need to combine into an evolved corporate architect. Sony, with its blend of Eastern harmony and Western individualism, to a large extent, represents such a combination. However, a fully functioning enabling company, crossing national and business boundaries, still needs to be formed.

Fourthly and finally, in the same way as transcendent and transformative cultures need to be combined, within a potent 'nuclear' company, so do the innovator and adventurer need to combine into an all-powerful visionary. Both the Bank of Credit and Commerce (Agha Hasan Abedi and John Hillbery) and Bodyshop (Gordon and Anita Roddick) to a large extent represent such combinations.

BCC places more emphasis on spiritual transcendence and Bodyshop on material transformation. Moreover, both are relatively young for all their maturity in outlook, and therefore not yet fully developed. This brings us on to the question of individual and institutional development, over time.

Temporal domains

Development, for managers and for organizations, is discontinuous, circular and accumulative rather than smooth, linear and discrete. In other words, there is often a need to regress backwards before progressing forwards, and you retain bits of your past within your future. In fact, we evolve successfully, as managers and as institutions, by progressively reintegrating the different parts of ourselves over time, rather than by leaving them behind us. So, as youth turns into adulthood, successfully established individuals and organizations become more responsible, but retain their youthful vigor. 3M or the Mondragon cooperatives, by implication, adopt formal structures and strategies, but retain their youthful entrepreneurism and shared values.

All too often, in fact, individual managers and business organizations either fail to develop, or, in duly making a transition, leave their old selves behind them. While Tom Peters holds on just a little too much to his youthful exuberance, Peter Drucker somewhat overdoes his adult responsibilities, leaving the instinct and enterprise of youth too fully behind him.

The same, and more, goes for many an animateur or entrepreneur, who fails to grow up, and for many an executive or change agent, who forgets what it was like to be a child. In a parallel context, small and free enterprises fail to grow large and accountable, and large organizations become sluggish dinosaurs.

Secondly, as adulthood turns into midlife, companies that successfully renew themselves not only retain their youthful vigor and their practical intelligence, but they successfully transform both through newly evolved insights.

All too often, established organizations either become increasingly bureaucratized, or else they revert, under stress, to a trumped up form of primal enterprise. Under these circumstances a new and heroic leader takes the rein, usually in the guise of a tough-minded, entrepreneurial manager, rather than as a genuine corporate architect. Similarly, a responsible executive may, under times of stress, either dig his heels in or else go 'back to basics'.

Sony, on the other hand, had the insight, in midlife, to create a new design center for its operations, rather than reverting to a youthfully decentralized operation. Within that consciously designed 'architectural' context it continues to encourage new ventures and a family feeling, as well as soundly based strategies and structures.

Thirdly, and finally, as midlife turns into maturity, companies that successfully transform themselves not only retain their entrepreneurism and shared values, their order and freedom, their harmony and adaptability, but also – and most importantly – create a new spirit and vision for themselves.

Both BCC and Bodyshop have such a mature vision, but because of their relative youth they have still to develop, and to integrate, many of the immature parts. Both lack, in particular, the degree of order and freedom that a well established adult organization, with appropriately soft and hard edges, would possess.

Unfortunately and finally, both for individual managers and for business institutions around the globe, there are very few examples of well integrated development. In the West youth is overvalued; in the North adulthood; in the East midlife; and in the South maturity!

Conclusion

In the beginning of this text was the end and at the end is the beginning!

From beginning to end

I began at the outset, to establish a set of global management principles, via four domains of management: primal, rational, developmental and metaphysical.

Whereas the primal ground covers the new and popular concepts, and the rational ground the existing and conventional wisdom, the developmental and metaphysical ground has only begun to become visible. For large enterprises, however, these last two domains are the most significant.

Each of the four domains is marked out by different cultures around the globe – East/West/North/South; by different ages in your management development – youth, adulthood, midlife and maturity; by different stages in a business' development – independent, consolidated, 'enabling', and 'nuclear', and by different sets of individual capabilities – instinctive, intellectual, intuitive, and imaginative.

The object of this whole exercise has been to establish a set of management principles that, on the one hand, drew out your personal and cultural individuality, and, on the other hand, enabled you to recognize and harness that very diversity. In other words the aim has been to draw out both your managerial individuality and your global management reach.

From end to beginning

At the same time I fully recognize that the end which I have reached, through this text, is only a beginning. For the all important business functions – most notably operations and marketing, financial and human resource management – remain substantially untouched by at least two out of the four domains.

Management theory in finance and accounting, and in technology and operations, is almost entirely rationally based. Marketing management spans both the primal and the rational, and just occasionally touches upon the developmental. The human resource function is the only one in which theory has touched all four of the domains, albeit that most of the theory is rationally founded.

Finally, business strategy and policy, the capstone course on most MBA programs, is strongly founded on rationality, with a recent primal emphasis changing the orientation, but only somewhat. The developmental and metaphysical domains have been left out completely in, you might say, the strategic cold.

The net result of this is that the business functions serve the middle-sized, adult organization well enough, but fall somewhat short as far as the pioneering enterprise is concerned, and totally bypass the underlying realities of large-scale enterprise, in midlife and in maturity.

By further implication, of course, business and management theory is richly endowed with European and American influence, but does no more than touch base with the East and South. We obviously, and globally, have a very long way to go. The future, you might say, is in our hands.

Reference

1. E. Jantsch, *Design for Evolution*, Brazillier (1975), p. xxi.

Index